American Justice on Trial
1968–2016

As I write this, the nation is still reeling from multiple shocks in July 2016. First, as the month began, came yet two more videotaped incidents of police shooting to death black arrestees after many other such widely-publicized incidents over the previous several years. The day after the Fourth of July holiday, disturbing footage went viral of Baton Rouge police outside a convenience store firing repeatedly at 37-year-old Alton Sterling while two white policemen already had Sterling pinned face down on the ground. A day later, a thousand miles away in a suburb of St. Paul, Minnesota, the quick-thinking girl friend of Philando Castile used her cell phone to capture a local policeman still waving his gun outside Castile's car window as Castile lay bleeding to death seated beside her following a traffic stop. This graphic image was followed within days by breaking news of a horrific sniper attack on Dallas policemen who were monitoring one of many Black Lives Matter protest rallies prompted by the deaths of Sterling and Castile. Then, on July 17, 2016 came another attack, this time on Baton Rouge police.

The carnage and proliferation of demonstrations and hostile reactions in the aftermath have drawn renewed national focus to fractured police-community relations in cities across country, the very issue that gave rise to the Black Panther Party a half century ago. Indeed, the day after video footage went viral of Castile dying from gunshot wounds following a traffic stop, AlterNet reporter Alexandra Rosenmann drew a direct comparison to the sensationalized 1968 murder trial of Panther Party co-founder Huey Newton. Rosenmann titled her web article, "Gun Rights, Police Brutality and the Case of the Century: Philando Castile's tragic case of police brutality pulls one of the most famous cases back into focus."[1]

The two incidents did start out in similar ways. In the early morning of October 28, 1967, Oakland policeman John Frey stopped the car Newton was driving to write a ticket for an unpaid traffic fine. A shootout ensued that left Officer Frey dead and Newton and a back-up

officer seriously wounded. Newton claimed to have been unarmed and the victim of an abusive arrest; no gun belonging to Newton was found. His death penalty trial the following summer drew international attention to whether any black man could get a fair trial in America.

Before the deadly July 2016 incidents occurred, interviewees for this book had already noted the remarkable relevance of the 1968 Newton case to current events. Among them is William "Bill" Patterson, a former President of the Oakland NAACP and the first black foreman of the Alameda County Grand Jury: "It does resonate today. A young man [Oscar Grant III] being killed in the BART station by BART police and how that played out. The Florida case . . . again another young man [Trayvon Martin] shot to death. These situations continue to emerge and if we are not careful, we will find history repeating itself."

In the past several months, both champions and critics of the Black Lives Matter movement have drawn parallels to the split among Americans in the turbulent 1960s. The comparisons reached a point where President Obama felt compelled to reassure the world, on July 9, 2016, that most Americans are not as divided as we were fifty years ago: "When we start suggesting that somehow, there's this enormous polarization and we're back to the situation in the '60s, that's just not true. You're not seeing riots, and you're not seeing police going after people who are protesting peacefully. . . . We've got a foundation to build on . . ."[2]

President Obama himself symbolizes the profound change in the fabric of our nation over the past half century. So, too, do black police chiefs like Dallas Police Chief David Brown. Chief Brown's reaction to a black gunman ambushing randomly chosen white officers on the evening of July 7, 2016, captured the sentiments of most Americans: "We are heartbroken. There are no words to describe the atrocity that occurred in our city. All I know is this must stop: this divisiveness between our police and our citizens."[3]

This book scrutinizes the 1968 Newton trial and its context and poses the same questions President Obama and others have recently addressed: what has changed in this country in the last half century and what has not? How do we best move forward?

— *Lise Pearlman*
Oakland, California
September 2016

Comments on the book
from trial participants and observers

Lise Pearlman's account of the tinderbox setting enveloping the trial of Huey Newton perfectly captures how much can be at stake for an entire community — even a nation — in a single trial and the exceptional role played by twelve everyday men and women we trust to decide each case. For those, like myself, who recall this case from our youth, Lise has done a wonderful job in both capturing a movement and its historical context. But anyone interested in history, courtroom drama, or criminal justice should read this gripping account of an all too often forgotten chapter of the 20th century.
Barry Scheck, PROFESSOR OF LAW
BENJAMIN N. CARDOZO SCHOOL OF LAW
Co-Director, The Innocence Project

The definitive book on the 1968 Huey Newton death penalty trial.
D. Lowell Jensen, NEWTON PROSECUTOR

A clear recognition and exposition of the quest for justice and equality by one man for all people within the parameters of a trial that illuminates the racial divide of a nation.
Melvin Newton, PROFESSOR EMERITUS
ETHNIC STUDIES, MERRITT COLLEGE
(older brother of Huey Newton)

Lise Pearlman's book about the trial of Huey Newton captures the tumultuous times, the personalities, the fighting defense lawyers, including Charles Garry, in a way that makes it eminently worth reading. Garry's jury selection dealing with race was one of the best pieces of trial work done by anyone. Loved the book.
James Brosnahan, SENIOR PARTNER, MORRISON FOERSTER
Rated among the top 30 trial lawyers in the U.S.
(San Francisco federal prosecutor in 1968)

I began my long career as a criminal defense lawyer in the mid-60s in Oakland, California, and witnessed many of the legal events Lise Pearlman describes. I find her account of the 1968 Newton murder trial and its political context accurate and fascinating. Fans of famous trials will thoroughly enjoy this fast-paced, well-researched book. If "THE" trial of the 20th century can be measured, her argument for People v. Newton *heading the list is a strong one.*
Penny Cooper, MEMBER OF THE STATE BAR OF
CALIFORNIA TRIAL LAWYERS HALL OF FAME
(Alameda County Deputy Public Defender in 1968)

Lise Pearlman is also the acclaimed author of

The Sky's the Limit:
People v. Newton, the REAL Trial of the 20th Century?
[Regent Press 2012]

A history of the American 20th century that compares the Newton trial to other headline trials from 1901 to 2000.

The Sky's the Limit won:

U.S. BOOK NEWS 2013
First Place: Law

IBPA AWARD BENJAMIN FRANKLIN 2013
Silver Award: Multiculturalism

INTERNATIONAL BOOK AWARDS 2013
Finalist: U.S. History

Praise for *The Sky's the Limit*:

This thorough text stands apart from other case histories for its comparative nature as well as its focus on this particular trial. It deserves a place on the shelf of anyone interested in legal studies, the radical social movements of the 1960s, or African American Studies.

Alyssa Vincent, THE LIBRARY JOURNAL
VOL. 137, ISSUE 3, P. 116, FEBRUARY 15, 2012

Racism is ingrained in America's birth, and it has been a long fight against it ever since. [In] The Sky's the Limit: People v. Newton: The Real Trial of the 20th Century?, former Judge Lise Pearlman argues that this court case . . . allowed America to eventually elect its first non-white president . . . a fascinating look at this very important case of the twentieth century.

James A. Cox, EDITOR-IN-CHIEF,
MIDWEST BOOK REVIEW,
WISCONSIN BOOKWATCH, MARCH 2012

I was born in Oakland a generation before the mass migration of African-American families to the Bay Area from the South during World War II. I later experienced the highly polarizing 1968 prosecution of Black Panther Huey Newton. Lise Pearlman has written a powerful account of both that trial and its place in our country's political history. I truly believe that had Newton received a death sentence, we would not have Obama in the White House today. Read this wonderful book.

Morrie Turner (1923–2014), AWARD-WINNING CREATOR
OF "WEE PALS," THE FIRST INTEGRATED COMIC STRIP

What a phenomenal book! I strongly recommend The Sky's the Limit *to high school history and social studies teachers as an essential resource. Focusing on important trials in the classroom provides an excellent basis for engaging their students in exploring key social questions of the past century.*

Deborah Menkart, EXECUTIVE DIRECTOR,
TEACHING FOR CHANGE, WASHINGTON, D.C.

Judge Pearlman breathes life into historical topics that remain highly relevant today. Her well-researched content on a full span of 20th century trials—many of which involve labor-related cases—reminds us of the enduring nature of the underlying social and economic issues that they raise.

Richard Trumka, AFL-CIO PRESIDENT

Judge Monroe Friedman watching Huey Newton testify before a packed courtroom.

Historic jury selected for 1968 Newton death penalty trial, including seven women and four minorities. Jury members: Linda Aguirre, Ronald Andrews, Marian Butler, Mary Gallegos, Jenevie Gibbons, David Harper, Helen Hart, Thomas Hofmann, Jr., Harvey Kokka, Eda Prelli, Joseph Quintana and June Reed. The lone African-American, banker David Harper (pictured on the cover of this book), is seated third from the left in the second row between Thomas Hofmann, Jr. and Harvey Kokka.

AMERICAN JUSTICE ON TRIAL

P E O P L E *v.* N E W T O N

LISE PEARLMAN

REGENT PRESS
BERKELEY, CALIFORNIA

Copyright © 2016 by Lise Pearlman

PAPERBACK:
ISBN 13: 978-1-58790-369-4
ISBN 10: 1-58790-369-5

E-BOOK
ISBN 13: 978-1-58790-370-0
ISBN 10: 1-58790-370-9

Library of Congress Catalog Number: 2016949475

Front Cover photos: photo of pioneering Newton jury foreman David Harper in the late 1960s courtesy of David Harper. Newspaper photo of Huey Newton and arresting officer taken on the morning of Oct. 28, 1967 © 1967 *San Francisco Examiner,* reprinted courtesy of San Francisco Media Company. *Back cover photo:* photo of Huey Newton *Oakland Post* Collection, MS169, African American Museum and Library at Oakland, Oakland Public Library, Oakland, CA.

This book is based in part on interviews conducted for *American Justice on Trial: People v. Newton,* a documentary project of Arc of Justice Productions, Inc., Oakland, California. www.americanjusticeontrial.com. Quotes from such interviews are published here with permission from the Board of Directors of Arc of Justice Productions, Inc.

Special thanks to the family of Rosalie Ritz and to the Bancroft Library, University of California, Berkeley, for permission to include in this book copies of original courtroom drawings of the Newton trial by CBS artist Rosalie Ritz (1923-2008). To see full color copies of Ritz's original Newton trial sketches reproduced in black and white in this book, see www.lisepearlman.com.

Printed in the U.S.A.
REGENT PRESS
Berkeley, California
www.regentpress.net
regentpress@mindspring.com

DEDICATION

This book is dedicated to the memory of
two extraordinary men who died in 2014:

my good friend, "Wee Pals" cartoonist Morrie Turner, who
devoted his life to spreading a gentle, humanitarian message
celebrating diversity and promoting equality, strongly encour-
aged my retelling of the story of the 1968 Newton trial, and
always urged me to "keep the faith"

and

author Gilbert Moore, who recognized the historic significance
of the Newton death penalty trial when covering it for LIFE
magazine and quit his job to write the classic book A Special
Rage *— capturing for posterity both the racial tensions the*
trial exposed and the inner workings of its ground-breaking,
diverse jury.

CONTENTS

INTRODUCTION

You can jail a Revolutionary,
but you can't jail the Revolution.

You can kill the Revolutionary,
but you can't kill the Revolution.

— FRED HAMPTON
(CHICAGO CHAIRMAN, BLACK PANTHER PARTY, 1969)

American Justice on Trial revisits in light of current events *People of California v. Huey P. Newton*—the internationally-watched 1968 murder case that put a black militant on trial for his life for the death of a white policeman accused of abuse. The trial put our nation's justice system to the test and created the model for diversifying juries "of one's peers" that many of us now take for granted as a constitutional guarantee. In the process, protesters orchestrated by the defense generated a media frenzy that launched the Black Panther Party as an international phenomenon. Using this trial as their platform, the Panthers took aim at entrenched racism in a democracy founded on the principle of equality. They put their sights on toppling white male monopoly power, and they convinced many followers to pay it forward. They also prompted an extraordinary backlash from those in power. The ramifications of this decades-old conflict continue to unfold today.

The year 2016 marks a half century since Huey Newton and Bobby Seale founded, in Oakland, California, a small militant group that they named the Black Panther Party for Self-Defense. Like Black Lives Matter, Black Youth Project and other civil rights activist groups today, Panther members were predominantly in their late teens or early 20s when they took to the streets, challenging the nation's criminal justice system and making bold accusations of abusive policing. Today almost everyone recognizes the image of Black Panthers in iconic black leather

jackets and berets, their fists raised in defiant salutes. In 1967, that fledgling organization would likely have disappeared quickly if not for one
riveting murder trial. Now — a half century later — is an especially good
time to take a fresh look back, to reexamine what may very well be the
most pivotal criminal trial of the 20th century and ponder what it tells
us about the importance of diversity, if we want to improve some of the
most glaring shortcomings in our beleaguered American justice system.

* * * * *

2016 began with intense populist attacks on the federal government from both the Left and the Right. Republican presidential candidate Donald Trump promoted a nationalist agenda that promised to
"take America back" to an idealized earlier conservative era of white
Christian domination, while disenchanted youth rallied in response
to a call for political revolution against economic inequality by Bernie
Sanders, a Democratic Socialist who came of age in the turbulent 1960s.

2016 also began with an armed takeover of a federal wildlife refuge in Oregon by a small contingent of militant white ranchers who
sought to instigate a broader revolt against the United States government. The response of the FBI says a great deal about race relations
today. Back in 1993, federal agents engaged in a deadly gun battle with
white religious cult members in Waco, Texas, when the agents were
denied access to a private compound to search for a stockpile of illegal
weapons. A 51-day siege ended in the fiery deaths of 76 more people,
including women and children inside the Branch Davidian compound,
amid widespread public criticism of the Department of Justice's handling of the confrontation.

On the second anniversary of the Waco siege, white army veteran
Timothy McVeigh and co-conspirators took revenge through the devastating bombing of the Oklahoma City federal building — the dead-
liest act of domestic terrorism our nation has ever experienced. The
explosion killed 168 people, injured many more and caused extensive
damage to hundreds of nearby structures. The unprecedented bombing at first sparked fears across the country that it was the act of Arab

terrorists. The FBI embarked on a nationwide manhunt, and after collecting tons of documentary evidence and conducting 28,000 interviews, found the death and destruction to be the work of homegrown bombers. They arrested McVeigh and Terry McNichols, another member of the same rightwing survivalist group; a third man turned state's evidence for a reduced sentence. University of Missouri constitutional law professor Douglas Linder maintains a website dedicated to famous American trials. He is among experts who assert that the closure of the Oklahoma Bombing case left many questions unanswered, including why the government failed to prosecute anyone else "despite considerable evidence linking various militant white supremacists to the tragedy."[1] Indeed, white supremacists celebrate McVeigh as a martyr to the cause of a rightwing overthrow of the federal government.[2]

The Southern Poverty Law Center (SPLC) tracks domestic terrorism. It has noted a sharp rise in terrorist incidents since Barack Obama became President. In 2009, the heads of the FBI and the Department of Homeland Security told Congress they considered homegrown terrorists as much of a threat as foreign terrorists. By the end of 2015, the monitoring of hate-mongering internet networks by the SPLC revealed a significant uptick — its annual Spring Intelligence Report characterized 2015 as "a year awash in deadly extremist violence and hateful rhetoric from mainstream politicians."[3]

In January 2016, federal agents took a careful and measured approach to the Oregon armed takeover of public land. Unlike the siege at Waco, the Oregon siege ended after 41 days with only one death and the surrender of the other white militants, who then faced criminal charges. What repercussions would there have been if the Oregon takeover of public lands had instead been perpetrated by a small band of Arab jihadists or by black militants? Journalists immediately speculated that racism played a major role in political reaction to the Oregon standoff.[4] Many Americans would never have expected, or tolerated, a similar restrained FBI response if the militants were not white.[5] Reaching back half a century to compare the illegal armed seizure of public lands in Oregon to an infamous Black Panther protest in Sacramento in 1967, one commentator wrote:

> [Unlike] what's happening in Oregon right now, [the Black
> Panthers] entered the state Capitol lawfully, lodged their com-
> plaints against a piece of racially motivated legislation and then left
> without incident. But for those who see racial double standards at
> play in Oregon, the scope and severity of the 1967 response — the
> way the Panthers' demonstration brought about panicked head-
> lines, a prolonged FBI sabotage effort and support for gun control
> from the NRA, of all groups — will serve as confirmation that race
> shapes the way the country reacts to protest.[6]

Young people today may find it hard to believe that the nation
was in fact more polarized over race in the 1960s than it is now. What
has changed in race relations since that tumultuous era? What hasn't?
Consider the radically differing reactions to the 1968 Mexico City
Olympics and the 2016 Super Bowl halftime show. In October 1968
African-American Olympic track medalists Tommie Smith and John
Carlos shocked observers around the globe with an emphatic civil
rights gesture during their awards ceremony — each raising a black-
gloved fist in a classic "Power to the People" salute. They were promptly
banned from the Olympics for life.[7]

In 2016, during halftime at Super Bowl 50, more than 110 million viewers witnessed megastar Beyoncé's dance troupe perform a
similar raised-fist tribute to the Black Panthers, whose own fiftieth anniversary year coincided with that of the Super Bowl. Just a day earlier
Beyoncé released a new video, "Formation," which paid homage to the
Black Lives Matter movement. Beyoncé's polarizing halftime message
triggered a barrage of negative tweets and blogs as well as calls from
conservative politicians, talk show hosts and police to boycott her per-
formances, all of them unlikely to diminish the entertainer's enormous
fan base.[8]

The Super Bowl incident is just one illustration of hot-button race
issues that have recently dominated the airwaves. In the last few years
— unlike prior eras in American history — deaths of unarmed blacks at
the hands of police have garnered as much news coverage as killings of
officers. Technology advances are the primary reason race issues today
take place in a particularly volatile context: the near-constant presence

of smart phone cameras has turned millions of Americans into potential on-the-spot documentarians.

In 2013 director Ryan Coogler made the acclaimed film *Fruitvale Station* about the last 24 hours of the life of Oscar Grant III, which ended violently on New Year's Day 2009. Cell phone videos captured a white Bay Area Rapid Transit (BART) police officer shooting Grant while he was handcuffed and lying face down on the platform of an Oakland BART station. Like the onlooker's video seventeen years before of Los Angeles police viciously clubbing black cab driver Rodney King after King was stopped for speeding, the clip of officer Johannes Mehserle killing Grant was replayed over and over to a shocked public. The outraged reaction to Grant's death was immediate. Although the rioting and looting in downtown Oakland never came close to the scale and impact of the devastation following the acquittal of white policemen who had thrashed Rodney King, vandals in 2010 caused extensive damage to hundreds of Oakland businesses and parked cars. Black Panther co-founder Bobby Seale, then in his early seventies, was among those who spoke out to restrain the senseless violence.

Mehserle claimed he only meant to use his Taser, but the Alameda County District Attorney concluded that Mehserle's behavior was reckless and charged him with murder — making him the first California law enforcement officer to face such accusations in decades. Mehserle's lawyer won a change of venue to Los Angeles after an opinion poll showed a sharp racial divide between whites and blacks in Alameda County over the presumption of Mehserle's guilt and the likelihood of violence if he were to be acquitted. In 2010, a Southern California jury with no black members convicted Mehserle only of involuntary manslaughter; he served less than two years for that crime.

On March 21, 2009, Oakland again made grim national headlines when two policemen stopped an ex-felon in broad daylight for a routine traffic violation in a crime-ridden section of East Oakland's flatlands. Lovelle Mixon was armed with a semi-automatic hand gun and an AK-47. Desperate to avoid returning to prison for parole violations, the 26-year-old Mixon opened fire on the surprised motorcycle cops and fled the scene. Cornered soon afterward, Mixon killed two members of a SWAT (Special Weapons and Tactics) team before being gunned down himself. It set a chilling record — the worst single day of police fatalities in the violence-plagued city's history, adding an ironic and bitter coda to a year in which the number of police officers killed nationwide by gunfire in the line of duty had reached a fifty-year low.[9]

President Obama sent his and his wife Michelle's somber thoughts and prayers to the policemen's families and the community, expressing the nation's gratitude "for the men and women in law enforcement who . . . risk their lives each day on our behalf" and condemning "the senseless violence that claimed so many of them."[10] Three days after the shootings, Oakland's then mayor, former Congressman Ron Dellums, expressed the city's grief at an evening vigil. Many police officers still despised Dellums for identifying with the Panthers as a young Berkeley politician in the '60s and early '70s when the Panthers were at war with the police. In that earlier time, in February 1968, Dellums had stood on the Oakland Auditorium stage in solidarity with revolutionary black leaders who pledged vengeance if Huey Newton were executed for killing Oakland Police Officer John Frey.

In 2009, a much more somber and reflective Mayor Dellums expressed the city's "shock and sadness" at officers who paid the ultimate price in service to community: "We come to thank them. We come here to mourn them. We come here to embrace them as community."[11] In the view of law enforcement, Officer Frey's death was in the same category as the four officers killed in 2009 — men who heroically gave their lives for public protection. The names of the four officers killed by Mixon and their date of death have since been chiseled into the memorial at Oakland Police headquarters where John Frey's name also appears among other Oakland officers killed in the line of duty since the city's founding. Every year local officials join members of the department and surviving family of the officers in a formal ceremony to honor their sacrifice.

Such tributes to fallen officers reflect enormous societal appreciation for their dedication to public protection, as we saw again with the outpouring of support for the five Dallas officers murdered on July 7, 2016, and their wounded colleagues — the most casualties for law enforcement in a single incident since September 11, 2001. Before he died, sniper Micah Johnson claimed he targeted policemen on duty at the Dallas protest in retaliation for deaths elsewhere of black arrestees.

The shooting death of Michael Brown in Ferguson, Missouri, in August 2014 triggered renewed attention to allegations of abusive police conduct, intensified by more recent deaths of unarmed arrestees elsewhere across country. Months later a passerby's cell phone in North Charleston, South Carolina, shocked Americans with footage of a policeman shooting African-American Walter Scott in the back as Scott started to run away following a routine traffic stop. The officer has been charged with murder. That same month in Baltimore, a cell phone caught police handcuffing Freddie Gray. When the 25-year-old African-American died of injuries after bouncing around the back of the police van en route to being booked, the incident sparked the worst riots in that city in almost five decades.

Unlike the police force in Ferguson, the officers in Baltimore were racially diverse and operated under a black police chief and mayor. The dysfunction in Baltimore has been traced all the way back to riots in 1967 and 1968 from which the impoverished city never recovered.[12] Baltimore still lacks resources for sufficient beat cops and suffers from high crime, drug addiction, joblessness, underfunded schools and urban blight. While Baltimore quickly replaced its police chief and undertook a new approach to police training, the Ferguson city council only agreed to sweeping reforms proposed by the Department of Justice when threatened with a civil rights suit in federal court. Federal District Judge Catherine Perry approved the Ferguson settlement "in everyone's best interest and . . . in the interest of justice." The mayor of Ferguson promised swift progress under the agreement as "an important step in bringing this community together and moving us forward."[13] The settlement agreement requires police officers to undergo diversity training, to track arrest records and use of force, to wear body cams and to be monitored for compliance on an ongoing basis. In other cities across the country, accusations of racist policing are also moving from protests in the streets to resolution in court.

Ultimately, the Department of Justice reinvestigation of Michael

Brown's death agreed with the Ferguson Grand Jury's decision not to indict the officer who killed him. All charges against the six Baltimore peace officers who faced prosecution for Freddie Gray's death were also dismissed, but the mayor requested a Justice Department review that resulted in a highly critical report documenting systemic racism. Major reforms have been promised. Investigations into several other highly publicized incidents are ongoing. Inflammatory clips widely circulated at the outset may or may not reflect the whole picture that emerges on thorough investigation.

How will this play out? Chance footage filmed by passersby feeds suspicion that widespread mistreatment of minority suspects would be revealed if only there were more transparency. Unlike officers' deaths, fatalities caused by the police have not systematically been tracked over the years. Going forward, that is already beginning to change. As we consider proposed solutions to the current divide between police and minority communities, what can we learn from how media-savvy activists drew an international audience to a murder trial that turned the tables and put the American justice system itself on trial nearly a half century ago? And how did it all start?

* * * * *

West Oakland was a tinderbox long before the Black Panther Party came into being — a ghetto suffering from two decades of high unemployment, overcrowded housing and heavy-handed policing. The black community considered patrolmen an occupying army. In their view, whenever a crime was committed, the police seemed too eager to blame it on a black man. Although "shoot to kill" was not official policy of the Oakland Police Department ("OPD"), in practice patrolmen could kill fleeing burglary suspects with impunity. Black and other minority residents feared officers imposing their own death penalty on the streets with no trial, no judge and no jury. Even in the courts a "jury of one's peers" for black defendants still too often resembled the *12 Angry* [white] *Men* in the 1957 classic Henry Fonda film.

By the late 1960s, the Vietnam War had created yet another societal fault line in America, splitting the country between war hawks and doves. The division fell largely along generational lines, with college students among the most vociferous opponents of the war. Eighteen-year-olds could be drafted and killed in war, but could not vote. "Never trust any-one over 30" became a popular slogan. The tense political situation in Oakland mirrored the nation as a whole. Older white men maintained a lock on the power structure, including the courts. The established press remained almost exclusively white male. Black and Latino youths disproportionately faced shipment overseas for an unpopular war from which they might easily come home disabled or in coffins.

In the midst of increasing unrest, in October 1966 Huey Newton and Bobby Seale launched the Black Panther Party for Self-Defense with a 10-point program that included demands for decent jobs, edu-cation and housing, exemption from the draft, trial for those accused of crimes by a jury of true peers, and an end to police brutality. Huey Newton welcomed to the Panther Party other street toughs who, like him, had criminal records and a reckless streak. Despite sympathy among liberals for many of the Panthers' demands, the Panthers' hos-tile rhetoric and ostentatious display of guns alienated and threatened far more Americans than they attracted to their cause. Older residents of Oakland's flatlands found the Panthers too confrontational. The Panthers scared them with their open display of weapons. Even sympa-thizers worried the Panthers would precipitate nothing but their own deaths at the hands of the police. Yet many young blacks welcomed the brashness of the Panther Party and wholeheartedly embraced its call for armed self-defense.

In August 1965 devastating riots had raged for days in the Watts area of Los Angeles. In their aftermath, the anxious Johnson administration sent experts from Washington to tour ghettos across the country. They concluded that Oakland was "one of the most likely to be the next Watts."[14] "Some believe[d] . . . any incident [could] spark an explosion."[15] Oakland surprised observers by remaining quiet during the long, hot summer of 1967, even while race riots erupted in Detroit, Newark and other cities across the country. Following those riots, FBI Chief J. Edgar Hoover ordered agents in his Counter Intelligence Program (COINTELPRO) to step up operations against black nationalist "hate groups."

COINTELPRO was a top-secret coalition put in place in 1956 dur-ing the Cold War and officially disbanded in 1971 when exposure of its unconstitutional, Gestapo-like tactics appeared imminent. It used against Hoover's domestic targets, no-holds-barred techniques that had originally been developed for wartime use against foreign enemies. The FBI director first used COINTELPRO to disrupt and neutralize suspected American Communists. In the 1960s, Hoover employed COINTELPRO with similar zeal to go after other targets labeled subversive, including the New Left and broadly defined "black hate groups." The shocking details later came to light through a 1970s Senate investigation — illegal wiretaps, agents provocateurs, blackmail, physical coercion of informants, and smear campaigns through FBI-friendly media. It also included murder plots and suicides goaded by threats of exposure of defamatory private information.[16]

Hoover did not consider anyone he labeled "subversive" to have constitutional rights deserving respect. In fact, he kept secret dossiers on politicians and celebrities of all stripes in case he felt the need to destroy their careers, too. In the mid-1960s, Malcolm X and the Nation of Islam were targets, as were Dr. Martin Luther King, Jr., and the Student Nonviolent Coordinating Committee (SNCC) formed as an offshoot of Dr. King's Southern Christian Leadership Council.[17] Equal rights for blacks threatened the status quo; Hoover spread word though sympathetic newspaper, radio and television reporters that these were all Communist fronts. Communists had, indeed, lent their support to civil rights movements for decades because they saw racism as America's Achilles' heel; but very few of Hoover's targets in the civil rights movement fit that description.

By the early 1960s, civil rights champions focused on suppression of voting rights in the South as a major rallying cry; it was SNCC leader Stokely Carmichael who first used the black panther logo for an Alabama voting rights group he headed. In June 1966, Carmichael sent shock waves across country when he publicly split with Dr. King and disavowed civil disobedience in favor of championing "black power." In her book *Imprisoned in a Luminous Glare: Photography and the African-American Freedom Struggle,* U.C. Berkeley African-American Studies Associate Professor Leigh Raiford notes that inner city militants quickly adopted "black power" as "both a rallying cry and a declaration of war."[18] Allying themselves with the growing anti-war movement sweeping across college campuses, they linked racism at home with allegations of a racist foreign policy exemplified by the war in Vietnam.

In the summer of 1967, Oakland's Black Panther Party had only just begun to attract Hoover's attention as an upstart organization. The FBI was then still primarily focused on Dr. Martin Luther King and SNCC leaders like Carmichael and H. Rap Brown. Brown faced federal prosecution for inciting a Baltimore crowd to riot that July by announcing: "If America don't come around, we're gonna burn it down."[19] Rioters then set fire to local stores and began a looting rampage. Unrepentant following his arrest, Brown electrified the press by announcing that America was "on the eve of a black revolution."[20] From his parents' living room in Oakland, Huey Newton observed television coverage of police brutally responding to rioters. Newton saw "spontaneous rebellions" by frustrated and angry youths "throwing rocks, sticks, empty wine bottles and beer cans at racist cops" as futile acts of desperation bound to result in "terrible casualties." He published an essay in a newly-launched Black Panther Party newspaper in June 1967, arguing, "There is a world of difference between 30 million unarmed, submissive black people and 30 million black people armed with freedom and defense guns and the strategic methods of liberation."[21] At the time, the paper had barely begun to circulate locally.

It was in May of that year that the tiny new Black Panther Party for Self-Defense shocked the world by making an armed debut at the California State Capitol, protesting a proposed law to prohibit most citizens from carrying loaded weapons within city limits anywhere in the state. In early August 1967 the *New York Times* magazine profiled Oaklander Huey Newton as an alarming new radical leader who promoted violence against the establishment, including the execution of policemen as an act of preemptive self-defense.[22]

The response among many in power to both the escalating protests against the war and more urgent demands for civil rights was to become increasingly heavy-handed in attempts to crush them. In reaction, more mainstream supporters emerged in support of the constitutional rights of those the government sought to suppress and for policy changes to address the underlying issues that fueled the dissidents' anger. Amid the heightened tension in cities across the country following the summer riots of 1967, it was all but inevitable that a spark would trigger another major clash over police brutality. The 1965 Watts riots had themselves started when angry onlookers erupted at the sight of a single, commonplace incident — a white policeman pulling over yet another black driver and impounding his car.

Less than three months after the profile of Huey Newton ran in *The New York Times* came headlines of an early morning shootout in West Oakland in which patrolman John Frey died and Newton and another police officer were severely wounded. Frey was the first officer killed by gunfire in Oakland in two decades. Were the Panthers signaling to inner city blacks across the country that the time had come for armed revolt? Sensing a great propaganda opportunity, the American Communist Party quickly offered to raise funds for Newton's defense. A public relations battle soon followed, with the establishment press on one side and the underground press on the other, over who was the victim and who the aggressor, while the Panthers exploited the publicity to gain support for their revolutionary agenda.

Pioneering black media professionals like San Francisco TV reporter Belva Davis and print journalist Gilbert Moore, who covered the trial for *LIFE* magazine, found themselves caught uncomfortably in the middle. The Panthers' 10-point program resonated with them even though they both disagreed with the Panthers' extremism and glorification of violence. The Panthers soon began to attract wealthy leftist celebrities like Marlon Brando, Jane Fonda and Leonard Bernstein — among the elite later ridiculed by author Tom Wolfe as indulging in "radical chic" by embracing the Panthers' cause. The implication was that these celebrities were naïve and silly, considering it trendy to dabble with extremists they knew little about. On the other side of the political spectrum, 1968 presidential candidate Richard Nixon focused on black militants as the target of his "Law and Order" campaign, vying with Independent segregationist George Wallace for the support of fearful white voters. The 1968 "Law and Order" campaign marked the start of the Republican Party's famous "Southern Strategy" which has been the GOP's electoral mainstay ever since.

Tension surrounding the upcoming Newton trial escalated after Dr. Martin Luther King's assassination in the first week of April 1968 prompted riots in cities across the country. President Johnson called out 60,000 National Guardsmen; the evening news reported that Mayor Richard Daley in Chicago ordered police to shoot to kill black rioters. A *Wall Street Journal* headline proclaimed that the nation was at a crossroads, with King's death threatening a "Lasting Rift in American Society." Its front page story noted that nonviolent efforts to bridge the racial gap were imperiled and asked: "Can America avoid two societies — one black, the other white, separated by a chasm of hate?"[23]

Just two days after King's death, a group of Panthers led by ex-felon Eldridge Cleaver ambushed two Oakland policemen. The armed confrontation ended with Cleaver and his young companion Bobby Hutton attempting to surrender unarmed. Hutton died in a barrage of gunfire that also caused extensive property damage in the neighborhood. The police said they mistakenly believed Hutton still held a weapon; the Panthers claimed the police murdered the young Panther in revenge for Officer Frey's death. The black community reacted with outrage at the police and City Hall; the press backed the angry mayor's call for stronger police action, polarizing black and white Oaklanders even more.

Could Huey Newton get a fair trial for the death of Officer Frey under these circumstances? With a traditional white male "jury of one's peers," Panther supporters assumed the answer was: "Hell, no!" Nearly everyone believed Newton was headed for the gas chamber. The trial judge rescheduled his death penalty trial for mid-June of 1968. Then, the week before the trial was set to begin, the nation again reeled with news of Senator Robert Kennedy's assassination while campaigning for President in Los Angeles. The judge postponed the Newton trial once again to July. All the while, growing opposition to the Vietnam War helped turn Newton into an anti-war icon and the Newton trial into a cause célèbre for radical groups and anti-war activists. What followed was a media frenzy amid high security never before seen at the Alameda County courthouse.

Reporter Belva Davis likened the Newton trial to a Hollywood film with perfectly cast top-notch lawyers. Each day one could expect a packed courtroom, many hundreds of demonstrators, and media from across the continent and beyond clamoring for press passes. Bay Area television and radio stations broadcast the highlights daily. National media and international papers followed the proceedings closely. *LIFE* magazine reporter Gilbert Moore experienced an epiphany while watching the prosecution and defense paint starkly different pictures of the confrontation that resulted in Officer Frey's death: "Conditioned by history, both sides blinded by myth and images, moved by rage and fear . . . each in their own blind way incapable of seeing each other as human beings . . . was a tragedy in the making."[24]

Hollywood could hardly have invented a more compelling movie script. A deeply politicized death penalty case with countercharges of racism against the police and prosecution witnesses makes for terrific theater, promising great division among spectators. Throw in the counsel on both sides receiving death threats and extraordinary precautions taken to safeguard the courtroom and the deliberating jury. Envision COINTELPRO wiretapping key Panthers and infiltrating their ranks with informers the whole time. Assume that hordes of police and National Guardsmen must be put on alert to quell anticipated riots. Picture the defendant as an emerging folk hero capturing the imagination not only of downtrodden members of his own race but athletes, singers and songwriters, liberal professionals, college students and anti-war activists, who have adopted him as a leftist icon. The 1968 trial of twenty-six-year-old Huey Newton was just such a screenwriter's dream.

In the extraordinarily volatile year of 1968 the message of black militant leaders — decrying police brutality and linking it to racism in general and the quagmire of the Vietnam War — resonated the most with those outside the establishment who got their news from the underground press. Here were the Panthers bragging that they were the vanguard of the revolution. The hordes of counterculture reporters who converged in Oakland to cover the trial served an audience of impoverished urban blacks, the Old and New Left, college students, and a growing coalition of war opponents. These were "the people" Newton was talking about when he proclaimed, "I have the people behind me, and the people are my strength."[25]

In mid-July 1968, when the proceedings began, one underground newspaper ran a blaring headline proclaiming "Nation's Life at Stake." The article explained:

> History has its pivotal points. This trial is one of them. America on Monday placed itself on trial [by prosecuting Huey Newton].... The Black Panthers are the most militant black organization in this nation. They are growing rapidly. They are not playing games. And they are but the visible part of a vast, black iceberg. The issue is not the alleged killing of an Oakland cop. The issue is racism. Racism can destroy America in swift flames. Oppression. Revolt. Suppression. Revolution. Determined black and brown and white men are watching what happens to Huey Newton. What they do depends on what the white man's courts do to Huey. Most who watch with the keenest interest are already convinced that he cannot get a fair trial.[26]

Nationally renowned trial lawyer James Brosnahan was then a local federal prosecutor: "This trial occurred at a time when Oakland was deeply divided and entrenched, and the white community controlled almost everything, certainly controlled the press, certainly controlled all of the facilities; the courts and all of that . . . It was reasonable to believe that he couldn't possibly get a fair trial. . . . Friction between the police department and the Black Panthers . . . had burst out in a number of different ways. All that created an atmosphere, a sort of cauldron of bias against Huey Newton." What happened when that sea of bias was roiled by a tidal wave of American youths already alienated by the ongoing Vietnam War?

Innocence Project Co-Director Barry Scheck was a freshman at Yale in 1967–68 who then counted himself among the fast-growing hordes of Panther fans. Scheck had been campaigning hard for Robert Kennedy for President that spring: "We thought we were going to change the world." Like millions of other Americans, Scheck found himself reeling from the twin shocks of Dr. King's assassination and Kennedy's just two months later. Looking back, Scheck asks: "How much more

destabilizing do you want a political situation to become? . . . Many of
us who had been involved in the presidential campaigns of McCarthy
and Kennedy began to feel like . . . we have to take direct action. We
have to go to the streets. We have to organize." By the summer of 1968:

> This trial is suddenly emerging to have enormous political signifi-
> cance in the country . . . You cannot understand the Huey Newton
> [trial] or the campaign against the Black Panther Party without
> really getting the feeling that the whole country was coming apart;
> that there really could be a revolution. . . certainly could be an
> insurrection of black militants . . . with weapons .. . in the streets
> of America. And so, many people took a look at the Black Panther
> Party and were terrified of it; others were inspired by it. . . . Who
> knew? If he was somehow acquitted of these charges [maybe] he
> would emerge from jail like some kind of militant Nelson Mandela.

Indeed, as demonstrators called the world's attention to Newton's
prosecution, observers of the trial got far more drama than they
expected. The two sides painted starkly different scenarios of what transpired — murder or self-defense? What seemed an open and shut case
to mainstream reporters quickly proved otherwise. The jury sat spellbound when Newton turned the packed courtroom into a lecture hall
on racism in America. They paid close attention when the defense produced several African-American men from West Oakland who attacked
Officer Frey's character by describing how abusive and racist he had
been when arresting them for minor offenses. The jury had a choice: to
accept prosecutor Lowell Jensen's methodical case against a cop-hating
revolutionary who gunned down a police officer making a routine traffic
arrest, or Garry's passionate closing argument comparing Frey's behavior to the Gestapo tactics of the Chicago police, just seen on television
bashing heads at the 1968 Democratic Presidential Convention.

The political defense that Newton and his leftist lawyers mounted
became the cornerstone of the Panther Party's recruiting efforts.
Newton's older brother Melvin Newton, now the retired Chair of Ethnic
Studies at Merritt College, witnessed that trial. He marveled as his
brother turned the tables and put America itself on trial for its history

of racism. At the time of Huey's arrest, the Panthers were few in number and most of them were in jail as a result of their bold Sacramento escapade. The Party even lacked an office. Melvin Newton believes to this day that, had it not been for Huey's widely-covered murder trial, the Black Panther Party would likely have disappeared within a year of its formation. Instead, it expanded rapidly, with branches popping up across country, prompting J. Edgar Hoover in September 1968 to declare the Panther Party the number one internal threat to national security — replacing the late Dr. King.

* * * * *

Since the escalation of the Vietnam War in 1965, the New Left Students for a Democratic Society (SDS) had played a central role in galvanizing national student revolt. SDS grew to over 100,000 members as it led successful efforts to greatly expand the "Stop the Draft" Movement. Sitting in his prison cell since the late fall of 1967, Newton became a heroic symbol of oppression not only to young blacks across country, but to white student activists in SDS and other anti-war organizations. Both the New Left and liberal college students alike admired the Panther Party's vehement opposition to the war and racist policies at home. "Free Huey" buttons and posters quickly spread from Bay Area protesters to hundreds of thousands of others across country then railing against the establishment. By the spring of 1969, student anti-war demonstrations had erupted at 300 college campuses amid thousands of protests nationwide.

In the summer of 1969, the most militant members of SDS split off, calling themselves the Weathermen. They incited unprecedented attempts to interfere with national commerce by acts of arson, explosions and violence reported almost daily in the media. J. Edgar Hoover focused COINTELPRO on dismantling the Weathermen and the increasingly fractious remaining SDS members. By the year's end, the Weathermen went into hiding to continue acts of guerilla warfare as the Weather Underground while SDS officially disbanded. In the meantime, with greater ferocity, the FBI was targeting the Panther

Party for extinction. By 1969, COINTELPRO agents had infiltrated the Party across country; they ratcheted up acts of sabotage against branch offices of the Party. At the FBI leader's direction, agents made sweeping arrests, and, in December of 1969, orchestrated an armed invasion of both the Party's Chicago and Los Angeles offices. Ostensibly, it was just Chicago police who killed Chicago Panther Party leader Fred Hampton in the predawn raid, but the highly suspicious circumstances raised alarms among both the conspiracy-minded Left and a growing number of mainstream Americans who considered respect for constitutional rights the hallmark of our democracy.

Then, in April 1970, national focus turned to the tens of thousands of demonstrators descending on New Haven, Connecticut, from across the country to protest Panther Party Chairman Bobby Seale's upcoming murder trial on charges his supporters believed to be politically motivated — just as his recent prosecution in Chicago for inciting riots at the 1968 Democratic Convention had been. Seale was the eighth co-defendant in the internationally-followed Chicago conspiracy trial prosecuted by the federal government to jail leaders of the growing anti-war effort. History buffs know it as the Chicago Seven trial because Judge Julius Hoffman had Seale bound and gagged for backtalk and ordered that Seale be tried separately from the seven other defendants. But first, Seale would be tried for allegedly ordering a murder while passing through New Haven on a speaking tour.

Yale had never seen such activism on campus as that in opposition to the upcoming Seale trial. The instigators were anti-war Youth International Party ("Yippie") leaders Abbie Hoffman and Jerry Rubin, joined by SDS leader Tom Hayden and other "Chicago Seven" defendants, whose own circus of a trial had just ended. In response to the Yippie-led pilgrimage to New Haven to protest the prosecution of Bobby Seale and New Haven Panther leader Ericka Huggins, President Nixon mobilized armed National Guardsmen from as far away as Virginia. J. Edgar Hoover sent agents provocateurs.

On April 15, 1970, police had confronted protesters and vandals at Harvard Square in Cambridge, resulting in extensive damage and hundreds of people injured. In an effort to defuse the situation in

New Haven to prevent a repeat of what happened at Harvard, Yale's President Kingman Brewster decided to shut down the Ivy League university for a week of voluntary teach-ins. Brewster then told the faculty, "I am appalled and ashamed that things should have come to such a pass in this country that I am skeptical of the ability of black revolutionaries to achieve a fair trial anywhere in the United States."[27] His remarks created a storm of controversy that instantly put the Mayflower Pilgrim descendant on President Nixon's growing "enemies list."

Although the approach at Yale won praise in some quarters as a model for incorporating the Panthers into peaceful college protests,[28] angry editorials from conservative papers throughout the nation called for Brewster's resignation for daring to voice skepticism of the American justice system. Articulating the opposite concern, Los Angeles Police Chief Ed Davis viewed the national situation in the same dire light as did J. Edgar Hoover. Testifying before a Senate committee, Davis asserted, "we have revolution on the installment plan . . . going on every day now."[29] But Brewster considered something far greater to be lost when Americans rationalized the abandonment of their core values as a society. He echoed Yale Law School Dean Eugene Rostow's reflections eight years earlier: "The quality of a civilization is largely determined by the fairness of its criminal trials. . . ."[30]

So, was Brewster's skepticism justified?

While under intense pressure from the media and polarized political factions, a trial judge, prosecutor and jury did their best to provide a fair trial to a black revolutionary in the summer of 1968. *People v. Newton* involved one of the most scorned revolutionaries of his day in an extremely volatile and bloody era. Was he guilty of murder as charged, or set up for a failed police ambush? By the late sixties, juries in mixed-race communities were ready to consider either possibility.

The objective of Newton's innovative defense team was to seat as many women and minorities on the jury as possible, recognizing they would likely be most open to his side of the story. The defense lawyers broke new ground in eliminating potential jurors for bias and wound up seating — *with the prosecutor's agreement* — seven women and five men, including four minorities. The defense tactics were captured in a handbook that soon became criminal defense lawyers' "Bible" for jury selection for minority defendants nationwide.[31]

What did that diverse Oakland jury do with the prosecution claim of a police officer martyred by an itchy-fingered black revolutionary? How did they respond to the defense argument that the early morning shootout was just one more example in a long history of racist police brutality? Why, with the extraordinarily high tension surrounding the trial, did no urban violence erupt in its wake, as had occurred so often in the prior year? And how did the jury's astonishing choice of African-American banker David Harper as their foreman influence the outcome of the deliberations? Harper was the first black foreman of a major criminal trial in America, a role that would still be unusual in a death penalty case today.

The Newton trial had all the ingredients to fit historian J. Anthony Lukas's definition of "THE" trial of the century: "a spectacular show trial, a great national drama in which the stakes [are] nothing less than the soul of the American people."[32] *LIFE* reporter Gilbert Moore soon quit his prestigious job to write a book about the newly discovered rage inside him from his childhood in Harlem that Newton and the Panthers had tapped into. The *Los Angeles Times* hailed Moore's insightful chronicle *A Special Rage* as "a classic document in the literature of the black-white experience in the 20th century."[33] Two decades years later it was reissued under the shortened title *Rage*, with a new foreword and afterword by award-winning author Ekwueme Michael Thelwell, then the University of Massachusetts' first Afro-American Studies chairman. Thelwell was himself once a leading SNCC activist. He found Moore's observations equally relevant to the next generation. The back cover blurb summarized why:

> The Panthers represented something new on the American political landscape. Lionized by the liberal cultural elite, spied on, shot at, and jailed by the police, they brought hope to some Americans and frightened many others. Revolutionaries, outlaws, pawns, they were a cultural bridge between urban street gangs and organized civil rights groups. They filled a dangerous void. They were the militant, articulate expression of the anger and aspirations of poor

young black men. That critical void exists as much today as it did
in the late 1960s.[34]

Another 25 years later the Panthers' mark on American history
remains indelible. As historian Jane Rhodes observed in her 2007
book, *Framing the Black Panthers: The Spectacular Rise of a Black Power Icon:*
"The passage of time has not eroded the strength of their symbols and
rhetoric — the gun, the snarling panther, the raised fists, and slogans
such as 'All power to the people' and 'Off the pig.' Today, representa-
tions of the Black Panthers linger in diverse arenas of commodity culture, from news stories to reality television to feature films and hip-hop,
as they function as America's dominant icons of Black Nationalism."[35]
Nine years later, interest in the Panthers is far more widespread than
when Professor Rhodes published her book. In 2014 the high-energy
musical *Party People* began playing to sold-out audiences in theaters
across America. With "REVOLUTION" in blazing lights as the backdrop, it engaged new generations with the fierce activism of both the
Black Panthers and the contemporaneous Puerto Rican Young Lords
Party in New York.[36]

Over the intervening decades, the ground-breaking accomplishments of Newton's sensational 1968 death penalty trial fell into relative
oblivion. Its absence from the pivotal 20th century cases listed by most
journalists and historians prompted me to publish, in 2012, *The Sky's the
Limit: People v. Newton, The REAL Trial of the 20th Century?* That book compared the extraordinary nature and enormous stakes of the Newton trial
to the significant features of other headline trials from 1901 to 2000. I
also addressed why I believe it nevertheless slipped from general public
consciousness and wound up all but forgotten by most experts analyzing
candidates for "the" trial of the American 20th century.[37]

Huey's brother Melvin has a short answer: "Huey was a threat. . . .
His actions were so raw and so challenging . . . his desire to be an agent
for social change. . . . Dr. King wasn't honored when he was alive and
even when Dr. King was looked to as a model [it was] . . . because there
were more threatening models out there . . . Huey is someone that
proper authorities would like to forget. . . ."

It is gratifying that, after reading my 2012 book, more legal experts now agree that the 1968 Newton trial truly deserves to be considered one of the most pivotal trials of the 20th century. Certainly, its focus on entrenched racism in the justice system resonates today. Activists still question whether — absent video proof — juries will believe a black arrestee charging a police officer of abuse, let alone whether a black militant accused of killing a police officer can get a fair trial anywhere in America.

As we approach the 50th anniversary of the founding of the Black Panther Party, we are once again in a polarized setting. In the past year, civil rights enthusiasts in cities across the country flocked to see Stanley Nelson's film *The Black Panthers: Vanguard of the Revolution*. A million more saw it on public television. (I had a cameo appearance in that film as an expert on the Newton trial.) Nelson likens the Party's mixed legacy to the parable of the blind men and the elephant — each man describing only one feature of a complex animal.

Among other Panther-related movies in the works is a more narrowly focused documentary project for which I am on the film-making team; the project is called *American Justice on Trial: People v. Newton.* www.americanjusticeontrial.com. Since July 2013, award-winning film director Bob Richter and I have interviewed surviving participants and observers of the 1968 Newton death penalty trial, who offer new insights on that ground-breaking trial from every perspective: from the Panthers to journalists to witnesses, the prosecution, the police and interested bystanders. This new volume incorporates quotes from these interviewees, some of whom had never been interviewed about the trial before. I have focused here solely on the trial itself, no longer including numerous comparisons to other "trials of the century" from 1901 to 2000 as I felt compelled to do in the 2012 book. Current events have illuminated the Newton trial's true historic significance.

In May of 2015, *TIME* magazine featured on its cover heavily-armed Baltimore police chasing a black suspect. Its editors asked America to consider what has changed and what hasn't since 1968.[38] President Obama recently readdressed that same issue. I invite you to read this volume and consider that question yourself.

1. FREE HUEY NOW!

Pushed into the corner
Of the hobnailed boot,
Pushed into the corner of the
"I-don't-want-to-die" cry,
Pushed into the corner of
"I don't want to study war no more,"
Changed into "Eye for eye,"
The Panther in his desperate boldness
Wears no disguise,
Motivated by the truest
Of the oldest
Lies.

— LANGSTON HUGHES, "BLACK PANTHER"

A newspaper photographer wormed his way past police guards into the Kaiser Hospital emergency room and snapped a quick photo before being ejected. That afternoon's front page displayed black militant Huey Newton lying bare-chested, a bullet wound in his abdomen, his hands shackled to a hospital gurney. A nurse stood in the background. The original photo showed another figure before it was cropped for publication. In front of Newton stood one of his police guards, dazed by the unexpected click of a camera. On the morning of October 28, 1967, Oakland police had put out an all-points bulletin for Huey Newton following a pre-dawn shootout in West Oakland's red light district. As co-founder of the Black Panther Party, Newton was already well known to local law enforcement,

infuriating them with his official title, Minister of Defense. Police immediately suspected Newton of killing Officer John Frey and wounding
Officer Herbert "Cliff" Heanes, who now lay hospitalized in critical
condition with gunshot wounds in the chest, knee and one arm. Police
headquarters released pictures of the young policemen to the press and
mentioned that both were fathers: Frey had a three-year-old daughter;
Heanes had a two-year-old and ten-month old.

The police stormed Newton's parents' home in Oakland looking for
Huey to no avail before they got word the Panther leader was at Kaiser
Hospital. Shortly before dawn, Newton had staggered into the emergency room with a bloody rag clutched to his stomach. The middle-aged
blond nurse on duty, Corinne Leonard, heard a car door slam and the
car drive off, but did not see who deposited Newton outside. The police
later thought that it might have been Newton's girlfriend. They knew
that a young black woman later stopped by the hospital, but left before
she could be questioned.

The police had confiscated the tawny 1958 Volkswagen sedan registered to LaVerne Williams that Newton was driving early that morning
on Seventh Street when Officer Frey pulled him over. At first, the police
assumed LaVerne was the male passenger who had accompanied Huey
in the car and fled the scene with him soon after the shooting. The next
day, Oakland attorney John George told the police that he represented
aspiring singer LaVerne Williams, Newton's 22-year-old girlfriend, who
worked at an office of the newly-established Job Corps. LaVerne acknowledged she was the young woman who had visited Newton in the hospital,
but had only learned of his whereabouts from an anonymous phone call.

Newton's passenger still remained a mystery. At the hospital,
Newton quickly created a stir by shouting for prompt medical care
while refusing to sign hospital forms. Although he was in agony from
the bullet wound, Newton had mustered the energy to withdraw some
notes from his wallet, tear them to pieces and throw them in the trash.
It had not been his idea to go to the hospital. He had wanted to die
among his close friends in the neighborhood. Though the bullet in
his abdomen had not hit any large blood vessels, it had punctured
his intestine. Nurse Leonard did not realize that peritonitis would kill

Newton if the doctors did not operate on him immediately. The small size of the wound caused her to underestimate the seriousness of his condition. Frightened by Newton's belligerence, she called the police before she summoned a doctor.

The police arrived at the hospital emergency room less than half an hour from the nurse's call, shortly after the doctor arrived and had Newton placed on a gurney. Newton screamed in pain and spat blood as the officer slapped handcuffs on his wrists, shackled him to the gurney and recited his *Miranda* rights. Newton was still shouting obscenities at the police as the doctor wheeled him off to surgery, while barking at Newton to shut up. Listed in fair condition following surgery, Newton was transferred to Highland Hospital and placed under 24-hour guard by six policemen armed with shotguns.

Meanwhile, after the startling police invasion of his home, Huey's father, Walter Newton, got dressed and headed over to his son Melvin's apartment in North Oakland. That insistent early morning knock on his door was something Melvin would never forget. Melvin found the news shocking, but not a surprise. Huey had been involved in armed confrontations with police before. By then, Walter Newton knew that Huey was headed into surgery at Kaiser Hospital following a shoot-out with two policemen at Seventh and Willow streets. Since it was a Saturday when Walter roused Melvin, Melvin did not need to head to his job supervising Alameda County social workers. He immediately got dressed and went down to the scene of the shooting, not sure what he expected to find. Melvin walked through the area, but found nothing. He soon learned of Huey's transfer to Highland Hospital. Melvin and his father visited Huey in a recovery room there — awake and complaining that police had shaken his bed and threatened his life.

Panther recruiter Earl Anthony was listening to soul music on the radio before dawn on the 28th when the announcer interrupted with a bulletin about the shootout. Anthony's assumption was that the "lousy Oakland police . . . had tried to set up brother Huey."[1] Anthony had accompanied Newton on the evening of October 26, two nights before the deadly incident. They started off at the Cleavers' apartment where Newton made a comment Anthony would never forget. They were talking about a passage from the book *Look Homeward, Angel* in which author Thomas Wolfe wrote about crossing a river and not being able to return. That struck Huey as similar to dedicating yourself to fight for black liberation and never being able to accept inferior status again.[2] The two left the Cleavers to go see writer James Baldwin, who was then in town, and provide him with several copies of the *Black Panther* paper. They ended up bar-hopping in Oakland before Newton drove him back to San Francisco. Anthony would not see Newton on the streets again for more than a decade.

Emory Douglas had often traveled around with Huey Newton and David Hilliard over the preceding three weeks, organizing support for the Panthers at bars and social events. At the time, Douglas was not yet devoted full-time to the Party. On the night of October 27, 1967, both he and David Hilliard begged off. Douglas had already agreed to monitor a dance. Hilliard had set up a late-night poker game fund-raiser for Party Chairman Bobby Seale's bail to gain Seale's release from jail after serving his sentence for the minor charges resulting from the Panthers' armed trip to Sacramento in May. Newton got another good friend to accompany him instead. The next morning Douglas woke up to a predawn call from Hilliard; Newton had been shot and a policeman was dead. Douglas was stunned. He hoped Newton would hang on, but also realized the bleak prospect that would attend his survival. Newton would face murder charges and likely execution. Emory Douglas also had to know how close he came to winding up in the same predicament.

Panther recruit Janice Garrett first heard about Newton's shootout on her car radio crossing the Bay Bridge to San Francisco from Oakland with her roommates. "We were in shock. . . . We went right to our apartment. We didn't know how extensive his wounds were . . . couldn't get any information. Everything was very chaotic and we were very scared at the time because we didn't know what the police were going to do." They soon found out that Huey was in the hospital with a stomach wound, but had survived the attack. By then, they also knew that one of the policemen was dead and another wounded. For Garrett, it was "very, very upsetting to see him [in the newspaper photo] in that position handcuffed to the bed because we knew he had to be in excruciating pain." As foot soldiers for the Party, they knew "we had to get busy and contact other Party members so that we could find out what the next strategy was, how are we going to get help for Huey." The answer from David Hilliard and Eldridge Cleaver was to get their side of the story out in the *Black Panther* newspaper as soon as possible — that Newton had been set upon by the police — and remind their readers what the Black Panther Party stood for.

Eldridge Cleaver had secretly joined the Black Panthers in the spring of 1967 as its Minister of Information, while pretending to cover the group solely as a reporter for *Ramparts*. At the time, Cleaver could not publicly admit his membership because he was still on parole and prohibited from associating with "undesirables" like the Panthers. In the early predawn after the October 28 shootout, Cleaver took the risk of declaring himself the acting head of the Black Panther Party. Bobby Seale, co-founder of the Party, was still behind bars at the Santa Rita County Jail. By October's end when Newton was arrested, the fledgling group was in near total disarray, lacking even a headquarters.

San Francisco Lawyers Guild member Beverly Axelrod, a former white volunteer for the Congress of Racial Equality (CORE), was then Eldridge Cleaver's fiancée and the first person he called for legal help. Eleven years his senior, the intense brunette from Brooklyn was a divorced mother of two teen-aged sons. She had made civil rights and social justice her life's passion. A brilliant and gritty lawyer, she risked jail to register black voters for CORE in Louisiana in 1963. After she returned to San Francisco, she became the lead defense attorney in a lengthy 1964 criminal trial of protesters arrested for picketing employment discrimination by San Francisco's Auto Row and Sheraton Palace Hotel.

Axelrod met Cleaver when he was still at Folsom Prison reaching out for legal assistance to win parole. While incarcerated, Cleaver had taught himself to read political books critically and to write on social issues. Influenced by the work of Malcolm X, Cleaver got the idea of marketing his own autobiographical essays from the publishing success of convicted rapist and long-time death row resident Caryl Chessman. Chessman was known as the Los Angeles "Red Light Bandit" for kidnapping at gunpoint couples stopped at traffic lights. Chessman became a

cause célèbre for death penalty opponents during the dozen years he
spent on death row, publishing four best sellers during the time before
his execution in 1960.

Cleaver systematically wrote to lawyers listed in a professional direc-
tory offering the prospect of future royalties from the marketing of his
own manuscript as legal fees for anyone who helped him to gain his
freedom. Axelrod responded enthusiastically. She arranged to have
parts of Cleaver's manuscript and letters he had written to her critiqued
by Pulitzer Prize–winning author Norman Mailer and then published in
Ramparts magazine, a leftist literary periodical based in San Francisco.

Axelrod engineered Cleaver's release from Folsom in December
1966. By then the confessed serial rapist had served nine years behind
bars. Cleaver's political essays gained him a national following and a
job offer as a full-time staff writer for *Ramparts.* In the spring of 1967,
Ramparts republished the essays as a book, *Soul On Ice,* which Cleaver
dedicated to Beverly "with whom I share the ultimate of love." Because of
her relationship with Cleaver, Huey Newton had come to trust Axelrod as
a close friend. She hosted many Panther gatherings at her San Francisco
home. Newton posed in the wicker chair in Axelrod's living room for the
now-iconic photo used to adorn the new, ten-cent newsletter the Black
Panthers began publishing in the spring of 1967.

When Cleaver contacted Axelrod with news of Newton's arrest
early on the morning of October 28, Axelrod knew there was no time
to waste. She called her friend Charles Garry, a prominent leftist lawyer
in his late fifties who specialized in defending murder cases. Axelrod
had previously collaborated with Garry on Lawyers Guild cases. Both
lawyers had long been on the FBI's list of subversives. Coincidentally,
Garry's friend Dr. Carlton Goodlett, publisher of the African-American
newspaper *The San Francisco Sun Reporter,* happened to be hosting that
same week legendary black civil rights activist William Patterson. When
Patterson heard of the shooting incident, he immediately asked to
meet Huey Newton's family.

Patterson was president of the American Communist Party and
already had close ties to East Bay civil rights lawyer Bob Treuhaft and
his wife Decca Mitford. Both were stalwarts of the "Old Left" — activists

for social change in the 1930s and 1940s who also included rough-edged trial lawyer Charles "Charlie" Garry and his scholarly law partner Barney Dreyfus. At 76, Patterson was nearly a generation older than most of his Bay Area leftist colleagues; what was left of his receding hair had turned white. They had all met through Bay Area Communist Party educational programs in the '40s. Since then, the Oakland firm of Treuhaft & Edises and the San Francisco firm of Garry, Dreyfus & McTernan had become the only two prominent white law firms in the Bay Area that represented black working class clientele. Patterson wanted to offer Huey Newton help from the American Communist Party. He had not seen a politically-charged case with such enormous potential for almost two decades. As a young lawyer he worked for International Labor Defense (ILD), the legal arm of the Communist Party, which placed Patterson on the appellate defense team for some of the most famous political prosecutions of the 20th century.

Patterson's first opportunity involved the widely-publicized appeals in the mid-1920s following the death sentences of anarchist immigrants Nicola Sacco and Bartolomeo Vanzetti on charges they participated in a bold 1920 payroll robbery-murder in the Boston suburb of South Braintree, Massachusetts. Upper-class judge Webster Thayer had both men caged during the trial. They were tried before a hand-picked jury that excluded any Italian-Americans, the most disfavored minority group in the area at that time. The judge openly ridiculed the defendants' radical political views. The evidence of guilt was hotly-contested: the prosecution put on a number of eyewitnesses; the defense countered with numerous alibi witnesses. At the end, Judge Thayer instructed the jury to do its patriotic duty — indicating the pair deserved execution simply for dodging the draft during World War I, which had nothing to do with the charges against them.

Years of appeals followed, most of which came for hearing before the same biased judge. Hundreds of demonstrators came to the prison to protest their execution; Patterson was among more than 150 whom the police arrested. Sacco and Vanzetti were viewed in many countries as martyrs of the working class; their deaths triggered attacks on American embassies and other violent anti-American incidents around the globe. The heavy-handed behavior of the prosecutor and judge toward these two dissidents acquired its own derogatory name — "Thayerism." It severely damaged the reputation of the United States' justice system for many years to come. Growing political opposition to Thayerism also helped usher in major reforms. Patterson believed that, live or die, Huey Newton could ignite similar anger around the world, if enough people viewed his cause as a race and class fight for justice.

The opportunity to use the Newton defense to ask whether any black man could get a fair trial in America also reminded Patterson of the historic Scottsboro Boys' appeals he worked on in the 1930s. Like Newton, the Scottsboro Boys faced the death penalty. In their case, it was based on false charges they gang-raped two prostitutes on a freight train passing through Alabama. The trials were about as unfair as one could imagine, which made them an ideal vehicle for holding American injustice up to international scorn. The original criminal complaint involved an inter-racial brawl that forced several white youths off the train. The white boys got the sheriff to deputize a posse to "capture every Negro on the train."[3] Some of those who had been in the fight had already fled the train by then. The deputies hauled off nine black teenagers aged 12 to 19 they found on board in five different cars, threw them all on a flatbed truck, and took them to the local jail where the terrified teenagers were held for assault with intent to commit murder.

The sheriff's men also hauled in two young prostitutes whom they found in a different car from any of the boys. The older one, Victoria Price, was twenty-one and made up a gang rape charge to avoid prosecution for taking an under-aged girl across state lines in violation of the federal Mann Act.[4] The claim quickly brought a lynch mob to the jail demanding the boys be turned over for hanging. The sheriff refused. Officials only dispersed the angry crowd by calling in the National Guard to protect the prisoners with machine guns and bayonets, accompanied by the promise of quick trials "to send them to the chair."[5]

The trials became the star attraction at the Scottsboro County Fair. The boys were all from out of state, illiterate and not even permitted to contact their families. The nine of them had not all even met each other before they were arrested. Yet after being beaten, the first one tried swore he witnessed the others commit gang rape. That false testimony was supposed to spare his own life at the others' expense — but the prosecutor asked for and got the death sentence for him anyway. In fact, there was no physical evidence that either of the young prostitutes had sex on the train in the time frame the gang rape was alleged to have happened. Represented by incompetent counsel, all but the youngest of the Scottsboro Boys were sentenced to die after back-to-back daylong trials before the same vengeful, all-white male jury. When the packed gallery heard the first boy's death sentence, the spectators burst into applause. Outside, a band struck up, "There'll be a Hot Time in the Old Town Tonight."[6] The trial of twelve-year-old Roy Wright was last. All but one juror voted for the death penalty even though, in view of his age, the prosecutor only asked for life imprisonment. The judge had to declare that one a mistrial.

As eight of the teenagers endured the miseries of death row, national newspapers reported the outrageous details of their prosecution that the ACLU had gathered post-trial. The Scottsboro Boys immediately became a cause célèbre for civil rights advocates. The Communist Party saw great recruiting potential in embarrassing the American system of justice as it had done through the martyrdom of Sacco and Vanzetti just four years before. The ILD quickly signed the boys up as clients, acing out the NAACP and America's most famous defense lawyer, Clarence Darrow. Darrow felt the ILD lawyers "cared far less for the safety and well-being of those poor Negro boys than the exploitation of their own cause."[7] The legal battle turned into a test of endurance. Alabama prosecutors subjected the Scottsboro Boys to more retrials than in any other criminal proceeding in American history; hard-fought appeals and multiple trials saved their lives.

In the second trial in a different county, the ILD brought in a nationally known defense lawyer, New Yorker Samuel Leibowitz, a master of cross-examination reputed to nearly match Darrow in his prime. The younger prostitute changed her story and agreed to testify for the defense. The chief prosecutor was the son of the Alabama Supreme Court justice who had found nothing wrong with sending the Scottsboro Boys to the electric chair after the first mockery of a trial. Unhappy with all these interfering Northerners, the prosecution asked the all-white-male jury: "Is justice going to be bought and sold in Alabama with Jew money from New York?"[8] The jurors quickly reached a guilty verdict and another death sentence. Yet in this case, Judge James Horton found the gang rape testimony of the prosecutor's star witness simply not credible. He set aside the jury's verdict only to lose his seat at the next election for his courageous action.

After the prosecutor got Judge Horton removed from the case, the newly-assigned judge refused to request state troops to protect the defendants, and Alabama's governor declined to order any. Panicked, Liebowitz cabled President Franklin Roosevelt to urge federal intervention to prevent the "extremely grave" risk of a massacre.[9] During the retrial, this judge showed open hostility to the Northern lawyers. Another all-white male jury convicted the defendants and sentenced all but one to die. More protests followed in Washington, D.C. and cities in the North. Ultimately none of the defendants was executed, and appeals of the Scottsboro Boys trials led to two hugely important Supreme Court decisions — the right of poor defendants to have competent counsel appointed in death penalty cases and the right of African-Americans to be included in the jury pool. Meanwhile, all of the defendants spent at least six years in traumatizing prison conditions with devastating effects on their lives.[10]

Three decades later, in the late 1960s, the right of black people to be in the jury pool in America still did not mean blacks got selected for criminal juries "of one's peers." Black defendants across the country still routinely faced conviction and execution at the hands of overwhelmingly white-male juries. The reason was that each side in a criminal case had — and still has — a certain number of discretionary "peremptory" challenges to eliminate qualified jurors. Historically, the vast majority of prosecutors used these peremptory challenges to systematically dismiss any blacks from their juries. With politically-motivated counsel to defend Huey Newton, Patterson sensed enormous potential for the charismatic black militant to draw attention to how the criminal justice system stacked the deck against black men accused of crime. Of course, unlike the Scottsboro Boys, the circumstances of this case made Newton's innocence questionable. But that had been true of Sacco and Vanzetti as well. Their martyrdom worked better, from the Communists' perspective, than if the pair had been spared execution. So had the infamous execution of Mississippian Willie McGee, charged with the unpardonable sin of raping a white woman.

Patterson had worked with Robert Treuhaft in the late 1940s on McGee's highly politicized death-penalty appeal. Other leftist lawyers in the Civil Rights Congress participated, too, including future Congresswoman Bella Abzug in her first civil rights case. What they zeroed in on was Mississippi's blatant double standard on rape prosecutions. The state had a history of executing black men for rape of white females, but not for white rapists convicted of ravaging white women. While white men got shorter sentences for raping white women, white men raped black women and young girls with little or no fear of *any* consequences. Other states in the Deep South had similar abysmal records.[11]

The charge that a black man had raped a white woman was guaranteed to make Southern white men's blood boil. McGee barely escaped lynching as he awaited prosecution. In another egregious example of how black lives didn't matter to the Southern justice system, his rape trial lasted only half a day. The alleged victim, 32-year-old housewife Willette Hawkins, claimed that the handsome, married truck driver crossed the tracks dividing blacks in Laurel from whites, broke into her home and raped her while threatening her baby at knife point. McGee did not testify in his own defense. The jury was all white men — blacks were theoretically permitted by law, but excluded in practice, and women were categorically banned from jury service by statute until 1968. (Mississippi was the last state to drop that prohibition.) The all-white-male jury deliberated less than five minutes before agreeing on McGee's death sentence. On appeal, Civil Rights Congress lawyers won him a new trial in which the jury again voted for the death penalty. Due to more errors, McGee faced yet a third trial, which resulted in another all-white-male jury imposing the death penalty. Meanwhile, rumors around the black section of town were that McGee and Hawkins had been having an affair for a couple of years and got caught.

In that Cold War era, mainstream media considered Communist support for McGee's appeal to the United States Supreme Court "the kiss of death."[12] The Supreme Court refused to touch the death penalty sentence. By then, famed Mississippi author William Faulkner and internationally renowned scientist Albert Einstein were among many prominent people who petitioned President Truman to pardon McGee or commute his sentence; Truman declined to act. Crowds gathered in New York City chanting "Jim Crow must go." The day before his scheduled electrocution, McGee wrote to his wife: "Tell the people the real reason they are going to take my life is to keep the Negro down in the South. They can't do this if you and the children keep on fighting."[13]

The State of Mississippi played into the Communists' agenda with its callous handling of the execution. State employees set up the traveling electric chair at the local courthouse; a thousand people came to celebrate Willie McGee's execution. Two local Mississippi radio stations broadcasted it live so everyone outside could hear when 2,000 volts of electricity surged through McGee's body.[14] Black parents got the message loud and clear. They warned their sons: "Don't mess with white girls. You see what happened to Willie McGee."[15]

Bob Treuhaft's work on McGee's appeals helped earn him, in 1951, a place on Senator Joseph McCarthy's short list of the most subversive lawyers in America. Treuhaft and his British wife, famed author Jessica Mitford, considered the distinction a badge of honor. The two joined Patterson and singer Paul Robeson in formally protesting America's sorry record of racial injustice before the new United Nations in a lengthy petition they gave the incendiary title: "We Charge Genocide." It included the fate of Willie McGee among its examples. The United States made sure the petition gained no traction, treating it as a gross exaggeration and effort to distract attention from the devastating atrocities committed by the Soviet Union. American mainstream media gave it little coverage. Patterson and Robeson soon had their passports revoked so they could not repeat their accusations in speeches overseas. Yet the charges reached a wide, receptive European audience and had broad dissemination in other parts of the world.

Patterson sensed that Newton's trial presented a similar rare political opportunity to deeply embarrass the United States again in the eyes of a mostly nonwhite world for America's continued mistreatment of racial minorities. Indeed, in the summer of 1968 the Panthers would present a new grievance petition to the United Nations, listing the denial in the Newton case of trial by a jury of true peers among its current examples of racism in the American criminal justice system.

Patterson knew just the lawyer he would like to see steer Newton's case. First, Patterson had to convince Newton's family. Wearing his customary suit and tie, the balding, bespectacled Communist was old enough to be Melvin Newton's grandfather. Patterson talked Melvin and his sister Leola into meeting Charles Garry. Garry practiced in San Francisco with three partners and a couple of associates. Huey Newton's two siblings came away quite impressed. Garry always dressed for success in the most fashionable suits. He greeted them warmly and assured them he had tried more than a score of capital cases and never lost one client to execution. But Garry expected the cost of the trial to reach $100,000, a staggering amount at the time. Melvin and Leola told Garry they did not have anything close to that kind of money, but they planned to establish a Huey Newton defense fund and Patterson had agreed to help obtain contributions. To the pair's delight, Garry said he could wait. He also told them it would probably take three years to get Huey freed, assuming their best bet was only after an appeal. Melvin shared what he learned with David Hilliard, who liked what he heard: "We decided that Garry would be the lawyer because we wanted the very best. Huey's life was at stake. . . . Left to the devices of the state he would have ended up dead in the gas chamber in San Quentin, because that's where he was headed."

Melvin took the responsibility of informing his parents and other siblings that he and his sister had found Huey a veteran death-penalty lawyer willing to start without them paying him a dime. Despite Beverly Axelrod's strong endorsement of Charlie Garry, the Cleavers' and Hilliard's blessing and that of the Newton family, other Panthers were outraged. They lobbied for Huey to retain a black attorney. Meanwhile, Garry and Axelrod rushed to Newton's bedside at Oakland's Highland Hospital, where he had been transferred following surgery. On their first visit, on November 1, 1967, the two lawyers knew they would have to talk their way past the police to get access to their new client. They came dressed formally, as Garry always did, but Beverly Axelrod only did when in her work guise. When representing clients, she would put on a skirt suit and heels and push back her bangs in a hair band, her long hair folded into a loose bun overhanging the nape of her neck. But at home, the way Huey would have seen her with Eldridge Cleaver, she often wore a loose hippie dress and sandals with her long, brown hair dangling free. It left her unimpeded as she danced to rock music blaring on the record player.

Garry and Axelrod encountered a platoon of heavily armed police in the hospital corridors. They had to convince a hierarchy of belligerent officials to let them see Newton. When they arrived at their client's room, he looked extremely vulnerable. An IV dangled from his arm; a tube remained in his nose. Under sedation since his arrival, Newton had lost a lot of blood, and appeared to be in great pain. Without asking any questions Garry felt right away that "this man was totally and completely innocent." Beverly Axelrod's presence was important. As Huey Newton's trusted confidante, she introduced Charles Garry to him as someone he could also completely rely on. Knowing that his brother Melvin had vetted Garry, Newton was even more at ease. He painted a grim picture of his ordeal to the two white lawyers, recounting different police guards' taunts: "Nigger, you are going to pay for this." One officer threatened to cut off the tube "so you will choke to death, so that the state won't have to bother trying you or gassing you."[16] Newton said he awoke once to see a shotgun pointed at his face and heard a policeman joke that they should get a razor to kill him with and say it was suicide.

Newton's complaints alarmed Axelrod. She called a close friend from the Lawyers Guild, Alex Hoffmann, in Berkeley. Hoffmann, a slightly-built, Viennese-born lawyer, was four years Axelrod's junior, with a brilliant legal mind and the same unbridled enthusiasm for radical causes as Axelrod. He looked like the product of the '50s Beat Era that he was, a chain-smoking intellectual fond of jazz, his dark hair already receding. With Hoffmann in tow, Axelrod immediately set off to find Oakland Police Chief Charles Gain and demand that Newton be allowed nursing aides round-the-clock at his defense team's expense. She and Garry had no doubt that the threats had occurred — the hatred the Oakland police felt for Newton was palpable. For the better part of a year, armed Panthers had been tailing officers around black neighborhoods, calling them "pigs" and challenging their authority.

The Panthers had first set foot on the world stage in May, less than six months earlier. Over twenty armed men (plus several unarmed friends along for support) marched into the State Assembly in Sacramento to assert their Second Amendment rights in opposition to pending gun control legislation. They also used that media platform to read a confrontational statement about their party's opposition to the Vietnam War and racism in America. Shocked by the gun-toting visitors, the Assembly members passed a new "Panther Rider," which specifically prohibited most civilians from openly carrying loaded weapons in any public place or street. That law made California the most restrictive state on gun control; it remains in effect today, in sharp contrast to permissive gun carry laws in many states where "Stand Your Ground" and "Open Carry" laws prevail.

During the next six months, Oakland police often invoked this new gun restriction when stopping Black Panthers with or without cause. The early morning shootout on October 28, 1967, marked the first exchange of gunfire. Now they had Newton in their custody facing potential execution for killing one of their own — the first Oakland officer shot in the line of duty in over twenty years. The police not only wanted revenge, they wanted to put an end to the growing popularity of the Panther Party platform. It addressed racial exploitation in fighting wars, in housing, education and employment. But the Panthers were best known for their angry and sometimes violent pushback against perceived police misconduct and racism in the criminal justice system. Impatient for results, the Panthers prepared an aggressive set of demands:

WHAT WE WANT NOW! . . .

7.   WE WANT AN IMMEDIATE END TO <u>POLICE BRUTALITY</u> AND <u>MURDER</u> OF BLACK PEOPLE.

8. WE WANT FREEDOM FOR ALL BLACK MEN HELD IN
    FEDERAL, STATE, COUNTY, AND CITY PRISONS AND
    JAILS.
9. WE WANT ALL BLACK PEOPLE WHEN BROUGHT TO
    TRIAL TO BE TRIED IN COURT BY A JURY OF THEIR PEER
    GROUP OF PEOPLE FROM THEIR BLACK COMMUNITIES.

WHAT WE BELIEVE . . .

7. WE BELIEVE WE CAN END POLICE BRUTALITY IN
    OUR BLACK COMMUNITY BY ORGANIZING BLACK
    SELF DEFENSE GROUPS THAT ARE DEDICATED TO
    DEFENDING OUR BLACK COMMUNITY FROM RACIST
    POLICE OPPRESSION AND BRUTALITY. [17]

The police resented being viewed as a "white army of occupation"[18] that the black community needed the Panthers to protect themselves against. Unbeknownst to the Oakland police at the time Frey
confronted Newton, the Panthers numbered only about a dozen members, in and out of jail. Newton's arrest and prosecution sparked what
would become a dynamic expansion of the Panther Party. In November
of 1967, a white hippie commune loaned Hilliard a psychedelic double-
decker bus so the Panthers could drum up support in local neighborhoods to "Free Huey!" With a bullhorn, they repeatedly blasted the
question: "Can a black man get a fair trial in America . . . defending his
life against a white policeman?"[19]

Within a few months' time, a new Panther chapter opened in Los
Angeles. Even then, the two branches totaled about 75 people who identified themselves as Party members. The Oakland police would have
been far more incensed had they seen what was coming; galvanized by
the campaign challenging Newton's imprisonment over the next year
and a half, the Panther Party would burgeon to over 40 chapters, nearly
5,000 members, numerous community programs and a nationwide
newspaper with a six-figure circulation. This rise was fast and precipitous. A year and a half after the Panthers' spectacular Sacramento debut
in the spring of 1967, J. Edgar Hoover listed the Party as the highest

internal threat to national security of all black nationalist "hate groups."

By the time they formed the Black Panther Party, Newton and Seale had developed a strong friendship based on a shared belief — the time had come for aggressive political action against entrenched racism. In his introduction to *Rage,* Professor Ekwueme Thelwell — then a recent advisor to the acclaimed civil rights TV series *Eyes on the Prize* — described Newton and Seale as combining the spiritual values of their hard-working, rural Southern parents in "uneasy tension with another incompatible current: the in-yo-face, up-against-the-wall-motherfuckah, quasi-criminality and macho violence of the urban street-gang culture."[20] The deliberately calculated "in-yo-face" strategy of young armed blacks looking "boldly into the eyes of white authority" took the breath away from observers on both sides of the racial divide. Newton and Seale were determined to lead by example "above ground," ostentatiously waging "ideological and material battle in plain view."[21] They quickly became known as "the baddest niggas on the scene,"[22] a reputation that new recruits found irresistible.

Front page of the San Francisco Sun Reporter, *October 1, 1966 featuring the riots that followed the killing of unarmed sixteen-year-old Matthew Johnson in the Haight-Ashbury district of San Francisco by a local policeman on September 27, 1966. Huey Newton and Bobby Seale formed the Black Panther Party for Self-Defense in Oakland within weeks of this incendiary incident.*

2. OAKLAND —
THE MAKINGS OF A
RACIAL TINDERBOX

*"The Negro's sounds of NOW! are not irrational
demands or threats; they are a cry of desperation."*
— AUGUST 1965, EUGENE FOLEY, ASST. SEC'Y OF COMMERCE
IN CHARGE OF ECONOMIC DEVELOPMENT[1]

What made Oakland in 1966 the next likely Watts? Alameda County, the seventh largest in California, occupies 821 square miles to the immediate east of the San Francisco Bay. Since 1873, Oakland has been its county seat. In 1852, when Oakland was incorporated with fewer than 1,500 people, most settled by the waterfront. After 1869, when Oakland became the terminus for the transcontinental railroad, the population began to expand exponentially, with large numbers of immigrants from Europe, most of them from Portugal and Ireland. The new arrivals also included a small percentage of Italians and Germans, African-American and Chinese railroad workers, Mexicans and Japanese immigrants. After the calamitous 1906 San Francisco earthquake and fire, West Oakland experienced another major growth spurt with thousands displaced from their homes across the Bay, including famed author and social activist Jack London, who had lived in Oakland as a child. Jack London Square on the waterfront now bears his name.

For entertainment, starting in the late nineteenth century, Oaklanders frequented a theme park in vice-ridden Emeryville — West

Oakland's industrialized neighbor to the north, nestled between Oakland and Berkeley. In just two square miles, the city of Emeryville managed to pack in railroad yards, saloons, gambling, dance halls and whore houses. Starting in 1903, Oaklanders could travel on Key System streetcars — the predecessor of today's AC Transit — for work or play. Their new minor league baseball team, the Oakland Oaks, in the Pacific Coast League, was conveniently located at the Key System's Emeryville hub, at the site Pixar Studios now occupies.

For the first few decades of the twentieth century, Oakland's white population kept growing. The 1940 census listed just over 302,000 residents in Oakland, almost all of them whites of European ancestry. Until 1940, the black populations in Berkeley and Oakland remained relatively tiny; even fewer lived in San Francisco. This is not surprising given the historic dearth of good jobs. By 1940, Oakland listed a total of 8,462 blacks, up less than a thousand from 1930. They made up only 2.9 percent of the general population. All other minorities combined added up to only another 5,765 people.

In 1940, most minorities still lived in essentially the same areas they had occupied since the turn of the century, alongside poor white families in the flatlands of industrialized West Oakland, between Emeryville to the north and Oakland's main business district. The only non-Caucasian racially homogenous neighborhood was Oakland's Chinatown, one of the oldest in the country, which occupied sixteen blocks between Lake Merritt and the Oakland waterfront.

The historic white monopoly in the Oakland power structure derived from wealth and conservative politics. The well-to-do lived in upscale neighborhoods in the city's center by Lake Merritt, on the Berkeley border to the north and in the Oakland hills to the east. Many of the most influential businessmen actually lived in Piedmont, an affluent all-white bedroom community completely surrounded by the Oakland hills. In the late 19th century, Piedmont's white residents had simply refused to have their community absorbed by the larger city as towns like Brooklyn, Montclair Village, Fruitvale and Melrose had done.

Within Oakland itself, a Republican machine held enormous sway in politics — and the engine for that machine was the city's newspaper of record, the *Oakland Tribune*. When its publisher, Joseph Knowland, added a twenty-two story tower to the Tribune building in 1923, it became for decades the tallest structure in the city. His detractors began to call Knowland "The Power in the Oakland Tribune Tower." The anti-union lumber baron was extremely active in both state and federal politics. Knowland served as a Congressman for 11 years along with future Governor and Chief Justice of the Supreme Court Earl Warren, who became a family friend. Joe Knowland's son Bill served in the state legislature before World War II. After the war ended, Governor Warren appointed veteran Bill Knowland to a vacant Senate seat. Senator Bill Knowland would take over the reins of the *Tribune* in 1961 and inherit his father's role as "the central figure in the Oakland 'power structure'."[2]

Through the 1960s, control of Oakland rested in the city council, elected citywide by the white supermajority. Joe Knowland hand-picked most of the council's members. The councilmen chose a part-time mayor from among their group, but his function was largely ceremonial; under the city's charter, a professional city manager oversaw all departments and reported directly to the City Council. Those who wanted to get ahead in Oakland had to make their business and political connections through the Chamber of Commerce, which Bill Knowland headed in the late 1960s, or finagle an invitation to join a prestigious service club. The club members gathered regularly for breakfast or lunch, made handshake deals and launched charitable and civic projects like the Shriners' sponsorship of the "Necklace of Lights" around Lake Merritt strung up in the business boom of the 1920s. For most of the 20th century, practically all of the city's power brokers met and interacted regularly in those clubs.

Since 1915, the most exclusive social club was the Athenian-Nile Club on Fourteenth Street, not far from the Tribune building. For the next several decades the Athenian-Nile Club earned its reputation as the city's "shadow power base."[3] It was one of several "old boy" social networks like the Shriners, the Elks and Moose Lodges and Knights of Columbus. Since 1909, Oakland also had an invitation-only Rotary Club for local businessmen — just the third one organized anywhere in the world. Oakland also boasted the first Lions Club west of the Rockies.

In 1933, a group of Oakland businessmen launched the Lake Merritt

Breakfast Club (LMBC) and made every mayor thereafter an honorary member. Hundreds of members representing various professions and businesses in the community got together weekly for breakfast to network and socialize at a restaurant overlooking the lake. LMBC members launched Oakland's Children's Fairyland theme park in 1950 (the main inspiration for Disneyland) and later spearheaded the restoration of the "Necklace of Lights" that had gone dark during World War II — "Oakland's jewel," which has become the city's iconic image ever since.

For decades, West Oaklanders had no seats at the table. The business and community leaders LMBC welcomed to its roster resembled the membership of other elite men's clubs in town. As of the late 1960s there were only one or two Jewish members, one pioneering Japanese-American city councilman (a Republican) and no blacks. Steve Hanson, a fourth generation Oaklander and future president of LMBC acknowledges that "the club had its political agenda, which was very conservative," even in the midst of the turbulent sixties. No women gained membership in any of these old boys' clubs until the late 1980s — and only after the courts stepped in to outlaw their male-only policies.

* * * * *

In the decades preceding World War II, West Oakland's Seventh Street was a bustling place. Before completion of the Bay Bridge in 1936, the electric Key Train System carried commuters along Seventh Street to a ferry to San Francisco. Black professionals opened up offices along Seventh Street, but at night, vice predominated. Near the railroad yards bordering Seventh Street were pawn shops, houses of prostitution, blues clubs, bars, barbeque joints and gambling establishments. The renowned Pullman porters, many of whom lived nearby because the railroad had its terminus in Oakland, called their gambling parlor "The Shasta." Until the 1960s, only black men served as Pullman porters. These were much-coveted jobs. Among their leaders was C. L. Dellums, the uncle of Ron Dellums, longtime East Bay congressman and, from 2007 to 2011, Oakland's mayor. In 1925, overcoming stiff opposition, C. L. made history, along with A. Philip Randolph, when they established the Brotherhood of Sleeping Car Porters, the nation's first chartered black union. The porters played a pivotal role in launching the black middle class in America and setting the groundwork for the civil rights movement. That history of local political activism would also make West Oakland fertile ground for the Panther Party.

Among the movers and shakers in West Oakland between World War I and World War II, one especially colorful entrepreneur stood out: Charles "Raincoat" Jones, a veteran of both the Spanish-American War (as an infantryman) and World War I (as a cook), who made most of his fortune moneylending and running gambling rooms. By the late '20s, Jones (who always wore a mackintosh) reputedly owned the entire block of buildings abutting Seventh and Willow, the corner where the October 1967 shooting would occur. Jones and a small group of successful business friends made it a point to support enterprises that the black community needed, such as by providing start-up money for a pharmacy or a timely loan to help save *San Francisco Sun Reporter* publisher Dr. Carlton Goodlett from having to close his newspaper's doors.

Before World War II, vice peddlers like Raincoat were able to maintain a "live and let live" relationship with the police. Raincoat was happy to pay protection money, which his attorney, Leonard Richardson, then the most prominent African-American lawyer around, hand-delivered by messenger directly to a police captain in City Hall each Friday.[4] Whenever police raided Raincoat's gambling room, he pulled out his wad of bills and bailed out whoever got arrested. But that peaceful coexistence rested on a relatively stable minority population that did not threaten the status quo.

As Bay Area industries geared up for the war effort in 1941, black-white relations began to change for the worse in a hurry. White unions collaborated with management to freeze black workers out of steady jobs. Discrimination became so pervasive that local black labor organizers joined with white civil rights leaders to plan a march on Washington to compel equal job opportunities. Roosevelt had wooed African-Americans from their traditional home in the Republican Party with his New Deal programs. He avoided the embarrassment of a major civil rights protest by issuing Executive Order 8802 in 1941, an unprecedented presidential decree that forbade discrimination on grounds of race, color or national origin in hiring workers for the national defense program. Kaiser Shipyards then recruited heavily in the South, encouraging a mass migration of blacks.

Some hailed Roosevelt's order as "the breakthrough of the century in the Negro's battle for civil rights"; others recognized it as but one of many hard-fought milestones over the prior several decades.[5] Unequal pay and other discriminatory employment practices in the defense industries continued despite the executive order. Yet conditions in Oakland were far better than in the South. In the first three years of the war, over 320,000 blacks migrated to the Bay Area. Berkeley created an Emergency Housing Committee to help find lodging for the new arrivals. Civil rights advocates like African-American pharmacist William Byron Rumford went further. They formed an inter-racial welcoming committee to help families from the South adjust to their new environment.

Many came from the rural south by the trainload and, for the most part, found housing only in the most undesirable locations. In Berkeley, that meant the flatlands below Shattuck Avenue. In Oakland, they poured into similarly neglected neighborhoods, mostly in West Oakland. Low-rent housing complexes first opened in West Oakland in 1941 as a wartime redevelopment project, but they were woefully inadequate. West Oakland "began to overflow." One Oakland resident remembered: "We'd go down to the 16th street station after school to watch the people get off the trains, and it was like a parade. You just couldn't believe that that many people would come in, and some didn't even have luggage; they would come with boxes, with 3 or 4 children with no place to stay . . . and they would ask everyone if they had any place to stay or could they make some space into rooms."[6]

A race riot broke out on a Key System train in downtown Oakland in 1943. It was inspired by the "Zoot Suit" riot in Los Angeles, where white servicemen had attacked Mexican-American immigrants wearing the showy, wide-lapelled Zoot suits with padded shoulders that first became popular with African-American and Italian men. The amount of cloth that went into Zoot suits was considered extravagant during wartime and criticized as unpatriotic. Similar "Zoot Suit" riots occurred in other cities, involving white soldiers attacking blacks. The Oakland riot grew to a mixed race mob of 2,000. A local newspaper, *The Observer*, commented:

> That riot on Twelfth Street the other day may be the forerunner of more and larger riots because we now have (a) a semi-mining camp civilization and (b) a new race problem, brought about by the influx of what might be called socially-liberated or uninhibited Negroes who are not bound by the old and peaceful understanding between the Negro and the white in Oakland, which has lasted for so many decades, but who insist upon barging into the white man and becoming an integral part of the white man's society.[7]

By 1945, four times as many blacks were counted in the official Oakland census as in 1940. Shortly after the war's end, a professor at the University of California's School of Social Work observed that "Negroes are rapidly becoming the most significant minority group in California."[8] The Oakland establishment not only feared the mass of new black residents; it had for decades waged a running battle with white labor unions. There had been major bloody strikes during the Depression, but a moratorium on strikes during World War II. Then in early December 1946 several hundred women retail clerks picketed two downtown Oakland department stores for equal pay and a union contract. The Alameda County Central Labor Council followed up with a call for a walkout by all of its members until union demands were met. Over the next two days, strike supporters went on a self-declared "work holiday" mushrooming to over 100,000 people enjoying a respite from work — more than a quarter of the city's population. Within 24 hours, the walkouts shut down most businesses in downtown Oakland, leading the City Council to declare a state of emergency and put tough-minded Mayor Herbert Beach in direct charge of the police and fire departments.

The heavy-handed treatment of these hordes of protesters would be mirrored in the 1960s, for similar reasons — Mayor Beach saw this general strike as an attempted revolution. He quickly hired beefy strikebreakers to supplement the police. "[S]ome 200 Oakland and Berkeley police, many in riot gear, swept down the street. They roughly pushed aside pickets and pedestrians alike as they cleared that block and the surrounding eight square blocks. They set up machine guns across from the stores, while tow trucks moved in to snatch away any cars parked in the area." Standing protected on the sidelines, nodding their approval, were the key local men in power, bent on crushing this populist uprising: the police chief, city council members, representatives of picketed department stores and, of course, the anti-union group's acknowledged leader, Joseph Knowland of the *Oakland Tribune*.[9]

It would be Oakland's last general strike. Yet Mayor Beach's temporary dictatorship caused a backlash. It ushered in a change to Oakland's charter to have the mayor elected directly by Oakland's citizens, independent of the city council. Even so, the mayor's role remained largely ceremonial. West Oakland still lacked any influence as businessman Clifford Rishell won the 1949 election and became known as "Ambassador of Goodwill for Oakland" and "Oakland's Super Salesman" — the man who brought in the Oakland Raiders football team. Meanwhile, Mayor Rishell and the city council ignored the growing slums of West Oakland.

During World War II the government constructed temporary housing for black shipyard workers and their families near the Navy Yard in the island city of Alameda, a nearly all-white town separated from Oakland by the Oakland Estuary. Shortly after the war ended, that government housing was bulldozed, forcing most of the suddenly unemployed black workers to relocate to West Oakland, which was already overcrowded. The project was billed as "urban renewal" but West Oaklanders knew it as "Negro removal," intended to reestablish the city of Alameda's nearly all-white status.[10]

The situation only got worse in the 1950s when ground broke for the double-decker Cypress Freeway, designed to connect the San Francisco Bay Bridge to the Nimitz Freeway in Oakland. The new connector bisected West Oakland and separated it from the city center. City Hall had no compunction about razing homes and displacing West Oakland residents to accommodate this progress. Nor, over most of the next two decades, did the City Council concern itself with addressing that broken community's chronic unemployment, dilapidated housing and overcrowded, underachieving schools. The problem required too much money for locals to address on their own in any meaningful way, and the officeholders did not consider government the answer.

In the 1940s, members of Oakland's growing black middle class opened their own branch of the NAACP to address community concerns. By the 1950s, the NAACP was inviting black youths to the West Oakland community center to plan their own activities. The adult council focused on gradual empowerment. They taught the teenagers Robert's Rules of Order to conduct their own meetings and reminded them that Oakland's Juvenile Hall was just across the street. Kids could either learn how to work within the system to make change or wind up in Juvenile Hall.

The Oakland branch of the NAACP did not just challenge discrimination in the courts. It also organized picketing of City Hall to call attention to blatant exclusionary practices by white businesses and homeowners in their own backyard. Much as in the South, blacks could not eat in most restaurants in downtown Oakland or shop at a dime store or sit at a lunch counter, much less buy or rent a home in a white neighborhood — their movements were almost completely circumscribed. Bill Patterson, who later became President of the Oakland NAACP, moved to West Oakland from Arkansas in the early 1950s, a teen-aged athlete who took the long train ride to join relatives in Oakland to fulfill his ambition to go to college. Now in his eighties, he vividly recalls what it was like back then: "The police department . . . if you traveled outside of your sector, you got stopped. Today they have a new name for that — they call it profiling — but it happened back then as a regular thing, because in neighborhoods that were all white, there was fear, you know, of black people. . . . Many of them just didn't know black folk."

Essentially, blacks needed a passport to get into white enclaves. In the early 1960s, the Oakland NAACP president was a rare black who still lived in the adjacent City of Alameda. Whenever he invited visiting civil rights leaders to his home — including the Reverend Martin Luther King, Jr. — he called the police ahead of time so the visitors would not be stopped for questioning as they crossed the bridge from Oakland.

Wall Street lawyer Amory Bradford, author of *Oakland's Not for*

Burning, was a former Ford Foundation consultant whom the Johnson administration tapped, in late 1965, to help launch a multi-million-dollar pilot jobs-program in Oakland. He and his colleagues from the Economic Development Agency (EDA) had as their mission to prevent another ruinous riot like the one that had just devastated Watts. When Bradford arrived from Washington, D.C., with other EDA emissaries, he could see that "a dangerous deadlock had developed between the Oakland ghetto, which was demanding a better way of life, and the business and government establishment, which was determined to maintain order in Oakland and to improve its economy, but was unable to provide the resources to meet ghetto needs. Without outside help, this deadlock seemed certain to produce an explosion. . . . The community had become fragmented into hostile, distrustful [warring] groups."[11]

Bradford met early in 1966 with Oakland's "leaders in business, in the city and in the port . . . men with the power to solve Oakland's problems if the federal government provided key resources." He noted, "This group was Republican, mostly conservative . . . Chamber of Commerce–oriented [and] . . . instinctively distrustful of Federal spending programs . . . ." These local powerful men were extraordinarily sensitive to outside criticism. National media from the *Wall Street Journal* to *TIME* and *Newsweek* had already zeroed in on Oakland as "a failed city plagued by racialized poverty and unemployment."[12]

There was much to resent in these disparaging accounts. In 1962, Oakland had expanded the capacity of its 35-year-old port. In the process, it became the first city on the Pacific Coast where container ships could dock. The port was soon handling the second highest tonnage of cargo shipments worldwide. By 1966, two mammoth construction projects were taking shape along Seventh Street in West Oakland: a new transbay tube to San Francisco for the Bay Area Rapid Transit (BART) rail system and a huge new main post office. Yet, many homes and businesses were razed in the process, leaving gaping construction zones adjacent to dilapidated Victorians that reflected a long-gone, more prosperous era.

Among the recent building projects was also a new multi-story police headquarters at Seventh and Broadway. Black youths arrested on the streets of West Oakland became all too familiar with its base-ment jail cells. Civil rights lawyer John Burris was a local teenager at the time: "Back in the 1960s . . . what you really had was this sense of white officers . . . occupying the African American community in law enforce-ment . . . . You did not trust the police at all."

Morrie Turner — a protégé of "Peanuts" cartoonist Charles Schultz — would become world-renowned in the 1970s for creating the first integrated comic strip, "Wee Pals." Turner was the son of a Pullman porter. He made his living in the 1960s as a rare African-American clerk in the Oakland Police Department. At night, Turner followed his pas-sion, penning civil rights cartoons for African-American newspapers and magazines and sketching signs for the local NAACP. By day, Turner typed up police reports from white officers who described African-American arrestees as "male, nigger." Morrie would correct them, repeating "male Negro" as a form of protest. There was no question in Turner's mind — the police he worked with were bigoted. Once he took a phone message meant for a white co-worker — "The niggers are taking over Oakland."

When Turner's co-workers looked out the window and saw NAACP picketers, they would call to him to come see the Commie protestors. Turner wisely did not mention that the signs they carried were his design. Too often police reports described male suspects who had to be physically restrained or shot. He could not imagine so many arrest-ees had invited such harsh treatment. He concluded that the officers simply backed each other up as cover stories to justify so many bruises and injuries to the black men they hauled in or, occasionally, to explain away their deaths.

By 1966, Oakland's population was over one-fourth black and thirty percent minority. White flight had turned much of North Oakland into transitional neighborhoods with black residents moving in and whites moving out. African-Americans still occupied West Oakland; East Oakland remained dominated by people of Portuguese descent as it had been for several decades. One exception was the Fruitvale District two miles southeast of Lake Merritt, which was becoming mostly Mexican-American. A large area near the 40-year-old Oakland airport was in the process of turning into another black ghetto. Starting in the early '60s, whites began moving to more homogenous communities further south in the county and blacks from West Oakland moved in.

Like Seventh Street in West Oakland, East 14th Street became the main thoroughfare through East Oakland. By 1966, East 14th Street had become a "garish strip of shops, bars, poolrooms, and dance halls" attracting young Latino and black clientele. To Ivy-Leaguer Amory Bradford, these youths seemed "poised on the edge of trouble."[13] Bradford saw some hope for salvation with job creation; most police on the beat simply saw them as budding juvenile delinquents.

The divide between police and minority communities was exacerbated by police patrolling in cars rather than walking beats on foot as they had once done. When Bradford and other white federal officials first met with black neighborhood leaders in West Oakland in early 1966, Bradford noticed how "the introduction of the 'prowl car' widened the gulf between police and people." The mixed race group of adults had gathered on a sidewalk while awaiting a key to the hall where they had come to discuss the proposed new jobs program. Bradford saw his black companions grow tense as a patrol car circled the block a number of times studying them, never stopping to ask what was the problem or to offer assistance.[14]

For Mexican-Americans the situation in East Oakland's flatlands was similar. Future Alameda County Judge Leo Dorado recalls, as a teen, policemen stopping him on his bicycle headed across the bridge to a public beach in the town of Alameda: "I was clearly stopped because I was a brown face from Oakland in Alameda... It was ... the way it was ... I was very aware that Alameda was completely white." Dorado explained: "From the time I was young... the Oakland police ... had a very strong presence in all of my neighborhoods. Everyone had stories. .... It wasn't all negative, but the lines were clearly drawn that the Oakland police were in charge of what was going on in the neighborhoods. And as long as you didn't get on their bad side, their wrong side, then you're okay. If you did, then you are in trouble . . . you are going to be physically handled before they took you to where they were going to take you."

In the spring of 1966 minorities in both East and West Oakland had a somewhat sympathetic new mayor who promised to listen to their concerns. John Reading was a self-made millionaire who had moved to Oakland as a young teen. Reading worked his way through the University of California ("Cal") before spending six years in the Army Air Corps, where he rose to the rank of lieutenant colonel. After World War II, Reading expanded his father's grocery business, which became famous for its frozen "Red's Tamales" packaged in company plants in Mexico and East Oakland. In just a couple of years Mayor Reading would become the Panthers' chief nemesis, but when sworn in in April 1966, his first instinct was to convince West Oaklanders that someone at City Hall would finally work with them to support major improvements in their community.

Reading's Republican fellow council members elected him in February of 1966 when the incumbent John Houlihan abruptly resigned after being caught embezzling from a law firm client. Houlihan later spent two years in prison. Reading figured the other council members valued his problem-solving skills and business success. He did not consider himself a career politician, but was willing to devote himself full-time to the "thankless job" of mayor, which offered only token part-time pay and little power.[15] His predecessor Houlihan had been a lawyer for the *Oakland Tribune*. Houlihan's gruff manner probably resembled that of his father, a San Francisco policeman. Black leaders considered Houlihan "an arrogant, impatient man" who enjoyed imposing the will of "the power structure" on the powerless.[16]

Reading promised dubious West Oakland leaders a new "open door" era at City Hall and vowed to "listen to anyone who wants to come in and talk to me." To launch his new policy of free-flowing communications between City Hall and West Oakland, Reading agreed to an interview with a new African-American newspaper, *The Flatlands*, started by two enterprising young women. Its motto was "Tell it like it is and do what is needed." Its first issue presented a grim and angry picture of the city: "Welcome to Oakland, the all-American city; welcome to Oakland, the 'city of pain.' Most of the well-to-do whites and a small number of well-to-do Negroes live in the Oakland hills . . . They look down onto a patchwork of grey . . . where the flatlands are. . . spilling over with people. The flatlands stink with decay. . . The flatlands people have had no one to speak for them."[17]

Mayor Reading gave honest answers in his interview. Critics coming to voice concerns at City Council meetings would be afforded "respect, dignity and courtesy," a decided change from mayors past. Reading understood the urgency of the situation in the spring of 1966 and squarely addressed the issue on so many people's minds: "Is Oakland going to blow?" The Mayor acknowledged: "Unless more is done, quickly, we can have real trouble here in Oakland, anytime."[18] He admitted to the paper's editorial board that, as a member of the establishment, he expected them to view him with suspicion.

Of course, the real power lay in the City Council majority, which remained intransigent. Nonetheless, Reading began to make inroads, working closely with African-American urban planner John Williams, the talented head of Oakland's Urban Renewal Agency. Reading also tried to broker a compromise when Oakland's Poverty Council and its community relations chair Judge Lionel Wilson first proposed an advisory police review board. Appointed to the bench six years earlier by Governor Pat Brown, Wilson was still the only African-American judge in the county. He had started out as a political protégé of East Bay Assemblyman William Byron Rumford, the first black elected to the state legislature. Judge Wilson's proposal for community police review went down to defeat at the hands of the adamantly opposed City Council majority. Not until 1980 would such a review board be established — during Wilson's tenure as Oakland's first black mayor.

While Oakland remained free of any major incidents in the summer of 1966, riots broke out in San Francisco as well as Chicago, Brooklyn, Cleveland and Louisville. As in Watts in 1965, what prompted four days of looting and burning of warehouses in San Francisco's Hunter's Point and the Fillmore District that September was a single inflammatory incident. This time it was the death of an unarmed sixteen-year-old named Matthew Johnson, whom a policeman had shot as a suspected car thief. When officers arrived to stop the looting that followed, they faced sniper fire. Rumors spread that militant blacks in Oakland were stockpiling homemade Molotov cocktails and stashes of arms to launch similar violence. Federal officials worried that it might not prove feasible to save Oakland from exploding next.

West Oakland community leader Curtis Baker was among the original doubters who came to trust Mayor Reading to represent the community in convincing the EDA and Department of Commerce in Washington that devoting federal resources to a multi-million dollar jobs program in Oakland was worth the risk. Baker distributed mimeographed flyers urging others to keep the faith. *The Flatlands* paper soon folded for lack of funds, but the federal jobs program went forward. In the summer of 1967 when riots erupted in cities across country, remarkably, none happened in Oakland. At about the same time, Mayor Reading lured a major league baseball team, the Kansas City A's, to Oakland beginning with the 1968 season, and decided he would run for election.

The widespread riots during the "long, hot summer" of 1967 prompted President Johnson to order a blue ribbon panel to study its root causes. Chaired by Illinois governor Otto Kerner, the commission and the report it produced were both commonly referred to by his last name. *The Kerner Report*, which became a best-selling book, zeroed in on the lack of diversity in police forces across the country as a major societal problem. The panel placed most of the blame for urban unrest on "[w]hite racism . . . for the explosive mixture which has been accumulating in our cities since the end of World War II." [19] The panel also criticized the press for reporting the news through "white men's eyes." It warned that the nation was "moving toward two societies, one black, one white — separate and unequal" and proposed controversial major investments in the nation's inner cities like the pilot jobs program in Oakland. [20]

Lyndon Johnson made the war on poverty a top priority, but the home front was only one crisis he faced in the fall of 1967. The other was escalating opposition to a war in Vietnam that was looking less and less winnable. What grew most worrisome for Washington was the convergence of the two anti-establishment movements — mostly white war protesters and mixed-race civil rights demonstrators. FBI Director Hoover became especially alarmed in April 1967 when Reverend King called for the United States to declare a unilateral cease fire in Vietnam and bring the troops back home to promote justice and "the service of peace."[21]

By this time, Hoover considered the gifted orator the most danger-ous man in America. Now King was openly using his moral authority to pressure the federal government to end the war and redirect those same resources to address longstanding civil rights grievances at home. More radical activists, including SNCC leader Stokely Carmichael, echoed — and amplified — the sentiments of King's speeches. Carmichael derided the war as "white people sending black people to make war on yellow people in order to defend the land they stole from red people."[22] In their first public statement in May 1967, the Panthers similarly con-demned the war as an act of racist colonialism mirroring centuries of genocidal practices at home.[23]

Starting in the fall of 1964 when protesters on the Berkeley cam-pus launched the Free Speech Movement ("FSM"), students joined with outside activists to turn the public against the war in Southeast Asia by staging numerous sit-ins, marches and teach-ins. They also plotted aggressive action to disrupt the arrival of troop trains at the Oakland Army Terminal. All the while, the FBI was not only tracking FSM lead-ers closely, it had embedded agents in the Movement. Journalist Seth Rosenfeld's best-selling 2012 book, *Subversives: The FBI's War on Student Radicals and Reagan's Rise to Power,* focused particularly on the FBI's activities at the University of California vis-à-vis the FSM in the 1960s. Rosenfeld says: "One of the most surprising findings in my research was the extent to which the FBI had infiltrated every level of the campus community, from student organizations to faculty to administrators to the Board of Regents."

The lead lawyers later involved in Huey Newton's defense were among the radical members of the Old and New Left the FBI had already been tracking. In the early sixties the FBI focused on East Bay's Friends of SNCC, headed by Jessica Mitford's daughter. It was one of the primary fundraisers for SNCC in the country. The FBI also main-tained a file on the San Francisco Lawyers Guild, which sent lawyer volunteers to help staff Freedom Summer in Mississippi and Alabama in 1964 to register black voters and defend arrested civil rights workers. So when the Free Speech Movement began in the fall of 1964, the FBI was already keeping dossiers on the activists who would lead it.

The Free Speech Movement started out nearly all white — in Berkeley, you could then count African-American student activists on the fingers of two hands. Students on college campuses across the country soon began staging hundreds of their own protests, as did activists in the nation's largest cities. Filling a role that radical bloggers would assume several decades later, new underground newspapers like *The Berkeley Barb* and San Francisco's *The Movement* ran stories that countered, and often ridiculed, establishment media coverage of erupting anti-war activity.

The third week of October 1967 marked a major, two-pronged initiative. In coordination with a planned march on the Pentagon, a coalition of Bay Area activists launched "Stop the Draft Week" — several days of massive demonstrations designed to shut down the Oakland Induction Center, one of the largest such facilities on the Pacific Coast. The police geared up too, with all officers assigned to 12-hour shifts for 24-hour coverage in anticipation of a major assault on the induction center. On the first day, some three thousand protesters blocked the center's entrance, leading to more than a hundred arrests. The following day twice as many demonstrators blocked the doorway and the surrounding streets. An estimated 250 Oakland police, sheriff's deputies and highway patrolmen broke through and dispersed the crowd, spraying mace and swinging batons in a bloody confrontation that injured many protestors.

The stand-off with white students amazed West Oakland blacks who had thought head-bashing was not something police did to whites. It also surprised them to see privileged college students standing up to the police to risk injury for a cause they believed in. Belva Davis covered the melee as a young reporter for a San Francisco TV station. She knew she was witnessing history: "The Bay Area felt like ground zero in a generational battle for the soul of the country."[24]

City officials were just as indignant as the protesters; while the crowds railed against injustice, the city's leaders ranted about the disruption and chaos. Businessmen at their club breakfasts and lunches deplored Oakland's growing notoriety. District Attorney Frank Coakley

brought conspiracy charges against key planners of the anti-war protest; the county's top prosecutor D. Lowell Jensen would eventually try
them together as "The Oakland Seven." A team of three defense lawyers, headed by Lawyers Guild veteran Charles Garry, quickly assembled. The defense team audaciously planned to invoke the Nuremberg
Principles as their clients' justification for blocking entrance to the
induction center. They wanted to make the case that the Vietnam War
was a crime against humanity — and put the war itself on trial.

It was hard to imagine at the time that another Oakland arrest would
generate enough coverage and controversy to drown out the noise surrounding the "Oakland Seven," while pitting the same lead counsel
against one another — with the police and establishment on one side,
and anti-war activists joined with civil rights protesters on the other. Just
two weeks after "Stop the Draft Week" came the spark Hoover dreaded
that would merge two protest movements on a shared goal: the synergy
of anti-war and civil rights activists that Dr. King urged in 1967 on a
national stage got a powerful boost from a single bloody confrontation
in the very same city where the Oakland Seven would be tried.

In his book *Oakland's Not for Burning*, published in mid-1968,
Bradford noted: "Oakland, to its credit, came through 1966, 1967 and
the first half of 1968 without a serious [race] riot. But, like all our cities, it will remain in precarious balance, on the edge of violence, until
far more than is now in view can be done to improve life for those
who dwell in the ghetto."[25] Bradford omitted from his book any reference whatsoever to the headline-grabbing West Oakland shooting on
October 28,1967, which left Officer John Frey dead and Huey Newton
and one other officer seriously wounded. At a time when the FBI was
treating the Panther Party as a growing threat to national security,
Bradford gave the Panther Party only brief mention in his book on
fragile race relations in Oakland, calling the Panthers a "militant group
of young Negroes, which had become active in Oakland in 1967, operating patrols to follow police cars and to advise those arrested in the
ghetto." Bradford referenced only a single shootout between a dozen
or so Panthers and the police in April of 1968 that "seemed likely to
trigger a riot," but did not.[26] The shootout was the one that ended with

the police killing unarmed teenager Bobby Hutton.

Bradford's omission from his book of the polarizing Newton murder case was telling. The looming outcome of that death penalty trial — covered daily on the front pages of local papers and on the evening news — was a glaring and obvious source of enormous tension. Bradford had to have seen the historic security measures at the courthouse where uniformed Black Panthers in their late teens and early twenties urged on unprecedented crowds of mixed race protesters with chants like "Revolution has come. Time to pick up the gun." Black youths from the flatlands had found a voice they felt spoke for them, a seemingly fearless voice backed up with arms and ammunition.

With full-throated support from the business community and the *Oakland Tribune*, Mayor Reading repositioned himself on one side of a new and bitter chasm dividing City Hall and the black community, the police and the Black Panther Party for Self-Defense — vanguard of the revolution. Amory Bradford published his book, not in triumph that the federal government's intervention had averted another Watts, but in guarded hope that Oakland truly was not for burning.

Huey Newton, co-founder of the Black Panther Party.

3. THE PANTHERS' ROOTS

We're hip to the fact that
Superman never saved no black people.
— Bobby Seale

What made revolutionaries Huey Newton and Bobby Seale tick? How did they develop ideas that later attracted huge numbers of adherents? Robert George Seale was born on October 22, 1936, in Dallas, Texas, the first son of George and Thelma Seale. By the time Bobby turned seven, he had already learned how to shoot guns. He likely got his first practice on his grandparents' 168-acre farm in Jasper, Texas, in the heart of the state's historic Ku Klux Klan territory. Bobby's mother, born Thelma Traylor, was an identical twin, one of sixteen farm children whose work ethic Bobby inherited along with her athleticism. Thelma was a star athlete at Jasper High School when she started dating George Seale.

Like many black youths of his generation, George Seale had dropped out of school after eighth grade, but he was good with his hands and became a master carpenter; he would pass those skills on to his two sons. George Seale often had trouble making ends meet and became abusive toward his family as his own father had been toward him. When Bobby was six, his father thrashed him for no good reason, an offense that he never forgot. Bobby also got his first lessons in exploitation from his father, who never paid him for any work he asked Bobby to do.

Thelma Seale left George more than once, raising her three surviving children with her twin sister and her sister's son Alvin. Early in

World War II, they moved from Dallas to San Antonio, where Mrs. Seale found work as a clerk at Kelly Airfield. By then George was back with the family. They decided to join the Great Migration, the mass movement of African-Americans from the rural south into big cities in the north. Bobby turned seven the year the family resettled in 1943 in subsidized rental housing in the Berkeley flatlands, just a few miles north of Oakland.

The Seales arrived in the Bay Area the year before the worst disaster of World War II to occur on continental United States soil: munitions improperly loaded by overhead nets onto cargo ships in nearby Port Chicago suddenly ignited on July 17, 1944, destroying two ships and adjacent docks. Five thousand tons of ammunition exploded less than twenty-five miles from where the family now lived, rattling windows fifty miles in every direction. The devastating accident annihilated 320 men, almost two-thirds of whom were African-American, and wounded over 400 others. It accounted for fifteen percent of all African-American casualties suffered on naval duty during the war. Outraged members of the African-American community believed the Navy and the U. S. government considered the workers to be expendable. The highly undesirable and manifestly dangerous task of handling explosives was assigned largely to untrained, predominantly black sailors in segregated units, working in conditions that many likened to a slave labor camp.

Hundreds of sailors, both white and black, refused to return to active duty in Port Chicago after the devastating explosion. Many of the resisting white sailors were transferred; none were prosecuted. Fifty blacks were tried for mutiny, a federal crime that could be punished by death. All were found guilty, but sentenced to hard labor and 15-year prison terms rather than death, most likely in light of the scathing national publicity stirred up by NAACP lawyer and future Supreme Court Justice Thurgood Marshall, who sat in on that controversial court martial. The trial had taken place just west of Oakland on Treasure Island in the San Francisco Bay. Outraged by what he saw, Marshall arranged to represent the convicted seamen on appeal. After the war, he succeeded in getting most of their sentences reduced significantly; it would take fifty years before the last surviving mutineer received a presidential pardon for his felony conviction. Yet behind the scenes the appalling incident quickly became a catalyst for change. As one historian put it, "U.S. government officials realized their ability to promote democracy among people of color around the world was seriously hampered by racial injustice at home."[1] The Navy began desegregating its units in 1946.

Bobby Seale was ten as this momentous change in the armed forces got underway. His mother Thelma was his biggest early influence. As a former military-base employee, she must have rejoiced along with other civil rights advocates in the East Bay at how Marshall had triggered this major step forward toward racial equality. Thelma vividly recalled an event that she had witnessed firsthand at age eleven in Texas that provoked great despair — a "race riot" in her home town of Jasper. It was one of the many bloody attacks across the country by whites against blacks that history books recorded as the infamous "Red Summer of 1919." It would remain the worst year of domestic violence in the 20th century until the late 1960s. Thelma Seale lived to see Jasper become infamous once again in 1998 when three white racists dragged 49-year-old hitch-hiker James Byrd to his death behind their pickup truck. The notorious incident instigated passage of the Texas hate crime law and also led to enactment of the federal Matthew Shepherd/James Byrd Hate Crimes Prevention Act signed into law by President Obama in 2009.

Once settled in Berkeley, George Seale opened a cabinet store in Oakland. Thelma Seale worked in San Francisco as a sandwich-maker and later found employment as a domestic worker. The family was always short of funds. As a young teen, Bobby made a little pocket change carrying groceries and mowing lawns. He tried out for two sports teams at Berkeley High. Both teams snubbed him; Seale blamed the slight on racist coaches. In the early 1950s, the high school's student body remained overwhelmingly white. The largest minority were Asians; there were very few blacks and Latinos. In his mid-teens Bobby joined one street gang and then another.

Seale's first awareness of injustice came around age sixteen when he learned of widespread and repeated mistreatment of American Indians that never made it into approved history books. He felt this injustice personally because he had Indian ancestry; Seale would not seek a better understanding of African-American history for several years. Seale quit high school and joined the Air Force, where he began studying history in earnest through books available at the library and an encyclopedia he purchased. While in the Air Force he learned to be a sheet metal mechanic. In his spare time, he started playing drums in a jazz band and splurged for a $600 set of drums on time payments, but got behind. A collection agency tracked Seale down at Ellsworth Air Force Base in South Dakota. By coincidence, his commanding officer was a relative of the bill collector and took it upon himself to hound Seale for payment of the arrears or go to jail. Seale had a melt down, ripped a phone out of the wall, cursed at his commander and prepared to go AWOL. Instead, he was court-martialed and ended his three years of service with a bad conduct discharge.

By the 1950s, after living in subsidized housing for many years, Mrs. Seale purchased a home on 57th Street in the North Oakland flatlands. After his discharge from the service Bobby came home and obtained a high school degree. His mother's motto was: "Whatever job you hold, be the best at it."[2] He got job after job as a sheet metal mechanic at different aircraft companies, only to be fired by all but the last one as soon as his bad conduct discharge caught up with him. At Kaiser Aerospace his boss kept him on a missile project despite learning of his ouster from the Air Force because Seale had developed expertise that was hard to replace.

In 1960, while still working for Kaiser Aerospace, Seale started taking classes in his spare time at Oakland City College (later renamed Merritt College). This was when Seale first focused on his African heritage. He grew his hair into an Afro and now wore a moustache. As Seale became more politically aware, he quit his job because he did not want to be helping the war effort. A natural extrovert, tall and broad-shouldered, Seale had occasional success as a stand-up comic getting people to laugh about things that oppressed them. He sometimes worked as a mechanical draftsman; he was good at reading blueprints. Though his original ambition in attending Oakland City College was to become an engineer, Seale had abandoned that goal by the time he met Huey Newton in September 1962. By then Seale was getting frequent gigs doing dark-humored stand-up comedy, and he hoped to make a career of it. He had also joined as one of its first members a new West Coast chapter of the Revolutionary Action Movement ("RAM"), a secretive East Coast organization that advocated guerrilla warfare. The underground group was not sanctioned by campus officials.

RAM took as its inspiration a new book, *Negroes with Guns*, whose author, black activist Robert Williams, was a strong proponent of armed self-defense. The former NAACP leader had fled to Cuba in 1961. Since then, with Fidel Castro's blessing, Williams regularly broadcasted his militant views to blacks in the South via "Radio Free Dixie." When Seale started to dedicate himself to taking action, he once again took his mother's advice to heart — if revolution was his goal, he would do the best job he could. His new young friend Huey Newton matched his zeal.

* * * * *

Like the Seale family, the Newtons were hopeful World War II transplants from the violent and unfriendly rural South. Huey's father Walter Newton was born in Alabama and worked for several years in Arkansas before he and his wife Armelia Johnson Newton moved to her home state of Louisiana. Walter held a variety of factory and farm jobs to support his seven children. Huey Percy Newton, born February 17, 1942, was the youngest. Walter Newton also preached every Sunday at a local Baptist church. One day in 1944, he could no longer stomach verbal abuse from the white overseer of the farm where he worked as a sharecropper. By talking back, Walter earned the label "crazy nigger."[3]

Every black in Monroe, Louisiana — like everywhere else at the time in the Deep South — knew you put your life at risk if you did not accept Jim Crow as the law of the land. For his own safety, Walter Newton took off for Northern California where war-time jobs were advertised. He found work in the new Alameda Naval Air Station. The rest of the family joined him the following year, when Huey was three. The family of Belva Davis — who became the first African-American woman TV journalist on the West Coast — fled at about the same time from the same Monroe, Louisiana, community that the Newton family left behind.

They escaped for a similar reason: her uncle had the audacity to sue a meat plant after he was seriously injured on the job; a white lawyer won a judgment for him, but none of it got paid. Instead, her uncle and his family were targeted for tar and feathering for being too uppity.[4]

By the time the Newton family moved to West Oakland their oldest children were adults. The new environment was like a foreign country where blacks occupied a segregated city within a city — one with its own culture, schools and entertainment. Melvin Newton was seven when they arrived and recalls its isolation: "It was like a traditional Jewish ghetto, only it was a black people's ghetto because that's where we had to live . . . in order to protect the white people being contaminated by the rabble that had migrated here from the South."

After the war, Walter Newton left his first job as a longshoreman and worked as a handyman and truck driver. He also volunteered again as an assistant minister at a local Baptist church. The Newtons moved several times to different parts of the Oakland community and ultimately settled in a racially mixed, working-class neighborhood in North Oakland. At Walter's insistence, Armelia Newton never looked for work outside the home as a domestic or otherwise. The couple doted on Huey. His older sisters — Myrtle, Leola and Doris — also favored him. Melvin was the next youngest boy, four years older than Huey, whose responsibility was to look after and protect his baby brother. Melvin knew that Huey was "kind of the darling of the family."

A very bright but shy child, Huey did not take to academics like Melvin did. While Melvin would enjoy spending weekend days in the nearest library, Huey favored the streets like his older brothers Leander "Lee" Edward and Walter, Jr., nicknamed "Sonny Man." But Huey later confounded anyone trying to pigeonhole him. He was a quick study with a phenomenal memory and obvious potential. He pleased his mother by his willingness to clean the oven out for her whenever she asked, yet at school most teachers found him uncooperative. Melvin Newton recalls the exception after they moved to the house Walter Newton bought in North Oakland: "[Huey] wound up having a teacher called Ms. McLaren. . . . It was the only time we had the same teacher. . . . When he entered her class, she told him that she knew me and she remembered me as his brother and what a fine student I was, and she expected the same out of him. That was the only teacher that didn't have any problems out of Huey."

Huey never got involved in sports. Nor did he learn to dance or carry a tune, but he did display talent for playing the piano. His parents then arranged for three years of classical training, and he became a lifelong fan. His cultivated taste in music would later impress his opera-singing fiancée LaVerne Williams and his lawyer Fay Stender, an accomplished concert pianist, to whom he described fond memories of playing Rimsky-Korsakov's "Flight of the Bumblebee" and selections from Tchaikovsky's *Nutcracker Suite.*

To impress the girls in junior high, Huey memorized and recited poetry and passages from Shakespeare's *Macbeth.* His parents still hoped Huey would follow Melvin's dogged pursuit of higher education and a steady job. At their urging, Melvin was one of the rare black students at Oakland Tech to take college preparatory classes. Melvin became the only one of Huey's siblings to get a college degree. Only one other finished high school.

Growing up, Huey felt severely handicapped by his light complexion and medium build, with a Caucasian nose inherited from a white grandfather who had forced himself on Walter Newton's mother. Newton's handsome bi-racial features, coupled with a high-pitched voice and a funny name, were serious liabilities on the streets of Oakland. Kids on the block may not have heard of Louisiana's demagogue Governor Huey P. Long, for whom he was named, but they teased Huey "Pee" Newton unmercifully.[5]

Black students were in the minority at his junior high school, where Huey quickly developed a thin skin. Despite the best efforts of his devout parents and brother Melvin, Huey became an indifferent high school student, often skipping school to spend hour upon hour in the pool halls. Melvin only realized later, when he read Huey's book *Revolutionary Suicide,* that Huey wanted to get thrown out of class so he could avoid being exposed for "not learning what was supposed to be learned." In high school, Melvin saw the dual track system for white and black students as a challenge to overcome; Huey took the teachers' low expectations of black kids "as a battle while he was still in school, to the neglect of the academic program. So you have two boys from the same family, handling the impact of race and racism very differently." Melvin later studied martial arts and realized that he and Huey illustrated how you "take the impact of something and you ride with it in another direction and then you'll bring it back. . . I didn't understand it academically like that, but that's in fact what I was doing." While Melvin tuned out those who discouraged him from pursuing his academic potential, "Huey was taking it on directly, and it was like a clash."

The rougher elements of Oakland acted as a magnet to Huey, as they had with his oldest brother, Lee, who had already served a jail sentence. Huey also hung out with his brother Sonny Man, a Korean War veteran employed at the Naval Air Station, who spent much of his spare time at the race track. Sonny Man impressed Huey and his friends with his street smarts, teaching Huey how to aggressively defend himself against local hoodlums. Huey had admired professional boxers since the age of five when his father encouraged him to defend himself against bullies. Ever since, Huey had numerous fights with neighborhood toughs, establishing a formidable reputation on the street.

His childhood friend David Hilliard explains the contradictions people always noticed in Huey:

> Growing up, Huey was greatly influenced by four strong male role
> models. He would eventually become an amalgam of all four: his
> father, a "strict disciplinarian" with "strict sense of moral character
> . . . deeply rooted in Old Testament values"; his "oldest brother
> Lee Edward . . . [who] taught Huey the meaning of standing up
> and holding his ground"; Walter, Jr. (Sonny Man), a ladies' man
> who "represented the excitement of the street"; and "Melvin
> [who] would influence Huey on the importance of education." . . .
> Throughout his life, Huey maintained a delicate balance of all four
> figureheads — [his father] Walter's values, brother Lee's strength,
> Sonny Man's street smarts, and Melvin's intellectual prowess.[6]

While Huey was a rebellious teen, Lee and Sonny Man influenced him the most. Constantly worrying his parents, Huey disguised

his reading and learning disabilities by acting out. As an adult, doctors would diagnose him as bipolar. Misbehavior in class and truancy
got him suspended from Oakland Tech in his sophomore year. In his
junior year, his parents enrolled him in Berkeley High. Not long afterward, there was an incident that got Huey suspended from Berkeley
High and referred to juvenile court. A gang of black kids attacked him;
the next day Huey retaliated against one of them with a hammer he
had brought from home. Placed on probation, Newton returned to
Oakland Tech, where he managed to obtain a degree; he graduated in
the bottom third of his class. Newton escaped the 1963 Vietnam War
draft with a 1-Y psychiatric exemption; he attributed it to his outspoken
criticism of racism in the military. Still, with a military exemption, a
high school degree and family support, Huey was better off than many
of his classmates. One-third of young black males in Oakland were
unemployed high school drop-outs, six times the national average.

Much to his parents' dismay and distress, Newton grew a scruffy
beard and quit the family home to share a flat near the Oakland City
College campus with William Brumfield, a.k.a. Richard Thorne, a co-
founder of the Sexual Freedom League and later the cult of Om Lovers.
Though Newton enjoyed sharing the favors of the young women
Brumfield attracted, Newton had his own ambitions. In high school,
Newton was told he was not "college material." Under the tutelage of his
brother Melvin, Huey began reading Plato's *Republic*. For the first time in
his life, he felt engaged by the written word. Perhaps to burnish his outlaw legend and self-made-man mythology, he would later claim that he
was completely illiterate until then and had faked the ability to read and
write in high school. As he pursued a social science degree at Oakland
City College, Newton focused on the study of philosophy and militant
politics, particularly the recent Cuban revolution and guerrilla leader
Ernesto "Che" Guevara. Newton had liked alcohol since he was a young
teen; in a show of solidarity, he made "Cuba Libre" his drink of choice.

By age twenty, in 1962, Newton had become a well-known figure
on the Oakland City College campus. He joined the Afro-American
Association, an informal group that met regularly at the home of a brilliant local lawyer and scholar named Donald Warden, who later changed

his name to Khalid Abdullah Tariq al Mansour. At the time, Warden also hosted a radio program called the Afro-American Association. Among the study group's members were Ron Dellums, future congressman and Oakland mayor, and Thelton Henderson, who became the first African-American to head the federal court in the Northern District of California. Henderson remembers Newton well: "A very bright young man. A very respectful young man . . . He came to learn and he was a quick learner. He contributed a lot, and I've always imagined that many of the ideas he got for the Panthers' philosophy and some of the interest areas that they had, came from those meetings at the Afro-American Association."

Warden had been a class ahead of Henderson at the U.C. Berkeley law school, known then as Boalt Hall. In the fall of 1963, Warden invited Henderson to do some legal contract work, making occasional local court appearances that helped Henderson pay his rent. Henderson had just returned to the Bay Area after getting sacked from his first job, a plum assignment in the Justice Department under Attorney General Robert Kennedy investigating civil rights abuses in Alabama. Henderson was sent to Birmingham after the church bombing that killed four girls in Sunday school in September 1963. He stayed at the only hotel in Birmingham that offered lodging to blacks, which was where Reverend Martin Luther King, Jr., also stayed. One night, out of concern for King's safety, Henderson loaned King's driver his car because King's had a faulty tire. Henderson did not realize that state agents working for the FBI were tailing King everywhere he went. Henderson's unapproved favor made headlines, and the Justice Department fired him for misuse of government property.

Believing that his career was in tatters, Henderson returned to Berkeley. Later he would be proud of his generous impulse — if King's car had been disabled by the roadside after dark, his life could have been at grave risk that night. Several months after Henderson went back to California, three Civil Rights workers — James Chaney, Michael Schwerner and Andrew Goodman — disappeared in Philadelphia, Mississippi. National outrage prompted a massive FBI search over the summer of 1964 which ultimately turned up their bodies. Years later, investigators identified the KKK culprits, including a sheriff's deputy, who tailed the civil rights workers' car and kidnapped and killed them.

In rebuilding his life after being fired for loaning Dr. King his car, Henderson welcomed the chance to join Donald Warden's study group:

> We'd learn about our heritage. The premise of the Afro-American Association was that blacks should not accept the white historical version of a Negro. . . [The name] Afro-American was very consciously decided to reflect our African heritage, rather than whatever a Negro had come to mean. So we started studying our heritage and read a bunch of very, very interesting [books] that I had never read . . . Marcus Garvey, W. E. B. Dubois, E. Franklin Frazier [Author of *The Negro Family in the United States*] . . . It was a very exciting and eye-opening period for me.

At first, Newton relished the group's focus on the works of Leftist political writers like W. E. B. Dubois, James Baldwin and Jean-Paul Sartre. He also liked the way the association promoted the wearing of dashikis and the teaching of Swahili. Soon, however, he was getting restless. Since the fall of 1962, Newton had been holding forth frequently at a lunchtime speaking forum adjacent to the Oakland City College campus on Grove Street — known as the Grove Street orators. Newton liked to expound on the Cuban revolution, hand out "Fair Play for Cuba" flyers and criticize President Kennedy's Cuban blockade and the history of American colonial power.

It was when Newton gave speeches on Grove Street that he first caught Seale's attention. Newton tapped into Seale's inner anger and frustration: "The experience of things I'd seen in the black community, killings that I'd witnessed, black people killing each other — and my own experience just . . . trying to make it . . . came to the surface."[7] Soon Newton's roommate Brumfield introduced the pair to each other at an Afro-American Association rally. Seale already found Newton's speeches impressive. Seale impressed Newton, too. Newton learned that Seale owned guns and was an expert marksman, and had been trained in the military to take apart and reassemble an M1 carbine blindfolded.

At the time they met, Seale was still secretly active in RAM. Seale soon suggested that Newton join, too. But when Huey applied for membership in RAM, he was rejected because he resided with his parents in a "bourgeois" mixed-race Oakland neighborhood. His home was outside the *lumpenproletariat* flatlands — the poorest area of the city, where pimps, hustlers, prostitutes and thieves abounded.[8] RAM's view did not match that of traditional Marxists. Karl Marx expected the working class to rise up to take ownership of their own labor, but placed no trust in the criminal class. Marx coined the term *lumpenproletariat* for outcasts in rags and low-level lawbreakers he doubted would ever attain class consciousness. Marx actually considered them "bottom-feeders" — obstacles to his dream of a classless society because of their dependence on the labor of others for their survival. In Marx's view, even if they became true believers in revolution, the *lumpenproletariat* remained far more vulnerable to arrest and coercion into becoming informants. That very problem would later be the Panthers' undoing.

When RAM snubbed him, Newton was surprised that RAM embraced a stand-up comic (Seale) but rejected a more serious Leftist philosopher like himself. Newton later scorned RAM members as just "phony armchair revolutionaries."[9] Ironically, at the same time RAM rejected Newton as unfit, RAM had unknowingly accepted as charter members undercover policemen intent on keeping a watchful eye on their activities.

Between 1962 and 1965, Newton and Seale saw each other only occasionally. During this time, Newton often took seasonal jobs at the Del Monte cannery in nearby Emeryville, where two of his sisters were employed. From time to time, Newton hired on as a construction worker or longshoreman or street cleaner for the City of Oakland, though he never held any job for long. Meanwhile, Newton secretly supplemented his legitimate income with petty burglaries from unlocked cars, parking lot robberies, selling stolen property and, for several months, pimping.

Huey's reckless streak was patent. He liked to scare friends by racing his car across the railroad tracks to barely beat an oncoming train. At five-foot-ten, he did not intimidate anyone by sheer size, but he still cultivated a fierce reputation on the street. Shortly after his twenty-first birthday, Newton was arrested for stealing a book. He managed to talk his way into an acquittal. Arrested in Berkeley for burglary a year later, he again persuaded the police to let him go. Arrested once more on five counts of burglary in early May of 1964, he got the charge reduced to petty theft.

Newton had his first serious brush with the law in the late spring of 1964, when he attended a birthday dinner party and got into an argument with a scar-faced bully named Odell Lee he had never met before. Lee was so hostile and aggressive, Newton acted first. He picked up a steak knife and stabbed Lee, which got Newton arrested for assault with a deadly weapon. He cockily decided to represent himself once again. This time, after a two-day jury trial, Newton was convicted. Tom Broome, who years later became Huey's probation officer, coincidentally had been present at the birthday party. Broome thought "there was so much provocation that a third-grade attorney could have beaten the case or at least had it reduced. Huey didn't know how to go about it, made a fool of himself and wound up with a felony conviction to boot."[10]

This conviction would be significant in Newton's prosecution for the death of Officer Frey. Newton served six months in jail at Santa Rita before his release on three years' probation. En route to Santa Rita, the 22-year-old spent one month in an isolation cell in the Alameda County jail, infamously known as "the soul breaker."[11] At Santa Rita, Newton received similar punishment in the "cooler." In December 1964, he watched from the Santa Rita prison yard as busloads of arrested Free Speech Movement demonstrators from U. C. Berkeley arrived for a brief stay. The political statement they made by joint action impressed him greatly.

Upon his release from Santa Rita, Newton returned to Oakland City College to take a few courses. Newton mainly wanted to use the college as a political base. From his perspective, Oakland City College's location in a run-down flatland neighborhood was ideal for recruitment. Newton figured knowledge of the law would come in handy. He signed up for a course on California criminal law taught by Assistant District Attorney (and Ronald Reagan's future Attorney General) Edwin Meese III. Huey quickly showed himself to be an apt student, particularly when the subjects were the constitutional rights of suspects and the dos and don'ts of California's open-carry gun laws.

Newton's parents must have been extremely pleased with his new devotion to studies and his new girlfriend, LaVerne Williams, an aspiring opera singer. Williams participated in a Miss Bronze Northern California competition co-sponsored by radio and TV journalist Belva Davis and won the talent competition. Williams introduced her boyfriend to Davis, praising his love of music, poetry and philosophy. Walter Newton knew Davis's father from the days both families lived in Monroe, Louisiana. Davis was shocked when, only a few years later, the quiet young man she had met as LaVerne's boyfriend morphed into a symbol of armed revolt.

When Newton was released from the Santa Rita jail, one of the most active and highly respected leftists on campus was Richard Masato Aoki, an eight-year army veteran. Huey already knew him as a fierce streetfighter from the late 1950s when Aoki's family moved to West Oakland after their World War II internment. As a teen, the third-generation Japanese-American had hung out with Huey's oldest brothers. At Oakland City College, Aoki started a chapter of the Young Socialist Alliance of the Socialist Workers Party. The Socialist Workers Party espoused Soviet Union co-founder Leon Trotsky's view that Communism should spread across the globe through continuing revolution. Aoki invited Bobby Seale as a speaker and became good friends with Seale as well as Newton. Aoki transferred to U. C. Berkeley and continued his activism there, while keeping in close contact with his Oakland college friends.

In 1965, Newton and Seale were searching for a new base on campus. They joined disaffected blacks who founded the Soul Students Advisory Council. One of the group's leaders was Ken Freeman, a self-educated expert on African history and editor-in-chief of a new radical political and literary magazine called *Soulbook*. Also among the Advisory Council's founders was one of *Soulbook*'s writers, leftist scholar Louis Armmond. Armmond grew up on the East Coast before attending U. C. Berkeley, where he had become one of the handful of black activists in the early Free Speech Movement. At Armmond's instigation, the Council opposed the drafting of black soldiers for the Vietnam War and organized hundreds of people to attend a rally — one of the largest such protests on the Oakland City College campus up to that time. The Council also increased awareness among blacks of their heritage and of the ways in which they had been relegated to colonial status. They lobbied for courses in black history and pushed for the hiring of African-American faculty.

Malcolm X's assassination in late February 1965 hit Seale hard. That same day Seale took some bricks from his mother's garden, broke them in two and started hurling them at every passing car driven by a white person. He later said, "I was ready to die that day."[12] Instead, he focused on learning more about one of the principal sources of Malcolm X's political consciousness — the late Afro-Caribbean revolutionary Dr. Frantz Fanon. Dr. Fanon had participated in the successful Algerian overthrow of French colonial rule, an insurrection that began in 1954 and took until 1962 to achieve its goal of independence from France.

Louis Armmond introduced Fanon's books to his friends in the Bay Area. The members of the Soul Students Advisory Council studied them like the Bible. Here was a blueprint, taken from recent successful experience, for how a liberation movement could be started from a condition of perceived total subservience. Dr. Fanon called violence "a cleansing force." He wrote in *The Wretched of the Earth*, "It frees the native from his inferiority complex and from his despair and inaction. It makes him fearless and restores his self-respect."[13] If violent revolt could work against the French in Algeria, why not for American blacks? Seale read and reread Dr. Fanon's *The Wretched of the Earth* and recommended it enthusiastically to Newton.

Newton was the first among the Grove Street orators to go public with the new revolutionary ideas being discussed among the members of the Council — the connection between the Algerians' overthrow of an oppressive regime and what might be possible for blacks struggling in Oakland. Newton drew a rapt audience. Seale later pointed to the moment in 1965 when the two focused on the impact of Dr. Fanon's writings as the true genesis of the Black Panther Party.

In March 1966, Berkeley police arrested Seale for disturbing the peace by standing on a chair on a Berkeley street corner loudly reading revolutionary poetry to passersby. Huey Newton was with him and scuffled with one of the officers, resulting in Newton's arrest as well. Soon afterward they used Soul Students Advisory Council funds to make bail. When other members objected, the pair quit the Council. The incident caught the attention of Max Scherr, the radical lawyer who owned the Steppenwolf bar in Berkeley where activists regularly gathered. In 1965, Scherr had started publishing an underground newspaper, *The Berkeley Barb,* to cover the Free Speech Movement and anti-war activities in Berkeley from a leftist perspective. Scherr later claimed the distinction of being the first to report on the political activities of the two, then unknown, black militants, Huey Newton and Bobby Seale, in the form of the *Barb's* account of their 1966 arrest for disturbing the peace.

That same summer of 1966, Bobby Seale was hired to oversee neighborhood youths in the new federal jobs project Oakland had obtained in the wake of the Watts riot. Local activist Mark Comfort was likely instrumental in bringing Seale into a leadership role in the jobs program. Two years older than Seale, Comfort had worked with Stokely Carmichael on voting rights in Alabama in the early '60s and returned to Oakland to become the head of the Oakland Direct Action Committee. At home among black youths in the streets, Comfort wore a tilted beret and a large gold earring. From day one, the EDA officials who arrived in Oakland from Washington considered Comfort an effective, natural leader. He established such a personal rapport with EDA's head, Assistant Secretary of Commerce Eugene Foley, that Foley went out of his way to visit Comfort when he was jailed at Santa Rita in the summer of 1966 on a questionable charge of misconduct in a peaceful protest of minority hiring practices at the *Oakland Tribune.* At the time, Comfort had just competed unsuccessfully in the Democratic primary for the state assembly.[14]

Given the opportunity, Seale brought in Newton to assist him at the North Oakland Anti-Poverty Center, where Seale supervised eighty at-risk high school students in work programs. Newton's elementary school classmate Paul Cobb became a neighborhood youth coordinator for West Oakland. (Cobb would years later become the publisher of the regional African-American weekly paper, *The Oakland Post.*) Judge Lionel Wilson headed the jobs project as Chairman of the Oakland

Economic Development Council.

Seale and Newton could see racial progress occurring, and not just from the new federal jobs program. By the mid-1960s, Oakland High School was thoroughly integrated: about a third of the students were black; almost a third were Asian; and the rest were white. Meanwhile, Seale and Newton were among the young men who met at DeFremery Park with Oakland Parks and Recreation Department manager Bill Patterson. A protégé of Judge Wilson who worked his way up from part-time playground director to head of the department, Bill Patterson was then in his thirties and already beginning to gain admirers for nurturing the careers of many future professional superstars, including baseball's Ricky Henderson and Joe Morgan and basketball's Bill Russell. Lionel Wilson himself had been a former star tennis and baseball player before becoming a lawyer. In a major move toward integration, when Patterson rose to head of the Oakland Parks and Recreation Department, he integrated all of the city swimming pools in one summer.

Both Mark Comfort and Curtis Baker, who also wore a gold earring and beret, provided the most inspiring examples to Seale and Newton. Neither was afraid to assail police brutality and directly confront white authority figures with the hatred that might easily explode into another Watts if West Oakland did not get immediate redress for longstanding governmental neglect. Baker ran the "West End Help Center" and helped start a group demanding jobs for black applicants for jobs at the new Bay Area Rapid Transit Authority. Yet the progress being made was nowhere near fast enough or broad enough for impatient young radicals like Seale and Newton in the mid-1960s. They wanted major change now.

In September 1966 Seale attended a conference headed by *Soulbook* magazine publisher Ken Freeman, who had led the Soul Students Advisory Council at Oakland City College. The hot topic was Stokely Carmichael's June 1966 call for black power organizations to replace traditional civil rights groups. A front page story in *The Movement* newspaper described Carmichael's Lowndes County Freedom Organization. That voting-rights effort in Alabama used a Black Panther logo and embraced a right of armed self-defense. The

Alabama group adopted the panther as its symbol because animal mascots were traditional in Alabama for every political party, and the panther was said to defend itself vigorously, but not to engage in unprovoked attack. By August of 1966, with Carmichael's support, the Panther logo was beginning to be used by organizers of black militants in cities across the country.

At the end of the three-day conference, the group announced the formation of the Black Panther Party of Northern California. Almost immediately, Seale and Freemen had a falling out. Seale quit the group and shortly afterward shared the materials he had received with Huey Newton. Both were still part-time students at Oakland City College. They began planning their own more militant organization in Oakland. Meanwhile, after the police shooting of teenager Matthew Johnson in San Francisco, SDS held a Black Power conference in Berkeley with Stokely Carmichael as the key speaker and Mark Comfort among others on the panel. Flyers describing the Lowndes County Freedom Organization with its black panther logo were distributed on campus.

In forming their own organization, Seale and Newton decided to use the same black panther logo, but added the words "For Self-Defense" to the group's name to emphasize their more aggressive approach — carrying loaded weapons. They got together on creating the Party platform with Richard Aoki, who was now at U. C. Berkeley. Together, the three radicals hammered out a 10-point platform for their new group using the Nation of Islam's "What We Believe" as a model. They refined the program at Seale's home near campus and at work. Then they took it to Newton's older brother Melvin, who was then a graduate student at Berkeley, to have him polish its language. The finished platform included a lengthy quote from the Declaration of Independence justifying the right to overthrow "absolute Despotism" after "a long train of abuses and usurpations." Seale's wife Artie and Huey's girlfriend LaVerne both worked on typing up the platform. Then Newton and Seale surreptitiously made 1,000 copies late at night on the Anti-Poverty Center's mimeograph machine. Melvin thought their proposal a timely cry for change to meet the needs of the black community, but he resisted their efforts to get him to join them. What good would carrying guns accomplish? It was probably Mark Comfort who first told Carmichael about a couple of Oakland friends using the symbol and the Black Panther name to start their own group. The SNCC leader did not think much would come of it.

As the two budding revolutionaries sought to establish their own organization, they still disdained white students at Oakland City College. But, unlike SNCC and cultural nationalist groups, Seale and Newton recognized the benefits of strong alliances with white radicals. They readily accepted money from Bob Scheer, a Peace and Freedom anti-war candidate for Congress in 1966, to help them organize support on campus. Other black student organizations on campus rejected outright Newton's insistence that the time had come for defending the black community with guns. They considered it suicidal. So did Newton.

Taunting police to join him in a life-or-death game, Newton expected not to live more than a year, but found the prospect exhilarating. He often likened the sensation to the "deep flow of play" Buddhists characterized as the essence of life.[15] The Eastern philosophical term struck a chord; it matched the sense of peace Newton felt after coming to terms with his own mortality. His older brother Melvin still hoped to persuade Huey to behave with caution; he warned his little brother the police were already digging his grave.

THE BLACK PANTHER

BLACK COMMUNITY NEWS SERVICE

VOLUME 1   APRIL 25, 1967   NUMBER 1

P.O. BOX 8641 OAK. CALIF. EMERYVILLE BRANCH

PUBLISHED BY THE BLACK PANTHER PARTY FOR SELF DEFENSE

WHY WAS DENZIL DOWELL KILLED

APRIL FIRST 3:50 a.m.

"I BELIEVE THE POLICE MURDERED MY SON" SAYS THE MOTHER OF DENZIL DOWELL.

Brothers and Sisters of the Richmond community, here is the view of the family's side of the death of Denzil Dowell as compiled by the Black Panther Party for Self Defense, concerned citizens, and the Dowell family. As you know, April 1st, 1967, Denzil Dowell (age 22), was shot and killed by an "officer of the Martinez Sheriff's Department", so read the newspaper.

But there are too many unanswered questions that have been raised by the Dowell family and other neighbors in the North Richmond community. Questions that don't meet the satisfaction of the killing of Denzil. The Richmond Police, the Martinez Sheriff's Department, and the Richmond Independent would have us Black people believe something contrary to Mrs. Dowell's accusation. That is, her son was "unjustifiably" murdered by a racist cop.

There are too many questionable facts supporting the Dowell family's point of view.

These questionable facts are as follows:

1. Denzil Dowell was unarmed so how can six bullet holes and shot gun blasts be considered "justifiable homicide"? (Con't Page 2)

WE BLACK PEOPLE ARE MEETING SATURDAY 1:30 AT 1717 SECOND STREET LET US SUPPORT THE DOWELL FAIMLY EVERY BLACK BROTHER AND SISTER MUST UNITE FOR REAL POLITICAL ACTION

First Issue of the Black Panther Party Newspaper, April 25, 1967.

4. TAKIN' CARE OF BUSINESS

Some people say we've got a lot of malice
Some say it's a lot of nerve
But I say we won't quit moving until we get what we deserve
We have been bucked and we have been scorned
We have been treated bad, talked about as just bones
But just as it takes two eyes to make a pair, ha
Brother we can't quit until we get our share.
— JAMES BROWN, "SAY IT LOUD"

Newton and Seale's new revolutionary party started out slowly. At the invitation of their friend Richard Aoki, the two fund-raised in the fall of 1966 by hawking copies of the quotations of Chairman Mao for $1 apiece at anti-war demonstrations on the U. C. Berkeley campus. They figured, correctly, that inner city blacks would do brisk business with white radicals when they offered them Mao Tse-tung's *Little Red Book*, with sayings like "Political power grows out of the barrel of a gun." At seventy-cents' profit per copy, the proceeds mounted quickly. They used them to purchase guns as an inducement to enroll new Panther Party members.

Aoki had started wearing the same black leather jacket and tilted beret as the Panther leaders, his eyes shielded by dark glasses. With his moustache, practiced grimace and sunglasses, he exuded a fierce image despite his slight stature. Seale and Newton gave the 29-year-old Japanese-American the title Field Marshal, the only non-black who would ever achieve any rank in the party. Newton had told him "The struggle for freedom, justice and equality transcends racial and ethnic barriers. As far as I'm concerned, you black."[1] After all, Aoki's entire family had endured worse violation of his civil rights than almost anyone else Newton knew — Aoki spent years as a child prisoner of war in a Utah internment camp with no indoor plumbing or heat, his parents scorned as enemies despite the fact they were both born and raised in America. Aoki had quit the army because he did not want to kill Vietnamese civilians. The ex-GI still bore the psychological scars of his family's mistreatment. Before their relocation, his grandfather ran a successful Oakland noodle company. Internment split up his parents. On their return, they found the family home vandalized; his father became a hardened criminal. As a teen in West Oakland, it was easy for Aoki to identify with disaffected black hustlers on the street.

Aoki earned his title of Field Marshal by supplying Seale and Newton with their first weapons; he also gave Newton and new recruits like young Bobby Hutton firearms training. Unbeknownst to either Seale or Newton or anyone else in their circle, since 1961 Aoki had been a government informant helping the FBI track Communists and other dissidents.[2] Aoki told the FBI he did not support the Soviet Union and would help them unmask Communists; he became a key informant on the Free Speech Movement at Cal. The shocking revelation of Aoki's duplicity would not occur until almost five decades later as the accidental byproduct of Freedom of Information Act requests by investigative reporter Seth Rosenfeld, author of the 2012 best-seller *Subversives: The FBI's War on Student Radicals and Reagan's Rise to Power*. When the news went public, Bobby Seale refused to believe it was true. A lifelong friend of Aoki's from the days when they were both young radicals found it just as astonishing, but realized that Aoki had long led a compartmentalized life.

The FBI was focused on Communists when the bureau originally recruited Aoki. When he started taking classes at Oakland City College, it was the FBI that suggested he open a chapter of the Trotskyite Student Socialist Alliance. Over the next fifteen years, Aoki secretly reported to the FBI on various leftist groups, including the Panthers. But when Aoki first joined Seale and Newton in 1966 to help write their party platform, the FBI did not have any interest yet in either Seale or

Newton. No evidence would ever emerge that the FBI used one of its standard provocateur tactics to put Aoki up to offering the Panthers weapons and weapons training in 1966 to lure them into confrontations with the police. Aoki may have provided the weapons out of genuine desire to abet their new venture; he had witnessed the brutality of police in West Oakland firsthand.

Aoki graduated from Cal in 1968 with a sociology degree and, after obtaining a master's degree in 1970 in the same field, went on to a 25-year career as a teacher and administrator at Merritt College (formerly Oakland City College). When Rosenfeld interviewed Aoki in 2007 for his book about the Free Speech Movement, Rosenfeld stunned Aoki with news that an FBI agent had identified him as a long-term informant listed in their records as T-2. The ex-GI at first retreated into silence; then he offered a denial with a cryptic explanation: "It is complex. Layer upon layer."[3] Three years later — before Rosenfeld's discovery went public — Aoki committed suicide at his home. On the bed near where he shot himself he had carefully laid out his Panther regalia and his freshly ironed Army uniform.[4]

Many informants led two lives. At Cal in 1966, Aoki become one of the most active Asian students lobbying for ethnic studies. He invited his good friends Seale and Newton to campus and provided Seale with a speaking opportunity. John Burris was an undergraduate that fall and became an early fan of Seale's oratory. But Burris disagreed with the Panthers' overall strategy: "There was a call for all black men to be armed. . . . My sense is if you have guns then you might be placed in a position to use them. . . . I was not a person who believed in violence and so I would not put myself in a position to harm anyone or to have anyone harm me . . . and I would not own a gun, and carry a gun, promote . . . any activities of that kind. . . . I didn't think that was realistic. . . . I had a real sense of the power of the U.S. Government . . . and that you could be wiped out, a whole mass of people could be wiped out."

Burris was not alone in his squeamishness about packing a gun. Most of the Cal students who gravitated towards the Panthers likely had a similar reaction. Newton headed off campus to recruit more street-wise acquaintances. The promise of guns quickly lured neighborhood toughs and high school truants to Newton's lectures about his new party's philosophy. The Panthers' first recruit, sixteen-year-old Bobby Hutton, had been one of Seale's charges at the Anti-Poverty Program in Oakland. Newton routinely carried a pump-action shotgun, Hutton carried an M3 carbine, and Seale a .45 automatic in a holster. As they gained off-campus supporters, the Panthers started to become an intimidating force.

By 1966, the whole atmosphere at Oakland City College had already become racially polarized. Many black students became campus bullies. Unofficial taboos kept most whites from using a particular water fountain the black students favored, maybe in retaliation for Southern "whites only" drinking fountains. Whites began to feel extremely uncomfortable if they congregated with black students in the hallway outside of classrooms; blacks also monopolized the snack room. White students who made eye contact with black males while walking around campus often generated icy stares; whites who were not radicals faced derision as "honkies." Graffiti on campus included death threats against honkies. When members of the new Black Panther Party brought rifles on campus, the open display of weapons intimidated and frightened many students while inspiring and empowering others.

* * * * *

Meanwhile, Seale and Newton had begun to tap into simmering black community outrage at chronic police abuse, a well-documented and long-standing problem. Back in 1949, the local branch of the left-wing Civil Rights Congress had investigated charges of Oakland officers regularly beating up black residents. Oakland-based civil rights lawyer Bob Treuhaft and his wife, Decca Mitford, had searing memories of that eye-opening experience. Decca spent long hours assisting in that research: "[Our investigation disclosed] monstrous beastliness, authority cloaked in nightmare garb . . . On Fridays . . . police would regularly lie in wait outside the West Oakland bars that served as banks for the cashing of pay checks, arrest those emerging on charges of drunkenness, and in the privacy of the prowl cars beat them and rob them of their week's pay en route to the West Oakland police station."[5]

The scathing report led to a legislative inquiry into police brutality in Oakland, one of the first official inquiries ever undertaken of any major police department for alleged abusive treatment of minorities. These days, such findings would be national news and would provoke mass demonstrations, but in those years before the Civil Rights Era, the report drew little media coverage and no meaningful state action. The continuing racial divide between the black community and the OPD greatly exacerbated the situation.

The first noticeable progress occurred in 1951 when Treuhaft and his law partner Edises amazingly obtained the reversal of a death penalty conviction in a highly publicized murder case involving a local black shoe-shine boy, Jerry Newson. (From 1930 to 1960 half of those executed in California were black.) Newson had been accused of murdering a white pharmacist and his assistant. In his defense, Newson testified that the police pressured him into making a false confession under threat of facing "the hard boys" of the department who would otherwise beat a confession out of him.[6] On remand from the California Supreme Court, the case was tried twice more, but both trials ending in hung juries. Newson eventually went to jail for an unrelated robbery. As a small boy growing up in Oakland, Newton had heard all about the Newson case. Huey considered Bob Treuhaft and Bert Edises two of his childhood heroes. They offered the black community a glimmer of hope that police misconduct might sometimes be redressed.

For more than two decades after the war, the black community believed the OPD deliberately cultivated a racist police force, mostly from the South. Black policemen were rare in the 1940s. A few more were hired in the 1950s, maybe 15 in all. By the late 1960s, when blacks were the largest minority group in the city, of 658 sworn police personnel in the OPD, only 27 were nonwhites — and only 16 of those were black. With the exception of one of 95 sergeants and one of 11 captains, the leadership was entirely white. Curtis Baker, who ran the West Oakland Help Center, became a strong advocate of creating a civilian police review board. He testified before the California Civil Rights Commission in June of 1966 at a hearing on police community relations:

"Oakland must stop hiring Ku Klux Klansmen and Mississippi hillbillies to do their killing. "We (Negroes in Oakland) are living in a cage."[7]

Seale's and Newton's revolutionary friend Louis Armmond, who introduced them to the writings of Dr. Fanon, agreed with that stark assessment. When the Panthers were first launched, "We found that community monitoring of the police and . . . methods of self-defense in Oakland, were just as necessary as . . . armed self-defense in . . . Mississippi and Louisiana in the '60s during the civil rights movement. But we knew that in Mississippi, the Klan and the police and the sheriff were the same. In Oakland, there were more or less formal separations, but the official police actually carried out the same methods in many ways as the Klan would do unofficially in the South."

A decade later, a black elected official in the East Bay described local law enforcement in the 1960s the same way — just as brutal as "the most rabid, cracker police force in a small Mississippi town."[8] That was quite an indictment. Mississippi and Alabama provided such horrific evidence of racist policing in the early '60s that they became the major catalyst for passage of the Civil Rights Acts of 1964 and 1965. Louisiana and rural Florida police employed similarly bigoted tactics, but Alabama took center stage in 1963 when national television showed shocking footage of police under Birmingham's Commissioner of Public Safety Eugene "Bull" Connor siccing attack dogs on freedom marchers and using fire hoses on children as well as adults. On "Bloody Sunday" — March 7, 1965 — people across the country again saw with their own eyes vicious beatings by police in Selma, Alabama, clubbing peaceful marchers unconscious for joining a freedom walk to Montgomery led by Reverend Martin Luther King. Future Georgia Congressman John Lewis was among the hospitalized victims.

Oakland's Police Chief strongly objected to this odious comparison; he vigorously disputed that his recruiters discriminated against minority applicants or actively sought Southern racists. Actually, the OPD conducted a nationwide recruitment effort during the years after World War II, focused on a combination of military veterans and graduates of four police academies, including one at Berkeley. These efforts to find top applicants netted dedicated criminology majors like George Hart at

Cal, who would rise through the ranks to become chief in 1973. And yet that did not entirely refute charges of racist police recruitment.

Two of the four academies that OPD hired from were located in the Deep South — one in Florida and one in Louisiana. Those recruitment efforts, as well as newspaper ads in hubs like Atlanta, attracted many white applicants to the OPD from communities that routinely turned a blind eye to mistreatment of blacks and to "unsolved" lynchings in which off-duty police were themselves often complicit. Throughout the South in the Civil Rights Era, the FBI fed slander to daily newspapers many of whose publishers gladly labeled Reverend King an "unspeakable extremist agitator," who associated with Communists. The press likewise derided Northern voting rights volunteers as "miserable street rabble."[9] Growing up in communities with such little regard for the rights of blacks who lived across the tracks, it was no wonder that many Southern recruits to the OPD drew fierce criticism from West Oaklanders for the way they handled their jobs in the similarly segregated city of Oakland. (Under pressure from the black community, the OPD later abandoned its national recruitment efforts and focused on hiring more locals.)

In doing research for his 1999 book, *Blue v. Black: Let's End the Conflict Between Cops and Minorities*, civil rights lawyer John Burris concluded: "The culture of the department in Oakland was such that, even if an officer came with good intentions, he could be co-opted by the department itself, by the culture of the department. And good officers in fact, even if they didn't turn into bad officers and turn to brutality, will nevertheless not speak up about it." Guy Saperstein, author of *Civil Warrior: Memoirs of a Civil Rights Attorney*, noticed that other local officials were complicit as well. When he worked with young black kids in an Oakland playground in the 1960s before he became a lawyer, he reported to his superiors that he had seen policemen repeatedly drive onto the playground just to harass the children. The only upshot was that Saperstein was considered a troublemaker and transferred to a different location.

An experience like Saperstein's at that time was unfortunately par for the course. If accused of any misconduct, the police department could then always count on the strong backing of both an irate City

Council and the *Oakland Tribune*. When the Poverty Council sought civilian oversight of the police in 1966, the City Council defended the department's professionalism and the majority rejected out-of-hand either creation of an advisory police review board or Mayor Reading's suggestion of an ombudsman to investigate citizens' complaints.

The City Council pointed to an official report detailing an incident in East Oakland that could have erupted into a riot but was defused by local police. "Police officials met behind the scenes with Negro teenage leaders to discuss rumors of police brutality and rumors of plans for further violence, and felt that these talks helped to improve the atmosphere."[10] But citing one instance of the police seeking to reduce potential conflict in East Oakland did not address the misery still experienced by the black community of West Oakland. The mainstream press compounded black communities' sense of oppression. Oakland and San Francisco reporters for major papers maintained their long-standing color code for news stories, leaving ghetto murders and beatings largely unexamined and unreported.[11]

In this toxic environment, most black Oaklanders felt helpless and resentful — not Newton and Seale, who seized the opportunity for direct action. They looked for an easy-to-find storefront, where they could boldly advertise their name for all passersby. On January 1, 1967, using paychecks Seale, Newton and Hutton received from the anti-poverty program, the Panthers opened their first office in North Oakland near the Berkeley border. A large sign in their window at the corner of Fifty-sixth and Grove streets proclaimed, "Black Panther Party for Self-Defense." (Grove Street is now Martin Luther King, Jr. Way.)

Today, most Americans recognize *Miranda* warnings from crime stories on television and in the movies. Police routinely tell suspects before interrogating them that they have a right to remain silent and a right to an attorney. These constitutional rights stem from the Fifth Amendment right not to incriminate oneself and the Sixth Amendment right to counsel in criminal proceedings. But such warnings were not required in California or other states when Huey Newton had his first brushes with the law. They were the controversial product of the Warren Court in the mid-1960s. When Newton took law classes, he learned about these new protections. In 1964, in a five-to-four decision in a case arising out of Illinois, the United States Supreme Court invalidated a confession obtained after the suspect asked to speak to an attorney and was denied that opportunity. The decision in *Escobedo v. Illinois* (1964) 378 U.S. 478 generated a lot of confusion about exactly when a suspect should be told he has a right to remain silent under the Fifth Amendment guarantee that no person "shall be compelled in any criminal case to be a witness against himself." It also left unresolved whether a suspect first had to ask for an attorney in order to benefit from the Sixth Amendment right to "have the assistance of counsel for his defence" before answering questions from the police.

The California Supreme Court addressed the Sixth Amendment question the following year, reviewing a death penalty case from San Quentin to decide if an inmate's confession should be thrown out even though he had not first asked for a lawyer. In *People v. Dorado* (1965) 62 Cal. 3d 338 the California court divided four to three in reversing the inmate's conviction based on *Escobedo*. Then, in June 1956, came the decision of the United State's Supreme Court itself on when suspects must be told of their right to remain silent and their right to council. The high court had before it several criminal convictions from various jurisdictions and made its famous ruling in all of them under the name of the lead case, *Miranda v. Arizona* (1966) 384 U.S. 436.

Miranda was another highly controversial five-to-four ruling. The majority recognized the inherently intimidating nature of a police stop and how that severely impacted a suspect's free choice. It also considered the question of whether those unschooled in the law should be required to first ask for an attorney in order to receive the protection of that Sixth Amendment right. The high court took notice that the FBI already had a practice of giving warnings to suspects at the outset of a criminal interrogation that they had the right to remain silent and the right to consult an attorney. The majority saw no good reason why such warnings should not be required of state and local police as well, where the vast majority of criminal prosecutions took place. The burden was minimal and outweighed by the benefit to individuals entitled to constitutional guarantees. The *Miranda* ruling was issued just a few months before the Panthers formed. The Oakland Police Department regularly monitored court decisions affecting its practices and quickly implemented mandated changes by special order and department training bulletins. Huey Newton saw this major new requirement as a perfect teaching tool to educate West Oakland arrestees on what their rights were and to put abusive cops who might not be following the new mandates on the defensive.

Starting in January 1967, the handful of members of the newly-formed Black Panther Party for Self-Defense began tailing Oakland police, pulling their cars over to observe firsthand when the police stopped to arrest someone in the neighborhood. Aoki went with them on their "shotgun patrols." "We had cameras and tape recorders to chronicle what was going on."[12]

The Panthers knew this was a major provocation. The basic idea of keeping tabs on police behavior toward ghetto blacks was not new — a Community Alert Patrol had been established with federal funding in Watts following the historic 1965 riots in that largely black Los Angeles district. But in Watts they just used tape recorders and notebooks. A clandestine, armed group of black war veterans had formed in Louisiana in 1964 to defend their neighborhoods from the Ku Klux Klan. But brandishing loaded weapons in public gave the Black Panthers a distinctive, more threatening aspect.

Amid the buzz created by their boldness, Newton began holding weekly meetings at the Panther office for walk-ins who learned they would get weapons training if they could sit still long enough through lectures in political theory. Armed Panthers continued to monitor black neighborhoods in Oakland, following testy police around on their patrols. To establish a unique identity, besides carrying weapons, the Panthers adopted uniforms for themselves: black pants, a powder blue shirt, a black leather jacket (which most of them already owned), black shoes and socks and a black beret like that worn by Mark Comfort, Curtis Baker and others modeling themselves after Che Guevara and the French Resistance. Jean Genet later proclaimed that the Panthers "attacked first by sight."[13] At the time, Thelton Henderson was running a legal aid office in East Palo Alto. The Panthers came to town recruiting and spreading their message. He recalls the first time he saw members representing the Party: "It was a very impressive show of . . . military-style discipline. When they left, they had a lot of people that said, 'Hey. This is good. This is the kind of thing that East Palo Alto could benefit from.'"

Newton commuted to San Francisco Law School to take another course in criminal law and spent many hours studying in the law library above the Poverty Center. He kept a copy of California Criminal Laws in his car, prepared to read policemen chapter and verse about the constitutional right to bear arms, as well as the rights of arrested citizens. This was all part of the two-pronged approach: radical action on the one hand, and savviness about "the system" on the other. Newton sometimes brought a gun to work at the federal jobs program and put it on his desk. He liked to explain how California gun law allowed the carrying of loaded weapons. His friend Paul Cobb from elementary school who worked with Newton in the jobs program had no interest in picking up a gun. When Lionel Wilson discovered that both Seale and Newton brought guns to work, they were fired. Newton sometimes got too cocky — to his detriment.

In January of 1967 Newton and Seale found an opportunity to proselytize at a black power rally in Golden Gate Park where more than 30 speakers were invited. They brought along copies of the *Little Red Book* to sell. Eldridge Cleaver had just gotten out of prison the month before and attracted a large crowd to hear the famous author, now publishing his essays in *Ramparts*. Afterward, Newton and Seale tracked Cleaver down at a radio interview and introduced themselves. Cleaver then invited the pair to a meeting at a rented Victorian in the Haight Ashbury district of San Francisco. The new cultural center Cleaver cofounded with other local black authors was called Black House. Parties were held there every Saturday for literary and political gatherings of black radicals. Cleaver told Newton and Seale planning sessions would start soon at Black House for a memorial celebration for the second anniversary of Malcolm X's death. The Panthers' 10-point program was just the unifying agenda he was looking for. Cleaver's aim at the time was to unite all black militants under one umbrella.

Seale and Newton showed up at the first planning session with several new recruits, all in uniform and all armed. They stood at attention together on one side of the room as Cleaver urged the other attendees to adopt the Panthers' 10-point program. Law student Earl Anthony, who had been to many meetings of black nationals before, had never seen anything like the Panthers. Anthony himself led the Independent Action Movement that had recently launched a highly successful public housing rent strike in San Francisco. The attendees that night surprised Cleaver by adopting the 10-point program without discussion or dissent. Many remained wary, especially the Black Panthers of Northern California, whom Seale had broken with in the fall. The Black Muslims Cleaver invited had little interest in anything Cleaver might orchestrate; they mistrusted him for having a white girlfriend affiliated with Communists. Like Stokely Carmichael, the Black Muslims no longer wanted anything to do with white radicals.

The Malcolm X event would last for several days in late February with his widow Betty Shabazz a star attraction. The other focal point would be a memorial service for Matthew Johnson, the unarmed teenager killed by police in San Francisco in September 1966. Cleaver tapped both the San Francisco Panthers and the newer Oakland Panther Party for Self-Defense to meet Betty Shabazz at the airport and escort her into the city. Seale and Newton and their new recruits shocked observers by showing up at San Francisco airport on February 21, 1967, carrying carbines, shotguns and pistols. The Black Panthers of Northern California showed up, too, without loaded weapons. Police had also arrived in large numbers, apparently alerted ahead of time to the reception awaiting Betty Shabazz's arrival. The combined entourage of Black Panthers then escorted her to an interview with Eldridge Cleaver at *Ramparts* headquarters in North Beach, with the police following them.

On the street outside the *Ramparts* offices, about a hundred policemen confronted the black militants before they entered the building. Eldridge Cleaver enjoyed the tableau from inside his office. Newton accused one of the policemen of having an itchy finger and dared him to draw. Seale immediately realized how close Newton had then come to a shootout: "If just one of them had gone for his gun, he would blast him, because Huey had his gun at a 45-degree angle to the ground and he was ready. He had the barrel of the gun in his left hand. His finger was on the trigger, he had knocked the safety off, and had jacked a round into the chamber."[14]

The police backed off, but they recognized that this was an ugly sign of more local armed confrontations to come. Incidents were occurring with greater frequency across the country. In June, a group of whites in Prattville, Alabama, would empty their rifles into homes in a black neighborhood, prompting SNCC leader, H. Rap Brown, to call for "full retaliation." Brown characterized Alabama as the "starting battleground for America's race war."[15] Brown also encouraged violent confrontations elsewhere, repeating before various audiences his strong support for armed self-defense: "If America chooses to play Nazis, black folks ain't going to play Jews."[16]

In April 1967 came another catalyst. In nearby Richmond, California, Mark Comfort saw an opportunity for action — the recent killing by a sheriff's deputy of unarmed 22-year-old Denzil Dowell. Comfort alerted Seale and Newton, who attracted hundreds of angry residents to a protest rally. Large numbers of police stood safely at the crowd's edges. The deputy had insisted he was justified in shooting Dowell for fleeing arrest for attempted burglary. The family cast doubt on the deputy's story: by their tally, three times as many shots had been fired as officially reported and two patches of blood on the ground indicated that Dowell's body had been dragged to where it lay when found. The attending doctor told them that the angle of the wounds indicated that Dowell's arms were raised when he was shot. The family got nowhere with their complaints to authorities so armed Panthers in uniform marched in to speak first with the district attorney and then the sheriff. They got nowhere either except to escalate the already tense stand-off between the Richmond police and the local black community.

Before forming the Panthers, Seale had already been working for a few years at community-building in North Richmond, which, even more dramatically than Oakland, had become a breeding ground for deep resentment toward local police. At the beginning of World War II, fewer than 300 blacks lived in the city. Richmond's black population increased over 5,000 percent in seven years as Southern transplants

were lured into overcrowded neighborhoods to work on defense contracts and in shipyards.

In light of Denzil Dowell's death, Cleaver suggested they start a
newsletter with the Richmond killing as the lead story of its first issue. It
ought to prove as much of a lightning rod as Matthew Johnson's death
had been in San Francisco's black community. Beverly Axelrod helped
them craft two mimeographed pages in her living room while Bob
Dylan's 1964 album *The Times They Are A-Changin'* blared on the pho-
nograph. The Panthers took to playing Dylan's 1965 album *Highway
61 Revisited* every time they gathered to put out the paper. Newton
particularly enjoyed the anti-establishment lyrics to "Ballad of a Thin
Man," which included the line "Something is happening here, but you
don't know what it is, do you, Mr. Jones?"[17] Having the Black Panthers
congregate in her home to launch their new party's messages of defiance against police brutality exhilarated Axelrod. She was deeply in
love with Eldridge. Her circle of leftists had just celebrated the pair's
engagement at a publication party for his book *Soul On Ice*. This was the
revolutionary relationship she had always coveted.

The first issue of the paper was fairly basic and crude-looking, with
a simple layout. Everything about the issue suggested amateurs at work,
much like the first issue of the underground *Berkeley Barb,* which would
soon achieve the highest national circulation for any newspaper of its
kind. What mattered is that they got the word out from the outraged
community's perspective. Twenty-three-year-old San Franciscan Emory
Douglas had joined the Panthers in mid-January of 1967. As a teenager
he had worked in a printing shop while serving a sentence in a juvenile detention facility in Southern California. He later studied graphic
design at San Francisco City College where he was active in the Black
Student Union. When Douglas saw Bobby Seale working on the primitive first issue of the *Panther* newspaper, Douglas told Seale he could
improve on the graphics. Douglas took over production of later issues
with the title "revolutionary artist" and later Minister of Culture.

By the second issue in mid-May, they launched a far more profes-
sional-looking *Black Panther* newspaper, published biweekly in a print
shop under Douglas's guiding hand. As he began to help Douglas with

the paper, Anthony came to understand that the Communist Party was financing the paper for mass distribution. All the Panther members distributed papers to tell their story and promote their 10-point program. Sales soon regularly exceeded 100,000 per issue; proceeds from the sales of the newsletters became the Panthers' primary source of income. They raised the price first to fifteen cents, then a quarter apiece. Each edition included blistering criticisms of racist policing and plenty of pictures and cartoons to communicate their message through imagery. Huey Newton had asked Douglas to be aware that "basically, the African-American community wasn't a reading community. They learned through observation and participation."

The Panthers were the first to popularize the term "pigs" for police, based on a postcard cartoon Beverly Axelrod had passed on to them. The first images Emory Douglas did were pig drawings, meant to be a symbol of police oppression — a "low-natured beast that bites the hand that feeds it." Douglas put a badge on the pig and sometimes gave it a number — that of Oakland Officer John Frey, who had a reputation in the community for mistreating blacks on his West Oakland beat well before his fateful encounter with Huey Newton on October 28, 1967.

Douglas, Newton and Seale had a new assistant in their all-night efforts to get out the *Black Panther* newspaper every couple of weeks: Earl Anthony. Anthony became the eighth official member of the Black Panther Party. To show force in San Francisco and Richmond earlier in the year, the Panthers had bolstered their numbers by inviting along armed friends who just dressed for the occasion without being members of the Party. Cleaver had been suspicious at first of Anthony because of his ties to Maulana Ron Karenga, founder of the black nationalist group "US" in Los Angeles and Anthony's association with Black Muslims in San Francisco. But Anthony was a "renegade" Black Muslim, the label applied to Black Muslims who took drugs and womanized, a subgroup Cleaver could identify with. He had been a Black Muslim himself in prison. Anthony broke with his own rent-strike organization to join the Panthers after seeing them in action in San Francisco.

Other black militants Anthony knew were now shunning white alliances. SNCC had recently purged whites from its Atlanta headquarters.

The Black Muslims in San Francisco suspected that Axelrod funneled money from the Communist Party to pay for Black House; that was not who Black Nationalists wanted interfering with their own agenda. What Anthony did not tell anyone is that two FBI agents whom he used to know from his old school sports teams had recently contacted him. Anthony came from a middle class family. In college at the University of Southern California, he had been a young Republican. The two fair-haired, white ex-Marines who showed up at his San Francisco apartment out of the blue warned Anthony that Eldridge Cleaver was associating with Communists and asked him to keep a look out. At the time, Anthony took it as a friendly warning.

When the pair of FBI agents later asked Anthony what he knew about the sudden disappearance from the Bay Area of the San Francisco Panthers that spring, he told them that Cleaver had scared them off. Maybe he had pistol-whipped a few first; Anthony would not always tell the FBI men all he knew. Meanwhile, the Panthers were becoming a subcultural force that increasing numbers of blacks admired. Anthony had driven Huey Newton to the Richmond gathering in honor of Denzil Dowell. Anthony had been involved in both the Watts riots in 1965 and the San Francisco riots in 1966, but had never witnessed anyone take charge of a crowd like Seale and Newton did that day. Watching the police look on in apprehension from the sidelines demolished their previous aura of invincibility.

For many black students at San Francisco State it took slightly longer than it took Anthony to embrace the Panthers' militarism. When Janice Garrett first saw the Panthers on campus, the sight of them marching in uniform was intimidating. But like her friends, Garrett now wore her hair in an Afro, part of the statement they were making as they became active in establishing a pioneering Black Studies department. When Bobby Seale came to the campus to speak, Garrett and her friends in the Black Student Union invited Seale, Cleaver and Newton to conduct political education classes in the large flat Garrett shared with several other students. Among her roommates was Judy Juanita who would later write the novel *Virgin Soul*, fictionalizing their entry into the Panther Party. The first Panthers they saw were all male. Beverly Axelrod's role in the Party was unofficial. The first female recruit to the Black Panthers was Tarika Lewis, a 17-year-old Oakland high school student. Janice Garret and her friends would soon quit school to join, too.

The Panthers had already attracted attention from the local mainstream press for their rally in Richmond and armed escort of Malcolm X's widow into the city from the airport earlier in the year. The Sunday San Francisco paper on April 30, 1967, ran a blaring headline — "Oakland's Black Panthers Wear Guns; Talk Revolution" — accompanied by photos of the two armed Party leaders.[18] San Francisco State was only one of many new platforms the Panthers sought to broadcast their views. The Black Panthers took over Black House from the Black Nationalists that spring as well. In April of 1967, after the Richmond rally, a local radio station invited Newton to speak on a call-in talk show. When he read the 10-point program on the air, an irate Assemblyman from Piedmont named Don Mulford phoned in to announce to the radio audience his sponsorship of a new bill in Sacramento to ban carrying loaded guns in public and to prohibit unapproved instructors from teaching the use of firearms. Newton came up with a bold and immediate response to this threat. Looking for volunteers, Seale shared Newton's plan with Garrett and her roommates. Seale would lead an armed group of Panthers and members of the Dowell family on an eighty-mile drive to the State Capitol in early May to oppose the bill and introduce the Panther Party and its 10-point program to the world.

Emory Douglas joined Seale in that historic trip as did Mark Comfort. They packed loaded guns in the trunks of their cars, planning to display them on arrival. Cleaver went along with no gun, on official assignment to cover the event for *Ramparts* magazine. Newton wisely accepted the recommendation that he stay home — he remained on probation, and they anticipated trouble. On May 2, 1967, 24 men and 6 women — most dressed all in black — emerged from six cars driven in a caravan to Sacramento. Many of them wielded rifles, 12-gauge pump-action shotguns and Magnum .357s. Seale also sported a .45 caliber pistol on his hip. Some had slung on bandoliers of ammunition. Following Newton's strict instructions, they kept the weapons pointed straight up or down at the ground as they marched toward the Capitol building.

Like Newton, those on parole could not carry hand guns, nor could Hutton, who was still under age. At the time, carrying loaded weapons in plain sight and not directed at anyone was legal. Still, Newton counseled Seale that, if fired upon, he should shoot back.

As the attention-getting entourage approached their destination, Governor Ronald Reagan happened to be standing on the lawn with a group of visiting school children. Members of the press corps were already on hand to cover events at the Capitol. At the startling sight of an armed squadron of black militants, Reagan broke into a trot in the opposite direction. Stunned cameramen and reporters followed the unknown group of black militants as they made their way into the Capitol building.

Caught off guard, the security detail let the expanded entourage of Panthers and media head upstairs to the Assembly much like any other visitors. All the while TV cameras were rolling and photos were snapped. The guards stopped a few of the Panthers in the building and took away their guns, but afterward gave the weapons back and let them go. On prior occasions when white NRA members had worn guns into the building the guards had not relieved them of their weapons. Reportedly, a few Second Amendment hardliners had already shown up that day in the visitors' gallery wearing holstered hand guns. But a squadron of armed blacks boldly exercising their right of protest alarmed legislators as white gun owners had never done. Cameramen kept filming as the proceedings abruptly came to a standstill at the intrusion. Then, to the immense relief of the Assemblymen, Capitol police quickly ushered out their unexpected visitors without any violence. One of the surprised freshman was San Francisco Assemblyman Willie Brown, at the start of his long political career. He would soon become a Panther lawyer and ally.

On both the way in and out of the Capitol building, Seale stood on the Capitol steps to read to the media Newton's "Executive Mandate Number One," which attracted immediate television coverage. It accused the California legislature of seeking to keep the black community "disarmed and powerless" while police repression increased throughout the country. The statement echoed the new bellicose direction of SNCC

since the spring of 1966 in asserting the American black power movement as part of an international struggle against imperialism, linking
U. S. domestic policy to the "racist war of genocide in Vietnam."[19]

Safely observing television coverage of the breaking news out of
Sacramento from his parents' home in Oakland, Newton reacted with
glee at the success of what he called 'shock-a-buku' — sudden moves
that keep the enemy off balance."[20] The story hit the next front page
of all major newspapers in the state with headlines like "Armed Men
Invade Assembly," "Guns in Capitol" and "Armed Foray in Assembly Stirs
Wrath."[21] It made Melvin nervous: "It got a lot of press, which was Huey's
object. He wanted . . . a colossal event, and the colossal event really was a
recruitment effort. . . . [But] to go to Sacramento with the guns [was] a
two-edged thing. . . . [I]t got the publicity and the attention of the youth
that wanted to be Panthers . . . . The other side of it was that it . . . drove
some people in the opposite direction. . . . I would not have done it, but
it was done. . . . I'd never thought the guns served a good purpose."

As the Panthers drove out of Sacramento, they were arrested on a
variety of minor charges and taken to the city jail. During the next few
days, the media deluged the Panthers with inquiries as the *London Times*
and other international papers featured their spectacular political confrontation. To Barry Scheck, as a politically aware high school senior in
New York, the Panthers suddenly sprung "out of nowhere . . . into the
news . . . going to Sacramento, carrying guns, with the black berets and
the black leather. . . This was a very powerful message . . . These were
people that were not going to get beaten and . . . hosed by police in the
streets" like the nonviolent civil rights marchers following Dr. King's
approach.

The governor's office immediately demanded tighter security at
the Capitol. As chief of staff, Ed Meese already had open channels
to the FBI from his days as chief prosecutor of protesters in the Free
Speech Movement. He could easily find out what Hoover knew about
this revolutionary group calling itself the Black Panther Party for Self-
Defense. Shocked newsmen raced to report the incident as an armed
invasion, though the Panthers had never actually threatened anyone
and were surrounded the whole time they were in the Capitol building

by reporters, camera crews and school kids with tales to tell of their most unusual civics lesson.

At first, no one in the media could concentrate on anything other than the guns, but as coverage continued, TV reporter Belva Davis proposed a new angle. As the first African-American woman hired by KPIX-TV in San Francisco, she had a different perspective than her white colleagues. She suggested that they look at the Panthers' motivation for the stunt. She told her boss they aimed to get publicity for their 10-point program to change society for the better. The Panthers wanted to improve education for kids in black communities; they dreamed of starting school breakfast and lunch programs and their own school. With persistence, Belva Davis got the background story on the air — one she believed would otherwise never have been broadcast.

By the time of the Panthers' startling May debut, *Soulbook* magazine contributor Louis Armmond had already left for the East Coast fully committed to armed revolt. He had seen hundreds of thousands of protesters marching in the streets in the past couple of years. Armmond and a number of militant colleagues "thought at that time that there was going to be a general insurrection in the United States." While he kept his plans secret, Armmond and some of his radical associates were then determined to head to China for training in guerrilla warfare to be better prepared for the coming uprising of American college students. "We had studied in detail guerilla warfare movements in Vietnam and Philippines and all over. So I wanted to go — many of us wanted to go — to get . . . further training."

Armmond was in New York visiting his mother and father to say good-bye — expecting he might never return home — when he read the newspaper headlines about the armed militant blacks who showed up at the California Capitol talking of revolution and carrying guns. Soon he and his friends decided against heading to China. "We didn't want to miss the revolution in the U. S." He expected it to happen soon and then the borders might be clamped down, preventing their return if they went to China. So Armmond headed to work in Mississippi instead, and the revolution never came. Neither Armmond nor fellow revolutionaries he plotted with expected the Oakland Panthers to be the vanguard of their revolution. Huey's brother Melvin thought Huey actually had a view similar to Armmond's. Huey envisioned the Panthers' role as symbolic leaders: "He saw the guns as something that was spectacular and something to draw attention and to draw people in. He didn't see it as something that would be used to take on the United States." Eldridge Cleaver had different ideas.

* * * * *

Not surprisingly, the Panthers' opposition to gun control only strengthened support for Assembly member Mulford's "Panther" bill. Until it passed, California gun laws had been extremely permissive. Rifles and shotguns could be obtained by anyone. The only people not allowed to buy handguns were convicted felons, drug addicts, minors and people not yet citizens. But the NRA's then moderate leadership envisioned no curtailment of hunters' rights in Mulford's bill and gave Governor Reagan their blessing to sign it into law in June of 1967 as emergency legislation. To this day, the Mulford Act remains one of the nation's most restrictive gun laws.

The widespread publicity garnered Newton his first paid speaking engagement at San Francisco State College. With the $500 speaking fee, Newton and his close childhood friend David Hilliard then bought a pound of marijuana, which they broke up for sale on the street to raise bail money for those arrested in Sacramento. Newton had not yet recruited Hilliard to become a Black Panther. Hilliard had a family and a good job as a longshoreman. But they considered themselves practically family since they had lived around the corner from each other in sixth grade. As they drove through Oakland with matchboxes of weed in their car, Hilliard spotted policemen on patrol and asked: "Hey, Huey, what are we supposed to do if the police stop us?" Newton laughed and responded, "We shoot them. You know, we fight" — a response that remained etched in Hilliard's memory less than six months later when Newton had his near fatal encounter with two Oakland police officers.[22] Fortunately, in May the police car drove on by.

Shortly afterward, Seale and Newton had words with policemen on a street corner outside Panther headquarters. The confrontation resulted in several minor charges against Newton: brandishing a weapon, possessing an illegal knife and disturbing the peace, including using profanity in public. In 1967, just wearing a "Fuck the Draft" jacket on the street was considered sufficient grounds for an arrest. It was why Newton thought it wise to call police pigs and got the Panthers to use the phrase "off the pigs" — words that did not amount to profanity.

When Janice Garrett dropped out of college and joined the Panthers that June she did not tell her parents in the Midwest. She knew that television coverage of the Panthers' Sacramento debut scared them. Janice joined the Panthers together with her boyfriend, which was the most common way for women to become involved in the Party. All of her roommates joined also. Women were expected not to have boyfriends outside the Party; the men could sleep with whomever they chose. In the early days, women had key roles, although its culture was decidedly macho. Garrett acted for a short time as Bobby Seale's secretary. Judy Juanita helped Emory Douglas with the paper. Over time, as more recruits came on board, the founders realized the women faced harassment and the organization would spin out of control if they did not establish strict rules of behavior. Some new Panther men also undermined the Party's mission by getting drunk or high on drugs while wielding guns or by committing crimes against people in the black community. This was not surprising, given Newton's aggressive recruitment efforts in pool halls and taverns.

The Panthers adopted rules inspired by those of Black Muslims which they then enforced by threats of expulsion. The rules included exclusive allegiance to the Party as a military force, following orders, and learning the 10-point program and rules by heart. Members were not to possess any drugs while on Party business or engage in unnecessary use of a firearm. That must have relieved Beverly Axelrod, whose teen-aged sons had often witnessed Panthers waving guns in her living room as points of emphasis. The rules banned commission of crimes against blacks (no mention of barring crimes against whites). They also prohibited possession of a weapon while under the influence of narcotics, "weed" or alcohol. Members were officially urged to speak politely, "not to take liberties with women and not to hit or swear at people."[23]

Bobby Seale was then serving a short sentence for the charges lodged against him in Sacramento. Represented by the Treuhaft firm, Seale and several other Panthers who had no prior police record had pled guilty to disturbing the peace so others who already had records would not have to serve any jail time. Earl Anthony felt Seale's absence more than he had expected. Seale provided leadership talents that were sorely needed. Newton liked to play hard when not devoted to Panther business. At night, he often partied with more than one woman, took speed pills and smoked a lot of marijuana between bar-hopping to down Cuba Libres while chatting with friends. At Newton and Cleaver's request, Anthony traveled to other cities to recruit new members. Not much seemed to be happening in Oakland or San Francisco, with their small ranks decimated by those jailed after the Sacramento excursion. Cleaver told Anthony not to worry: "The Party is going to take over California in 1968."[24] That was not COINTELPRO's view. Oakland had been quiet while other cities rioted that summer; J. Edgar Hoover considered the Black Panthers a local problem that would quickly fade away.

Maddeningly to the Oakland police, over the summer of 1967 the Panthers' aggressive watchdog behavior quickly turned Newton and Seale into neighborhood celebrities. Word spread about what Huey told the San Francisco policeman who pulled a gun on him, "If you shoot, I'm shooting back and you'll die just like I do." David Hilliard was among those impressed: "For the first time the playing field was level."[25] Not exactly. Two policemen guarding public housing in San Francisco got killed that August. Earl Anthony had been traveling at the time. He had dropped out of law school and his draft board in Van Nuys, California called him up. Once there, the new Panther boldly told the board to draft him at their peril — if he got sent to Vietnam he would likely shoot his white superiors. The practice known as fragging was then growing increasingly common in Vietnam — unhappy black GIs who began tossing hand grenades at detested white sergeants or other superiors.

The week after Anthony appeared before the Van Nuys draft board, someone bombed it. Shortly afterward, Anthony had another visit from the two ex-Marine, Vietnam War veterans who had approached him earlier that spring. This time, FBI agents Kizenski and O'Connor beat

him unconscious. When he came to, they told him he would face prosecution for the Van Nuys bombing and as a co-conspirator to murder in
San Francisco unless he turned informant. Anthony disclaimed knowledge of the bombing; as far as he knew, the Panthers also had nothing to do with the San Francisco cop killings. But that was irrelevant.
Hoover had proof of Anthony's radical connections and had no compunction about securing false evidence to convict those he considered
subversives — that was how he ensured that Ethel Rosenberg got the
electric chair for treason at the height of the McCarthy Era.

Anthony knew that if the murder charge stuck he would face the
death penalty. He agreed to weekly predawn meetings at a designated
isolated location South of San Francisco. Anthony would later fear for
his life from both sides. In his 1990 tell-all, *Spitting in the Wind: The True
Story Behind the Violent Legacy of the Black Panther Party*, he revealed that,
starting in August of 1967, FBI agents Kizenski and O'Connor, elite
members of COINTELPRO, "had me by the balls and they squeezed
hard and long."[26] Among other useful information Anthony could tell
them about was Eldridge Cleaver's new black girl friend, Kathleen Neal
from SNCC in Atlanta, who came out to visit Cleaver in July. The agents
figured it was only a matter of time before Cleaver would split from
Beverly Axelrod, lose Communist backing, and the Black Panther Party
would die for lack of funding. They urged Anthony to egg Cleaver on
to turf wars with black nationalists.

J. Edgar Hoover did not let most FBI agents or local police know
COINTELPRO even existed. At first, Kizenski and O'Connor were
based in Washington; they soon relocated to the West Coast. As the
FBI kept a closer eye on the Panthers, local leftists started to take
notice of the Panthers, too. Muckraker Decca Mitford counted herself
among their earliest fans. She later observed, "I admired the idea of
the BPP since its origin. I felt such an organization was badly needed in
Oakland, based upon my experiences and observations . . . during the
1950s and 1960s."[27]

Melvin Newton recalls, "it was not unusual for a black person [even
for a low level] misdemeanor arrest [to] receive a good beating before
making it into the jail." As a rare black clerk in the OPD, Morrie Turner

came to the same conclusion — something needed to be done about police abuse. If you were a trigger-happy officer "you could shoot . . . prisoners or suspects, and the department would back you up, they were on your side." But that was before Chief of Police Charles Gain took office in 1967 and implemented what changes he could to the culture he had inherited.

Chief Gain grew up in a working class neighborhood in Oakland in the 1930s and made strong friendships in the black community, including among local leaders of the NAACP. Gain empathized with their frustration. John Sutter, who served on the Oakland City Council in the early 1970s when Gain was chief, notes: "When Charles Gain became the chief of police in the late '60s . . . he [had a] much more liberal inclination than most police chiefs and more so actually than our mayor and city manager. So he ran into conflict with his bosses. But he was . . . more concerned about community response to what the police [department] was doing. And, of course, that meant that . . . some people . . . thought that he was too soft on crime and others who were very supportive of him . . . ."

Among his first acts as chief, Gain issued an order making it punishable for officers to use racial slurs. His predecessor had prohibited use of derogatory language, but to little avail. Gain created a specific list of banished words so there would be no doubt as to what he meant. Gain also began to address the problem of racism in training and in policy statements. Turner considered Chief Gain a man ahead of his time who could not alter the culture singlehandedly. As Burris observed: "Those same officers were still there. Chief Gain was in the process of trying to control the department, but it already was steeped in a certain kind of culture . . . he could not change. . . ."

Morrie Turner, then in his mid-forties, lived two blocks from Panther headquarters and would frequently stop to talk with Bobby Seale to learn more about the Party. Seale won Turner over as a supporter sooner than many of his generation, though Turner totally opposed the use of guns. A veteran of World War II, Turner had almost lost his hand when a soldier accidentally discharged his weapon in the barracks. The bullet whizzed within inches of Turner and barely avoided crippling Turner's chances for a future livelihood as a syndicated cartoonist.

Aside from carefully managing their confrontations with police and engineering media events, the Panthers built community support by lobbying for traffic signals at dangerous intersections and acting as crossing guards. The black middle class may have not wanted to associate publicly with the Panthers, but neither did they completely back away, in part because the Panthers were providing a free and desperately needed community service. As Belva Davis observed, "Better education, food for the kids that go to school and . . . not to have to go to school hungry. I mean, they were just fundamental rights and to deny that the things that they were asking for were needed would have been hypocritical." Other black community leaders began taking a look at the Panthers' 10-point program and came to a similar conclusion: the Panthers' demands largely echoed their own wish list for fair treatment.

By August, the Panthers became sufficiently mainstream in the local black community to be asked to patrol a Juneteenth Day celebration in West Oakland's DeFremery Park commemorating freedom from slavery. DeFremery was the largest park around, a favorite gathering place for the locals. Oakland police were officially asked not to monitor the August 1967 festival. Entertainers and speakers were all African-American, including San Francisco Assemblyman Willie Brown (later Speaker of the State Assembly and then Mayor of San Francisco) and State Senator Mervin Dymally (later Lieutenant Governor of California) as well as Berkeley's new anti-war Council Member Ron Dellums, who would go on to a long career in Congress capped by serving as Mayor of Oakland. The police were affronted that the Panthers were the chosen event security, but acquiesced. It turned a new page in local police-community relations.

5. THE DEFENSE TEAM

THE ONLY CLIENTS OF MINE THAT GO TO SAN QUENTIN ARE THE ONES WHO LIE TO ME.
— Sign on Charles Garry's desk

Everything about the Newton case would be unusual, starting with the first hearing. Charles Garry walked with determination as he made his way back to Huey Newton's Highland Hospital room through the heavily-guarded corridor. At 58 and balding, he was still trim and muscular. Garry came smartly dressed as always in a fashionable suit and tie. Because of Newton's condition, the court had ordered a special bedside hearing to announce the formal criminal charges. Lanky prosecutor Lowell Jensen was just 39, nearly twenty years Garry's junior. Jensen had enough experience trying violent felonies that he took this case in stride. Yet the Newton trial would be Jensen's first exposure to trying a case against Garry, whom Jensen knew mostly by reputation as a formidable criminal defense lawyer favored by radicals. By the time they met, Jensen was also already scheduled to try the Oakland Seven against Charles Garry, which was expected to take place shortly after the Newton trial ended.

They stood near the bed as the court reporter made the record. It did not take long for Municipal Court Judge Stafford Buckley to formally transfer Newton to county custody on charges of murder, assault with a deadly weapon, and kidnapping. This was too early for Newton to have to enter a plea, but it was the first step toward his possible execution — and it was over in minutes.

Following the arraignment, sheriff's deputies took over guard duty from the Oakland police. Newton was now a county prisoner. Still fearing for Newton's life, Garry asked Judge Buckley to order that Newton not be moved, a request the judge took under submission. Meanwhile, at a Catholic church not far away, the slain young policeman, John Frey, who had only served on the force for a year and a half, received the special treatment reserved for fallen heroes. His funeral included a twelve-man honor guard, a long procession of private cars and a squad of motorcycles, with over 150 colleagues participating. Officers' wives showed up for the emotional funeral service as well, each acutely aware it could have been her own spouse's funeral they were attending.

All the officers in attendance likely thought as Commander George Hart did: "There but for the grace of God." It was the first policeman's funeral Hart had attended since he joined the force in 1956. He would endure ten more during the remainder of his tenure in the OPD — each a gut-wrenching experience. "It rings real close to home." Honorary pallbearers at Officer Frey's funeral included Police Chief Charles Gain, County Sheriff Frank Madigan, the city manager, a Superior Court judge, a Municipal Court judge and Assemblyman Don Mulford from Piedmont, author of "the Panther bill." The *Oakland Tribune* gave the funeral extensive coverage.

The situation looked grim for Newton. Garry later described the case as "the most complex, emotional, fascinating case I've ever tried . . . Huey was the kind of person I immediately felt a warmth and friendship with; his charisma and his openness and frankness just came right through, even while he was lying in a hospital bed with a tube through his nose."[1] Garry was married, with a mistress as well, but no children. This self-described streetfighter in the courtroom related to Huey as the son he never had.

Unlike Oaklanders who had been following the emergence of the combative Panther Party over the past year, when Charles Garry first agreed to represent Huey Newton, Garry knew virtually nothing about the Panther Party. After he obtained Newton's rap sheet, he viewed Huey as a scrappy warrior like Garry himself was. Garry believed that the job of the "Movement" lawyer was to expose the system as rotten, and "tie it up."[2] The only clients Charles Garry could never imagine defending were Nazis or fascists. His empathy for Newton was reinforced by reading the revolutionary literature Newton assigned him as homework: if one viewed the black community as a colony oppressed by its mother country, then crimes like those Newton was charged with were either self-defense or self-liberation.

Garry instantly realized that any chance of winning the case required him to orchestrate two high-powered defense strategies: one, a traditional defense relying heavily on research and writing assistance; two, and more importantly, a political defense of the Panthers as peacekeepers protecting their community from police oppression. As Garry planned his public relations campaign, he knew the audience he really needed to convince was an as-yet unpicked panel of jurors, likely unfamiliar with life in black ghettos. In the crucial jury selection process, he would need help from experts as well as top-notch support staff. The best person to ask was right there in his office.

Now thirty-five years old, Guild lawyer Fay Stender had been a part-time associate at Garry's firm since 1961. Working for clients she believed in put the five-foot-eight, dark-haired Jew in an enviable position — few established local firms then hired any women lawyers, or Jews for that matter. Stender was the only woman lawyer ever hired by the firm. Women were considered especially unsuited for criminal trial practice, especially among old war horses like Charles Garry. Yet, after six years, Stender had become Garry's right hand for legal research and briefing. The son of immigrant Armenians fleeing Turkish massacres had never fully mastered English syntax and had little interest in paperwork.

For Garry — unlike his far more genteel partners — it was not unusual to instruct his secretary to "get that motherfucker in here to pay his child support." Uniquely structured phrases became "Garryisms" fondly repeated in the office.[3] Recently, in light of landmark Supreme Court rulings, court practice had evolved. Defendants now had more procedural rights. Instead of the shoot-from-the-hip style Garry was used to at trial, defense lawyers were starting to file strategic pretrial motions ahead of time to preclude the prosecutor from calling challenged witnesses to the stand in front of the jury or to prevent the admission at trial of improper testimony or illegally obtained evidence. If Stender's sexist mentor had had his way, the former Supreme Court clerk would have stayed his assistant for her entire career.

With her two children now both in elementary school, Stender had just begun working full time. When she started at the Garry firm in 1961, she had much preferred library research and writing that she could do on a flexible schedule. At the time, Stender was recently separated from her husband Marvin, and needed to race back from San Francisco each work day to relieve the patchwork of babysitters she had cobbled together for her toddler daughter and three-year-old son. By the late fall of 1967, the Stenders had been reunited for the better part of three years. Fay Stender was eager to take on new challenges at work to prove she was partnership material.

Though she had little criminal trial experience, Stender had honed her knowledge of the law by assisting Garry's highly demanding partner Barney Dreyfus on several death penalty appeals. Garry considered Stender's skills essential to this difficult defense. He popped his head into her tiny cubicle as the dowdily dressed lawyer pounded away on her typewriter. Stender typed faster than any secretary in the office and prepared all her own filings. When Garry asked Stender to join him when he made his next visit to Newton, she instantly realized this might be the career break she was looking for.

Stender had some background handling civil rights cases and had even spent a week in Mississippi during the 1964 Freedom Summer, but by 1967 had made her niche representing draft dodgers. Over time, she had grown disenchanted. "I knew for every one I handled [for a white, middle-class male], there were many Third World people who really needed a lawyer and couldn't get one."[4] Here was Charles Garry offering her the type of satisfying challenge she much preferred. Instead of yet another white middle class draft dodger, Stender would be right at the center of the hottest Movement case around, with the client's very life dependent on their efforts.

Like everyone else, Stender had heard about the Panthers' bold appearance in the Assembly months earlier. She had also met Eldridge Cleaver when he came with Beverly Axelrod to the book release party for *Soul On Ice* in the spring of 1967. Stender had joined in a toast to their engagement. Like Axelrod, Stender was passionate about social justice. She had worked together with her husband, Axelrod, and other local leftist lawyers a couple of years back in a group they called the Council for Justice. As volunteers, they took on anti-war clients and politicized cases for Cesar Chavez and the farmworkers until the group folded for lack of funding. Whatever Garry needed her to do, Stender was game.

* * * * *

By the fall of 1967, though the police viewed the Panthers as thugs, they were beginning to appreciate that the Party was unlike any street gang they had previously encountered. It unnerved them to see pig graffiti on the walls of West Oakland with messages of "off the pigs" scrawled alongside. The defense soon found out that the OPD began furnishing patrol cars with a list of known Panther vehicles to stop on any pretext. Anyone who lived in East or West Oakland could see deadly conflict ahead.

One of those people was teenager Leo Dorado. Back in the days before it ever crossed his mind he might become an Alameda County prosecutor let alone a pioneering Latino judge, Dorado starred in basketball and baseball games played all over the city. He made it a point to know where trouble might lie. The tall Mexican-American had his eyes fixed on getting into Cal and not getting mugged or arrested first for being in the wrong place at the wrong time. That had happened to too many of his friends. So, when Dorado first heard of this new, armed, black gang following police around in West Oakland, he paid attention. When news hit that the Black Panthers had shown up armed at the State Capitol, Dorado thought it could only mean they were bent on becoming martyrs.

That fall at Cal reinforced Dorado's assumption: "We heard a lot about how . . . extremely militant they were. . . . The general feeling was they weren't going to last very long because they were going to step over lines . . . Oakland police . . . were a very, very strong police department, and they would meet force with force. . . . all the force

and violence they needed to put them down. . . . If it was a matter of
them getting hurt and injured and killed, then that was going to happen . . . they would get killed." When word spread of the October 28,
1967, shootout, Dorado assumed that Newton had just stepped forward
as the first martyr. There was no question in Dorado's mind — or the
mind of anyone he knew — that Newton would get the death penalty.

Charles Garry had the opposite reaction — not if there was anything he could do about it. He could not wait to have an opportunity to
speak to his new client alone in the hospital. The veteran trial lawyer's
first advice to Huey as he lay recovering from surgery was what Garry
told all of his clients: "Make no statements to anyone." Garry had to
make sure Newton did not blow whatever chance he had of avoiding
the gas chamber by bragging about offing a pig to his friends or saying
anything at all about the incident that could come back to haunt him
at trial. Newton's chances of success were low enough already. Even a
good friend or relative, not to mention a cellmate, might be forced to
reveal anything Newton said about the case.

After Garry came back from visiting his brother, Melvin Newton
asked Garry, "Did he do it?" Garry said he never asked. Melvin also
decided against asking his brother to tell him what happened on
Seventh Street that morning — there wasn't much Melvin could do
with the knowledge one way or the other. In his short acquaintance
with the Panther Party, Melvin had already learned not to ask questions
that would lead to answers he could do nothing about.

Like Charles Garry, many criminal defense lawyers don't want their
client's story. The defendant has a right not to testify on his own behalf
and knowing what he has to say could limit the array of defenses. In fact,
Garry did not seek any information from his client about the shootout
until a few days before Newton took the witness stand in the middle of
the trial. When asked why not, Garry later explained, "I wasn't particularly interested."[5] Garry's primary aim matched that of Huey Newton
himself — to conduct a political defense, painting a picture of a racist
establishment that itself should be on trial. The Panthers reminded
Garry of some of his most militant union clients decades before, whom
he felt had been even more vilified by society. Garry saw in the Panthers

"a kind of cohesion of all the things that the labor movement originally started out in the '30s fighting for."[6]

The timing of the breaking story was excellent for gaining leftist political support. The Bolivian army captured legendary guerrilla leader Che Guevara in early October 1967 and executed him just a few weeks before Newton's arrest. Only a few months before, Berkeley's community-supported station KPFA broadcasted a daring live interview with Che in South America. Radicals like KPFA station manager Elsa Knight Thompson rushed to champion the cause of Huey Newton as a revolutionary like their martyred hero Che.

Though Garry would immediately proclaim his client's innocence to the press, the prospects of Newton's acquittal at that point looked slim to non-existent. When Newton's arrest for murder hit the front pages of local papers, two totally unrelated police shootout cases were set for trial the following week. Having three local cases involving police shootings in the news at one time was extraordinary. But Newton's case drew by far the most coverage. The attorneys in both of the other cases told the judge that they needed a delay of their clients' trials in light of the mounting hostility in the community over Officer Frey's death. Otherwise, the lawyers expected the jury box would fill with folks ready to throw the book at anyone accused of killing a cop. Although judges generally frown on delaying trials already set, the delays were granted. This underscored what Charles Garry already knew — shooting a police officer is a crime that packs an oversized emotional impact on the entire community. Suddenly everyone feels less safe.

Garry needed to counteract the negative publicity as quickly as possible. He pounced on an opportunity that just got handed to him: a local physician contacted Garry after seeing the newspaper photo of Newton handcuffed to his gurney before surgery. She was flabbergasted that doctors at Kaiser Hospital would allow police to stretch out the arms of a man with a serious abdominal wound. Garry asked Stender to quickly draft a complaint charging Kaiser with medical malpractice. Meanwhile, they obtained the original uncropped photo of Newton on the gurney showing the startled police officer in the foreground. They used that photo on the cover of a new pamphlet their new white allies put together for wide distribution, accompanied by the caption, "Can a black man get a fair trial?"

The lawyers' stated aim was to get Newton the impartial jury of his peers promised in the Bill of Rights, but never delivered to minorities in practice. The defense brochure also focused on a fair trial. Yet the "Free Huey" chant adopted as the Panthers' mantra at pretrial hearings focused instead on rousing support for his release regardless of the evidence. Most of Newton's militant associates assumed he did what he was accused of. The Panthers considered Newton amply justified in killing an oppressor and wanted their leader out of jail by any means available. Many radicals thought Newton had just started the revolution. As Cleaver later wrote: "We all knew that it was coming. When, where, how — all had now been answered. The Black Panther Party had at last drawn blood, spilled its own and shed that of the pigs! We counted history from Huey's night of truth."[7]

A front page editorial in *The Black Panther* newspaper appeared with a half-page headline "HUEY MUST BE SET FREE!" The article placed the shooting squarely in the context of historic race relations, emphasizing that it occurred in a black ghetto between a black resident and white cops who lived in the white suburbs:

> On the night that the shooting occurred, there were 400 years of oppression of black people by white people focused and manifested in the incident. We are at the cross roads in history where black people are determined to bring down the final curtain on the drama of their struggle to free themselves from the boot of the white man that is on their collective neck. . . . Through murder, brutality, and the terror of their image, the police of America have kept black people intimidated, locked in a mortal fear, and paralyzed their bid for freedom. [Newton] knew that the power of the police over black people has to be broken if we are to be liberated from our bondage. These Gestapo dogs are not holy, they are not angels, and there is no more mystery surrounding them. They are brutal beasts who have been gunning down black people and getting away with it. . . . Black people all over America and around the world . . . are glad for once to have a dead cop and a live Huey . . . we want Huey to stay alive . . . we want Huey set free.[8]

Belva Davis was sure that someone with Huey Newton's reputation could not shoot an Oakland police officer and expect to get off. "Everyone thought that surely he would be convicted of first-degree murder." Just a little over six months earlier the media had covered the first execution on Governor Reagan's watch after Reagan had handily won office as a strong believer in the death penalty. An African-American man named Aaron Mitchell was on death row when Reagan was sworn in, convicted of killing a white policeman in a shootout after Mitchell attempted to rob a Sacramento bar in January 1963. Interviewed the day of his execution on April 12, 1967, the condemned man told reporters: "Every Negro ever convicted of killing a police officer has died in that gas chamber. So what chance did I have?"[9] Belva Davis thought Newton had no prayer of a different result.

Davis now faced her own dilemma. Here was "the mild-mannered, piano-playing, opera-loving Newton that I had met" likely headed to the gas chamber. The CBS affiliate where she worked in San Francisco had been the first station to bring on two African-American newscasters. She and Ben Williams talked about who would likely be assigned to cover this story. He was a much more seasoned reporter. She asked him to please volunteer: "This is not a good way to begin a career." Ben got the assignment to cover the trial and Belva Davis became his relief person.

The defense had already made a formal motion to Municipal Court Judge Buckley to order that Newton stay at Highland Hospital under armed guard, which his family would foot the bill for. They argued it was the only way to keep Newton safe. Judge Buckley had not yet ruled on that motion when the county transferred Newton to a cell on death row at San Quentin Prison. Similar transfers had occurred with a half-dozen or more other prisoners charged with serious felonies earlier that year as a cost-saving way for the county to ensure greater security.

Melvin Newton and his father visited Huey at San Quentin, extremely distressed that he was already on death row. His mother was too upset to come. It surprised them to discover that Huey was actually relieved to be left in isolation to recover peacefully from his surgery. But he told them that, whenever he was taken from his cell, a guard would lead the way to announce "Dead man walking" and another guard would follow behind him. Huey had been taken aback, but soon learned this was the protocol for every prisoner on death row. His family found it shocking — months before any trial, the justice system was treating Huey as if he were simply awaiting execution. The defense team vigorously objected to him being left there until trial. A few weeks later, the sheriff transferred Newton to a jail cell in the courthouse on the shores of Lake Merritt.

To bring Newton to trial, the prosecutor had alternative paths he could pursue: convening a grand jury or conducting a preliminary hearing in municipal court. A preliminary hearing would entitle Newton's counsel to cross-examine the prosecutor's witnesses in open court. In contrast, appearances before the grand jury were confidential. The defendant could not have counsel present. Grand juries were (and are) notorious for doing the prosecutor's bidding — they only hear one version of events. Not surprisingly, Lowell Jensen took the case to the grand jury. It had the added benefit of avoiding a media circus. Ten years later, the California Supreme Court ruled that choosing a grand jury provided the prosecutor with such a tactical advantage that defendants should have the right to ask for a preliminary hearing after an indictment is issued. In 1990, prosecutors went to the voters and won a change in the Constitution, taking that right away.

The grand jury convened on November 13; it issued its indictment against Newton by mid-afternoon of the same day on charges of murder, assault and kidnapping. The indictment also included one more allegation — that the crimes were committed at a time when Newton already had a prior felony conviction on his record. This could increase the penalty for the other crimes. What loomed over all was the death penalty for first-degree murder. One ray of hope for the defense emerged the next day when the California Supreme Court stayed two executions scheduled later that month at San Quentin prison, where Newton had just been held. The high court ordered the fate of all sixty men on Death Row placed on hold while it considered a constitutional challenge to the state's death penalty. By then forty countries had abolished capital punishment. By issuing the stay, the California Supreme Court was signaling its concern that it was time to abolish capital punishment as cruel and unusual. A coalition of death penalty opponents had presented the state's high court with statistics showing that the death penalty was "primarily inflicted upon the weak, the poor, the ignorant, and against racial minorities."[10]

This blanket stay by the state's high court was good news. If somehow Huey Newton did get the death penalty, the court would delay any execution and might reject it altogether. But Garry and Stender would not accept that as a goal — they wanted to get Newton acquitted and set him free. Stender immediately went to work day and night under the direction of Garry's partner Barney Dreyfus. Unlike Garry, Dreyfus was a constitutional scholar, thorough and meticulous in his research, under whose critical tutelage Stender had learned over the past several years to hone her own painstaking research. Dreyfus was a past president of the National Lawyers Guild, who shared with Garry a reputation as "a humanist who battles for the disadvantaged and the despised."[11]

Stender found working for Dreyfus a challenge. The product of an Irish-Jewish marriage, Dreyfus was a gentleman of the old school: he routinely opened doors for women, called Stender "little girl" and notoriously had his own mistress on the premises: the firm's office manager. But Stender appreciated her mentor's focus on perfectionism. Their first task was to prepare a constitutional challenge to the grand jury on the grounds it did not reflect a cross-section of the community, as the law required. Stender methodically gathered information on how the grand jury system operated. Each of twenty county judges submitted three names from county residents "personally known to them" to be good citizens. Not surprisingly, those selected were largely middle class, almost all white contemporaries of the judges.

The defense aimed to demonstrate that, in practice, grand jury panels systematically left out young people, blacks, the poor and low-income wage earners. This resulted not only from the way the grand jurors were chosen, but also from the hardship service imposed. Grand jurors were paid only $5 per day plus expenses. Service was for one year, a financial sacrifice wage earners could not afford. Exemptions were also given to mothers with preteen children. Stender obtained the current list of grand jurors to determine its racial composition. The Alameda County grand jury serving in 1967 had only one black member, who was not present the day Newton was indicted.

The date set for accepting Newton's plea was November 16, only three days after the grand jury convened. Before the hearing, the defense made a motion to obtain twenty-seven categories of information they believed the prosecutor had to turn over. Five years before, in *Brady v. Maryland*, the United States Supreme Court had ruled that the state violated criminal defendants' constitutional rights if it withheld evidence important to the defense of the case. The District Attorney's office would have to honor most, if not all, of these defense requests or risk reversal on appeal. The list Stender and the firm's co-counsel Alex Hoffmann prepared included the guns allegedly used, ballistics reports, the clothes worn by Officers Frey and Heanes, any files the office kept on the Black Panthers and police memos on their strategy for dealing with the Panthers.

Newton made his appearance at the November 16 hearing neatly dressed in slacks, a blue shirt and a green jacket. He appeared recovered from his gunshot wound, though he still complained to his attorneys of lingering numbness in his hands from the tight handcuffs used to shackle him in the hospital. Upon entering the courtroom, he raised a clenched fist salute to the gallery of mixed race supporters, who sat quietly throughout the short proceedings. Garry immediately requested a continuance for entry of Newton's plea, telling the court he had not had sufficient opportunity to talk with his client or to obtain the transcript of the grand jury indictment.

Heightened security was already evident. Three uniformed court bailiffs and three police in plainclothes patrolled the hallways directly outside the courtroom. Outside, demonstrators chanted "Free Huey, Jail the Pigs," while teenaged Panthers passed out leaflets, announcing one of several press conferences Garry had arranged. From the get-go Garry saw the value of getting the defense message out to the media and to people on the streets. In contrast, the prosecutor's office had no person designated to conduct public relations and issued no press releases. Jensen did not need to. The *Tribune* strongly favored the death penalty for Frey's death and that was the paper most people in the jury pool read. Other mainstream news was similar. Garry countered negative pretrial publicity by publicizing the Panthers' 10-point program and their focus on self-defense and not aggression. He also explained why the Panthers carried guns and tape recorders while patrolling black neighborhoods: to protect the residents from police harassment. Axelrod joined Garry in touting Newton as a selfless example of a courageous man deliberately hounded by the police for safeguarding his community.

The mainstream press that covered criminal trials was quite familiar with Garry's remarkable record of never losing a murder client to the death penalty. Many could also recall a decade earlier when the flamboyant leftist and his partners first opened the doors of their new office in San Francisco: three of its four principals were immediately subpoenaed to appear before a House Un-American Activities Committee (HUAC) hearing in San Francisco focused on exposing Communist professionals. HUAC and FBI head J. Edgar Hoover (who fed the committee its information) particularly wanted to destroy the career of Barney Dreyfus because he had taken the lead in opposing loyalty oaths and had recruited State Bar leaders to come to the defense of HUAC targets. Both Garry and Dreyfus were identified by a witness who had attended secret Communist educational programs in San Francisco with them in the '40s. The Bay Area hearings turned into a circus as a crowd of sympathetic onlookers cheered the uncooperative lawyers, who invoked the Fifth Amendment right not to incriminate themselves in response to every question asked of them. The FBI still kept a file on the Garry and Dreyfus firm.

In contrast to the streetfighter he was about to face, Democrat Lowell Jensen had risen through the ranks of the Alameda County District Attorney as a model of propriety. The tall, polite Mormon had grown up in the City of Alameda. His family moved there from Utah in 1928 shortly after his birth so his father could do missionary work. The family liked their new location so much they never moved back. Jensen generally only interacted with youths of different races in sports events. It remained etched in his memory when a Japanese-American Little League team he used to play against had all of its members sent to a World War II internment camp.

Jensen went to college in Berkeley and was the first in his family to go to law school. At Boalt Hall, there were three women in his class and no minorities. After passing the bar, Jensen did his deferred military service as a lawyer before the Alameda County District Attorney's office hired him. At the time, there was only one black lawyer in the office, Donald McCullum, a decorated Korean War veteran and civil rights leader. (McCullum later became a local judge.) There were women lawyers in the civil department, none doing criminal work. Two years after he joined the office, Jensen married. By the time of the Newton trial, he and his wife Barbara were the parents of three children.

Ironically, Jensen had started work as an Alameda County prosecutor just before the county's most infamous trial to date, one involving a white defendant and white teen-aged victim. In the mid-1950s the prosecution of Berkeleyite Burton Abbott for the rape and murder of fourteen-year-old Stephanie Bryan drew extraordinary press coverage. District Attorney Frank Coakley succeeded in convicting Abbott based solely on circumstantial evidence. The state executed Abbott in 1957.

At the time of Newton's arrest in October of 1967 a decade later, Coakley was still District Attorney, and had recently promoted Lowell Jensen to oversee all criminal trials in the county. By 1968, Jensen had thirteen years of experience, including five or six death penalty cases and several other murder cases. Relatively apolitical, Jensen made an odd sparring partner for Garry. Without lawyers in his family, Jensen had looked to mentors in the District Attorney's office for guidance. These senior lawyers had, in turn, learned their professional approach from Earl Warren when he was the Alameda County District Attorney for twelve years prior to World War II. Warren had then achieved the reputation as the state's best district attorney for his no-nonsense approach to crime and rooting out government corruption.

Backed by the powerful Knowland family that owned the *Oakland Tribune*, Earl Warren left the prosecutor's office in 1939 to become the state's Attorney General and then Governor. Two years before Jensen became a prosecutor, President Eisenhower appointed Governor Warren Chief Justice of the United States. Eisenhower was greatly surprised and disappointed when Warren then made history, guiding his court to a unanimous, historic decision in 1954 in *Brown v. Board of*

Education of Topeka that outlawed segregated public schools. Warren still kept up with his protégés in Alameda County when he visited California.

Jensen's mentors taught him a deep commitment to justice and playing by the rules. Veteran trial lawyer James Brosnahan tried a few cases with Jensen in the 1960s when Brosnahan was a local federal prosecutor. The experience left Brosnahan quite impressed with Jensen: "one of the most fair-minded people that I've ever met in any context." Morrie Turner liked him, too. As a subpoena clerk for the police department, Turner used to go to the District Attorney's office to get the names of witnesses. Despite Turner's low opinion at the time of the policemen he worked with, he felt Lowell Jensen respected him.

Jensen quickly noticed that Garry was far more aggressive than defense attorneys he had normally gone to trial against. Jensen thought maybe that was how defense lawyers practiced in San Francisco. Actually, Garry's hard scrabble background made him a far more assertive lawyer than most, if not all, of his legal contemporaries. He had always been called Charles or Charlie, but his feisty nature started with defending his birth name — Garabed Hagop Robutlay Garabedian. His parents were poor immigrants who fled Turkey for the United States after the Ottoman Empire began persecuting Armenians in the 1890s.

Charlie was five in 1914 when his father moved the family from Boston to farm a peach orchard near Fresno, California. In elementary school Charlie got into fist fights when other boys in the community called him a "goddamned Armenian."[12] As a teen, he honed his fighting skills while hanging out with semi-pro boxers. Later, as a factory worker and labor organizer, Charlie got into frequent brawls. He shortened his last name to Garry during the Depression to increase job offers. Self-supporting since he was a teenager, Garry worked as a drycleaner before he opened his own tailor and dry-cleaning shop in San Francisco. His passion for union rights led him to get a law degree at night school. He started out as a solo practitioner representing labor unions, trying personal injury cases and defending prostitutes. He became adept at jury trials after trying about three dozen cases a year.

Unlike Jensen's practice never to ask for anything from the court that Jensen did not consider reasonable, Garry routinely made outrageous demands. Penny Cooper observed Garry in the Newton trial and was awestruck at his technique. Garry "took the court by storm. . . . He didn't really care what the press thought, and he didn't really care what the judge thought." Instead of displaying deference like other lawyers, he stood up to the judge "to get his points across in a very vocal way." Garry recognized that judges have a tendency to split the difference between the parties' positions. In retrospect, Jensen realized that Garry's technique of over-reaching gave Garry a decided advantage by getting the judge to adopt a midway point much further in his direction than it would otherwise have been.

In addition to Garry and Fay Stender, the basic defense team included Yale Law School graduate Alex "Sascha" Hoffmann, two paralegals, and a volunteer from outside the mainstream black legal community, Carlton Innis. Most local black lawyers were still angry about the choice of Garry as lead counsel. They assumed the trial would inevitably result in Newton's conviction and wanted Garry to bear all the blame. The inclusion of Carlton Innis on the defense team did little to placate them. Innis had only five years of experience as a lawyer and was not highly skilled. In fact, at the time he joined the defense, Innis was under temporary suspension from law practice for failure to pay his bar fees and could only perform paralegal functions. (Years later, Innis would get in repeated trouble with the State Bar on more serious infractions; ultimately, he resigned.)

The malpractice claim against Kaiser Hospital already put the legal team on the political offensive in the public arena. It was helpful to counter adverse publicity, but it was a diversion from the criminal trial. Interested criminal lawyers and professors soon inundated the four lawyers with ideas on how the defense could best raise constitutional issues. Everywhere they looked, progressive attorneys and law professors wanted to help. The first step for the team was to read the grand jury transcript: it outlined the prosecutor's basic case.

The testimony before the grand jury included a police dispatcher who spoke early on the morning of October 28 with Officer Frey. Frey was then alone in his patrol car in the middle of his rounds in West Oakland's red light district on "the dog watch" a colloquial term for the nightshift. Spotting a Volkswagen sedan with two black men inside, Frey radioed in a request for a "rolling check" from police headquarters. The dispatcher looked up the license plate number and told Frey it was on a list of twenty "known Black Panther vehicles." Officer Frey told the dispatcher he was going to stop the car and ask the driver for identification. Frey asked for a report on any unpaid traffic fines and for a back-up patrol car, common practice when there were two people in the car about to be stopped. The dispatcher told Frey the car was registered to LaVerne Williams and had outstanding tickets.

Officer Heanes, just released from the hospital, made a dramatic witness. He told the grand jury he was Frey's backup. When he arrived, Newton was still in the driver's seat of the Volkswagen and identified himself by name. Frey was then standing behind the police car, writing Newton a ticket. After Heanes got out of his police car, Newton got out, too, and walked toward Frey. At that point, neither policeman had a gun drawn. Heanes had not seen one in Newton's hand either, but gunfire suddenly erupted from Newton's "general vicinity." Heanes then saw Frey and Newton wrestling. He recalled hearing a shot, being struck in the arm and then firing at Newton. Heanes heard other shots, was hit twice more, and "blacked out."

At the time, Dell Ross was sitting in his parked Ford convertible around the corner from the shooting. He testified that two black men kidnapped him and forced him to drive them away. One of the men was wounded and said, "I'd 'a kept shooting if the gun hadn't jammed, I'm too mean to die" and the other had replied, "You shot two dudes. You still got two dudes." Ross said the wounded man had a gun in his hand. After asking him to drive them to 32nd and Chestnut Street in Oakland, the two men instead left the car on Adeline Street, where the wounded man limped into a dark alley, aided by his companion. Ross later identified the wounded man as Newton.

Other police arrived at the scene to find Frey dying and Heanes seriously wounded. By then, the two men whom Frey had pulled over were gone, leaving their parked Volkswagen behind. A half-written ticket for driving without a license was found near Frey's body. Also found on the street near Frey was a blood-soaked copy of a law book with Huey Newton's name written in it. In less than fifteen minutes, police were circulating Newton's photo as the prime suspect, describing him as "armed and dangerous" and "last seen on foot . . . on Seventh Street in Oakland, wearing a light brown jacket and a dark hat." They were also looking for Newton's companion. Within forty-five minutes, an all-points bulletin went out to stop any male Negroes. When police heard Newton was at Kaiser Hospital, they sent officers to arrest him.[13]

Police technicians concluded three guns had been fired, though they found only Heanes's gun. A search of the Volkswagen turned up two small, penny match boxes of marijuana in a paper bag on the floor by the front seats. The search also turned up a live 9-mm bullet. The autopsy on Officer Frey showed he was shot five times, twice in the back at close range. It was unclear who started the shooting and the order in which the guns were fired, but both the bullet removed from Frey and the slug removed from Heanes came from the same weapon, which was not Heanes's revolver. The police still did not know the name or whereabouts of Newton's passenger. They interviewed Newton's twenty-two-year-old girlfriend, LaVerne Williams, who confirmed that it was her car Newton was driving when he was stopped, but she had not been with him that evening and knew nothing about the shooting.

While Garry's associates reviewed the grand jury transcript for holes in the prosecutor's case, a handful of Panthers and a growing number of supporters concentrated on building community support to "Free Huey." They announced ambitious plans to picket the courthouse four hours per day, seven days a week, until Huey was free. Stender had recently helped elect Berkeley City Council Member Ron Dellums. She persuaded him to bring before his colleagues a resolution condemning Newton's indictment by an unrepresentative grand jury.

Meanwhile, the Panthers' efforts to galvanize support paid off. Circulation of *The Black Panther* increased a thousand percent. At Newton's second court appearance on November 28, over sixty followers filled the public gallery. *The Sun Reporter* newspaper, run by Dr. Goodlett in San Francisco, actively drummed up defense funds, as did *The Berkeley Barb* and the *Panther* newspaper. This time, when Newton arrived in the courtroom in his new gray sharkskin suit, emboldened supporters stood up and greeted him with a clenched-fist salute. Newton returned the salute and invited the attendees to be seated. His usurpation of the judge's authority caused them to break into laughter.

Superior Court Judge Staats was not amused. He called for order in the courtroom, warning the crowd against any more demonstrations. His remarks only generated more derisive laughter. The judge quickly took control. He ordered Newton returned to his cell and used the recess to lecture Newton's supporters: "This is a courtroom and we require that people remain quiet and seated except for the counsel and principals involved. If you are not prepared to do that, we will ask to clear the courtroom. Is there anyone who will not comply?"[14]

Only after the crowd grew silent did the judge order Newton brought back. Newton then insisted that the judge call him "Minister of Defense" Huey Newton rather than simply by his name. The next time they were in court in December, the judge held an informal discussion in chambers with the lawyers for both sides. The judge asked Garry if he would seek a different trial venue due to the bad publicity the *Oakland Tribune* had already generated. Such a strategy only made sense if there were potential jurors in another California county Garry believed would give his client a better chance than an Alameda County jury would. The Black Panthers had their base among Oakland's now almost forty percent black population. Across the bay, San Francisco was at the time only 13.5 percent black and had only 3.3 percent blacks in its jury pool.

Garry already had a useful proxy to measure a community's entrenched racist attitudes — the vote on Proposition 14 in 1964. That ballot initiative proposed a state constitutional amendment to undo the impact of California's highly controversial Fair Housing Act of 1963. The Fair Housing Act was a crowning achievement of pioneering African-American Assemblyman William Byron Rumford — the Rumford Act was the first in the nation to prohibit discrimination by home sellers and landlords on the basis of race, religion, sex, national origin, ancestry or marital status.

Much like laws enacted today to allow refusal of services for gay weddings, Proposition 14 sought to amend the state constitution to protect landlords and sellers from suit if they refused to allow a black family to purchase or rent a home in an all-white neighborhood. In 1966, the California Supreme Court struck down Proposition 14 as unconstitutional; a bare majority of the U.S. Supreme Court affirmed that ruling in May of 1967 — just over six months before Judge Staats asked Garry if he might seek a change of venue. While Garry publicly charged no militant black could get a fair trial anywhere in the state, he knew Alameda County had rejected Proposition 14 by 54 percent of the vote, a better result than any other county. Garry responded to Judge Staats with his own question: where in California did the judge think Newton could get a fair trial? The judge joked "Orange County," a conservative white enclave in Southern California. Garry laughed and said he was thinking about some place in Cuba.

In these early days, Melvin Newton chaired the fund-raising effort. He worked with the Panther Party to organize community support, but still resisted joining the Party. Melvin admired their police patrols, but harbored serious concerns about where it would all end. At one point he told Emory Douglas, "I see a lot of blood with the guns."

Emory Douglas replied, "To the horse's brow."

Melvin responded, "Wow." He understood that meant a commitment to let flow whatever amount of blood it took.

Janice Garrett later talked about how the Panthers got ready for potential warfare: "We used to go to the Santa Cruz mountains and take target practicing, the women and the men, because it was very important that you understood the use of a weapon, that you just didn't carry a weapon. We were prepared and realized that we might have to give our lives in defense of our beliefs. . . . Everybody's life was expendable."

Hilliard thought the same way: "Anything might happen. You know, we would leave no stones unturned in trying to free our freedom fighter and leader."

As Huey's prosecution moved forward in November of 1967, Melvin Newton called a press conference to appeal for support. Naïve as he was, Melvin did not anticipate being asked if he was also a Black Panther. He quickly realized that if he said no, he would be asked for an explanation that might hurt his brother's case. So Melvin said, "Yes." He would remain a member of the Party for about a year before quietly withdrawing.

During this early phase of the Newton case, Bobby Seale had been transferred from a Sacramento jail to the maximum security wing of Santa Rita. As soon as Seale saw the front-page photo of Newton manacled to a gurney, he became consumed with getting Newton out. Seale knew from past conversations that Newton could not abide the mental torture of sitting on death row with an unknown execution date, waiting years while stays and appeals took their course.

During November, other Panthers visited Seale at Santa Rita, urging him to countermand Cleaver and get rid of Charles Garry. Their first choice to represent Newton was forty-seven-year-old Clinton White, long-time general counsel for the NAACP's Oakland office, who had just become its president. White was considered "the preeminent civil rights lawyer of his era." Tall and athletic with a booming voice and aggressive style, local lawyers and judges agreed that White was one of the most formidable criminal defense attorneys around. His colleague Willie Brown claimed, "If you wanted to learn how to cross-examine someone, no matter who you were, you had to watch Clinton White."[15]

The unhappy Panthers' distant second choice was John George. He had once negotiated a favorable compromise for Newton on an assault charge, but nobody had ever heard of him trying a death penalty case. Death penalty cases pose unique challenges and require expertise generalists in criminal law lack. George did not inspire confidence that he was up to it. Yet Seale already had serious reservations of his own about the choice of Charles Garry. As soon as he walked free on December 8, 1967, he would personally check Garry out. It was not just Newton's life that hung in the balance, but the future of the Black Panther Party. If Newton were found guilty, how would they justify having asked a white lawyer to represent the leader of the vanguard? What would they tell new recruits from the black community shouting, "Free Huey or else"?

128

Oakland Tribune headline story October 28, 1967, on the afternoon of the shootout, featuring pictures of the officers John Frey and Herbert C. Heanes. The officers' OPD photos are shown here larger than they appeared in the newspaper article.

6. WHO DO YOU TRUST?

The first lesson a revolutionary must learn
is that he is a doomed man.
— Huey Newton

Given his precarious position, Garry knew how important it was to keep Newton's morale buoyed and his lines of communication open to Panther leaders on the outside. But hand-holding was not Garry's forte. His busy law practice in San Francisco also kept him from scheduling non-essential visits at the Alameda County jail in November and early December of 1967. Newton could only have visitors from 1 to 3 p.m. three days a week. Newton did not hurt for company. The first day, his Panther friends filled the hallway waiting their turn to see him. His spirits were high. He told Earl Anthony that when he was lying on the gurney at Kaiser he kept telling himself: "I'm too mean to die."[1] Beverly Axelrod regularly crossed the Bay Bridge to visit Newton and bring messages back to Cleaver from the jailed Party leader. Her participation soon became too awkward. Axelrod was still head-over-heels in love with Cleaver. Less than a month after Newton's arrest, Cleaver rejected her.

* * * * *

When Axelrod first met Cleaver in the mid-1960s, she was already past forty. She had recently left her husband to marry her lover, Reggie Majors, a well-known African-American journalist and author of books on black liberation. But Majors had surprised Axelrod by then declining to divorce his wife, as he had promised Axelrod before her own divorce.

Greatly hurt, Axelrod had found solace in correspondence and jail visits with a new client. Eldridge Cleaver resembled Majors in height and athletic build. Standing tall and self-assured, Cleaver made a macho statement with his moustache and small beard. Axelrod believed Cleaver embodied what she had been searching for nearly all her adult life — a soul mate with the same radical, egalitarian goals.

When Cleaver left prison in 1966, he used Axelrod's brother's San Francisco house as his official residence to meet with his parole officer, though he actually often lived with Beverly. The couple bought a Volvo together, and Cleaver told his mother he and Beverly planned to marry. Already a celebrated author, Cleaver became a popular speaker after his release. He began cultivating friendships with local black authors and militants. He received invitations to address black nationalist rallies and promoted his book on radio shows. Cleaver also sometimes took to the road to conduct high profile interviews for *Ramparts.*

On Easter weekend at the end of March, 1967, SNCC scheduled a student conference at Fisk University, in Nashville, Tennessee. The small, highly prestigious black college counted civil rights leader W. E. B. DuBois, co-founder of the NAACP, among its early alumni. Cleaver received an invitation to serve on a panel with playwright Leroi Jones (later known as Imamu Amir Baraka), whom Eldridge had befriended in San Francisco, and frequently showed up at literary gatherings at Black House, the rented Victorian in Haight Ashbury.

SNCC also scheduled a higher profile conference early the following month at nearby Vanderbilt University, featuring the Reverend Martin Luther King, Jr., beat poet Allen Ginsberg and SNCC leader Stokely Carmichael. It was less than a year since Carmichael had sent shock waves throughout the country with his historic "Black Power" speech repudiating King's pacifist marches for civil rights. Now, Carmichael urged his followers to defend themselves against white supremacists. As soon as word leaked out of the invitation to Carmichael, Vanderbilt's administration cancelled it for fear of riots. Cleaver agreed violence was likely. That was what he was looking forward to: "We were dancing with death, and we knew it. But we did not call for the music to stop. Instead, we called for the band to play louder, stronger, and longer."[2]

Fisk immediately cancelled its own SNCC conference. A local minister offered his church social hall as a last minute substitute. Once
Cleaver learned his conference was back on schedule, he flew to
Nashville only to discover that a huge East Coast blizzard prevented all
other speakers from attending. But then he learned that Carmichael
had also defiantly headed for Nashville. Earlier that winter, Cleaver had
interviewed Carmichael in Chicago and Atlanta for *Ramparts*. The two
men decided to crash the April conference at Vanderbilt together. After
Carmichael addressed an angry crowd, police, students and activists
clashed in the worst violence in Nashville's history. The battleground
over the next few days engulfed Fisk and nearby Tennessee Agriculture
and Industry University. Students barricaded themselves inside their
dorms while police stormed the campuses. The violence quickly spread
to include armed confrontations with the police in the black community at large.

Even after the violence had subsided, Cleaver remained in Nashville.
Among the staff from SNCC headquarters in Atlanta that came to oversee the two conferences was Kathleen Neal, a beautiful young college
dropout recruited from New York. The red-headed, light skinned black
was tall and slender and wore her hair in a big, bushy Afro. She joined
SNCC in June of 1966 just two weeks after Stokely Carmichael's call for
Black Power. A fan of SNCC since she was in high school, Neal was now
living her dream life. When Cleaver met her in Nashville, he fell in love
at first sight. The feeling was not mutual. Cleaver became so infatuated
with the twenty-one-year-old that, when he learned she did not drive, he
chauffeured her around Nashville on SNCC errands in his rental car.

Axelrod grew so concerned by Cleaver's extended absence that she
flew to Nashville to find him. Showing up on the Fisk campus wearing
her hair loose, a California sun dress, sandals and long, dangly ear-
rings, Axelrod might not have been conspicuous if she had been twenty
years younger and black. She caught up with Cleaver as he was about
to transport several new young SNCC friends, including Neal, back to
Atlanta. Cleaver introduced Axelrod to his new friends in Nashville simply as "my lawyer," leaving them quite curious and Axelrod steaming.
He then followed Kathleen Neal to Atlanta and won her heart over a

chess game. After his return to California Cleaver and Neal kept up their romance with passionate letters and long telephone conversations on SNCC's dedicated Watts line.

Although Cleaver had recently moved into Black House, he still spent a lot of time with Axelrod. Both were helping launch *The Black Panther* newspaper. In April, Cleaver made a fiery speech at an antiwar rally in San Francisco, which he followed with his high-profile trip to Sacramento with the Panthers in early May. Not surprisingly, his parole officer told Cleaver that his speeches now needed to be vetted in advance and he could no longer travel out of the county.

Axelrod's suspicions were confirmed that summer. Anxious to see Kathleen Neal again, Eldridge invited her to visit him in San Francisco. Neal flew to San Francisco in early July and stayed with Cleaver for over a month. The FBI took note. Cleaver was restricted to traveling within the city, so Black Panther members came several times to Cleaver's apartment for meetings. That was when Neal first met Huey Newton, finding him fast talking, always on the move and intense. His "pretty boy" looks did not attract her like Cleaver's rugged machismo. By then, Neal was madly in love. Still unable to drive, she depended almost totally on Cleaver to take her places, though the Panthers took her once across the Bay to visit their headquarters in Oakland.

Once Cleaver disappeared for a couple of days and then called Neal to come by taxi to pick him up at Beverly Axelrod's house. It had been an awkward scene. During the several weeks that Neal stayed at Cleaver's apartment, Axelrod often parked her Volvo outside the apartment, spying on them. Axelrod was greatly relieved when Neal left in early August, unaware her philandering fiancé had proposed to Neal the second day of her stay.

When David Hilliard called to alert Cleaver the morning of October 28, 1967, that Newton had been shot and a policeman was dead, Cleaver called Beverly Axelrod first for legal help. He next reached out to Kathleen Neal. He was extremely upset. Not only was Newton gravely wounded, but it was clear Newton faced the death penalty. Cleaver told her, "You have to go out here and help us." Neal was an experienced fund-raiser who could help Melvin Newton with the

"Free Huey" campaign. Neal could also help organize demonstrations on Newton's behalf. Neal immediately started soliciting contributions while still at SNCC headquarters in Atlanta. She then moved to the Bay Area in mid-November, as David Hilliard was gathering supporters for Newton's next hearing.

As soon as she arrived, Cleaver took Neal to a meeting with other Panthers. Unlike her visit in the summer, they no longer had an office, they had no supplies and no money. The organization she had observed in July had essentially collapsed. Just a few men showed up. Among them was skinny, seventeen-year-old Bobby Hutton with his pork pie hat and glasses and the Panthers' 24-year-old newspaper publisher Emory Douglas, the Panthers' cherubic Minister of Culture. It took Neal aback — counting herself and Eldridge, it was a very small group to try to support Newton. Neal settled for good in Cleaver's apartment and began strategizing how to build a coalition. Her suggestion was to arrange demonstrations outside the courthouse to draw attention to Newton's trial and fill the courtroom with supporters. She was drawing upon civil rights techniques used by SNCC that had drawn a lot of press coverage in the South to protect demonstrators against retaliation. The SNCC trials had been for minor violations like willfully obstructing public streets, disturbing the peace or violating local parade ordinances. None had involved a serious felony of any kind, let alone the toxic atmosphere surrounding a trial for the death of a cop.

Neal suggested to Hilliard that they get a flatbed truck with a loudspeaker to play music to draw attention to their message and then call on people to attend hearings in Huey's case. The Peace and Freedom Party loaned them a truck and they started playing the popular 1965 single "Shotgun" by Junior Walker and the All Stars. They recruited in Berkeley and Oakland, using the loudspeaker to ask "Can a black man get a fair trial anywhere in America?"[3] and declare "Come see about Huey." When they handed out leaflets, people often responded, "He is going to the gas chambers." "He is done for." Neal was determined to take on that universal assumption — to make Huey Newton the symbol of every black man railroaded by the system.

It was true that this case was markedly different than any other shooting case that people had heard of. When one of the gunman was a police officer, past incidents always featured a dead black man and a cop who never faced prosecution. Such incidents were all too common. The national attention to Huey Newton's arrest showcased the opposite — a dead policeman and a live black man. It was the proverbial "man bites dog" news story — an unusual twist on a commonplace event. Neal wanted to take it a step further. She sought to foment outrage that an oppressive policeman and a rigged system were about to doom Newton before he even had his day in court, just like every other black defendant before him.

No one knew what happened when Officer Frey stopped the Volkswagen and suddenly realized he was about to arrest "the great Huey Newton." Kathleen pictured the male rivalry of two men about the same age, one with a reputation as a bully and the other as a street-fighter. All she knew is that "Huey survived and Frey didn't." The Panthers wanted "to transform the way police behaved and we wanted community control of police. We wanted 'point 7' — an end to the police murder and killing of black people." If a black man did not have the right to self-defense, then he did not have the right to live. Kathleen's attitude was as fierce as Eldridge's: "We had a sense we are going to change the world or we are going to die trying."

Meanwhile, Neal and Cleaver made wedding plans for late December. Shortly after Neal's arrival, Cleaver had an ugly falling out with Beverly Axelrod, telling her he could no longer associate with white women. Cleaver then named his newly disclosed fiancée the Party's Communications Secretary, the only woman in the Party with a title. Axelrod was deeply wounded. On her visits to Newton at the Alameda County jail, he empathized and offered to decree her an honorary black woman. But the rift between Axelrod and Cleaver made it impossible for her to continue to serve as a go-between. When Cleaver visited Newton in jail in late November, Newton told him he was convinced that if he went to trial, he would die in the gas chamber. In Cleaver's words, "His preference was to be broken out, to have a red-light trial, with the red lights flashing."[4] Newton agreed to let Cleaver try to address the situation. Both knew that meant Cleaver would openly risk having his parole revoked for publicly associating with the Panthers.

At Earl Anthony's urging Eldridge Cleaver sent Anthony down to Los Angeles to address "Free Huey" rallies, fund-raise for the defense and promote the Party in the media. In December, Cleaver introduced Anthony to Cleaver's prison friend Alprentice "Bunchy" Carter so the two could form a Southern California Panther office. Before Bunchy Carter spent four years behind bars for robbery, he had a fearsome reputation as "the Mayor of the Ghetto," head of the Slauson Renegades. The Slauson Renegades were the most militant members at the heart of a huge gang operating on Slauson Avenue in South L. A. In early 1968, Carter would open the Party's first branch outside of Oakland with John Huggins, a Vietnam veteran, and his wife Ericka among the first members. By late June of 1968, at Cleaver's instigation, the Central Committee named Anthony Deputy Minister of Information in Los Angeles despite developing tension between Anthony and Bunchy Carter over Anthony's dedication to the Party. Anthony agreed to take on responsibility for conducting political education classes for new recruits.

Cleaver and Carter had no knowledge that Anthony was regularly reporting to COINTELPRO on their activities or that the idea for opening that L. A. office actually came from COINTELPRO. Hoover wanted Anthony to instigate a turf war in Los Angeles between Ron Karenga's US and the Oakland-based Panther Party.[5] Anthony immediately began inciting Cleaver to order Bunchy Carter to "roll over Karenga." Though "US" stood for the community of "us black people," the Panthers derided it as short for "United Slaves." Cleaver and Carter were hot-headed enough to precipitate several violent incidents until the High Command in Oakland forged a temporary truce with Karenga. Anthony's handlers were most unhappy — their goal was to see members of both groups annihilate each other.[6]

* * * * *

As the tense rivalry developed in L.A., back in Oakland, the Panthers' focus was on getting large numbers of picketers to the courthouse. From the first hearing in November, when Huey Newton had introduced himself in court as the Minister of Defense for the Black Panther Party, Garry had encouraged that brazen approach. Together, they were launching the first Movement murder trial. Even the Scottsboro Boys and Sacco and Vanzetti did not draw protesters to their trial proceedings — they primarily attracted political support in places outside the incensed community where the crime occurred, and only after their juries imposed death sentences. Garry had no intention of letting things get to that desperate stage.

Meanwhile, local black lawyers still lobbied hard for an experienced black criminal lawyer to replace Garry as lead counsel for Newton. John George and Clinton White remained under consideration. The discontented group also considered Donald Warden, Newton's former mentor at the Afro-American Association, but were leery of Warden's track record — too many convictions. Seale had also heard rumors that some unhappy former clients felt Warden had sold them short. The gossip from disgruntled inmates Warden had represented made Seale uneasy. Seale knew of Clinton White's extraordinary reputation and could not fathom how the family chose Garry instead.

When Seale met Garry at his law offices in December of 1967, Seale immediately asked how much money it would cost. Garry responded, "Let's not worry about that." Garry explained how he handled political trials and tried to reassure Seale of his leftist credentials and philosophy. Seale remained dissatisfied and went to see White, who asked for $10,000 to $12,000 in advance, which the Panthers did not have. Given White's reputation for taking many cases without pay, one colleague later guessed White wanted the Panthers to look elsewhere. White would not have promised or delivered a political defense as Garry was planning. The NAACP leader likely felt quite relieved that this polarizing, high-profile trial was in someone else's hands. But it was also possible that the savvy trial lawyer simply realized the high cost to his practice involved in assuming that death penalty defense. It promised to be all-consuming and White might even risk bankruptcy if he took on such a huge case without substantial payment up front. He would not want to wind up pursuing the Black Panthers for his fee.

Seale confirmed Garry's personal record of winning some two dozen murder trials. Garry had in fact first gained fame in the early '50s representing an African-American named Bob Wells, the feisty Armenian's first death-penalty case. Wells was originally caught stealing a $26 suit as a teenager in the late 1920s. Garry painted his client as a reincarnated Jean Valjean, the fictional French hero popularized in *Les Misérables.* A series of increased penalties for altercations in prison resulted in Wells getting a life sentence. Then, a nonlethal assault on a guard put Wells on death row. Looking back three decades later, Garry called Bob Wells "the first Black Panther"[7] because of his feisty attitude toward his jailers. Psychiatric evidence of Wells' unbalanced mental state caused by beatings, hosings and repeated isolation in the "hole" helped Garry win delays in Wells' scheduled execution. One writ was issued when Wells was only thirteen hours away from death. A successful public-relations campaign eventually convinced Governor Knight to change Wells' sentence to life without possibility of parole.

In 1959, Garry and Benjamin Dreyfus persuaded the California Supreme Court to consider the issue again in *People v. Gorshen,* another death penalty case. Their client had admittedly committed homicide; the question was the penalty. They succeeded in reducing Gorshen's sentence, too, based on his mental state at the time of the killing. As shorthand in legal circles, the mitigating factor of "diminished capacity" then became known in California as the *Wells-Gorshen* rule. Proof of impairment would not result in getting off entirely, but conviction only of a lesser-level crime. A defendant who acted with diminished capacity would not merit a first-degree murder conviction. That required proof beyond a reasonable doubt of premeditation, deliberation and specific intent to kill.[8]

When Seale met Garry, he was still working periodically to secure Wells' release, a long-term project finally realized in 1974. With funding offered from the Communist Party and Garry's impressive record as a radical defense lawyer, Seale reconsidered his first instincts and decided that the best course was to accept Garry. Other Panthers remained vehemently opposed to any white lawyer. Garry himself later admitted: "I thought I knew something about Negro America because some of my intimate friends are Negro professionals who have been accepted partially in our great white society. . . . It wasn't a week or two weeks after I got into this case, I came to the conclusion I knew absolutely nothing about black America."[9]

Seale and Cleaver repeatedly argued to other Panthers not to judge Garry "by the color of his skin."[10] What better option did they have? Clint White was too expensive, Warden and George too risky. George was also too cautious for their taste. When representing the rival Black Panthers of Northern California, George had advised them to walk around carrying unloaded weapons. Newton and his friend Hilliard had taken to calling them "paper Panthers." Seale, Cleaver and his new bride Kathleen remained unable to convince all doubters. Some quit the defense committee. Local black lawyers took their grievance to the press, arguing the legal work should have gone to a black brother. And so it was that America's black Che Guevara came to be represented by a white radical lawyer few Panthers trusted.

Ironically, Garry's law firm paid a high price for taking on Newton's representation, just as Clint White had anticipated. As the firm's principle rainmaker, Garry had been bringing in $20,000 to $30,000 per month in personal injury fees before he took on the Newton case — but no longer. The firm's support for the Black Panthers also did not sit well with some of its other clients. A large labor union, which new partner Al Brotsky had just brought to the firm, took all of its legal work elsewhere. As the Panthers' debt to the partnership grew, Seale realized that many of the black lawyers who wanted a piece of the action would not have held on anywhere near as long without getting paid. He did not regret his decision to endorse Garry or the equally controversial decision he and Eldridge Cleaver made to keep strong ties with the white radical Peace and Freedom Party. As Seale saw it, the only road to success required allying themselves with like-minded whites.

7. HONKIES FOR HUEY

They took away Sacco, Vanzetti,
Connelly and Pearse in their time
They came for Newton and Seale

— FROM "NO TIME FOR LOVE" BY
THE IRISH POLITICAL-ROCK GROUP "THE MOVING HEARTS"

White radicals working for *The Movement* monthly newspaper had rushed to report on the first Newton hearing in November. Having started as a voice for SNCC, *The Movement* staff recognized that a highly-politicized death penalty case attacking the racist justice system was front-page fodder. *The Movement* had also just played a key role in orchestrating "Stop the Draft Week," whose leaders were now facing criminal charges in the same courthouse. In the small world of leftists in the Bay Area, it was not too surprising that Newton's lawyer, Charles Garry, headed their defense team as well. Beverly Axelrod and her colleague Alex Hoffmann had also been among the first attorneys to represent demonstrators arrested during "Stop the Draft Week." The boyfriend of *Movement* staff reporter Karen Jo Koonan was now jailed as one of the Oakland Seven; she knew that she could easily have been named as an eighth defendant.

Koonan and other reporters for *The Movement* found direct connections between the two cases: "It was the same government that turned its back on the sharecroppers in the South that [was] dropping bombs in Vietnam." Stokely Carmichael's close ally Muhammad Ali had linked the abhorred domestic and foreign policies more succinctly in famously resisting the draft in the spring of 1967: "No Viet Cong ever called me a nigger."[1] Ali's forfeiture of his soaring boxing career while he fought imprisonment for refusing induction on religious grounds had made him a rock star of the antiwar movement.

The value of an alliance that fall with the Black Panthers was obvious to the "Stop the Draft" steering committee: "The way that the police were targeting the Black Panther Party [and] the underlying issues of racism and poverty in the black community [mirrored] the issue of African-Americans being drafted and sent to Vietnam." The Panthers call for "Power to the People" also applied to frustrated white youths protesting the draft. The white anti-war activists arrested during "Stop the Draft Week" had also impressed the Panthers. Arrangements were soon made for Hilliard and Seale to attend a meeting of the activists to seek support for Newton from the coalition already rallying behind the Oakland Seven. After that meeting, Koonan recalls, "Many of the same people participated in some of the early rallies in support of Huey and there were a lot of discussions . . . between the 'leaders' of the antiwar movement and the leadership of the Black Panther Party."

Only one *Movement* reporter, Karen Wald, had conventional press credentials. She was quickly deputized to visit Newton at the Alameda County jail. Meanwhile, among the prominent picketers at the December hearing were Free Speech Movement Leaders Mario Savio and Jack Weinberg, as well as Bob Avakian, the radical son of Judge Spurgeon Avakian, the most liberal judge on the Alameda County Superior Court. These three white activists were then leaders of the Peace and Freedom Party. Like the staff of *The Movement*, the leadership of the Peace and Freedom Party viewed the Newton trial as a great opportunity to cement an alliance with some radical blacks. By then, both SNCC and Black Muslims shunned all ties with white radicals. The Peace and Freedom Party passed a formal resolution calling for Newton's freedom and offered $3,000 towards his defense costs, a show of solidarity demanded by the Panthers which came at the expense of badly-need money the Peace and Freedom Party was also seeking to help defend the "Oakland Seven."

It was during a jail visit to a defendant in the "Oakland Seven" that Axelrod introduced Alex Hoffmann to Huey Newton, then held in a nearby cell. Hoffmann had been curious to meet Newton since the day he had helped Axelrod confront Police Chief Gain to obtain permission for twenty-four-hour nursing care for Newton to protect him against revenge by the police. Hoffmann then joined the Newton defense team in Axelrod's stead as she abandoned her California practice and fled the state for New Mexico.

By December of 1967, Axelrod had found herself unable to remain any longer in the Bay Area following her devastating rejection by Cleaver. Before she left, she exacted payback by drafting an agreement for Cleaver to sign, granting her 25 percent of the net proceeds of his book *Soul On Ice* "in perpetuity"[2] — that percentage had been her promised legal fee for helping him get out of prison. Axelrod showed up at Cleaver's apartment to get his signature while Neal looked on silently from the bedroom. The two women would not formally be introduced to each other until Eldridge Cleaver's memorial service thirty years later.

For the December hearing in the Newton case, demonstrators first conducted a rally on the Berkeley campus and then moved to the Alameda courthouse, shouting "Free Huey" and "Support the Oakland Seven." By then a plan was in place to have protest demonstrations scheduled every time Newton went to court. Bobby Seale made an impassioned speech on the courthouse steps, his first since he had been released from prison. Kathleen Neal found Seale extraordinarily impressive. Cleaver told her, "Yeah, that's why he is the chairman."

The first-floor corridor and entrances of the courthouse were blocked by about 400 Black Panthers, Peace and Freedom Party members and other demonstrators, including a large turnout of a new white radical support group, "Honkys for Huey," who hauled down the American flag at the courthouse and re-raised it upside down as a distress signal. Kathleen Neal and David Hilliard looked at each other in disbelief as police stood by and allowed vocal protests without incident. Both hailed originally from Alabama where civil rights demonstrators risked beatings or worse for far more peaceful protests outside a courthouse. Only in Oakland did it seem Neal's strategy was possible — much as the two of them could read the frustration in the eyes of the officers on duty. Many years later Eldridge Cleaver would admit to grudging appreciation of the Oakland police: "I'm telling you after I ran into the

Egyptian police and the Algerian police and the North Korean police and the Nigerian police and Idi Amin's police in Uganda, I began to miss the Oakland police."[3]

Inside the courtroom, Garry argued that the evidence before the grand jury was not enough to hold Newton on the murder charges. The audience cheered, drawing a strong rebuke from Judge Staats, who ordered them to remain silent. Garry said the witnesses had not seen Newton holding any weapon in his hand, nor had the prosecutor even identified the murder weapon. Garry suggested that Officer Heanes might have killed Frey accidentally. The judge was not persuaded; Garry would have been quite surprised if the ruling were otherwise.

At this early stage of the proceedings, Newton was kept in the same cell block within earshot of defendants in the Oakland Seven case. Concerned officials moved Huey to an isolation cell on the tenth floor. To keep his spirits up, he kept a dog-eared copy of *The Wretched of the Earth* in his cell, which he reread between visitors. Newton had to enjoy the alarmed account in a local paper of Seale firing up supporters in Richmond by calling the prosecution "trumped up charges by the white racist, Gestapo pig cops. That was no murder in Oakland. That was the execution of a pig cop."[4] The small cell often grew unbearably warm. Newton peeled off his flannel jail uniform and paced naked. He could sometimes hear cries of "Free Huey" from the sidewalk below.

During this time, it was Janice Garrett's job to follow Seale around to take notes and to arrange more speaking opportunities. Garrett was arrested once: "I was in a Black Panther 'known vehicle' and we were stopped by the police and taken in to the Oakland police department. I was carrying a briefcase at the time as Bobby's [Bobby Seale's] secretary. And they took us down and confiscated all of our belongings, held us for 24 hours and then let us go the next day — without charges."

At the next hearing in January of 1968, Garry arrived with a briefcase overflowing with more than two dozen motions Stender and other defense team members had feverishly assembled over the past few weeks. The motions sought disclosure of police reports and the names of all witnesses whom the D.A.'s office might call to testify against Newton. They included a request that the prosecutor identify all other evidence he intended to rely on. Garry also asked the judge to allow the defense to subpoena former grand jurors who had recently testified before a State Assembly committee in Sacramento on major flaws in the grand jury system.

As soon as he took the bench, Judge Staats revealed that he had received a gold-embossed invitation to a fund-raising cocktail party for Newton. As the judge started to say he did not consider it appropriate to attend, Newton interrupted, telling the judge it was too bad, because he would have enjoyed himself. The circus atmosphere had begun. Outside were many young black picketers who chanted loudly enough to be heard inside the room: "Huey will be set free! Free Huey now! Down with Gestapo pigs! Black power!"[5]

Garry won permission to subpoena only one person — the superior court judge who had chosen the 1967 grand jury. Garry would be allowed to quiz the judge on his selection process. Judge Staats set January 26, 1968, for argument of the constitutional challenge to the grand jury. He also took under submission all the other motions Garry had made. The judge then asked Garry for his client's plea on the pending charges. On Newton's behalf, Garry pled not guilty to all counts. He also told the judge he would challenge the 1964 assault conviction because Newton had never received any legal counsel in defending against that charge. Outside, after the hearing, Seale urged the boisterous crowd to return to the next hearing in late January and asked each to bring two more picketers.

Ironically, the very same day, the *Oakland Tribune* featured the passing of 89-year-old "Raincoat" Jones, the city's most flamboyant black resident of the past half century. Due to his declining health and fortunes, no one had seen "Raincoat" Jones for years on the blocks of Seventh Street he once owned. The overflow bi-racial crowd of mourners at Jones' funeral ranged from high-level city officials and West Oakland businessmen to hustlers and regular patrons, all of whose lives had been touched by the unforgettable old-timer. It was unlikely that reporters describing his casket generously strewn with flowers realized that their papers were already covering the first stages of the next, far more transformative era of community-police relations.

Back in his cell, Newton continued to receive visitors thrice weekly.

The visitors had to strain to hear him through a three-by-twelve-inch window in his isolated cell. During the first week of January, a Kaiser Hospital lawyer sought to take Newton's deposition under oath about his claim for malpractice. In mid-January, Newton gave an exclusive interview to white radicals from *The Berkeley Barb*. In it, he talked about how he and Garry thought the Kaiser lawyers were acting at the bidding of the D. A. to induce him to make incriminating statements. Instead of focusing on the manacles that held the wounded Newton to the gurney, the Kaiser lawyer had asked about the shooting that had occurred before Newton reached Kaiser, a line of inquiry both Garry and Newton considered highly suspect. A representative of the prosecutor's office had recently appeared at a hearing on the Kaiser suit, pressing for similar details.

Rather than risk having Newton explain his version of the shooting, which could be used against Newton in the murder case, Garry dismissed the malpractice action. By then, the civil suit had served its true purpose of generating positive publicity for Newton and rallying supporters to his cause. Garry realized a bit late that he should not allow any press unfettered access to Newton, even if it was a friendly underground paper, because anything Newton said could be used against him. Shortly after *The Berkeley Barb* interview, Garry issued ground rules that no interviews with Newton would take place without an attorney present. This not only brought any future statements Newton made to the press under his attorneys' control, but provided a more civilized setting for all future interviews — an attorney-client meeting room with table and chairs.

Another large crowd of supporters attended the January 26, 1968, hearing. Late that night the defense team got a crank anonymous call describing Garry as a "Nigger lover." Upon learning that Garry had gone home to bed, the caller left a chilling message: "Hope you keep on sleeping forever and soundly."[6] Staff kept this threat and others received afterward in the case file for later disclosure to the judge. The prosecutor also collected threats received by witnesses and the police: an anonymous male caller had dialed the home number in San Francisco of Dr. Thomas Finch, the first physician to treat Huey Newton at Kaiser Hospital, and threatened the doctor's life if he returned to Oakland. The hostilities this case generated had only just begun.

8. THE SMELL OF REVOLUTION

We counted history from Huey's night of truth.
— ELDRIDGE CLEAVER

With money from Cleaver's advance for *Soul On Ice*, the Panthers decided to open a new storefront office in North Oakland. Back in late June of 1967, the Panthers had built on the momentum from Sacramento by another dramatic announcement. As their Second Executive Mandate, Newton and Cleaver sought to link the Panthers to SNCC by calling a press conference to proclaim Stokely Carmichael as their new "Field Marshal . . . [with authority to] establish revolutionary laws, order, and justice . . . [East of the Continental Divide]."[1] Carmichael was handed the scroll while he was visiting in Northern California and shared it with others at SNCC headquarters on his return. At the time, Carmichael raved to Kathleen Neal about the Panthers as the first and only group to implement Black Power in an urban setting. He was thrilled and so was Neal — on the eve of her own trip West to see Eldridge Cleaver again and meet the Panthers herself in July of 1967.

Shortly afterward, H. Rap Brown replaced Carmichael as head of SNCC and Carmichael headed off on an extended speaking tour of Cuba, China, North Vietnam and Africa. After Carmichael returned to the United States, Cleaver and Seale talked the Peace and Freedom Party into paying their expenses to go to Washington, D.C., to convince Carmichael to come to the Black Panthers' aid. The pair were planning a major fund-raiser to be held at the Oakland Auditorium on

Newton's twenty-sixth birthday, February 17, 1968. The city had initially refused to rent the facility to discourage the possibility of riots, but the Panthers had brought an attorney with them who obtained the venue by threatening to go to court to enforce their First Amendment right to peaceably assemble.

When they met with SNCC officials in Washington, D.C., Cleaver and Seale ran into further opposition for hiring a white attorney to defend Newton and for forming a coalition with the mostly white Peace and Freedom Party. The two Panthers assured SNCC leaders that the alliance was tentative and limited. They convinced a skeptical Carmichael to make his first major public address since his return to the country and also lured H. Rap Brown and James Forman of SNCC to Oakland as well.

Forman was now living with Decca Mitford's daughter, Friends of SNCC organizer Dinky Romilly, one of the few whites to still have any association with SNCC. Forman objected to the Black Panthers' plan to name Carmichael its Honorary Prime Minister. He suggested H. Rap Brown, revealing a rift between Carmichael and other SNCC leaders that the Panthers had not previously appreciated. The Panthers decided instead to give all SNCC leaders positions of importance in the Party. These were all the Panthers' heroes, and titles were cheap, even if their scope was ill-defined. The Panthers thought this would cement a SNCC-Panther alliance with access to SNCC's national infrastructure, not realizing it was then crumbling.

Just before the rally, Carmichael made a quick visit to Newton in the Alameda County jail, telling him that the only way he would get out was "armed rebellion culminating in race war." Newton disagreed. Carmichael then told Newton he had no faith in the Black Panther alliance with the Peace and Freedom Party, warning Newton "that whites would destroy the movement, alienate Black people, and lessen our effectiveness in the community."[2] But Newton rejected Carmichael's argument as weak and misguided.

Police Chief Gain contacted Cleaver in advance of the rally to offer traffic supervision for the anticipated crowd. Cleaver turned him down. The event attracted three generations of people from the black

community as well as radical white longshoremen, students and professionals, all carefully searched for weapons by Party members before
entering. Adults paid $3, students $2 and the unemployed half-price. In
addition to speakers, the organizers promised a performance from the
top soul-music singing group "The Impressions." Networks had inquired
about coverage of the event, but refused to pay $1000 each for the privi-
lege. The next day the Panthers would draw another huge crowd to the
Los Angeles Sports Arena, featuring most of the same speakers flown
down from Oakland, joined by two busloads of Panthers traveling to
Los Angeles as well. The Panthers raised $10,000. The defense funds
were sorely needed; the entire Garry firm was then working "round-the-
clock," with at least $30,000 of time billed on the case so far.

To the surprise of the police, the standing room only fund-raiser
turned out to be well-managed and peaceful — an unprecedented
multi-racial gathering, as Eldridge Cleaver called it, of "the biggest lineup of revolutionary leaders that had ever come together under one roof
in the history of America."[3] (Colonial insurgents in the 18th century
obviously being excluded.) SNCC leaders had only reluctantly agreed
to share the podium with Bob Avakian of the Peace and Freedom Party.
The Panthers, in turn, let Forman include Maulana Ron Karenga, head
of US and the leading black nationalist in Los Angeles, recently known
for founding the holiday of Kwanzaa. Bunchy Carter came, too, as head
of the new Panther branch in Los Angeles, then still in an uneasy truce
with US. Berkeley City Council member Ron Dellums joined SNCC
leaders on stage with Seale, Cleaver and Bunchy Carter. During the
program, Huey's mother, Armelia Newton, mounted the stage briefly
to speak on behalf of her son, the first time she had addressed any
group outside of church.

Carter started the rally off by reading the crowd the classic poem "If
We Must Die" by Jamaican-born poet Claude McKay, one of the founders of the Harlem Renaissance. McKay wrote the poem nearly a half
century earlier following the brutal race violence across the country of
the Red Summer of 1919:

> If we must die—let it not be like hogs
> Hunted and penned in an inglorious spot,
> While round us bark the mad and hungry dogs,
> Making their mock at our accursed lot.
> If we must die—oh, let us nobly die,
> So that our precious blood may not be shed
> In vain; then even the monsters we defy
> Shall be constrained to honor us though dead!
>
> Oh, Kinsmen! We must meet the common foe;
> Though far outnumbered, let us show us brave,
> And for their thousand blows deal one death-blow!
> What though before us lies the open grave?
> Like men we'll face the murderous, cowardly pack,
> Pressed to the wall, dying, but fighting back![4]

Throughout the rally an empty wicker chair sat center stage — the same one in the photograph featured in almost every issue of the *Panther* newspaper, depicting a seated Huey Newton holding a spear and a shotgun with African shields on either side of him and a zebra rug under his feet. Ironically, Newton had begun to hate that primitive image. He considered it cartoon-like. But Newton had used similar symbolism himself in speaking of the fear that the man who invented the spear had engendered in people, until the shield was invented to protect them from its use.

It had been Eldridge Cleaver's idea to match the Panther Party's vision of armed self-defense with ancestral culture, putting resistance in the context of African heritage. Now, Newton, the wicker chair and the accompanying props symbolized for Party members and their supporters "a shield for black people against all the imperialism, the decadence, the aggression and the racism in the country."[5] Copies of the poster soon adorned the walls of all new Panther branches and dorm walls on college campuses across America. Bobby Seale and the Cleavers, SNCC leaders and other surrogates like Earl Anthony used both that image and the one of Huey arched in agony on the hospital gurney to build up an aura of a charismatic leader of superhuman value to the Movement — once he was freed.

Actually, behind bars facing the death penalty was where Newton's usefulness to the Movement rose to its peak. With the empty throne as backdrop, many speakers talked of Newton in the past tense as already having given his life for the cause. Armelia Newton refused to consider that possibility — the heartsick mother could not believe her youngest son would be found guilty. Rap Brown railed against his listeners as "chumps" for buying into a white society. He called recently-appointed Supreme Court Justice Thurgood Marshall a "Tom of a high order" and condemned the status quo for blacks in America. Garry was the only lawyer invited to speak. Despite his best efforts, the audience did not share Garry's faith in securing Newton's acquittal if his lawyers could just get an impartial jury impaneled. They knew little or nothing about the law. Either Newton was going to be freed through a trial or they would go and break him out of prison.

Over the past year both Seale and Newton had repeatedly exhorted their followers to "off" oppressive cops. Many were aware of *The New York Times Magazine* profile less than three months before the Oakland shooting, which featured Newton boldly stating that "every time you execute a white racist Gestapo cop, you are defending yourselves."[6] At a planning meeting for the Free Huey Celebration in Los Angeles, James Forman suggested that they agree to retaliate if any of their leaders were killed. He pegged his own life as worth "one hundred lives of the enemy, plus ten police stations wiped off the map."[7] So what value should be the price for losing Newton? His followers believed that Newton was indeed willing to give his life to inspire a coordinated uprising across the country. Speakers at the birthday rally expected him to be sentenced to death for murdering a cop. If that occurred, Forman warned, "The sky is the limit."[8] Bobby Seale had severe misgivings about that threat, but went along with the overwhelming sentiment of the others. By then Newton represented the Party's soul.

Janice Garrett Forte recalls this birthday fund-raiser as by far the largest gathering to date. When Forman spoke: "It was a pretty dire time . . . We were pretty certain that he would get the gas chamber if he did not get a fair trial. . . They had the chair that Huey took his infamous picture in . . . and it was sitting there empty on the stage to let people know that this is where he belongs and that it's empty for now but we have to get him back in this chair. . . . If he were not given a fair trial . . . if he were killed during that process, that the sky is the limit. We would do anything necessary to avenge."

Garrett and other Panther recruits knew exactly what "the sky's the limit" meant: "We would resort to warfare on the streets, against the establishment . . . we didn't want it. But we felt that it would push us to the brink of fighting in our communities against the oppression . . . And this meant the use of weapons . . . against the establishment, the police department, whatever the United States government was going to put on us . . . to defend ourselves the best ways that we could. And that meant armed — being armed to do this. Everybody in the Black Panther Party during that period of time carried a weapon. We all had weapons."

After Forman pledged "the sky's the limit" in reprisals, Carmichael followed with his own incendiary speech. He changed into an African robe for emphasis before taking the podium to urge other blacks to reject Communism and socialism in favor of an ideology solely for black people. Many other blacks in attendance wore dashikis. Carmichael ended by proclaiming, "Brother Huey belongs to us." His exclusion of anyone not black alienated many of the radical whites in attendance. Carmichael continued, "He is flesh of our flesh, he is blood of our blood . . . Brother Huey will be set free — or else."[9]

Oakland Post publisher Thomas Berkley used his own bully pulpit to respond as forcefully as he could. In his next editorial, he declared that despite all of the militant rhetoric at the Newton fund-raiser, "black citizens of this community have not and are not going to declare war on the white citizens here . . . for they know better than anyone that he who lives by the sword will die by the sword." Yet Berkley had already heard repeated predictions that the summer of 1968 would produce worse violence than the summer of 1967. Only time would tell who had the better handle on the mood of young inner city blacks. All Berkley could do was hope for the best and warn his readers "the hard truth . . . that nothing of consequence will be gained by such a tragedy."[10]

9. CLIENT
OR COMRADE?

*He is a truly great man. Huey is a loving, gentle,
kind person. . . . He has a righteous force,
a fierce combination of moral outrage and anger.*
— FAY STENDER

For the political defense Garry was planning, Newton
gave his attorneys background on the origin and purpose of the Black Panther Party, as well as a reading list.
At his suggestion, Garry and Stender were now studying the writings of
Malcolm X and the revolutionary Frantz Fanon, among other authors.
Unlike SNCC, Newton and Seale still welcomed white support for their
revolutionary efforts.

In the new year, Stender began visiting Newton more regularly in
jail. Nowadays she was dressing chicly and making sure her fingernails
were painted and her lipstick was on when she met with her charismatic
client. Stender had found herself attracted to Newton at first sight of
him, bare-chested under armed police guard in a hospital room. Now
she found herself even more captivated by Newton's courage and intelligence. She was but one of a growing number of his new female devo-
tees. Stender took no warning sign from the ugly termination of Beverly
Axelrod's relationship with Eldridge Cleaver as her client.

Garry charged Stender with putting together a motion to have
Newton released on bail, which they expected Jensen to vigorously
oppose. She needed to gather personal information to show Newton

posed little risk of flight prior to trial. With gentle persistence, the deceptively soft-spoken lawyer learned from Newton that a tutor taught him to play classical music. When asked for favorite pieces, he told her he grew fond of Tchaikovsky's *Nutcracker Suite.* It touched her heart — classical music was her first passion, now her second one after social justice. Stender shared some of her life story with Newton, too, leaving out parts she considered too personal or that he would be unlikely to relate to.

Stender was born Fay Ethel Abrahams in San Francisco in March of 1932, the older of two daughters of an ambitious middle-class Jewish couple. She had been a child prodigy at the piano. The family spent much of its time and discretionary funds from her father's successful career as an asbestos expert to focus on developing Fay's talent. At age fourteen, after ten years of private lessons, she received an invitation from the San Francisco Symphony to showcase her talent in a solo performance. Shortly afterward, she rebelled against her parents and the rigors of concert training. By the time she graduated college, she was radicalized by a Marxist professor she had fallen recklessly in love with. By then, she had abandoned any thought of music as her career. Fay Abrahams aspired instead to become a lawyer to challenge the inequities in the world. She wanted desperately to wield the power to change things.

Abrahams met her future husband, Marvin Stender, in law school at the University of Chicago where he graduated two years ahead of her. Their rocky marriage of more than two decades had involved more than one separation, but both remained dedicated Lawyers Guild members devoted to Movement causes. Even when apart, they socialized as well as worked in the same leftist circle of activists. Newton knew of two of them — Jessica "Decca" Mitford and Bob Treuhaft. Of course, he also knew Beverly Axelrod and had just met Alex Hoffmann, who was alternating with Stender in visits to Newton at the jail.

Stender asked Newton for more details that could help get him out on bail. He further impressed Stender by telling her that he learned to read for the first time after high school, by repeatedly tackling his brother Melvin's copy of Plato's *Republic.* It amazed her to learn that

Newton also had taken a criminal law course from Ed Meese, moonlighting from his job as assistant district attorney in Alameda. Meese now headed Governor Reagan's legal staff. Newton showed her only the side of him that was thoughtful and serious. Like his mother, Stender could not imagine the violent thug that police described.

With so many people counting on the defense team to keep Newton from the gas chamber, Stender was under enormous pressure. Although there was no realistic chance that the court would free Newton on bail while he faced charges of murdering a policeman, anything that could be attempted would be done. Garry encouraged such constant legal activity because it also helped keep Newton's supporters motivated and guaranteed sustained news coverage. David Hilliard got to know her well during this time. Stender earned his complete trust as someone you could always depend on.

Stender did her best on the bail motion. The standard she had to work with was provided by the California Constitution. It denied an arrestee release on bond in death penalty cases only "when the proof is evident or the presumption great."[1] Stender set out to convince the court that proof of first degree murder was not "evident" nor "the presumption great." There was no evidence of premeditation, no competent evidence Newton had a gun and no evidence he had planned a crime. The bail motion was denied, just after the Newton birthday rally.

The judge also rejected their attack on the grand jury. Pursuing that challenge on appeal and in the court of public opinion was also a key part of the political defense strategy — to expose the jury system for its bias against minorities. Looking back with admiration, Innocence Project Co-Director Barry Scheck notes: "It raised the specter that given the tenor of the times . . . a person like Huey Newton, a self-declared black revolutionary, could not get a fair trial. . . . In the great tradition of Clarence Darrow, Charles Garry was going to put the government on trial — to put the whole process on trial." Quite a tall order.

On January 16, 1968, the police had raided Cleaver's San Francisco apartment before dawn, kicking in his front door. On February 28, the Berkeley police invaded Seale's home, also without a warrant. The police found five people there, including Seale and his wife Artie, David

Hilliard, and Bunchy Carter from Los Angeles. The police charged all five with conspiracy to commit murder and unlawful possession of weapons. Judge Lionel Wilson would dismiss the sensational conspiracy charge; the minor weapons charges would be prosecuted. The bail roughly matched the net proceeds they had just raised at the birthday fund-raiser. The same day, three other Panthers were stopped for a minor traffic offense, searched and charged with violating laws prohibiting concealed firearms and carrying loaded firearms in public. The Panthers and their lawyers saw a pattern in these arrests — they evidenced a purpose to harass and crush the Party. Newton quickly issued Executive Mandate No. 3 ordering all Panthers to defend their homes with weapons against illegal searches or be permanently expelled from the Party.[2] A man's home might be his castle, but defending it with guns from police with arrest warrants was a dangerous course to take. Newton was inviting more bloodshed.

With the Panthers and the Oakland police heading toward open war, Garry wanted to avoid lighting the fuse with a disastrous result in court. If he were to have any chance of getting Newton acquitted, it was vital to delay the trial. Garry desperately needed breathing room while his office investigated the circumstances of the October shooting. While he focused on gathering evidence, it was Stender's job to exhaust all avenues for review of Judge Staats' ruling denying the challenge to the all-white grand jury. She prepared a detailed petition to the court of appeal, which was denied the very next day without opinion. The next step was a petition for hearing before the California Supreme Court. Barney Dreyfus oversaw her efforts as constitutional law specialists outside the firm provided a continuous stream of advice.

Stender and Dreyfus knew they had an uphill fight, but proceeded aggressively on several fronts. One was an attack on the institution of the grand jury itself as an anachronism lacking constitutional safeguards because of its secrecy, failure to permit cross-examination of witnesses, and denial of any advance warning to the defendant of the evidence to be used against him. Other angles included an attack on the statutes by which the grand jury was selected and the method by which judges picked the panel — not from a cross-section of the community, but from a short list of middle-class contemporaries of the judges, excluding blacks, the working class and the young. Their chances of convincing the appellate court something was amiss with the judges' selection method were exceedingly slim. Similar methods were still in use throughout the country — it was called the "key man" system because those chosen to serve were prominent members of their communities.

The defense team also argued that the grand jury acted too fast to have truly made any decision on the evidence in front of them. Reconstructing the grand jury's actions, Stender and Dreyfus concluded the grand jury had heard the evidence, gone to lunch and issued its indictment just under half an hour afterward, including roll call, the prosecutor's explanation of the law and the court's instructions. Where was there any time spent on deliberations? Lastly, the two lawyers argued that the grand jury had no reasonable basis to believe Newton murdered Officer Frey or assaulted Heanes because no one testified Newton had a gun in his possession and no such weapon was ever found.

The Attorney General's office answered each argument in turn. The grand jury system is centuries old and recognized in the Constitution. The limited record on the selection process did not demonstrate systematic discrimination by age, race or economic class; and, most importantly, there was ample evidence to support a determination of Newton's guilt. At this preliminary stage, the prosecutor needed only to demonstrate probable cause to go forward with the trial. "Probable cause" meant reasonable grounds to arrest Newton, a far lower threshold than the high standard of proof the prosecutor would have to meet at trial. Here, probable cause was easily demonstrated. The evidence before the grand jury showed an undisputed exchange of gunfire, one officer dead and Newton and another officer wounded. The bullets that killed Frey and wounded Heanes came from a different gun than the one found at the scene, which was Heanes' gun. In addition, the grand jurors heard the damning testimony of Dell Ross identifying Newton as one of two men who kidnapped him minutes later. Ross testified that the wounded kidnapper had a gun and that the pair mentioned the man had just shot "two dudes."[3] Stender was bound to lose this argument.

Meanwhile, trial preparation proceeded. The law firm subscribed to a news-clipping service to collect negative press about the case to bring to the trial judge's attention. Volunteers also reported biased radio and television coverage. Pretrial publicity in sensationalized murder cases had just become a hot legal topic. The American Bar Association asked a special commission to address the problem. Its report came out in February of 1968 with a startling statistic: adverse newspaper publicity often resulted in the disqualification of 99 out of every 100 potential jurors in a high profile murder case.

The commission suggested that courts should prohibit the media from publishing a defendant's prior criminal record, whether he had confessed, the identity of proposed witnesses, and most other material relating to the merits of the case. None of the ABA's recommendations would be in force for the Newton trial. Instead, it would be up to the trial judge to make his own orders, and no one had yet been assigned. In the meantime, city officials strongly supported the police in a publicity war with the defense attorneys. Prosecutor Lowell Jensen steered clear of the media fireworks.

During this time, more calls and letters poured in to the defense team with suggestions or information that they might want to follow up on, some of which proved quite useful. Cleaver left a message for Garry that Cleaver said was received from a source inside the Oakland Police Department. According to Cleaver, when the police learned Newton was at Kaiser, they were given an order to work him over. Treuhaft forwarded an inflammatory clipping from *Newsweek* describing Newton as a man with a "rage so blinding he can look on white America comfortably only through the cross hairs of a gun." The article quoted Newton as saying, "Guns are very, very political. A gun makes me immediately equal to anyone in the world."[4] The defense team also learned that a San Francisco radio station had started a recent broadcast with the title "Cop Killer Huey Newton." A local paper quoted an unnamed state legislator prejudging Newton's guilt. If the judge thought the bad publicity might taint the jury pool, Newton's lawyers might win a delay of the trial start date until things became calmer.

A tip came in for Garry of a witness who lived over a record shop near the Willow Street intersection where the shooting had occurred. The word was that the witness observed a very tall man do the shooting, not a man of five-foot-ten as Newton was. The firm employed investigators to assist Garry in tracking down this man and other witnesses. This involved interviewing a number of prostitutes who lived and worked in the area. The defense team was desperate to find someone, anyone, who could help them deliver on their mission to set Newton free.

As the trial date loomed menacingly, Garry took to walking at night in the run-down West Oakland neighborhood where the shooting took place, hoping to meet someone who could provide useful evidence for the defense. He could not bear to think of Newton becoming the first client he lost to the death penalty. Garry had once dug up the trial record of the infamous Julius and Ethel Rosenberg McCarthy era espionage case that ended in both of them being electrocuted despite international protests on their behalf. Garry convinced himself that he could have won their acquittal had he been their trial attorney. Freeing Huey seemed a far more formidable challenge.

Panther-led demonstration outside the Alameda County courthouse at January 1968 pretrial hearing in the People of the State of California v. Huey P. Newton. In the center foreground are Kathleen Neal Cleaver and Bobby Seale. Behind and between them, with his head lowered, is teenager Bobby Hutton, the Panthers' first recruit. Second from the left, profiled in the back row, is Eldridge Cleaver.

10. POWER TO THE PEOPLE

Free black panthers
Free humanism
Free black men
Free goodness & honor
Free Huey, now, and Free us all.
— SARAH WEBSTER FABIO

A death penalty case then pending before the United States Supreme Court offered a ray of hope. The defense attorneys in *Witherspoon v. Illinois* challenged the practice of judges disqualifying prospective jurors for bias simply because they opposed capital punishment in principle. The result of this practice was death-oriented juries. This was an issue on which Garry's firm had already undertaken extensive research in a California death penalty case then en route to its third death penalty appeal. *Witherspoon* was of huge importance to the Newton defense team, which would do everything possible to keep jurors opposed to the death penalty on the panel. Oral argument before the United States Supreme Court was scheduled for late April of 1968. At best, its ruling could be expected sometime toward the end of spring — another reason to push for as late a trial date as possible for Huey Newton.

The defense still wondered who would take the bench as the trial judge. Local rules provided that the presiding judge had to appoint a trial judge by forty-five days before the trial. Odds were that they would draw a white male since almost all of the twenty local judges fit that description. Lionel Wilson was still the only African-American superior court judge in the county, and the only woman on that bench was former prosecutor Cecil Mosbacher. Garry considered Mosbacher, a conservative hardliner on crime, a worse draw than most of her male counterparts.

On March 10, the defense team found out that the judge they drew was a political moderate, Monroe Friedman. The bespectacled seventy-two-year-old had a reputation as a stickler for organization and for strictly controlling his courtroom. They knew the draw could have been much, much worse. Judge Friedman was a Democrat Governor Pat Brown had appointed to the Superior Court in 1959, after Friedman's failed nomination to the federal bench by lame-duck President Harry Truman. By the spring of 1968, Judge Friedman was nearing retirement, and as such, the 1920 graduate of Berkeley's Boalt Hall could have easily declined the controversial and thankless assignment. Instead, the former presiding judge figured his one and only major criminal case would be as good a way as any to end his career. He set the trial for May 10.

Judge Friedman was not considered one of the sharpest judges on the local bench, but thorough, with a low reversal rate. Garry, the self-proclaimed streetfighter in the courtroom, did not relish the idea of Judge Friedman keeping him on a short leash, but Garry did not believe the defense had a realistic choice. Though he had the right to refuse Judge Friedman and get someone else assigned, Garry did not want to gamble and draw someone far worse whom he could not remove. It was a plus that Judge Friedman had practiced as a criminal defense lawyer before becoming a judge. If a particularly difficult judge were assigned — of which there were several Garry could name — Garry would have to risk contempt citations at every turn, hoping to lure the judge into committing mistakes that the court of appeal would feel compelled to reverse. To Garry's knowledge, only about one percent of criminal convictions were ever reversed on appeal. No, Garry would have to win this case at trial.

The defense pursued a strategy to convince Judge Friedman to delay the trial date for at least two months. To win more favorable public opinion, they published a declaration signed by forty-five members of the local black community describing Officer Frey's reputation as an aggressive and obstinate officer, a discredit to the Oakland Police Department. Meanwhile, Garry granted as many interviews with Newton as possible with left-leaning media. An early political interview of Newton in *The Movement* had already generated substantial interest. The authors were two Free Speech Movement arrestees whom Newton had first seen at Santa Rita in December of 1964. One of them, Joe Blum, had been a trusted friend of Newton's from Oakland City College. Newton shared with Blum his view that "The Black Panther Party is the beacon of light to show Black People the way to liberation."[1]

Now requests for additional interviews came in fast and furiously: Ray Rogers of the *Los Angeles Times*; *The Movement* reporter Karen Wald; Eldridge Cleaver for *Ramparts* magazine; Kennedy assassination conspiracy theorist Mark Lane; Joan Didion from *The Saturday Evening Post*; Collin Edwards and Elsa Knight Thompson from local public radio station KPFA; and even a black reporter from the decidedly unfriendly *Oakland Tribune.* The *Tribune* reporter had originally been denied access by the police. Publisher Joseph Knowland then exploded in anger and contacted the precinct to make sure the reporter got into the jail. What Knowland did not count on was that his reporter wound up writing a positive story about Newton, which the newspaper then refused to publish.

As armed deputies looked on through a thick glass partition, Newton enjoyed puffing on cigarettes offered by some of his visitors and educating the press about the party platform and its goals. Each interview required a separate permission slip signed by Garry and submitted in advance to the Alameda County Sheriff. Once approved, every reporter would be accompanied by a member of the legal staff, often Alex Hoffmann, sometimes Fay Stender, and, rarely, Charles Garry.

Meanwhile, the California Supreme Court declined to review the defense team's grand jury challenge. Notice of the ruling had simply arrived at the law office by a postcard, signed on March 28 by Chief Justice Traynor. Stender's quest for pretrial review temporarily exhausted, she lost no time moving on to her next challenge: finding sociologists to testify at trial. She already knew activist David Wellman, who had co-authored the favorable article about Newton in *The Movement.* They had met at a joint gathering of Friends of SNCC

and *Movement* staff in August 1964 when they were planning ahead for
Freedom Summer 1965. Wellman had reacted to meeting Fay Stender
in the same awed fashion as the students at "Legal Central" at Cal who
had coordinated lawyer assistance for their FSM friends arrested in
December of 1964. Wellman noticed how she drew people in with her
soft voice, but then could bowl them over with her insights. He recalled
her at the Friends of SNCC meeting quietly raising excellent points.
That impression was reaffirmed whenever their paths crossed.

Stender knew that Wellman was working on a Ph.D. in race relations at Cal. She asked him to bring a couple of his professors with
him to her home in Berkeley to have them help her strategize for trial
— then a novel concept. Today professional jury consultants are often
used in high profile civil and criminal cases, assuming the parties can
afford them, but back then the use of sociologists in the Newton case
was pioneering. Wellman still recalled four decades later how thrilled
he was. Here she was both a confirmed leftist and an articulate, well-
dressed woman lawyer. Wellman still knew of few women lawyers of any
political persuasion. Fay Stender seemed to have it all. She was married,
had two children, was physically attractive, intense and smart. Now she
was his access to a front seat at the Huey Newton trial. He would do
whatever she asked.

The first meeting at Stender's home included Wellman, Sociology
Professor Jan Dizard and Associate Sociology Professor Robert Blauner.
In the last few years, Blauner had made race issues his primary focus.
Stender explained that at trial, they would have a white male judge
and a white male prosecutor. The only thing they could affect was the
composition of the jury. Stender conveyed to the men the vital role they
would play in unmasking biased jurors.

Criminal defense lawyers like Stender's future partner Doron
Weinberg now know: "Who gets on a jury is very important . . . We all
have bias . . . And you try to neutralize these biases as much as you can
through the jury selection process." But back then, this was a revolutionary approach. As Weinberg explains:

> A lot of lawyers were the kind of cowboys who would get up there and say, I'll take the first twelve people in the box. That's fine if you're representing somebody who is of the same class and race as the jury. But when you are representing somebody who is a black person in a largely white community, a black militant, active, with very strong political views . . . somebody accused of shooting and killing a police officer. . . . You have to be really, really careful about who you can get to be thoughtful and fair. Who could conceivably think about Huey Newton's testimony against another police officer's testimony, and actually try to decide who's telling the truth as opposed to just assuming that the officer is telling the truth and this black guy is lying? Charlie Garry had an enormous challenge. How do you find those people? How do you get to those people?

Stender gave the experts a short lesson on the law and explained the grounds for challenging jurors for bias in criminal cases. Her aim was to use the professors' help to get as diverse a jury as possible and, if need be, to create a record for appeal. After a productive evening session exchanging ideas, Stender provided the experts with the intelligence test then given Alameda County prospective jurors and told them about a brand new trial court ruling which held the IQ tests unconstitutional. The timing could not have been better.

The victory was the brainchild of two deputy public defenders, Bob Boags, the first and still only African-American in the Alameda County Public Defender's Office, and one of his two women colleagues, Penny Cooper. Though Boags joined the office a year after Cooper did, he was considerably older than all the other deputies. Most, like Cooper, came directly out of law school or within a year or two of graduating. By design, the Public Defender's office represented arrestees who did not have enough money for private lawyers. With the racial disparity in arrests in the 1960s, most of their clients were underprivileged African-Americans. As Penny Cooper later recalled, "Not only were people being discriminated against [in terms of arrest rates], the people that were being tried were being discriminated against because they couldn't get any blacks on the juries. . . . Then we found out . . . the intelligence test that was being used in Alameda County, to qualify individuals for jury service, was prejudiced against black people."

The pair of criminal defense lawyers secretly strategized for over a year when to bring a test case challenging the IQ tests as racially biased. During that time, Boags gathered expert opinions and crafted motion papers to hold in readiness. Ultimately, Cooper spotted on the master calendar a low-stakes criminal case with a black defendant that the Presiding Judge assigned for trial to Judge Spurgeon Avakian. He was the only local judge they deemed liberal enough to give serious consideration to their proposed constitutional attack on the fairness of the standard IQ test. When Boags brought the motion in *People v. Craig*, he took the deputy prosecutor completely by surprise. Boags produced undisputed evidence that only 14.5 percent of residents of white middle class neighborhoods flunked the intelligence test, while 81.5 percent of those in the ghetto of West Oakland failed it. Judge Avakian could see why when he focused on questions like:

23. If a person asks you for something you do not have, you should:

    1) Tell him to mind his own business;
    2) Say you don't have it;
    3) Walk away.

25. If it rains when you are starting to go for the doctor, should you:

    1) Stay at home;
    2) Take an umbrella;
    3) Wait until it stops raining.

The judge did not believe a person's choice of one of these answers over another bore on their intelligence. Rather, the questions produced unrepresentative jury pools by focusing on vocabulary and presumed conventional wisdom not often shared by ethnic minorities. Judge Avakian concluded the test was both biased and of questionable use. Prominent East Bay attorney Tom Berkley, the publisher and editor-in-chief of The *Oakland Post*, applauded the ruling. The *Post* was California's largest black and Latino newspaper. Berkley noted that black lawyers considered the outmoded IQ test "absurd, misleading and wicked," measuring "moral and social attitudes and level of education rather than mental capacity" with an intrinsic cultural, educational and environmental bias.[2]

Though Judge Avakian's rejection of the IQ test was a good sign, Stender realized soon after it was issued that they would be hard-pressed to use the ruling to their advantage. In light of Judge Avakian's ruling, the Presiding Judge had just announced that the county was now dropping the IQ tests. The old policy would not have any effect on the jury pool for the upcoming Newton trial, still set for early May. Still, Stender asked the experts to review the analysis in *People v. Craig* and promised to let them know when their testimony might be needed. In the month of April, the professors heard nothing at all from Stender because the Garry firm's frantic trial preparations received a shocking last minute reprieve that shook the nation and increased the trial's stakes dramatically. On April 4, a sniper assassinated Martin Luther King, Jr., as the civil rights giant stood on the balcony of his motel room in Memphis, Tennessee.

From the Panthers' standpoint, until that fateful moment, King was an Uncle Tom like Justice Thurgood Marshall. Back in the summer of 1967 the Panthers had listed King in their newspaper's "Bootlickers' Gallery." In the past few months King's new focus on combining opposition to the war with organizing a poor people's campaign pushed his strategy closer to theirs, but the Panthers remained adamantly opposed to King's pacifism. From their perspective, the assassination proved they were right. His martyrdom could only swell their ranks with newly outraged blacks.

King's death was a game changer for national anti-war activists like Students for a Democratic Society leaders as well. On the heels of the assassination, SDS quickly embraced the Black Panthers as the quintessential African-American voice against the war and became full-throated supporters of the "Free Huey" movement.[3] Indeed, the murder of the country's most famous pacifist generated an immediate visceral response throughout the country, halting presidential candidates in their tracks as they absorbed the enormous impact of this tragedy. Its political consequences for the 1968 election would be huge. Just days earlier embattled

President Johnson had startled the nation by announcing his decision not to seek reelection. Demoralized by his dismal polls and the quagmire of the Vietnam War, Johnson already faced a primary challenge from Senator Eugene McCarthy. Johnson withdrew from consideration, leaving the Democratic field wide open.

After King's death, Johnson declared a national day of mourning and ordered flags flown at half-mast — the first time ever for the death of a black man in America, and only the third half-mast salute ever noted for any private citizen.[4] Gathering African-American leaders to the White House, the President vowed that King's dream had not died with him, but would become a blueprint for united action to assure young blacks that the "fullness of life" would not be denied them "because of the color of their skin."[5] A sea change was occurring in national race consciousness. Many white leaders were overcome with shame, blaming pervasive white racism for Dr. King's death and vowing to work together with black communities to address "the white problem."[6]

As President Johnson convened a special joint session of Congress to address new proposed legislation, coverage of the assassination of Dr. King trumped regularly televised shows. All three African-American megastars slated to perform at the Academy Awards on April 9, 1968 withdrew — Louis Armstrong, Sammy Davis, Jr., and Diahann Carroll. So did Sidney Poitier, the country's very first black matinee idol. To avoid appearing insensitive, the network then postponed the annual event for two days out of respect for Dr. King. Then Katherine Hepburn won an unexpected Oscar for best actress in *Guess Who's Coming to Dinner?*[7] The comedy drama, in which Hepburn played her last role opposite Spencer Tracy, revolved around liberal parents surprised by their daughter's announced engagement to a black doctor portrayed by Poitier. The stilted, groundbreaking film proved exceedingly popular at the box office, hitting the theaters the same year that the Supreme Court finally ruled anti-miscegenation laws unconstitutional.

Meanwhile, newspapers counted over twenty deaths from violence following King's assassination. Despite thousands of arrests for curfew violations, widespread looting and firebombing broke out in Chicago, Baltimore, Detroit, Kansas City and Washington, D.C., and more than one hundred twenty other cities across country. Over sixty thousand National and State Guardsmen were mobilized to keep the peace. Outbreaks of vandalism prompted Oakland and several other Bay Area communities with large black populations to close their schools.

Janice Garrett Forte recalls how excited the Panthers were at the opportunity to attract new recruits: "After Martin Luther King was assassinated, we felt that . . . more and more people would arm themselves and more and more people would align themselves with the Party because they were understanding, firsthand, how corrupt and how brutal the situation was here in the United States." The Panthers felt that soon "the whole country would erupt in a series of riots everywhere."

Yet Newton and Seale considered organization the first priority; chaotic uprisings at this stage would be counterproductive. They actively sought to discourage any vandalism or rioting in the East Bay. Hilliard said: "We were busy about running around in the community telling people not to riot and you shouldn't beat up and fight your white neighbors. This is Oakland, Berkeley, and we all live together and this is a solidarity movement that we're building. So we were with our bullhorns going around telling these young boys on the corner that, no, you don't start riots, you don't burn your community down . . . Come to our meetings. We're going to tell you just what to do. So we used that as a way to organize young people into . . . our ranks of our Black Panther Party."

Coincidentally, the day before the assassination a dozen Oakland police wielding shotguns arrived at the church of Huey Newton's pastor, Reverend Earl Neil. Two local clergymen, one of whom was black, accompanied the police. Apparently, the police asked the pair along to lend legitimacy to the intrusion. The police claimed they were searching for a fugitive, but Eldridge Cleaver assumed they were after him and Bobby Seale. The Panthers had recently switched to using St. Augustine's as a regular meeting place, having guessed correctly that the FBI had their own headquarters bugged. When the police arrived at the church, Cleaver had just left a meeting run by David Hilliard.

The young black pastor was already alarmed by a letter from a sympathetic black Berkeley policeman warning that Seale's and Cleaver's lives were in grave danger. Hilliard blocked access to the sanctuary, while the normally soft-spoken, bespectacled clergyman insisted that the police leave. Reverend Neil was so outraged that he immediately called a press conference to denounce the armed intrusion as a Nazi storm trooper tactic.

Coverage of King's death quickly dwarfed news of the Oakland church invasion. Memorial tributes came from all sectors of the community, including one from Oakland's Mayor John Reading, whom Governor Reagan had just designated to represent the state of California at the televised service for Dr. King in Atlanta, Georgia. The black community considered Reading's choice an affront. Yet Reading's appearance at the funeral undoubtedly helped calm some whites in Alameda County who harbored fear of race war. John Burris worked part-time in an Oakland store: "Immediately after [the news of King's assassination] white men [came] into the store. . . and they start buying guns. And it was like they were arming themselves in the event that something bad was going to happen."

Shortly afterward, the media reported that Stokely Carmichael was inciting all blacks to pick up guns and seek revenge in the streets against white America for killing "all reasonable hope" with the death of the Nobel Peace Prize winner.[8] At the time of King's assassination, David Horowitz was a radical leftist working as an editor at *Ramparts* magazine where Eldridge Cleaver had been hired. Though Horowitz later became a conservative Republican, he recalls: "The most refreshing thing about '60s radicals was their honesty. We want a revolution and we want it now. Up against the world, motherfucker, . . . "the sky is the limit". . . civil war . . . I didn't think that armed revolution was a very practical idea . . . I thought that it would just get people killed." Yet, after a few minor incidents, East Bay streets were surprisingly quiet. Seale publicly appealed to Black Panthers and their followers to refrain from any violent reaction that would bring the police out in force. He feared that all the community work he had done over the years would come to naught from senseless rioting that would just precipitate massacres of neighborhood youths. So Seale gathered two vanloads of Panthers, and the ten vigilantes put an end to any rioting they saw on block after block of North Richmond.

Like Stokely Carmichael, Cleaver vehemently disagreed with Seale's keep-it-cool strategy, particularly after Father Neil shared with him the warning letter Neil had received from a Berkeley policeman. Ever since Huey Newton's "night of truth" at the end of October 1967, Cleaver had been eager for an opportunity to prove himself as a member of the vanguard by offing his own pig. Cleaver considered that goal to exemplify "theory and practice rolled up into one."[9]

On Saturday evening, April 6, Cleaver told Hilliard he had an urge "to intensify the struggle . . . to organize people to avenge Martin Luther King's death." Inspired by all the riots across the country, Cleaver wanted "to do something more revolutionary" than the food delivery Hilliard and others had been planning that evening. Cleaver led three carloads of armed Black Panthers on a cruise of Oakland's streets looking for a confrontation. Hilliard went along, seated next to young Bobby Hutton. They parked in a West Oakland neighborhood and ambushed a patrol car, wounding both officers. Hilliard feared that Cleaver was leading them "down the path of destruction. . . . This whole thing . . . was totally against Huey Newton's orders. . . . I'm on the street having mad, crazy arguments with Eldridge Cleaver about this insanity. He totally ignored it."

Police were then working 12-hour shifts, anticipating violence in the wake of King's assassination. Perhaps, as Hilliard later suspected, they were already tipped off about Cleaver's plans by an informant. Backup officers quickly rounded up most of the fourteen Panthers who had been in the three vans, including Hilliard. Bobby Hutton and Cleaver took guns and barricaded themselves in a nearby home belonging to the godmother of Hilliard's son, who lived around the corner from where Hilliard lived in West Oakland. Police commander George Hart was on the scene and participated in the gun battle that followed. In the ninety-minute siege, Cleaver and Hutton originally ignored repeated orders to surrender. When the situation appeared stabilized, Hart left a senior patrol captain in charge while he left to focus on another hot spot.

The police then tear-gassed the home where Cleaver and Hutton still occupied the basement, forcing the two Panthers to emerge as a small crowd of neighbors looked on. Cleaver came out naked, limping. He had been shot in the buttocks and hit by a tear gas canister. He did not mind risking his life, but did not want to die in a fire. It was time to surrender. He knew the drill from prison searches and stripped to prevent police from claiming he was reaching for a gun as an excuse to shoot him. His arms were raised to show he held no weapon. Cleaver had warned Bobby Hutton to do the same, but the teenager was too shy. Hutton came out partially clothed, wearing pants and a coat. Cleaver later claimed that Hutton was already in custody when another officer pushed Hutton and told him to run toward an open door to a police car parked in the street. Someone yelled that Hutton was reaching into his pants for a gun. Officers on the scene said Hutton ignored a command to halt. They hit him with a barrage of gunfire — nineteen shots. The teenager died in the driveway, unarmed. Neighborhood onlookers reportedly began shouting "murderers, murderers."[10]

Paul Cobb witnessed the gun battle from a nearby telephone booth where he reported it live to a local radio station. From the booth, Cobb could see both the house and the policemen on the street. The police seized an arsenal of military-type weapons from the Panther vehicles. The woman who owned the house had been inside throughout the ordeal. The gunfire exchange destroyed her home. Cobb would soon coordinate 46 organizations into a Black Strike for Justice Committee to put pressure on law enforcement for indictments of the policemen who killed Bobby Hutton and for other reforms to the police department.

The casualties on the night of April 6 might have been much worse. Janice Garrett Forte remembers that evening vividly:

> It was on a Saturday night and a bunch of us had gone to a Black Panther Party member's sister's house to play cards and just to relax. . . . We didn't have a TV at the time at the apartment. But we had the radio on and we had heard that there had been a shootout with Black Panther Party members and the Oakland police. After that, the apartment . . . was surrounded by the Oakland police department and we thought at the time that they were going to kill us. . . . We didn't have any weapons to defend ourselves . . . and we

were just waiting to be killed. Literally, waiting to be killed . . . For whatever reason, they got in their cars and they left. . . . They knew where we were. So there had to be some surveillance . . . to know where different party members were.

The police immediately arrested on felony charges eight Black Panthers involved in the ambush, including Cleaver, who remained on parole for the 1958 conviction that had originally brought him to Beverly Axelrod's attention. That same night the Adult Authority revoked Cleaver's parole for possessing a gun, associating with persons of bad repute and failing to cooperate with his parole officer. No hearing was conducted; none was believed to be required. Police took Cleaver to Highland Hospital to get his wounds treated. As word quickly spread the night of the killing, either Melvin Newton or Father Neil contacted Alex Hoffmann around midnight to let him know that Cleaver was under arrest at Highland Hospital. Hoffmann had been with his housemate KPFA Program Manager Elsa Knight Thompson, celebrating her sixty-second birthday, but rushed downtown to police headquarters when he got the call. Hoffmann told the police he represented the arrest-ees without even knowing exactly who had been arrested. The police appeared to be playing games, and prevented Hoffmann from learning useful details. Hoffmann then briefly saw Cleaver at the hospital before Cleaver was whisked away to San Quentin and then to the State Medical Facility at Vacaville to recover from his wounds and then go back to prison. Cleaver urged Hoffmann to contact his wife Kathleen immediately to let her know what happened to him.

Cleaver had spoken at a gathering in Berkeley earlier that afternoon and then left Kathleen at a friend's house near campus, telling her only that he was headed to Panther headquarters and would come back for her. Hoffmann used a hospital pay phone, but could not reach Kathleen. He called his clients to tell them the news and tried but failed to reach Elsa Knight Thompson. Her home phone was suspiciously rendered inoperative, only to be quickly cleared the next morning. It was already obvious that Cleaver's home phone was wire-tapped. It made a clicking sound before anyone on the receiving end picked up.

Hoffmann ultimately reached Kathleen early in the morning. She had fallen asleep on the sofa at her friends' house awaiting Eldridge's call. In the meantime, Hoffmann tracked Cleaver to San Quentin and then to Vacaville. There, the official in charge told Hoffmann how shocked he had been to receive Cleaver with no accompanying paperwork. In his experience, that was not how the system had ever operated before. All prisoners were supposed to be duly accounted for with appropriately signed orders, not simply dropped off in the middle of the night.

On Sunday afternoon there was a pre-planned "Free Huey" rally at DeFremery Park on Adeline Street. Hoffmann had gotten no sleep. He arrived escorting a shell-shocked Kathleen Cleaver, who spoke in her husband's stead. The biggest Panther gathering so far became an impromptu memorial celebration for Bobby Hutton, with members of the Party eulogizing the young Panther as a martyr. Over 2500 community members would attend the teenager's funeral the following week — joined by actor Marlon Brando, who later accompanied some Panthers on a neighborhood patrol and offered $10,000 in bail for Hilliard's release. It was then that Hilliard first realized the Panthers had gained leftist celebrity status.

The death of Bobby Hutton also galvanized the established black community to support the Panthers in their opposition to the police. The Panthers honored him as their first martyr — the real beginning of their movement. Suddenly far more youths arrived at their headquarters interested in joining the Panther Party, church congregations began to pass the hat and women in the black community started to collect money for their support. Panther members were already aware that the FBI was making records of everything they did, including pictures. But Hutton's shooting suddenly escalated the stakes. Janice Garrett Forte recalls: "It became very real at the time after Little Bobby was assassinated that the police department had an agenda, and that was to assassinate as many Black Panther Party members as they could. So there was a directive that came out that you have to be very careful of what you did and where you were. . . . There was a great fear that whatever you did and wherever you were that this could happen to you, too." The deadly incident prompted an abrupt change in strategy.

She remembers: "After the shootout with Little Bobby Hutton, we were given a directive to stop carrying weapons. . . . Because too many police-men were stopping Panthers and knowing they carried weapons, they would start shooting. . . . So there was a directive that went out to stop carrying weapons so that that would not give them the excuse to kill us."

In the Alameda County jail, police permitted Newton to conduct his own memorial service for Hutton with other more recently arrested Panthers. Upset by Cleaver's recklessness and the death of Li'l Bobby Hutton, Newton took Hilliard aside and named him Chief of Staff, in charge of the Party's programs. Hoffmann had already contacted Barney Dreyfus, who promised that his firm would take on the defense of Cleaver and seven other Black Panthers arrested following the April 6 shootout. At this point, Garry assumed he would have little trouble convincing Judge Friedman to postpone Newton's trial. No one could question the extremely negative racial climate in Oakland amid so much front-page coverage of the recent bloody confrontation. Garry immediately assigned Stender to set a motion before Judge Friedman, asking for at least two months' more preparation time. A great deal of pretrial investigative work remained to be done. Garry also felt it was urgent that they free Cleaver from prison so they could send him on a speaking tour. Cleaver's celebrity as a best-selling author and his proven oratorical talents were critical to their fund-raising and for rallying widespread support for the "Free Huey" campaign.

Kathleen Cleaver played a key role, meeting with Garry and Hoffmann frequently to strategize. The young activist had already demonstrated her exceptional organizational skills in helping launch the "Free Huey" Committee. She quickly put her talents to work with even greater zeal on her husband's behalf, working with a new "International Committee to Release Eldridge Cleaver." The co-chairs were Sandra Levinson of *Ramparts* in New York and Nathan Schwerner, father of the martyred civil rights worker Michael Schwerner. The committee immediately set to work raising money and inviting celebrity supporters to attend Cleaver's upcoming hearing.

Though Kathleen Cleaver had met Garry before, she had not noticed Fay Stender until the spring, when Kathleen came frequently to his office. Stender entered her consciousness as a very striking woman, her black hair set off by a black dress with a square cut neckline, her smile highlighted in red lipstick. Stender seemed much younger and more vibrant than the other lawyers in the office. Soon Stender had no time to spare for the efforts to free Eldridge Cleaver. It took precious hours from necessary preparations for Newton's trial.

Stender and Garry turned back to their primary goal, leaving Alex Hoffmann to lead efforts to help the Cleavers. The defense had already been put on notice that Jensen intended to rely at trial on key witnesses not presented to the grand jury. Garry wanted their names, to investigate and possibly interview them. Jensen told the court that his witnesses' lives had been threatened, causing the prosecutor's office to place at least one of them in a safe location unknown to the defense. Judge Friedman was receptive to both of their arguments. He pushed back the trial date one month, until June 10 at 10 a.m. He granted Lowell Jensen's motion to keep his remaining witnesses undisclosed until two days before they testified at trial.

Stender put her long-planned family vacation to Europe and Israel on hold. The trial would now likely go through June into early July. In the meantime, the defense team felt that police propaganda had poisoned the local atmosphere. To offset its impact, they gathered signatures from prominent citizens. Volunteers wearing "Free Huey Newton" buttons distributed the flyers door-to-door throughout Oakland. Named the "Oakland Tribunal" in mockery of the *Oakland Tribune*, the flyer described how the Black Panther Party arose in response to police harassment. It accused the local police force of attempting to eradicate the Party and urged that the charges against Newton be placed in the context of historic crimes against the black community.

A "Racism in the Law" conference in early May featured both Charles Garry and Clinton White reporting back from the front lines. The Peace and Freedom Party formally named Newton its candidate for Congress, and urged write-in votes for the imprisoned Black Panther leader in the upcoming June 4 primary. Yet not all members of the Peace and Freedom Party remained comfortable with their alliance with the Panthers. Mario Savio became concerned that the Panthers demanded unconditional support no matter what kinds of activities they were involved in, some of which he found troubling. He soon backed away from the Peace and Freedom Party.

Meanwhile, the Panthers were taking old *Panther* newspapers and posters and started plastering them throughout the community on available walls. Emory Douglas viewed the community as his gallery. Volunteers helped distribute "Free Huey" flyers invoking left-wing martyrs of the past — Sacco and Vanzetti, the Scottsboro Boys, the Rosenbergs and Malcolm X. Though women had become the backbone of the Party, unattached women increasingly endured harassment by male recruits. Some of the men nicknamed the women "Pantherettes" after the Raiderette cheerleaders at Oakland professional football games. Marriage had not stopped Eldridge Cleaver from aggressively pursuing other females he found attractive; he would soon alienate many women supporters by urging them to exercise their "Pussy Power." A number of Panther sisters later quit the Party rather than be treated as sex objects.[11] To discourage such conduct, the Party started calling members who repeatedly indulged in unrestrained, boorish behavior "renegade Jackanapes" whose "antics" involved attempts to "bogart down the brothers" or "gorilla a sister" for sex.[12] Maintaining Party discipline would always be an issue.

Both the political and legal fronts of the defense were going full bore. Stender assisted Dreyfus with an ambitious federal class action filed on behalf of all blacks living in the Northern District Court of California. They named as defendants the City of Oakland, the Mayor, the Chief of Police, the District Attorney and the Superior Court. Filed in mid-April, the complaint alleged that the state prosecutions of Newton and other Black Panthers violated the new federal Civil Rights Act. The attorneys wanted the federal court to step in and delay Newton's trial in June and the as-yet unscheduled trials of Black Panthers involved in the April shootout — a creative request, most unlikely to happen.

The defense team had asked in their filing for a three-judge court to hear the case, hoping that would slow the process down, but the federal panel responded quickly, scheduling the first hearing for May 21. Dreyfus argued the case for the defense. The panel issued its decision with uncharacteristic speed a week after the hearing. It refused to delay any of the contemplated state trials and dismissed the Superior Court and the City of Oakland as defendants to the case. However, in a small victory for the defense, it held that a potential claim was stated against the Mayor, the District Attorney and the Chief of Police.

Delay of the June 10 trial date set by Judge Friedman was still deemed critical. Stender immediately began work on an even longer shot — a new legal brief addressed to the United States Supreme Court seeking direct review of the three-judge court ruling. Stender then turned back to gathering information on the jury pool to share with her expert witnesses. They held a long planning meeting on May 1. Professor Dizard at Cal provided the defense with his national and local research on race discrimination by white Americans. He concluded more than half of whites had feelings of prejudice against blacks. Dizard had also gathered local statistical evidence on the skewed source of the jury pool: 85 percent of all eligible adults were registered to vote in Alameda County, but only 60 percent of eligible blacks, and only 52 percent of blacks in West Oakland.

On May 27, Fay contacted Dizard again to alert him that, despite their best efforts, the trial would likely proceed on June 10. The defense intended to file a motion to disqualify the entire jury panel the week before. She had quickly redrafted his report as a legal memorandum arguing for the unusual step of having each juror examined individually for prejudice while all other jury panel members were excluded from the courtroom. Stender prepared a list of questions for Garry to ask Dizard; she also prepared a memo on what Garry should include in an offer of proof to the court if Dizard were not permitted to testify. Her argument was that by using the voter registration list as the sole source of trial jurors the county disproportionately excluded racial minorities and lower-income citizens. Bob Treuhaft, with nearly twenty years of experience in handling East Bay race discrimination cases, again offered help, calling attention to the requirement that jurors be available for sixty to ninety days, which effectively excluded workers not reimbursed by their employers for jury duty.

Stender prepared declarations supporting the motion from several sociology professors, including Bob Blauner from Cal and Dr. Bernard

Diamond. (Dr. Diamond had been Garry's favorite forensic psychiatrist since the '50s, when Garry and Dreyfus had successfully established the *Wells-Gorshen* diminished capacity defense.) Stender had already begun working closely with Bob Blauner, who was helping prepare the analysis of the skewed juror pool. Like Fay Stender's husband Marvin, Blauner had gone to the University of Chicago as an undergraduate. He obtained his Ph.D. in sociology at Cal, focusing on problems of the working class. In 1964–65, as a young faculty member, he participated in the Free Speech Movement. That was what inspired the confirmed Marxist to switch his focus to race relations. Though he was excited to be involved in Newton's defense, he did not share David Wellman's infatuation with Fay Stender.

After a Memorial Day weekend camping trip with her children, Stender returned to file two quick motions, seeking more pretrial discovery and another continuance of the trial for sixty days. Garry argued that the defense needed time to depose Officer Heanes, District Attorney Coakley and Police Chief Gain in the pending federal suit. Not surprisingly the motion was denied, but they did win a key ruling — the District Attorney had to make the personnel records of Frey and Heanes available.

Judge Friedman also modified his May 8 order to force Lowell Jensen to disclose the names of prosecution witnesses immediately after the jurors and alternates were picked, instead of 48 hours before the witnesses were to testify. This would give the defense more time to investigate the witnesses for cross-examination. Still, Garry pressed Stender to come up with reasons for further delay. He felt it was urgent to get Eldridge Cleaver released from the State Medical Facility at Vacaville to travel on an international book tour and fund-raise for the Panthers. Kathleen Cleaver and Garry also worried about Eldridge's state of mind. He had taken to saying that he "died with Bobby Hutton" at the April 6 shootout and only a ghost remained to haunt "racists of America."[13] (Mental health issues actually ran in Cleaver's family.)

With guidance from experts in the field, Hoffmann prepared a writ petition challenging the Adult Authority's revocation of Cleaver's parole. The hearing was set to take place on June 3 in the town of

Fairfield, an hour northeast of Oakland, in the same county as the
Vacaville Medical Facility. To underscore its importance, Garry asked
Kathleen Cleaver to cram the courtroom with supporters. Kathleen
delivered in style, bringing in, as part of the crowd, best-selling author
Norman Mailer, Stokely Carmichael and black comedian and actor
Godfrey Cambridge. Kathleen sat up front, strangely calm after two
frenzied months of activity. She had been so distraught and worn out
from the intensity of hearing preparations and from lack of sleep that
she took tranquilizers for the first time in her life. She later reflected it
was very lucky she was not asked to testify.

The defense felt fortunate to draw a liberal Democrat, Judge
Raymond Sherwin, who permitted an unusual three-hour hearing for
the high profile case. Garry argued forcefully that the state based the
revocation in part on Cleaver's exercise of free speech. The police had
targeted the Panthers as a political threat; the parole revocation was
payback for Cleaver's inflammatory publications and prominent association with the Black Panther Party. Garry also challenged the entire
premise of automatic parole revocation. Why shouldn't a man being
sent back to prison get a hearing first? He pointed to Cleaver's prior
unblemished parole record and his parole officer's earlier recommendation that Cleaver be taken off parole for good behavior by the end
of the year. Garry also touted Cleaver's success as an author, his job at
Ramparts and recent marriage. Alex Hoffmann added charges of inter-
ference with the defense, citing instances in which Cleaver's communications with his attorneys had been censored and delayed.

The state lawyer for the Adult Authority was ill-prepared to counter this barrage of arguments. Exercise of the discretion of the Adult
Authority had seldom, if ever, been successfully challenged in the past.
There was little question that, if the Adult Authority had not drawn
a line in the sand and instead had held a hearing to revoke Cleaver's
parole, the judge would have had ample evidence to support the decision to send him back to prison. The Oakland officers involved in the
April melee had already testified before the local grand jury, resulting
in Cleaver's indictment for attempted murder. Since then, the police
had obtained confessions from all of the arrested Panthers except for

David Hilliard. The confessions implicated Cleaver as the instigator of the shootout. But in the Fairfield proceeding in June, Cleaver was sworn as the only witness to the April 6 shootout. He denied all of the allegations against him and swore that the Panthers were ambushed by the police, not the other way round. All he had done was defend himself and surrender as his teenage companion Bobby Hutton was cold-bloodedly murdered on the street. Judge Sherwin took the case under submission.

Though she would have loved to be present, Stender could not attend the Cleaver hearing. She was too busy filing the notice of appeal from the three-judge federal ruling that same day in San Francisco. That very afternoon the Supreme Court issued its landmark ruling on death penalty juries in *Witherspoon v. Illinois.* The seminal case had drawn "friend of the court" amicus briefs on both sides: state attorneys general supporting the State of Illinois and various organizations on behalf of the appellant, including the ACLU and the NAACP. Banner headlines in Monday's afternoon papers proclaimed "Hanging Jury Declared Illegal." A majority of six justices found that the state of Illinois had violated its role as a neutral by categorically excluding potential jurors for their philosophical opposition to the death penalty. The high court cited studies showing that more than half of Americans and roughly half of the potential local jury panel opposed the death penalty. By culling out the majority of people who "harbored doubts about the wisdom of capital punishment," the state of Illinois had denied the defendant a jury drawn from a cross-section of his peers, producing instead "a jury uncommonly willing to condemn a man to die."[14]

The Supreme Court indicated that the impact of *Witherspoon* on other capital cases would have to be determined on a case-by-case basis. Its decision drew immediate cheers from prisoners on death row throughout the country and angry ridicule from district attorneys. Both groups anticipated that the new ruling would dismantle "Death Row, U.S.A." by sparing the lives of most of the nearly 500 prisoners then awaiting execution, 77 of them at California's San Quentin.[15] Under the mandate of *Witherspoon*, the penalty phase of all capital cases would have to be retried if jurors expressing only general opposition to capital punishment had been automatically excluded from the defendant's original trial.[16]

Fay Stender wasted no time getting a copy of the *Witherspoon* opinion. Its wording would be critical to their upcoming jury selection. A footnote in the Supreme Court decision had included Professor Hans Zeisel's preliminary unpublished summary of the results of a long-term University of Chicago study that her husband Marvin Stender had worked on after law school. Zeisel had reached the firm conclusion that: "A jury consisting only of jurors who have no scruples against the death penalty is likely to be more prosecution prone than a jury on which objectors to the death penalty sit." The study had also drawn a corollary: "The defendant's chances of acquittal are somewhat reduced if the objectors are excluded from the jury."[17] Stender contacted Professor Zeisel immediately, realizing he could prove crucial to the Newton team. After all, the Supreme Court of the United States had just expressly relied on Zeisel's findings. Who better to convince Judge Friedman that he would need to delve further into the mindset of jurors who opposed the death penalty? Under the new mandate, Judge Friedman could now only dismiss for cause potential jurors who: "made unmistakably clear . . . that they would automatically vote against the imposition of capital punishment without regard to any evidence that might be developed at the trial of the case before them."[18]

The *Witherspoon* opinion was extraordinarily promising news, but still, the defense team needed more time to investigate potential witnesses to the charged crimes. They were nowhere close to ready to begin trial the following week. On June 4, they filed another of Stender's motions for continuance; it repeated the argument that white racism in the community and prejudicial statements continually disseminated by the media prevented a fair trial.

The moving papers challenged the entire jury panel of 1900 citizens as unconstitutional on the grounds that blacks, low-income and culturally different persons were systematically excluded and underrepresented by the use of voter registration lists as the sole source. They had a good point; more recently other sources have been consulted as well, including Department of Motor Vehicle records. As a member of a militant subgroup of blacks, Huey Newton was "virtually a stranger to most of the white American voters who will make up the jury under prevailing practice. They are not his peers. . . ."[19] The papers relied heavily on the declarations of the experts Stender had met with and on analogies drawn to the intelligence test rejected by Judge Avakian in April in *People v. Craig*, which she attached to the motion. Jensen characterized the motion for continuance as frivolous. He saw no evidence demonstrating white racism in the selection process.

Stender had some breathing room in her schedule and made a short trip to Los Angeles on June 4, the day of the California Democratic primary for President. There, she met her close friend Bob Richter outside the Ambassador Hotel where the Kennedy campaign had its headquarters. Richter now worked with Walter Cronkite at CBS television in New York and had flown in to cover Senator Bobby Kennedy's campaign for President. That night, Kennedy won the primaries in both California and South Dakota. The California victory gave Kennedy much-needed momentum following a setback the prior week in the Oregon primary. It put Kennedy in a strong position to challenge Vice President Hubert Humphrey for the Democratic nomination. The key to Kennedy's victory in the California primary had been a huge minority turnout on his behalf, enthused by his pledge to focus on education, housing and jobs.[20]

It was well past midnight when Kennedy made an upbeat speech to supporters, cheering his twin victories. The senator then walked through the hotel's kitchen to glad-hand staff. Suddenly, gunfire erupted and pandemonium broke out as the crowd learned that Kennedy and members of his entourage had been shot. Kennedy was gravely wounded and taken to the hospital by ambulance. His prospects were grim. Kennedy died the following day without ever regaining consciousness. The news horrified President Johnson. He had himself received over 1,000 death threats a month by then. Johnson immediately issued an order for all other presidential candidates to begin receiving Secret Service protection. The fact that the victim was President Kennedy's younger brother magnified the impact of Senator Kennedy's assassination immeasurably. The intense media attention on his grieving widow Ethel, mother Rose Kennedy, widowed sister-in-law Jackie and lone surviving brother

Ted also brought renewed focus on the shocking death of his older brother less than five years earlier.

The Pope offered special prayers for Senator Kennedy's family and for his country. Condolences poured in to the family from world leaders on both sides of the Iron Curtain, while ordinary citizens in the U.S. and abroad grieved openly as President Johnson proclaimed another national day of mourning. People could not fathom that this had occurred while the country was still reeling from the assassination of Reverend Martin Luther King. Indeed, news of Senator Kennedy's death shared headlines with the capture by Scotland Yard of King's alleged assassin James Earl Ray in London, England, where he was traveling under a forged passport. Network radio and television coverage of these two stories was almost nonstop for the next few days, dwarfing all other news.

The Panthers reacted with cynicism. They considered Kennedy just another untrustworthy politician with false promises to black communities. But Kennedy's death had come as a huge blow to most minorities. Mexican-Americans viewed his assassination as "La Muerte de una Esperanza" — the death of a great hope. Most blacks throughout the nation also reacted with extreme bitterness and shock at this second assassination in the space of two months. In May, on the Mall between the Washington Monument and the Capitol building, Martin Luther King's followers had built a shantytown "Resurrection City" as the culmination of King's recently proclaimed "Poor People's Campaign." Resurrection City quickly drew a population of poor, mostly black activists from around the country, together with other minorities and a few supportive whites. Following news that Bobby Kennedy had been shot, Reverend Ralph Abernathy addressed a crowd gathered at Resurrection City. The successor to the presidency of the Southern Christian Leadership Conference did not mince words, viewing Senator Kennedy's assassination as evidence of a racist conspiracy to eliminate leaders supportive of the poor. Another speaker captured the mood of the angry audience with a similar observation: "You noticed that every time we get somebody willing to speak out for the black man, they cut him down?"[21]

The same despair overtook hordes of liberal whites who were

working for civil rights and economic equality and had already been shaken profoundly by King's assassination. Prosecutor James Brosnahan headed Bay Area Lawyers for Kennedy. He found the two shocking murders life-altering. So, too, did Barry Scheck among many college student activists who had flocked to join Kennedy's presidential campaign to carry out King's agenda: "We really had power we thought to change American in profound ways. . . [Kennedy] could unite blacks, Latinos, white working class, along with the anti-war movement, with a lot of white middle class people in a very, very powerful political coalition and when he was shot, that fell apart." Seeing bleak prospects for achieving social change through traditional means, white activists like Scheck became more receptive to the Panthers' message: "We began to feel like why are we even bothering with electoral politics. . . . There's going to be real revolutionary activity . . . 'Pick up the gun,' 'by any means necessary'. . . . a very powerful message . . . and the leader of the Black Panther Party . . . in prison. Right? Facing trial." The idea the Newton death penalty trial could spark a general insurrection became far more plausible after Kennedy's assassination.

The intense gloom and despair across the nation stoked anxiety at Oakland's City Hall over the city's already high potential to explode in violence in the aftermath of Bobby Hutton's death. The City Council took up a proposal the next day to order an independent study of the turbulent race issues in Oakland, focusing on both the difficult relationship between the police and the black community and more general issues regarding white control of the city's administration. Local Democratic members of the State Assembly introduced a bill to implement tough gun-control laws as columnists and panelists contemplated whether violence and assassinations were "the American Way."[22]

On June 7, the day after Senator Kennedy died, Garry and Jensen appeared before Judge Friedman on the renewed motion for continuance. In that highly charged political atmosphere, Garry argued there was no way that the murder trial of Huey Newton could be expected to proceed on Monday, June 10, if they were to try to seat an impartial jury. Reporting on that hearing, *Oakland Post* editor Tom Berkley said Charles Garry had set himself a more difficult task, "looking for a jury, presumably white or black, without race prejudice" than the fourth century B.C. Greek Diogenes who "spent a lifetime looking for an honest man."[23] Judge Friedman announced that he would move the trial date to July 8 to give himself time to analyze the impact of the *Witherspoon* death penalty case. Though the judge had practiced criminal law back in the 1950s, he had not handled many criminal cases on the bench. In such a high profile trial, he needed to fully understand how to apply this new mandate for qualifying death penalty juries. At last, here was some breathing room for the defense.

The following Tuesday, Judge Sherwin issued his ruling on Cleaver's challenge to his parole revocation: "The uncontradicted evidence presented to this court indicated that the petitioner had been a model parolee. The peril to his parole status stemmed from no failure of personal rehabilitation, but from his undue eloquence in pursuing political goals. . . . Not only was there absence of cause for the cancellation of parole, it was the product of a type of pressure unbecoming, to say the least, to the law enforcement paraphernalia of this State."[24]

The court had already set Cleaver's bail on the attempted murder charge at $50,000. Judge Sherwin ordered Cleaver's release on a token amount of additional bail. The Attorney General's office expressed total shock at the decision, calling it "unprecedented and amazing . . . far out of line and contrary to law."[25] Garry immediately posted the entire sum, $50,027.50, at the Solano County Courthouse so Cleaver could be released the next day. Garry and Kathleen drove out to retrieve Eldridge on the afternoon of June 13 for a triumphant press conference in Garry's San Francisco law office.

That evening the defense team and friends celebrated their incredible victory with champagne. Cleaver was back on the streets. He could return to lead the Free Huey Movement and fund-raise for the mounting costs of Newton's defense. The symbolism of Cleaver's release could not be overstated. Thorough preparation and a passionate plea by his lawyers before a courtroom full of supporters had won them that ruling — the first time they had ever heard of the Adult Authority losing a parole revocation case. The Attorney General's office filed an appeal the following morning. Upcoming hearings on Cleaver's and other

Panthers' arrests still posed major challenges to overcome. Hundreds of hours of work still remained to prepare for Newton's murder trial. But for the moment, the defense team reveled in their success.

Copy of memorial program for Bobby James Hutton held in Berkeley, California, April 12, 1968, at the Ephesian Church of God in Christ. Among the eight pall bearers were Emory Douglas, Bobby Seale, George Murray and June and David Hilliard.

11. THE QUEST FOR A JURY OF HIS PEERS

If you kill this man, you are killing your wife kids and mother.
We will kill all white dogs—stay in the open
and be shot dog! A brother!
— Anonymous letter sent to the Oakland police

Dear Nigger Lover: . . . I hope that race war they
are always threatening would start right away. We
outnumber the blacks ten to one so guess who will
win, and a lot of damn nigger lovers will be lying
there right beside them. I wish Hitler had won.
Then we could have finished off the sheenies and
started in on the coons. KKK
— Anonymous letter sent to Charles Garry

Pretrial publicity for the Huey Newton murder trial flooded the newspapers and local news in June and early July of 1968. The case always evoked an intense gut reaction, pro or con, since Newton had catapulted to international attention. To many in the United States, he was a homegrown terrorist; to many others, at home and worldwide, he was a political prisoner and a symbol of oppression of American blacks, linked with charges of a racist war in Vietnam. By the summer of 1968, the Panthers' high visibility as a revolutionary party elevated it to public enemy number one in the eyes of FBI Director J. Edgar Hoover — a movement to be stopped at all costs. Hoover was particularly incensed at wide distribution of the *Black Panther* newspaper. The June 10, 1968, issue included a cartoon captioned "Free Huey Now." It showed a smiling pig standing on his back two hooves. The pig wore a badge and had flies encircling his head. Douglas also drew an angry black man with a pickaxe. Douglas viewed the message as obvious to readers and non-readers alike: the black man was "fixing to bash the pig in the head."

Public awareness of the upcoming Newton trial extended well beyond the media. The Cleavers, Bobby Seale and David Hilliard recognized the tremendous spotlight it gave them. As Hilliard says, "Huey Newton's trial for shooting one officer and killing another was the centerpiece, the cornerstone of our Black Panther Party movement." Treating the trial like a political campaign, Panther supporters posted signs on telephone poles and store windows throughout the community and distributed bumper stickers as well. Bus riders could expect to see fellow passengers displaying "Free Huey" buttons and hear responsive murmurs of "Right on."[1] Eldridge Cleaver soon published an article claiming that Newton had set a bold example for others in defense of the black community by taking justifiable action against murderous police. Despite protests from Huey's family that Cleaver would help send Huey to the gas chamber, the jailed revolutionary fully supported Cleaver's efforts to credit him with offing his first pig. Newton saw the boast as a useful recruiting tool and relished playing the contradictions to the hilt, fully aware that Cleaver's claims on his behalf were not admissible in court against him.

California would soon be documented as one-third minority, the largest minority population in the nation. Yet judicial proceedings, like other governmental functions, were still almost universally controlled by whites. In his editorials, *Oakland Post* owner Tom Berkley expressed great skepticism about Newton's innocence and open disdain for the militancy of the Panthers. Yet the underlying issue raised by Newton's trial reverberated with him as well: "It is impossible for a minority to receive justice in a Court that 99 times out of 100 consists of a white judge, white clerks, white bailiffs, white opposing counsels and white jurors."[2]

Galvanized by the killing of Bobby Hutton in West Oakland in April of 1968, pressure escalated on city officials for community control of the police, an issue that had first been formally proposed and emphatically rejected by the City Council two years earlier. A number of innocent victims of the April 1968 shootout brought suits against the police for negligence, alleging that more than a thousand rounds of ammunition had needlessly been fired in the April confrontation with the Panthers, damaging many West Oakland residents' parked cars. The community pressure on public officials grew exponentially after the county grand jury exonerated the Oakland police of any wrongdoing simply on the testimony of members of the force. A group of law professors at U.C. Berkeley's Boalt Hall Law School petitioned the United States Department of Justice to conduct an independent inquiry. The county bar association also requested an impartial review since all of the Panthers at the bloody confrontation declined to testify before the grand jury. Hearing only from the police could have easily skewed its findings.

On another front, the "Blacks Strike for Justice Committee" picketed Oakland businesses to once again urge community review of the police. Black ministers lobbied the Oakland City Council and the office of the mayor to the same end. The mayor called the economic boycott blackmail. The *Oakland Tribune* reacted with a full-page ad which characterized the picketing as "coercion and extortion." The inflammatory ad ran "with a picture of a gloved hand aiming a pistol out at the reader, asking: 'What would you do in a case like this?'" Two *Tribune* staffers resigned in protest: an African-American reporter who viewed the ad as an incitement for whites "to riot" and a white editor, who likewise believed the ad was "an open invitation to violence."[3]

Police Chief Gain responded to criticism by claiming it was difficult to find qualified black men to hire as officers, but he did impose a moratorium on the use of mace as a crowd control. Oakland lawyer John Sutter, a former colleague of Lowell Jensen's in the District Attorney's Office, recalls that: "a lot of the rank and file policemen did not appreciate those changes. And the city manager and mayor did not appreciate those changes. But a lot of people in the community did." However, as far as the Panthers and supporters like John Burris were concerned, the change in the policy as to when deadly force was to be employed "was a philosophical change. It wasn't a practical change. Because in practice, the police were still killing people and shooting people. . . ."

Reading's own grocery, run largely these days by his wife, was affected by the economic boycott. He became increasingly vocal as the Panthers and Peace and Freedom Party gathered signatures to put on the ballot the creation of separate police districts within the city, permitting blacks and whites to have officers of their own race patrolling their neighborhoods. Mayor Reading soon began openly talking of not seeking reelection. He gave an exclusive interview in a local Sunday paper in which he cited the Panthers and the pending Newton trial as major factors. With blacks now 46 percent of the city's population and more than half of all students in its public schools, speculation grew rampant that should Reading retire, several prominent African-Americans might throw their hats into a wide open race.[4]

As the city grew increasingly polarized, Garry prepared for a preliminary hearing in late June representing several Black Panthers facing charges from the alleged April 6 ambush. Meanwhile, Stender flew out to Chicago to consult Dr. Zeisel, who offered to donate his time to testify at the trial. Dr. Zeisel even agreed to advance his own costs because money for the defense was so scarce. Stender tried to convince other experts from the East to come to California at their own expense. They declined, but offered to mail her sworn statements if the court would accept them. Locally, Stender worked with the volunteer experts she had already recruited. They helped her draft some 300 questions to ask potential jurors to smoke out evidence of racism. She learned from Penny Cooper in the Public Defender's office that the Alameda County D.A.'s office had the voter registration of every juror. Unlike Stender, Cooper had accumulated substantial trial experience by then, though Cooper was only thirty, six years Stender's junior. That was one of the benefits of going to work for the Public Defender. But in her three years in that office Cooper had experienced firsthand the downsides of working for a conservative Public Defender who only reluctantly hired women.

In the 1950s, there had been only one woman in the public defender's office. She was openly ridiculed by some of the prosecutors and investigators, one of whom told her at an office party that she should be home with her kids. A decade later, female deputies like Cooper would remain scarce. The Public Defender considered himself on a mission to protect women from embarking on such a seamy practice, telling interviewees in the mid-1960s that the job was "like going down a sewer in a glass bottom boat." Cooper realized her days in that office were numbered after the Public Defender pressured her unmercifully to recant her anti-war views. When he did not succeed, he followed up with a series of undesirable assignments.

A decade earlier, Stender herself had quit working as a law clerk for an ultra-conservative justice on the California Supreme Court when she realized the extent of his bigotry. Back in the 1920s when he was elevated to the high court, Justice Shenk had supported "Oriental exclusion." He still used the term "the yellow hordes" to describe Asian-Americans and had written a scathing dissent to *Perez v. Sharp*, the landmark 1948 ruling making California the first state in the nation to strike down anti-miscegenation laws. Shenk fervently believed there was scientific proof that: "The amalgamation of the races is not only unnatural, but is always productive of deplorable results."[5]

Identifying with a kindred spirit, Cooper eagerly informed Stender that the D.A. knew whether any potential jurors had ever been arrested, and, if so, he had a copy of the arrest sheet. District Attorney Coakley's office also had information on any juror who had served on a jury before, including how the juror voted. Cooper had just recently learned of the list and had promptly requested access to the D.A.'s jury file in a few of her own assigned cases. But even the liberal judge Sparky Avakian denied Cooper's requests. Judge Avakian reasoned that the same information the D.A. had accumulated would be available to the defense if they put investigators to work on digging it out. Cooper told Stender that this was not in fact the case — some of the information the District Attorney had accumulated on potential jurors was from a Sacramento Central Intelligence data bank, which was not accessible to defense investigators. Stender wanted Garry to make a motion for its discovery, putting the issue on the record even if Judge Friedman was likely to deny their request. But Garry had other priorities.

In late June Garry interviewed a forensic medical expert who analyzed Officer Frey's and Newton's bullet wounds. The expert had been puzzled by the multiple directions of the wounds to Officer Frey, but concluded that the fatal shot had been fired at close range through Frey's back. Immediate treatment would not likely have saved him. This was not going to be particularly helpful. Garry had been hoping to get the medical expert to say the fatal wound could have come from Heanes' gun, shot from thirty feet away. No such luck.

As the date for the Newton trial approached, the media covered the liberal response to racial violence following the twin assassinations, increased civil rights activism and new gun control efforts, and the even stronger backlash. Alabama's Governor George Wallace entered the 1968 presidential campaign as a candidate on his own American Independent Party ticket. A proud white supremacist, Wallace threatened to take a majority of the Southern states as a base to build a larger coalition he hoped to use to direct the outcome of the presidential election. Some political analysts feared that Wallace's growing support among Northern blue collar whites could force the election to be decided by the House of Representatives. Republican candidate Richard Nixon responded by making veiled appeals to racism central to his own campaign, coupling images of violent urban protests with promises to restore "law and order."[6] Meanwhile, Senator Eugene McCarthy reached out to black youths, proclaiming that resolution of urban racial problems was of paramount national concern, trumping the Vietnam War.

Just before the Newton trial was to begin, the *Oakland Tribune* also gave front page coverage in early July to congressional hearings in Washington, D.C., on Associate Justice Abe Fortas's controversial nomination for Chief Justice. A lame-duck nominee of President Lyndon Johnson, the New Deal scholar from Yale would have replaced Chief Justice Earl Warren. The local paper reported relentless questioning of the Jewish Democrat by Senator Strom Thurmond, one of many Republicans disgusted with the Supreme Court's recent record of overturning criminal convictions based on police conduct found to be unconstitutional. Like other critics, Thurmond considered liberals on the high court to be too concerned with mere legal technicalities.

Of greatest impact locally was a hotly contested ruling on July 8 by Alameda County Superior Court Judge George Phillips. Judge Phillips declared a mistrial in an Oakland criminal prosecution against five black inmates of Santa Rita accused of attacking a white inmate. Judge Phillips based his ruling on arguments that the prosecutor had used his peremptory challenges improperly by removing every non-white from the jury panel. The prosecutor had also used a few of his peremptory challenges against prospective white jurors. Generally speaking, peremptory challenges could be used to strike anyone that a lawyer did not want on the jury, with no explanation necessary.

An opposing attorney wishing to show that a peremptory challenge was used improperly had to meet an extremely high threshold of proof. But Judge Phillips ruled that the threshold was met in the case before him. He concluded that the deputy district attorney had demonstrated a systematic, conscious intent to exclude African-Americans as a class, depriving the defendants of a fair trial by an impartial jury of their peers drawn from a cross-section of the community. Not wanting the delighted defendants to read too much into his ruling, the judge added that he was simply delaying their day in court, intoning, "You will be tried for this alleged crime."[7]

The mistrial made front page news. District Attorney Coakley sharply criticized Judge Phillips for holding that a member of Coakley's office had acted in a racially discriminatory manner. Coakley immediately announced he was exploring an appeal: the ruling gave his office a black eye in the community at a very sensitive time, with obvious implications for the imminent Newton trial. Coakley himself still smarted from charges of racism that Bob Treuhaft had levied when he ran for office against Coakley two years earlier.[8]

As racial tension peaked in the community, Garry faced the added distraction of ongoing issues related to Cleaver's continued freedom. The Adult Authority had ignored Judge Sherwin's June 12 ruling in Cleaver's favor and set a hearing on the charge of parole violation for July 8, 1968, at San Quentin prison in Marin County — the same date Judge Friedman had reset the Newton trial. But then Judge Friedman moved the Newton trial one week later, to July 15. Despite a new order from Judge Sherwin not to do so, the Adult Authority then proceeded with the July 8 hearing, ignoring the judge's threat to hold the state agency in contempt. The impasse was temporarily resolved when the court of appeal issued an order leaving in place Judge Sherwin's ruling. As a result, Cleaver remained free on bail pending an appellate decision in the matter. The review court set a date in late September for its own hearing. Eldridge told Kathleen that if he was ordered back to prison, he was determined not to go.

Meanwhile, the Cleavers tried to generate international support for Huey Newton by filing a complaint with the United Nations alleging human rights violations. Eldridge Cleaver also took advantage of his current freedom to make a number of public appearances both to support Newton and to attack the police for persecuting the Panther organization. Wearing dark sunglasses, the leather-clad revolutionary told audiences he was convinced that on April 6 he had been marked for death along with Bobby Hutton. He claimed that the police only stopped short of double murder because there had been so many black people from the neighborhood crowded around as witnesses. Cleaver's rhetoric and that of most Panthers had evolved in the past few months. Influenced by the Peace and Freedom Party, Cleaver abandoned black nationalist positions and was now talking about the need for white and black unity in fighting capitalism. The Peace and Freedom Party then announced its plan to run Eldridge Cleaver as their candidate for President of the United States, while Newton remained their candidate for Congress. They added Kathleen Cleaver as a candidate for State Assembly.

Thanks to the efforts of the Peace and Freedom Party, the door was now open for anti-war candidates to topple the incumbent Democrat in California's Seventh Congressional District. In 1966, *Ramparts* journalist Bob Scheer had paved the way by running as a Peace and Freedom candidate in a grassroots anti-war campaign that won him forty-five percent of the primary vote. But that opportunity was thrown away by running Huey Newton for that congressional office. Newton enjoyed the notoriety of running for office from his jail cell. But with no chance of success, the Peace and Freedom Party approach all but guaranteed another split among the left-leaning voters of Berkeley and North Oakland.

Democrats like Ron Dellums on the Berkeley City Council and congressional candidate John George felt thwarted by the radical Left just

as the East Bay finally seemed ready to vote for more politically mainstream African-American candidates. Cleaver did not care. He knew
he was not going to get elected to anything. He told audiences, "I'm
a Black Panther and a madman . . . a symbol of dissent, of rejection."[9]
He despised the white power structure and wanted to build support
for the Black Panther Party wherever he could find it. He suggested
that women refrain from sex as an incentive to their men to take arms
against oppression. He got crowds to yell that they would free Newton
"by any means necessary." Cleaver declared, "I've been watching those
pigs railroading Huey. If they kill Huey P. Newton, they're going to have
to kill us all first."[10]

Cleaver met with representatives of The American Communist
Party. For the first time since 1940, the Party openly supported a candidate for President of the United States. Its platform was twofold:
freedom and justice for blacks and an end to the Vietnam War. The
Communist Party now estimated its membership at 14,000 to 15,000
people nationwide, of which twenty percent were black. The FBI had,
by now, not only assigned operatives to cover Panther leaders, but had
begun to strategize on how to implode the Panther organization with
a campaign of dirty tricks. In the spring of 1968, Alex Hoffmann had
publicly documented the government's disabling of his home phone in
connection with the April 6 arrest of Eldridge Cleaver. The FBI was listening in on other telephones of Panther officials as well, evidenced by
a tell-tale click. They also planted false documentation, seeking to sow
suspicion among the Panther rank and file that Stokely Carmichael,
David Hilliard and Newton himself were government agents.[11]

On the evening of July 3, Cleaver and Seale were invited to address
an emergency session of the Berkeley City Council on which Dellums
sat. It drew a crowd of over a thousand people to the 3,000-seat Berkeley
High School auditorium. The specially-called meeting capped several
tumultuous days of violence and strict citywide curfews. Seale appeared
haggard and unkempt. Cleaver looked in command of his audience.
They used the podium to rail against racist "pig" cops as the council
debated a controversial motion to close several blocks of Telegraph
Avenue for a massive Fourth of July gathering, permitting rallies by

hippies, Yippies, Black Panthers, Peace and Freedom Party members, and other anti-war activists. Though renewed violence was threatened, the holiday celebration on Telegraph Avenue turned out to be peaceful. Cleaver urged the Berkeley crowd to rally for Newton's release from jail, but the audience was dominated by flower children more interested in enjoying a warm summer afternoon than in his political passion.

Cleaver's busy calendar of appearances at rallies was part of a defense strategy to draw a huge group of spectators to the Newton trial. Stender filed a motion the second week of July to have the trial moved to a different venue capable of seating a much larger audience of spectators, together with the more than one hundred media representatives expected to cover the trial. She could find no precedent for the unusual motion except that Newton was entitled to a public trial. Her moving papers argued that a larger space would more readily satisfy widespread interest in the case. Of course, the logistics of such a move would have also meant more delay in order to put necessary security precautions in place. The defense team would have welcomed any further postponement they could obtain.

Tom Berkley of the *Oakland Post* assumed that no further delays would be seriously entertained by the court: "Barring something unforeseen up the sleeve of wily defense counsel Charles K. Garry, Huey Newton, baby-faced guru of the Black Panther Party . . . will go to trial Monday morning."[12] Thelton Henderson recalls his foreboding as an interested observer: "As I read the press . . . covering the events leading up to the trial, I had very little hope for Huey that he would not be convicted. I think that anyone who read the paper closely, you'd have to conclude that, the way it was reported."

At the end of that second week of July, spectators filled only about two-thirds of the seats in the small courtroom where the Newton pretrial hearing was set. Many other interested parties stayed away, not anticipating anything exciting to happen until the trial actually started the following week. Friday morning's spectators included court officials, lawyers, the press and a dozen or so Black Panthers who stood to salute Huey Newton with de rigueur clenched fists as he strode into the courtroom. Garry told Judge Friedman of worldwide interest in the trial as he suggested it be moved to the Oakland Auditorium theater, the Veterans Memorial Building or, if available, the presiding judge's oversized courtroom.

Reporters from the *Boston Globe* and *New York Times* were expected along with those from local dailies, a London reporter, network and local television and radio crews, and representatives from the wire services, *TIME, Newsweek,* and *LIFE* magazines, and from some underground papers. Among reporters already watching the proceedings that Friday was Gilbert Moore, one of two African-Americans on the staff of *LIFE* magazine. The seventy-two-year-old judge who held Newton's life in his hands impressed Moore as a man with "the demeanor, the gentle forbearance, the myopia of an aging beagle."[13] Unpersuaded by the hoopla, Judge Friedman denied Garry's motion to move the proceedings: "The court of justice is not a place for entertainment or amusement."[14] The media reacted in disbelief — only a fraction would receive passes from the sheriff's office. They would need a different pass each day, first-come, first-served. Moore now urgently wanted to be among them.

* * * * *

Gilbert Moore had originally been assigned in late June to do a story "on Eldridge Cleaver, the Panthers in general or on Oakland: a tinderbox about to explode."[15] He had accepted the task quite reluctantly, not relishing the idea that his race automatically made him the right choice to cover the story. Raised in Harlem and Jamaica by conservative West Indian parents, the thirty-three-year-old New Yorker had never set foot in Oakland. All that he knew at the time of his new assignment was that a man named Huey Newton headed a "bizarre bunch of California niggers, talking bad and occasionally shooting someone."[16]

LIFE's San Francisco bureau chief had turned the assignment down as "sticky at best and dangerous at worst."[17] It was his suggestion that the story be assigned "to a Negro." The only other black *LIFE* reporter at the time specialized in science issues. Gilbert Moore handled general news. Moore's bad experience a year earlier covering the notorious Blackstone Rangers gang in Chicago made him especially wary of this new assignment. The Rangers had viewed him suspiciously from the get-go. Moore had wound up hightailing it out of Chicago without a story after coming to the conclusion the Blackstone Rangers were a dangerous "loose coalition of armed hustlers" and that he had nothing a mainstream magazine could print because he had been "caught in a crossfire of conflicting hustles."[18]

On his arrival in California, Moore first met up with freelance photographer Howard L. Bingham from South Los Angeles. Eldridge Cleaver liked Bingham's work and had only agreed to a *LIFE* interview on the condition that the magazine would hire Bingham to photograph it — Bingham's first major assignment for *LIFE*. Bingham was a low-key dropout from Compton Junior College whose photographs already included many celebrities and politicians. He most enjoyed being an eyewitness to black history. Bingham began snapping photos of his friend Cassius Clay back in 1962 when Bingham was just twenty-one — two years before Clay abandoned his "slave name" for the Muslim name Muhammad Ali. Bingham had since covered Martin Luther King, Jr., Malcolm X and the Nation of Islam. Unlike Moore, Bingham was comfortable around radicals like Bobby Seale and SNCC leaders Stokely Carmichael and H. Rap Brown. Bingham had recently completed a photo shoot of Ron Karenga and US in L.A.

The plan was to work in tandem on the Newton trial, hanging out with the Panthers "day in, day out." At first, Bingham found Moore intense and visibly uptight. But Moore enjoyed Bingham's "jes' plain folks" attitude — the signs of a transplanted Mississippi country boy. Bingham thought the two of them seemed like a black version of the "odd couple." Moore carried a briefcase everywhere; Bingham was always draped in cameras and related equipment. The very first time Moore called Eldridge Cleaver's apartment, he could hear a noticeable click that signaled a wiretap. Despite Bingham vouching for Moore, Cleaver greeted Moore and his constant note-taking with suspicion, calling him to his face an FBI "pig" informer masquerading as a reporter.[19] Moore then spent a couple of weeks learning the rudiments of the multi-step, Black Panther handshake ritual, ending with a finger snap of African tribal origin, so he would be more welcome among the brothers. Eldridge Cleaver quizzed him on whether he had ever before written about the struggle for black liberation. Moore said, "Yes, of course I have."[20] Bingham found Moore's discomfort and efforts to gain Cleaver's trust quite amusing.

Moore interviewed Newton in jail. He and Bingham toured the cramped and disorganized Panther headquarters. They watched kids feast at the Party's free breakfasts, visited still wary Eldridge and Kathleen Cleaver at their apartment in San Francisco's Haight-Ashbury District, and tagged along after the Cleavers and Seale at rallies and education sessions. They noticed that Eldridge was always on the move. After three weeks, Bingham had snapped thousands of pictures — sometimes risking assault by Panthers who assumed they were a pair of "pigs" or "bootlickers."[21]

Moore soon accumulated more than enough information to write the story he was assigned. He also realized none of the Panther leaders "gave a rat's ass whether *LIFE* magazine did a story on the movement or not."[22] His impatient editors demanded an explanation for his delayed return to New York. But Moore knew he was witnessing a major happening on a global stage. He overcame their skepticism with assurances the Huey Newton trial would have "very wide political implications" which he felt compelled to cover firsthand.[23] He and Bingham had already met media correspondents from around the world who had flown to Oakland to cover the extraordinary goings on.

* * * * *

The hearing on Friday, July 12, 1968, addressed a far more basic concern than spectator space in the courtroom. Before the trial began, the defense team wanted to seek review in both state and federal court on an issue Garry deemed critical to the defense — expunging Newton's prior felony conviction for assault. They fully expected to lose the issue before Judge Friedman. On that assumption, Stender had prepared a writ raising the same issue later that morning before another Alameda County judge. If this petition was also denied, an appeal to the state appellate court was already planned, together with a request for an order postponing the trial date until the appellate court ruled.

The motion was deemed critical because the status of Newton's prior conviction greatly influenced Garry's trial strategy. He thought his handsome client would make a persuasive, articulate witness on his own behalf. If Newton explained the Panther platform, he might win the sympathy of at least some of the jurors. Garry definitely wanted to consider that option, though Newton had the constitutional right not to testify at all. But the prior conviction was a powerful disincentive, a sword of Damocles dangling over Newton's head. If it remained unchallenged, Jensen would focus the jury's attention on it, prejudicing the panel against Newton. The prosecutor would even be entitled to have the jury instructed that Newton's prior criminal conduct was reason enough to discredit his testimony on *any* subject. Unlike witnesses in general, felons could be presumed dishonest.

Garry was also concerned about the impact of Newton's no-contest plea to the charges that had been filed against him for the incident in front of Panther headquarters the prior spring. In November, after Newton had been jailed on the murder charges, John George had entered a plea on Newton's behalf for the May 1967 incident and obtained a sentence of fifteen days' jail time, to be served simultaneously. It had seemed a reasonable deal at the time. George had since been persuaded to ask the court to reinstate the original charges against Newton and to set a hearing for late July on those minor charges. On Garry's advice, Newton now wished to plead innocent and have his day in court. George accommodated them by informing the court he had entered the original plea without Newton's approval.

After Judge Friedman denied the motion to expunge the conviction, Judge Lercara, the judge assigned to hear the other petition raising the same issue, took an unusual step to accommodate the parties and the press. Normally, he would have used his own courtroom several floors below. Instead, he simply took the still-warm bench as soon as it was vacated by Judge Friedman. Then he quickly told the parties he had read the petition and response and did not want to hear arguments.

Within just minutes of his arrival, Judge Lercara denied the petition, giving the defense time the same day to seek review in the court of appeal. Part of the defense strategy had been to ask Judge Friedman for another continuance while awaiting review of his ruling on Newton's prior felony conviction. They had hoped the possibility of reversal would persuade him. Not so. Judge Friedman remained firm. Unless another court ordered otherwise before Monday morning, that was when trial would commence. Stender scrambled off to file the appeal as Garry announced, "We're prepared to go to the U.S. Supreme Court if necessary."[24]

When the media left the hearing on Friday, they realized they had obtained a preview of precautionary measures they could expect at trial on Monday. Cameras would be relegated to a makeshift press room on the sixth floor, temporarily converted from a jury room. Reporters figured that they had better plan to arrive early Monday morning to allow time for court personnel to process everyone entitled to enter. No one wanted to be left out. Judge Friedman might believe that a court of justice was not an entertainment venue, but show time was about to begin.

The court of appeal quickly denied the defense request for review; that same afternoon Stender filed a similar petition with the California Supreme Court. She worked all weekend preparing other legal briefs, including a federal petition in the event the California Supreme Court declined to act, and a renewed motion to present to Judge Friedman challenging the jury panel. Garry planned to call the expert witnesses Stender had prepared on this issue before starting the trial in earnest.

While the legal work was being churned out, the "Free Huey" committee kicked into high gear. On Sunday, July 14, a huge mixed-race crowd of Panther supporters and curious locals of all ages gathered at DeFremery Park for a four-hour picnic and rally. (By then many in the community called the site "Bobby Hutton Park," though no official name change was permitted under the terms by which the wealthy family had deeded the land and Victorian mansion to the city back in 1910.) Helmeted Oakland police circled the block in patrol cars, on foot and in hovering helicopters that reporter Gilbert Moore believed were "awaiting a signal to declare open war upon the savage citizens below."[25] Melvin Newton addressed the crowd along with SNCC's James Forman, Bobby Seale and the Cleavers. Eldridge again stood out among the militant speakers, urging members of the audience to show up in force at the trial. Even as Cleaver rallied the troops, Garry hoped against hope that Stender could pull off a miracle and get another court to temporarily postpone the trial.

On Monday morning, July 15, 1968, the *Oakland Tribune* proclaimed that the city's main courthouse looked like a "besieged fortress."[26] Sheriff Frank Madigan had responsibility for the historic security put in place for this polarizing trial. Most steps leading to the building were covered with netting. Armed deputies stood outside every entrance; they had also been supplied with walkie-talkies, mace and batons. The National Guard provided reinforcements as did the Oakland police. A multi-racial mass of Panther supporters in the thousands — many with children in tow — circled the building and overflowed onto the street, impeding traffic until they were dispersed by the police. Patrol cars circled the blocks around the courthouse, advertising the officers' readiness to jump into action at any signs of trouble.

All but one of the entrances to the building were locked. At the 12th Street doorway a guard required everyone who approached to show identification — couples applying for marriage licenses, attorneys and parties to other cases, as well as county employees. Such high security precautions had never before been implemented in the county. Equally strong security measures were evident inside the courthouse. Special passes obtained at the sheriff's office on the second floor allowed those authorized to attend the trial access to the seventh floor where Judge Friedman's sixty-two-seat courtroom was located. A few eager spectators had begun lining up at 5 a.m. Friends and family of Huey Newton complained they were singled out for photographing and fingerprinting before receiving passes.

Doors permitting seventh-floor access to the stairwells leading to the sixth and eighth floors were temporarily sealed. One elevator with its own armed guard was assigned exclusively for persons headed to the Newton trial. Veteran Judge Cecil Mosbacher could not hide her irritation when the long-time elevator operator on the basement floor turned down her request to let the judge board. She would have to take another elevator to her own courtroom on the seventh floor. No exceptions whatsoever were being made to the tight security arrangements.

That morning, when members of the jury pool arrived at the courthouse they were promptly sequestered while thousands of Newton supporters gathered outside — black, white, "Brown Beret" Chicanos and Asians. The Panthers had hoped to conduct a mass march through downtown Oakland that morning for the trial's start, but too few supporters had shown up at the designated assembly point. Instead, they all met at the courthouse where Black Panthers in full regalia — sweltering in leather jackets and berets — defiantly led the crowd in chanting, "Free Huey Now," "Free Huey, Off the Pigs" and "Black is Beautiful." Signs lofted above protesters' heads warned, "The Nation Shall Be Reduced to Ashes," "Free Huey or Else" and "If Anything Happens to Huey, the Sky's the Limit."[27] A few in the crowd likely wore "Gas Reagan" buttons, which started selling after Governor Reagan refused to grant clemency to cop killer Aaron Mitchell in the spring of 1967.

Though most unsympathetic onlookers held their tongues, reporter Moore heard a few from time to time saying things such as "Jesus Christ, what is this country comin' to? Free Huey — my ass! They oughta burn the son of a bitch!" while others wondered exactly what was meant by "Free Huey": "Is it a command, a request or an exhortation — or perhaps all three? Does it mean, examine the evidence, go through the court rituals and then free Huey? Does it mean storming the Alameda County jail and freeing him by force of arms? Or what?"[28] Lowell Jensen was concerned about seating a jury under these circumstances. He realized that the political context might be "more difficult and more tense than it had ever been before."

Somehow, though most white males in the crowd wore long hair and beards, Judge Friedman circulated among them unobtrusively, gauging the situation for himself. The din made it almost impossible for court staff on the first floor of the building to perform their work. Outside the courthouse, Peace and Freedom Party leader Bob Avakian ascended the flagpole and cut down the American flag as other demonstrators yelled, "Burn it." The sequestered jurors could hear the shouts through the windows of the courthouse high above the sidewalk. Police rushed out of the building and immediately arrested Avakian for petty theft, flag desecration and malicious mischief.[29]

Several times the police also disrupted the demonstrators circling the courthouse. They arrested some of them and dispersed the rest of the crowd. But those who were chased away simply returned later and started to chant again. Janice Garrett was among them: "They saw that they couldn't stop us." Eventually, the police just let them picket the courthouse. The demonstrators only knew what was happening inside the courthouse from getting reports once in a while from someone who went inside. Their job was to keep the chants going, and they did so from the heart.

From the very first day, armed guards patrolled the courthouse corridors. Two stood guarding the door to Judge Friedman's locked courtroom. Inside, the bailiff inspected the underside of all chairs and tables. Once they exhibited identification and were allowed entry, spectators and media, on opposite sides of the central aisle, overflowed all available seats, spilling into the hallway. FBI agents in white shirts posed as press with notepads; they were accompanied by cameramen. Plainclothes members of the District Attorney's office and undercover policemen also spread out among the spectators, attempting to blend inconspicuously into the crowd. To the discerning eyes of Panther supporters, they might as well have been wearing neon. Yet the Panthers' radar had not picked up insiders like Aoki and Anthony already on COINTELPRO's payroll from their first days in the Party. Paranoia about agents provocateurs and informants would come later.

As expected, no photographers were permitted in the courtroom, but artists employed by the media busily sketched the high-ceilinged room with wood-paneled walls where the drama of the trial would be staged: the raised bench; the judge's empty leather chair with a huge American flag hanging on the wall behind it; the jury box on the right and the clerk's desk on the left. The Gettysburg Address was framed on one of the courtroom walls. The two counsel tables were positioned in "the well" beyond a gate segregating the players from the spectators. The prosecutor's table sat nearer to the jury and the defense table to its left.

Unaware of all the last minute machinations, Blauner had obtained his trial pass as a designated defense expert witness on race bias in the jury pool. He showed up on Monday morning flushed with excitement at the unfolding drama. To his dismay, Stender and Garry arrived late, looking exhausted. By then Stender was routinely putting in twelve-hour days and had had no weekend break. She sat down in the front row dressed for court in a tailored skirt suit, accompanied by Alex Hoffmann, who wore a suit as well — the lawyers' uniform. (In those days, both courts and established law firms refused to permit women to wear pantsuits as unbecoming their sex.) Their seats were right behind Charles Garry at the defense table, where Ed Keating from *Ramparts* magazine also sat, attired in a suit. David Horowitz was an editor for *Ramparts* at the time, and one of the best-known radicals later to flip 180 degrees and become advocates of neoconservative Republican politics. Though he did not attend the trial himself, he recalls, "My circle of political comrades was very, very involved in the Newton case. . . . This is where the Left devised a strategy . . . that you don't try the case, you try the system."

After learning Ed Keating wished to cover the trial for *Ramparts*, Garry had offered to designate Keating as his co-counsel. Unlike other reporters, Keating would have automatic access to the proceedings. Eager to have such a birds-eye-view of the historic event, Keating reactivated his little-used law degree and offered help in the nature of a paralegal. He had no expertise in criminal law and had not practiced in years. Freelance reporter Karen Wald also managed a ringside seat embedded with the defense team, the first political trial she had ever witnessed from start to finish. Over its course, she would write several lengthy articles for *The Movement* and *The Guardian*.

It quickly became evident to all present that the trial would not begin right away. Garry had persuaded Judge Friedman to agree to a late morning start in case the California Supreme Court or the federal district court granted a temporary stay. When no stay order materialized, the tension in the room was palpable. Twenty-eight credentialed reporters sat in the courtroom ready to chronicle the current trial of the century, leaving another seventy reporters outside due to insufficient space. Gilbert Moore and his new friend Rush Greenlee had both obtained coveted seats. Greenlee was a black reporter covering the story from a human interest angle for the *San Francisco Examiner*. He often collaborated with a more senior white colleague assigned daily responsibility for reporting on the high profile case. The Panthers castigated Greenlee as part of the "spineless black bourgeoisie."[30]

The *Oakland Post* characterized the stakes for the American system of justice to be as high as those involved in the 1920s' Sacco and Vanzetti trial. Its reporter Almea Lomax expressed amazement that a "self-confessed small-time hood" like Newton could transform himself into a hero with "new-found socialist convictions."[31] The *Post* was not Huey Newton's only local black media critic. Early in the trial, the Berkeley campus student newspaper, the *Daily Californian*, featured a caustic editorial column entitled "The Paper Panthers" by an African-American graduate student. He derided the paramilitary organization's "vacant generalities and absurd manifestoes," its lack of "plausible short term goals" and reliance on pistols as "sex symbols." The author lambasted Newton's organization as the source of much wasted newsprint in the liberal and radical press as well as wasted time and energy of people in the ghetto.[32] In contrast, the alternative press viewed the trial as a pivotal point in the nation's history of racism that was on the eve of engulfing the nation in flames — "Oppression. Revolt. Suppression. Revolution."[33]

As the trial officially began, Garry asked Judge Friedman to have the court reporter prepare a daily transcript of proceedings for both the prosecutor and the defense. It would be costly, but essential to have the ability to review each day's testimony for use in cross-examination and for summing up the evidence in closing arguments. Garry also requested that the judge list his entire firm as Newton's counsel of record. Everyone in the Garry partnership had by now been mobilized as reinforcements. With Fay Stender in the courtroom, Garry's partner Frank McTernan was back in the office readying appeals to the Ninth Circuit and the Supreme Court, if the pending petitions were denied.

Jensen asked Judge Friedman to exclude from the courtroom any persons expected to be called as witnesses, a common order designed to prevent anyone who might be taking the stand from hearing what others had already attested to. Otherwise, the later-called witnesses might be tempted to tailor their testimony accordingly. Two exceptions to the order were requested and granted: an inspector from the District Attorney's office was allowed to stay and Newton's fiancée, LaVerne Williams, who was seated with Newton's siblings and his minister. Everyone else — reporters and interested observers — remained seated. Jensen also asked the court to prohibit any display of support for Newton in the courtroom, including leaflets, buttons and signs. Garry, in turn, objected to the unaccustomed security measures. He charged that they created an atmosphere of fear and intimidation that gave members of the jury panel the impression Newton was a dangerous killer before the trial even began. Following his cautious custom, the judge took both motions under submission, though the likelihood that he would abandon the extraordinary security precautions was virtually nil.

It was close to 11:15 a.m. when the clerk called the names of forty-five prospective jurors for *The People of the State of California versus Huey P. Newton.* Kathleen Cleaver was astounded that the state got to call itself "The People." She thought the protesters were "the people." On the few occasions it was her turn to come inside to watch part of the trial, Kathleen found the proceedings in the courtroom mystifying. So did most of the other Panther demonstrators, who turned out day after day on the sidewalk, yelling themselves hoarse calling attention to their cause. Most of them were under twenty-one, too young to vote and thus not yet eligible for potential inclusion in any jury pool. Their job was to increase mobilization around the courthouse, attract more press coverage and create a political environment in which it would be extremely difficult for Huey Newton to get the death penalty. The legal strategy to pick a jury and persuade the panel of the righteousness of Newton's case was in his lawyers' hands; the protesters were focused on "the people" strategy to accomplish radical change in a biased justice system. Inside the courtroom, it might be business as usual. Outside felt like a giant picnic or happening.

In the packed courtroom, all but two prospective jurors acknowledged their presence when their names were called. Some were seated on folding chairs that had been brought in, some were allowed to sit temporarily in the jury box. Many shivered in the sixty-degree courtroom. Out of that group only six were non-white. Newton then entered from a side door, accompanied by a bailiff. Looking cheerful and relaxed, he created a remarkable first impression, with a new haircut, a sharp gray suit and black turtleneck chosen for him by his streetwise brother Walter. As he made his way to the defense table next to Garry, Newton raised his fist to greet supporters.

Out of sight of the spectators, Newton had just been escorted in handcuffs down a stairwell from the tenth floor into a hallway leading to the courtroom. At the side entrance, his cuffs were removed to avoid prejudicing potential jurors against him. For a similar reason, he had been allowed to dress in a turtleneck, slacks and jacket for the court proceedings. Once he returned to his tenth floor cell, he had to change immediately into his loose, county-issued jail clothes. The same ritual was repeated each court day. Sometimes spectators could get a glimpse of the officers re-cuffing Newton's wrists behind his back as they headed into the stairwell.

After the court clerk called the names of all the potential jurors in the first group, he told them they could leave and report back the next morning. As soon as they departed, thirty more spectators streamed into the courtroom. Judge Friedman dismissed the panel of potential jurors for the rest of the day because he needed the time to address several preliminary issues Garry had raised. These included a motion Stender had just prepared based on Judge Phillips' recent ruling. She anticipated that Jensen might use his jury challenges improperly, both to eliminate all black jurors and to exclude anyone with scruples against the death penalty. Garry told the judge he intended to call several witnesses in support of these motions, which the judge would need to rule upon before any jurors were selected.

Judge Friedman called both sides into his chambers. Jensen got up from his chair and started to enter the chambers by himself. Though he had lots of backup from attorneys in the office, the only other person he had helping him every day in court was an investigator from his office. When Garry rose to join Jensen, so did Ed Keating, Fay Stender,

Alex Hoffmann and Carleton Innis. Jensen did not feel outgunned. However, the judge looked askance and promptly advised Garry that he had a rule that only two attorneys could represent one side in chambers. Though Jensen had never tried a case in front of Judge Friedman before, Jensen thought the judge made the rule up on the spot. Without hesitation, Garry summoned Stender to join him, leaving the others in the courtroom. In Jensen's view, that decision was a ringing endorsement of her vital role in the case. It made quite an impression: "This was the first time I'd ever seen a woman representing a defendant in a case so serious that it included even the notion of capital punishment."

Garry was among the vast majority of trial lawyers who considered their practice an exclusive men's club, but he was also extremely practical. The decision who would accompany him into chambers was not even close. He could not handle this case without Fay Stender; everyone else was dispensable. Belva Davis thought Stender's role was "remarkable. . . . There she was sitting in the second chair, visible, smart, and some people knew just how smart and how important she was to this case . . . the research, the work, the backbone."

By the end of the first day, Garry's feisty attitude already irked Judge Friedman. Among all the other issues he had dumped on the judge's plate, Garry raised a complaint from Newton's family that they had been discriminated against in being photographed and fingerprinted to obtain trial passes. The judge shouted in reply that Garry needed to file proper papers if he wanted the issue considered. He then emphatically announced, "This court is in recess" and left the bench.[34] When the court session ended, Garry and Stender quickly learned from their office mates that the Ninth Circuit had acted that afternoon to deny review of the federal district court's ruling on a technicality. In their hurry, they had not provided proof they had given notice of appeal to the Alameda County District Attorney. Their last hope was the United States Supreme Court. Frank McTernan filed that petition for review Monday night.

On Tuesday, hot weather reduced the crowd around the courthouse to a few hundred, a fraction of the crowd that had gathered on Monday. The flagpole on the ground remained bare on Tuesday, but another on the courthouse roof still waved its state and national flags. Standing outside all day, marching and shouting, took its toll. One of the Panthers fainted from the heat. But the remaining crowd still demonstrated noisily. Inside the courtroom, Newton wore the same black turtleneck and gray suit on Tuesday as he wore on Monday. He complained to his counsel that he was chilly, but they were unable to convince the judge to adjust the air-conditioning.

Newton often turned to smile at the spectators in the courtroom, particularly SNCC's leader James Forman, who was seated prominently in the audience. Forman, then in his late thirties, could be easily spotted. Dressed in an African tunic with his graying hair uncombed, Forman looked somewhat like a modern-day version of fiery abolitionist Frederick Douglass. Forman made himself even more conspicuous as the only person in the courtroom who remained seated when the judge entered, rising only after Judge Friedman glared at him. Back in 1964, Forman had gained a reputation for his in-your-face attitude toward authority with an angry challenge: "If we can't sit at the table of democracy, we'll knock the fucking legs off."[35] Ironically, Forman was not deemed militant enough for SNCC's new leadership and that of the Black Panthers, who considered him paranoid and unstable. He and Decca Mitford's daughter Dinky Romilly now had a one-year-old son. His ongoing relationship with her may have contributed to his impending political ostracism from SNCC. Other whites formerly integral to the organization had already been ousted from its power structure. This trial appearance was Forman's last show of public affiliation with the Party. SNCC now intended to sever its relationship with the Panthers and look to the Black Muslims for protection.[36] But on the second day of trial in mid-July, Forman seemed to offer his full support to Newton.

The first witness Garry called was the County Jury Commissioner to explain how the master jury panel was selected solely from registered voters. Every six months, the county drew the names of 7,000 prospective jurors. From that number, the county used a "working panel" of 1,600 potential jurors selected at random from nearly 1,200 precincts in the county. The master panel for the Newton case had instead been a 900-member emergency panel created after the springtime ruling in *People v. Craig.* The new panel avoided the constitutional problem that Judge Avakian had addressed; none of the 900 panelists had been required to pass a juror intelligence test.

Next came Professor Vizard, who analyzed the voter registration of various county districts. He noted that Oakland's highest ratio of voter registration, 83.6 percent, was in the hilly Montclair district, which had only a minute percentage of blacks. Vizard also testified that low-income blacks were often apathetic about voting. It presented no meaningful opportunity to them, since they had little, if any, political power. On cross-examination, Jensen got the professor to admit that in South Berkeley most blacks did vote. The professor attributed this phenomenon to much higher education and income per capita compared to other black neighborhoods.

On Tuesday afternoon, Garry called his co-counsel Ed Keating to the stand. Keating had overseen a review Monday night of the jury commissioner's office records to analyze the number of potential jurors who had been excused and the reasons why. On cross-examination by Jensen, Keating conceded that almost twice as many juror forms were returned from West Oakland as undeliverable than in the county as a whole. On Wednesday, as a record heat wave continued, Panthers outside the building wisely left their leather jackets home, showing up in matching blue tee shirts instead. Inside the courtroom, Garry called Alex Hoffmann to the stand to report on his examination of juror records on Monday night. Seventy percent of potential jurors from West Oakland had been excused, while sixty percent were excused from Montclair. Reporters began to yawn — the showing of disparate treatment was hardly dramatic.

Garry continued a parade of experts, including Professor Blauner. The bearded academic answered questions for half an hour, describing the results of his research, including his work as an adviser to the California commission that investigated the 1965 Watts riot that left in its wake 34 dead, over 1,000 injured and $40 million in damages. Blauner addressed the problems of racism in the country and how the jury might prejudge a black man accused of killing a white police officer. Blauner found that he enjoyed sparring with Jensen on cross-examination. Blauner fully supported Garry's position that only poor residents of the Oakland ghettos would constitute a true jury of Newton's peers and freely admitted that he himself held residual racist attitudes. The experience was a first for Jensen. He had never seen a defense attorney produce experts on racism before.

Garry also called Dr. Nevitt Sanford, one of the principal authors of *The Authoritarian Personality*. The book focused on the type of personality predisposed to convict defendants, the phenomenon the Supreme Court had been troubled by in the *Witherspoon* case. As with the other experts, Stender had prepared the outline for Garry to use. One of the key points she wanted Dr. Sanford to mention on the stand was how few people would admit to prejudice when directly questioned. This was a major reason why the defense deemed it critical to question potential jurors individually, out of the presence of the other panelists.

Reticence to admit prejudice was mentioned again by Dr. Diamond. Reporters might have noticed that he bore a strong resemblance to the then-prominent Hollywood actor, Canadian-American Raymond Massey. Dr. Diamond startled Judge Friedman by saying it was impossible to select a totally impartial jury, even with extensive questioning designed to expose latent racism. He told the judge he would need close to fifty hours alone in his clinic with each prospective juror to attempt such a task. The judge had been planning at most fifteen minutes per prospective juror. Dr. Diamond, like Professor Blauner, admitted that he himself held residual racist attitudes, prompting Judge Friedman to ask if Dr. Diamond considered himself to be a good potential juror. Dr. Diamond said "No," leaving the judge to wonder who would.[37]

From the point of view of the press, the star witness on Wednesday was Dr. Hans Zeisel from the University of Chicago. Many were already aware that Dr. Zeisel's seminal work on *The American Jury* had influenced the United States Supreme Court in issuing the landmark *Witherspoon* opinion. Short and balding, with a heavy Austrian accent, the expert exuded an air of authority as he lectured the judge from the witness chair when prompted by Stender's questions. Dr. Zeisel testified that white males were most likely to favor the death penalty — about fifty-five percent in his studies — followed by less than half of white women,

while the percentages of black men and black women who supported
it declined to the mid to low thirties. He went into other statistics his
researchers had derived. Judge Friedman tried to get to the essence of
Dr. Zeisel's testimony, asking "Are you trying to say it is your opinion a
white jury is more likely to wrongfully convict a Negro?" Dr. Zeisel spread
his hands to underscore his response: "It's rumored it has happened."[38]
As he concluded his testimony, Dr. Zeisel was taken aback when the judge
asked him his own personal views. Zeisel wondered if his objectivity was
undercut when he honestly responded that he opposed the death penalty.

Newton was pleased with Zeisel's testimony and asked Stender to
thank the professor for him. Zeisel, in turn, told Stender he had been
impressed with how remarkably attractive a person her client appeared.
"Not only attractive . . . courageous and intelligent," responded Stender
as she promised Zeisel reimbursement for his $250 in travel costs.[39]
She took great pride in how Newton impressed both experts and activists with the righteousness of his cause, his obvious inner strength and
extraordinarily handsome appearance. She likely was unsurprised
when one Oakland woman who saw Newton in jail in early July compared his charisma to that of Jesus Christ or Lenin.

Reverend Jesse Jackson, the highly touted, new heir-apparent to
Dr. King, wired Newton a supportive message: whether found innocent
or guilty, he represented "the disenchanted and degraded" against
whom "unjust men" could not "render justice."[40] The same theme had
pervaded the testimony of the expert defense witnesses who had come
forward to defend their conclusions that overt and subtle racism was
pervasive among white jurors.

The timing for seeking court permission to ask jurors an extensive list of introspective questions could not have been better. Whether
from perceived heightened national interest or out of a sense of guilt,
or both, national television was for the first time showcasing programs
like *The History of the Negro People*, *Black Journal*, and *Of Black America*,
narrated by comedian Bill Cosby. Suddenly, other prominent African-
Americans were also featured commentators. Locally, since the late
spring, the *San Francisco Examiner* had been running a series of articles
on "Negro History in California."

Poet Maya Angelou hosted a ten-week television program, *Black, Blues, Black,* seeking to educate white viewers on contemporary black culture and the current unrest among fellow African-Americans: "The hostility that some blacks are expressing now is just a stage we have to go through. The black person has always been pictured as either sub-human or superhuman . . . We have to arrive at the stage where we're just human."[41] The distance to that goal was exemplified by a popular new show on Broadway in San Francisco's North Beach district. Already famous for its topless go-go dancers, the neon-dominated street now featured a marquee drawing patrons to a "nude inter-racial love dance" until the police arrested the manager and a naked performer.

The point made by all of the experts Garry called to the stand was that the community as a whole was exceedingly far from treating its black members as just "fellow humans." In the late 1960s there even remained strong disagreement on the subject of self-identification. Almost forty percent still preferred the term "Negro." Twenty percent favored "Colored People," though thirty percent despised that term. Close to twenty percent had warmed to the term "Black," but twenty-five percent considered that terminology the most distasteful. Ten percent preferred African-American and a roughly equal number found that nomenclature least appealing. Very few, however, did not care.[42]

Garry himself had just undertaken a crash course on the subject of racism from the sociologists Stender had gathered. The professors were surprised at Garry's own lack of sensitivity on the subject and his arrogant assumption he had little to learn. Among his long-established black clientele was an African-American doctor then serving as a member of the San Francisco Police Commission. Much to the irritation of the Oakland Police Officers Association, Garry liked to flaunt the gold star the doctor had just bestowed on him, designating his longtime friend as an honorary member of the San Francisco Police Department.

Garry was persuaded by Stender and the experts to spend more effort educating the judge on this issue since his role in the upcoming jury selection phase of the trial would be crucial. To this end, the defense team wanted to offer the affidavits Stender had obtained from additional experts back East to bolster the expert testimony Judge

Friedman had just heard. Garry then took a gamble. He had not decided yet whether to call Newton as a witness at trial, but he summoned his client to the stand at this stage to testify that he was penniless. Some of the press in the audience misinterpreted this development. They thought it was another ploy for delay, assuming Newton would seek to have court-appointed counsel, instead of Garry. But Garry had no such thought in mind. He wanted to impress on Judge Friedman that Newton could not afford to bring experts from the East Coast to the trial, hoping that the judge would then accept the declarations of the additional experts instead of requiring their live testimony.

Judge Friedman, taken by surprise, warned Newton that anything he said on the stand could be used against him at the trial and that the prosecutor might ask him questions unrelated to his financial status. But Jensen accepted the limited purpose for which Newton had been called and focused his questions solely on Newton's finances and not on the charged crime. Secretly, Garry admired Jensen as a worthy adversary with strong notions of fair play. Jensen could be counted upon to follow "Marquess of Queensberry" rules in court — like the traditional good sportsmanship rules that governed boxing. Jensen was well known by then for trying the most inflammatory cases — like the Free Speech prosecutions — without injecting politics or being disrespectful to opposing counsel. Jensen could be counted on to approach the Newton trial in the same conventional way. No one who was familiar with him was surprised. An unapologetic street fighter, Garry came from a different mold. He did not respect rules that interfered with his overall objective.

Newton then testified he had no savings, property or money held in trust. The defense fund in his name was not under his control, and he did not know how much was in the fund or how it was being used. Newton elicited titters from the packed courtroom when he turned to the judge and said, "I probably could get the names if the court would permit me to be free for a couple of days."[43] Actually, as Garry well knew, Newton's brother Melvin was in charge of the Newton Defense Fund set up with guidance from William Patterson of the American Communist Party. All that Garry acknowledged in court was that some $12,000 of the

defense funds had been paid to his firm to date, primarily for cost reim-
bursements. Jensen still objected to the admission of the expert affidavits since the authors were not available for cross-examination. Judge
Friedman agreed with the prosecutor and declined to consider them.

Outside of court, much of Stender's recent work on the case had
been dedicated to preparing the expert witnesses and drafting the
trial motions on weekends and evenings. In court, Stender alternated
between sitting next to Garry at the counsel table or just behind him
in a row of seats inside the barrier separating the audience from "the
well" where counsel tables were located. She could usually be seen
intensely scribbling notes and sometimes passing them forward to
Garry or reviewing them with him at a break. Reporter Gilbert Moore,
attending regularly, saw how Stender's dedication equaled Garry's. He
described her as the street fighter's "nervous, hard-working assistant,
like her boss passionately in love with lost causes."[44] Moore had to have
numbered among the sympathetic reporters joining Stender for lunch
at the Court Lounge restaurant. She had little opportunity to express
her zeal as an advocate in court.

Whenever David Wellman attended the trial, Garry impressed the
Cal graduate student as an overbearing egotist who seemed largely unap-
preciative of Fay Stender's remarkable talents. Cooper thought Garry
undervalued Stender, too. Stender not only oversaw all the research,
"Fay was the brains behind the legal issues in the Huey Newton trial."
Despite the vital motion work Stender performed, Cooper noticed the
back seat Stender often took in the courtroom. This was because when
Keating came to court, he always took his place next to Garry at the
defense table, despite his far lesser role in Newton's defense. When
Cooper spoke with Stender at a break in the proceedings, Stender
gave her the clear impression that she would like to have much more
responsibility if she could make it happen. Had his chief collaborator
been a male, it is doubtful Garry would have bounced him back and
forth from the counsel table in such fashion. As it was, Garry remained
oblivious to Stender's ever-increasing dissatisfaction.

After the lunch recess on Wednesday, July 17, Stender addressed
the court briefly on a procedural matter. She reported to Judge

Friedman that the United States Attorney's office had communicated an objection to one of their experts, Dr. Hunter, being called to testify before they completed a review of a government report he had prepared. There could be privileged information, which it might wish to protect from disclosure. But since the government had not obtained a restraining order, Judge Friedman let Garry proceed with his questioning of Dr. Hunter. Stender sat back down in her role as note-taker.

When the parade of experts concluded, Judge Friedman, like Garry, felt he had just taken an advanced crash course in sociology. The defense topped off their successful day of race-bias sensitivity training by granting interviews with Newton on the tenth floor of the courthouse to all the reporters who could squeeze into the small, green interview room with Newton and his attorneys. Amazingly, sandwiched like students into a telephone booth, sixteen had done so. Newton thrived on the attention. Asked to assess Judge Friedman, Newton was blunt: he did not believe the man presiding over his capital case was "very well versed in the law." He told the gathering that Garry sought to accomplish a "revolution in the courtroom" by obtaining a nontraditional jury, ideally from his same socio-economic background and race. Newton also welcomed younger white jurors who understood black culture in ghetto communities like West Oakland.[45] Actually, Newton's lawyers likely had heard from Penny Cooper that in the relatively rare instances when two or three African-Americans had sat together on a jury in a criminal case in the county, the case predictably ended in a hung jury split along racial lines.

At every recess on the first three days, reporters rushed past the rail dividing the attorneys from onlookers to be the first to obtain quotes from the calm prosecutor and cocky defense counsel. By Thursday, Judge Friedman halted this practice. During the trial breaks, no reporters would any longer be allowed into "the well" where the attorneys sat. For Jensen that was a benefit. He did not relish talking with the press. Nor did they ever get much from him except who was his next witness or other procedural information. Belva Davis noticed that the media often left the prosecutor out of the headlines "because the defense had captured the attention of the world."

On Thursday morning, Judge Friedman denied the pending defense motions. A jury of Newton's peers did not mean a jury of blacks from his neighborhood. Otherwise, a white truck driver defendant could argue that he was entitled to exclude all blacks from his jury and other defendants could make similar demands based on their race or ethnicity. Judge Friedman did rule, based on the United States Supreme Court decision in *Witherspoon*, that challenges for cause based on potential jurors' objections to the death penalty would be limited to those who could not set aside their personal views and consider imposing the death penalty in appropriate circumstances.

The rulings were all that the defense could realistically have hoped for. Stender's long hours preparing all the expert witnesses and briefing the issues of racism and prejudice had rendered Judge Friedman far more aware of the centrality of these issues to the defense's case. The judge would wind up allowing a substantially longer jury questioning process to weed out racists than he had originally intended. He would also bend over backwards to keep in the case jurors opposed to capital punishment who said they would consider imposing the death penalty if the specific facts warranted it. The time had come to see who would have Huey Newton's life in their hands.

12. A MINORITY OF ONE

I who am left here as . . .
passive eye in the center of a terrible storm.
— ANNE CHRISTINE D'ADESKY

When proceedings continued after denial of the pretrial motions, Professor Blauner surprisingly abandoned the role of disinterested expert and became a front row spectator for the duration of the trial. Like the other experts, Blauner had not charged for his testimony. He provided continued consultation on jury selection free as well. For a specialist in race relations with an open summer schedule, it was far too exciting an opportunity to pass up. Sitting next to Fay Stender and Alex Hoffmann, Blauner got into the habit of taking copious notes, thinking he might write a book about the racially charged case when the trial was over. The three enjoyed long lunches every day at the Court Lounge restaurant across the street from the courthouse. They often dined with Karen Wald and Newton's minister, Father Earl Neil, who was sitting in on the trial with Newton's fiancée and family. Other reporters friendly to the defense also joined them from time to time. Sometimes Ed Keating, who also planned to write a book about the trial, sat in, and occasionally Garry would join them for lunch as well, if he wasn't too busy working during the noontime break.

Professor Blauner's expertise came in handy during the jury selection process, which the legal world calls by the phrase "voir dire." On the other side, Lowell Jensen had no such help. His office had never used experts for voir dire. Jensen's approach was basically the same as he had developed in other trials: to try to keep jurors who would pay attention to the evidence and decide the case on the facts and the law and excuse those who manifested that they could or would not do so. He often did not use all of his challenges. Jensen realized that in this case the heavy security and racial setting would be added factors, as would the extraordinary political context. He hoped those called for jury duty would not feel too intimidated to serve. For his part, Jensen wanted to reassure the world that Huey Newton was getting a fair trial.

The lawyers would examine nearly 160 prospective jurors under oath during the question-and-answer selection process over the next two-and-a-half weeks as they picked twelve jurors and four alternates. From the master panel of jurors, the bailiff escorted a group of up to fifty to the courtroom at one time. There, the clerk would spin a wheel to randomly select people from that group to sit in the jury box for voir dire. The very first person questioned was a Hayward dental technician named Orville Miller, who announced that he had read accounts of the killing in the *Oakland Tribune* that made Newton's guilt appear an open-and-shut case. Yet Miller believed he had since "sort of become unbiased."[1] Garry would soon get Judge Friedman to dismiss Miller for cause.

The first batch of potential jurors included six blacks. The first who sat for questioning was Leroy Steveson, a 70-year-old retired waiter who had worked for the Pacific Railroad. He said he could not impose the death penalty. Observers may have wondered why Garry then asked if his views might change if someone brutally murdered his own child. Surely, Garry did not want to persuade this juror that Newton might merit the death penalty. Actually, Garry hoped to save Steveson from automatic dismissal, counting on Steveson never actually to vote for the death penalty when and if the time came. Steveson wasn't taking the hint — he said he could never apply it under any circumstances. The judge dismissed him.

As the days wore on, many potential jurors, including a high percentage of minorities, insisted that they could not ever render the death penalty; the judge then excused them for cause. This troubled Stender, who felt that minorities who took an absolute anti-death-penalty position confirmed how racism worked. These jurors clearly believed capital punishment was so skewed in its use, they could never support it. She hoped they would not have to wind up arguing on appeal that Newton's life should be spared because skittish minorities had voluntarily removed themselves from the jury pool, thus making his conviction more likely.

When she was preparing for trial, Stender had learned that the jury commissioner questioned members of the jury panel about their views on capital punishment. She added that as an area of inquiry. She was very proud to have collaborated with the sociologists on nearly 300 questions designed to draw out biased answers to get a juror excused for cause. They included asking about the panelists' views of the Black Panther Party, "fair housing" and "Black Power." The list even included asking how they reacted to the best-selling "Kerner Report," attributing urban blight to white racism. Predictably, Jensen objected to most of the questions. Judge Friedman would not let Garry ask how the jurors voted on Proposition 14, which rejected the fair housing law, or how they perceived race issues generally. The judge restricted questioning to each juror's own state of mind or conduct on race issues. Yet the defense realized all they had to do was reword the questions to meet that concern. It was okay to ask "What feeling does 'Black Power' bring to mind?" instead of "What are your views on Black Power?" The reporters settled in for a long and tedious selection process.

Yet, after all the effort they had put into preparing the probing set of jury questions, Stender and the sociologists were the ones who quickly grew disappointed. Garry had no intention of reading the entire list of questions to each potential juror. As an old-fashioned trial lawyer, he trusted his gut and had no patience for their new scientific approach. In his experience, questioning potential jurors in voir dire was not just to expose disqualifying bias. His object was to obtain a feel for the jurors' personalities. Garry did not want to bore the friendly jurors to death or spend more time than he felt he needed to smoke out an unwanted juror. Dapperly dressed, the former tailor proceeded to woo middle-aged women jurors, and joked and tried to develop a rapport with many of the others. He could be warm and sympathetic one minute with a friendly juror and openly hostile and intimidating to the next panelist, hoping to force disqualifying responses. He put on quite a show, sometimes waving his glasses for emphasis of a particular point.

Quickly, Garry discovered that almost everyone had heard of the case and that some insisted they could put any preconceptions aside; that most of the white panelists had little interaction with blacks in their lives; had never heard of the "Kerner Report" commissioned by President Johnson; had heard of Black Power, but did not know what it meant; and had never heard the term white racism. Wellman only attended the trial sporadically, but could see how Garry ignored most of their hard work in his jury examination. Wellman also noticed that Garry's ego often got in the way. All too often, Garry seemed to be showing off, flaunting his own skills, sometimes at the expense of a candid response.

Jensen appeared artless compared to Garry, but effective in his sincerity. He was more rough-hewn in appearance and not a showman by nature. As for his suit, it looked like something he'd bought straight off the rack; its sleeves were too short for his long arms. His strategy also had little in common with Garry's. The lanky prosecutor steered clear of most political questions, focusing on the specifics of the case. His approach was far more earnest and respectful of all jurors and relatively devoid of emotion. To some observers, he appeared unfeeling, but sitting at the defense counsel table every day, Keating sized Jensen up as a top-notch trial lawyer who took his role as a champion of law and order very seriously. Jensen tried a little humor himself, but looked uncomfortable competing with Garry in that fashion; usually, when he tried to make a joke, the attempt fell flat.

It was clear what Jensen was concerned about. He mostly wanted to gauge the juror's level of commitment and then ferret out anyone with strong anti-establishment views or obvious dislike for the police and those unable to apply the death penalty. If he could not get them dismissed for cause, they would go on his own discretionary list for dismissal. Garry wanted to try to save from dismissal anyone with qualms about the death penalty and all members of minority groups. He generally favored white women over white men. Otherwise, he used his intuition to guide him in deciding whether to engage in tough questioning or lighten up.

The first person seated as a potential juror was a black man employed as an Alameda Naval Air Station aircraft cleaner. He denied ever hearing of the Panthers or Huey Newton and vowed that he could apply the death penalty, if need be. By lobbing easy questions to minorities, Garry took a calculated risk. He wanted to create the impression that every member of a minority group would understand his client's perspective better than whites, but he knew better. Even most blacks in the Bay Area had varied reactions to the Panthers, viewing them with "a mixture of fear, embarrassment and admiration."[2] Other minorities often shared the fear and not the admiration.

When conservative whites took the stand, Garry might probe them on any affiliation with the right-wing John Birch Society or their views on the Warren Court, or ask direct questions designed to elicit race bias. A registered Republican surprised Garry when he had a ready response for a question Garry had asked many others: whether he would relocate his family if black families moved into his neighborhood. The retired Air Force supply sergeant replied that he had moved his wife and six children *into* a mostly black neighborhood in Oakland's flatlands the year before. Garry still did not trust him.

Using a similar strategy, Lowell Jensen moved to reject potential jurors the defense favored. The Peace and Freedom Party member from Berkeley with a "Free Huey" bumper sticker on his car — who made pottery and got his news from *The Berkeley Barb* — did not stand a chance of remaining, despite his solemn promise to be impartial. Jensen also rejected the ex-wife of a Berkeley police inspector who, perhaps out of bitter experience, seemed too eager to point out that police were no better than anybody else.

When the prosecutor used a peremptory challenge to excuse the African-American aircraft cleaner, Garry stood up and pointedly noted his race for the record. Garry would repeat that announcement each time Jensen challenged a black person, though Garry eventually drew an admonition from Judge Friedman that both the prosecutor and defense had the same right to dismiss jurors of their choice. Everyone could see that Garry had used his own peremptory challenges primarily for jurors from the white suburbs, but Jensen never remarked on this. Jensen knew Garry was making a record for appeal in case no blacks made it onto the jury. Due to sheer numbers, some white jurors would make the panel no matter what — and Jensen was not one to play tit for tat.

Garry did get a rise out of Jensen when a supermarket clerk from unincorporated Castro Valley took the stand. In answering Jensen's questions, Wesley Kissinger had mentioned his past experience as a reserve deputy sheriff who still knew several high-ranking members of the police force. Given his turn, Garry immediately went on the attack: "We plan to show that the police instigated and plotted the incident that brought Huey Newton here." Jensen's heated objection forced Garry to rephrase the statement as a question: "Would you find it hard to believe that police would plot and instigate an incident against a defendant?" As reporters scribbled notes of the day's highlight, the clerk answered, "Yes".[3] But, try as he might, Garry could not get Kissinger disqualified by the judge for cause and had to use his thirteenth peremptory challenge.

Despite all his efforts to eliminate jurors predisposed to reject his theory of a police conspiracy to get Newton, Garry felt strongly that the entire panel was less than satisfactory because of a pro-prosecution tilt. He had been forced to use his very last peremptory challenge after prolonged questioning of a man from the city of Alameda, who belonged to a health club that barred Negro members. The assistant bank manager said he thought the club's "whites only" policy was wrong. He acknowledged that one of his handball partners at the gym was an Oakland police officer, but promised that relationship would not influence him when he evaluated the evidence.[4] Judge Friedman saw no reason not to take him at his word. Garry assumed Hitler himself would lie about his racist beliefs if asked about them in a polite and respectful manner, the way judges were wont to do with jurors — "Do you have an open mind? Can you be fair?"[5]

LIFE reporter Gilbert Moore empathized with Garry's unusual burden in defending a revolutionary: "[I]f Lowell Jensen had had only twenty and Charles Garry had had two hundred peremptory challenges at his disposal, it still would not have been enough."[6] If jurors seemed unsympathetic, Garry tried to force a reaction with questions such as, "If the charge were made in this courtroom that white racism was responsible for most of the problems of black people, would that make you mad?" Though Garry might not elicit a knee-jerk response from the juror he was questioning, other panelists would sometimes have an audible reaction. Hearing this question, three potential jurors in the back row hissed loudly; the defense team noted their identities and made sure that none of them were selected.[7] Some of the challenges had been easy, like the prospective juror who published a newspaper that criticized the Black Panthers, the one who was a close family friend of the District Attorney or the man who was a local auto mechanic for the FBI. Every successful challenge for cause meant one less peremptory challenge that had to be used. Garry viewed each of his twenty challenges as if Huey's life depended on it. It may well have.

Judge Friedman took his role in ensuring fairness seriously. In deference to the new Supreme Court ruling, he did not excuse jurors for cause who said they opposed the death penalty but under some circumstances might apply it. Stender realized that under this new ruling, Jensen had to use up more than one of his valuable peremptory challenges on jurors whom judges used to dismiss automatically. Also, by persuading the judge to permit juror questioning in far greater depth than usual, the defense team obtained far more information about the jurors than usual.

Garry had another reason for lengthy, repetitive questioning of some jurors he figured were hostile. He was using the opportunity of voir dire to put all of the white panelists on the defensive about any latent racism, and to alert all of the panelists to key, negative facts about Newton before Jensen raised them. Garry figured that if he mentioned the prosecutor's best arguments first, they might lose their punch. So he asked potential jurors if evidence of Huey Newton's felony conviction would affect their view of his credibility. Or whether they would assume that if Huey Newton testified, he would be motivated to lie because his life was on the line. He also asked whether they would be resentful of Newton and the Panthers for referring to police officers as "pigs." One prospective juror, June Reed, a married secretary with three children, took offense at the derogatory Panther term for policemen — the same reaction she had to hearing "white people call colored people niggers."[8] She was uncomfortable that anyone carried guns for self-protection. Reed admitted that she might harbor some residual racist attitudes; she conceded, for example, that she disapproved of inter-racial marriage. Another prospective juror, Jenevie Gibbons, was married to a fireman. Gibbons herself was a factory worker. She said she had no trouble with the term "pigs." "People used to call them 'the fuzz' and that didn't bother me either," she said.[9] Both made it onto the jury.

As was customary, though Garry had requested otherwise, all of the potential jurors were present as the rest of the panel was interviewed. Each could absorb what the others said. The judge dismissed one man who heard a frightening rumor that the Black Panthers would seek revenge on any person who convicted Huey Newton. The man said, quite frankly, that he assumed a juror who rendered a guilty verdict would have to plan to leave town. That was the kind of reaction that worried Jensen. Who would be courageous enough to serve? Others in the room probably felt as this man did. In contrast, a white Hawaiian refused to participate because he had an inter-racial son who was unfairly blamed for neighborhood pranks. He emphatically stated, "I have seen with my own eyes how colored people are treated in California . . . So I don't want no part of this."[10] Two blacks who were dismissed said they were friends of the Newton family or their kids went to school together. One pointed out that Huey had always been a nice kid.

The judge dismissed a woman who admitted that she moved out of her Oakland neighborhood after her other white neighbors left because too many black people had moved in. They had resettled in the white suburb of San Leandro. Another woman prompted Newton to laugh when she said she could not be sure of her impartiality because she sympathized with both the police and the Black Panthers. Jensen issued a peremptory challenge to excuse her from the jury. Most of those who were discharged displayed visible relief. Jury duty is a heavy responsibility in criminal cases, even without the extraordinary drama that this particular murder trial presented. That is why judges thank jurors profusely for their valuable service. Back then more people considered the summons an important obligation to fulfill than do now

— but not this particular case. Reporters could see how many of them jumped at the dismissal slip offered by the court clerk and scurried from the courtroom with a perceptible lilt in their steps.

Blauner did not always agree with Garry's approach. He shared his views frequently with Stender and Hoffmann. Sometimes he spoke to Garry during breaks to make suggestions for alternative wording of questions. He thought Garry asked too many directed questions that led to uninformative responses. Blauner favored open-ended questions that might reveal honest, prejudiced answers. He would have asked a juror, "Tell me what feeling Black Power brings to your mind" rather than "Black Power, does that create a revulsion in your mind?"[11] Anyone would be expected to say no to Garry's wording. But Garry was less interested in the actual answer to that question than in the body language with which the answer was delivered. Representing a militant client accused of murdering a policeman, Garry never expected to achieve a truly impartial jury. He merely hoped for one with a few favorably disposed jurors and others who were too intimidated to favor the prosecution.

Judge Friedman expressed interest in Blauner's view of the ideal white juror. Blauner told the court that even the least racist white person would acknowledge some degree of race prejudice. That person would know something about Afro-American culture, would interact with blacks daily and support the fight against discrimination. Newton had found his testimony "out of sight" and invited the highly flattered professor to meet him in his cell.[12] But voir dire was not designed to find and keep the people Blauner would have considered most receptive to Huey Newton's defense. Blauner would have kept the middle-aged woman who was the last to leave her neighborhood in Oakland for an all-white enclave in San Leandro. Her honesty had impressed him as he watched Garry get her excused for cause.

On Thursday of the first week, the defense filed a renewed motion to exclude Newton's prior conviction from the jury's consideration. They had just obtained the transcript from that assault trial where Newton had acted as his own attorney. They pointed out to Judge Friedman that Newton had told the court at the beginning of that proceeding, "If possible, I would like to have a legal advisor, but I would like to speak for myself."[13] They argued that the judge in that case had been too quick to deny Newton legal assistance.

On Friday at noon, the trial adjourned for the week. Judge Friedman said he wanted to use the afternoon to research the motion he had just been handed. By then, Judge Friedman had issued a new ruling for the media — from now on twenty-five seats would be reserved for the local dailies, the two wire services, television and radio, with only three seats guaranteed for all other reporters, first-come, first-served. Reporters who were guaranteed seats realized that the second week promised more repetitive questions along the same lines as what they had already witnessed. Despite Garry's feisty approach, they would be in for a fairly boring couple of weeks until jury selection was over. Seventeen jurors had been eliminated for cause out of the twenty-four questioned, leaving seven jurors tentatively chosen — subject to later rejection by either attorney using their remaining challenges.

The *Oakland Post* reported that the Alameda County Courthouse was not "where it was at" on Monday and Tuesday, July 22 and July 23.[14] But they meant nothing exciting was happening *inside* the courtroom. Kathleen Cleaver thought otherwise on Monday morning when it came to her cheerleading role *outside* the building. Using a bullhorn on Monday morning, she orchestrated the handful of Panthers and twenty or so children chanting and shouting in Swahili and English until her voice went hoarse. But the small crowd on Monday dispersed by noon and no one except Kathleen showed up on Tuesday, amid rumors of a planned rally elsewhere. Kathleen was all set to go to the rally to help keep the energy going, when her husband told her to go home instead to unpack boxes. They had just moved to new rental accommodations. Kathleen was furious, but ended up doing his bidding.

Reporters left to fight over the last three seats fumed at Judge Friedman's decision to skew access in favor of the mainstream press, leaving most representatives of underground papers and freelance journalists outside the locked courtroom. They desperately wanted to experience firsthand Newton's counsel putting America on trial. They filed a complaint asking the judge to reconsider. Although they did not convince him, it wound up not mattering. Far fewer reporters sought entrance the next week than the number of allocated press badges. Some seats remained empty as the jury selection process wore on. Yet as the trial progressed, *LIFE*'s Gilbert Moore was taking no chances; he rose as early as 2 a.m. on key days to make sure he was a daily fixture in the courthouse. He was obsessed with the absurd theatricality of the event. Moore realized the potential jurors felt otherwise: among the hundreds of mostly white, middle-class voters called to serve, "almost none of the 'talent' wanted to be in the show."[15]

All in all, through Jensen's methodical questioning and Garry's alternately hard-hitting and playful questioning, 41 people of the more than 150 panelists called were removed for cause. Of those, most admitted that they had some preconception of Newton's guilt, low regard for the Black Panthers or high regard for police that they could not set aside. Throughout Newton remained cheerful. To keep up the best impression he could with the jury, Newton relied on his brother Walter's taste in clothing. Newton looked as dapper with his brown suit accompanied by a mustard-colored turtleneck as he had on day one in sharkskin gray.

One juror, a Hayward technician named Strauss, said that for the last ten months he had assumed that Newton was guilty, but believed he could set that aside and be impartial as instructed by the judge. Jensen argued that the juror should be allowed to stay since "virtually every resident of the county" had some exposure to the sensational murder.[16] Judge Friedman then let Garry probe further. The particularly impressive interchange later made its way into legal textbooks. It began when Mr. Strauss indicated that "to a certain extent" he had already formed an opinion about the case from the pretrial publicity and the fact that the officer was dead. Under further questioning, he professed willingness to decide the case solely on the evidence presented. Garry's intuition told him otherwise. Ruling in Jensen's favor, the judge denied Garry's challenge for cause, but acceded to Garry's request to ask Mr. Strauss just a few more questions.

> **Q:** As you sit there right now do you believe that
> Huey Newton shot and killed . . . Officer Frey?
> **A:** I don't know whether he shot him or not. That I cannot say.

The judge then instructed Mr. Strauss on the presumption of innocence:

> **The Court:** So, therefore, as it stands right now, do you believe he is guilty before you hear any evidence?
> **A:** No.

Garry then questioned Mr. Strauss again, only to hear him repeat that he would apply the presumption of innocence and look solely to the evidence presented at trial. Garry remained unsatisfied that he was getting a straight answer, so he pushed it one step further:

> **Q:** As Huey Newton sits here next to me now, in your opinion, is he absolutely innocent?
> **A:** Yes.
> **Q:** But you don't believe it, do you?
> **A:** No.
> **The Court:** Challenge is allowed.[17]

On the issue of race prejudice, Garry still felt dissatisfied with most of those in the remaining pool whom he could not get to make disqualifying statements. Writing for *The Guardian* radical weekly newspaper, freelance reporter Karen Wald described his frustration: "Garry was able to eliminate 'for cause' only the most flagrant racists . . . But if a prospective juror knew the right answers, as quite a few did,"[18] he then had to consider how best to use the remainder of his twenty peremptory challenges. He eliminated those with obvious ties to law enforcement, racially exclusive clubs or conservative political causes. Then he followed his gut in using some of them on liberal whites who seemed to think too deeply about race issues, attributing some of the civil rights problems to black racists as well as white racists.

After two weeks of questioning, Stender and Blauner would have accepted the jurors then seated in the jury box, although the defense still had three of its original twenty peremptory challenges left. Wellman again noticed Garry's arrogance as he dismissed Stender's input and that of the sociologists. It made Wellman angry. But Garry trusted no one's instinct but his own and was still not satisfied. Moore described Garry's jury selection efforts as a man "stuck in the apple orchard with a taste only for oranges."[19]

Wald reassured readers of *The Guardian,* "While the lawyers play a legalistic chess game with jurors, the political nature of the trial is always there." Watching the voir dire every day, Wald observed how Garry "never let [the prosecutor and the judge] forget" the political context by repeated questioning of jurors on their familiarity with white racism, Black Power and the Black Panther Party.[20] In the entire three-week jury selection process, Garry had not objected to a single minority, reinforcing his argument that race and class affiliation were central to the case. In the meantime, the defense team noticed that Jensen had challenged every black working class panelist. Garry also used the time to remind the jury panel that reality was not like the popular *Perry Mason* television show. It was not Huey Newton's burden to prove who killed Officer Frey and have the true killer confess on the stand. Garry had continued to exhaust all of the remaining peremptories and to challenge other potential jurors for cause until he "finally accepted a jury with a few people on it I would not want to have lunch with let alone let them decide Huey's fate."[21] Garry later insisted that he would have eliminated "at least six of the jurors if I had had any peremptory challenges left."[22]

Jensen always kept a close eye on how many challenges both sides used in the all-important jury selection process; he breathed a sigh of relief when Garry exercised his last challenge. An invisible but undeniable cloud hung over the court proceedings like a pending thunderstorm. The polarizing pretrial publicity, the militant demonstrators outside and the extraordinary security protecting the building weighed heavily on the willingness of many citizens to do their civic duty. For over two weeks, Jensen had feared that they would not be able to seat twelve jurors. He dreaded having to repeat the grueling process in Oakland a few months later amid another set of intimidating protesters. Worse yet was the prospect of the lengthy murder trial having to be rescheduled somewhere else in the state with all the complications that entailed. Jensen knew one thing: "I didn't want to end up with a situation where we were unable to pick a jury . . . and we would have to go back and start it all over again." He blessed those local citizens

who completed the jury and hoped that they would remain committed
enough through the trial's end to reach a verdict on all the charges —
deadlock could itself force a retrial.

Jensen had a good feeling about the commitment of the jurors now
seated in the box. Friedman had removed a total of fourteen jurors for
cause on Jensen's objection because they stated they could not apply
the death penalty. Belva Davis was amazed at the jury's composition:
"There were so many things that we were not accustomed to seeing in
a trial where there is a black accused of a heinous crime that we did
not quite know how to report it." Of the twelve jurors who were finally
selected on Monday July 29, there were seven women and five men. At
the time, it did not fit most observers' image of a felony jury panel, let
alone one charged with considering the death penalty. Looking back,
jury selection expert Karen Jo Koonan of the National Jury Project
describes the diversity of that jury as "absolutely pioneering . . . it just
was unheard of."

Across the country, juries still looked much more like the "twelve
angry men" in the classic 1957 Henry Fonda movie. Originally both
women and minorities were barred from serving on juries. Under
British common law, women were categorically excluded from jury
service in all but a few specialized types of cases due to a "defect of
their sex." This practice continued in the colonies and the United
States, with each state mostly free to decide for itself what restrictions it
imposed on jury qualifications. The high court ruled in 1879 that states
could no longer exclude black men or other minority men from the
jury box after passage of the Fourteenth Amendment. But the Supreme
Court made it clear the states could still impose other restrictions,
such as requiring persons of good moral character and able to pass
IQ tests. The high court also gave its approval to keeping women off
juries altogether — which all states then did with varying justifications.
Suffragettes assumed that when they won their battle to get the vote,
jury service would follow as a matter of course. Not so. In California,
women got the right to vote in 1911 and still had to lobby another six
years for a state law allowing women to serve on juries. It turned out to
be a Pyrrhic victory — the state's judges treated the law as permissive,

not mandatory, and systematically excluded women from jury service for another quarter of a century.

Men in state legislatures used a number of arguments to defend the practice of excluding women from criminal juries or severely curtailing their eligibility for service. As summarized by an ACLU lawyer: "[Women's] primary obligation was to their families and children; they should be shielded from hearing the details of criminal cases, particularly those involving sex offenses; they would be too sympathetic to persons accused of crimes; and keeping male and female jurors together during long trials could be injurious to women."[23] This last argument was actually more specific — legislators in Southern states were livid at the hypothetical prospect of white women sitting next to black male jurors for any length of time even though as a practical matter prosecutors kicked almost all black jurors out of the box. Feminists and civil rights groups persisted and states started gradually and grudgingly added women to the jury pool — with a double standard.

In many places women had to preregister for service to opt in to jury panels, while men were automatically eligible to serve. Of course, few women signed up. When women did get called, misogynistic lawyers like Clarence Darrow routinely knocked them off the panel. Darrow believed the civic-minded feminists who navigated their way into the jury pool were too fastidious in applying the law and thus less susceptible to his emotional closing arguments. He practiced mostly in Chicago where — until the Supreme Court nixed the practice in 1941 — women could only serve on criminal juries if they were on a League of Women Voters list limited to those who completed a jury service course taught by the local prosecutor.

It also took a long time before judges began randomly selecting juries. Until the Supreme Court decreed otherwise, judges in California, like Webster Thayer in the Sacco and Vanzetti case in Massachusetts, often just pulled all-male juries in from private clubs or from blue ribbon panels. Even as of 1961 — seven years before the Newton trial — the nine male traditionalists on the Supreme Court reiterated that exempting most women from jury service was permissible because women were "still regarded as the center of home and family life." The court decreed that laws exempting most women from jury service were still valid despite the "emancipation of women from the restrictions and protections of bygone years, and their entry into many parts of community life formerly considered to be reserved to men."[24]

As a result, even by the late 1960s in many states women rarely served on juries.[25] In fact, not until 1975 did the still all-male United States Supreme Court hold that women constituted such a "distinctive group" from men that double standards keeping most women exempt from jury service violated the Sixth Amendment right to be tried by a jury of one's peers. The high court came to the belated realization that women on juries mattered because "community participation in the administration of criminal law . . . is . . . critical to public confidence in the fairness of the criminal justice system."[26] Both the defense team and the prosecutor in the Newton case had figured that out already.

As ground-breaking as the female majority was in this high-profile death penalty case, it was mind-boggling that four of the twelve jurors in a death penalty case were minorities. One, Harvey H. Kokka, seemed to flash a smile at almost every opportunity. He was a married Shell laboratory technician in his mid-thirties who generally disfavored the death penalty, but agreed he was able to apply it in an extreme case. A month earlier he would have been excused for cause. Two women had Spanish surnames, but Mary A. Gallegos was actually Portuguese by birth and had become an American citizen when her family moved to Oakland when she was a child. The department store bookkeeper took her husband's last name in 1967 when she married a Hispanic construction worker. She was sure she could apply the death penalty if it was called for, although with some reticence.

Linda M. Aguirre, a Latina, who worked as a junior executive secretary for a paper company in San Francisco had no reservations about applying the death penalty. A third minority juror was Joseph Quintana, a well-traveled Cuban immigrant machinist with two children, who admitted to having limited English skills, but felt he could understand the testimony. He might also have failed the stringent test for death-penalty qualification just a month earlier. This trio represented most of the non-black minorities in the entire set of prospective jurors called to the courtroom.

The last non-white on the jury was David Harper, a middle-class married black man with six children, who was the only one among twenty-two black voters called for service to make it onto the panel. The defense team assumed that Jensen would have excluded all blacks as his colleague had done the week before in Judge Phillips' courtroom, if Jensen had not been concerned about its legality. If given the choice, why would Jensen not just act like most other prosecutors to seat as many white law-and-order types as they could in order to ensure Newton's execution for the death of a policeman? Actually, Jensen had no such intention. Years before Judge Phillips made his mistrial ruling, the law already forbade intentional dismissal of jurors based on race. What had made headlines was that Judge Phillips found proof of prejudice when the vast majority of judges would have given the prosecutor the benefit of any doubt.

It had been Jensen's practice before the Newton trial to select jurors who appeared fair-minded regardless of race or gender. He just saw mostly white men in the jury pools. He flatly rejected the notion that "you could not have an African American who was a fair juror for a case like this. It's the same for an African American as it is for a white, so the question is will they be fair in terms of their handling of the case." Jensen also kept in mind the charges of racism Garry repeatedly made against this high profile prosecution: "My ultimate decision was that if it ended up that the jurors who were potential people to serve on the jury . . . included an African American juror, that would be of some value in terms of the overall case. . . . That was a part of my considerations."

Jensen had previously selected women for jury service as well as minorities, though in the past they were a much smaller percentage of the jury pool. The IQ test for jurors that was outlawed in April of 1968 for socioeconomic bias had screened out most minorities from poor neighborhoods. Until June 1968, the automatic exclusion in death penalty cases of service by anyone with doubts about capital punishment had forced dismissal of many other minorities and women. Yet, when faced for the very first time with a far more diverse death penalty pool than he had ever seen before, Jensen felt no compulsion to use all of his challenges despite the remarkably different demographics and the high stakes. In fact, Jensen was quite comfortable with women jurors and was glad that this high profile jury would include several minorities. The jury's diverse composition could only improve the chances for community buy-in to the verdict of murder that Jensen believed he could achieve. Unlike Garry, Jensen had often left some of his challenges unused. Yet, he flabbergasted the defense when he accepted a jury with seven women and a total of four minorities when both sides were keenly aware that the rest of the pool was Caucasian and mostly male. "I could have challenged some of the people who were already there who were not white men, on the notion that I would add to that pool. I did not see any reason to do that. . . . My assessment of the people who were there [was that they had] made a commitment to provide a fair trial, and that was what I was concerned with."

Leo Dorado later tried some very challenging cases as an Alameda County prosecutor and found Jensen's decisions in the jury selection for the Newton trial amazing. "He could have had more of a white male jury. He could have eliminated some of the women, some of the ethnics. He also could have eliminated the one black man. . . . The dynamics of a jury are very, very important. The fact that he decided not to exercise those peremptories and assure a jury that resembled more Alameda County, and even more Oakland, was an amazing decision on his part, showing incredible strength of character."

For Doron Weinberg, who attended Stanford Law School at the time, the seating of a diverse jury for the Newton trial was an eye-opener. Over his career in criminal defense, Weinberg would learn: "The single most important question about a trial is who's on your jury. The composition of a jury has more to do with the result than anything. More important than the judge's role, more important than the brilliance or the failure of the lawyer, more important than the audience is the question of who those twelve people are in the box."

The women were mostly middle-aged, three were married, and two — landlady Mrs. Eda Prelli and airline caterer Helen Hart — were widowed mothers. The two remaining males were Ronald L. Andrews, an over-forty married engineer with three grown children, and Thomas R. Hofmann, Jr., a young, single bank trust officer. Hofmann lived with his parents in Berkeley and said he knew very little about the Panthers. Andrews professed to be free from racism, at least as far as he knew. He looked to be the likely choice for jury foreman.

The selection of alternate jurors took a few days more. Now that the entire rest of the pool was white and mostly male, Garry was extremely careful with his questioning. In a long trial there is always a concern that a juror might at some point get sick or become otherwise unavailable. Then an alternate juror would take that person's place to prevent a mistrial. Garry did not want to risk having one or more of the twelve jurors replaced by someone who was pro-conviction. Jensen was also careful not to seat someone as an alternate who seemed unwilling to follow the law. Among those dismissed for cause the chief reason was again strong opposition to the death penalty. One woman from Berkeley announced to the courtroom her view that capital punishment was "legalized premeditated murder."[27]

The lawyers selected three men and one woman, Mary Anderson, a bank secretary from Oakland who was the married mother of two children. The men were twenty-six-year-old Berkeley surveyor, James H. Jackson; Richard L. Roberts, an Oakland aircraft maintenance technician; and Edgar A. White, a thirty-six-year-old salesman at a Berkeley camera shop. One of the alternates had been a student at Oakland City College. When the last one had been picked, Judge Friedman sent all of the jurors and alternates home until the following Monday morning. Despite seating a pioneering diverse jury, Garry immediately renewed his motion that the judge dismiss the entire panel since it did not consist of Newton's peers from the flatlands. He also made a motion for mistrial on the basis that Jensen excluded blacks as alternates. Not surprisingly, Judge Friedman denied both motions.

David Harper, the only black man seated on the jury, quickly became the subject of great speculation as to whom he might favor. He had handsome features, somewhat resembling an older, more heavy-set version of Huey Newton. Harper was a veteran of the Air Force and worked at the Bank of America as a lending officer where his wife worked as head of security. Impeccably dressed in a suit and tie, he made quite an impression. There was a reason no one in the courtroom had ever heard of a major bank hiring a black executive — he was the first in the nation. At night, he also taught college business courses. Harper wore his hair long enough to look like a modified statement — halfway between an Afro and the conservative, short cut one would expect at the time of a man in his line of work.

During voir dire, Harper admitted he had "reservations" about the death penalty but in a proper case could consider it.[28] He said he could decide the case solely on what was presented in the courtroom and believed he could be fair to both sides. He had heard of the Panthers and read about the shooting in the local papers, but had not discussed the case much with anyone. Harper explained that his colleagues largely steered clear of the subject, just as they had pointedly refrained from talking to him following Martin Luther King's assassination a few months earlier. When asked if he harbored any feelings against the Black Panthers, he said, "Not at all." He had never formed an opinion from media coverage that Huey Newton had killed Officer Frey.[29]

The defense team thought Jensen had made a mistake in keeping Harper on the jury. But the prosecutor was privy to the bank executive's recent service on three other jury panels, including an armed robbery prosecution and could tell he took this obligation very seriously. Garry and Stender began to notice that, on occasion upon entering the courtroom, Harper appeared to nod slightly as a greeting to Newton's minister, Father Neil. But when Harper passed Newton at the defense table, he invariably kept his face expressionless. Reporters gazed at him intently, and sometimes noticed Harper looking fleetingly back in their direction. He maintained an enigmatic expression as they searched for clues to the lone black juror's thinking.

Huey Newton Trial Judge Monroe Friedman.

240

Unprecedented security at the Oakland courthouse

Members of the underground press at 1968 Newton trial, who had to remove their buttons before entering the courtroom.

Prosecution witness Dell Ross, alleged kidnap victim of Huey Newton.

Emergency Room nurse Corrine Leonard testifying on August 13, 1968.

Prosecutor Jensen examining ballistics expert John Davison.

Bus Driver Henry Grier, chief eye witness for the prosecution of Huey Newton.

Police dispatcher Clarence Lord, first witness for the prosecution in People v. Newton, *playing the tape of Officer John Frey calling in that he was about to stop "a known Panther vehicle" early on the morning of October 28, 1967.*

Officer Herbert Cliff Heanes being cross-examined by Charles Garry in the July 1971 retrial. (Ritz did not sketch Heanes in 1968 when he wore his uniform while testifying.)

Charles Garry dramatically pointing to his client Huey Newton.

246

Huey Newton in his cell awaiting the verdict of his 1968 penalty trial.

13. ON TRIAL — NEWTON OR AMERICAN SOCIETY?

I'll be judge, I'll be jury, said cunning old Fury.
I'll try the whole cause and condemn you to death.
— LEWIS CARROLL

On his way into the courthouse during July and August, prosecutor Lowell Jensen often endured ironic shouts of "Power to the People" from the protesters gathered outside. As a career public servant, Jensen officially represented "the People" in *The People of the State of California v. Huey P. Newton.* Yet which people? Newton's defense team pointed to serious flaws in a governmental system that ostensibly derived its authority from the democratic process, but had historically excluded large segments of the population from meaningful participation.

Jensen strove to be absolutely dispassionate and by-the-book in seeking justice for the county in this murder case, as he acted in all other cases he handled. Yet he knew that the defense team's message of prosecutorial bias resonated with some local citizens. What was his view of "The People" on whose behalf he acted? To Jensen, it meant, "not only the police and the Panthers . . . everybody who lives there who expects that the criminal justice system will work." He understood that achieving justice required not only a fair-minded judge and prosecutor, but a dedicated jury. Jensen was pleased to see enough citizens brave the threatening circumstances to do that civic duty and "committed to

. . . doing it in a fair fashion because they represent, in its basic sense, the people or the community."

Jensen believed he had ample evidence to support the murder charge and reason to feel confident that none of the impaneled jurors were predisposed to be anti-establishment — he had weeded out the few who turned up in their jury pool. Jensen expected that his usual careful presentation, coupled with a reminder of the jury's role in pre-serving law and order, would win the Newton jury over just as that strat-egy had prevailed with so many other panels in his career.

Methodical by nature, Jensen put on as simple a case as possible: a policeman had been killed in the line of duty at the hands of a felon fearing imminent arrest for violating the terms of his probation. The shooting was intentional and necessitated the death penalty. Behind the scenes, law enforcement pressure on Jensen was intense. The Oakland Police Department expected a first-degree murder conviction to send an unqualified message that no one — particularly the head of a militant organization that vilified police as "pigs" — would get away with murdering a cop.

Governor Reagan had campaigned on his support for the death penalty and had already denied clemency to one cop-killer executed a few months after he was sworn into office. Governor Reagan had an even stronger interest in the Newton case from day one after his shock-ing personal introduction to the Panther Party in May of 1967. He had relished signing the Mulford Act as emergency legislation in June of 1967 precisely to reduce the chances of any officers getting killed in confrontations with the Panthers. Reagan wanted Newton to pay with his life for Officer John Frey's death, to serve as an example to other would-be revolutionaries. The governor believed wholeheartedly in the death penalty as a deterrent and viewed the Panthers as an even greater threat to democracy than the FSM activists he vehemently abhorred. Newton's conviction and execution would have huge symbolic value to Governor Reagan and other champions of law and order in this chaotic time. As Governor Reagan's Legal Affairs Secretary, Jensen's former superior Ed Meese was also personally interested in its outcome: he knew most of the players and acted as a liaison between the Governor's office and J. Edgar Hoover, who was also keeping a close eye on the potentially explosive situation in Oakland.

For his part, Garry would try his best to paint the prosecutor as a vengeful old Fury and his witnesses as biased and untruthful. He and Jensen both worked through weekends getting ready to do battle in court. As the first day of trial testimony approached, tensions ran high. Eldridge Cleaver, covering the trial for *Ramparts* magazine, had made news a week earlier by publicly warning that if Newton were found guilty of murder, the state could only execute him "over our dead bodies."[1] Earlier that month Cleaver had held a press conference in New York predicting the likelihood of open warfare in the streets of California if Huey Newton were sentenced to death. He expected the carnage to spread quickly across the country. David Hilliard agreed: "In a six-month period you had more than 150 rebellions or riots . . . across America. It was a very volatile time. We had chapters in at least 30 or 40 cities so we were pretty . . . fired up about the possibility of doing some things if Huey was given the electric chair. We said . . . 'Free Huey Newton or the sky is the limit.' You are not going to take this leader of ours and take his life without having a response from people in the street, especially the Black Panther Party."

Only the underground press saw fit to publish these threats. If any rioting happened, mainstream media expected a heavy police response as had occurred in April after Martin Luther King's assassination. COINTELPRO had so many wiretaps in place and informants among the Panthers that J. Edgar Hoover was confident the FBI would know ahead of time about any proposed concerted action by the Panthers. At this point, Hoover assumed nothing would happen until the trial ended. Cleaver would then have his probation yanked and go back to prison, Newton would get the gas chamber and Governor Reagan could handle any outbreak of violence from remaining Panthers by having state police back up local squadrons as the governor did in October of 1967 to put an end to protests at the Oakland Induction Center.

The mainstream media were not sure what to make of Cleaver's boasts, but came to the trial knowing the county sheriff had prepared the courthouse for a siege and the Panthers remained unintimidated.

The media had never seen a trial with stakes this high. Yet they could not see how Newton had any prayer of acquittal, given the circumstances of the shooting as they appeared from the grand jury report and the usual pool of voters from which the lawyers would pick a jury. Even so, based on Garry's reputation for never losing a death penalty case, reporters expected plenty of fireworks inside the courtroom.

Radical freelance reporters soon reiterated their complaints of favoritism in the allocation of seats. The mainstream press received up to three badges per agency, including a courtroom artist. Though there was a 9:30 a.m. cut-off for picking up reserved badges, it seemed that the reporters for local dailies could get in no matter when they arrived, while many reporters from underground papers skulked through the hallways, looking indignant as the testimony continued behind locked doors. It was easy to tell one group from the other. Representatives of major media were mostly clean-shaven men with short haircuts who wore suits and ties; the few women reporters or sketch artists wore their hair neatly styled and came to court in dresses or skirt suits, nylon stockings and heels. Representatives of the underground press basically looked like the activists they were — both men and women wore their hair longer and dressed more casually, with men favoring bell bottom jeans. Many wore "Free Huey" buttons that had to be removed to enter the courtroom. The men also tended to have moustaches or beards. (In 1969, the Broadway megahit *Hair* would capture the "us v. them" dividing line between the establishment and anti-war activists in one four-letter word.) Some members of the alternative press lobbied Garry to petition the court again to move the proceedings to a larger venue to accommodate all of the media, but Judge Friedman remained firm.

By Monday, August 5, Stender had worked hard to ensure that all eyes of the Movement were upon them. Among those carrying press passes in the packed courtroom was award-winning author Kay Boyle, blacklisted in the '50s and now a prominent anti-war activist. Boyle had sent Stender a draft of the article she was writing for *The Progressive* magazine on the jury selection phase of the trial and asked Stender to point out any glaring factual errors. Though she was already working long hours that left little time for her family, Stender had been eager to accommodate Boyle. Stender considered such assistance as essential to her job in this political trial as what she prepared for court.

Judge Friedman began the August 5 session with the jury still sequestered while he announced rulings from the bench that could have a significant effect on the course of the trial. He had previously decided not to exclude reference to Newton's 1964 conviction, rejecting the argument that it was obtained in violation of Newton's constitutional right to counsel.

In a last-ditch effort the prior Thursday afternoon, Stender had submitted a brief arguing that Newton's prior assault conviction should be reclassified as a misdemeanor instead of a felony. If so, the defense could achieve the same result they had sought in attempting to strike the felony conviction. The prosecution could not mention a misdemeanor to the jury. Newton had in fact only gone to county jail for six months, a typical misdemeanor sentence, not a year or more in state prison, as felony convictions permitted. But on Monday morning Judge Friedman rejected this latest argument. Regardless of the much shorter time he actually served in county jail, Newton was a convicted felon. If Newton took the stand, the prosecutor could use his status as an ex-felon to undermine his testimony.

Judge Friedman also announced that the lawyers for both sides were worried that various people associated with the trial might come to harm — Huey Newton himself, spectators, and witnesses called by the prosecution. The judge decided that tighter security was called for. Over the objection of the defense that searches would be a means to harass Newton's supporters, Judge Friedman declared he was now ordering that everyone but counsel and the jury — whether they were "black, white, brown or yellow" — be frisked for weapons daily before being permitted entry into the courtroom.[2] The order would take effect after lunch that same day. After this series of disheartening rulings against the defense, the bailiff sat the jurors in the jury box. The trial itself would finally begin, three weeks after the July 15 official start date and almost three months after the first trial date of May 10.

As prosecutor, Lowell Jensen went first because he had the burden of proof. In his much-awaited opening statement, Jensen informed the jury it was their duty to decide the facts for themselves from the courtroom reconstruction of key events alleged to have occurred. The veteran prosecutor gravely summarized the incriminating evidence he intended to present, and expressed his confidence that Newton would be found guilty. Although he limited himself to a brief account of the events of the early morning on October 28, 1967, the day of the shooting, he took pains to describe Newton ominously, as a man with a history of violence and known animosity toward the police.

Jensen told the jury that the fatal incident had happened very quickly after Officer Frey made a routine stop of Newton in a car with outstanding traffic violations. Marijuana found in two matchboxes in the car Newton drove provided a specific motive for the shooting — Newton feared being caught with contraband. Garry jumped up and objected that Jensen's remarks were highly prejudicial. Garry demanded a mistrial. He pointed out heatedly that Newton had not been charged with marijuana possession and asserted that Newton had no knowledge whatsoever about the contents of the matchboxes. The judge let Jensen continue, but instructed the jury that opening statements were not evidence in themselves. The jury needed to wait to determine what proof was offered at trial.

Jensen plowed ahead with confidence. He asserted that Newton knew he was still subject to parole restrictions for a prior felony when Office Frey stopped his car. Conviction for "knowing possession of marijuana" would have constituted an automatic parole violation, forcing Newton back to prison to serve the rest of his suspended 1964 felony sentence for assault. Jensen continued his chilling narrative. Shortly after Officer Heanes arrived, Newton decided on a bold surprise move, pulling a gun on Officer Frey, who grappled with him as it went off. Newton then wrested Frey's own gun from Frey, killing him with his own weapon and wounding Officer Heanes with that same weapon in the resulting exchange of gunfire.

The jury then heard how Jensen expected to prove that Newton and his passenger had escaped on foot with both his own and Officer Frey's weapons, commandeered a nearby car at gun point and were driven away. Only a short time later, wounded in the stomach, Newton would turn up for treatment at Kaiser Hospital, where he was arrested for murder. Jensen dramatically promised the jury that, in addition to the kidnap victim, he would produce an eyewitness to the shooting, a bus driver who would identify Newton as the killer. The media reacted with surprise as Jensen made this revelation. Newton and Garry immediately huddled together in whispered conversation, though they already knew about this bombshell. Before they had adjourned on Thursday, August 1 — the day jury selection was completed — Jensen had provided the defense team his list of thirty anticipated prosecution witnesses. That was when the defense finally learned the identity of Jensen's key surprise witness for the trial, an African-American municipal bus driver named Henry Grier. Grier was now safely sequestered in an unidentified location under police protection, which Jensen had arranged the day Grier's name first surfaced.

At the same time he disclosed Grier's identity, Jensen had provided the defense with a transcript of Grier's tape-recorded statement to the police. Grier's statement identified Newton as the civilian he saw with a police officer when driving his bus route early that morning. The statement said that Grier observed the civilian pull a gun from inside his jacket or coat, spin around, and struggle with the officer. The gun went off, hitting another officer, who fired his own gun. The civilian then fired several shots at the first officer, who fell forward. After summarizing Grier's expected testimony, Jensen concluded there was proof beyond a reasonable doubt that defendant Huey Newton was the civilian Grier saw shooting the fatal bullet into Officer Frey's back and was guilty of first degree murder. One local reporter expressed surprise that Jensen did not then ask for the death penalty, forgetting that the jury would only face that issue in a separate hearing if Newton were first found guilty of premeditated murder. From the extensive questions on capital punishment at voir dire the jury already knew that they might be asked to vote for Newton's execution.

Spectators knowledgeable in criminal trial procedure wondered whether Garry would respond immediately with his own opening statement or wait until Jensen completed his case-in-chief and give the defense opening statement at that time, probably two weeks down the road. But those who knew Garry well could harbor no doubt that he would ever seriously contemplate the option of waiting a fortnight to educate the jury on his view of a death penalty case.

Given his turn, the streetfighter stood up and jabbed back. The prosecutor had zeroed in on the morning of the shootout. Garry gave it the back of his hand. Spectators noted his confident demeanor as he claimed Newton was not guilty of any of the charged crimes. At times, he would take his glasses off and wave them in his hand for emphasis. Garry dwelt upon Huey Newton's life history, his decision to join the Black Liberation Movement and then form the Black Panther Party with Bobby Seale. Reporters observed Seale in the courtroom for the first time that day, seated among several other Panthers. Garry read the jury the Black Panther Party's 10-point platform and asserted that because of their stand against police brutality, the Panthers had been singled out for persecution. Jensen repeatedly objected to Garry's charges of police harassment, but Garry was allowed to continue. Garry told the jury that Officer Frey was a known racist with no justification for stopping Newton that October morning. Frey had done so only to abuse the Panther leader yet again. Frey then mistreated Newton and precipitated the shootout in which he died.

Garry reiterated the death threats Newton received from police officers while in the hospital, strung with obscenities such as "nigger" and "Black bastard." The veteran trial lawyer then emphatically summed up what he intended to show in defense of the murder and assault charges: Newton did not fire a gun at any time on that date. He did not kill Officer Frey. He did not shoot Officer Heanes, and he had no knowledge of any marijuana in the car. The jurors listened intently to both opening statements — the two lawyers had just laid out two starkly contrasting versions of the underlying incident for them to consider, and Huey Newton's life hung in the balance.

As one of the few blacks among the reporters present, Gilbert Moore was torn by conflicting reactions: Newton was too smart to have shot Officer Frey in cold blood when he knew the police watched his every move. But then Moore pictured the early morning scene with Newton facing an oppressive enemy spewing hatred. Where did all the bullets come from that resulted in one dead and two wounded participants? Given the context, Moore could not believe the Panther leader had not fired a shot. He thought to himself, "You can bullshit the judge and the jury and the press all you want to, but I'll bet a million dollars you shot John Frey." Raw emotion then bubbled to the surface as he pondered the huge flag behind the judge: "Do I really give a damn? I hope to God he did shoot him. Shoot him, Huey! Shoot him dead! Kill him for me, Huey, kill him for us. Revenge is ours, saith the Blacks."[3]

Stopping by occasionally to observe the trial as she pondered her own future career path, Penny Cooper found the Newton case fascinating. As far as she could tell, the case "captivated the entire nation." Watching Garry's brilliant voir dire of the jury had opened Penny Cooper's eyes. She thought he had probably won over the lone black juror on day one.

When court adjourned after opening statements, Rush Greenlee singled out Huey's graying father for a reluctant interview. Walter Newton made his very first appearance in the courtroom seated in the front row with his six other children, Huey's fiancée LaVerne Williams and Reverend Earl Neil. Huey's mother had been too upset to attend. Greenlee noted that Walter Newton greeted Greenlee's request with suspicion and disgust, claiming that newspapers always printed lies. When asked to express his view of the charges his son faced, Walter Newton exclaimed: "Now that's a damn fool question. Of course, I don't think he's guilty. When I raised my boys I never even let them get a near a gun, much less learn how to shoot one."[4]

The enormous problem facing Newton's lawyers was that two key prosecution witnesses were African-American men. Despite Garry's air of confidence, the defense team agonized over what they could do to attack Henry Grier's anticipated testimony. How in a trial that was predicated on racism did you refute a black, presumably neutral, eyewitness to the shooting? At least they had a three-day weekend to get a head start. Stender and Keating immediately prepared a subpoena for the bus driver's employment records at AC Transit and the company's daily log for the morning in question.

Stender obtained another lead from Garry's veteran expert witness

Dr. Diamond, who suggested that she check out a rumor that Grier's sons were involved in a bicycle-thief ring. If so, perhaps, some deal had been cut with the D.A. for leniency that would call into question Grier's motivation. There was so much ongoing leg work for the defense to do behind the scenes during the trial that the firm could not handle it all even with the help of volunteer experts. The defense team delegated some of the overwhelming workload to members of the Black Panthers, to private investigators, law students and other, largely unpaid, trial assistants.

Prosecutors always go first because they have to establish evidence of a crime. Late on the afternoon of August 5, Jensen started by asking Oakland police dispatcher Clarence Lord to play a dramatic tape-recording made less than half an hour before Officer Frey's death. It revealed Frey calling in over his police radio to another dispatcher. Jensen wanted the jury to identify with Officer Frey as the crime victim. The jurors and courtroom audience strained to hear Frey ask the dispatcher for a "rolling 36" auto license check and backup support for stopping a car on Seventh and Willow Street. First, Officer Frey identified himself as "1A." Then Frey said, "I'd like a quick rolling 36 on Adam Zebra Mary 489." A rolling 36 was a vehicle check on a license.

Less than a minute later the dispatcher responded, "1A we got some P.I.N. information coming out on that."

Frey said, "Check, it's a known Black Panther vehicle." The dispatcher's response was garbled. Frey said, "I'm going to stop it at Seventh and Willow; you might send a unit by."

The dispatcher responded, "OK. Check. Seventh and Willow."

Officer Clifford Heanes then entered the conversation, "2B is en route."

A few minutes later, the dispatcher's office identified the car's owner as a "man" named LaVerne Williams, on whom they had no further information. Frey told the dispatcher he thought the driver gave him something "phony."[5]

Jensen then had Lord fast forward to play the tape of Officer Heanes shouting the "940B" code for an officer needing immediate assistance. The dispatcher sent all units to Seventh and Willow. Next, the tape skipped to the radio transmission from the officers who arrived at the scene to find Officer Frey dying on the street and Officer Heanes wounded. When they arrived, Heanes was slumped inside his parked police car. On cross-examination, Garry replayed the entire tape and focused the jury's attention on Frey's identification of the car he stopped as a Black Panther vehicle. Garry pointed to time lags in the tape to indicate the stop was far from routine and that Frey was deliberately harassing Newton. The dispatcher conceded the Oakland Police kept a list of Black Panther vehicles in their radio room.[6]

Jensen next called pathologist Dr. George Loquvam, who had performed the autopsy on Officer Frey. Dr. Loquvam demonstrated on a model torso the path of five bullets that he concluded had struck Frey, one of which Dr. Loquvam found still in Frey's body and gave to the coroner's office to turn over to the police. Dr. Loquvam attested that Frey bled to death within five to ten minutes of the shooting. Garry realized that lengthy cross-examination of this witness would gain nothing and quickly guided Dr. Loquvam to admit that it was possible that there had only been four bullets that hit the officer, leaving those in attendance to wonder what difference that would make. Jensen then introduced into evidence an envelope containing the bullet removed from Frey's body.

Thelton Henderson followed the trial closely in the major Bay Area newspapers: "I think that they tended to make it look like Huey Newton was the bad guy. And it wasn't a neutral presentation, ultimately, I think anyone reading it, reading the papers . . . then going on to sit on a jury, would have had a tough time going in, thinking that Huey didn't do what he was charged with." Henderson would have enjoyed seeing part of the trial, but "the word was that it was impossible to get into the trial, so I never made an attempt to go. I had some friends who went to see the trial, and they thought it was a very exciting thing. . . . The 'Free Huey' movement was . . . big in the black community and among the crowd that I ran with. . . . And one of the raging debates of the day was, 'Was Huey getting a fair trial? Did he shoot the cop or was he being . . . picked on by the police?' It was a raging discussion back then."

John Burris was among black college students deeply interested in this trial's outcome: "The question did he shoot the officer in self-defense? . . . I kind of wondered what the facts were. I had to believe that Huey Newton would not just try to kill a cop without having a basis to do it. But he did have a right to self-defense. . . . At the time I was sympathetic to what was happening to the Panthers, as well as what was happening to Huey. So to me, this was a major, major event. . . . The cop himself could have created the environment that caused this to happen." Yet, Burris assumed a black revolutionary like Newton would surely be convicted of murder. "I didn't have a view that a black person could get a fair trial in Oakland. . . . So if you pushed it out even further [to consider the issue of whether or not a black revolutionary like Huey Newton could get a fair trial in Oakland], then my argument would be, no! Hell, no!"

On Tuesday morning, August 6, Jensen called Officer Gilbert De Hoyos to the witness stand, the first officer to respond to Heanes' call for assistance after the shooting. The Oakland policeman described how he had just returned from the jail where he had transported a drunk arrested earlier that morning by Officer Frey when De Hoyos' police radio announced a "940B" emergency call for help at Seventh and Willow. Already back cruising the neighborhood on Eighth, he came upon the scene of the shooting in less than thirty seconds. There, he spied the three parked cars, hit his brakes and rushed to the side of Officer Frey lying in the street, still alive, pleading for help. De Hoyos covered him with a blanket. De Hoyos saw another officer, Thomas Fitzmaurice, arrive behind him. Fitzmaurice heard moans coming from the first police car and went to the aid of Officer Heanes, collapsed in its front seat.

The audience stirred in anticipation as Jensen called Officer Heanes as his next witness. He came dressed in his uniform. But before Heanes testified, the jury was temporarily excused while Judge Friedman listened to arguments over whether the fact that Heanes suffered acute depression following the shooting would be fair game for Garry to pursue on cross-examination. Garry argued that hospital records of Heanes' emotional state following the shooting could shed light on his mental state prior to the shooting. Judge Friedman denied Garry that latitude, as every other judge on that bench would no doubt have done. The jury returned and Heanes testified that he arrived as backup for Officer Frey's traffic stop and was told by Frey that the driver identified himself as LaVerne Williams.

Heanes then said he walked to the Volkswagen, and the driver himself told Heanes that he was Huey Newton. Newton was, in fact, well known to many cops on that beat. Heanes continued his testimony, explaining that Officer Frey then joined Heanes by the driver's side of Newton's car. The two officers asked Newton to get out of the car where Frey planned to arrest him for falsely identifying himself to a police officer and failing to carry his license. Heanes added that they both suspected Newton "might have something in the car he didn't want us to see."[7]

Heanes recalled that Newton had not appeared belligerent. Newton emerged from the Volkswagen and walked "rather briskly," followed by Officer Frey, back to the second of the two parked police cars. But when they reached the rear of Officer Heanes' car, Heanes told the jury that Newton "turned around and started shooting." Heanes identified Newton in court as "the gentleman in the gray coat," pointing to the defense table. When Garry objected, Judge Friedman asked Officer Heanes to step down from the stand and touch the man he saw that day. Jensen had never seen defense counsel use such an intimidating tactic before. Fearful as he was, Heanes dramatically walked over and placed his hand on Huey Newton's shoulder as Newton remained motionless.[8]

On cross-examination at the end of the day on Tuesday, Garry startled Heanes by his first question: "Did you shoot and kill Officer Frey?"

Heanes froze in shock, suggesting that he did not know the answer. He then said, "No, sir, I did not." He recalled only firing one shot and didn't see anybody fall.

Garry continued, "There were two shots expended, were there not, sir?"

Heanes replied, "I have been told this, yes."

Garry then asked him, "What happened to the other shot?"

Heanes answered, "I have no idea, sir." He then admitted he never saw a gun in Newton's hand, but had heard gunfire from Newton's direction.[9]

On Wednesday morning August 7, testimony was delayed as Garry requested that the judge reconsider the scope of cross-examination.

This time, Judge Friedman relented and decided to allow questioning of Heanes regarding his depressed emotional state following the shootout. Heanes retook the stand. On further cross-examination, he testified that during the incident, out of the corner of his eye, he spotted the former passenger in Newton's car, standing on the curb. Stender quickly scribbled a note for Garry, pointing out that there were no street lights on then and a nearby fence was so close to the Volkswagen that Officer Heanes should not have been able to see the passenger standing there.

Responding to further questions from Garry, Officer Heanes described how he turned and aimed his gun at the man on the curb, who raised his arms in surrender and declared that he was not armed. Heanes described to the jury that he shifted his glance from the surrendering passenger to see Officer Frey and Huey Newton wrestling with each other on the trunk of Heanes' police car. After being shot in the right arm, Heanes switched his gun to his left hand, firing one shot at Newton's mid-section. Both Frey and Newton were still standing after he fired. Heanes was later told that the gun found in his hand at the scene had fired two cartridges.

Garry had earlier obtained from the prosecutor a pile of clothing; Heanes said the items appeared to be what Newton wore that morning. Garry made sure the courtroom saw the ripped shirt, its front covered with an enormous bloodstain. Garry also showed the witness a blood-stained law-book. Heanes could not recall that Newton had the book under his arm when he ordered him out of the car for questioning. Garry then stunned everyone present by asking Heanes and Newton to reenact where they had stood in relation to each other and Officer Frey at the scene of the shooting. Garry portrayed Officer Frey. Reporters could not believe their ears as Garry's questions to Heanes suggested yet another surprise person at the shooting, a gentleman about five feet tall. Heanes had not seen such a person. He concluded his testimony by revealing that he now constantly feared attack by the Black Panthers. Though he had never received any death threats, since the shooting, even in the hospital, he slept with a gun under his pillow.

The cross-examination of Heanes had been remarkable in its

boldness and its ability to diminish the persuasiveness of a star prosecution witness. Garry had masterfully begun to create doubt that Huey Newton had shot Officer Frey. Was there another man on the scene that the police had ignored in their zeal to "get" Huey Newton? Had Heanes, in the confusion, killed Frey by mistake?

Heanes' testimony was followed by that of Officer Fitzmaurice, who had arrived at the scene shortly after De Hoyos. Fitzmaurice testified that he had found Heanes sprawled on the front seat of the car, with his head down, the gun still in his hand. Fitzmaurice asked him if he was hurt and by whom. Heanes weakly responded, "My leg, my leg . . . Huey Newton did it."[10] Just before he fainted, Heanes added that he had shot back at Newton, but did not know if he had hit him. Fitzmaurice took Heanes' gun, put it in his own belt and used his police radio to call in Heanes' description of Newton as the perpetrator. An ambulance had already been summoned; they now needed two, which were quickly demanded by the beat patrol supervisor, Sergeant Ream. Ream had just emerged from another police car, after rounding the corner at full speed with siren blaring and red light flashing — announcing to the world a "Code 3" situation.

At 2:30 on Wednesday afternoon the drama heightened as Jensen called his surprise witness, forty-year-old AC Transit bus driver Henry Grier. The six-foot-one, two-hundred-pound Navy veteran had closely cropped hair and a trim moustache. Calm and straightforward, Grier testified that he had started at the transit company two years before the incident. Early on the morning of October 28, 1967, he drove his No. 82 express bus on his accustomed route between Hayward and Oakland and arrived at the stop at Seventh and Willow about 5 a.m. Though the early morning was overcast, he testified that he had a clear view of two policemen and a male civilian in a light shirt and dark coat. One of the policemen was facing him, apparently tugging the man under the arm as they walked toward the rear of a parked police car with its light on about thirty feet away. The other police officer followed "about ten paces behind."[11]

As had occurred with Officer Heanes, Grier's examination was interrupted to have him get up from the stand and place his hand on the shoulder of the man whom he saw in the shootout with the policeman the morning of the crime. Grier then rose from the witness stand, walked over to the defense table and touched Newton's shoulder. Newton remained expressionless. Before a rapt courtroom, Grier returned to the stand and answered further questions from Jensen. The bus driver said the scene was illuminated by the headlights of his bus. Grier saw the civilian whirl and pull a gun from inside his shirt while the officer grabbed the civilian's arm. The gun fired and another policeman, several yards away, fell. Grier radioed his dispatcher for help and saw the civilian crouched over the first officer, firing "at least three or four shots" into his back. The man then fled across Seventh Street.[12]

As Garry rose to cross-examine Grier, he planned to be thorough and aggressive. In part, he wanted to stall for time so that Stender and Keating would have time to rifle through all available papers, looking for anything contradictory that could impeach the credibility of Jensen's star witness. If Garry proceeded slowly enough, they could have the evening to search for more ammunition to paint Grier as a liar. After court closed for the day, Stender obtained the daily transcript and spent hours on a detailed comparison of Grier's statement to the police an hour-and-a-half after the shooting to his direct testimony. She highlighted discrepancies for Garry to use in cross-examination and headed her outline: "GUTTING OF HENRY GRIER."

On Thursday morning, Garry again started the day with motions before the judge, outside the jury's presence. He asked the judge to strike Grier's testimony and for a mistrial on the grounds that the defense did not have access to Grier before he testified. Lowell Jensen pointed out that he had offered to allow Grier to be interviewed in the District Attorney's office, which Garry had rejected as inadequate. Garry made a second motion for mistrial on different grounds, arguing that the unusually heavy security around the courthouse could not help but prejudice the jury against his client. Both motions were denied.

When the jury was brought in and Garry resumed his cross-examination of Grier, he noted that Grier originally had only tentatively identified Newton's photo for the police as resembling the civilian he saw. In court he was positive. Using Stender's comparison chart of Grier's inconsistent statements, Garry pointed out that Grier had also told the police the man he saw was a light-complexioned pygmy, no more than five feet tall and about 125 pounds. In the statement, Grier said he first saw the incident from thirty to forty yards away. In court, Grier said he saw it first from just fifteen to twenty feet.

In his original statement, Grier said the civilian wore a light tan jacket, dark shirt and dark hat. Now he was unsure about any hat. Grier had also changed his mind on the stand to say the jacket he saw on the civilian was dark, not light, and that the civilian reached into his shirt for the gun, not the jacket as he had first told the police. Grier's description now matched the bloody shirt and jacket in the pile of clothing Officer Heanes had earlier identified. Garry assumed that Police Inspector McConnell had influenced Grier's changed description of the civilian.[13] When on the stand, Grier further denied that he had seen the gunman run off through the nearby post office construction site, as he had originally told the police.

Garry dramatically asked to have Grier step down from the stand to reenact the position of the gunman he saw. This time, Garry asked a surprised Alex Hoffmann to play the fatally wounded Officer Frey, summoning Hoffmann from his seat in the front row of spectators without any prior warning. The diminutive Hoffmann was much smaller than Frey, a heavy-built man about the same height and weight as Grier. Instead of landing on his back as Grier had told the police, Grier now demonstrated the officer falling on his stomach. In an aggravated tone, Garry inquired if Grier knew what an Uncle Tom was. Jensen rose with a quick objection, but Garry had finally succeeded in rattling the bus driver's composure. How could Grier be sure the five-foot-ten-inch, 155-pound defendant was the same man he saw wrestling with the officer? At this point, to some observers, Grier seemed overconfident and a bit too self-righteous.

Grier was dismissed. He went home exhausted from the experience and lay down on his couch. When he resumed his route, his superiors at AC Transit authorized him to carry a weapon for self-protection, the only driver so authorized in the entire system. Grier believed he was an easy target if the Panthers wanted revenge. When Grier had

first cooperated with the police in describing the civilian gunman he
happened upon on his route, the Hayward resident had no idea that
the man his testimony might send to the gas chamber was a leader of
Oakland's Black Panther Party. Now Grier had to go back to driving
a municipal bus each day under the cloud of being labeled an Uncle
Tom. No serious threats emerged.

Meanwhile, back in court, Lowell Jensen called Sergeant Ream to
the stand to attest to the evidence he found at the site of the shooting, including the bloodstained uniforms of the two officers, Frey's gun
holster and both officers' bullet pouches. On cross-examination, Ream
revealed that the officers in his command had seen pictures of Black
Panther Party members and had been briefed on the Panthers after
their armed appearance at the State Assembly chamber in May of 1967.
Ream denied that orders had been given to pull over Panther-owned
vehicles on sight or that his office singled out the Panthers for persecution. Rather, the Panthers were only one of several organizations that
the police considered possibly armed and dangerous.

On Thursday afternoon Jensen followed Sergeant Ream by calling
a police technician who detailed other evidence found at the site: two
fired 9-mm shells; a brown leather button and a small black button that
may have come from Newton's clothing; a police citation book on the
front fender of Frey's car with a partly written ticket; and, near the pool
of blood surrounding Officer Frey, a blood-stained California criminal
law book with Newton's name inscribed in it. Garry stipulated that the
book belonged to his client.

Because used 9-mm shells were found at the site and similar live
bullets were found on the floor of the Volkswagen, the police concluded that Newton had a 9-mm Luger concealed in his shirt or jacket
when he was arrested by Frey and discarded the weapon after he and
his passenger fled the scene. They had questioned Bobby Seale about
the 9-mm pistol they had previously seen him with, hoping to get Seale
to confess he had supplied the presumed murder weapon to Newton,
but got nowhere.

Proof of a concealed gun on his person would automatically make
Newton guilty of felony murder either in the first or second degree,

resulting in a long prison sentence or death. For Charles Garry, it was critical to sow doubt that Newton was packing a weapon when he was stopped. Garry focused on the 9-mm shells. Though a Luger was not a standard-issue hand gun that Officer Frey would have normally carried, the police witness could not say whether Frey might have carried more than one gun or bought his own non-standard ammunition, such as the 9-mm bullets.

Friday, August 9, was a much-needed break from the court proceedings. The jurors got to go back to their regular jobs for the day with a warning not to discuss the case. Judge Friedman adjourned the court until Monday. By Saturday, August 10, the defense team had used the prosecutor's witness list to locate a passenger on the bus, Tommy Miller. Garry dispatched Alex Hoffmann to interview him and made a key discovery — Miller disputed the driver's vantage point and ability to see what transpired on the early morning of October 28. On Monday August 12, Jensen called his second star eye-witness, the alleged kidnap victim, Dell Ross. Here was the man Jensen told the jury had been sitting in his parked convertible near the corner of Seventh and Willow when Newton and his companion leaped in and ordered him at gunpoint to drive them away.

The media representatives' antennae perked up again. They were well aware of Ross's devastating grand jury testimony identifying Newton as the shooter and assumed Ross would clinch the prosecutor's case. Ross, in his mid-thirties, came to court colorfully dressed in dark pants, a red sweater and an azure sports jacket. His eyes were hidden behind dark sun glasses. When Jensen asked Ross his first question, "Where were you on the morning of October 28, 1967?" Ross shocked the judge, onlookers and Jensen by refusing to testify on Fifth Amendment grounds of potential self-incrimination.[14]

Ross, a migrant laborer with a low IQ, had somehow developed a sophisticated new strategy of non-cooperation sometime after appearing before the grand jury. He had been accompanied in court that morning by his own counsel, Doug Hill, a radical Berkeley lawyer in partnership with Peter Franck, a close friend of Stender's from the Lawyers Guild. Hill then sat down unannounced at Garry's counsel table. When Hill rose to address the court, Judge Friedman, surprised by Hill's presence, harshly informed Hill that he had no authority to speak since he was not an attorney representing any party in the case. Actually, the judge was wrong; however rarely it comes up, a witness is entitled to have the services of his own counsel.

Disconcerted, the judge then temporarily halted the proceedings, sequestered the jury and heard arguments from the lawyers on the novel issue. Jensen was uncharacteristically irate. He could not fathom how a kidnap victim could claim he would expose himself to prosecution if he testified. Hill argued that Ross might be subject to prosecution for being an accessory after-the-fact to murder. Jensen suggested he could resolve the issue by offering Ross immunity from prosecution. The judge took the issue under submission and dismissed proceedings for the day before noon as news representatives ran from the courtroom to report the stunning trial development.

On Tuesday morning, August 13, Judge Friedman granted Ross immunity from prosecution, and Ross retook the stand before the jury. He again refused to give any details of the morning in question on Fifth Amendment grounds. With growing exasperation, Judge Friedman explained to Ross that he no longer faced any possible criminal jeopardy for his testimony because immunity had been granted. What Ross now risked was a citation for contempt of court. While he could not go to jail for any crime that his testimony revealed, Ross could be sent to jail for refusing to testify. Hill objected that his client would be entitled to a separate hearing on ten days' notice, but the judge had his dander up. In his entire career, Judge Friedman had never sent anyone to jail for contempt, but he had no problem making Ross his first. Ross said, "Send me to jail then."[15]

Jensen appeared to have another way out of the impasse. He asked Ross if he remembered the events of the October morning of the shooting. Ross said that he could not remember. Jensen showed Ross the grand jury transcript and asked him to read it. Ross replied, "I can't read." Jensen then started reading aloud Ross's damaging grand jury testimony as a means of attempting to refresh Ross's recollection. The prosecutor started with Ross's earlier testimony that he was sitting in his black and white Ford convertible at the intersection of Seventh and Willow with a friend around 5 a.m. When they heard gunshots, his buddy fled, leaving the car door wide open. According to Ross's prior testimony, two men had then jumped into the car. The one in the back carried a gun and threatened to kill him if Ross did not do as he was told. The backseat passenger then said, "I just shot two dudes. I'm shot." Jensen read to the jury how Ross had earlier identified a police photograph of Newton as that person.[16]

Garry repeatedly objected that this reading was improper because defense counsel had been precluded from participating in the grand jury proceeding and had no means of cross-examining Ross at the time. These were valid points, but Judge Friedman, like Jensen, assumed that Ross would have his memory refreshed by this reading and could then be cross-examined by Garry on all of these prior statements. It would have been far wiser for the judge to have sequestered the jury after Ross said he could not read. Jensen could have attempted to refresh Ross's memory by reciting the challenged testimony to Ross outside of the jury's presence. Then, if Ross still professed no memory of the events, the jury would not have heard inadmissible grand jury testimony. But Judge Friedman overruled Garry's objections, allowing the jury to hear Jensen read Ross's entire damning grand jury testimony.

On the stand, Ross claimed that he still could not recall any of the events of that morning. Garry asked that the jury be instructed to ignore the grand jury testimony and moved for a mistrial on the ground that the jury was prejudiced by hearing Ross's prior statements. Judge Friedman denied the motions. Despite having been sandbagged by Ross's sudden lack of cooperation, it looked to the press like Jensen had won a key battle. The prosecutor had backed Ross into a corner, the *Oakland Post* reported, "like a rat in a trap."[17]

When it was time for cross-examination of Ross, Garry rose and asked Ross if he recalled being in Garry's law office in San Francisco in late July. Ross also professed to having no memory of that very recent interview. Garry then announced to a flabbergasted courtroom that he had tape-recorded Ross at his office on the evening of July 28. He obtained the judge's permission to play the tape to refresh Ross's recollection, as Jensen had just been permitted to do with Ross's grand jury testimony. Garry also produced a written transcript of the recently taped interview for the jury.

The jury, press and spectators listened intently and heard a man's voice on the tape, which Garry identified as Ross. The man explained that he had been a witness before the grand jury and had also given a statement to the police and that both were "not true." Ross stared at the ceiling while the recording played. The voice on the tape said he feared the police and had gone along with suggested testimony implicating Newton because the police had a warrant outstanding against him for a parking violation. He specifically recanted seeing Newton holding a gun and that Newton had spoken at all on the morning of the shooting. "He was kinda out" in the back seat of his car. Garry could also be heard on the tape advising Ross that when he came to court he would be entitled to be represented by his own attorney.[18]

When asked about these taped statements on the stand, Ross repeated, "I don't know nothing." He claimed that he could not recognize his own voice on the tape, or that of Charles Garry. Jensen, convinced that Garry had tampered with the witness, could barely contain his fury. When Garry concluded his cross-examination, Jensen questioned Ross on redirect. How had he gotten to Garry's office? Ross responded that he did not even know where Garry's office was. Jensen pointed to Doug Hill and asked if he was Ross's attorney. Ross identified Hill as his lawyer, but when Jensen asked whether Ross obtained Hill as his lawyer before or after he visited Garry's office, Ross replied, "I just can't remember." When asked to identify his signature on the police statement, Ross said: "I see some writing here, but I don't know what it is." Stymied, Jensen excused Ross as his witness.[19]

The next day, Wednesday, August 14, Jensen shifted gears and produced Oakland Police Crime Laboratory Director John Davis, a ballistics expert. Davis was a highly respected scientist whom Jensen knew well from using him as an expert in prior cases. Jensen expected Davis to be one of the most important witnesses in his case against Newton. The jury paid rapt attention as Davis testified matter-of-factly that unburnt gunpowder deposits on Frey's clothing revealed that he had been shot in the back from a distance between six inches and one-and-a-half feet.

Illustrating his testimony with color slides, the soft-spoken expert explained to the jury that the slug removed from Officer Frey's body appeared to come from the same gun as the bullet that wounded Heanes. It was his opinion, however, that neither one of the slugs could have been fired from Heanes' gun, the only one recovered at the site of the shooting. The ball powder around Frey's wounds indicated that the fatal wounds most likely came from Officer Frey's gun, matching live bullets remaining in his holster. So much for Garry's theory that Heanes might have accidentally shot Frey.

Davis identified two buttons found near Frey's body as similar to those on Newton's jacket. On the other hand, he admitted on cross-examination that his office had not run any tests on Newton's hands to determine whether he had recently fired a gun. The criminologist explained that his office had not subjected Newton to tests it had previously conducted in other cases because the test results would likely have been inconclusive. Jensen also put on the stand Officer Robert Fredericks, the police officer who arrested Newton at Kaiser Hospital.

After Jensen elicited a matter-of-fact account from Fredericks on direct examination, Garry jumped up and angrily accused Fredericks of manacling the wounded Newton to the gurney "because you hated him and wanted to see him die." Fredericks responded that an officer had the right to protect himself if he felt his life was in danger, to which Garry countered that Fredericks had been armed. "So was Officer Frey" was the icy reply.[20]

Next came Dr. Finch, the emergency room doctor whose life has since been threatened. Dr. Finch admitted having told Newton to "shut up" as he was hysterically spewing invective at the police from the hospital gurney. Dr. Finch explained that he was trying to shock Newton into silence. Garry asked him to identify Newton's scars, and Newton stood up, lifting his shirt and turning to allow the jury to see both the entrance and exit wounds. The hole in his abdomen and in his back dramatically underscored to the jury Garry's focus on Newton as a victim. Nurse Corinne Leonard, the person in charge of the hospital emergency room when Newton arrived, was next on the stand. She made a very poor impression with her bleach-blonde hair, excessive make-up and brand-new, spiked heels. Garry treated her with hostility as he questioned her delayed treatment of a gunshot victim while they had argued over whether he was a patient of the medical plan. Visibly upset by his questions, she snapped that Newton's wound had appeared slight with no hemorrhaging and that he had called her a white bitch. She said, "I'm not there to have people swear at me and call me names."[21]

Jensen objected that Garry was yelling at the witness, but Judge Friedman announced, "Counsel can ask questions in any tone of voice he wishes."[22] On August 15, Garry made one more effort to keep Newton's felony conviction from the jury, but committed one of his famous Garryisms by telling the court that the conviction "far outweighs the prejudicial harm it can do." Garry had meant the opposite — that the jury should not be told about Newton's prior conviction because of the prejudicial harm to his client. Jensen called the mangled phraseology a Freudian slip. Garry's motion was denied.[23] By the end of the day that marked exactly one month into the trial, Jensen completed his case. His last two witnesses were brief, but powerful in impact. Huey's probation officer set off loud whispers among the spectators when he said the probation officially ended three years from October 29, 1964, on October 28, 1967, the day of the shooting, not the day before as the defense contended. On cross-examination of the probation officer, Garry had gotten him to admit he didn't know what date he had told Newton his probation ended.

Then a chemist for the Police Department identified the contents of the two matchboxes found in the car as marijuana and also attested to having found tiny amounts of marijuana in the right front pocket of Newton's pants. In total, Jensen had called 26 of the 30 witnesses he had originally listed. When Jensen announced in a flat tone that "the People rest," he seemed deflated. The defense team read Jensen's body language — so different from the confidence he exuded on the first day of trial — as recognition his presentation had fallen well short of its goal.[24] Garry then jumped up and asked the court for acquittal on all three pending charges. The routine motion asked the court to evaluate the prosecutor's case. If Jensen had not put on enough evidence on a particular charge, no defense to that charge would be necessary. The jury would be directed accordingly. Garry had no serious expectation that the judge would grant the motion in its entirety. But Jensen knew the motion had merit with respect to the kidnapping charge. He told the judge he would not object to dismissal of that charge since the sole witness, Dell Ross, refused to testify and denied remembering anything. Judge Friedman indicated he would hear argument and rule on the motions for acquittal on all three charges before Garry was scheduled to begin his defense on Monday morning.

Garry was in a good mood when he reached the elevator at the same time as Jensen. Knowing he would be overheard by others in the hall, he playfully told Jensen, "I'm going to call you for my first witness."

Jensen replied, "Can I take the Fifth?"

Garry said, "You better get yourself a lawyer."

Jensen retorted, "I'll be up to your office Sunday night to give you a statement."

At the press conference that followed, a reporter asked Garry who his first witness would be, and he answered "Lowell Jensen."[25] Though he was obviously being facetious, the implication was clear: if Jensen were put under oath, Garry could elicit facts that would destroy the prosecutor's whole case.

272

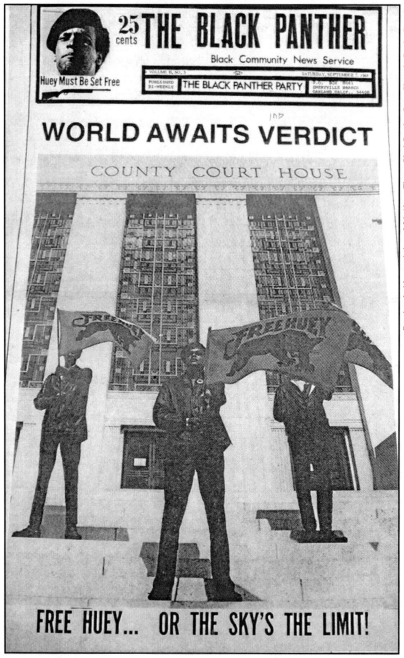

Front page of the Black Panther newspaper on Saturday, September 7, 1968, the third day of jury deliberations in the death penalty trial of their leader Huey P. Newton.

14. THE BURDEN SHIFTS

Even though the judge will tell the jury, the state has to prove its case beyond a reasonable doubt, when a defendant takes the stand, often the question becomes — and certainly in a case like this . . . the jurors would just assess a defendant . . . do I believe him? Do I not believe him?
— BARRY SCHECK

Once Jensen rested his case on Thursday, August 15, the defense team faced a daunting list of tasks. They needed almost every moment of the three-day recess before they returned to court. Stender had completed 125 hours of work on the case in the last two weeks, and yet she eagerly started her latest to-do list:

- Talk to the hospitalized prisoner who could describe officers beating Huey when he was a wounded patient at Kaiser.
- Check whether a friend of Huey's could corroborate that Huey was celebrating the end of his probation on the evening of October 27, 1967 [that would refute the prosecutor's claim Huey knew he was still on parole when stopped by Officer Frey].
- Follow up on a possible witness in Sacramento.

Stender also needed to research cases for Garry to rely on during Monday's arguments. He would seek Newton's acquittal on first-degree murder charges on the grounds that Jensen had failed to produce evidence of premeditation or malice. This was the only charge that carried the death penalty. If she could find persuasive cases, she harbored a slim hope that the judge might direct the jury to acquit Newton on that murder charge, just as he was planning to dismiss the kidnapping charge. Stender planned to outline the examination of two witnesses for Garry and to contact a third witness and tell him when to appear. She reminded herself to have the Panthers conduct a background check on Tommy Miller, the passenger on Grier's AC Transit bus. Lastly, she wanted to follow up on the rumor passed on to her by one of their witnesses that Grier's children might be involved in a bike-stealing gang. With her client's life at stake, she would pursue any avenue — no matter how unlikely — that might undermine the credibility of the prosecutor's star witness. But this idea never bore any fruit.

The court day on Monday, August 19, started with the jury sequestered as the defense moved for acquittal. Garry boldly asserted there was no basis in the record for the jury to convict Newton on the murder charge, citing Stender's federal case research. Jensen may never have seen a claim that audacious. The argument rested on two points: Heanes did not see a gun in Newton's hands and Grier had not identified Newton positively in his original police statement. But this only looked selectively at two pieces of evidence, not the totality of circumstances Jensen had presented. The judge's job was to look at the whole picture and decide if the murder charge could stick if the jury accepted the prosecution's view of the facts.

If the jury believed Heanes, then the first shot came from the direction of Newton and hit Heanes in the arm, which was when Heanes fired back, wounding Newton. The jury could decide that Newton grabbed Frey's gun, used Frey as a shield and then fired at Heanes and killed Frey. The jury could also decide Newton packed his own gun. Grier had testified that he saw a civilian pull a gun and draw first. Garry had made Grier walk over to the defense table to identify that civilian as Newton. The fact that Grier was not sure when he first spoke with the police on the day of the shooting whether he could identify that civilian was just evidence the jury could weigh in the balance, not proof that the bus driver lied in court or was mistaken. Huey Newton was in fact that wounded civilian. The only question was did the bus driver see him pull a gun. Some of the stray bullets found at the scene corroborated Grier's testimony — they were not police issue. Jensen's expert John Davis also testified that the bullets that killed Officer Frey were fired into his back from under two feet away. Judge Friedman agreed with Jensen that the jury had ample evidence to consider both the murder and assault charges.

As expected, Judge Friedman granted the motion to dismiss the kidnapping charge. Everyone agreed that Ross had never been cross-examined on his grand jury testimony. Ross claimed he could not recall having given that testimony. Ross also insisted that Jensen did not refresh his memory by reading passages of it in court. That made the grand jury testimony inadmissible — the judge had to strike it from the record and tell the jury to disregard what they heard Jensen read from that transcript. Without it, there was no evidence at all that Ross had been kidnapped by anyone. Reporters were impressed that Garry managed to make the kidnapping charge evaporate and were eager to see who Garry planned to call as defense witnesses. Many wondered out loud about the still unidentified "mystery man" who had accompanied Newton in the car. Would he show up as a defense witness? Would Newton take the stand on his own behalf?

As his first witness, Garry called AC Transit passenger Tommy Miller to the stand. Miller was a young black employee of the Alameda Naval Station. He testified that he had boarded the bus at the corner of Seventh and Willow at about 5 a.m. on October 28 after spending ten or more minutes at the bus stop. While waiting for the bus, he saw some activity about a block away that he had trouble making out since it was very dark at the time.

Miller said the bus driver was making change for him from a five-dollar bill as they pulled out into the street. A passenger who boarded behind Miller then paid the bus driver as Miller took his seat. The bus immediately slowed to a stop, and Miller heard shooting. He looked out the window, but could not see what was happening. He was sure the bus had passed the police cars before the shooting took place. He could see an officer tussling with a man, but it was impossible to see their faces.

Court recessed for the noon break with Miller still on the stand.

After the jury left for lunch, Garry apologized to Judge Friedman for bringing the subject up again, but felt compelled to read two racist death threats that he had received into the record. He asked again for a mistrial, arguing that community hysteria made it impossible for Newton to receive a fair trial. He presented to the court a menacing note from four retired Marines and another purportedly from a member of the KKK. The second one, addressed "Dear Nigger Lover," assumed that Garry would get "that murdering coon off because the judge, jury and witnesses have all been intimidated . . . It's too bad we ever stopped lynching."[1]

Garry reported that the Panthers were temporarily providing him with a 24-hour bodyguard, and he had turned the threatening notes over to the FBI. Lowell Jensen reported to Judge Friedman that he, too, had received death threats. He considered death threats to come with the territory. Jensen did not mention the police protection being provided for his own family or his suggestion to his sister that she might want to leave town for her own safety. Jensen kept a stoic attitude in court, still vainly seeking to try the case as if it were not a political bombshell.

Makeshift security screening rooms had already been set up the week before in a small room across the hall from Judge Friedman's courtroom. Back then, this was an extraordinary precaution. Everyone emptied their pockets. Armed male deputies patted down male courtroom attendees, searching for concealed weapons. On one occasion, they found narcotics on a spectator, but released the man after he told him that he had borrowed his jacket from someone else. Female employees carefully searched women attendants, reviewed the contents of their purses and confiscated any sharp objects, including nail files. A reporter for the London-based *Daily Telegraph* observed that the unusual tight security matched that of the Israelis when they tried Nazi Adolf Eichmann in Jerusalem.

Though he obtained some press coverage of the death threats, Garry was not surprised his oft-repeated motion for a mistrial had been denied. After Jensen concluded his cross-examination of Miller, Garry called to the stand as his next two witnesses a woman and male friend of

Newton's who had seen Newton relaxed and celebrating the end of his parole earlier on the evening of October 27 at Bos'n's Locker, Newton's favorite Oakland bar. Both witnesses were called to refute the prosecution's theory that Newton shot Officer Frey because he was under parole restrictions and was desperate to avoid jail. The male friend made an especially good impression. He was a Ph.D. candidate from Cal.

Garry also called ACLU attorney Marshall Krause, whom Newton had approached three years earlier to appeal his 1964 assault conviction. At the time, Newton had been concerned that he would lose his voting rights, and Krause had told him that would not be the case. Krause informed Newton that the crime would be treated as a misdemeanor due to the short county jail sentence. Apparently, Krause's advice was admitted to show what Newton mistakenly thought at the time; Judge Friedman had already ruled that the conviction was a felony, not a misdemeanor.

Jensen raised a successful objection when Garry tried to put on the stand an inmate who had been a patient at Kaiser after the shootout. The man was called to testify about police threats to Newton's life when Newton was in the hospital recuperating from his wounds. Judge Friedman agreed that evidence of police misconduct after October 28, 1967, was irrelevant. Tempers flared as Jensen also won a heated dispute with Garry over three other proposed witnesses. Garry had wanted to get on the record a conversation the three people said they had with an investigator for the D.A.'s office. It was just as irrelevant as the charge of police misconduct after the shooting. When Garry kept arguing, Judge Friedman had reacted angrily, shouting, "I will run this court in my own way."[2] But Judge Friedman overruled Jensen's objections to a parade of witnesses that Stender and other members of the defense team had assembled to testify that Officer Frey was a racist who abused other black arrestees. The defense inverstigation, of course, ignored other evidence of acquaintances who would vigorously defend the good character of their friend John Frey. That would be for the prosecutor to develop.

Frey grew up in neighboring Contra Costa County. At the time of his death he was just four years out of high school. He was born John

Favreau and later took his new stepfather's last name. In the fall of
1967, Frey lived in a mixed-race neighborhood, where he welcomed
kids like his Chinese-American paperboy to hang around as he worked
on detailing his Austin Healy sports car. Frey also maintained a cordial
relationship with several black neighbors. Back in Clayton Valley High
School he had been on the wrestling team; after school he had worked
for an ambulance service. From the defense perspective, it was more
useful to learn that he collected guns and had specifically requested
assignment to West Oakland's red light district.

The black men Frey arrested just prior to the incident with Newton
had been difficult to find. Some moved and had to be tracked down at
their new addresses. The evidence was also tricky to get admitted in the
face of Jensen's vehement objection: Frey was no longer available to
defend himself against such charges, and how Frey had behaved toward
other arrestees did not necessarily match his conduct vis-à-vis Newton.
Yet it did have a bearing on the defense argument that Frey might have
provoked the shooting. Garry considered it critical to get these allegations of racism before the jury for the same reason Jensen wanted them
kept out — to recast the dead man as a villain and Newton as a victim.
At the same time, Garry contended that Newton's primary defense was
that he had no gun and was innocent of the shooting charges. The
judge focused on the most serious charges and concluded that the
theory of Frey's aggressive racism on the beat could affect the degree of
murder if the jury found that Frey had provoked Newton into a lethal
response. This was a major victory for Garry.

The defense then put on the stand Daniel King, a teenager arrested
the night before the early morning shootout. King testified that Frey
called him a "nigger" and a pimp and then left him to be beaten up
by a white man who claimed he had just been robbed. The irate crime
victim had been dressed only in a shirt and underwear; he claimed
King had stolen his pants. Another man, Calvin Hudson, whom Frey
had stopped for speeding, testified that Frey called him a "black motherfucker." Belford Dunning, a black insurance agent, received a ticket
a couple of days before the shootout. He came forward to say that
Officer Frey was the assisting officer at the scene and boasted "I am the

Gestapo."[3] These negative accounts of Officer Frey's behavior came as a surprise to Jensen. (He would later put on the stand one of Oakland's few black police officers, who contradicted Dunning's account of abuse from Officer Frey.)

Stender also tracked down a high school student, Tom Parson, who heard Frey give a talk to his class about choosing police work as a career. Parson had told her that Frey used the word "nigger" at least once in his talk. But when called at trial, the teenage witness became nervous and hesitant and denied hearing Frey use the word. Garry felt he had no choice but to call Stender next to the stand to challenge the credibility of Parson — his own witness — by having her repeat to the jury Parson's out-of-court statement. Garry also called the teacher to the stand to say that he heard Frey start to use the word "nigger" and then correct himself. While various witnesses testified, Newton often appeared disengaged, apparently lost in his own thoughts.

After portraying Officer Frey as a racist prone to using inflammatory slurs, the defense team considered it absolutely essential to educate the jury on the Panthers' own use of explosive terms. They offered two experts, including Dr. Herman Blake, a black professor of sociology, to explain that rhetoric like "off the pigs" had a different, non-literal meaning in the black community; he argued that this threatening figure of speech resonated differently for whites and blacks. For whites it sounded like a death threat; for black youths in the inner city it signaled frustration and anger not meant to be taken as an actual call to violence against cops. The judge did not have much patience for this novel argument and originally denied the request. Later, Judge Friedman allowed Garry an opportunity to reargue the linguistics issue in a lengthy hearing outside the presence of the jury.

As Dr. Blake testified before Judge Friedman on how to interpret Panther slang, Professor Blauner's mind was on a breaking story with global consequences. On August 20, 1968, Soviet tanks rolled into Prague, reigniting the dormant Cold War. Shocked observers saw the Soviets kill a hundred people and arrest local Communist Party leaders. The purpose of the invasion was to crush their "Prague Spring" experimental reforms of free speech and freedom of assembly. The developing

Czech crisis had been front-page news for a month. A long-time Leftist, Blauner was deeply upset about the Soviet massacre of the Czech reformers. On the morning of August 21, he turned to Stender, who was sitting next to him at the trial, and said "The Russians are pigs, too." She did not respond. He found her lack of reaction disquieting. Blauner had joined the Communist Party as a student in the '50s, but quit when Stalin's bloody purges came to light. Stender would soon come to agree with Blauner about the abhorrent Soviet tactics. In 1969, she hung in her new office a prized poster by artist David Lance Goines of a man confronting a Russian tank on Prague's city streets. "QUI TACET CONSENTIT" was written in large print underneath: "He who is silent consents." In the summer of 1968, Blauner believed whole-heartedly in the Black Panthers, but decades later, in an interview, he expressed regret about the way he and other activists had rationalized the Panthers' guns and violent rhetoric and downplayed their dangerousness. Stender reached a similar conclusion by the mid-1970s — but not yet.

When the jury returned, Garry called to the stand another African-American, Gene McKinney, who, like Hilliard, had been a friend of Huey Newton's since boyhood. The press was amazed to hear that McKinney was the mysterious, previously unidentified passenger who had accompanied Newton in the Volkswagen sedan when Officer Frey pulled up behind it that fateful October morning. McKinney had fled the scene with Newton. In all the months since the shooting McKinney's name had never before surfaced. Shortly after the shootout, the police advertised in the newspaper their desire to speak with Newton's passenger. They let the community know the mysterious passenger was not considered a suspect. Garry had kept McKinney's identity so closely guarded that even some members of his own legal team were taken by surprise.

Like Ross, McKinney had taken the unusual precaution of coming to court with his own lawyer, an African-American named Harold Perry. Garry liked the symbolism of this gesture, but he'd had a hard time finding a black lawyer to represent McKinnney. Among all the other black lawyers around, no one but Carleton Innis wanted to associate in any way with the case after Garry became Newton's lead counsel. After McKinney responded to a few preliminary questions, Garry dramatically asked McKinney the same question he had asked Officer Heanes — whether he had shot the deceased officer "by chance or otherwise."[4]

On Perry's advice, McKinney refused to testify further about the incident on the grounds that it might incriminate him. Jensen vigorously objected that the witness could not start to testify and then invoke the Fifth Amendment. Garry suggested that Jensen offer immunity to McKinney as Jensen had offered Ross. Jensen wisely declined to do so — who knew what Newton's good buddy McKinney would say if granted immunity? To Jensen's surprise and dismay, Judge Friedman then ruled that Jensen could only ask McKinney about the few statements McKinney made before invoking the Fifth Amendment. McKinney still invoked the right not to incriminate himself, even to explain how he first came in contact with Newton that morning. This time Judge Friedman made good on his threat; for the first time in his judicial career he held a witness in contempt. McKinney was hauled off to a tenth floor jail cell. He would be incarcerated for six weeks before an appellate court ordered his release (for Judge Friedman's failure to employ proper procedures). Garry's office helped Perry with that appeal.

At this point, the jury had seen two different black men — other than the defendant — who were at or near the scene of the shootout. Both claimed they could be incriminated if they answered questions about the events of the morning of October 28 that led to Officer Frey's death and Huey Newton's arrest for murder. Following the spectacle of McKinney's brief and extraordinary appearance, Garry escalated the drama by calling Huey Newton as his next witness — intended as a signal to the jury that the defense had nothing to hide. The following day, Jensen's efforts to keep the trial focused narrowly on the shootout rather than on politics and race would face its biggest challenge.

Garry considered it crucial for Newton to tell his life story and political philosophy to place the shooting incident in context. Allowing Newton to testify, of course, was part of what Garry alluded to when he later said this was one of the most complex and fascinating cases he ever tried. Garry's claim puzzled his partner Al Brotsky, who had visited Newton with Garry in jail early on. Brotsky thought, like Jensen, that the case would be a rather straightforward one. But Garry considered that approach too dangerous. He was willing to gamble on having Newton testify only within the context of a strategy shifting the jury's focus to the broader picture of police brutality and Panther persecution.

Garry knew what any veteran defense lawyer knew: when a defendant chooses to take the stand the burden of proof switches to the defense despite the fact the judge instructs the jury otherwise. O. J. Simpson "dream team" member Barry Scheck has no doubt about the high stakes involved when lawyers let the defendant testify and be grilled on cross-examination. How credible is he? Scheck says, "That becomes the issue in the case, not whether the prosecution has proven its case beyond a reasonable doubt." The risk in Newton's case was magnified even further: the judge would instruct the jury that they could disbelieve everything Newton said simply because he had a prior felony conviction — it is okay to assume someone who committed a prior serious crime would lie about anything.

Stokely Carmichael (now completely disassociated from SNCC), Eldridge and Kathleen Cleaver, and Bobby Seale were all in the courtroom to hear Newton's testimony. Eldridge Cleaver now drew more publicity than ever — the California Peace and Freedom Party had just announced him as its candidate for President of the United States.[5] In a recent report, an FBI agent had noted the rivalry between Cleaver and Seale for leadership of the Panthers. He also saw how devoted Kathleen Cleaver was to furthering Cleaver's more aggressive, openly threatening agenda. The agent suggested in his next report that Kathleen might split from Cleaver if the FBI gave her reason to believe Cleaver was having an affair. Eldridge's sexual misconduct was common knowledge among Party leadership; the Central Committee had already called on him to respond to a serious allegation: a mother's irate claim that Cleaver had raped her fourteen-year-old daughter. Under the Party's rules, that charge could have justified his expulsion. Cleaver admitted having consensual sex with the girl. His only response to her age was that he wished she were 12 years old.[6] The Central Committee took no action.

By 6 a.m. on August 22, crowds again surged outside the courthouse, which had far more security guards stationed outside than any

day since the trial began. Gilbert Moore of *LIFE* magazine was thrilled
to be on hand to witness the scene. Anger erupted as he heard a few
blacks confront whites who arrived first. One of them wanted to know
"what the fuck" white boys were doing in the front of the line.

The latecomers asserted their own priority. One of them said, "We
been standing on line for four hundred years."[7]

The crowd pushed its full weight against the double glass doors.
A panel of glass broke as everyone pressed to be among those lucky
enough to see Huey Newton take the stand.

Gazing upon a full courtroom from the witness chair, Newton was
obviously pleased with the strong show of support — the friendly faces
in the crowd counterbalanced the increased numbers of plainclothes
policemen. Before he began to answer questions, he shivered, perhaps
from the temperature in the chilly courtroom. He spoke in a conversa-
tional tone with no quaver in his voice and focused his gaze on the one
black man on the jury. Every day so far, Newton had carefully observed
David Harper for signs of his inclinations, but could not take his measure. Was the banker an Uncle Tom like all the other Panthers then
thought he was — "blinded by the crumbs the system offered him"[8]
— or a brother who, like the Panthers, seethed at the unfairness of
a racist society? Newton considered his testimony an opportunity to
address Harper one-on-one, hoping he could develop a bond.

As Garry began the questioning, Huey flatly denied shooting either
officer. He knew the police kept a list of Black Panther vehicles and that
he risked being stopped at any time. Newton had in fact, by his count,
been accosted by police forty to fifty times before. That was one of the
reasons he kept his law book handy, as he did that day. Newton told the
jury that when the officer told him to get out of his car that morning the
book was all he held. He never carried a handgun because that would
be in automatic violation of his parole, as would the use of marijuana.

The pants Newton wore had been purchased secondhand from
Good Will. He claimed he had no idea there was marijuana residue in
the pocket because he never checked the pockets. He also claimed that
he was unaware of any marijuana in the car. He insisted that the only
gun he ever carried was a shotgun, which the law allowed. He also said

he only carried his shotgun when he was on one of his police patrols. Newton added that he could be expelled from the Panthers if he ever carried a gun when he wasn't on one of those patrols, or if he was ever caught with narcotics. (When McKinney pleaded the Fifth Amendment right not to incriminate himself, he knew they had weed in the car — a fact he would own up to long after the statute of limitations had passed.)[9]

The defense team was well aware that if the jury believed Newton knowingly transported marijuana, Jensen had his motive for killing Officer Frey. If Newton carried a concealed handgun when stopped by the police, that would also constitute a felony violation of his parole. Under California law, possession of a forbidden gun would automatically have rendered Newton guilty of second degree murder of Officer Frey under the felony-murder rule. Any death, even an accidental one, caused by a felon with an illegal gun constituted second degree murder. All the prosecutor needed to prove was that Newton had a hidden gun in his possession when he was frisked. And that was exactly what bus drive Grier testified that he saw.

Only four minutes of Newton's direct testimony concerned the early morning shooting. The defense theory was tricky, given that Newton denied killing Frey. As alternatives, they still hoped to convince the jury that it was possible Newton acted in self-defense or with diminished capacity. By putting Newton on the stand, Garry gave Jensen the opportunity to cross-examine him at length on the events of that fatal morning. If they had exercised Newton's right to remain silent, Jensen could never have called him as a witness.

Newton relished his familiar role as lecturer, having gotten plenty of experience in his years drawing crowds as one of the Grove Street orators at Oakland City College, and in addressing weekly meetings of new recruits at Panther headquarters. He talked at length on direct examination about hundreds of years of oppression, interrupted several times by Jensen's objections to the judge that this history lesson was not relevant to the proceedings. But Judge Friedman was fascinated and overruled the objections. Newton then told a hushed courtroom that blacks were the most brutalized people in the country. Penny Cooper realized, as Lowell Jensen did, that most other judges in the county likely would not have allowed this to go on. Garry knew that, too. He was extremely grateful for the latitude Judge Friedman accorded him. From his perspective nearly five decades later, Barry Scheck is impressed with the judge's willingness to allow Garry "to bring out the history of race problems in the United States as a predicate for understanding the defendant . . . in the context of a political trial." Scheck considers the decision a key ruling for the defense that "not all judges would do . . . even to this day."

As a federal judge looking back, Thelton Henderson later observed:

> I think Judge Monroe Friedman, who presided over this trial, did something unusual, and I thought courageous in his . . . evidentiary ruling that Huey Newton could talk about racism as it affected him, as it affected his life, and his view of the world, and his behavior. It was courageous to do it. . . . It was unusual. . . . I don't think there are many judges who would have made that ruling. I think it was the right ruling because I think that one's perception, one's life experiences that affect them deeply and from birth, if you're black, your racial experiences start as soon as you're interacting with . . . other human beings. I think he made the right ruling, but it was a rare ruling in those days.

The jury appeared rapt as they marveled at Newton's dignified and scholarly account. Watching from the spectators' gallery, Hilliard was greatly impressed with Huey's performance:

> Because then the trial is not a trial. It's actually a classroom for people in court. . . . He would swivel around from the D.A. and start talking to the jury. He would be educating the jury about our movement, because Charles Garry would say, "Well, why did you create the Black Panther Party?" So he turned the chair around. He's not talking to the D.A. He is talking directly to the jury . . . about how we got here . . . a history lesson in the oppression and economic subjugation of black folks in America, and Huey was very, very adept. . . . The jury, nobody there had seen anything like that before. . . . So the jury members would be glued to what he's

saying . . . He used the courtroom as a forum to validate our just
cause for freedom, equality and justice."

Newton explained that when he and others sought to organize
members of the black community, they realized they needed to unite
with all people who were oppressed. He said that the Black Panther
Party was not a racist group and formed alliances with many cultural
minorities, as well as disillusioned youths in the white majority. Newton
also explained to the jury that the Black Panther Party had adopted
rules against drinking or drug use among its members and advocated
only peaceful methods of achieving their goals. (While that was the
rule, it was one Newton honored in the breach. He often went bar-
hopping, including the night of October 26, 1967, with the Panthers'
Minister of Information Earl Anthony.) While Newton gave testimony
about the Party's commitment to nonviolence, outside the courthouse
beyond the jury's hearing, demonstrators shouted, "Revolution has
come — Time to pick up your gun" and "Off the pigs."[10] Those carrying "Free Huey" and "Off the Pigs" signs included more than three
dozen white protesters from the Citizens Committee Mobilized for
Huey Newton, headed by an Oakland housewife.[11] Jensen was fighting
a losing battle to treat the shootout in a vacuum.

The jet-lagged Stokely Carmichael had been seated near the front
of the spectators during Newton's extraordinary testimony, but had
fallen asleep. Refreshed by his nap, Carmichael conducted a press conference during the noon break. He characterized the proceedings as
a political "trial of a black man . . . trying to liberate his people."[12]
Overseas press loved this angle. In London, the *Sunday Telegraph* had
just published an in-depth article for its two million readers, analyzing
the case in political terms.

Yet by dwelling on Newton's political philosophy, Garry opened the
door wide for Jensen to cross-examine Newton on the virulent anti-
police rhetoric in his writings. That was Garry's greatest fear in eliciting
Newton's testimony — a risk that Garry felt he had to take. It was one
of the reasons he considered this case so complex to try. Now Jensen
could ask Newton directly why he urged his followers to "off the pigs"

and see how the jury reacted. Garry actually had no choice — Jensen could have introduced those writings anyway. If Newton's hate-filled essays were not placed in political context, Garry considered them inflammatory enough to convict Newton of murder. Garry could best explain the purpose and background of these writings with Newton on the stand, testifying on his own behalf. But Garry still desperately wanted to convince Judge Friedman to let the jury hear Dr. Blake's more benign interpretation of the Panthers' frequent exhortation to followers to "off the pigs."

Jensen had all weekend to finish preparing his proposed cross-examination on Monday, August 26. He planned to take Newton through all of his movements on October 27, starting from his speaking engagement on the future of the black liberation movement at San Francisco State College that afternoon. Jensen started off with softball questions designed to put Newton at ease. He was then hoping to draw Newton's ire with tougher tactics so the jury could see Newton's explosive temper, but Huey had been forewarned and kept his irritation largely in check. He testified he had earned $75 for two hours of his time as a speaker. He then described going to his fiancée LaVerne's home because they had a date to celebrate the end of his probation, but she felt ill and instead loaned him her car.

Newton went to his favorite bar, Bos'n's Locker, where he had one rum and Coke and then left to attend a party at a church social hall where he linked up with his friend Gene McKinney. When they left the party, they went to Seventh Street, intending to stop at an all-night restaurant. They were looking for a parking space when they were pulled over by Officer Frey. Newton described for the jury how Frey had frisked him abusively, feeling his genitals. He held out his law book and told Frey there had been no reasonable cause for stopping him, but Frey called him a "nigger" and told him "to take the law book and stick it." Frey then "straight-armed" Newton, who stumbled.

The audience perked up when Newton asked Jensen's permission to demonstrate what he meant by being straight-armed. He got off the stand and pretended he was Frey. Newton then pushed Jensen back with his hand extended to Jensen's chin, using obvious restraint to avoid causing the prosecutor to lose his balance. Newton then said, "This is the way it happened. Excuse me," and resumed his seat on the witness stand.[13] Newton then testified that Frey drew his revolver and Newton felt a sensation "like hot soup." He heard explosions, and the next thing he remembered was crawling onto the concrete platform outside the emergency entrance to Kaiser Hospital.[14]

Shifting to the *Black Panther* newspaper and Newton's prior writings, Jensen sought to repulse the jurors by the Panthers' philosophy. Jensen pointed out that Panthers listed the late Dr. Martin Luther King in a "Bootlickers' Gallery." Newton said that characterization changed when Dr. King came out against the Vietnam War. Jensen then called specific attention to an article Huey had published in the *Panther* newspaper the summer before, called "The Correct Handling of Revolution." Newton had written it as a critique of the Watts riot and more recent urban riots. It included a potentially very damning passage.

It started with a description of the Panther Party as the vanguard of the revolution:

> The Vanguard must provide leadership for the people. It must teach the correct strategic methods of prolonged resistance through literature and activities. If the activities of the party are respected by the people, the people will follow the example.

It then explained that the revolution would start:

> When the people . . . see the advantage in the activities of the guerrilla warfare method . . . when the Vanguard group destroys the machinery of the oppressor by dealing with him in small groups of threes and fours and then escapes the might of the oppressor, the masses will be overjoyed and will adhere to this correct strategy.

Jensen must have paused for effect before he finished reading the passage:

> When the masses hear that a Gestapo policeman has been executed while sipping coffee at a counter, and the revolutionary executors fled without being traced, the masses will see the validity of this type of approach to resistance.[15]

Newton's supporters all considered him a hero for such fiery rhetoric — it was "off the pigs" taken to its logical conclusion. How would

Newton convince the jury that he had not acted on his own words? Newton had a ready explanation. The article was referring to an unspecified revolutionary time in the future. Conditions had not yet risen to the level of impasse where peaceful struggle was fruitless and revolutionary tactics were appropriate.

Jensen also confronted Newton with a poem he had published in the *Black Panther* newspaper the summer before. It was called "Guns Baby Guns!" and elaborated on the same theme as his essay:

> Army .45 will stop all jive
> Buck shots will down the cops
> will open prison gates
> The carbine will stop the war machine
> A .357 will win us heaven.
> And if you don't believe in playing
> You are already dead.[16]

Jensen had Newton read the poem aloud to the jury along with the list of weapons on the same page of the newsletter that the Panthers advocated as necessary for self-defense: an Army .45 pistol, a 12-gauge shotgun, an M-1 carbine, a .357 Magnum pistol and a .38-caliber police revolver. (Gilbert Moore had heard that "when a bullet from a .357 hits you, you feel like you've been struck by lightning."[17]) The jury already knew that Frey had apparently been killed with his own .38 caliber revolver after struggling with Newton. Newton repeatedly stated the Panther Party was an organization for self-defense working to combat violence. When he gave speeches on black liberation in which he advocated "taking care of business" through guerrilla bands on the streets, it did not include executing policemen. He claimed he had been misquoted in a *Ramparts* magazine article by Eldridge Cleaver entitled "The Courage to Kill" that portrayed him as unequivocally advocating bloodshed.[18]

Instead of focusing on Jensen, Newton shifted to look at the jury when he launched into long answers. At the end of one such lecture, Newton turned back and, to his surprise, Jensen was no longer standing there. Newton said, "Where is he?" before he turned his head and spotted Jensen sitting at the prosecution table. Newton then said, "Oh.

There you are. I thought you had left."

Jensen said, "No. I'm still here." Laughter erupted in the court-room, quickly stopped with a rebuke from Judge Friedman.

As Garry had dreaded, Jensen then examined Newton regarding his prior assault conviction, inquiring whether racism was involved. Jensen knew that Odell Lee, the victim of the assault, had been black. But Newton surprised Jensen by claiming that ethnicity may have been a factor. Lee had used a Chinese greeting at the party where they met; Newton replied with a Swahili salutation he had learned from cultural nationalists. The two had then gotten into an argument. Newton had seen a scar on Lee's face that indicated Lee had a violent streak. Newton considered their conversation over and went back to his dinner. Lee tugged insistently on Newton's arm to continue their argument and reached into his pocket. Newton then grabbed a steak knife and stabbed Lee; he told the court that he had acted in self-defense. However, when he went to court without a lawyer, the jury had not seen it that way.

Jensen then asked about Newton's arrest in Berkeley in March of 1966, when two policemen sought to arrest his companion, Bobby Seale. Jensen began most of his questions, "Isn't it a fact." Newton sparred with Jensen, recalling that Seale was reading poetry from a chair on a street corner when the police harassed him. Newton denied he had tried to grab the policeman's gun as the arrest record indicated. He then turned to ask Jensen, "Isn't it a fact" the plainclothes officer accompanying the uniformed policeman had been drunk at the time? His sarcastic attempt at role reversal brought angry intervention from the judge, causing spectators to laugh out loud. Garry quickly asked for a mistrial. Much subdued, Judge Friedman responded, "Your objection is noted."[19]

One sympathetic lawyer in the gallery told Eldridge Cleaver during a break that he thought Newton was being crucified on the stand like Jesus Christ. Cleaver had responded instinctively, "Yes, Huey is our Jesus, but we want him down from the cross."[20]

The Panthers and the defense team had engineered the enormous turnout that day of some eight hundred Newton supporters — a crowd second only to that on the first day of trial. About a fifth of them wore Panther uniforms and circled the courthouse. Kathleen Cleaver led the women shouting, "Revolution has come — Time to pick up your gun," which alternated with the men yelling, "Off the pigs." Of the remaining crowd waving "Free Huey" signs and related slogans, more than half were white. A noticeable contingent was Asian. One banner read, "Yellow Peril Supports Black Panthers."[21]

All the jurors except David Harper had taken to entering the courthouse through an underground tunnel from the garage to avoid the crowd. Harper refused to be intimidated. During the trial, threats were received against his wife. He had then been offered police protection for his home in the lower hills of East Oakland, a middle class neighborhood by the Oakland Zoo. The Harpers declined because his wife feared the police as much as the Panthers. He parked in the same garage as the other jurors each day of the trial, but then walked outside to cross the street and walk past the demonstrators up the steps of the courthouse. Once inside, he silently shared the elevator to the seventh floor with other trial attendees. None of the jury panel could altogether avoid hearing the loud chants: "The sky is the limit"; "Free Huey, off the pigs"; "No more brothers in jail"; "It's time to pick up the gun and use it."

At the day's end Garry was relatively upbeat. He was convinced that Newton had handled himself exceedingly well. Bob Blauner, like everyone else on the team, was impressed at how brilliant and articulate Newton had shown himself to be. Belva Davis realized that getting on the stand helped Newton. The jury was left to ponder Newton's makeup: "His intellect on the one hand, his blending in . . . embracing white society through classical music and the philosophy of those non-blacks that he admired. But on the other hand, he was this gun-toting black guy that was out to shoot cops. . . People had trouble putting the two Newtons together. . . . If anything, he certainly was not a typical man whose skin was brown. So the stereotype just didn't fit him."

Even Lowell Jensen later conceded that it had been a smart move for Garry to put Newton on the stand in his own defense. Dr. Blake, sitting in the audience, was almost moved to tears watching Newton testify. There he was with his life on the line, carrying the banner of the black revolutionary. The professor wrote Newton shortly afterward,

"You were absolutely beautiful. Your manner and presentation on the witness stand were the highest manifestation of the integrity of the black experience. I shall never forget what I saw and heard, regardless of the outcome."[22] After two days of watching Newton being cross-examined on the stand, trial observers all appeared in agreement that he had handled himself impressively. In chambers, Judge Friedman confided to the lawyers, "He could have been a fine young man, It's really too bad. . . ."[23]

The *San Francisco Examiner*'s Rush Greenlee relished covering the remarkable feat that Garry and Newton had achieved: "[T]he political nature of the Black Panthers seemed to have transcended the stark events of 5 a.m. last Oct. 28. The jury must still decide the fate of Newton — whether he lives or dies, remains imprisoned or is set free — not the question of his politics. And yet in the back of the minds of the jurors, what he stands for may loom large, perhaps larger than the murky evidence pointing to his guilt or innocence. . . . He wishes to stand or fall on the validity of his cause." Greenlee's article proved Garry's strategy had worked — the extraordinary political overtones lent an atmosphere of unreality to the courtroom battle over what exactly happened in the morning shootout: "The testimony inside the courtroom and the evidence outside show all too plainly that the case is at least in part one of people who feel they have been discriminated against and who are not willing to take it any longer."[24] It was not the type of observation to *The Examiner*'s readers that Greenlee's white colleague would likely have made.

Garry brought in a forensic chemist to testify that the police failed to perform tests that could have determined if Newton had fired a gun that morning. Garry sought to plant in the jurors' minds the idea that the omission was not an oversight — it was a deliberate decision because tests would have proved his client's innocence. Introducing this idea after bringing in strong evidence that Frey's aggressive, racist behavior might have provoked Newton to shoot him did not bother Garry in the slightest. Consistency was not his problem; it was Jensen's.

15. THE DAY OF RECKONING ARRIVES

This is not a threat. We are four retired Marines USA. We . . . do not see why any attorney would see fit for a fee to defend Huey P. Newton. We all knew Policeman John Frey. So, to make this short and to the point, you or Newton will not be alive ten days after this trial is over. Makes no difference which way the jury disides [sic].

— ANONYMOUS LETTER TO CHARLES GARRY,
TURNED OVER TO THE FBI.[1]

Throughout the trial Garry counted on juror confusion. As long as there was no proof beyond a reasonable doubt that Newton committed any of the charged crimes, he should go free. Garry originally wanted to argue self-defense: that if Newton did fire the gun that killed Frey, it was only after Officer Frey put Newton's life at risk. But Garry dropped this theory at trial as inconsistent with Newton's insistence that he had not shot the second officer and had not killed Frey. Deprived of the self-defense theory, Garry raised the question whether Heanes shot both Frey and Newton. But John Davis, the ballistics expert, established convincingly that Heanes was too far away to have fired the fatal shot. Garry also pounced on bus driver Grier's original description to the police of the civilian he saw grappling with Officer Frey. Grier said the man was about five feet tall. The defense then raised the possibility that a pygmy stranger had killed Frey and escaped unobserved. Or maybe the shooter was Newton's friend Gene McKinney, who pleaded the

Fifth Amendment right not to incriminate himself when asked if he had shot the officer.

Garry himself spent many nights in the months before the trial following up leads to potential eye witnesses. With suggestions from the Black Panthers and volunteer law students from Boalt Hall in Berkeley, Garry interviewed numerous prostitutes in the whorehouses and cheap hotels on Seventh Street. One prostitute tried to convince him she had seen the whole thing, including the mysterious killer who got away. Garry had found her version of events so inconsistent that he reluctantly concluded she would not be worth calling as a witness at trial.

On Tuesday, August 27, Garry called as his last witness Dr. Bernard Diamond, the veteran forensic psychiatrist he had successfully relied on in prior cases to prove diminished capacity. Dr. Diamond testified for the defense as to the reflex shock reaction and state of unconsciousness commonly caused in combat by bullet wounds to the abdomen. His credentials were impeccable: Dr. Diamond was a criminologist on the faculty of U.C. Berkeley; his resumé included more than a decade of experience in the Army Medical Corps and listed two dozen articles published in medical journals.

Over Jensen's objection, Judge Friedman let Dr. Diamond answer Garry's hypothetical question based on a summary of Newton's testimony. Dr. Diamond was asked to assume Newton had little or no recall of what transpired after he felt a hot flash from the bullet he took in the stomach. Dr. Diamond told the jury that shock of that nature was "fully compatible with a penetrating gunshot wound of the abdomen."[2] Garry also asked Dr. Diamond whether most people were more credible in their first recollections of an event than when they reconstructed it later. He was trying to discredit Grier's trial testimony in favor of his earlier statement to the police. Judge Friedman upheld Jensen's objection, instructing the jury that credibility determinations were solely their job. After Garry rested the defense, Jensen had the opportunity to present four rebuttal witnesses from local law enforcement. These included two Berkeley officers. One testified about arresting Newton in high school after he hit a fellow student with a hammer in 1958. The other arrested Newton in 1966 for punching an officer who was in the process of arresting Seale and for trying to grab that officer's gun from its holster. Garry hoped the jury believed Newton when he denied that he had made a bold move for a Berkeley policeman's gun in the past; otherwise that arrest would support a conclusion something similar occurred when Officer Frey confronted Newton.

When it came Garry's turn, Judge Friedman announced some welcome news: the defense would be allowed to present novel expert testimony on ghetto slang. At last, Dr. Blake could explain to the jury that the violent language used by Newton and the Panthers in their newspaper signified something different to the black community than the white community. Stender worked closely with Dr. Blake in preparing his testimony. He explained that a phrase like "takin' care of business" had multiple meanings depending on the context. It could refer to politics, sex or a variety of other subjects. "Off the pigs" was not intended literally, but figuratively, as an exhortation to free the community from police oppression. That would have been news to Panthers like Janice Garrett chanting "off the pigs" outside the courthouse. To her, it meant "kill the pigs, kill the policemen. We viewed the police department as our enemy, and they were trying to kill us and it was up to us to defend ourselves. So when we used verbiage like 'off the pigs,' it was if they come at you, then you defend yourself and you shoot back at them."

Garrett and other Panther demonstrators continued waving their revolutionary placards and chanting outside while Professor Blakely testified inside the courtroom that graphic phrases like "buckshot will down the cops" and "carbine will stop the war machine" were similarly figurative expressions of the desire for an end to police brutality and for peace.[3] Though some observers remained quite skeptical, Dr. Blake considerably softened the impact of the Panther rhetoric — maybe they used provocative language just for dramatic effect. The jury would likely give some deference to an African-American professor's benign interpretation of Newton's writings, undermining Jensen's argument that the hate speech provided strong evidence of Huey's motivation to kill Officer Frey.

Melvin Newton also came forward as one of Garry's rebuttal witnesses, explaining away his kid brother's juvenile record. After describing his own education leading to a master's degree in social work, Melvin corroborated Huey's testimony that the Panther co-founder had been functionally illiterate in high school. (Huey had been at his least credible when he told the judge he graduated from high school unable to read or write even simple words like "cat.") Melvin also described how badly beaten Huey had been in his junior year the day before his rash use of a hammer against one of his assailants from Berkeley High.

When Melvin Newton finished his testimony on August 28, the jury was dismissed for the day while the judge heard defense motions. Judge Friedman invited the lawyers to his chambers to decide what jury instructions he would give. The informality of the judge in chambers contrasted with his manner on the bench. He liked to doff his robes as soon as he could and then relax in his shirt sleeves, smoking a cigar. He offered his couch to visitors as they chatted off the record. Judge Friedman would have cause to regret this particular instance of informality.

In chambers, Garry raised the defenses of unconsciousness and diminished capacity, i.e., that the jury should be instructed that Newton had not deliberately shot Officer Frey, but maybe he did somehow shoot him unknowingly. He argued that if Newton did shoot Frey, it was after he had been hit first. Either Newton was not conscious of his acts when he then picked up and fired a gun or had diminished capacity to appreciate what he was doing due to his own wound. Officer Heanes had similarly testified about his own lack of memory after he was wounded. The trial judge agreed to give the diminished capacity instruction, but not the instruction on unconsciousness. It was decided that the trial would resume the following week.

Meanwhile, people watching the news were glued to national coverage of the confrontations between police and demonstrators at the Democratic Convention in Chicago. Mayor Richard Daley had taken unprecedented security precautions, including denying parade permits, so the planned gatherings would all be illegal. Not dissuaded, ten thousand anti-war demonstrators converged on Grant Park in the city's Loop, not far from where the convention was underway. Their ranks were actually swelled by more than a thousand federal and local undercover agents. (It was later estimated that one of every seven people at the various protest rallies was a mole gathering evidence to be used against the organizers.) The Panthers had asked Earl Anthony to speak at that rally, but he was forewarned by O'Connor and Kizenski that Mayor Daley intended to "come down hard on white radicals and Panthers" and Anthony's best option was to flee the country. He made up an excuse to visit a friend in Rome.[4]

Largely at President Johnson's unseen direction, Mayor Daley amassed 12,000 uniformed policemen backed up by 6,000 armed National Guardsmen and teams of firemen prepared to snuff out any arson attempts at the Convention Hall. Rancor was on display within the Convention as well. Four-fifths of primary voters had voted for anti-war candidates. Barry Scheck attended as a former delegate for the late Robert Kennedy, among those pushing unsuccessfully for an open convention and a plank in the platform to end the war. On August 27, viewers had seen police roughly handling some attendees and reporter Dan Rather on the convention floor, and heard Connecticut Senator Abraham Ribicoff condemn such "Gestapo tactics."

A confrontation between the police and demonstrators erupted on August 28. The agitated crowd headed out into the city streets where the police tear-gassed and sprayed mace on just about anyone in their path. Scheck and his friends were in the streets and got gassed. Television news cameras captured more than fifteen minutes of chaos outside the luxury hotel where Vice President Hubert Humphrey was awaiting his nomination for President. Outside the Convention Hall demonstrators shouted, "The Whole World Is Watching"; a motto that Occupy Wall Street protestors would echo in September of 2011. By the time the 1968 Democratic Presidential Convention ended, about a hundred protesters and 119 police officers had been injured. Nearly 600 people were arrested. Everyone involved in the Newton trial had a long weekend to absorb the mind-boggling anarchy in Chicago and ask themselves, "What's next?"

Attention to the Newton murder trial reached its peak starting the Tuesday after Labor Day. At last, the polarizing case chronicled almost daily in the papers and nightly news for the past eight weeks would come to its conclusion. The question on most people's minds was how violent the reaction of the Panthers would be once the jury condemned their leader to die. Surely the police could contain whatever outbreak of rioting occurred, but at what price in carnage? Then what would happen? Would the city face havoc like in Chicago or like the destructive race riots that had occurred in Detroit and Baltimore and other cities in the summer of 1967 that Oakland had narrowly avoided?

The sheriff agreed with the chief of police on a show of overwhelming force to deter any violence. Reinforcements arranged for the trial's end began arriving to multiply the number of police stationed outside the building. Penny Cooper made a point of being among the lawyers with business on the seventh floor of the courthouse who made a break in their schedule to come watch all or part of the closing arguments. None of the press wanted to miss this either. How convincing would Jensen be that Newton deserved the death penalty? Was Jensen about to light the fuse triggering major riots? Would Garry live up to his reputation as a melodramatic orator like a present-day Clarence Darrow? How would he navigate his way around the prosecution's case? Or would Garry fail and Newton become the legendary defense counsel's first client lost to the chair?

In his final arguments on Tuesday morning, Jensen appeared confident. By all appearances, the protests going on outside the building had no impact on him at all. He used no notes. With restrained indignation, he called John Frey "a forgotten man."[5] Frey had no chance to tell his own story on the witness stand because he had been murdered in the line of duty, only to face character assassination in court. Jensen sensed the jury's rapt attention and stayed clinical in his approach, reviewing the forensic evidence in detail to convince the jury that only Newton was close enough to fire the bullet that cut down Officer Frey.

Jensen pointed to the torso of a mannequin propped up next to him. His expert witness, John Davis, had testified that the killer had shot multiple times from a distance of about a foot, and marked the entrance wounds on that mannequin. Davis also pointed out that the fatal bullets did not match those from Heanes' gun. Jensen then explained to the jury that premeditation and malice were required for a verdict of first degree murder. This was not the sort of premeditation that had to unfold over weeks or days. If Newton had taken a brief moment to choose whether to kill Frey, the killing would meet the definition of premeditated murder.

Jensen referred to the partially written traffic ticket at the scene of the shooting, which showed that Newton had given Frey a false name and had not produced his driver's license. When Officer Heanes arrived, Newton had only identified himself because he realized the two officers would figure out who he really was in short order. At times, Jensen spoke softly as he paced in front of the jury. At other times, he sounded sarcastic when he described Newton's political posturing, his self-appointed status as a protector of the black community and an alleged victim of police abuse. Jensen vigorously denied any police conspiracy to "get Huey Newton" and rebutted Garry's insinuations that Jensen or the police had coached any witnesses to distort the truth and frame Newton. Jensen intoned: "Actions speak louder than words."[6] A convicted felon, Newton was "no stranger" to violence. Caught with marijuana in his car and in his pants pocket, he had a strong motive to take deadly action against Frey; he did not want to be caught in possession of drugs in violation of parole.

Jensen argued that on a number of prior occasions, Newton had demonstrated patent hostility toward the police, and looked for an excuse to kill one. He had been caught once before, trying to take a policeman's gun from him. Jensen pointedly relied on Grier's testimony as an eye witness. Brushing aside as minor all the discrepancies that Garry had shown between Grier's testimony and his prior statement, Jensen called the jury's attention to Grier's original statement to the police — "I did get a clear view of his face."[7]

After lunch, the veteran prosecutor explained the law the jurors would have to apply. He needed them to understand the circumstances that would make one killing murder, another a kind of manslaughter and the various "degrees" involved. Jensen reminded the jurors that not every killing was a crime; it depended on the circumstances. To make the degrees of murder as understandable as possible, he suggested that they compare the situation to a driver running down a pedestrian. If the luckless walker stepped out suddenly in front of a car that could not stop in time, it would not be the driver's fault. But if the driver were speeding or drunk, he or she could be held criminally responsible for manslaughter. If the driver deliberately ran the pedestrian down, it would be first degree murder. Second degree murder was a death caused by reckless disregard for human life. He told the jurors to assume the same driver had raced wildly through a busy intersection and crashed and killed a bystander. Jensen then told the jurors the trial had reached "its moment of truth."[8] He ended with a request that they find Newton guilty of assault upon Officer Heanes and first degree murder of Officer Frey — premeditated murder with malice.

Jensen's presentation had been methodical and extremely persuasive. Taking no apparent pleasure in his task, he said that it was "a sad and melancholy truth that Huey Newton . . . is a murderer."[9] Most of the reporters assumed the prosecutor had the jury convinced. Gilbert Moore wrote that when Jensen finished his remarks, "you could feel the noose tightening around Huey Newton's neck; you could well-nigh sniff the gas chamber fumes seeping up through the floorboards."[10]

When Jensen sat down, all eyes turned to Garry, who stood and opened his final argument with a quote from *Alice in Wonderland*: "The King said, 'The evidence first, and then the sentence.' The Queen said, 'No. The sentence first and then the evidence.'"[11] Garry quickly became animated and emotional, focusing primarily on all the discrepancies in Henry Grier's testimony and the contrasting testimony of the bus passenger, Tommy Miller. Garry noted that the police who arrived within minutes of the incident did not mention seeing a bus stopped nearby.

Garry quoted Heanes' testimony that he never saw a gun in Newton's hand and reminded the jury that no paraffin test was done. He suggested that the police could have planted the small traces of marijuana found in Newton's pants pocket. He also intimated that the pot might have been lying in the pants pockets before Newton picked them up at the second-hand store. "You have seen exposed his entire past. Frankly, I wish my own past was as clean as his was. Did you see in any one of the things, the difficulties that he had ever gotten into, where he had stolen so much as a loaf of bread, a pencil?" Newton had never been convicted for any of his parking-lot robberies or petty burglaries, so none of those arrests had been referred to at the trial. Gary continued, "Did you see anything about his past, his juvenile record was even brought in, which is supposed to be sacred."[12]

Referring to Newton's high school hammer-wielding incident, Garry suggested to the jury: "This youngster sought some way of defending himself. Every one of you would have done the same thing. . . . Huey Newton doesn't ask very much for himself. Huey Newton, in my opinion, is a selfless man. I am sure that came out in his testimony. A man who is not interested in himself as a person; he is a devoted man; he is a rare man. Mr. Jensen tried to make this man a liar. He says he [Newton] talks about love and he preaches violence or words to that effect."[13]

Garry then compared Huey Newton to Christ in the Gospel according to Luke, telling his disciples to defend themselves. (It was enough to make the plainclothesmen in the gallery roll their eyes and impress all the Panthers in the audience with Garry's nerve.) He reminded the jurors of the findings of the *Kerner Report* on white racism, of Malcolm X, of the prevalence in the English language of words denoting white supremacy, like a white lie versus a black one, of the pejorative "blackball" and "blacklist" as opposed to the benign term "whitewash." He spoke of Dr. Frantz Fanon and Dr. W. E. B. DuBois. Garry wove in reference to the massacre of his Armenian relatives and the genocide of six million Jews in World War II as he defended the black ghetto fighting for its right of survival. He then exclaimed, "This case is a diabolical attempt to put an innocent man into jail or into the gas chamber."[14]

To make his case, Garry had to take bus driver Henry Grier on directly, but it still shocked the courtroom when he castigated Henry Grier as "either deliberately lying or . . . a psychopath."[15] Highlighted among the discrepancies was Grier's shifting description of the clothing he thought he saw the perpetrator pull a gun from — a tan jacket on the morning of the shootout and a dark one at trial. The one at trial had been stripped off Newton at the hospital. Officer Heanes had identified it in court as what Newton wore when stopped by Officer Frey. Garry demonstrated to the jury that the dark jacket police had confiscated from Newton at the hospital had pockets far too shallow to hold a gun.

Garry then focused on key features of Newton's testimony: that he had been subjected to a degrading, complete frisk and had a law book, but no gun in his hand when he was shot. He spoke generally about discrimination, racism and ghetto life; he highlighted the actions of Mayor Daley and the Chicago police in the riots that had dominated the news that past week in the coverage of the Democratic Presidential Convention in Chicago. Garry had the courtroom spellbound, the jurors in rapt attention, as he ended almost three-and-a-half hours of final argument, brushing back tears.

Emotionally exhausted, Garry embraced Newton's shoulders with one arm and haltingly urged the jury to find his client innocent of all charges. Newton looked equally teary-eyed. Judge Friedman appeared moved and offered Garry time to compose himself. Garry thanked him and told the judge he had "said all I have to say."[16] Jensen jumped up in rebuttal, livid at Garry's accusations of perjured testimony and a police frame-up. Garry had impugned his own integrity as well as that of the state's chief witness. Any discrepancies in Grier's testimony were the product of honest mistakes. With those last words from the prosecutor, the trial itself was over. The jury would be instructed the following day.

Onlookers marveled at Garry's legerdemain: reporters, lawyers who had dropped by for a glimpse of the trial of the century, and even the most skeptical Black Panther supporters who had lobbied for a black lawyer for their leader. They had just witnessed a master magician in the courtroom. Newton was both a tough and articulate revolutionary hero and a hapless target of police brutality. Kidnapping victim? I'll make him disappear before your very eyes. Mysterious passenger? Now you see McKinney, now you don't. Eyewitness story, impossible to penetrate? Shot full of holes. Like Houdini, Garry made his showmanship appear relatively effortless as Stender and others labored mightily behind him, often out of sight. Outside, under constant surveillance by a deputy sheriff, Black Panthers stood in military formation, waving black and blue Party flags. Some Panthers remained behind at the courthouse, continuing their vigil, as others left for their headquarters on Grove Street or headed for a planned 5 p.m. rally at DeFremery Park. The Peace and Freedom Party had planned its own courthouse vigil, but they cancelled those plans when fewer than two dozen people showed up.

After forty minutes of instruction on the morning of Thursday, September 5, the jury began its deliberations in a locked jury room on the eighth floor of the courthouse. The room was not large: it contained two small tables, chairs and a blackboard and had its own private bathroom. The window of the room was too high up for anyone from the street to see inside. An old cigar carton sat on one of the tables, presumably for paper ballots. The alternate jurors were sent to a separate room accompanied by a bailiff and frustratingly told not to discuss the case. The alternates would only play a role if one or more of the jurors took ill or otherwise could not participate in continued deliberations. If that were to occur, the alternate or alternates chosen to join in deliberations would be disqualified if they had discussed any of the evidence with any of the alternates who were not selected.

Meanwhile, the reporters, defense lawyers and Newton's family moved to the sixth-floor press room and hallway, where the media representatives engaged in a free-flowing analysis of the trial. A few placed wagers on the anticipated verdicts, favoring first or second degree murder. That same day in San Francisco, Eldridge Cleaver held a press conference and then left to give a luncheon speech to the Barristers Club as the Peace and Freedom candidate for President. When a young lawyer at the Barristers Club asked him about the Newton case, Cleaver declared ominously that "consequences" would be "inflicted" on whites if Newton were "railroaded," adding, "then all the strings will be cut . . . ." Bobby Seale delivered a similar message on the steps of the Alameda County Courthouse: "The sky's the limit around the world" if Newton were not freed.[17] Later that day, Newton told skeptical reporters that "the sky is the limit" was merely a symbolic statement meaning the Panthers would "exhaust all judicial and political resources throughout the world."[18]

Shortly after 6 p.m. Thursday evening, everyone piled into court again. They had just been alerted that the jury was returning. Hearts sank among some of Newton's supporters. A quick verdict usually meant conviction. But once in session, the judge revealed a signed request from David Harper, as the newly selected foreman of the jury.

Harper asked for a copy of Grier's statement to the police as well as a rereading of Grier's testimony and that of Officer De Hoyos, the officer who had first responded to the scene of the shooting. The jury also asked to see Newton's wounds again. With the judge's permission, Newton walked to the jury box, removed his coat and pulled out his shirt. Garry helped Newton once again display the scars of the entrance and exit wounds.

Thelton Henderson had already been impressed that Garry had succeeded in seating an extraordinary number of women and minorities on the jury. He considered a black foreman on the jury "completely revolutionary."

Belva Davis reacted the same way: "The selection of the jury foreman was absolutely a surprise, a shock, and of a trial, a high profile trial like this . . . highly explosive international trial. All I could think about then, this is a brave man because he's entering an arena where either side is used to guns, and one never knows what kinds of emotions are going to be provoked by a verdict." Newton's family was happy to see this development, but the Panthers took no pleasure in learning of Harper's selection as foreman. They assumed from his successful career and suburban lifestyle that he must be a bootlicker. Yet the jury's questions and the opportunity for this second viewing of Newton's wounds, lifted the defense team's spirits.

Until this point in the trial the jurors had gone home each night. Now they were sequestered until they completed deliberations. They had each been told to pack a suitcase to bring to court that day, but Harvey Kokka forgot to do so. A bailiff was sent to his home to fetch a packed suitcase from his nervous wife. The jury continued deliberating all day Friday and through the weekend, accompanied by armed bailiffs or sheriff's deputies every time they left for lunch or dinner or to retire for the night. As a safety precaution, the jurors slept at a different, undisclosed hotel each night. Most of the reporters remained holed up at the courthouse, afraid they would miss a scoop if they left. Many crammed into the sixth floor press room, sleeping, eating and playing cards. They occasionally left to check out rumors, which often proved unsubstantiated. Gilbert Moore, Fay Stender and Bob Blauner were among those who passed some of the time playing chess on the floor while they awaited the verdict. Tension mounted as the jury deliberation continued. By Friday, all of the reporters had taken sides on the outcome and began trading speculation on suspected government or rightwing plants at the trial.

The local police began preparing for rioting when the expected murder verdict was announced. In London, the week before, an angry demonstration had broken out after a false announcement that Newton had been convicted and sentenced to die. A much larger, violent reaction was expected locally if the jury found him guilty of first degree murder. A group of white radicals, the Berkeley Socialist League, announced that it would hold a vigil and undertake retaliatory action within two days of an adverse verdict. The Panthers had the same thought in mind. Hilliard recalls that if the jury came back with the death penalty, "We're going to come and take him out of the state's hands and we're going . . . to make sure that we mobilize our constituency to make certain that you don't take his life. . . . He wasn't going to die in the gas chamber. That was our mandate. That if you kill Huey Newton then, 'The sky is the limit.'" The phrase had become their mantra.

The county had already paid tens of thousands of dollars in overtime for extra deputies. In anticipation of rioting, several hundred police officers were immediately placed on extended duty, augmented by members of the California Highway Patrol. There were eighty-two extra units of law enforcement, primarily from the CHP, arranged to work from Thursday to Tuesday on the assumption the verdict would occur during that time period. Thousands of National Guardsmen remained on alert surrounding the city of Oakland, equipped with helicopters. A large contingent of the police was hidden from public view in the basement parking lot of the Oakland Museum, then in the midst of construction across the street, half a block from the courthouse.

Inside the courtroom the defense felt the intensified pressure — they asked themselves if there was anything else they could do to reduce the chance of a first degree murder conviction or strengthen their position if they had to appeal. Suddenly, it occurred to them that the jury had requested a copy of bus driver Grier's original statement to the police. What the jury got — and what had been offered at trial — was not anything Grier had written, but a transcription of a tape-recorded oral statement. The defense realized that they had never received the original police tape of the bus driver's interview. At their request, Jensen produced the tape itself along with the transcript that had been produced in court on Friday morning. The defense team then obtained Judge Friedman's permission to double check its accuracy.

Fay Stender needed to stay at the courthouse in case the jury came back. She pressed her husband Marvin into service right away; he left with Ed Keating to find an expert to re-transcribe the tape for the defense. They hurriedly obtained a new transcript that had an easy-to-miss but highly significant wording difference from the transcript provided at trial. On the tape, the driver had said he "didn't" get a good look at the civilian. The transcript said he "did" get a good look.

The defense team quickly contacted the judge and Jensen to schedule immediate argument on this newly disclosed issue. They considered it a bombshell — evidence the prosecutor had engaged in deliberate deception. On Saturday afternoon, the jury remained sequestered while the judge heard highly charged arguments on both sides. Judge Friedman then himself listened to the tape and heard the word "didn't." Yet he refused to reopen the trial as Garry angrily demanded. There was no indication that the error in the transcription was purposeful. Jensen had indicated he was as surprised as everyone else, but he also considered the issue less important than Garry did in light of all the other evidence. Jensen persuaded the judge that to call the jury back for the sole purpose of reading the corrected version of Grier's statement — "didn't get a good look" — would overemphasize the significance of the change. Newton never denied being at the scene — he had in fact identified himself to Officer Heanes, testified to being shot in the stomach and identified the law book he left behind. Judge Friedman's solution was to allow the correction of Grier's prior statement to be transmitted without comment to the jury as it continued its deliberations.[19]

That same day the Panthers got out the latest edition of their newspaper. At the top was the usual head shot of Huey in a beret wearing a grim expression on his face. Underneath the photo was the caption "Huey

Must Be Set Free" underscored with the image of a rifle. Covering the entire front page below the logo was a photo of three militant Panther Party members on the steps of the Alameda County courthouse. The trio stood at attention in full dress uniform waving "Free Huey" banners emblazoned with the panther emblem. In bold print above the building were the words "WORLD AWAITS VERDICT" and, ominously below the photo, "FREE HUEY . . . OR THE SKY'S THE LIMIT!"

At quarter to eight that evening, the jury created a stir by asking to return to court. They had already been back in the morning for a lengthy rereading of testimony. Reporters again wondered if there was a verdict, but the jury only wanted to have the instructions on the degrees of homicide recited to them again along with the definition of assault. Two of the women jurors looked like they might have been crying. It appeared that a decision was imminent. But the jurors ended Saturday, September 7, at 9:45 p.m., with a request that they be escorted to their hotel for the night, with no indication a decision had been reached.

It meant one more night for police on overtime, anxious that they likely would soon have a major riot on their hands, one more night of uncertainty for the press and the lawyers as well as for Newton and the Panthers. Eldridge Cleaver expected the jury verdict to trigger guerrilla warfare and made plans accordingly. Kathleen Cleaver thought "it would not necessarily come to that, but if it did, people weren't going to back down." In the event Newton was headed for execution, the decision had been made to break him out — or die trying. Jensen had to wonder, too: What was the jury debating? How long would they remain out? Would it end in a stalemate with one or more hold-outs and require the case to be retried?

On Sunday, the jury started deliberations again at 10 a.m. and returned to court immediately, asking the judge to slowly reread the definitions of murder and manslaughter. After Judge Friedman got part way through, the foreman signaled they had heard what they needed to hear. The jurors retired once more to the jury room. After having all but ruled out first degree murder on Saturday, the reporters in attendance felt overpowered with gloom. They concluded that the jury deliberations had actually come down to a choice between first and second degree murder — their original assumption when the trial began. Newton's surprisingly effective testimony had lulled a few of them into thinking otherwise, but none now believed he would be acquitted.

Newton's family remained apprehensive. They all fervently wished for Huey's acquittal, but Melvin knew that might be too much to hope for. His biggest fear was that Huey would be found guilty of premeditated murder and sentenced to die. Melvin could not bear thinking of his parents having to endure the pain if his mother's baby was headed for the gas chamber. It might kill her. Kathleen Cleaver could not imagine that result. She and the other protesters were pushing so hard for Newton's freedom they would not accept death as the verdict.

In his office, Lowell Jensen noted the eerie calm in the city, like the prelude to a major storm. He and his staff remained unavailable to the press. It amazed Jensen to hear from the police that crime in the city was at an ebb as even would-be burglars awaited the jury's verdict. Belva Davis remembers her own trepidation at the time: "I think the only thing that those of us who were watching from the sidelines dreaded was a verdict that could act as the flint to ignite a fire of resentment and frustration . . . because of the way our society was structured . . . we feared what could happen. We'd seen people hurt and injured, and none of us wanted to see that again. Nor did we want to see our city going up in smoke."

As head of Oakland's Parks and Recreation Department, Bill Patterson had his pulse on the mood of youth in the flatlands: "Oakland was a powder keg, it could've blown up." Mayor Reading and other city officials expected violence, too. All of Oakland seemed to grind to a halt awaiting the verdict. As the nerve-racking weekend wore to a close, Garry, KPFA program director Elsa Knight Thompson and Alex Hoffmann spent Sunday afternoon and evening closeted with Newton at the jail, with Fay Stender, Blauner and others coming in and out during their extended vigil. Thompson had the surreal experience of flying back to await the verdict in the Newton case after covering the chaotic Democratic Convention and demonstrations in Lincoln Park in Chicago. There, even television network crews and newspaper photographers had been targeted with billy clubs. She had seen the confrontations escalate as police and National Guardsmen responded to sporadic rock and bottle throwers by spraying everyone they saw on the streets — bystanders included — with mace or tear gas before they dragged them into paddy wagons off to jail.

Elsa Knight Thompson was herself a veteran World War II BBC radio announcer. She had relished witnessing firsthand the brutal tactics of Chicago police captured on camera with ninety million Americans watching. The overreaction exceeded the Yippies' expectations when they set out to provoke Gestapo-like repression. The Chicago police were doing a great job helping them galvanize revolutionary fervor among their followers.[20] Thompson stopped off on her way back to Berkeley from Chicago to visit Beverly Axelrod in New Mexico and brought Axelrod's well wishes to Newton. As Newton knew, his good friend was now working on major land rights issues for Reies Lopez Tijerina, a militant New Mexico counterpart to Cesar Chavez's farm workers' organization in California. Tijerina had come to California twice earlier in the year to speak at rallies for Newton.

Newton enjoyed the distraction of Thompson's travel tales. Thompson was amazed at the calm in the small, tenth-floor visiting room at the Oakland jail. Newton acted as if he were entertaining guests in his living room rather than awaiting a life or death verdict from jurors sequestered two floors below. Newton even joked that: "If they come in with an acquittal, I'm going to ask to poll them individually."[21] He thought the others would enjoy his gallows humor — if the foreman reported that all twelve jurors agreed he should go free, someone should test to see if they each really meant it. It was the prosecutor who would want to poll each juror individually in the event of an acquittal, not the defense.

Thompson had a sixth sense that the jury had just reached a verdict shortly before a knock on the door summoned them back to the courtroom late Sunday evening. Foreman Harper had sent a note out to the judge that the jury had completed the verdict forms. Their adrenaline flowing, only a couple of dozen rumpled and unshowered members of the press still waited on the sixth floor of the courthouse. They answered the call to the courtroom along with a few spectators, the cheerless, exhausted lawyers and Newton's nervous family, leaving a large number of empty seats. Newton arrived dressed in olive drab slacks and a green shirt, looking dour but determined. He told reporter Rush Greenlee, "No matter how it goes it's not the end of the road. I've prepared myself."[22] When everyone was inside, Judge Friedman took the bench and announced that the doors to the courtroom would be locked and stay locked until the verdicts had all been read and the jury dismissed. That precaution had not been taken before. Sheriff's deputies remained on guard at the building's entrances and in its abandoned hallways. The atmosphere was eerie; the audience in suspense. Moore felt the room seem to shrink "as though we had all been stuffed into some malodorous bottle. The stench of death was everywhere."[23] When the jurors entered a side door and sat down, they, too, looked bedraggled and exhausted. None looked at Newton as they walked past him, which veteran reporters considered a sure sign of a murder conviction.

Judge Friedman then asked for the verdicts. The tension in the room heightened even further as Harper handed the verdict to the bailiff, who brought it to the judge. The judge reviewed the form silently. His expression revealed nothing. He then passed it to the clerk, who read it aloud as Newton stood at the counsel table waiting to hear if the moment had come that would send him back to San Quentin with all the other men on death row. First degree murder — not guilty. Sighs of immense relief escaped from the defense team and Newton's family. Second degree murder — not guilty. Members of the press were astounded. Lowell Jensen was stunned, but showed no emotion. He had assumed that if the jury did not come back with first degree murder, they would find Newton guilty of second degree murder. The loss was difficult to understand. Would Newton win acquittal?

Voluntary manslaughter — guilty. Jensen sensed a compromise. So did many others. Most of Newton's family had trouble accepting even that lesser conviction. Panther supporters in the audience, who had been ecstatic at the murder acquittals, were not sure how to react to that unexpected news. Newton swallowed hard, but remained impassive as the reading of the verdicts was completed. Assault upon Officer Heanes — not guilty. People thought the announcement was over, but not quite. The clerk had one more verdict to read. The jury had also followed instructions to determine for themselves if Newton had been convicted of a prior felony. Their affirmative vote on that issue automatically increased the penalty.

Jensen tried not to show his severe disappointment as the most dramatic case he had ever tried came to an end without the anticipated first or second degree murder conviction. "The police were not happy with the verdict and the Panthers were not happy with the verdict. . . ." Above all, Jensen had wanted to avoid either a hung jury or the perception of race bias — those hurdles looked overcome, which was a source of no small comfort.

Though Newton's life had been spared, and he had avoided conviction for a capital crime, this was not enough for most of his loved ones. They had hoped he would be freed altogether, and right on the spot. His family struggled with conflicting emotions. Most of Newton's family looked stunned that he was not acquitted of all charges. Huey's sister Doris Godfrey collapsed in shock. Melvin Newton rejoiced that his mother would not have to face her baby being sent to the gas chamber. Stender squeezed Newton's hand. Charles Garry consoled Karen Wald with a hug and whispered, "This is a victory." As soon as word got outside, the Panthers who had demonstrated every day were jubilant. Janice Garrett later said: "We were totally shocked when we heard the verdict that Huey was found innocent of murder. . . . We could not believe it because this was the first time that an armed black man was in an altercation with the police department and was vindicated." Actually, not totally vindicated.

The jury verdicts had surprised nearly everyone. The press was amazed. Looking back, Belva Davis summed up the nearly universal reaction: "Huey Newton, a black man with a gun, who shoots a white policeman, was tried by a jury in this country, in the court, and for reasons that many Americans say they still don't understand, was judged . . . not guilty of first-degree murder. I can't think there are very many places where life would come together in such a fashion. That you could find a jury and foreman, and a prosecution and a defense, coming together and get a verdict that was for anything other than death penalty, but it happened right here."

The police could not see how the jury got to voluntary manslaughter. Neither could many members of the press. The jury found that Newton had shot Frey, but it must have decided Newton did not possess his own gun. By now, all of the press knew that possession of a concealed firearm, a felony itself, would have automatically rendered Newton guilty of second degree murder. The jury must have concluded that Officer Frey had pulled out his gun, that Newton had wrestled it away from him, and that Newton only shot Frey after Heanes shot Newton in the stomach.

Each juror was polled individually on all three counts and affirmed that he or she agreed with the verdict. Judge Friedman, dabbing his brow with a handkerchief, thanked and dismissed the jury for their hard work and expressed his appreciation to the alternates for standing by in readiness. The bailiff then led them out by the side door. To the jurors' surprise, none of their cars remained in the enclosed garage. The police had impounded them for safety and reparked them on the street. The whole experience had to seem surreal as they parted ways to resume their lives after several weeks of high-stakes drama since the jury had first been seated. The next day police patrolled the streets in front of each of their homes, but nothing happened.

Garry had a clear victory that day, but he was only part way to his goal. He pressed onward, immediately filing three motions: for a new trial, for Newton's release on bail and for the sentencing to be delayed. The defense team would have their work cut out for them to accomplish all of these in short order. Judge Friedman set a date for that Thursday, September 12, to take testimony on the bail request, set the hearing itself for September 27 and then adjourned the proceedings. As bailiffs escorted Newton from the courtroom, his minister raised a fist up high with an emphatic "Power to the People," and Newton responded in kind.

When the brief Sunday evening court session concluded, bailiffs opened the locks on the seventh-floor stairwell for the first time since the trial had begun almost two months earlier. The reporters were as jumpy as corralled mustangs about to be let loose. Everyone rose at the clerk's order signaling the close of the proceedings. As soon as the judge left the bench, the reporters rushed for the telephones in the building and for quotes from the lawyers, Newton and Newton's family — each on deadline trying to get a read on which side felt it had won. Some also sought out the jurors before they left the building, but they were protected by armed security guards as they left. No opportunity arose to see if any of them would discuss their decision with the press.

After Garry spent half an hour with him in his cell, Garry reported that Newton believed he had been "sold down the river by a white racist society."[24] But the legal team had in fact buoyed Newton's hopes that the low-level verdict could make him a likely candidate for release on bail pending appeal. Freeing him on appeal had been what they told him to expect all along.

Belva Davis had all kinds of unanswered questions: "The Newton trial was as unconventional as one could get in looking at justice within a courtroom. Everything was unusual. The number of women on the jury, the foreman." She also noticed Fay Stender had been "one of the most underreported persons during the Huey Newton trial because Charles Garry was such a big personality. He commanded all of the attention. It was only those who dug deeper that found out what her importance had been to the verdict."

Newton instructed Garry to tell Seale to get word out immediately on the street "to keep it cool." Newton wanted no uprising in response to the verdict that would spoil his chances for release.[25] Seale felt the same way — there was no point to giving the police an excuse to bash heads and make mass arrests. Seale got on the phone and then jumped in his car to spread Newton's message. Hilliard understood that Huey did not want any of the Panthers "to do anything crazy and there is not going to be any riots. . . . Our charge was to make sure that Oakland didn't burn." Panther Party Field Marshall Donald "DC" Cox was livid. Based on prior instructions from Party leaders, Cox had been all set to assault the jail with his men and liberate Newton. The change of plans rankled long afterwards, causing Cox to side with Cleaver when the Panthers later split.[26] Yet even Cleaver saw merit in holding off revolution in the streets — at least for the time being. Everywhere Seale went, he passed caravans of police and highway patrolmen in riot gear.

Upon hearing the verdict, most members of the defense team were in a celebratory mood. They all knew that the result was far better than it could have been, though Alex Hoffmann, who had spent the most time keeping Newton company in jail, still found the voluntary manslaughter conviction traumatic. The sensitive lawyer may have secretly been in love with Huey, though it would be many years before Hoffmann acknowledged his homosexuality. Fay Stender — another hopelessly passionate devotee of Huey and his cause — also remained unsatisfied at anything short of complete exoneration. In her view, it would have been unthinkable for the jury to find Newton guilty of first degree murder and subject to execution.

Federal prosecutor James Brosnahan had closely followed the progress of the case. Garry's aggressive approach to jury selection impressed Brosnahan as some of the best jury work he had ever seen. But he saw the verdict more as a major shift in community thinking: "A symbol that Oakland was changing. . . . It couldn't happen in the '50s. Charlie Garry or not, it would not have happened in the '50s." Garry would have debated Brosnahan on that. He remained convinced he could have saved Julius and Ethel Rosenberg from execution, too.

Civil rights lawyer Ann Fagan Ginger, a Lawyers Guild colleague of the defense team, wryly noted: "The concept that the jury could listen to the facts and decide he was innocent of first degree murder in effect proved that the Black Panthers were wrong in thinking everything was bad. So it was a kind of a contradictory situation. . . . The Panther insistence that racism was present every minute couldn't be true. The white community could say we did a fair thing." Ginger decided the picking of that historic jury needed to be chronicled in a handbook. First published in 1969, *Minimizing Racism in Jury Trials: The Voir Dire Conducted by Charles R. Garry in People of California v. Huey P. Newton* would quickly become a well-thumbed "Bible" for criminal defense lawyers nationwide.

Barry Scheck notes: "What's extraordinary about the trial is it changed people's approach to jury selection, and the issues of race in jury selection. And it really proved that, even in the most high profile incendiary kind of political case in the United States, you could get a fair trial. There could be an assessment of the evidence . . . and that some-body in Newton's position could take the witness stand and be believed by the jury essentially, and that was not self-evident to anyone at the time."

True to form, Lowell Jensen refused to publicly second-guess the jurors, out of respect for their efforts. He later said, "The verdict that was rendered shows that this jury was fully capable of listening to the evidence that was introduced, and deciding the case on the basis of the evidence, rather than on any racist considerations. As far as I was con-cerned . . . they were very conscientious . . . [and] should be respected."

Privately, as soon as he heard the manslaughter verdict, he assumed the jurors had compromised on the result. Even diminished capacity usually reduced premeditated murder to second degree "reckless" mur-der, not voluntary manslaughter. (Eleven years later in San Francisco, a jury instructed on what became known as "the Twinkie defense" — impaired judgment from too much junk food — would come back with a similarly surprising voluntary manslaughter verdict. In that famous case with both a white defendant and white victims, the defendant Dan White was a politically conservative former supervisor charged with assassinating liberal San Francisco Mayor George Moscone and the city's first openly gay supervisor, Harvey Milk.)

While Jensen deliberately kept his thoughts to himself, Garry pos-tured to the press that the verdict was a disappointing, "chicken shit" compromise. After he met with his attorneys, Newton told reporters the same thing — that the jury had reached a compromise unsup-ported by the evidence. Most other observers subscribed to that view as well. But on his way out of the courthouse, Garry poked reporter Gilbert Moore in the ribs and whispered, "We got 'em. We got 'em."[27] He shouted to another supporter, "It is a victory, buddy, it's a victory!"[28]

102-160 2M 7/61 (Rev.)

SUPERIOR COURT OF THE STATE OF CALIFORNIA IN AND FOR THE COUNTY OF ALAMEDA

ABSTRACT OF JUDGMENT
(Commitment to State Prison)

The People of the State of California, Present:

vs.	Present: Hon. **MONROE FRIEDMAN** Judge of the Superior Court **D. Lowell Jensen** **Asst.** District Attorney **Charles R. Garry** Counsel for Defendant
HUEY P. NEWTON	
Defendant	

This certifies that on **Sept. 8, 1968** judgment of conviction of the above-named defendant was entered as follows:
(1) Case No. **41266** Count No. **One of the Indictment.**
On his plea of **not guilty**
he was convicted by **verdict of jury** of **a felony, to wit: voluntary manslaughter, a violation of Section 192, Subdivision 1 of the Penal Code of the State of California, a lesser and included offense within the offense charged in Count One of the Indictment.**

with prior felony convictions charged and proved ~~committed~~ as follows:

Date	County and State	Crime	Disposition

On October 29, 1964, in the Superior Court of the State of California in and for the County of Alameda, defendant was convicted of a felony, to wit: assault with a deadly weapon, a violation of Section 245 of the Penal Code of the State of California under the name of Huey Percy Newton, and pursuant to said conviction, sentence was suspended for three years, during which time he was placed on probation.

~~Defendant ... charged with and proved or admitted ...~~
~~(c) Defendant ... adjudged an habitual criminal within the meaning of ...~~

(3) IT IS THEREFORE ORDERED, ADJUDGED AND DECREED that the said defendant be punished by imprisonment in state prison of the State of California for the term provided by law and that he be remanded to the Sheriff of the County of Alameda, and by him delivered to the Director of Corrections of the State of California. **California Medical Facility, Vacaville, California.**

F I L E D

SEP 27 1968

JACK G. BLUE, County Clerk
BY K. L. FAGRE

(4) To the Sheriff of the County of Alameda and to the Director of Corrections at the **California Medical Facility, Vacaville, California.**
Pursuant to the aforesaid judgment, this is to command you, the said Sheriff, to deliver the above named defendant into the custody of the Director of Corrections at the **California Medical Facility, Vacaville, California,** at your earliest convenience.
Witness my hand and seal of said court **September 27, 1968.**

JACK G. BLUE, Clerk

(SEAL)

By **K. L. Fagre** Deputy.

State of California, } SS.
County of Alameda,

I do hereby certify the foregoing to be a true and correct abstract of the judgment duly made and entered on the minutes of the Superior Court in the above entitled action as provided by Penal Code Section 1213.

Attest my hand and seal of the said Superior Court this

(SEAL)

The foregoing instrument is a **27th** day of **September,** 196**8**.
correct copy of the original
on file in this office   JACK G. BLUE,
County Clerk and ex officio Clerk of the Superior Court of the State of California in and for the County of Alameda.

Monroe Friedman ATTEST: SEP 27 1968
Judge of the Superior Court of the State of California in and for the County of Alameda

By **K. L. Fagre** , Deputy.

JACK G. BLUE, County Clerk and ex officio Clerk of the State of California in and for the County of Alameda
DEPUTY

EXHIBIT A

Courtesy of Department of Special Collections and University Archives, Stanford University Libraries, Green Library, Dr. Huey P. Newton Foundation, Inc. Collection.

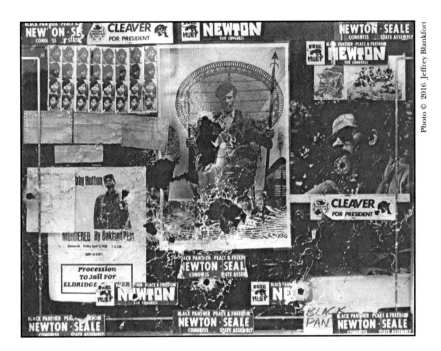

Panther headquarters shot up by two Oakland policemen early on Tuesday morning, September 10, 1968 in response to the jury verdict.

318

Eldridge Cleaver, 1968

Huge demonstration outside the federal building in San Francisco, May 1, 1969. Huey Newton was in jail and Eldridge Cleaver had fled the country.

Police confront a small part of the crowd of thousands outside the Alameda County courthouse awaiting Huey Newton's release on the morning of August 5, 1970.

Huey Newton bares his chest in the heat, standing atop his attorney Alex Hoffman's VW Beetle outside the Alameda County courthouse, celebrating his release from prison August 5, 1970.

Huey Newton and Fay Stender

Charles Garry, Huey Newton and Fay Stender conducting a press conference in the library of Garry's San Francisco office on the afternoon of Newton's August 5, 1970, release.

16. AFTERMATH

"I just hope we did the right thing.
We certainly tried. "
— NEWTON JUROR EDA PRELLI

J ust before turning in their verdicts, the jurors made a pact to keep their deliberations shrouded in secrecy, to let them go on with their lives unmolested by curious media. Two of the women changed their minds the next day and spoke to the press. The day after the ordeal ended, an *Oakland Tribune* reporter interviewed Mrs. Gibbons, the factory worker who was the only juror chosen the very first day. She described how the jurors were anxious to reach agreement and decided that they could only convict Newton for assault of Officer Heanes if they concluded that Officer Frey's death was premeditated murder. During deliberations, one of the jurors brought up the threats made by demonstrators, "Huey must be free or else." They decided it was not their problem and focused instead on reaching the result the evidence supported. The jurors believed that Officer Frey had stopped Newton for no reason, that he had called Newton a "nigger" and frisked him abusively. They found no malice in Newton's reaction, but did find him culpable of manslaughter. Mrs. Gibbons said no ballot was ever taken on first or second degree murder, and no one took a hard line position on finding him guilty of first degree murder.[1]

Mrs. Eda Prelli, the widowed landlady on the jury, gave a somewhat different version to Rush Greenlee of the *San Francisco Examiner*. She revealed her own strong belief a fifth person had been present at the shootout and that Huey's passenger Gene McKinney might have known more than the jury heard. Two of the women strongly favored second degree murder, but Mrs. Prelli started out for acquittal. She later joined with David Harper and Tom Hofmann, the bachelor bank officer who lived with his parents, when they switched from acquittal to manslaughter.

Examiner reporters interviewed many Oaklanders for their reactions and found them divided on racial lines. Most blacks believed Newton "got a raw deal"; most whites thought he should have no complaints about a result many considered better than he deserved. Clinton White — whom Bobby Seale interviewed for chief defense counsel — was more evenhanded. He had anticipated acquittal, but thought the jury conscientiously applied the law and "may have believed part of Newton's story and part of bus driver Grier's testimony." The acquittal of Newton on the charge of shooting Heanes might simply reflect that the jury believed Heanes was hit accidentally by errant gunfire during a struggle between Frey and Newton.[2]

San Francisco Examiner editor-in-chief William Randolph Hearst, Jr., held his tongue until the Newton trial was over, but could wait no longer to observe that the murder trial raised issues that "will long echo." The concerns raised were ironic, coming from the flagship paper run by the Hearst media conglomerate. William Hearst was the son of the man who built his empire on yellow journalism, sensationalizing "trials of the century" with sometimes tragic results. The central question raised in his September 10, 1968, editorial was: "Did the big 'Free Huey' demonstrations around the courthouse while the trial was in progress amount to attempted intimidation of the judge, jury and prosecution witnesses?" The editorial noted that, if the courthouse had been surrounded by a hanging mob, the result would have been a mistrial—a conclusion only very recently reached by the U.S. Supreme Court after decades of circuslike national coverage of dramatic trials. Hearst's editorial concluded:

> [If] American justice is to be done, the judge and jury must be
> as free from attempted intimidation by those who want to free a
> defendant as those who want to hang him. . . . [S]ociety [must]
> maintain a system of justice functioning in an atmosphere of calm

detachment, not one surrounded by demonstrators, bullhorns, paramilitary forces shouting allegiance to the defendant, armed sheriff's deputies at every courthouse door, physical searches of courtroom spectators, cries of "pigs" yelled at police, and big banners proclaiming in fierce rhetoric that "the sky's the limit" if anything happens to the defendant.[3]

Though it represented a total turnabout for one of the nation's most ardent First Amendment rights' champions, the editorial had a point. Within two years the state legislature would enact a criminal law to prevent a recurrence of potentially intimidating demonstrations circling courthouses. But heightened courthouse security heralded the new norm, and, as Hearst well knew, "Free Huey" rallies could be held at a nearby park with no repercussions. The editorial also failed to mention that, to the embarrassment of law enforcement, two drunken policemen had just committed the only violence by shooting up Panther headquarters. Most glaring in its absence from the editorial was its explosive context: an overwhelmingly white establishment in open confrontation with a broad coalition of anti-war activists who embraced Newton as an icon; a black community seething over decades of abuse; and skewed *Oakland Tribune* coverage of the shootout making the Panther leader's murder conviction look like an open and shut case before the trial had even started. These were only a few of the factors impeding "calm detachment" — an unattainable goal for a trial of a black revolutionary in 1968 in Oakland or anywhere else in America.

Looking back as a veteran lawyer, John Burris considered the jury verdict fair. "Huey, in my view, was stopped as to who he was, not because of anything he had done. And so that meant there was no probable cause for the stop. . . . The same thing that happens in stop and frisk, people are stopped and frisked based upon who they are and not what they have done." Yet, Burris says, "In . . . retrospect, having a chance to understand the law a lot better, the manslaughter verdict makes a whole lot more sense than any other verdict . . . because it was a spontaneous act. Huey was not looking for the officer, the officer stopped him. . . . Something happened between those two men, and the officer could have been . . . yanking on him, pulling on him, assaulting him, and Huey could have very well believed that his life was in danger. . . . If only one of them has a gun, it strikes [me] that you can't have a complete self-defense in a situation like that, if it's the officer's gun."

Barry Scheck also thinks "Newton got a fair trial . . . an incredible trial . . . a political defense [that] also brought to bear some pretty creative legal strategies, particularly around the jury selection. . . . The prosecutor was a fair guy. . . . You compare it to some of the other political trials where the prosecutors were . . . determined and hell bent to get a conviction no matter how they got it. . . . Lowell Jensen was different."

In hindsight, Lowell Jensen concurs that justice was done. "Justice is a function of the process. . . . As far as the process in this case was concerned, this was a fair trial under difficult circumstances, and I think that's justice."

* * * * *

In March of 2016, District Attorney Ken Thompson of Brooklyn, New York, made headlines for showing similar mettle under extreme political pressure. Thompson is the borough's first black District Attorney. In February, Thompson had convicted Chinese-American policeman Peter Liang of manslaughter for firing his gun one night in November 2014 in a poorly-lit stairwell in a New York housing project. The ricocheting bullet killed African-American tenant Akai Gurley. Comparable situations in the past had been dismissed as accidents, but Black Lives Matter protestors led demands for Officer Liang's prosecution. Meanwhile, watchdogs tallied five times as many unarmed blacks killed by police in 2015 as unarmed whites.[4] The Liang jury of seven men and five women included eight whites, one African-American and three Latinos. After they reached their guilty verdict, an older white man on the jury told reporters, "I come from a family of cops. I have to face them tomorrow. They are here to protect us. It was a very tough decision."[5]

Liang could have received a similar manslaughter sentence to Huey Newton's — up to fifteen years in prison. Instead, District Attorney Thompson wrestled with his conscience and recommended no jail time at all, telling the judge, "There are no winners here." In a front-page story, the *New York Times* noted that neither the police nor the outraged black community could claim victory. Former federal prosecutor Alan Vinegrad was asked to comment and gave a Solomon-like answer: "Who was the winner? You could argue it was the justice system."[6]

After a claim of juror misconduct arose, black community members applauded the trial judge, Justice Danny Chun, when he refused to order a new trial for Liang. Chun was also a pioneer — the first Korean-American appointed to that trial bench. The following week, the same group did an about-face and lambasted Justice Chun for his next ruling. He decided that the jury made a mistake in convicting Liang of manslaughter instead of merely criminal negligence, pointing out that Liang did not even know Gurley was in the stairwell. Justice Chun then sentenced Liang only to probation and community service. Once more the case made front-page news as "dueling groups of protesters erupted into chants and debates" outside the courthouse — Black Lives Matter supporters versus the Police Benevolent Society and Asian-American activists.[7] Each faction claimed the exclusive right to define what justice meant under the circumstances.

New York Times reporter Alan Feuer looked at it from a broader perspective: "The politically contentious case . . . highlighted concerns over police accountability . . . but never neatly fit the narrative of other killings by law-enforcement officers around the country."[8] Déjà vu. The circumstances differed but the raw emotions on both sides were similar, with a prosecutor, judge and jury searching their souls for their own definition of justice for "what happened in the moment" that gave rise to the charges. As Lowell Jensen says, "justice is a function of the process." He sought two retrials of Newton and ultimately dismissed the charges when three juries disagreed with his view of the case.

D.A. Thompson has vowed to appeal the reduction of Liang's crime to criminal negligence so a higher court will have a chance to weigh in. But Thompson's critics on the Left were so irate at Thompson for not seeking any jail time for Liang that they took their protests to his home, demonstrating loudly in the middle of the night, accusing Thompson to his neighbors of complicity in murder. As with the Black Panthers and their supporters in the Huey Newton case, the dispute over justice in the Liang case "reflects a clash of perspectives that has surfaced . . . after police killings. . . . Activists, particularly black ones, look at these killings through the long lens of history, in which specific facts dissolve into an overarching narrative of continuing abuse and lack of accountability. But that, of course, is not the lens through which a district attorney, weighing evidence and making legal judgments, looks."[9] Indeed, wanting to send a strong message to a class of people regardless of the facts was what motivated lynch mobs and kangaroo court trials in the past. Justice in a civilized society requires a fair process for each defendant. In the long run, we should all see why neither political pressure from the Left nor from the Right ought to sway a dedicated prosecutor from doing what he considers to be the right thing in a difficult case.

* * * * *

Observing the drama of the 1968 Newton trial was a career-altering experience for reporter Gilbert Moore. When he returned to New York, he brought back 36 notebooks full of the notes he took. Bingham had accumulated a staggering 10,000 photos. The photographer later said, "We turned in a big fat story. But the great irony is that *LIFE* magazine, after spending all that time and all that dough to get a Panther story" refused to run the submission as written.[10] Moore tried one more draft. He felt "caught in the middle between my editors and the Panthers." He had no intention of becoming "the *LIFE* editors' Negro instrument for chastising the party," nor would he write "a Panther puff piece, trying to make them come off like Boy Scouts in leather."[11]

The upshot was that *LIFE* magazine's editors opted to publish nothing at all. Instead, Bingham kept his photo shoot for future use and Moore left his job to write a book about the deep anger the Panther leaders had stirred inside him: "cursing them for raising ten thousand questions and answering none of them."[12] Moore soon realized his own phone was now being tapped and that some of his friends appeared to be spying on him, presumably reporting to government "pigs."[13] The experience only increased Moore's empathy for the Panthers. He began to dig more deeply into the story of the trial and set out to track down the enigmatic jury foreman.

At the time of the trial, David Harper had been on a fast track up the Bank of America corporate ladder — the first black trust officer the corporation had ever hired, or any national bank had hired for that matter. A top student in college at Arizona State (only the second black undergraduate there to earn a degree in accounting), he had since earned a master's degree and taught business classes at night at Golden Gate University in San Francisco and at Peralta Community College in the East Bay. Harper was on an advisory committee working with Vice President Hubert Humphrey to get Fortune 500 companies to hire black executives; he also encouraged black colleges to start business departments to train qualified applicants and counseled students on how to prepare their resumés.

Harper did not know much about the Black Panthers before trial except what he read in the *Tribune* and other dailies. For him, Oakland was a bedroom community: "I was one of the first [blacks] that moved into the hills because I didn't care if people didn't like me." His white colleagues at the bank all thought he was crazy to sit on the Newton jury. But Harper believed justice would not likely be done otherwise: "Up until that time, if you were black and you killed a white person, especially a cop, you died. You simply died. Hands down. You're not going to survive."

Harper ignored the letter his superiors sent him that suggested if he did the right thing he and his family would be transferred anywhere in the world for their safety. Harper assumed they expected him to vote for the death penalty and wondered if the message originated from the police or perhaps the FBI. No one was going to intimidate him: "Let the cards go where they may."

Though aware before the trial of Newton's reputation for aggression, Harper found himself profoundly affected watching the Panther Party co-founder on the stand. It stung when Newton said, "About two percent of our people are middle class . . . They realize that the only reason that they advanced is when the blacks pushed from the bottom, when the blacks caused disturbances . . . . But the black who actually was the perpetrator of the disturbance gets nothing but maybe a jail sentence."[14] Harper later recalled "that . . . really affected me . . . that their enemy was not the police, their enemy was not the white community, their enemy was middle class blacks. . . . He was looking right at me when he said that, and he said because middle class blacks are leaving the community." Within a year of the trial, Harper quit his job to move to Detroit to start a new bank to help the city recover from its 1967 riots. (Harper would be named man of the year for those efforts.)

When Gilbert Moore located Harper in Detroit, he found the banker immensely proud of his accomplishment in the Newton trial. During voir dire, Harper gave short answers that downplayed how much he wanted to serve on that jury. He had no such compunctions when talking to Moore. Harper puffed on a cigar as he recounted the details. He had observed Oakland's political tensions rising to the bursting point before the trial: "Oakland was divided. We had blacks down, in the flatlands. We had . . . white people . . . in the hills. I'm sitting right in the middle. And if there's a war — which looked like it could easily be a war over this trial — I didn't have any place to go . . . so I decided that I had to be . . . on this jury and decided, I had to be a foreman of that jury, to get justice." That was months before he received notice he was in the Newton jury pool. (In fact, around January of 1968, Harper told his oldest son, who was then in college at Cal, of his premonition he would be called to serve on that jury). Harper had served in juries before and believed he could follow the law and be fair to both sides.

Watching two weeks of voir dire before he was put on the stand, Harper saw many other minorities in the jury pool jump at the chance to say they could never apply the death penalty and then leave the courtroom as soon as they could: "Nobody wanted to be on that jury . . . because it was so dangerous. . . . It was a no win situation. . . . If he's guilty, the jurors — the panel — is going to be in trouble. If he's not guilty, they're going to be in trouble. At Bank of America . . . people told me, you know you made a big mistake, you're gonna die. 'Cause there's nothing you can do. You're going to be trapped one way or the other. And I said, 'I don't think so,' because I felt that if we had justice . . . they would recognize justice."

When questioned, Harper had taken the most care in answering whether he could apply the death penalty. (He had originally studied in a seminary for the priesthood.) He said he had some reservations about the death penalty, but they did not prevent him from considering it (an answer that would have kept him off the panel before the U.S. Supreme Court decided the landmark *Witherspoon* case in June of 1968). He told Gilbert Moore that what mattered to him most was to prove enough progress was being made so that "a black guy could be part of the legal system and come out with something fair. . . . If he dies, he dies for what he did — in a fair trial."

Once selected for the jury, Harper followed through on his plan to become foreman, though he let the other jurors think it was their idea. He realized that among the twelve of them there was a natural choice for foreman: "The white guy with the gray hair, fifty-year-old engineer, he would have been selected because he's the father figure. . . . But I'd be the last one, I think would be selected." Harper decided that, while sitting through the trial prohibited from talking about it, he could maneuver himself to be a top candidate for foreman: "I had time to establish leadership, and I knew how to establish leadership." He focused on strong women in the jury, "outspoken, in their forties. . . . They played cards . . . so I decided to play cards with them. And I could beat them. . . . I began to become the leader of the group." It also did not go unnoticed that he braved the picket line outside the courthouse each day instead of taking the underground tunnel from the garage, as the rest of them did.

Once the jury was sequestered, the choice of foreman took less than ten minutes. He already stood out to the women for his leadership skills and professionalism; Harper figured the four men on that jury appreciated how he had managed to get the strong-minded women to defer to him. It also occurred to him that a few of the jurors likely just wanted a scapegoat. Drawing on his prior jury experience, Harper declined to conduct a formal vote right away. He told the group they first needed to review all of the evidence together and see how much they could agree on what happened. Harvey Kokka, the Japanese-American lab technician, had taken copious notes, which came in handy. Linda Aguirre, the young Latina secretary, had also taken notes in shorthand that she shared with the group.

During the trial, Harper was careful to follow the judge's instructions not to communicate with anyone about the case, read newspapers, watch television, listen to the radio or discuss it with other jurors. Riding up the elevator, he sometimes found himself standing next to belligerent Panther leaders like Bobby Seale and Kathleen Cleaver on their way to the spectators' gallery. No words were exchanged, but he thought to himself, "You guys want justice, you got to allow me to do my job." While listening to all the evidence, Harper did his best to completely suspend judgment on Newton's guilt or innocence, but when closing arguments ended he knew which way he strongly leaned. During deliberations, Harper kept his opinions close to the chest, concerned that if he revealed his position too early, he would no longer be persuasive. As the defense had guessed, Harper was favoring acquittal. (His wife thought so, too, though he did not discuss the case with her until after the trial ended.)

All of the jurors thought the judge had done a good job and praised the professionalism of the lawyers on both sides. They were also impressed by Newton and how well-dressed, handsome and articulate he was in court. Tom Hofmann was about Newton's age. He thought Newton's testimony showed that he was "a leader in his own way." David Harper believed that Newton was particularly persuasive in describing why he founded the Black Panther Party: "He sold me on his ideology." Not so for several of the others, including Mary Gallegos, who thought to herself Huey Newton was trouble and she could readily envision the police acting as they did toward him. She felt sorry for Huey's parents. All the jurors except Harper admired the bus driver Grier's courage. Harper considered Grier an Uncle Tom, though he never told the other jurors that for fear of losing credibility. All of the jurors found the ballistics expert, John Davis, highly credible.

Several members voiced doubts that Newton was telling the truth about being shot first. Harper himself thought Newton was a "hothead" trying "to read the law to a hothead arresting policeman" and "didn't have . . . sense enough . . . to know when to be respectful to the law." Harper would lead the group in a discussion of every piece of testimony and let each juror say what he or she thought it meant: "We would serve

. . . five or six different scenarios based on one piece of evidence and then we would vote. And the way the judge told us, we should vote on the ones most in favor of the defendant. Which one of these five things most favored the defendant? So we would . . . select that one. Then we go on to the next step, in terms of the process. . . . Yes, he did get out of the car with a law book, he didn't get out of the car with a gun." How else could you explain why Officer Frey found no gun when he frisked Newton immediately after Newton got out of his car? The bus driver could not have had a great vantage point in the predawn and must have mistaken the book for a gun.

Harper got the others to focus on Newton's wound. He suggested that if Newton were already on his knees when he was shot — as Newton claimed — the bullet would have entered Newton's abdomen at a higher point than it exited through his back. That was why the jury had returned to court asking to see the wound again on Thursday afternoon. The exit wound was lower than the entrance wound, supporting Newton's version of the shootout.

Not until Saturday did they take their first formal blind vote, using scratch paper brought in by the bailiff and the cigar box already at hand. Harper anxiously tallied up the votes. They were split three ways: three for acquittal, four for voluntary manslaughter and five for first degree murder. To his dismay, three-quarters of the panel believed Newton was criminally responsible for the death of Officer Frey, disagreeing only on whether the killing was provoked or premeditated. After two days of painstaking efforts to reconstruct the shootout, five of them were prepared to consider sending Newton to his death and just two thought like Harper did that Newton should walk free. How was he to bridge that extraordinary gulf?

Harper had an idea what direction the deliberations would have taken if he had not served on the jury — a stalemate. (That was the outcome his wife would later tell him she expected to see.) Harper thought maybe the five hardliners could be persuaded, as the other seven were, that the police had instigated the shootout by their own abusive conduct. He led the panel back through their analysis. They discussed again the conflict between Newton's version of what happened and that of Grier and Heanes. Most now decided Heanes was not telling the truth. They believed Heanes shot first and that only after Newton was wounded did Newton wrestle with Frey and then kill him with Frey's own gun. But still positions did not budge.

As the third day of deliberations wore on, the jurors' tempers started to fray. Whenever factual disputes came up, Linda Aguirre would whip out her notes to read aloud. She insisted they were accurate. David Harper told her she got some of her notes wrong and they would review the evidence again or go back to court to get clarification. The most difficult person was the factory worker, Mrs. Gibbons. She always cut off any argument by saying Newton "did the dirty deed."[15] The fiery Cuban, Joseph Quintana, favored acquittal, but could not persuade anyone of his reasoning. Mrs. Reed, who disliked hearing police called "pigs," was the most insistent on a murder conviction. Trying to move the discussion forward, engineer Ron Andrews appealed to them all to consider their decision as if they were in Newton's shoes. Harper found that demoralizing — he assumed that had been their charge from the outset.

On Sunday, when reasoned discussion had all but evaporated, Harper threatened to send a note to Judge Friedman asking for a reminder that they were required to be dispassionate in their deliberations. Some of the other jurors took offense, particularly Mary Gallegos, the dark-haired Portuguese-American. The pretty 28-year-old newlywed had not spoken up before. Harper was taken aback. No note was sent, but Harper was now feeling at his wits' end:

> One of the fellows was saying . . . let's have a recess, let's have a break. . . . I said, you know, I can resign as foreman. . . . "We don't want you to resign." . . . But around five o'clock . . . I thought I wasn't going to be able to pull it off and I went into the restroom and felt like I was going to throw up . . . So I straightened up and came back out as poker as I've always been and as friendly as I've always been. And said, we've got to finish this job. We cannot go to mistrial; we've got to finish this. So, I buckled back down and went through this whole thing . . . trying to come up with some kind of agreement, in terms of applying the law that would justify the verdict.

Harper had thought Heanes acted nervous on the stand and might not have remembered the actual order in which events had transpired. Heanes reminded him of the television actor Don Knotts, who played Deputy Barney Fife on the popular *Andy Griffith Show*. They all agreed that the ballistics showed Newton was shot first by Heanes as Newton was being pushed down by Frey. Only then had Newton grappled for Frey's gun and started firing. Harper was originally convinced that this chain of evidence exonerated Newton. Now a few other jurors persuaded him that, even though Newton was shot first, he should not have grabbed Frey's gun to shoot the officer twice in the back: "You don't empty a gun on a guy's back and call it self-defense."

Then, Harper had the jury face the next question: "Is it first degree murder, second degree murder, or manslaughter? . . . And that's when it got tough." Mary Gallegos never thought it was first degree murder, so her decision had always been between second degree and manslaughter. Everyone knew that Mrs. Prelli, the widowed landlady, had many low-income black tenants. Linda Aguirre said that Mrs. Prelli would never vote for first degree murder, so she would have to do so herself. In frustration, Harper told the young secretary that none of the jurors wanted to know anyone's vote, but not to base her decision on how she thought Mrs. Prelli planned to vote. Privately, he thought Mrs. Prelli would have preferred not to serve on this jury at all, but had not been clever enough to realize how to get excused.

At a quarter past nine that Sunday evening, another vote was taken with ten for manslaughter and two for murder. Harper had changed his own vote from acquittal to avoid a hung jury and convinced the other two favoring acquittal to do the same. The prospect of coming that far and not reaching agreement weighed on them all. "So at that point . . . people got together and started talking. And then they said, we'll take another vote."

Harper recalled that Tom Hofmann, the bachelor who lived with his parents, had favored murder, not acquittal, as the landlady Mrs. Prelli thought. Hofmann then switched to make it eleven to one for voluntary manslaughter. At that point only Mrs. Reed still voted for first degree murder. She went to the bathroom while the final tally was taken. Upon hearing the new results, she called her change of heart out from behind the closed door. It was 10 p.m., Sunday night, and they had a verdict! Greatly relieved their ordeal was over, the men all shook Harper's hand and the women kissed him. It was the first jury Tom Hofmann and Mary Gallegos ever served on, but both felt they reached the right result. They would still feel the same way looking back nearly fifty years later. Gallegos said: "For me, being as young as I was, I really put my heart and soul into it, and I wanted to come up with the right decision. . . . I listened very carefully and it was easy for me to reach . . . I stood by my decision then and I stand by it now. . . . What's wrong is shooting people and breaking the law. . . . You are going to jail. If we didn't have that, where would we be?"

After eight weeks of trial, Hofmann recalled being asked by one friend about his experience. "There wasn't any way I could convey all of the facts and deliberations. . . . I said, how much time have you got? . . . That just killed [any] discussion." Hofmann later served on a number of juries over his lifetime, including another murder trial, and strongly believes in the importance of that service. It bothers him to see so many people make up excuses to avoid jury duty. Looking back in his seventies at the 1968 Newton trial, he realized that, in the end, consensus on the verdict had not been hard to reach: "Analyzing each and every question . . . and coming to a conclusion. [It did not end up being] beyond a reasonable doubt. . . . We just eliminated anything people might have had preconceived thoughts about . . . . We built up where everybody could agree based on the facts and bouncing it off one another, and we discussed this for quite some time . . . . We eliminated a lot of uncertainty. . . . It was just the process of law." Unlike David Harper, as a first-time juror who grew up in Berkeley Hofmann had not realized how ground-breaking their jury was: "I was one of twelve."

At the time, all of the jurors recognized how instrumental Harper was in achieving consensus. His wife was surprised he had not hung the jury by insisting on acquittal, but Harper rejoiced when he saw the *Oakland Tribune* headline. The paper trumpeted Newton's manslaughter conviction as a victory for the prosecution. Meanwhile, the black community was amazed: for the first time anyone could recall, a black man accused of murder did not die. "This was a celebration as far as I was concerned . . . in both the white community and black community. . . . That was the end of the news. . . . The verdict in the black community was, 'we won.' The verdict in the white community was that 'we won.' It was no news after that."

Harper did not follow what happened in the Newton case on appeal. He just went on with his life. Yet, looking back in his eighties, Harper recognized "historically, it has brought about a lot of change." He considers his role as jury foreman the most significant accomplishment of his life:

> I was of the opinion that I had the kind of ability and power to bring about justice and, being involved with . . . eleven more people that I didn't know . . . I thought it would be reasonable enough to work together and to come up with the right answer. And whether it was guilty of first degree murder, or whether it was innocent . . . it had to be just based on the evidence, just based on our process. . . . That could have been a dangerous situation for me . . . with the confrontation that was created by the Black Panther Party surrounding the courthouse — 'The sky is the limit.' It was a very dangerous situation. . . . But it was a call for justice, and I think we did that.

Last fall, as his extended family gathered around him, Harper received a proclamation from current Oakland Mayor Libby Schaaf, decreeing November 10, 2015, David Harper Day in the retired banker's honor. He also received an award from Congresswoman Barbara Lee for his courage, and a similar proclamation from Peralta Community College, where Harper had taught business courses at night in the late 1960s — organizational management skills that came in quite handy in overseeing the difficult Newton jury deliberations.

Yet, when interviewed in 2013 for the documentary project *American Justice on Trial: People v. Newton,* Harper revealed an incident that occurred in the mid-'60s that many lawyers would have used to keep him off the Newton jury. He had been wearing a sweat suit with a hoodie, jogging at night in his almost all-white neighborhood in

Oakland. It was after nine p.m. on a Sunday evening and he had not
shaved that day. Harper realized he was being followed and turned to
see a slow-moving police patrol car. Harper went over to the officer.
When asked for ID, he could not produce any. The officer did not
believe that Harper lived in that neighborhood or worked as a banker.
He took Harper with him back to police headquarters for further
questioning.

Apparently, it never occurred to the officer simply to drive Harper
to the house in the neighborhood where Harper said he lived and see
if the person who answered the door was a middle-aged black woman
who vouched for him as her husband. Harper could have then also produced his ID if still required. As it was, the officer never gave Harper
an opportunity even to call his wife. Hours later, the officer finally
accepted that Harper worked for the Bank of America and lived where
he said he did. It was past midnight when Harper was told he could go
home — a walk of several miles from police headquarters. As Harper
started to leave, the officer told him it was a good thing he had stopped
jogging when he spotted the police car. If Harper had instead sped up
his pace, the officer would have shot him in the back.

George Hart had been on the Oakland police force for about a
decade by the mid-1960s. Looking back, he notes that if the jogging
incident occurred as Harper described it, "the circumstances didn't
exist at the time that it would have been justified to shoot a person."
Yet Harper realized that people reading about such an incident in the
newspaper would likely have believed the policeman was simply protecting the neighborhood from a would-be burglar. Harper never ran
again at night.

When Harper got called to jury duty in the Newton trial, his own
experience brought home the need for careful review of the evidence.
Veteran civil rights lawyer Bryan Stevenson of the Equal Justice Initiative
notes: "If you had some of the experiences that the jury foreperson had
in the Newton trial, if you had some consciousness that people can be
treated badly, presumed guilty because of their race, then you're going
to want to see evidence . . . and I think that's an important necessary
function for a fair system of justice. . . ." Yet most prosecutors would

likely have dismissed Harper from the jury in this high-stakes case had they been aware of the prior incident.

How was it that neither Garry nor Jensen asked David Harper if he had any prior negative experiences with the police? When Garry sensed that a white juror was biased, Garry would keep asking questions to try to get the juror removed. In contrast, Garry made it a point to examine minorities lightly precisely to avoid drawing out disqualifying answers. In Harper's case, Garry gambled that the Panthers were wrong in assuming the banker was an Uncle Tom.

Sitting there for over two weeks listening to probing questions and qualifying or disqualifying answers from other prospective jurors, Harper sensed why both sides would want to leave him on the panel. He watched Garry making race an issue every time Jensen dismissed an African-American and knew that he was Jensen's best prospect to appear unbiased. As it turned out, Harper was also the last black questioned in the jury pool. By Harper's turn, more than 160 people had been interrogated. Garry could not afford to challenge him. Nor could Jensen.

Jensen surely knew that Harper had no arrest record. His office had ready access to that type of information on jurors. Jensen could certainly have asked a broader question about any interactions Harper might have had with the police if Jensen saw a good reason to do so. Alameda County Judge Leo Dorado once worked as a deputy public defender and later in the district attorney's office. Over four decades, he has participated in hundreds of jury selections. Judge Dorado says that if prosecutors questioned city residents in detail they could probably keep most of them off juries: "One of the easiest ways . . . to get a juror to respond so they disqualify themselves is to ask whether or not they themselves or anyone close to them, family or friends, have ever had unpleasant experiences with the police or the justice system or the D.A.'s office. That kind of open-ended question would have clearly resulted in any number of responses where [Jensen] could have then argued that [Harper] wasn't qualified. . . . In Oakland, that's just naturally . . . what happens. You see people, you see things that aren't necessarily fair."

That was Judge Dorado's own experience growing up in two poor Latino neighborhoods in East Oakland: as a teenager in Fruitvale and,

earlier, in a district called "Jingletown," next to the estuary dividing
Oakland from the city of Alameda. Dorado was the only one of his
friends even to go to college. He knew many who wound up in state
prisons; others died from drug overdoses. If asked to talk about negative experiences with the police, he could readily envision himself
kicked off a jury.

In the recent prosecution of ex-NYPD officer Peter Liang, potential jurors were asked under oath if they had any close relative who was
ever arrested. A white male carpenter in his sixties who said "no" made
a startling revelation after the trial ended. The juror's own father had
been convicted for an accidental shooting and sentenced to prison for
several years. When the defense sought a mistrial, the juror said he had
not lied. He grew up in orphanages and boys' homes and had never
been close to his father. The defense made a motion for mistrial. The
trial judge ruled no misconduct was shown.[16]

In more recent years, judges have often allowed lengthy questionnaires to be given to jurors before they go on the stand. In California
today standard-form questionnaires for criminal cases include asking
the panelists if they or family members were ever victims of crime,
witnessed a crime or: "Have you, your spouse, any person with whom
you have a significant personal relationship, or relative ever had any
contact with law enforcement, including but not limited to being (A)
stopped by the police? (B) accused of misconduct whether or not it was
a crime? (C) investigated as a suspect in a criminal case? (D) charged
with a crime? (E) a criminal defendant?" After a series of follow-up
questions, the juror is asked: "Is there anything about that experience
that would make you question your ability to be fair and impartial in
this case? If so, please explain."[17]

Back in the days when lawyers frequently sat the first dozen people
whose names were called, the Newton trial was unusual for the length
of time spent questioning potential jurors. After a good many repetitive
rounds, both Charles Garry and Lowell Jensen often used shorthand to
ask if any questions put earlier to other panelists triggered a memory
that might interfere with a juror's service. They assumed most jurors
had read something about the widely-publicized shooting and certainly

were aware of the huge crowd of Panther protestors on the street below and the high security surrounding the packed proceeding.

If Harper had wanted an excuse to be discharged — as his colleagues urged and other blacks called for jury duty had appeared quite eager to do — he had an easy way out. He could have brought up the jogging incident and claimed it left him with bad feelings about the Oakland police. But Harper's own wife was the head of security at an office of Bank of America and he did not feel that he was prejudiced against law enforcement. Nor did he consider himself biased against Newton, despite living in a neighborhood near where the Panthers were active and thinking their behavior toward police was brash and likely self-defeating. When asked if he could set aside whatever he had heard before, Harper had no hesitation in agreeing to do so. That was exactly why he thought someone like him should serve on this jury.

Judge Dorado emphatically agrees: "It is so important not to have people disqualified that way. . . . Knowing how good Lowell Jensen [is] and how intelligent he is, he could have easily done that had he wanted to. . . . He could have had a very different makeup of his jury had he wanted to." Judge Thelton Henderson later served nearly three decades with Jensen as his colleague on the federal bench: "I have rarely met a man who, in my view, is fairer than Lowell." Looking back at the 1968 trial, Henderson is proud to say: "Lowell gave Huey as fair a trial as Huey could get from a prosecutor."

Actually, had Jensen gone further in questioning Harper it is easy to imagine the prosecution ending in a mistrial. Charles Garry would undoubtedly have pounced on Harper's revelation as another example of police abuse. Harper's experience was far closer to home than the aggressive Chicago police Garry pointed out to the jury in closing argument. Even if Harper was then dismissed from the panel, the remaining jurors would have heard about a trigger-happy Oakland policeman ready to shoot a man just for jogging while black in his own neighborhood. How do you unring that bell?

* * * * *

Nearly two decades after the Newton trial came another racially charged case that shows how impractical it can get to avoid seating jurors who have had similar experiences. The prosecution in 1987 of New York "subway vigilante" Bernhard Goetz started a national debate on violent crime and self-defense. The Manhattan trial judge called it the "most difficult case of our time."[18] Since 1966, violent crime in New York City had tripled — all too often perpetrated in the city's then poorly patrolled subways. Over the next decade, the Big Apple's reported crimes would greatly exceed those of any other city in the country. In this setting, a blond, bespectacled white man in his thirties became the symbol for states later adopting "Stand Your Ground" laws.

Goetz was raised in upstate New York, the son of a Jewish mother and German Lutheran father. In 1981 the willowy entrepreneur lived and worked in Greenwich Village when he was attacked by three assailants in a lower Manhattan subway station. The assault left Goetz with a permanent injury to his knee and an abiding grudge against blacks and Hispanics. The one attacker police caught faced only a criminal mischief charge. Following that mugging, Goetz applied for a permit to carry a concealed weapon. His request was denied. Goetz bought a revolver anyway and carried the Smith and Wesson every day concealed in a special, quick-draw holster. From this point on, Goetz stopped wearing gloves in the winter so he would always be ready to pull his gun on any would-be mugger. At the time, the city was in the midst of an unprecedented explosion of crack cocaine use, which increased the homicide rate among teenage blacks nearly fivefold.

One afternoon shortly before Christmas of 1984, Goetz entered the rear of a subway car at the 14th Street station in New York's SoHo District. There were fifteen to twenty other passengers. Most were seated toward the front, distancing themselves from four rowdy blacks in their late teens in the back. One was sprawled across a bench; the other three were seated nearby. Goetz chose to sit across from them. Three of the teenagers rose to intimidate him, sensing an easy mark.[19] Though none displayed any weapon, one of them demanded $5 from Goetz. A high school dropout, the youth later testified that he had a crack cocaine habit since he was thirteen that cost $50 a day to support. All four came from notorious Bronx housing projects. Later, it would come to light that two of them carried in their pockets sharpened screwdrivers they intended to use to pry open coin boxes at the video arcade they were heading toward that day.

On prior occasions Goetz warded off would-be robbers simply by showing his gun. This time Goetz stood up, whisked out his revolver and fired four shots in rapid succession at the three youths' mid-sections. Goetz then stood over the fourth seated teenager and fired twice more at close range. All four suffered wounds. Luckily, none of the other petrified passengers was hurt by a bullet ricocheting off the wall. A few prostrated themselves on the subway car floor in fear as soon as the shooting started.

When the subway came to an emergency stop, most of the passengers fled, including Goetz. Police circulated a sketch of the gunman on wanted posters, which some locals decorated with halos. As one New York journalist put it, "In . . . telephone conversations and exchanges in bars, on street corners, in beauty parlors, in pool halls, and wherever . . . people met, from the too rich to the very poor, there was a collective emotion that cannot be described as anything other than jubilant."[20] After more than a week's manhunt, Goetz turned himself in and confessed that his intention was murder. He wanted to "to make them suffer as much as possible."[21] Many fans wore tee shirts picturing Goetz with the title "Thug Buster." The Guardian Angels helped furnish his $50,000 bail. The only youth who never recovered from his wounds was the one who had remained seated. Darrell Cabey was now a brain-damaged paraplegic.

At the bail hearing for Goetz in February of 1985 people inside could hear the shouts of over 100 protesters on the sidewalk: "Bernhard Goetz, you can't hide; we charge you with genocide" and "We want justice."[22] Yet it took over two years and an appellate court ruling to get a grand jury to indict Goetz for attempted murder of the four black teenagers and reckless endangerment of other passengers on the subway car. A *New York Times* survey showed locals mostly supported Goetz because crime was the worst feature of city life. Nearly a quarter reported a family member had been a victim of crime in the prior year. Forty percent thought muggings and holdups had become so bad that New York "have a right to take matters into their own hands." The frustration crossed color lines. People were just fed up with "predators who roamed New York looking for people to bully and mug or rape . . . young, crude, obnoxious, sullen, elbowing people on the subway, making vile statements to women, cursing anywhere and as loudly as they could."[23]

As in the 1968 Newton murder trial, the 1987 jury selection took several weeks. Ultimately, the panel included ten whites and two blacks, six of whom had been victims of crime themselves. Goetz exercised his right not to testify. His defense attorney kept calling the four shooting victims "thugs." He got into evidence their criminal records both before — and after — the subway incident. (In contrast, Judge Friedman had excluded evidence offered by Garry of alleged police misconduct after the shooting.) Even more prejudicial to the prosecution, one youth was brought to court to testify dressed in prison clothes, again unlike Newton who was allowed to wear street clothes when he sat in front of the jury.

After four days of deliberation the jury returned to the crowded courtroom. Spectators gasped as the foreperson rattled off verdict after verdict of "not guilty" through seventeen acquittals. Then came the final verdict — "guilty" only of the illegal possession of a firearm. The proceedings adjourned to loud applause. Guardian Angels in red berets escorted Goetz through the hordes of onlookers. Many shouted congratulations. One raised a handwritten sign praising Goetz for winning one for "the good guys" while an African-American shouted "Goetz is a Nazi!"[24] Congressman Floyd Flake, pastor of the Greater Allen Cathedral, displayed outrage at the blatant double standard: "I think that if a black had shot four whites, the cry for the death penalty would have been almost automatic."[25]

Reverend Al Sharpton and Manhattan Borough President and future Mayor David Dinkins worried that it was now "open season" on young black men.[26] NAACP head Benjamin Hooks urged that a federal criminal case be brought against Goetz for violating the youths' civil rights. He considered the jury verdict "inexcusable. It was proven — according to his own statements — that Goetz . . . went far beyond the realm of self-defense. There was no provocation for what he did."[27] But Assistant U.S. Attorney Rudy Giuliani had already investigated the case and determined Goetz was motivated by crime, not race. No federal charges were initiated.

By itself, the illegal gun possession could have resulted in a seven-year sentence. Instead, Goetz's original sentence was six months' jail time, plus one year of psychiatric treatment, a $5000 fine, 200 hours of community service and five years of probation. His jail sentence later was increased on appeal to one year. He wound up serving eight months. It was not until 1996 that lawyers for Darrell Cabey finally succeeded in bringing to trial a federal civil rights case in the Bronx on his behalf. From the mostly minority jury pool, the lawyers picked a panel of six: four blacks and two Hispanics. This time Goetz took the stand. The jury heard about the racial slurs he used and how he admitted shooting to kill. They rejected his claim of self-defense against Cabey who had never left his subway seat. The panel issued a largely symbolic award of $18 million in compensatory damages and $25 million in punitive damages. Goetz then filed for bankruptcy. Though the judgment could not be discharged, eight years later he claimed he had not paid Cabey a dime.[28] Meanwhile, Goetz became a cult figure. Characters mirroring his vigilantism appeared in a number of television shows and movies, popular songs and raps. He also sparked a movement to relax state laws restricting concealed weapons — a movement that has mushroomed in recent years.

Starting around 1990, New York City began dramatically reducing its crime rate. Successive mayors — including Dinkins and Giuliani — made it their highest priority. Some attributed the crime reduction to Mayor Giuliani's tough-on-crime policy. Goetz claimed that armed vigilantes like himself were a major factor. Others gave substantial credit to the city's investment in many more police patrols, a drop in the at-risk population, decline in crack cocaine usage and the advent of drug courts.[29]

Several books about the Goetz criminal trial include one by a juror that provides insights into the role of reasonable doubt in their deliberations.[30] In 2010, looking back on the *Goetz* case, one legal commentator observed:

Goetz was acquitted of every charge except not having a gun permit for his concealed weapon. Of the many cases of racial injustice . . . few have sparked as little outcry as the case of Bernhard Goetz. . . . This is a social misfortune because, in many ways, the Goetz case represents the epitome of society's racism and the dangerous consequences of the "fight violence-with-violence" mentality. Few have bothered looking deep at the case and what it says about our culture. . . . [T]he four young men [were not] innocent victims . . . . They indeed intended to rob or extort money out of Goetz and their criminal record speaks for itself. They were not nice kids. But the justice system doesn't defend nice people only. Our justice system is there for a reason. As egregiously flawed as it is, it is preferable to a self-righteous and emotionally unbalanced gunman taking the law into his own hands.[31]

* * * * *

In stark contrast to the *Goetz* case, perhaps no verdict caused as huge a cry of racism on both sides as the O. J. Simpson murder case in the mid-1990s. The 2016 made-for-tv saga *American Crime Story* acquaints a new generation (and reminds the rest of us) of the details. On June 12, 1994, police found the former football star's beautiful, blonde ex-wife Nicole and her friend Ron Goldman brutally stabbed to death outside her condo. O. J.'s bizarre behavior immediately after the grisly discovery helped make him the prime suspect. The case captured the interest of a hundred million viewers, hooked by the jarring criminal charges against the handsome sportscaster and former football superstar. The public became fascinated by the ugly reality underlying his picture-perfect interracial marriage and Hollywood lifestyle. They marveled at the tactics of his "Dream Team" of defense lawyers. How could gavel-to-gavel coverage not generate excitement when the trial focused on "sex, violence and power?"[32]

National magazines immediately focused on racial issues. O. J.'s attorneys noticed that when *TIME* magazine put Simpson's face on its cover, it darkened the color of his skin. *Newsweek* psychoanalyzed Simpson as a troubled black man who self-destructed when he "tried to be white."[33] Half of the country would eventually watch live coverage of one of the longest criminal trials ever held in the United States.

From the outset the case did not resemble any other domestic violence case or murder prosecution. First, Simpson did not face the possibility of execution — the prosecutors took that off the table on the assumption no jury would want to impose the death penalty on a celebrity.[34] District Attorney Gil Garcetti also made the unusual choice to file the case in mixed-race downtown L.A. rather than where the crime took place — the mostly white upper class community of Santa Monica. Presumably, Garcetti wanted to avoid accusations of jury bias, as happened after the acquittal of the officers who had been caught on tape beating Rodney King in 1992. The Rodney King riots had eclipsed the devastation of the 1965 Watts riots. Officials assumed that if — and when— Simpson was found guilty, riots might erupt again. It was another reason not to seek the death penalty. Third, unlike poor minorities, Simpson did not have to depend on an overworked public defender, but could afford the best private defense team money could buy. Fourth, the case was televised live — most judges do not allow cameras in the courtroom.

The prosecution team was carefully chosen. Instead of a traditional white male, the lead prosecutor was Marcia Clark — still a pioneering role for a woman as the century neared its end. Sitting in the second chair was African-American Chris Darden. How could anyone accuse the District Attorney of bias? It took two months to pick the jury from a pool that was 40% white, 28% black, 17% Latino and 15% Asian. After asking the panel questions related to a huge array of issues, the Dream Team managed to seat nine blacks, two whites, and one Latino; ten of the jurors were women. None subscribed to newspapers; most had only a high school education. Five jurors were impaneled despite reporting prior negative experiences with the police.[35]

The extraordinary gavel-to-gavel coverage included expert commentary on all the news shows to explain legal jargon and procedure to the vast majority of Americans unfamiliar with our criminal courts. John Burris was among those hired by Bay Area networks to comment nightly on that day's developments. Unlike in the Newton case, the defense never put O. J. on the stand to deny the killings. Instead, they relied on the jury to take to heart Judge Lance Ito's instructions that the prosecutor had the burden of proof beyond a reasonable doubt and that the defendant had the right to remain silent without that being held against him.

What the sequestered jury never knew — but the *National Enquirer* spread to the world — was that O. J. had wanted to testify against his lawyers' advice. They only dissuaded Simpson after bringing in top-notch criminal defense attorneys Penny Cooper and Cris Arguedas to put him through a grueling, mock cross-examination. Presumably, Simpson was convinced by this experience that he would not bear up well if subjected to penetrating questions from prosecutor Marcia Clark.

The Dream Team scored big when it obtained a tape-recorded prior interview of a key prosecution witness, Detective Mark Fuhrman. On the tape Fuhrman repeatedly used racial slurs. The defense charged that Fuhrman planted evidence at the crime scene to incriminate Simpson. Barry Scheck and Peter Neufeld, co-directors of the Innocence Project, raised doubts about whether incriminating DNA evidence actually came from the scene of the crime. In his closing argument, lead defense lawyer Johnnie Cochran pulled out all the stops: he compared Fuhrman to Hitler: "a genocidal racist, a perjurer, America's worst nightmare and the personification of evil."[36]

Still the police anticipated a guilty verdict and prepared for riots. Simpson's lawyers assumed that their best hope was a hung jury with one or two hold-outs against conviction. So they, too, were surprised when the African-American forewoman of the jury delivered a verdict of acquittal. Reactions to the Simpson verdict divided along racial lines. A Gallup Poll found that 42 percent of whites interviewed agreed with the acquittal, while 49 percent thought he was guilty as charged. In contrast, 78 percent of blacks thought the acquittal was proper; only 10 percent disagreed.[37] An NBC news poll ten years later found that 87 percent of whites thought Simpson was guilty of the murders, but only 29 percent of blacks.[38] In the meantime, the families of both victims won civil verdicts against Simpson and the rights to the proceeds of his controversial best-seller, *If I Did It.* By 2015, more than half of blacks polled believed Simpson had indeed killed his wife and her friend Ron Goldman.[39]

* * * * *

The Simpson jury's decision to acquit a celebrity based on distrust of the L.A. police did not come close to matching what was at stake back in 1968 when David Harper led deliberations on the fate of a black revolutionary. So how much of a difference did Harper make on the Newton jury? Veteran jury consultant Karen Jo Koonan notes that Harper "had a very important role in that deliberation but . . . it wasn't a one-person jury. And if it wasn't him on that jury, it might have been somebody else . . . who would have said, 'wait a minute before we vote. Let's look at [the evidence].'" Koonan notes that, "The opposite issue occurs . . . every day. Jurors come to court. They say they are going to follow the law. The law requires the prosecution to prove the case beyond reasonable doubt — to give the defendant the presumption of innocence. And our research shows — and survey after survey after survey — that huge percentages of people think that if someone is charged with a crime they must be guilty."

Judge Dorado agrees. He makes a point of telling all of his juries not to automatically credit prosecution witnesses more than defendants: "to make sure that jurors understand that anyone who comes to court, no matter what their position in life — doctor, police officer, civilian — comes to court as a witness and that no one at the outset deserves more credibility than the others. It's a very important part of my voir dire, and I have to make sure jurors understand that because I think it's also very important that police don't come in with . . . more credibility."

Excusing jurors simply for prior experiences like Harper's could also keep a huge number of black men from ever serving. Sixties radical Louis Armmond later went to law school and tried for years to serve on juries. Understandably, because of his background "and the fact that I have a brother-in-law who is a former police detective . . . I am always dismissed by one side or the other." But the dismissals cut a wide swath. In his recent best-selling book *Between the World and Me,* acclaimed African-American author Ta-Nehisi Coates (who is currently writing *Black Panther* superhero comics for Marvel) addressed the different prism of the hunted that blacks experience growing up in urban America. His father was a member of the Baltimore branch of the Black Panthers; the book takes the form of a long letter to his own teen-aged son. Coates describes how deeply disturbed he felt when an undercover officer stalked and shot to death a college friend whom the plainclothes cop mistook for a crime suspect. Criminal charges were never brought. It only made Coates more disillusioned to learn the policeman was black.

Gilbert Moore prided himself on his balanced journalistic outlook on life. But if asked on a jury panel if he was ever arrested, Moore had his own confession to make: years after he covered the Newton trial, he once spent a night in jail after uncharacteristically losing his temper when stopped by a state trooper. The arrest might have had something to do with Moore tapping into his inner Black Panther spirit to call the officer "a dirty white racist motherfucker."[40] Eldridge Cleaver would have laughed out loud.

Professor Bryan Stevenson has been called America's Nelson Mandela for his work heading the Equal Justice Initiative. Stevenson describes in his 2015 best-selling book *Just Mercy*, how he himself was badly mistreated by a policeman late one night while parked outside his own apartment listening to music in his car. The officer assumed he was a burglar. In July of 2009, Professor Henry Louis Gates, Jr., of Harvard made international news over a confrontation with a Cambridge policeman seeking to arrest Gates as he tried to unjam his own front door. Judge Thelton Henderson had friends in law school who told him they got stopped simply for walking or driving while black.

Bill Patterson (who became the first African-American foreman of the Alameda County Grand Jury in 1981) used to get stopped regularly by police in the 1950s when leaving "his sector" of Oakland. When Morrie Turner gave a friend a ride to a bus stop in the 1960s, he got treated roughly by a policeman who did not recognize Turner as a police clerk. The officer simply exhibited the same disrespect routinely shown to other blacks on his beat.

A nationwide Gallup poll taken after the death of Michael Brown in Ferguson, Missouri, in the summer of 2014 reinforced prior polls showing a huge disparity between white and black American adults' confidence in the police. On average almost three-fifths of whites polled trusted the police a lot; another nearly 30% trusted them some; and only 12% placed little or no trust in the police. In contrast, a quarter of blacks placed little or no trust in the police and only 37% had high trust in the police, 22% fewer than whites.[41] In the summer of 2013 — following widespread protests of vigilante George Zimmerman's acquittal for the death of black teen-ager Trayvon Martin — another national Gallup poll had yielded jaw-dropping news: almost a quarter of black men between 18 and 34 said they had a negative experience with the police just in the last 30 days.[42]

The videotaped shooting deaths in July 2016 of Alton Sterling and Philando Castile followed by a black sniper shooting police in Dallas shocked South Carolinian Senator Tim Scott. The only Republican African-American Senator came forward on the Senate floor to acknowledge: "There's a deep divide between the black community and law enforcement — a trust gap. I do not know many African-American men who do not have a very similar story to tell, no matter their profession, no matter their income, no matter their disposition in life."[43]

How do African-American crime suspects get a jury of their peers if so many black men have life experiences deemed likely to disqualify them? Stevenson says:

> It is more common than uncommon for people of color to have those kinds of experiences. And I think that consciousness, that awareness is really important when you are going to adjudicate the guilt or innocence of someone. That's why we want diversity so desperately in these courtrooms because that consciousness changes things. There have been studies that show that there are real differences between black and white people on whether they believe that police officers are telling the truth all the time. And if you have some doubts about that, then you are prepared to insist on evidence. And if you insist on evidence, you're going to get a much more reliable verdict than when you operate on this presumption of guilt, when you just assume that police officers never lie.

* * * * *

While the Newton jury was still deliberating, Police Chief Charles Gain prepared for a murder verdict. He put twice as many officers on patrol as normal, believing that such a strong show of force, combined with state highway patrolmen and National Guardsmen, would together deter any violence. Gain was well aware that the devastating six-day Watts riots three years earlier had escalated from a single incident: a policeman pulling over an African-American drunk driver and impounding his car in front of hostile neighborhood spectators.

After two bloody skirmishes between the Panthers and the police in the last year, Oakland was so on edge over the Newton trial that the slightest new confrontation could trigger horrendous consequences. After the Panther ambush in April 1968, police on patrol in the flatlands all kept alert for similar attacks. Panther newspapers urging followers to "kill the pigs" and "Sky's the Limit" placards and speeches left patrolmen in West Oakland increasingly jittery, especially after they heard that the Panthers were stockpiling ammunition. A *Los Angeles Times* reporter observed: "Frustration, fear and anger are straining the nerves of big city policemen close to the breaking point."[44]

On Sunday night after the verdict issued, calm prevailed. On Monday, Emory Douglas and other Panthers working on the newspaper in the Party's headquarters at 4451 Grove Street warily eyed policemen on patrol. The intensity of the officers' hatred was palpable. The staff decided to leave the office early in case some policemen sought revenge. When Monday evening ended peacefully as well, Chief Gain must have gone to bed breathing a sigh of relief. Then the telephone woke him before 2 a.m. with most unwelcome news. Around 1:30 a.m., two members of his force had driven past the Panthers' Oakland headquarters and fired a shotgun and a carbine repeatedly from their squad car at the portrait of Newton in the front window. By then, the building was empty. The barrage of bullets struck office furniture and shattered an interior room divider. The officers also damaged posters of Eldridge Cleaver and Bobby Hutton that hung on the wall. Three shots struck an adjoining café. One errant shot went through the roof of their own patrol car.

The first shots woke up neighbors, who saw the officers' car make a U-turn and the officers fire a second round. The neighbors wrote down the license number and called the police dispatcher. Gain wasted no time calling for an investigation. The patrol car was assigned to officers Richard Williams and Robert Ferrell. When stopped for questioning, breath and blood tests showed their blood alcohol at .19, well over the generous definition of a person "under the influence of alcohol."

Janice Garrett had been working in the headquarters earlier on Monday and came back the next day: "I remember very clearly . . . seeing the damage that the policemen had done when they had shot up the office, it was riddled — and we knew then that that was their expression [to] let us know that we are here . . . to disrupt and create havoc in your lives." A spokesperson told a reporter this was proof of what they always claimed: "The Oakland Police Department is racist and determined to wipe out the Panthers." Newton again sent out word to lay low and not give the police an excuse to come down hard on the community.

That same day, Mayor Reading issued a press release calling the policemen's behavior "most regrettable and deplorable." Meanwhile, Chief Gain urged locals not to impugn the department as a whole for the shooting spree.[45] Unlike the radicals, the police could not afford to look like they condoned lawlessness as a response to a disappointing trial outcome. Less than thirty hours after the jury's verdicts were announced, the rogue officers were arrested on felony charges of firing into an occupied dwelling. On Police Chief Gain's recommendation, they were immediately fired for gross misconduct. Commander George Hart agreed with their termination: "It was a totally inappropriate, unjustifiable . . . action, unexpected and intolerable. . . . The immediate response within the department was this is outrageous. It is not something we stand for, something we will not tolerate and stand by."

The Oakland Police Officers' Association refused to cover the fired men's legal fees. Most members were anxious to avoid putting themselves at risk. The organization's president lamented, "I can't think of anything worse they could have done. Policemen long after they're gone are going to have to live with this."[46] Gain's prompt action was credited with playing a major role in averting riots. The National

Guardsmen were sent home as radical militant supporters of Newton retreated to contemplate their next move after a day of reckoning that few if any had reckoned on.

17. WINNING NEWTON'S FREEDOM

Be wary what you wish for. You may get it.
— KATHLEEN CLEAVER

D espite the verdict averting a murder conviction, the Newton case was far from over. The aim of Newton's defense team had always been far more ambitious than just avoiding the death penalty. Garry and Stender had as their goal the same as that of the Newton family — winning Newton's freedom. It was also the stated aim of the Panther Party — to get Newton back to spearhead the revolution. Actually, the symbolism of his continued imprisonment served the Panthers as a superb recruitment tool. As long as Newton remained incarcerated, he still represented to his followers all black men victimized by a racist criminal justice system. The Black Panthers did not care about the technicalities of the law of voluntary manslaughter or murder. They wanted Officer Frey to stand in for all abusive white policemen and Newton to embody all black men railroaded since colonial days. The cry of "Free Huey!" stood in for freeing all political prisoners — all minorities the Panthers considered unjustly behind bars. As with the Sacco and Vanzetti case, the Scottsboro Boys and that of Willie McGee, the court of public opinion was what mattered most as the briefing process slowly progressed on the appellate docket.

Within three weeks after the jury convicted Newton of manslaughter, Fay Stender coordinated community volunteers to obtain 20,000 signatures in support of his release on bail pending appeal. Newton's parents, Walter and Armelia Newton, came to the hearing to vouch for their youngest son's good character and trustworthiness. Unlike Walter, who attended the trial, Armelia had spent most of the past eleven months since Huey's arrest in seclusion. The judge likely had never seen such an array of support for a prisoner's release as Stender presented to him, including an association of black clergy who vouched for Newton as a force for peace in the community. But the judge had to have looked askance at Stender's own observations that she had seen "a definite change in the defendant's personality" and strongly felt that he did not currently represent "even the mildest aggressive threat to others."[1] Stender had only met Newton while he was in custody.

The Panther leader's pastor, Rev. Earl Neil, took the stand and called Newton "the personification of what our American ideals are set up to produce in all of its citizens."[2] He told Judge Friedman that just a week before the verdict was reached — when Newton had no idea whether he might face execution — Newton had made a tape recording for students at Oakland's predominantly black McClymonds High School warning them against reacting violently to whatever the jury decided. Duly impressed, Judge Friedman turned and commended Newton.

Newton then took the stand. He told the judge that he had advised his own followers in advance of the verdict to "keep cool" no matter what resulted.[3] The judge questioned Newton at length about his prior record. Newton's negative probation report detailed a decade of serious run-ins with the law. It lent credence to Jensen's argument that Newton's repeated misconduct demonstrated "nothing but contempt for the rules that govern civilized men."[4] Jensen had fought hard for a verdict of first degree murder, but accepted the jury's role to decide the appropriate penalty for itself. He was now determined to see Newton stay in prison for that manslaughter conviction.

It surprised few besides Newton's family and most devoted advocates when Judge Friedman agreed with Jensen and denied the request for Newton's release pending appeal. A large segment of the local community believed, as the police still did, that Newton should have been sentenced to death for murder. Judge Friedman ordered Newton to begin his sentence even though he might easily wind up doing two years of prison time before the appellate court decided whether the conviction was valid. Reversal seemed most unlikely. Newton remained stoic about the prison time, which Stender single-mindedly opposed. Keeping him from the gas chamber was only part of her mission. Newton was now the symbol of every black man sold down the river by a racist system — his freedom was her goal. For now, Stender had to accept a setback. Newton's mother Armelia remained in denial — her baby could not have done what he was accused of. She screamed hysterically at the announcement of Newton's prison sentence. Moments after the hearing ended, police removed Newton to the Vacaville Medical Facility for evaluation.

Following Garry's orders, Eldridge Cleaver had not attended the hearing and took no action when he learned of its outcome. Local papers noticed that no "Sky's the limit" reprisals occurred for Newton's conviction of manslaughter instead of murder. When asked by reporters, Garry insisted that the "The sky is the limit" meant only that they intended to exhaust all the Panther leader's legal rights. A reporter for *The People's World* commented, "No doubt there are those in the black community for whom the slogan means more; a warning of the pent up frustrations and anger in an oppressed and exploited people, which might easily explode into violence if provoked by the power structure."[5] One reporter assumed that, for some Panthers, Huey would have made "a much finer martyr" if he were instead headed for execution.[6]

But the racial tension that served as a backdrop for the Newton trial had not dissipated in Oakland or nearby cities. The day after Newton's sentencing, without apparent provocation, a white policeman in San Francisco shot a black truck driver, who died. When he shot the trucker, the officer was wearing a homemade tie pin — "Gas Huey." To avoid sparking a riot, the chief of police quickly suspended the officer and arrested him on a charge of using excessive force. At the time of this new tragedy, Kathleen Cleaver had just made local headlines by rallying supporters, much as H. Rap Brown had done the summer before: "We have to civilize America . . . or let it burn."[7] She posed for *Ramparts* with a rifle at her side to broadcast to the world that she was prepared for armed self-defense. The photo was bound to provoke anger among local policemen. Yet both San Francisco's and Oakland's Police Chiefs had now sent strong messages they would not tolerate rogue cops inciting any armed retaliation from the Panthers.

Meanwhile, Newton headed off to prison. At the beginning of October, prison officials transferred Newton to the Men's Colony in San Luis Obispo, a medium-security facility four hours' drive south. It housed mostly white, nonviolent (and gay) convicts. Though the prison facilities were better than most, his time behind bars isolated Newton from Bay Area supporters, and right at the moment when his public profile had never been higher. Coincidentally or not, on October 3, two bombs went off in the Alameda County Courthouse where Newton had been tried, breaking one hundred windows. The administration called in a Navy bomb squad.

The guards and the isolated location took away Newton's ability to communicate directly with young supporters in the Bay Area and across the nation who had become his fan base. But on the inside he was also an instant celebrity, much to the warden's dismay. His fellow inmates at the Men's Colony adopted him as their new hero as news agencies all over the United States inundated the prison with requests for interviews, few of which were granted. Meanwhile, the impact of the Panthers was felt in the international arena. In mid-October, Newton was ecstatic to learn that Olympic medalists Tommie Smith and John Carlos had just lifted their arms in defiant power-to-the-people fist pumps at the 1968 Summer Olympics in Mexico.

By the end of the month, Newton launched his own protest. He demanded the minimum wage instead of working in the prison kitchen for "slave wages" of three cents per hour. The warden put Newton in lock-up for rule violations. As in the Alameda jail, Newton often paced naked in his poorly ventilated cell, roughly four-and-a-half feet by six feet. When the press again demanded access, exasperated prison officials permitted limited numbers of further interviews.

* * * * *

By late September 1968, Charles Garry resumed preparations for the upcoming Oakland Seven conspiracy trial for blocking access to the Induction Center in which Garry and his co-counsel ambitiously planned to put the Vietnam War itself on trial. Meanwhile, Garry handed to Fay Stender the tedious job of reviewing the 4,000-page trial record in order to prepare Newton's appeal. Stender knew that the appeal, like the trial, needed to remain the center of political attention so she also played a key role in expanding the "Free Huey" campaign. Stender squeezed in as many fund-raising and speaking events as she could and recruited celebrities to lend their names as well, helping galvanize more support for the Panthers and the "Free Huey" movement. The FBI sent an undercover agent to a keynote address Stender gave to a thousand students in San Diego. He noted for her growing dossier that the soft-spoken lawyer seemed surprisingly persuasive when she proclaimed that the Black Panther Party was the best thing ever to happen to African-Americans.

Belva Davis recalled travelling on vacation in Europe and seeing people wearing "Free Huey" tee shirts. Overseas support was growing rapidly. Meanwhile, in Washington, a congressional hearing on violence in late October 1968 generated more headlines about Newton's revolutionary agenda. Professor Herman Blake was among those called to testify. The linguist who had testified at the Newton trial provoked public controversy when he sparred with a Congressman over Newton's statement that blacks should go to war if necessary to overcome racism.[8] Then, a staff member from the Kerner Commission told the congressional panel that, in a jailhouse interview, Newton had predicted "future bloodshed." He alarmed the staffer with his belief that his own trial would become a "springboard that mobilizes the community."[9] Newton expected the Movement to mushroom to two million members in two years.

Newton was counting on the Panthers' alliance with the Peace and Freedom Party to help the Panthers gain political control of black ghettos throughout the country. SDS, the leading New Left organization, had aligned with the Panthers back in the spring, right after King's assassination. SDS leader Tom Hayden, who would become a co-defendant of Bobby Seale in the 1969 Chicago conspiracy trial, dubbed the Black Panthers "America's Viet Cong."[10] Hayden obviously viewed that nickname as a high compliment — equating the Panthers with Ho Chi Minh's

National Liberation Front currently battling American troops in the Vietnam War. In the eyes of the Nixon administration and patriotic supporters of the war, linking the Panthers with the Viet Cong made the Panthers traitors to America. Stender had already arranged for Newton to be featured in a new film, *Prelude to Revolution*. By November of 1968 the film was drawing crowds to black film festivals across the country.

As hard as Stender had worked during the trial, she continued at a similar incessant pace, often working late into the night from late 1968 through most of 1969. She welcomed offers of help pouring in from constitutional law professors, criminal law practitioners, and students who saw Newton's appeal as an important vehicle for addressing systemic racism in the justice system. The end product was a nearly 200-page opening "brief" and another lengthy reply "brief."

Almost every month, Stender drove her husband's Mercedes four hours each way on a weekend trip to the Men's Colony in San Luis Obispo to visit Newton to update him on her progress and to serve as a go-between for members of the Party denied visitation privileges. Alex Hoffmann alternated with her. The Garry firm footed the $10 gas bill for each round trip and occasional overnight stay at a nearby motel. Unlike other visitors, the attorneys met with Newton alone and unfettered. Guards only peered in occasionally through a window. Stender began smuggling in letters and photographs from friends to show Newton and bring back with her in her brief case when she left, to avoid having them discovered and confiscated. In talking with Newton, both Hoffmann and Stender tried to be very careful, realizing the room might be bugged. Stender whispered whenever she needed to convey critical information.

Between visits, Stender frequently wrote to Newton, assuming that all correspondence would be opened and read. That meant picking safe topics and saving sensitive Party business for in-person visits. Stender thought Newton would enjoy knowing that a photographic essay of "The Black Panthers" had opened at the De Young Museum in San Francisco. To cheer him up, she treated Newton as extended family. She included pictures of her kids and her house and relayed return messages from her client to her children. It never occurred to Stender back then that there should be any barriers erected between her family and her militant clients. Her affection knew no bounds.

Stender had another reason for frequent trips to see her client. Newton suffered from bouts of depression, which she believed were caused in part by deprivation of female companionship. With her special access as his attorney, Stender wanted to demonstrate her love for him and buoy his spirits in captivity. On one occasion, a startled guard reported seeing Stender bent down, apparently engaged in oral sex with Newton. The guard did not enter the room, but his report went all the way up the chain of command to Corrections Chief Raymond Procunier in Sacramento; Procunier later privately shared this with others. In a few years' time, Stender would encourage women in her prison law collective to boost the morale of men in maximum security by engaging in whatever sexual activity they could get away with. It was an act of defiance that brought a much-coveted taste of freedom to inmates subjected to conditions she considered inhumane. If Stender took that risk with Newton at the Men's Colony, it must have contributed to the bitter memory in her last days of the lengths she had gone to for her revolutionary client, only to be ultimately rejected.

The state's Attorney General would make a major public issue in the early 1970s out of Stender's exploitation of the attorney-client relationship when she and her associates represented George Jackson and other prisoners. The California Attorney General's focus was the misuse of privileged attorney-client communications to further criminal conduct by militant inmates. Although it brought bad publicity, Stender suffered no consequences to her license. Attorneys smuggling notes and messages in and out of prison would hit the headlines again in 2005 when Lynne Stewart, a New York radical six years Stender's junior, became another Lawyers Guild celebrity. Stewart challenged the constitutionality of federal laws that precluded her from using her status as lawyer for a convicted Egyptian-born terrorist to communicate messages from him to his Middle East followers.

Mike Tigar's legendary skills as a criminal defense lawyer could not prevent sixty-six-year-old Stewart from going to prison and suffering automatic disbarment. Tigar had known Stender since his undergraduate and law school days in Berkeley when he worked on Movement causes that she also was deeply involved with. In retrospect, Tigar saw no distinction in the conduct Lynne Stewart engaged in from that of Stender and her colleagues acting as go-betweens for Newton back in the late '60s and inmate George Jackson in the early '70s. It was only the rules that had changed.

Back in 1968 and 1969, Stender knew she and the Panthers were being closely monitored by the FBI, but felt the cause of freeing Huey was worth any personal risk. With the whirlwind of activity Stender generated, friends saw her as an irrepressible force on a mission for which she refused to consider failure a possibility. Given the slowness of the appellate process it was fortunate that Newton was in no hurry to get released. Though still subject to depression and mood swings in isolation, he felt safe in prison. It also gave him time to strategize while unprecedented clashes took place on the outside between militant protesters and the establishment, particularly on college campuses.

The chaos started at San Francisco State College in November 1968. Newton was proud that the Panthers figured prominently in the first and longest campus strike in American history. Aggressive lobbying for an African-American Studies Department and for the hiring of more black staff had taken a violent turn a year earlier when some students physically attacked editors of the campus paper for opposing the Panther-inspired demands for ethnic studies. Several students had gotten suspended as a result of that confrontation. In the fall of 1968 renewed protests followed the abrupt suspension of Black Panther Minister of Education George Mason Murray from the adjunct faculty of the English Department. The State College Board of Trustees had swiftly removed Murray from the faculty after learning that he had stirred up black students at a rally on another campus with an express call for armed revolt: "We are slaves and the only way to become free is to kill all the slave masters."[11]

Governor Reagan and the U.C. Regents were already angry about the demonstrators and campus unrest, but they became apoplectic in September when Eldridge Cleaver received invitations at U.C. Davis, U.C. Berkeley and Stanford to lecture that fall on the topic of urban unrest. More than ten thousand Californians lodged letters of protest with the governor. An equally irate State Superintendent of Public Instruction told reporters, "Mr. Cleaver certainly would be as well-qualified to lecture on urban unrest as Attila the Hun . . . on international mass murder and as Benedict Arnold to lecture on treason."[12] Not surprisingly, intrigued students had a very different reaction; the enormous controversy only induced more Cal students to enroll for the guest lecture series featuring Eldridge Cleaver — the Peace and Freedom candidate for President. Cleaver then surprised everyone with his first lecture, an unexpectedly serious talk about racism that was devoid of his trademark obscenities. In fact, some students found it a boring disappointment, provoking more yawns than protests. But in spite of the understated reaction to that first speech, the Regents took no chances, bypassing the campus administrators to cancel Cleaver's remaining nine lectures.

Across the bay, the San Francisco State student body then invited the ex-felon to their campus to speak. This time, Cleaver did not restrain himself. Eager to provoke the administration, Cleaver told the audience that "we have to throw this capitalist system into the garbage can of history." He urged listeners to harness "red, yellow, brown and even white power" and warned, "If Huey isn't freed, we're going to free him, and we're going to do it with guns." He then invited the students to listen to a poem he had just dedicated to the governor. To great applause, he recited a three-line chant, pausing for the audience to echo his words. "Fuck Reagan . . . Fuck Reagan . . . Fuck Reagan . . ." The students enthusiastically joined in a loud chorus. As an afterthought, Cleaver added, "Fuck the Regents — ten lectures to one."[13] Maligning the governor with obscenities and threatening armed revolt guaranteed more outraged headlines. Where would it lead?

For Cleaver, the no-holds-barred speech led to more opportunities to get his message across. In late October 1968 — just a month before his scheduled return to prison for parole violation — Cleaver gave *Playboy* magazine an interview at his lawyer Charles Garry's office in San Francisco. Relishing the limelight, Cleaver hinted darkly that the day of reckoning was coming soon: "We don't work on a timetable, but

. . . the situation is deteriorating rapidly. . . This isn't the 1930s. We're not going to play Jews,"[14] echoing a warning that H. Rap Brown had often made at rallies.

The fiery rhetoric that roiled the U.C. Regents and Governor Reagan did not have quite the same impact on J. Edgar Hoover. His COINTELPRO agents figured the Free Huey Movement had no future with Newton serving a potentially fifteen-year sentence and Cleaver headed back to prison soon, too. Plans already were underway for Seale to be among those prosecuted in Chicago for the recent riots at the 1968 Democratic Convention.

Hoover was also already at work sabotaging the Panthers' new breakfast program. A new Panther member in Sacramento prepared an inflammatory coloring book for kids featuring the Panthers killing white pig cops, which the Party's Central Committee rejected as distorting their message. But the cartoonist and his friends mimeographed and distributed unauthorized copies anyway, which the FBI then anonymously sent to corporate sponsors of the Panthers' breakfast program, including Safeway. The FBI also made sure the coloring book came to the attention of a Senate subcommittee focused on organized crime — the standing committee that had just played a key role in passage of both the Gun Control Act of 1968 and the Omnibus Crime Control and Safe Streets Act of 1968. The new laws included wiretap authority, increased funding for state police and the FBI, and major restrictions on interstate trade in handguns. The Panther leadership in the fall of 1968 thought the comic book distributors were off on their own lark; it did not occur to them until much later that the FBI was behind wide distribution of the coloring book — one of many efforts to undermine the Panthers in the community at large that wound up documented by a Senate investigation into Hoover's abuses of power against the Black Panthers.[15]

When Earl Anthony met with agents O'Connor and Kizenski in the fall of 1968, they told Anthony that the FBI was about to ratchet up efforts to "crush the Panthers." They would strike deals with petty criminals already used as FBI informants and pay them to become members of the Party "to start an internecine struggle to destroy the Party."[16] It was the same kind of tactic Hoover had used against the American

Communist Party in the mid-1950s — at one point an estimated thirty
percent of the Communist Party's shrinking paid membership consisted of federally-funded informants.[17] As part of his plan to destroy
the Panther Party Hoover wanted to put Anthony in the position to
head what remained of the Party after its existing leaders were imprisoned. The FBI agents urged Anthony to write a book about his life as
a Panther in order to promote his leadership. Anthony presented the
idea to the Panther Central Committee after he had already secured an
agent. He claimed his intentions were honorable and thought Cleaver
and Hilliard would welcome his initiative in seeking to publicize how
they had built the Panther Party as a political force. Instead, the Central
Committee reacted with immediate suspicion and put Anthony under
house arrest at Hilliard's home. At the time, Seale was just beginning
to dictate his own recollections of the Party's formation and political
agenda for the book *Seize the Time;* Anthony's decision to publish his
own book looked like a competing power ploy by an out-of-control
jackanape whose political views had already been criticized as out of
sync with those of the High Command. Anthony escaped his Panther
guards with help from renegade Muslim friends and fled to New York.
John Huggins was soon named Deputy Minister of Information in Los
Angeles in Anthony's place.

Meanwhile, the Panthers continued their run-ins with local police.
A few weeks after Cleaver threatened an imminent timetable for the
start of guerilla warfare, San Francisco police stopped a Panther newspaper delivery truck fleeing from a gas station convenience store
robbery. A gunfight then followed in broad daylight near police headquarters at the San Francisco Hall of Justice. Three officers were shot
and eight Panthers arrested. Seale believed the instigator was a provocateur. The Party's central committee refused to bail the suspected
government agent out.

Newton also learned from visitors to the Men's Colony that Cleaver
was making plans to barricade himself and supporters inside an
Oakland building to precipitate a final bloody confrontation with local
police just before Thanksgiving. To avenge Bobby Hutton's death and
go down in a blaze of glory, Cleaver wanted to repeat the gun battle he

had precipitated in April 1968. Cleaver later described how energized
he had been by the April exchange of gunfire with the Oakland police:
"That was the first experience of freedom that I had. I was free for an
hour and a half because during that time the repressive forces couldn't
put their hand on me because we were shooting it out with them."[18]

Outsiders who lumped Cleaver and Newton together as radical fire-
brands did not appreciate — or understand — the complexity of their
working relationship with each other or with other Panthers in leadership roles. After his arrest in 1967, while Newton professed his innocence in court, he supported Cleaver's efforts to advertise the killing
of Officer Frey as a bold first step toward general insurrection. Newton
also gave Cleaver the green light to have the Panthers storm the courthouse to try to break him out if he wound up headed for death row.
But by the spring of 1968 the two were far from united, appearances
to the contrary notwithstanding. While Cleaver found the foolhardy
April shootout with Oakland police exhilarating, it had been against
Newton's orders. Even as the Panthers publicly accused the police of
Bobby Hutton's murder, privately, Newton blamed Cleaver for instigating Hutton's death.

Although Newton himself was prone to recklessness, he now favored
strengthening political coalitions and community-building through
free breakfasts and health clinics before taking young followers to the
streets in armed revolt. Cleaver was far more impatient for the revolution to begin. The manslaughter verdict had changed Newton's mind.
With Governor Reagan and the FBI hell-bent on eradicating the Party,
Newton saw Cleaver playing right into their hands, sacrificing the lives
of many more recruits like Bobby Hutton for no good reason.

When word got to Newton about Cleaver's intentions to commit suicide by cop that Thanksgiving and take other Panthers with him, Newton
instead ordered Cleaver to flee the country, head for Cuba, and recruit
new international members to the Panther Party. Cleaver then failed
to show up for a final announced lecture at U.C. Berkeley and embar-
rassed his FBI tail by disappearing completely. (Disguised as a member
of a mime troop, he fled the country and turned up first in Cuba and
then months later in Algeria, joined by his very pregnant wife).

At the same time Cleaver disappeared, Earl Anthony fled, first to New York and then to Paris, to work on his book, fearing that the Panthers would have killed him had he stayed in the states. The Panthers would officially expel Anthony from the Party for life at the end of March 1969, among many Panthers purged from the Party in the wake of the assassination of Huggins and Bunchy Carter that January. Some of the Panthers in the Central Committee also mistrusted Mark Comfort by then, but he stayed in Oakland heading his own neighborhood youth group. By the spring of 1969, Stokely Carmichael had secretly turned against the Panthers and sought Earl Anthony's support to overthrow the Party leadership.[19] With all these fissures largely beneath the surface, the Panther Party nonetheless continued to expand across the country in 1969, its ranks growing with both hordes of young admirers and increasing numbers of informants.

While San Francisco State remained in turmoil, similar strikes and sit-ins erupted in 1969 at 300 college campuses across country. The escalating student unrest occurred at the same time as unprecedented attempts by militants to stop the nation's business as usual. Meanwhile, students at Oakland City College hosted a national conference aimed at converting its new campus already under construction in the Oakland hills into an all-black college renamed for Huey Newton. Exasperation of government leaders reached a new pinnacle in the Bay Area in April 1969 when veterans of the Free Speech Movement took possession of dilapidated university property near Telegraph Avenue on the south side of the Berkeley campus and planted trees and shrubbery for "People's Park."

In early April Governor Reagan gave a speech in which he vowed: "If there has to be a bloodbath, then let's get it over with. No more appeasement."[20] On the morning of May 15, 1969, he sent 250 highway patrol and police officers without notice to uproot "People's Park," install a chain-link fence around the property, and defend it with live ammunition. Three thousand students were gathered at Sproul Plaza for an unrelated rally that day. When told of the precipitous police action they became incensed. Student body president Dan Siegel then urged them to "Take the park." When they marched to confront the police guarding the new chain-link fence, a mélée ensued: the police shot thirty people, killed one and blinded a bystander.

Governor Reagan then declared martial law in Berkeley. For the next few weeks, helicopters circled the city and officers prepared to spray tear gas on any Berkeley residents who assembled. Coincidentally, Penny Cooper had quit the Public Defender's Office two weeks before the People's Park confrontation to go into private practice in Berkeley with her colleague Jim Newhouse. By precipitating so many arrests, Governor Reagan handed the duo a superabundance of clients to launch Cooper and Newhouse's new criminal defense practice.

Historians started describing the situation in 1969 as the worst violence since the Red Summer of 1919 when bloody race riots had erupted for months in cities across the country. In late June, *TIME* magazine predicted "Guerrilla Summer." The administration feared the role the Panthers could play in that tense environment. President Nixon's new Attorney General, John Mitchell, created a special unit just for Panther prosecutions. Meanwhile, Newton reassessed the Party's priorities even as Eldridge Cleaver, from his outpost in Algeria, remained intent on growing international support for open warfare in America's cities. Newton rejected the black nationalism Stokely Carmichael advocated, but Newton also saw that his followers were not ready for the revolution Cleaver wanted to start.

Newton preferred to buy time to build up a strong enough base. First, Newton needed to dispel the Panthers' image as "trigger-happy, gun-toting thugs."[21] Newton had to convince his followers to go in a new direction. He had always used the threats of violence as an organizing tool, but having seen the police and FBI decimate the Panthers — and the Panthers' recent loss of community support — he realized they needed to ratchet down their violent image. He directed David Hilliard to focus instead on expanding community programs. In Oakland and Los Angeles the Panthers were feeding thousands of children daily. Assembly Speaker Jesse Unruh (author of the state's pioneering 1959 Civil Rights Act) soon credited the Panthers with serving more meals to needy youngsters than the government was doing. In the process, the Panthers were building mainstream political alliances and luring large numbers of new recruits.

J. Edgar Hoover reacted to this Panther strategy with alarm. Back in August 1967, Dr. Martin Luther King worried him most. By 1970, a poll indicated that a quarter of blacks held the Black Panthers in high regard, including an eye-popping 43 percent of those under twenty-one.[22] (Kathleen Cleaver believes that poll vastly underestimated the true level of the Panthers' support among black inner city youths in 1970.) Hoover stepped up efforts to stymie the Panthers' attempt to foster a more wholesome image. He realized that the Panther paper served as a potent tool for attracting support for its revolutionary agenda. He also saw the great momentum the Panthers had already achieved by focusing on much-needed community programs. The FBI Chief warned his staff that the breakfast program "represents the best and most influential activity going for the BPP." That program made feeding hungry children "potentially the greatest threat to efforts by authorities to neutralize the BPP and destroy what it stands for."[23] Hoover invited local FBI offices to come up with more illegal techniques to isolate the Panthers from moderate blacks and whites, humanitarians, churches and suppliers for their breakfast programs.

The Panthers who ran the newspaper encountered a number of suspected informers, who would come in and hang around the organization. Panthers in cities across the country faced more frequent arrests on charges that were often later dismissed. Their office equipment was destroyed; their food supplies thrown away; their newspapers confiscated and tossed in trash bins. An appalled leftist commentator for *The Nation*, the country's oldest weekly news journal, wrote, "Panther arrests with charges later dropped, and bail in the millions, constitute an unprecedented national scandal which beggars the fifties." He quoted author and educator Donald Freed, who was then working on a play about Julius and Ethel Rosenberg, who both had been executed as spies during the McCarthy Era: "If what is being perpetrated against the Black Panther Party was being done to any white group, including the Nazi Party, the liberal establishment — from the ACLU to *The New York Times* — would absolutely refuse to tolerate it further."[24]

When the head of the FBI's San Francisco office balked at some of the tactics he considered unconstitutional, J. Edgar Hoover scolded him. In Hoover's estimation, the Panther breakfast programs represented a cynical ploy "to fill adolescent children with . . . insidious poison."[25] Several years later, the Senate investigation of "The FBI's Covert Action Program to Destroy the Black Panther Party" would document such misconduct as disrupting delivery of Panther newspapers, trashing the Party's branch offices, spreading malicious false rumors and sending forged letters and anonymous threats to instigate retaliatory killings by rival organizations.[26]

Meanwhile, the Panthers continued to ride the tide of campus protests against the Vietnam War. In the fall of 1969, opposition to the war grew exponentially among college students. The center of attention became the Chicago Eight trial where the defense would put the Vietnam War on trial as several other high profile war opponents had done in the past two years. The Chicago Eight Trial would indeed live up to its reputation as the "most incredible trial in American history"[27] — a symbolic battle between the political establishment and the entire anti-war Movement. The defendants had learned from the trial of Dr. Benjamin Spock, of the "Boston Five," convicted the year before. The trial of the famed author of *Baby and Child Care* (one of the most widely distributed books in the world) had received international attention, but Dr. Spock and his fellow defendants played by the rules and were precluded from introducing the morality of the Vietnam War into their criminal trial. In retrospect, Dr. Spock himself questioned his lawyers' strategy: "We sat like good little boys called into the principal's office. I'm afraid we didn't prove very much."[28] Yet their convictions were reversed on appeal.

There were also lessons to be learned from the highly publicized October 1968 trial of the "Catonsville Nine," led by religious anti-war activists who burned draft files to protest the continued killing in Vietnam. That trial of Catholic priests Philip and Daniel Berrigan and seven other defendants spawned anti-war demonstrations nationwide. William Kunstler, who later became one of the Chicago Eight lawyers, acted as lead counsel in defending the Catonsville Nine. Kunstler argued that the court should instruct the jury on the common law concept known as "jury nullification" — the name given to an acquittal by a jury that sympathizes so much with a guilty defendant that it renders a verdict clearly contrary to the facts and law. Kunstler wanted the trial judge to instruct the jury that it had the power to acquit the defendants if the panel agreed the war was immoral. Instead, following the court's instructions, the jury took less than two hours to convict all nine defendants, who were then sentenced to prison.

The most promising model for the Chicago Eight defense was the Oakland Seven case completed in March 1969. By then President Johnson had left office, while more and more citizens had become disillusioned over the wisdom of the ongoing war. The political make-up of the Oakland Seven jury pool was also closer to that of Chicago than the Catonsville Nine jury pool had been. The judge in the Oakland Seven case was Judge George Phillips, the same judge who had issued the landmark ruling barring deliberate dismissal of all black jurors by the Alameda County District Attorney's office the summer before.

Even though all of the Oakland Seven were white, Charlie Garry figured out how to inject race issues into the jury selection — he argued that jurors might be biased against the defendants for opposing a racist draft. Each time Lowell Jensen dismissed potential black jurors for opposition to the war Garry noted the juror's race for the record. Garry also tested the jury on their reactions to the Panthers to try to get those who disliked the Panthers kicked off for cause, leaving a more left-leaning panel. Garry had a plausible excuse for mentioning the Panthers, too, even though none of the seven white defendants belonged to the Panther Party. The Oakland Seven were allied with the Panthers in their opposition to the war and Garry himself had been in the news almost daily for much of the prior year when he represented Huey Newton. So Judge Phillips let Garry ask the panel what they felt about the Black Panther Party, and whether they bore any ill will to Garry as Newton's lawyer.

When it came time to put on the Oakland Seven's defense, Garry pulled a major surprise on prosecutor Lowell Jensen. Garry called a Stanford University physicist to the stand who admitted to organizing rallies on his campus for Stop the Draft Week, circulating flyers and coordinating busloads of demonstrators headed for the induction

center. The physicist had never been prosecuted or even, to his knowledge, investigated. After his testimony was completed, the defense team
abruptly rested their case in late March of 1969 without calling any
of their clients to the stand. Garry said Jensen's jaw dropped and "he
looked as if someone had just poured ice water over his head."[29] While
the jury was out, Garry entertained reporters and defense supporters by
standing on his head in the courtroom, as he often did at parties. After
three days of deliberation, the jury returned with acquittals of all seven
protest leaders. When a local reporter interviewed Garry, one of the
jubilant defendants asked Garry if he considered himself as good as the
fictional Perry Mason, who never lost a case. Garry quipped in reply,
"I'm *better* than Perry Mason. *All* of his clients are innocent."[30]

Garry had been Seale's lawyer of choice for the Chicago Eight trial,
but was scheduled for surgery and unable to get Judge Hoffman to
delay the trial's start until he recovered. Seale then insisted on representing himself. It had been somewhat surprising that Seale was named
as a defendant in the first place since he had only been a last-minute
substitute speaker for Eldridge Cleaver and could hardly have played a
major role in orchestrating the protests. When a journalist asked a representative of the Department of Justice what prompted the government to prosecute Seale, the official responded frankly, "The Panthers
are a bunch of hoodlums and we have to get this guy."[31]

Early in the trial Judge Hoffman, a former law partner of Mayor
Daly, lost his temper at Seale when the Black Panther leader repeatedly called the judge a "fascist dog," a "pig" and a "blatant racist." [32]
Tellingly, Judge Hoffman would issue nearly 160 contempt citations
against various defendants in that case and against their lawyers, but
saved the most draconian punishment for the only black defendant
— physically attempting to silence Seale. To the shock of liberals and
leftists across country, but to the delight of Nixon's law-and-order
supporters, Judge Hoffman ordered Seale bound and gagged. Seale
struggling to be heard through his gag became an instant symbol of
a broken criminal justice system. Under the circumstances, the jury
could no longer be expected to fairly evaluate the charges against him.
Seale's case wound up separated from the prosecution of the other

activists, who went down in history as "the Chicago Seven." (All the contempt citations were later overturned by the Court of Appeals.)

Yet all of their notoriety came at a high price as the Panthers faced one legal crisis after another. After he was removed as a defendant in the Chicago conspiracy trial, Seale was extradited to Connecticut on charges of conspiring to murder suspected FBI informant Alex Rackley. Members of the New Haven Panther Party had confessed to torturing and executing Rackley, but trying to prove that Seale ordered the killing was a stretch. Though New Haven's Police Chief would not say so publicly until much later, he believed the police had "no solid evidence" to link Bobby Seale to Alex Rackley's murder and was "astonished" when Seale was indicted by prosecutor Arnold Markle.[33] It was all part of FBI Chief J. Edgar Hoover's effort to kill off the "Free Huey" Movement so there would be no Party left if Newton ever got out of prison.

In November, nearly a million protesters gathered in Washington, D.C., to demand that America pull out of the war. That same month, David Hilliard used the podium at an anti-war rally before a quarter of a million peaceniks at Golden Gate Park in San Francisco to announce a brazen Panther Party proposal: that Eldridge Cleaver be authorized to negotiate with the Viet Cong for the exchange of POWs for Bobby Seale, Huey Newton and other Panthers. Then Hilliard lambasted American society as fascist and cursed President Nixon as an evil "motherfucker" who sent his "vicious murderous dogs" out to destroy the Black Panther Party children's breakfast programs. Hilliard boldly announced, "We will kill Richard Nixon."[34] Afterward, Charles Garry warned Hilliard that his statement would land him in jail. So Hilliard was not at all surprised two weeks later when federal agents surrounded his car and arrested him for threatening the President's life.

At the time of his arrest, Hilliard was the highest ranking Panther not in prison, but Hoover was far from through in making sure the Party remained leaderless. In early December 1969, COINTELPRO dramatically escalated its campaign against the Panther Party. They orchestrated a predawn raid on the apartment of Chicago Panther leader Fred Hampton with the secret assistance of Hampton's own bodyguard who had turned informant a year earlier in exchange for getting felony charges against him dropped. Hampton had proven himself a charismatic and effective community organizer. The FBI feared Hampton had potential to become the next Black Messiah after the late Reverend King. With a barrage of gunfire, plainclothes Chicago police officers stormed the apartment, and murdered Hampton lying in bed already drugged to sleep by his bodyguard. They also killed twenty-two-year-old Panther Mark Clark and wounded four other Panthers.

Four days later, the Los Angeles SWAT team conducted another predawn raid on the Panthers' Los Angeles headquarters and seriously wounded three members. Charles Garry forestalled a similar raid in Oakland by immediately calling a press conference where he charged that the Panthers were being targeted for annihilation. Many civil rights leaders and mainstream press echoed Garry's concerns that law enforcement was out to eradicate the Panthers, although skeptics discounted conspiracy theories as paranoid. No public information had as yet leaked about the existence of COINTELPRO and most Americans could not believe that the FBI Chief and the Nixon administration would go to such extremes. Fay Stender talked San Francisco Lawyers Guild members into spending a couple of nights at Panther Party headquarters in Oakland. One of the volunteers later admitted that the gun-wielding Panthers frightened him more than the police did.

In spite of their attempt to craft a new, community-building image, the Panthers had not strayed all that far from the militancy that engendered so much public fear. Yet worldwide support for the Panthers kept growing because they were seen as victims of extraordinarily repressive government tactics like those of Judge Hoffman in court and those of the Chicago police whom critics likened to the Gestapo. The horrifying news of the armed invasion of Panther headquarters in Chicago brought five thousand people from across the nation to attend Fred Hampton's funeral in December of 1969. Reverend Jesse Jackson proclaimed, "When Fred was shot in Chicago, black people in particular, and decent people in general, bled everywhere."[35] The Panthers and their outraged supporters renewed demands for a probe of the FBI and state police. From his safe haven in Algeria, Cleaver urged retaliation, but no further confrontations occurred.

Between his arrest for the Chicago Conspiracy trial and his trial in New Haven Seale used much of his time in jail dictating *Seize the Time: The History of the Black Panther Party and Huey Newton.* By then, the Party had been in the headlines for two years. One freelance reporter noted that the Panthers were "deeply revered in colonial and liberated, formerly colonial countries; Eldridge Cleaver is a household word, and the names Huey Newton and Bobby Seale are familiar in homes from coast to coast."[36]

Fortunately for Seale, Charles Garry was able to recover in time to head up Seale's Connecticut defense team. He planned to return to New Haven for pretrial preparations right after he and Fay Stender argued Newton's appeal in San Francisco. Meanwhile, the mainstream media were willing to cover the Panthers as long as they presented themselves in menacing fashion. At the beginning of 1970, *Newsweek* talked Panthers David Hilliard, Elbert "Big Man" Howard and D. C. Cox into posing for its cover in front of a poster of Bobby Seale. To make them look more sinister, magazine staffers insisted that the Panthers wear leather jackets. Never mind that the Panthers had already abandoned that look after concluding it invited police harassment. The fiercer look sold more magazines.

The oral argument on Newton's appeal took place in mid-February 1970, accompanied by a three-hour "Free Huey" rally at the adjacent Civic Center. The spectacle now required a lot more effort to put together. For some, the gatherings had grown old. Jaded white radicals wondered what difference it would really make if Newton were free. Still, nearly a hundred observers accompanied Newton's counsel into the appellate courthouse for the much-anticipated oral argument. A skeptical Panther reporter noted that the elevated bench seemed designed to make attendees feel as if they were "going before the throne of the Lord." He left the building convinced that "the pigs had no intention of allowing Huey to receive anything close to another trial."[37] Yet from the questions asked by the three-judge panel, Newton's lawyers emerged cautiously optimistic.

A heavily promoted birthday benefit for Newton the following week in Berkeley resulted in intense disappointment. The year before celebrations of Newton's birthday in major cities had drawn crowds of 3,000 to hear a taped messaged smuggled out of prison from the Party leader. This event was expected to generate similar funds to defray the costs of appeal. The speakers instead faced an echo chamber. Hardly anyone showed up.

This time, leftists were far more focused on the escalating war that Nixon had won office in 1968 promising to end. Instead, he expanded it. On April 30, 1970, President Nixon stunned the nation with the announcement that he had ordered bombing in Cambodia five days earlier. The news touched off student strikes and flag-burnings across the country. Nixon's announcement coincided with a large May Day gathering in New Haven already planned for protests of the upcoming Seale trial. A large number of civil rights advocates — including future presidential candidate Hillary Rodham — found cause for concern that the Seale murder proceedings demonstrated yet another example of the Panthers being systematically deprived of their constitutional rights. Rodham was already a nationally known student activist. She had started college as a Goldwater Republican and switched parties in 1968, inspired in part by a stirring speech given by Martin Luther King. Rodham helped found the Yale Law School *Review of Law and Social Action*. The new law review decided to devote an entire issue to constitutional issues raised in cases involving the Panthers.

Those who stayed on the Yale campus May Day weekend 1970 at Yale saw armed National Guardsmen poised to tear-gas both protest-ers of Seale's trial and students on the sidelines — even those remain-ing in their dorms. Barry Scheck was among the Yale student activists who witnessed the government's heavy-handed response firsthand and thought there really could be a revolution. Draft resistance had become far more widespread, while opposition to the war included a growing number of Vietnam veterans who were now revealing their own experi-ence of its horrors. Historian Clara Bingham, author of *Witness to the Revolution: Radicals, Resistors, Vets, Hippies and the Year America Lost Its Mind and Found Its Soul*, estimates that nearly a million radicals then saw themselves as revolutionaries.[38]

The *Chicago Daily Defender* praised Yale as the "focus for justice for the Black Panthers" and a leader in promoting social change. "Though a new force on the political horizon, the Panthers may provide the dynamism for the reformation of American society."[39]

Just days later, at Kent State in Ohio, National Guardsmen killed four unarmed student demonstrators and wounded nine others. Many at Yale assumed they had narrowly avoided a similar deadly incident. The Kent State massacre galvanized far more campus strikes, estimated to involve eight million students. At Jackson State in Mississippi, another lethal police response resulted in the deaths of two black students and the wounding of twelve others. That year of escalating campus protests and violent clashes with police likely had an impact on the care the California Court of Appeal took in reviewing alleged errors in the conviction of Movement icon Huey Newton.

By late May word leaked out that the court had written a lengthy opinion that would be released shortly. Newton's lawyers sent word to their client and debated what that meant. Stender panicked and feared the worst — a detailed explanation rejecting every argument she had made. But she soon had reason to rejoice. On May 29, 1970, the appellate court issued its unanimous fifty-one-page decision reversing Newton's conviction. The startling news spread immediately. Reporters tried to contact Newton by telephone for his reaction, but prison officials refused to bring him out of his cell. The Men's Colony prison yard erupted in glee while most of the country reacted with astonishment. Of Stender's many claims of error at trial, three gained traction. One was Judge Friedman's failure to instruct the jury about the correction of the taped statement of eye witness Henry Grier that he "didn't" get a good look at the perpetrator. A second assigned error was that the judge allowed prosecutor Lowell Jensen to read kidnap victim Dell Ross's damaging grand jury testimony in the presence of the jury. Since that testimony was then struck from evidence, the Court of Appeal ruled the jury should not have heard it in the first place. Maybe it improperly influenced them in finding Newton guilty on the manslaughter charge.

Third, the Court of Appeal blamed the judge for not giving another jury instruction Garry had offered about Newton's mental state at the time of the shooting. Newton had testified similarly to Officer Heanes: neither recalled what happened after being wounded, which Dr. Diamond testified often occurred as a shock response to abdominal wounds suffered in combat. The manslaughter verdict indicated that the jury found Newton had acted with diminished mental capacity when he fired the gun at Frey. The rejected instruction would have let the panel consider an alternative idea — Newton may have been completely unconscious of his actions. Would the jury have instead acquitted Newton if given an unconsciousness instruction?

Normally, both sides note their objections for the record if the judge rejects one or more jury instructions that the lawyers believe are warranted by the evidence. Yet, in this extraordinarily high profile case, the entire discussion of which jury instructions would be given and why others were rejected had taken place off the record in the judge's chambers.[40] Exhibiting irritation, the higher court held that Judge Friedman should have given the unconsciousness instruction on his own initiative even if Charles Garry did not insist upon it. "Although the evidence of the fatal affray is both conflicting and confused as to who shot whom and when, some of it supported the inference that the defendant had been shot in the abdomen before he fired any shots himself."[41]

As a result of the three cited errors, Newton was granted a new trial limited to manslaughter. Already acquitted of murder, he could not be tried again for that capital offense. The stunned prosecution immediately sought discretionary review of the decision by the California Supreme Court. Such relief was exceedingly rare and, not surprisingly, denied. Newton was then scheduled for release from custody following a bail hearing on August 5, 1970.

In his first interview, Newton credited the reversal in large part to "the pressure the people brought to bear on the case, as well as the work of my attorneys Charles Garry and Fay Stender . . ."[42] Both lawyers also paid homage to the unprecedented turnout of support for their client. The attention drawn to the case was obviously a factor, but the lawyers had both been brilliant. Penny Cooper realized that Garry had done a phenomenal job as the trial lawyer, but their ultimate success owed as much to Stender. It was her painstaking research and motion work at trial coupled with her exceptionally persuasive appellate brief that yielded the unexpected reversal on appeal. Criminal law specialists like Cooper had assumed the appeal was doomed. Stender's future partner Doron Weinberg recalls how impressed he was at such long shot results:

> Fay Stender was a superb legal writer . . . so persuasive . . . so impassioned. . . . [Yet] to get a reversal of conviction was pretty extraordinary . . .. In the early '70s, you could expect that an appeal would be successful in a criminal case maybe one out of twenty times, maybe one out of twenty-five. . . . So for her to have done that in a case as fraught with . . . implications as Huey's case was and in a case in which the . . . jury had been thoughtful, it was pretty remarkable.

Already unhappy that Newton escaped the death penalty for killing one of their own, the Oakland police could not believe that even the manslaughter charges had not stuck. Jensen prepared for another battle with Charles Garry, vowing to convict Newton again in a retrial. By then, Stender had left her dead-end role at Garry's firm. She was now a name partner and, at 37, the oldest member of a new leftist law collective in Berkeley. It had been put together by her Guild friend Peter Franck to represent Movement clients.

But Stender, whose career and confidence soared after the Newton trial, was about to enter into an ultimately fatal involvement with another radical client. Just months after joining her new firm, Stender became deeply involved in another major death penalty case. This time, the victim was a white prison guard at Soledad Prison. At Huey Newton's behest, Stender had taken on as a client a black militant inmate at Soledad, whom she turned into another international cause célèbre to challenge racial abuse at Soledad. By the spring of 1970 maximum security inmate George Jackson and two other black prisoners, Fleeta Drumgo and John Clutchette, were known worldwide as the Soledad Brothers.

From February to June of 1970 Stender and her co-counsel drew Bay Area demonstrators to conservative Salinas for pretrial proceedings in the Soledad Brothers case — protests modeled after those surrounding Huey Newton's 1968 death penalty trial in Oakland. By mid-June, a rattled Monterey judge ordered the first ever change of venue in his county's history. As a result, the Soledad Brothers death penalty trial was ordered to take place in San Francisco — exactly what the defense team had fought for. The ruling in Salinas came less than three weeks after the Court of Appeal opinion reversing Newton's conviction, propelling Stender to instant stardom among leftists. She credited all the Movement supporters who caravanned to Salinas from the Bay Area, creating pressure that traditional lawyering would never have generated.

Stender then turned to arranging Huey Newton's bail. She now referred to her most famous client as a political comrade. Stender proudly stated that in the past two years, her identity had become almost "anti-professional" in order to build her revolutionary clients' trust and promote their shared goal. She was alluding to ignoring the boundaries that lawyers are required to observe when representing their clients — to be their mouthpiece in court, but not to identify with them to the point of crossing ethical lines. Stender realized she was acting "anti-professionally" by conduct like engaging in sex with Newton, sneaking in contraband and illegally bringing his tape-recorded communications to cohorts on the outside. Her close personal relationships with both Newton and George Jackson impaired her professional judgment and recklessly risked her license. Ultimately, Stender would realize she put her own life and that of her family in jeopardy. Yet in July of 1970 Stender basked in the limelight and in the knowledge of her central role in freeing the Movement's most celebrated hero.

Charles Garry proclaimed that Newton's release would give a great boost to the American liberation movement. As both he and Stender knew, Huey Newton was not in a hurry to regain his freedom. Prison had been a place of refuge from potential assassination attempts by COINTELPRO and by Ron Karenga's rival US party. And this was no mere paranoia or conspiracy theorizing on Newton's part; he had cause for fearfulness on both fronts. In January of 1969 two US members had ambushed and killed Los Angeles Panther leaders Bunchy Carter and John Huggins at the suspected instigation of the FBI. (Internal records later showed that an FBI agent took credit for prompting their assassination, leading to his promotion.)

Prison was also a retreat for Newton from legions of new Panther recruits. Newton's glorified image quickly outpaced the more complicated reality. By then, the Panther ranks were far from united. Somehow, Newton, after prevailing in a court fight to spare his life, had gone from being the party's radical standard bearer to one of its more middle-of-the-road voices. Four days after the victory in Salinas, at a Juneteenth celebration of freedom from slavery, Panther Chief of Staff David Hilliard announced brazen plans for all Panther branches nationwide to send representatives to a constitutional convention in Washington, D.C., in December of 1970. Eldridge Cleaver had lobbied for this move, which Newton had only reluctantly endorsed. A planning session was scheduled for September in Philadelphia — the site of the original American Constitutional Convention in 1787. Meanwhile, Seale remained in jail in New Haven awaiting trial for his life; and the "Panther 21" in New York City faced an array of felony charges for allegedly conspiring to bomb the Botanical Gardens, police stations, railroad crossings and department stores.

In early July of 1970, a month before Newton's scheduled release, Garry and Stender arranged for best-selling author Mark Lane to interview Newton in prison for the *Los Angeles Free Press*. Lane publicized Newton as "America's authentic revolutionary" and vocalized Leftist fears for his life: "The administration considers Huey Newton to be the most dangerous man in America. . . . Huey's safety must be guaranteed. . . . For those who love peace and those who crave justice, Huey's leadership is crucial. He represents America's last, best hope for social change with a minimum of violence."[43]

Well before dawn on the morning of August 3, officials at the Men's Colony turned Newton over to two Alameda County sheriff's deputies, who drove him shackled hand and foot in the back seat of an unmarked car headed up the coast to the Alameda County jail. His bail hearing was set for Wednesday, August 5, at 9 a.m. Two thousand rabid Panther supporters, both black and white, gathered around the Alameda County courthouse early that morning yelling, "We want Huey! Where's Huey? Free Huey!" By 9:15 a.m. when the hearing before Judge Harold Hove began, a hundred people crammed into the sixty-seat courtroom, with hundreds more in the corridors or waiting outside.

The hearing lasted just half an hour. Newton, dressed in a loose khaki shirt and matching trousers, spoke just once to waive his right to be retried within 60 days. Garry made a show of arguing for Newton's release on his own recognizance, but already knew from Fay Stender's negotiations with prosecutor Lowell Jensen, that Jensen would recommend $100,000 bail. Jensen conceded that Newton had an obvious right to bail now that he only had a voluntary manslaughter charge pending. Judge Hove considered $50,000 reasonable and ordered Newton returned to a 10th floor cell until the money arrived. It took a few hours. When the crowd spied their hero exiting the building with David Hilliard and attorney Alex Hoffman, they exuberantly yelled, "Huey's Free! Huey's Free!"[44] The trio were headed to Hoffman's Volkswagen Beetle parked in front. They had hoped to rush Huey off, but that was not feasible.

There was a moment of regret that they had not gone out the back door. Hilliard said, "No, the people want to see Huey. 'You have got to say something. They spent their lives working for [you].' So he comes out . . . Now we've got to wade through the crowd to get to Alex's little Volkswagen." Newton's entourage kept the crowd from mobbing him as Newton, Hilliard and Panther branch leader Elmer "Geronimo" Pratt from Los Angeles climbed on top of the Beetle. The roof of the makeshift platform partially caved in under their weight.

Newton shouted, "Right on! Right on! Power to the people!" He punctuated his chant with repeated Panther salutes toward the sky above.[45] Then, to avoid fainting in the heat, he famously stripped off his khaki shirt, celebrating his freedom by showing off his muscular body to photographers and frenzied supporters. He then urged similar efforts to free the Soledad Brothers and Bobby Seale.

Hilliard was exuberant: "It was one of the greatest days of our life. We were victorious. It was a beautiful day. Two thousand people in the streets of Oakland saying, 'Free Huey or the sky is the limit.' Here this guy comes walking out of the court, the door. A great victory. . . . It was a very powerful moment I will never forget."

At Hilliard's suggestion, Newton told the crowd to move its rally to

Bobby Hutton Memorial Park (still officially DeFremery Park). Sheriff Frank Madigan was, in fact, looking for an excuse to crack heads if any problems arose at the courthouse demonstration. Madigan had seen demonstrators arrive that morning in a bus with a sign showing it belonged to the "Office of Economic Opportunity, Inc." It made Madigan's blood boil to think that Panther supporters got federal jobs they redirected to their own purposes. When asked, "Just how do we handle these foxes in the chicken coop?" Madigan had a ready solution. "Shoot 'em. You can always raise more chickens."[46]

To the dismay of the crowd, after suggesting the move to Bobby Hutton Memorial Park, Newton disappeared to change at Alex Hoffman's home for a press conference in San Francisco. There, eager reporters and photographers from underground newspapers and magazines soon surrounded Newton and Charles Garry in the cramped library of Garry's office. Fay Stender, who no longer worked there, stood beaming behind her client as his comments on their historic achievement were captured on at least a dozen different microphones.

At a party later in the evening, intoxicated Panthers declared that Newton needed to make up for lost time and suggested to Stender that she be his prize for winning his freedom. The two were ushered into a bedroom and the door closed behind them while others continued their revelry. Stender later bragged about the celebration to women colleagues at the Lawyers Guild, some of whom were aghast. She offered it as proof the rank-and-file Panthers and their leader recognized her as a true comrade. To the contrary, Newton was proving to the Panthers that the lawyer who won his freedom was just another woman he could use and then keep or discard at his whim. At the next Panther celebration several weeks later, Newton pointedly left Stender standing by herself, while he socialized with others. Stender was deeply humiliated. She would never forget the embarrassment she felt at that moment.

382

The front page of the San Francisco Sun Reporter, *Saturday, August 8, 1970 recapping the enormity of the accomplishment of Huery Newton's freedom on August 5, 1970, two years following his 1968 death penalty trial. Two pivotal trial figures are featured: chief defense counsel Charles Garry and pioneering African-American jury foreman David Harper. (No mention was made of the intervening shocking news — the aborted kidnapping at the Marin County courthouse on Friday, August 7, 1970 that resulted in the death of Judge Harold Haley and Panther George Jackson's younger brother Jonathan Jackson.)*

18. TO WHAT END?

The task is to transform society; only the people can do that —
not heroes, not celebrities, not stars.
— HUEY NEWTON

The *San Francisco Examiner* noted that Newton had become "something of a folk hero among militants and revolutionaries," but his appeal to younger generations in black communities and on college campuses was obviously far broader. He drew strong support from singer Harry Belafonte, comedian Dick Gregory and many other celebrities who championed civil rights; many curiosity seekers among the general public viewed him as a left wing rock star. His attorneys already had Newton booked to appear on *Face the Nation*, where Hilliard had previously been featured following the government raids on the Chicago and Los Angeles Panther branches. At the press conference, Newton threatened unspecified consequences if political prisoners, including the Soledad Brothers, were not freed. When asked for clarification, he did not rule out military action and warned that "the struggle is coming to a final climax."[1]

Privately, Newton realized full well that neither he, nor his Party, were anywhere near ready for a revolution. Like Bobby Seale he just saw too many of the Panthers headed for slaughter or prison if they did not first build enough support for their political agenda in the community. Newton left the press conference to see the new Panther headquarters in West Oakland and to walk his old neighborhood, exchanging salutes with the crowds who turned out to greet him. He also had a major decision to make. Earlier that summer, the Soledad Brothers had been transferred to maximum security in San Quentin prison in

Marin County, awaiting their upcoming murder trial in San Francisco. Newton learned that George Jackson and his cohorts were plotting to escape by forcing an exchange of themselves and other San Quentin inmates for hostages. Newton also heard that Los Angeles Panthers Geronimo Pratt and his men were intending to meet up with Jackson's younger brother Jonathan at the Marin Civic Center and seize the hostages at a pending criminal trial. The plan included a second group of Panthers who would head to San Francisco airport and commandeer a plane to fly the hostages to Algiers so Eldridge Cleaver could barter their lives for the release of Jackson and several of his militant San Quentin comrades.

Newton wanted no part of it. After members of US ambushed Bunchy Carter and John Huggins in January of 1969, Newton immediately suspected that the FBI had engineered their deaths. He had expelled Panther Party National Field Marshal George Sams later that year as a likely agent provocateur. It had been Sams' accusation that Bobby Seale ordered Sams to murder Alex Rackley that had Seale now facing his own death penalty trial in New Haven. The deadly invasion of Fred Hampton's apartment and the coordinated attack by police on the L.A. Panther headquarters provided strong evidence to Newton and Hilliard of an ongoing nationwide crackdown even as new Panther offices kept popping up in cities across country. Newton expected to discover more informers and the FBI laying more traps. No one really knew whom to trust. Hilliard had heard of an entire chapter of supposed Panthers in the Northwest that turned out to have been created by undercover agents bent on damaging the Party's image in that community. Upon discovery, it was disbanded.

Ex-Panther Earl Anthony was now back in the public eye doing television and radio appearances promoting his best-seller *Picking Up the Gun*, which the publisher advertised as the book the Panthers tried to suppress. Newton actually liked that book, which left out key details and gave no hint that Anthony was writing it at the behest of J. Edgar Hoover as a ploy to position Anthony to destroy the Party from the inside. In fact, Anthony wrote in his book that he did not share the paranoia of young black activists that the "Man" had the manpower to heavily infiltrate the Black Panther Party from the beginning. Anthony scoffed that "if any of those brothers we recruited in the early days in L.A. were the Man, I have to give credit to the FBI or L.A. police intelligence — because they're really recruiting brothers off the streets, or people who act so well that they should do it as a profession. Otherwise, it seems that the Man plays upon internal difficulties to induce those who are weak enough to become informers."[2] Anthony never went public with his duplicity until a year after Newton's death. After Anthony's book *Picking Up the Gun* came out in 1970, Newton would soon reconnect with Anthony when Anthony offered to supply Newton with high grade cocaine — obtained courtesy of Anthony's government handlers.

As fallible as Newton's judgment was on who still merited his trust, Newton had instantly suspected trouble ahead in the plans for the Marin County courthouse invasion. He immediately cancelled all Panther support for Jonathan Jackson's kidnapping plan.[3] Newton's suspicions were well-founded. By then, the FBI had many other infiltrators in place to undermine the Panthers from the inside who did not even know whether the folks whose activities they reported to COINTELPRO were revolutionaries or fellow informants. Among the informants was Louis Tackwood, the brother-in-law of George Jackson's close prison friend Jimmy Carr, whom Newton had later befriended in prison and recruited as his body guard. Tackwood would much later go public with his knowledge that the Los Angeles Criminal Conspiracy Section (CCS) planned to ambush the Panthers at the Marin County courthouse.[4]

Sensing a trap, Newton followed his instincts and ordered Geronimo Pratt and his cohorts to lie low. Newton then holed up in his new temporary home, the two-bedroom rental in Berkeley his lawyer Alex Hoffmann shared with KPFA radio's Elsa Knight Thompson. With Hoffmann acting as his scheduler and trusted confidante, Newton immediately began entertaining a parade of visitors from his fiancée to family, associates, reporter Karen Wald and his lawyer Fay Stender, whom Newton had not yet cast aside. Everyone came and went under the watchful eyes of plainclothes officers and obviously phony telephone repairmen perched for four days straight on a pole across the street from the Berkeley apartment.

In desperation, Jonathan Jackson decided to go ahead with the kidnap plot anyway without any Panther support. That Friday, August 7 — just two days after Newton's release — the determined teenager managed to sneak guns into the public gallery for the assault trial of San Quentin inmate James McClain at the Marin County Civic Center. In an era when most courts had yet to institute routine security checks, Jonathan Jackson simply hid guns in a satchel and under his raincoat. Wearing a raincoat into court should itself have looked suspicious to bailiffs on a clear summer day. When Jackson arrived, two guarded inmates, William Christmas and Ruchell Magee, were waiting to testify as witnesses. Jackson and McClain surprised everyone in the courtroom by grabbing weapons Jackson had brought and freeing and arming both Christmas and Magee. The kidnappers then seized and bound the trial judge, prosecutor and three jurors.

Jackson and his cohorts marched the hostages at gunpoint to a yellow van parked in the driveway. There, as Newton had anticipated, scores of law enforcement officers were already in waiting, hidden among nearby bushes. Once everyone was seated, the officers opened fire on the van and killed Jonathan Jackson, Christmas and McClain. The judge, who was tied to a sawed-off shotgun, was also killed; the prosecutor and one juror were wounded, as was inmate Ruchell Magee. (Magee was later convicted for his role in the aborted kidnapping; Angela Davis was separately tried as an off-site co-conspirator, but won acquittal in another extraordinary Movement trial drawing worldwide attention in 1972. Magee remains in prison to this day.)[5]

The week after the aborted kidnapping, a huge gathering of mostly white officials and community members mourned Judge Harold Haley at an elaborate funeral in Marin County. A similarly large gathering of mostly African-Americans in the East Bay attended the funeral of Jonathan Jackson at St. Augustine's Episcopal Church in Oakland. Though Jackson's family invited Newton to give a eulogy for Jonathan Jackson as a fallen hero, whispers spread that the family actually blamed Newton for Jonathan's death — because Newton had called off all Panther support for the kidnapping.

Shortly after the funeral, Newton gave his first political speech after his release. Pent-up demand had jacked up expectations for a fiery call to action. Instead, attendees received a lengthy lecture about the steps needed to establish a revolutionary "intercommunal framework" for socialism to thrive. Some left before Newton finished. By prearrangement, Newton then embarked for the East Coast with a full agenda: to visit Bobby Seale jailed in New Haven and fund-raise for his defense; to meet Panthers in several new branches opened while Newton was imprisoned; to promote his new ideas for the Party's future; to attend the Panthers' Revolutionary People's Constitutional Convention in Philadelphia; and to explore the idea of relocating the Party's headquarters to Harlem in New York or Atlanta, Georgia, where SNCC had been based.

On his return to Oakland in September of 1970, Newton opted to keep his Party's base where it started. For safety's sake, Newton resettled into a penthouse apartment overlooking Oakland's Lake Merritt. His new digs were paid for by wealthy white donors. The spacious accommodations on the twenty-fifth floor of 1200 Lakeshore on the south edge of Lake Merritt came with a doorman and space for a car in an enclosed garage. Under constant surveillance by COINTELPRO and wary of new recruits who might be moles, Newton took comfort in the security it offered from attack by enemies in rival militant groups.

The *San Francisco Examiner* soon ran an article describing Newton's fancy new apartment as a sign of his abandonment of his people — a story planted by the FBI with a reporter they had previously used to spread negative publicity about the Free Speech Movement. It worked. Fay Stender was among those advising Newton he was alienating many followers by moving to an opulent penthouse apartment. Newton ignored them all. Swearing off speech-making, he used the solitude to work on revolutionary writings, but quickly turned his gilded cage into a place of escape through drugs, alcohol and hedonism. These days he snorted cocaine from a silver platter and had beautiful women on hand to wait on him; other women threw themselves at the revolutionary rock star. Newton cultivated a coterie of white Hollywood patrons, including Donald Sutherland, co-star of the award-winning 1970 movie *M*A*S*H*; Sutherland's wife actress Shirley Douglas (the daughter of Tommy Douglas, the head of Canada's New Democratic Party); and actresses

Vanessa Redgrave, Shirley MacLaine, Jean Seberg and Mia Farrow.

Through Sutherland, Newton met *M*A*S*H* co-star Elliot Gould, then at the height of his career, and Gould's then wife, singer Barbra Streisand. The FBI kept close track of Hollywood stars who contributed large sums of money to the Panthers and made the donors targets of COINTELPRO themselves. Jean Seberg would become COINTELPRO's most famous victim of stalking and character assassination. Years later, her husband publicly blamed the FBI for her suicide.[6]

Soon to become one of Newton's chief benefactors was "New Wave" Hollywood producer Bert Schneider. Schneider had first gained fame in 1966 for bringing the Emmy award–winning *Monkees* to television as a take-off on the Beatles. In 1969, Schneider introduced Jack Nicholson to the public in the counterculture classic *Easy Rider*. In early September of 1970 Schneider had just released another ground-breaking film, *Five Easy Pieces*, with Nicholson in his first starring role.

COINTELPRO agents took special note after author Mark Lane introduced Newton to actress Jane Fonda, who had become a new-age sex symbol when she starred in the 1968 science fiction fantasy *Barbarella*. Fonda was even more prominent than the Sutherlands in the anti-war movement and had already fund-raised for bail and defense costs for Newton and other Panthers. By the time Fonda and Newton met in person shortly after his release from the Men's Colony, she was making plans to embark on a national fund-raising tour of college campuses with Vietnam Veterans Against the War, who named her their Honorary National Coordinator. In her speeches endorsing the Panthers, Fonda openly embraced rebellion and revolution. The military soon began calling her "Hanoi Jane," a traitor who supported the Viet Cong.

Alarmed at Newton's heady new Hollywood life style, Hilliard introduced Newton to a nineteen-year-old Party member Hilliard hoped would help Newton settle down. Gwen Fountaine did have some effect, but saving Newton from himself would prove too Herculean a task. By November, Hoover had Newton's penthouse broken into and bugged. Ironically, *Esquire* featured a several-page pictorial essay that month with the caption "Is It Too Late for You to Be Pals with a Black Panther?" The Panthers already knew that the FBI Chief was wire-tapping their headquarters and other Party members' and supporters' homes. By then the FBI and state police also had many informers infiltrating the Party, some of whom the Panthers discovered and some they did not.

Newton trusted few Panthers he had never met before. Invitees to the penthouse received instructions to take the elevator to the twenty-fourth floor, walk up one flight, and use a special knock to be admitted through the back door. On one occasion in 1971, an old friend brought a new buddy with him — an unshaven white guy in his early twenties. The two visitors both smelled like they had not had a shower in quite a while. Unbeknownst to Newton the two were rookie cops. Among the innovations Chief Gain had introduced was to have each new class at the police academy go ungroomed for two weeks and then spend one day on the streets with empty pockets to feel what life was like for beggars on their beats. Rob Stewart grew up in North Oakland and had black friends in high school. When a black fellow recruit took him to meet the great Huey Newton, Stewart came away extremely impressed — the Panther leader exuded charisma. Neither recruit ever mentioned this little side trip to their bosses.

Someone had given Huey a high-powered, standing telescope he kept in his living room, focused north across Lake Merritt directly on the tenth floor of the Alameda County courthouse. Back in July of 1970 on the eve of his release, Newton had told interviewer Mark Lane at the Men's Colony that people outside of jail were also prisoners, but under minimum instead of maximum security. Now Huey liked looking through his telescope across the lake at the window of the isolation cell where he had spent so many months before his 1968 trial. Alex Hoffmann asked if he was homesick. Newton admitted that he was having problems adjusting: life had been so much simpler when he was inside.

* * * * *

The FBI stirred suspicions between Cleaver and Newton with faked letters from Party members, helping to stoke a growing rift between the two. The feud erupted in public when Newton appeared on a San Francisco talk show on February 28, 1971. By prearrangement, the program hooked Cleaver up by telephone line from Algiers. Angry at recent Party expulsions, Cleaver called for the resignation of Panther Chief of Staff David Hilliard, who had only been carrying out Newton's agenda. Furious, Newton immediately expelled Cleaver from the Party. As the Panthers split into two factions, each accused the other of retaliatory killings, most notably the murder by Cleaver's followers of Sam Napier, the key distributor of Panther newspapers nationwide. Soon afterward, Stokely Carmichael proclaimed the Panther Party was finished. The Panthers had indeed become all but invisible in most major cities where the Party had recently operated chapters.

Meanwhile, Garry entered lengthy pretrial proceedings for the New Haven murder trial of Bobby Seale and Ericka Huggins. It took more than four months and interviews of over 1500 people to select the jurors — one at a time outside the presence of others (unlike in the Newton trial). Barry Scheck had been among the Yale student volunteers who checked out the prospective jurors by going to their homes to see if they had political bumper stickers on their cars. He vividly recalled watching Garry get straight to the point in questioning jurors from all-white neighborhoods: "You can't be fair to black people, can you?" And the juror would go, 'No!' because they were happy to have no part in that trial." The lawyers wound up seating seven women and five men; five of the women and none of the men were black. In May 1971, Garry obtained a hung jury that strongly favored acquittal of both Seale and Huggins.

The judge surprised everyone by refusing to order a new trial. Instead, he dismissed the case, stating that it would have taken "superhuman efforts" to find another impartial jury.[7] Having spent time in Oakland in the 1960s and at Yale in the 1970s, Panther associate Louis Armmond later noted that the situation Seale faced when prosecuted in New Haven in 1971 resembled the situation that Newton benefitted from in Oakland in 1968: "a trial where the community was involved, mobilized, informed, politicized. . . . So he did get a fair trial, under the circumstances. But they had to work at it. . . . If there had not been that mobilization, and the students of Yale played a very important part, I am proud to say, he would have . . . probably [been] executed."

Once the New Haven trial ended, both Garry and Seale then returned to the Bay Area, where Seale and Newton reunited as free men for the first time in nearly four years. Nevertheless, Seale's success was largely a Pyrrhic victory. The gory details of the murder of Alex Rackley by members of the New Haven Panthers alienated large numbers of former Party supporters. A similarly devastating high price-tag in diminished public opinion accompanied the acquittals that same month of "the Panther 21" in Manhattan.

Following Fred Hampton's death the year before, underground Weathermen had issued a "Declaration of a State of War" against the Nixon administration. The Weathermen then claimed responsibility for several bombing attacks on government buildings. When the Panther 21 openly aligned themselves with the Weathermen, Newton ordered the rest of them expelled, just as he had expelled Cleaver. Newton had come to the same conclusion as Bobby Seale. Cleaver was a madman and an anarchist who would lead his followers to death as he had led Bobby Hutton. Too impatient for results to listen to Newton, both the Harlem and New Jersey Panthers then split off to join the Cleaver faction. Geronimo Pratt sided with Eldridge Cleaver as well, prompting Newton to give orders "to wash everybody who's a Pratt man . . . right out of the Party."[8]

Newton had previously symbolized every black man confronted by racist police. It was the compelling story that grew the Party exponentially. But from the very first Cleaver had admired Newton's reckless confrontation with police more than any long term political strategy for achieving the Party's platform. It had served the interests of all Panthers to repeatedly urge Newton's freedom as a rallying cry while he remained under the white man's lock and key — but after his release, new recruits actually had to make a choice of which man's vision to follow going forward.

Be careful what you wish for. By August of 1970, Newton was free on bond, but what was left of the Panther Party was soon in near complete disarray and at each other's throats. As J. Edgar Hoover had hoped, the Panther Party was also broke from defending so many prosecutions. After the public feud erupted between Newton and Eldridge Cleaver in

February of 1971, another major public relations blow occurred on the first of March 1971 when Charles Garry debated journalist Edward Jay Epstein on *The David Frost Show*. Epstein had recently published in *The New Yorker* a widely read article: "The Black Panthers and the Police: A Pattern of Genocide?" which questioned Garry's charge that the government had murdered twenty-eight Panthers.

Epstein was just as persuasive on *The David Frost Show* in disputing example after example of claimed police murders as a shootout or unproved. Huey Newton would himself be invited on the show in mid-May, making a claim similar to Garry's. Though neither of them sounded credible in charging a government plot to annihilate the Panthers, the truth was already leaking out. On March 8, 1971, a group calling itself the Citizens' Commission to Investigate the FBI managed to burglarize a Pennsylvania FBI field office. They took a number of key files which they began sharing with the press. To limit the damage, J. Edgar Hoover soon declared that the COINTELPRO centralized program was at an end and that all future counterintelligence operations would be handled on a case-by-case basis. An outraged Senate Investigation Committee would later find substantial merit to Newton's basic claim of government persecution, but would tally fewer victims.[9]

In the meantime, the prosecution of Panthers continued. In the Party's punishing version of musical chairs, at the beginning of June 1971, it became Chief of Staff David Hilliard's turn to face prosecution for his role in the April 6, 1968, shootout that resulted in Bobby Hutton's death. Hutton had been featured on Garry's list of government murders. Panther supporters again filled the courtroom for the high profile trial, but Hilliard had no realistic chance of avoiding conviction. This time he was represented by another feisty leftist giant in the San Francisco criminal defense bar, Vincent Hallinan. Other Panther participants had already confessed to their roles in the April 1968 ambush of Oakland police that Cleaver had led. Hallinan had no convincing way of explaining the arsenal of weapons the police had found in the Panthers' van that evening as purely for self-defense. Still, Hilliard blamed the all-white jury for the verdict that sent him to prison for one to ten years, of which he would serve four. (The federal charge for threatening the President's life had by then been dismissed.)

Now it was Newton's turn again. The prosecution never learned that David Hilliard had information pertinent to the case against Newton. Huey and Gene McKinney had been at Hilliard's poker party at Hilliard's mother-in-law's house around 2 a.m. on October 28 where the Hilliards were raising money for Bobby Seale's bail from Santa Rita. Newton and McKinney left to get something to eat on Seventh Street. On the stand in 1968, Newton never mentioned the poker party when recounting his activities that night for the jury. Hilliard vividly recalled what happened not that long afterward: "The next thing I know I hear somebody banging on my door saying, 'Open the door. Huey has been shot. We've got to take him to the hospital.'"

Once he was helped inside, Newton argued with his friends not to bring him to the hospital. He feared that he would end up in the gas chamber. But they were not about to let him die. "So when he comes in my house all bloody . . . my brother and my wife are putting towels around him trying to stop the bleeding until we could get him in the car to take him to Kaiser Hospital, which happened to be only 10 minutes away. We were rushed to do that because he was bleeding and blanking out — just becoming unconscious. So we put him in the car, took him to Kaiser, drive to emergency. I go up and I bang on the door . . . and I'm screaming, 'There is a man dying out here. He's been shot. You have got to bring a gurney.' They bring a gurney, put Huey on it." The shirt and jacket Huey was wearing when dropped off were different from the ones Hilliard's wife had stripped off him at her mother's house.

Hilliard and his brother fled from Kaiser Hospital before anyone identified them. When he got back to his mother-in-law's home, he called Eldridge Cleaver. Cleaver spoke with Beverly Axelrod and then told Hilliard that Axelrod said to get rid of the clothes Newton had been wearing when he showed up wounded. In an oil barrel in the back-yard, Hilliard incinerated the bloody shirt, jacket and beret Newton had left behind. Had Newton's prosecutor had any clue of Hilliard's role it would not have done him any good — Hilliard could then have invoked the Fifth Amendment just as McKinney did.

In July of 1971, Garry defended Newton's retrial in Oakland

without Stender by his side. After Newton had ostracized and humiliated Stender the prior fall, there was no way she could continue as second chair in his defense. That was okay with Newton — owing his freedom to a woman had never squared with his macho self-image. Since 1968, Jensen had been elevated to District Attorney. He delegated the second prosecution of Newton to another veteran lawyer in his office, Donald Whyte. With the death penalty no longer an option — and competition from the higher stakes Soledad Brothers' case among other Movement causes — Newton's retrial was far less of a draw than his first prosecution in 1968, though it still attracted substantial attention.

Shortly before the retrial, *Ramparts* publisher Ed Keating published *Free Huey!* a skewed account of the 1967 shootout and 1968 trial that suggested there was still an unidentified midget on the loose, who had fled the scene after murdering Officer Frey. That description derived from bus driver Henry Grier's first account of the man he saw bent over, struggling with Frey. Regardless of discrepancies in Grier's description of the perpetrator, Huey Newton was the only person ever seen close enough to Frey to cause the bullet wounds that killed him. Newton himself admitted at the first trial that he grappled with Frey after being abusively frisked and that it was his bloodied law book police later found on the street.

Grier was once again called to testify that he saw a gun in Newton's possession, but no gun ever materialized. In the retrial Garry managed some more courtroom magic tricks, aiming to obtain a hung jury. (Garry also privately talked Fay Stender into providing him with additional legal briefs, for which she took no credit.) The proceedings lasted until early August. The panel of ten women and two men included one African-American woman. They deliberated for six days in a heat wave before they announced they were deadlocked eleven-to-one for conviction. Garry and Newton assumed that they had persuaded the lone African-American woman that the prosecution was part of a genocidal crusade against all blacks. But she was actually among those who did not buy Newton's story. The holdout was a Latina. Prosecutor Donald Whyte marched out of the courtroom "tight-lipped and grim" without talking to reporters.[10] Before the afternoon was out, District Attorney

Lowell Jensen promised a third manslaughter trial to avenge the death of the fallen officer. Meanwhile, Newton remained free on $50,000 bail.

Less than two weeks later, on August 21, 1971, radio and television stations interrupted their regularly scheduled programs with reports of another Marin County bloodbath in which six men died and a number were gravely injured. San Quentin Associate Warden Jim Park grimly announced to the press that George Jackson had been killed trying to break out. Somehow the maximum security prisoner surprised guards with a gun that had been smuggled in. Stender had been fired by Jackson months earlier for refusing to bring him a gun. Prison officials said Jackson had hidden the gun in his Afro. When he pulled it out, he reportedly declared, "The dragon has come." The statement invoked the memory of his hero North Vietnamese leader Ho Chi Minh. Jackson then overpowered his guards and freed other prisoners.[11] The inmates managed to slit the throats of several guards before the uprising was over. Jackson himself was shot down in the prison courtyard.

More than a thousand people attended George Jackson's funeral at St. Augustine's in Oakland, the same church where his younger brother Jonathan's funeral took place the year before. Tension was once again high between George Jackson followers and Newton. There was already bitterness over the fact that the Panthers had obtained Jackson's literary rights shortly before his death. Jackson had reassigned the royalties from his books to the Panthers when he rewrote his will to give the Panthers his estate to help finance weapons for the revolution. By the time of George Jackson's funeral, a rumor spread that Newton was socializing at Lake Tahoe with his patron Bert Schneider and the wealthy producer's girlfriend Candice Bergen when he learned that Jackson had been shot down in the yard at San Quentin.[12] Jackson's family and supporters believed Newton was trying to exploit Jackson commercially by negotiating through his Hollywood connections for a movie on Jackson's life. So began another major rift.

By summer's end a congressional report would conclude that the relatively small violence-prone Party, while "insidious and virulent," did not constitute a clear and present danger to the government's security — and never had. Several Republican committee members strongly disagreed.[13] So did Governor Reagan and the California prison administration. In October 1971 the surviving Marin County inmates involved in the San Quentin bloodbath would be charged with murder and prosecuted over the next several years as the San Quentin Six, with Charles Garry representing one of the defendants.

That fall, Newton accepted an invitation from Red China to visit as a guest of Chairman Mao's regime. (Newton's conditions of release on bail neglected to include travel restrictions.) Newton wanted to upstage President Nixon several months before his own recently announced historic visit to reestablish diplomatic relations with mainland China. On his trip overseas, Newton brought two companions: a bodyguard and his protégée and new lover, Elaine Brown. After Cleaver's defection, Newton had named Brown the Panthers' Minister of Information and editor of the *Panther* paper.

Newton and Brown first met in New York a month after his release from prison in 1970. She had been one of Eldridge Cleaver's early recruits to the Los Angeles branch of the Party in the spring of 1968. In 1969, David Hilliard arranged for the singer/songwriter to go to Motown to record her first album, *Seize the Time*. Newton used to listen to a tape of it over and over at the Men's Colony. He had been mesmerized by Brown's voice — Huey could not carry a tune himself. The album included a song for Eldridge Cleaver that the Party adopted as its anthem.

When she moved to Oakland in the fall of 1970, Brown had just returned from joining Eldridge and Kathleen Cleaver on a Panther good will tour to Communist countries — traveling illegally from Paris to Russia, North Korea, North Vietnam, Red China and Cleaver's headquarters in Algiers, before using her passport to head home. Newton figured Brown would be very useful to have along on his own trip to China in the fall of 1971. Plainclothes agents tailed Newton and his companions the whole circuitous way through Canada to China and back. Newton assumed the Nixon administration hoped he would accept the Chinese government's offer of asylum, but he returned after ten days.

Jensen authorized yet a third trial of Newton in December 1971. Stender would have no role in that trial, but the day before it was set to start, she visited Newton in his penthouse to negotiate with him over the Panthers' claim on George Jackson's estate. Before Jackson had rewritten his will he had previously authorized use of royalties from *Soledad Brother* for legal defense costs. Though Stender had left the Soledad Brothers defense team, the two young lawyers who successfully defended Jackson's co-defendants remained unpaid. Stender felt that if she confronted Newton on their behalf, he might do the right thing. She also urged him to put a stop to the criticism of his indulgent life style by moving to a less ostentatious home. It was undermining his standing in the Movement. Newton angrily rebuffed her. She wanted too much control. He insisted that the Panthers get all of Jackson's royalties — a book whose international acclaim owed much to Stender's uncredited editing. Stender left in tears. The FBI recorded the entire conversation.

The third trial also ended in a hung jury — despite prosecutor Whyte's best efforts to learn from the outcome of the second trial. Garry succeeded once more in impaneling a mostly middle-aged female jury. This time there were no black members. As before, Garry's defense included witnesses to Frey's abusive conduct during earlier arrests. The trial again featured expert testimony on Newton's impaired mental condition after being shot. On Saturday afternoon, December 11, 1971, the jury reported they were deadlocked six to six. At the end of the day, the judge declared another mistrial. All twelve jurors were convinced Newton shot Frey, but divided over whether he was conscious of firing the gun. Newton looked tired. A crowd gathered inside and outside the building.

The following Wednesday, twelve television crews set up in the press room as reporters and scores of Newton supporters grabbed seats in the courtroom. District Attorney Jensen visibly trembled as he rose to speak. He said that, after searching his conscience, he concluded that another trial would be futile and requested dismissal even though it would be "a frustration of justice."[14] The law contemplated dismissals only "in furtherance of justice," but Judge Hayes granted Jensen's motion. Both knew that public resources would likely be wasted if the District Attorney pursued the case any further — at some point there needed to be finality.

Fifteen minutes after the hearing began, Newton was a completely free man. Despite Garry's pleas to join him in a press conference, Newton stopped only briefly before descending the stairs out of the courthouse to utter a clipped, "No comment"[15] to the gathered reporters. He then raised his fist to those waiting to cheer him outside and headed off to his penthouse. Like Garry, Newton considered Jensen quite adept at his job; he had developed a good deal of respect for the prosecutor by the time the case was over. Belva Davis noted the irony: "They convinced young people that it was impossible to get a fair trial and here their leader, after three trials, found himself free, at home, in a[n] apartment overlooking the very county courthouse where he was tried, musing about his life and what this had all meant."

Garry held forth at the press conference, praising Jensen as "a perfect gentleman and a worthy adversary" whom he had misjudged as not having "the intestinal fortitude to dismiss a case like this."[16] But Garry once again bashed the justice system for forcing Newton through three long trials on charges that Garry claimed never should have been brought in the first place. That must have galled Jensen who still believed the first degree murder charge had been amply justified. Walter Cronkite announced the extraordinary result on the national news. Fay Stender was nowhere to be seen. Her pivotal role in securing Huey's ultimate freedom went unmentioned in the banner press that accompanied the ultimate dismissal.

Panther Janice Garrett Forte looked back proudly at her achievement as one of many idealistic young people with a steadfast goal:

> I was a part of helping the leader of the Black Panther Party get his freedom, when at a time in America, this was not possible. Huey was in a shootout, in which a white officer was killed. The chances of him coming out alive were very slim . . . So to see that we actually [did it] — not only through our demonstrations, but through all the work, selling the paper, making the public aware of what was going on with Huey and his trial, but what was going on throughout the United States with black people in general was something very, very significant and key.

Ironically, though partisans on both sides had criticized the first jury's result, that panel was the only one of the three juries able to reach a verdict — and the only jury to convict Newton of any crime. The first jury also included the highest percentage of minorities. Studies have since shown that diverse juries deliberate longer and come to more accurate results than juries of similar backgrounds who do not counterbalance each other's bias as they seek consensus.[17] Twelve ordinary men and women — a cross-section of citizens with different life experiences — defused a racial tinderbox and demonstrated why democracy places its trust in the people. A pioneering black foreman played a key role in achieving a just verdict. On reflection, even Huey Newton's mother, Armelia, thought so, too. In 1969, she and one of her daughters journeyed to Detroit to personally thank David Harper for his service.

* * * *

Looking back nearly five decades later, how much lasting significance did the Newton trial have? NYU Professor Bryan Stevenson believes the 1968 Newton trial was one of "three trials in the 20th Century that have really shaped our thinking about the challenges that our criminal justice system presents." Professor Stevenson lists the Newton trial alongside the Scottsboro Boys and the O. J. Simpson trial "because for the first time, we had in a post-civil rights era the issues of race and justice colliding. The consciousness, the presumption of guilt being presented in a courtroom, outside the South, where there were all of these systemic failures — the inadequacy of the jury system to produce fair and impartial jurors, bias by judges and others. All of that was shaping the parameters of that trial. And I think for many Americans, it was a glimpse on how far we had come since the *Scottsboro* case."

For Professor Stevenson, "the trial of O. J. Simpson [involved] someone who had an identity that had been largely embraced by the American people, and yet found himself in a situation where a very racialized prosecution was going to manifest itself and create a very significant divide in America about questions of guilt and innocence, fairness and unfairness." Professor Stevenson concludes that "if you look at those three trials, you learn a story about the American criminal justice system that still continues today. We have a system that treats you better if you are rich and guilty than if you are poor and innocent. We have a system where people of color are presumed guilty rather than innocent. And you have a system that hasn't quite yet found a way to protect everyone from the bias and bigotry that our narrative of racial difference has created."

Penny Cooper participated on the defense team for the O. J. Simpson trial. In her view, "the Huey Newton case historically was far more important than the O. J. Simpson case. . . . I think that the jury was swayed in the Newton case by arguments about economic and racial oppression. And that really was significant politically. . . . If you can measure such things, the Newton trial really was 'the trial of the 20th century.' . . . It was pretty ground-breaking."

Doron Weinberg sums up the reasons: "The Huey Newton trial had a greater impact politically, socially and legally than . . . not just the *Simpson* trial . . . but any of the other trials that are generally talked about as 'trial of the century' because on every level, inside the court-room, outside the courtroom, legally, politically, Huey Newton's trial had an enormous impact."

Morrie Turner had a different perspective: "The Newton trial did have a lasting impact, but . . . I think the impact is what didn't happen. . . . the results of the trial kept terrible things from happening . . . ter-rible and lasting — insurrection . . . and riots . . . definitely. . . . I'm just so glad that it turned out the way it did."

David Hilliard gives credit to the Chief of Police for firing the two policemen who shot up Panther headquarters after the manslaughter verdict: "Chief Gain . . . understood that at the local level and aborted that. Young people would have taken to the streets and Oakland would have had a whole different chapter in the history books . . . because that would have really, really turned the whole city into something tan-tamount to something happening in Birmingham."

Hilliard added: "I probably wouldn't be sitting here now . . . if Huey had been convicted [of first degree murder]. . . . Oakland would have been a different, much different place. It would have been a lot of bloodshed in Oakland. . . . If that Huey Newton thing had gone sour, I think that America would have been a police state. . . . We were able to curtail that. . . . We were anticipating having to defend our lives against more police repression. The police were kicking our doors down. . . . Black Panther Party members dead. . . . All of our money that we have in our programs . . . always being used for bail. . . . They would have intensified their activity against us and we would have been mandated to strike back. . . . There would have been blood to the horse's brow."

402

Huey Newton, in the early 1970s, pointing to the tenth floor jail cell in the Alameda County courthouse directly across Lake Merritt from the penthouse at 1200 Lakeshore Avenue, Oakland, that he occupied following his 1970 release. The jail cell was where Newton had been incarcerated from the late fall of 1967 through his 1968 trial.

19. REVOLUTIONARY SUICIDE

The concept of revolutionary suicide . . . demands that the revolutionary see his death and his life as one piece.
— DAVID HILLIARD WITH KEITH AND KENT ZIMMERMAN,
HUEY: SPIRIT OF THE PANTHER [1]

By 1973, Ann Ginger's 1969 handbook *Minimizing Racism in Jury Trials: The Voir Dire in People of the State of California v. Huey P. Newton* was in wide use by Lawyers Guild members across the country. In November 1973 Ginger published *The Relevant Lawyers: Conversations out of court on their clients, their practice, their politics, their life style.* It profiled a number of prominent leftist lawyers in the Bay Area dedicated to social change, including Fay and Marvin Stender and Charles Garry. It emphasised the groundbreaking work in the Newton trial as Garry's and Fay Stender's crowning achievement. The book inspired many college activists to go to law school, eager to implement reforms. Yet as the years passed, Ginger saw how other historians failed to acknowledge the impact of the 1968 Newton trial, and included it in a 2006 booklet for progressive law students as one of the *Landmark Cases Left Out of Your Textbooks.*

When Ginger's 1973 book on *The Relevant Lawyers* came out, Fay Stender had long since been fired by Huey Newton and by George Jackson. Back in the summer of 1973, she had also been forced to pull the plug on her latest project. When Jackson kicked Stender off his legal team, she expanded her work for inmate rights. In preparation for his trial, Stender had interviewed many prisoners in maximum security at Soledad. Their horror stories led Stender to broaden her mission from representing individual inmates to exposing entrenched racism and cruelty in the prison system. A commission specially convened at Governor Reagan's request issued a report in October 1971 blaming the killings at San Quentin two months before on a chain of events starting with bad press Stender had generated about Soledad Prison in 1970. Prison officials insisted Stender had egged on the prisoners' rights movement by spreading false and incendiary charges of inmate mistreatment and baseless lawsuits.

The report made no mention of the fact that conditions at Soledad had first been condemned in 1966 by Federal District Court Chief Judge George Harris, who had personally inspected strip cells. The jurist then made history by issuing an injunction ordering the prison to fix shockingly unsanitary conditions, poor ventilation, insufficient heat and light, and inadequate healthcare. By 1969, when the mandates of Judge Harris's order had not been met, five black prisoners filed another civil suit. They accused guards of letting white and Mexican trustees serve black inmates meals adulterated with cleanser, crushed glass, feces, spit and urine — charges later repeated in a complaint to the United Nations for human rights violations. Both the federal judge's order and the inmates' lawsuit preceded Stender's involvement in championing prisoners' rights.[2]

From early 1970 through the spring of 1973 Stender's persistent efforts to publicize conditions at Soledad and other prisons and her push for inmate rights statewide earned her the nickname "the dragon lady." Corrections officials scorned her as a "demon agitator" and "one of the greatest threats to security in prisons."[3] Compounding the enormous uphill battle she and other prisoners' rights advocates faced, since May of 1967 when the Black Panthers first stunned Governor Reagan by showing up at the state capital, the Governor had transformed the prison industry into California's Pentagon. Its budget would skyrocket over the next few decades with more state dollars aimed at building prisons than expanding higher education.

Stender's Berkeley-based Prison Law Project quickly won recognition as the largest such project in the country. Her staff of woefully underpaid lawyers and paralegals magnified their impact by coordinating volunteers from top law firms whom Stender convinced to donate their time. The Prison Law Project took the lead in filing constitutional challenges and class actions, while courting political support for prison reform.

As much longer penalties for crimes were implemented, Stender became totally disillusioned at the overwhelming scope of the problems inmates faced. By June of 1973, she was forced to close the doors of the Prison Law Project after public interest waned and funders disappeared. A *San Francisco Chronicle* reporter likened the shuttering of the Prison Law Project to the closing of a heavy prison door on the hopes of those inside. He noted that "hundreds, perhaps thousands of inmates" considered her a "heroic figure" and "almost a legend in places where women once were seldom seen."[4]

* * * * *

The same month that Bay Area Progressives celebrated the publication of Ginger's book *The Relevant Lawyers*, a new locally-based revolutionary group calling itself the Symbionese Liberation Army (SLA) sprang into the headlines. Its leaders saw a vacuum left by the demise of the Panther Party and sought to become the new vanguard of the revolution. Like US in Los Angeles, the SLA based its principles on Kwanzaa, but adopted as its symbol a seven-headed cobra. The SLA's aim was to unite all prisoners against the government, echoing point 8 of the Panther Party platform: "We want freedom for all black men held in federal, state, county and city prisons and jails. " But the SLA was ill-conceived and incoherent in its strategies and goals. Their leader was a black escaped convict, Donald DeFreeze, who called himself Field Marshal Cinque. Most members were white, though one of its other founders was another inmate, former Black Panther Thero Wheeler, who quit early on. Evidence later surfaced that caused some investigators to surmise DeFreeze was actually a double agent, working secretly for the Los Angeles Police CCS Squad.[5]

On November 6, 1973, the SLA assassinated Oakland's popular black school superintendent Marcus Foster, asserting that he embodied fascism because of a new rule requiring visitors to the city's schools to show ID.[6] Lowell Jensen prosecuted SLA members for Foster's death, but even with all the publicity surrounding that latest headline trial, Jensen still considered the Newton trial the biggest of his career.

While the SLA made a mockery of the goals of '60s radical groups, Newton was personally on his own downward spiral. Once freed from prison where his heroic image could have stayed untarnished, he undermined his own larger-than-life reputation with a blend of paranoia and entitlement. Newton remained in his secure penthouse apartment through mid-August 1974. With the landlord's consent, the FBI occupied a neighboring apartment from which they eavesdropped on Newton with secret authorization from Attorney General John Mitchell. The FBI followed developments closely as Newton invited to Oakland the remaining Panthers across the country who had won his trust. With much fanfare, Newton modified the Panther's 10-point program after his split with Cleaver, officially eliminating the call for all black people to arm themselves for self-defense.[7] In fact, the Party continued to stockpile weapons for an eventual revolution. Newton was trying to play it both ways. He knew the time was not right for armed insurrection, but it remained his ultimate goal as well as that of the Panthers who remained in his camp. Had he abandoned the notion of leading the vanguard on some date in the near future, he would have had few, if any, followers left.

Eldridge Cleaver was then threatening to return from exile in North Africa to start a guerrilla war. Newton heard that Cleaver had placed him on a hit list. "The Servant of the People" now openly scorned Cleaver as a "renegade scab traitor." He ordered the Party purged of Cleaver's followers. For his own protection, Newton created two teams of five or six highly trained hit men, whom he dubbed "the Squad." They modeled themselves after government SWAT teams like the Los Angeles CCS Red Squad. The Red Squad specialized in the most dangerous and stealthily authorized operations — such as the ambush of Jonathan Jackson and the other kidnappers in the driveway of the Marin County Civic Center in August of 1970. Newton rewarded his own Squad members with cocaine, liquor and women; they basked in the aura of "The

Supreme Servant of the People" or, by 1974, just "The Servant."[8] Melvin Newton "felt that now he really was a public figure and that the family really had lost their . . . little baby brother." His mother knew she had lost her devoted youngest child for good when she asked him to come clean the kitchen stove and he sent two underlings instead.

Team leader Flores Forbes later revealed that the Squad would do practically anything for the Party leader, even lay down their lives. (By the time he wrote *Will You Die with Me? My Life with the Black Panther Party*, Forbes had long since served time for attempted murder of an eye witness expected to testify against Newton in an upcoming murder trial.) By his own admission, Forbes and two other Squad members donned dark jumpsuits and ski masks for a late night home invasion that they botched by going to the wrong entrance of a duplex. When the landlady who lived there shot back, one Panther died at the scene. Forbes and the other Squad member fled underground both to avoid the police and to avoid retaliation from other henchmen of Newton for the failed hit.

Back in the early 1970s one or another member of the Squad always accompanied Newton in late night forays to nightclubs and bars. Critics charged that the Panthers began operating like a Mafia protection racket, shaking down businesses to support Party programs.[9] Newton actually modeled the Panthers on *The Godfather* after repeatedly watching the classic 1972 gangster film. He ordered all Party members to view it as well.

In 1973 the Panthers opened an alternative learning center featuring the Oakland Community School. The project was spearheaded by Newton's new leftist admirer David Horowitz, the former editor of the now-defunct *Ramparts* magazine. One of the directors of the Oakland Community School was Ericka Huggins. The widow of L.A. Panther leader John Huggins had returned West from New Haven after the charges against her and Bobby Seale for the murder of Alex Rackley ended in dismissal. Meanwhile, Newton remained largely sequestered in his penthouse library, dictating two books that would be published with the assistance of ghost writers: *To Die for the People* in 1972 and *Revolutionary Suicide* in 1973. Professor Herman Blake, who had testified on ghetto slang at Newton's 1968 death penalty trial, later demanded listing as a co-author of *Revolutionary Suicide*.

At Newton's urging, Bobby Seale ran for Mayor of Oakland in 1973 against incumbent Mayor John Reading. At the same time, Panther Minister of Information Elaine Brown ran for a city council seat. In addition to the school, the Panthers could now point to a number of community programs they operated beyond their signature free breakfasts for children and sickle cell anemia inoculations. To register residents in the flatlands, the Panthers gave away truckloads of groceries and shoes. Civil rights leaders endorsed their new fourteen-point program — even widow Coretta Scott King. (On Seale's campaign staff was a young political activist named Barbara Lee, who worked in the Panther community programs. She later succeeded Ron Dellums in his congressional seat, where she still serves.)

Although his Republican base had shrunk considerably by 1973, Mayor Reading still enjoyed popularity as the man who built the Coliseum Sports Complex — where the Oakland A's were now the reigning World Champions. Reading fended off Seale's challenge, but only in a run-off. Elaine Brown also lost her race, but would later help orchestrate Lionel Wilson's successful 1977 campaign to become the city's first black mayor — only the second African-American mayor of a major city on the Pacific Coast (after Tom Bradley of Los Angeles). Wilson was prouder yet that he was the first Oakland mayor in more than sixty years to win without the endorsement of the *Oakland Tribune*.

Wilson would serve three terms, ushering in a new era in city politics that the *New York Times* dubbed "a racial, cultural, economic and political revolution."[10] He filled many city positions with black applicants and steered contracts to black-owned businesses, but also worked closely with both Governor Jerry Brown and Republican businessmen to rejuvenate downtown Oakland with a building boom in new high rises. As an integral part of the plan, Wilson oversaw creation of 10,000 new jobs and hundreds of low-income housing units for West Oaklanders. Huey Newton viewed the popular liberal Democrat as a modern-day Dr. Sun Yat-sen, the revolutionary doctor venerated by both the Communist Chinese and Nationalists in Taiwan for establishing China as a republic.

* * * * *

Within days of Wilson taking office in the summer of 1977, Newton returned from three years of self-imposed exile in Cuba. Newton and Charles Garry brazenly held a press conference at the San Francisco airport before a huge gathering of Panther supporters, curiosity seekers and reporters. The now-bearded thirty-five-year-old surprised everyone by announcing that the Panthers would undertake as their new goal ridding Oakland of the menace of drug dealers. Crossing the San Francisco Bay Bridge back to Oakland, members of the Squad enjoyed a new experience — traveling in a joint caravan with the police as they escorted Newton to surrender himself for prosecution for two felonies.

Back in 1974, Newton became increasingly violent and paranoid. By July of that year he forced out of the Party Bobby Seale, David Hilliard and other Panthers from its earliest days. In Seale's stead, Newton elevated Elaine Brown to Party Chair. On a drug high, he reportedly bragged to a close friend that he was "the baddest nigger that ever walked" because he got away with killing a white cop.[11] Of course, Newton would have made that boast regardless of whether it was true. In August of 1974, Newton faced renewed prosecution on charges of pistol-whipping his tailor and shooting a young prostitute named Kathleen Smith. That was when Newton and his fiancée Gwen Fountaine fled to Cuba for an indefinite stay and left Elaine Brown in charge of the Party with backup from the Squad.

Four months after Newton fled the country, a Berkeley resident, Betty Louise Van Patter, went missing. On David Horowitz's recommendation, the former bookkeeper at *Ramparts* magazine had been working with the Oakland Community School as it faced an IRS audit. In January of 1975 Van Patter's bloated, battered body washed up from the San Francisco Bay. It sent chills through the local leftist community. The police suspected the Squad since the bookkeeper was last seen at the Lamp Post bar, a Panther hangout. Yet the murder was never officially solved. The grim discovery traumatized Horowitz, galvanizing his decision to quit working with the Panthers and to rethink his entire political outlook. He eventually emerged as the prominent neo-conservative author and political strategist he remains today, permanently disillusioned with radicals and the failure of their leadership to condemn Panther atrocities.

* * * * *

Though Garry had stood by Newton's side at the press conference when he arrived back from Cuba, Newton hired new counsel to represent him at his pending criminal trials. In 1977, Garry and a co-author published his autobiography, *Streetfighter in the Courtroom: The People's Advocate.* By then, his courtroom victories were behind him.[12] In 1978, the aging lawyer had his own personal nightmare to deal with — the worst American massacre before September 11, 2001. Garry barely escaped with his life in November of that year during the mass murder-suicide of U.S. citizens in Jonestown, Guyana, orchestrated by another client, San Francisco People's Temple founder Reverend Jim Jones. (Likely arranged through Garry, Jones had visited Newton in Havana in early 1977.) Over nine hundred people died at Jonestown, including Congressman Leo Ryan, who was gunned down as he arrived to investigate the strange cult at the urging of worried family members in his district.

Newton's new defense lawyers won his acquittal on the pistol-whipping charge when the tailor refused to testify. In his trial for the murder of Kathleen Smith, a mostly middle-aged suburban jury (nine women and three men) deadlocked ten to two in favor of acquittal after a key eyewitness recanted prior testimony and Newton took the stand to swear he was at home at the time of the shooting. After consulting with District Attorney Lowell Jensen, prosecutor Tom Orloff decided to retry Newton. The second trial before a jury panel of four men and eight women hung eleven to one for acquittal. Frustrated, Orloff then dismissed the case. As Newton rejoiced with his family, an *Oakland Tribune* reporter noted how few Panthers attended this last trial. The reporter realized that the Panthers were clearly in irreversible decline since Elaine Brown's departure in the fall of 1977.

With inside information supplied by David Horowitz, two freelance reporters wrote an in-depth article on the Black Panthers for the avant-garde magazine, *New Times*. "The Party's Over: How Huey Newton created a street gang at the center of the Black Panther Party" produced shock waves — the first time members of the Movement had written an exposé of the Panthers' history of violence. Reporter Kate Coleman took precautions to protect herself after Newton threatened her life. Meanwhile, Newton relocated to Santa Cruz to pursue a Ph.D. in the History of Social Consciousness.

* * * * *

By 1978 Fay Stender had distanced herself completely from the Panthers and from representing prisoners. The lack of appreciation she received for her prison work angered her, especially the way Huey Newton had treated her. Instead, for the past several years she had focused on furthering women's rights, starting with a test case on palimony in 1974 that gained national publicity. Stender also became one of the founding board members of California Women Lawyers. On Memorial Day weekend of 1979 an African-American ex-felon affiliated with the Black Guerrilla Family prison gang (BGF) invaded Stender's Berkeley home in the middle of the night. The BGF had many members on the streets of Oakland and Berkeley in the 1970s and 1980s who dominated the local crack cocaine trade. The BGF claimed George Jackson as its founder. Back in 1974, the BGF had put Fay Stender's name on a hit list along with Charles Garry and Huey Newton, among others. At gunpoint, Stender was forced to write a note saying she had betrayed George Jackson. Her assailant then marched her downstairs in her nightgown to her kitchen, where he shot her several times and fled down the street, leaving her collapsed in pooling blood on the floor.

It was their split from Newton and the Panthers following George Jackson's death that fueled the BGF's vendetta. They believed that Newton and the Panthers betrayed George Jackson by backing out of the Marin County kidnapping in August of 1970 and by seeking to profit from Jackson's book and life story. Stender and Garry were blamed for their legal work for Newton, but Stender was hated more because BGF members believed she exploited her relationship with George Jackson for her own aggrandizement and personal gain. Stender had in fact made hardly any money off of representing either Newton or Jackson. She had simply embraced both men and their goals too closely and been cast aside for trying to counsel them against self-destructive behavior.

Stender survived the murder attempt, but was permanently paralyzed and in constant pain. Her only motivation to live was to see justice done. For that she now needed the help of District Attorney Lowell Jensen, then in his tenth year in that office. Despite Garry's respect for Jensen, the Panthers still hated him for his efforts to get Newton executed for the death of Officer Frey in the 1968 trial. The Panther editorial staff put Jensen's photo on the back page of their paper in the center of a target and unsuccessfully sought to get him recalled from office as a racist. Back then, Fay Stender still totally identified with the Panthers, inspiring large crowds to support the Panthers and to rally to "Free Huey." Though it was now several years since Stender quit representing radical prisoners, both the Oakland police and many lawyers in the District Attorney's office still bore a grudge against her. Broken in body and spirit after the home invasion left her paralyzed, Stender had to wonder how Jensen would approach the twist of fate that had him tasked with the duty of pursuing her assailant.

Jensen assigned the case to one of his best prosecutors, Howard Janssen, maybe the only veteran attorney in Jensen's office besides himself who did not harbor ill will toward Stender for her contemptuous attitude toward law enforcement back when she represented black militants. Jensen demonstrated to both Stender and his staff that he wanted justice for her as much as for any other victim of violent crime. Stender identified Edward Brooks as the perpetrator after viewing him in a lineup. She then became the star witness for the prosecution, sequestered in an undisclosed location in San Francisco under 24-hour police protection until the trial, during which time she formed a strong bond with prosecutor Howard Janssen.

Much to the surprise of law enforcement, almost all of Stender's leftist friends and former colleagues, including Charles Garry, found themselves rooting for the prosecution in this new headline trial. They knew it could have easily been one of them who was targeted for violent reprisals. On his way out of court after Stender's riveting testimony, Charlie Garry whispered to a reporter. "She was a good attorney and now, a perfect witness."[13] After the jury convicted Brooks and he was sentenced to prison, Stender fled the country still in fear for her life from the BGF. The District Attorney's office continued to keep a close eye on BGF activity and alert her family to any known threats, but Stender never considered it safe to return.

Two months later, still wheel-chair bound and in constant pain, her melancholy overcame her. Despite strong emotional support from friends and family, she had grown increasingly despondent at how her passion for justice had jeopardized her life and put her family at risk. With her care giver in the next room, Fay Stender took an overdose of pills and left a suicide note in her Hong Kong hideaway, with instructions not to be resuscitated. By the time the ambulance arrived, it was too late anyway. Her 21-year-old son, who had also been a key witness against Brooks, had secretly been sent by his father to China for protection from the BGF. Heedless of any remaining danger, Neil Stender accompanied his mother's body back to San Francisco.

Amidst the hundreds of mourners at her funeral, there were almost no black faces. Among those profoundly affected was journalist David Horowitz. He considered Stender a kindred, disaffected spirit. In a lengthy magazine article, he and Peter Collier called her death "the end of an era." "Requiem for a Radical" later became the first chapter of their widely sold 1989 book, *Destructive Generation: A Second Look at the Sixties*. Horowitz had himself originally found Huey Newton an inspirational heroic figure representing all those wronged by the system, but Stender's death ended his beliefs "in the Left as a champion of black people." Back during the 1968 trial when Collier and Horowitz were *Ramparts* editors, both strongly favored Newton's acquittal on charges he murdered Officer John Frey. By the mid-1970s they had become disillusioned with the man behind the myth just as Stender did. Horowitz saw her death as the ultimate consequence of a misguided embrace of militant blacks. Horowitz recalls: "I was struck when I went to her funeral; there were 300-odd people there. But there were no blacks, there were no Panthers. And she had dedicated her life to saving and representing black prisoners."

Huey Newton was, of course, the most conspicuous of the absent Panthers — Newton, who owed his freedom primarily to Stender's dedicated efforts on appeal of his 1968 conviction. If the verdict of manslaughter had been allowed to stand — as almost everyone expected — Newton could still be doing his twelfth year of a fifteen-year sentence. Instead, he remained at large and increasingly dependent on cocaine and Courvoisier while he took graduate school classes at the University of Santa Cruz in its new History of Consciousness Department. The department chair let Newton's bodyguards accompany Newton around campus, but drew the line when Newton came to class obviously high on drugs.

The university endured a spate of negative publicity across country for conferring a doctorate degree on Newton in June of 1980 after just three academic years in which Newton acted increasingly strung out and had to commute back and forth to Oakland to face three separate felony trials. But the chair of the sociology department defended the quality of Newton's thesis. "War Against the Panthers: A Study of Repression in America" rested on FBI records Newton's lawyers had obtained under the Freedom of Information Act. Newton had a lot of sensational material to work with for his dissertation. When J. Edgar Hoover died in 1972 after more than 55 years with the FBI, his extraordinary abuse of power was already well-known. That was what prompted Congress in 1968 to change the law to limit Hoover's successors to ten-year terms.

Coverage of the Watergate scandal that led to President Nixon's resignation in 1974 for abuse of power also revealed Nixon's complicity with the FBI and CIA in the "Huston Plan," an executive order that purported to suspend the constitutional rights of its targets for reasons of national security. With Nixon's secret executive order as their fig leaf, the CIA and FBI engaged in burglary, illegal wiretapping and interception of mail of a list of targets and, in the case of the Panthers, physically destroyed office equipment, confiscated food for their breakfast program, tossed their newspapers in the trash and sprayed those for sale with a foul odor that smelled like feces. The CIA and FBI also framed some targets for murder, hounded others to commit suicide and themselves committed other violent crimes, including murder.

The Panthers topped the list of Huston Plan targets whose illegal persecution formed the basis of one of the articles of impeachment that forced President Nixon to resign. By then, Fred Hampton's death had already been the subject of a 1971 documentary, *The Murder of Fred Hampton,* and further exposed in a 1973 reinvestigation of his killing. The Commission of Inquiry into the Black Panthers and the Police, headed by NAACP executive director Roy Wilkins and former Attorney General Ramsey Clark, issued a scathing report that detailed a prior state and federal cover-up. None of the perpetrators ever got prosecuted for Hampton's murder. In 1983 — after more than a decade of legal wrangling — Hampton's family would receive an historic $1.85 million from the City of Chicago in compensation for his wrongful death.[14]

In April of 1976, Senator Frank Church's Senate Select Committee issued a scathing report on "The FBI's Covert Action Program to Destroy the Black Panther Party." It followed several other reports shocking the public with details of international assassination plots by the CIA and illegal domestic spying by the FBI. While Newton was still in Cuba, the Panther Party brought suit alleging $100 million in damages against the FBI, CIA and local police. The suit would end in dismissal. Yet all of the sordid details gave credence to Newton's thesis, placing the history of covert FBI and COINTELPRO operations against the Party in the context of historical repression of political dissidents from the 1880s through the 1970s. But skeptics had reason for criticizing U.C. Santa Cruz for awarding Newton a Ph.D. based on this scholarship: his paper recounted his own persecution by the FBI in the third person, which was not surprising to those who assumed it was also largely ghost-written.

Eventually, Dr. Huey P. Newton returned to Oakland, a caricature of his former self. He jested that those who treated him with racist derision would now have to call him "Dr. Nigger."[15] His abuse of intoxicants accelerated. In December of 1982, he totaled his car while driving under the influence and almost killed himself and his two stepchildren riding with him. His wife Gwen had had enough — she took her children, left the state and filed for divorce. In the fall of 1984 Newton remarried an old girlfriend, Fredrika Slaughter, the daughter of Panther realtor

Arlene Slaughter. He had dated Fredrika on and off since 1970. Her efforts to keep Huey clean through rehab failed. Relapses came with bouts of paranoia and cocaine delusions. He also faced mounting debt. Newton lost his house to an IRS foreclosure, and pleaded guilty to embezzling $15,000 from the Community School.

On the early morning of Tuesday, August 22, 1989, Newton went to a West Oakland housing project to meet a young drug dealer. Tyrone Robinson's father had gone to school with Melvin Newton. Huey knew his uncles, too. But Tyrone Robinson was now a member of the BGF who considered Huey Newton an enemy. Robinson viewed this encounter as a chance for glory. He shot the forty-seven-year-old icon three times in the head and left him to die on the sidewalk. As fate would have it, the incident occurred in the same neighborhood as the early morning shoot-out with officers Frey and Heanes almost twenty-two years before. In an ironic twist, one of the two Berkeley police officers who testified for the prosecution in the 1968 Newton trial about Huey's hammer attack on a fellow high school student was now both the County Sheriff and County Coroner. In his role as Coroner, Charlie Plummer made a personal visit to the morgue to assure himself the victim really was Huey Newton.

It was an ignominious but not unexpected end to a living legend in irreversible decline. The news was featured so quickly on television that the cameras caught the firemen hosing Newton's blood off the street. When Melvin Newton got notified, he said, "We always knew this was gonna happen. We just didn't know when."[16] The next day, the *Oakland Tribune* ran a three-page spread on the life and death of Huey Newton. The coverage was far more balanced than if the Knowland family had still owned the paper. For the past decade, the *Tribune* had been edited by acclaimed African-American journalist Robert Maynard, who became its owner in 1984. The extensive coverage included an article captioned: "Friends and foes remember Newton: 'visionary,' 'thug,'" which quoted, among others, Charles Garry and prosecutor Thomas Orloff. Garry said that his long-time client "should be remembered as a tremendous contributor to the quality of [life for] black Americans." Orloff bluntly disagreed: "The Newton I dealt with in the '70s was basically a gangster. There was nothing political about him."[17] Staff reporter

Brenda Payton called Newton "the face of black defiance" whose admirers, including herself, lauded a brash show of militancy that ultimately amounted to "little more than immature adventurism."[18]

Immature adventurism could also describe Robinson's attempt at fame for killing Newton as an enemy of the Black Guerrilla Family. When arrested, Robinson claimed Newton had pulled a gun first — just as had been the issue when Newton was accused of murdering Officer Frey back in 1968. But this time, unlike when Frey was shot, the police concluded that Newton had been an unarmed victim. By 1989, Lowell Jensen no longer headed the Alameda County District Attorney's Office. When Governor Reagan was elected President, Jensen's good friend Ed Meese from the District Attorney's office became Attorney General. In 1981, Meese invited Jensen to join the Department of Justice. Jensen rose quickly to Deputy Attorney General before President Reagan appointed him in 1986 to the federal bench in the Northern District of California. Among the judges already on that bench was Carter appointee Thelton Henderson.

So as it turned out, it was Jensen's successor Jack Meehan, who oversaw the prosecution of Robinson to get justice for Huey Newton. As a Deputy District Attorney Meehan had once prosecuted Newton. The jury returned a murder verdict against Robinson, who then received a 32-year sentence. In another quirk of fate, Robinson himself had participated as a child in a Panther free-breakfast program at a nearby Oakland housing project. Poet Carolyn Baxter captured the irony in "Huey P. Newton — The Frailty's and Flaws of a Man":

> Genius of an Innovator.
> Heart of a Black Panther.
> Spoken about on the News like a Criminal,
> mentioning Drug use.
> So much blood, from his head,
> they said covered almost 15 feet in diameter
> around his body,
> as Huey lay [in] eternal sleep on Concrete . . .
> Who killed Huey YO!?
> The same people he set out to feed, educate and free.

The "Servant of the People" had an elaborate funeral paid for mostly by myriad small donations. Over two thousand people attended the service at the Allen Temple Baptist Church, Oakland's largest black congregation, where Newton had become a member in his last years. Most of the crowd were black, but some whites and Latinos were also in the crowd. A caravan of white limousines accompanied the hearse carrying Newton's flower-bedecked wooden casket.

The entourage passed through blocks of buildings whose walls were newly covered with Panther slogans and graffiti silhouettes of Newton. The caravan then pulled up to the church decorated with Pan-African flags, Panther posters and an enormous banner proclaiming "Huey Lives." From the vehicles emerged Huey's widow Fredrika and son Kieron as well as a Who's Who of Panther stars in their heyday: Bobby Seale, Elaine Brown, Angela Davis, H. Rap Brown (now calling himself Imam Jamal Abdulla Al-Amin as head of an Islamic community in Atlanta) and David Hilliard. Though two black City Council members showed up at the service, noticeably absent was Oakland's Mayor, Lionel Wilson, then ending his third term and gearing up to run unsuccessfully for a fourth. (His successor was also African-American).

Upon learning how many ex-Panthers would be attending Newton's funeral, city officials feared an outbreak of violence. Actually, the surviving Party co-founder had become best known near the end of his long absence from Oakland for his popular 1988 cookbook, *Barbeque'N with Bobby, Down-Home Barbeque Recipes by Bobby Seale,* whose proceeds he dedicated to charity. Television cameras and a flock of reporters covered Newton's funeral procession. The only incident occurred when teenagers assaulted some cameramen. Not surprisingly, Kwame Ture (the former Stokely Carmichael), who lived in exile in Guinea, did not show up. Nor did Eldridge Cleaver, who had long since been expelled from the Panther Party.

By the time the Cleavers had returned to the United States from Algeria in 1975, Eldridge was totally disillusioned with the Left. He announced that he had undergone a religious epiphany and was now a born-again Christian. He was now enamored of capitalism and had developed an idea for a new commercial venture. Always proud of his manhood, he designed pants for men with a codpiece. The retro idea did not catch on. He then came back to the states and made a plea bargain regarding his 1968 parole violation and pleaded guilty to assaulting police officers back in April of that year. In exchange, he did no jail time. (The Panthers suspected that part of the deal involved Cleaver turning government informant.)[19]

By 1981, the Cleavers separated and Kathleen got a full scholarship to Yale. Eldridge then sought to recall incumbent Mayor Lionel Wilson for his ties to the Panthers and get himself elected the next Oakland mayor. Having let bygones be bygones since he had banished author/playwright Earl Anthony from the Panther Party, Cleaver gave Anthony a published interview with his new view that more black people should get involved in politics and "instead of hating the police department . . . join the police department and take control of [it] and make it our own."[20] Cleaver's campaign against Lionel Wilson went nowhere. Kathleen divorced Eldridge in 1987, and then pursued a Yale law degree and career on the Yale and Emory university faculties. In the meantime, Eldridge was baptized into the Mormon Church in 1984, registered Republican and endorsed his old nemesis Ronald Reagan for President. The former revolutionary then ran unsuccessfully in the California Republican Senate primary in 1986.

So no one expected Eldridge Cleaver to come pay his respects to Newton. The Servant of the People now lay with his beard shaved off, dressed in a gray suit, shirt and red tie, his legs festooned with roses and carnations in a well-designed, heavy wood casket — not the simple pine box Newton had once envisioned. It was somewhat of a surprise even to see Bobby Seale back in Oakland after fifteen years' absence. Following the violent row between the two Party founders that precipitated Seale's departure from the Party in the summer of 1974, Seale had never crossed paths again with Newton. Just before Seale took off for the East Coast, Seale had heard that local gangsters had taken out a contract on Newton's life after Newton had extorted money from them. Seale later told a reporter that "If I stayed around, I probably would have killed Huey myself."[21] Yet Seale donned a trademark Panther black beret to lead the eulogies in the three-hour service as if there had been no love lost between them. KPFA public radio in Berkeley covered the orations live. With a clenched fist salute to his co-founder, Seale recounted the major community programs the Panthers instituted. He told his audience that they tested more people for sickle cell anemia than all state and federal programs combined.

Congressman Ron Dellums told the audience that he first met Newton as a student at Merritt College when they were in a study group together. He pointed out that "the very same streets that [Huey Newton] tried to make safe for the children are the streets that took his life."[22] Hilliard challenged the audience to deal with drug and alcohol dependency before it brought down their whole race. Though Elaine Brown had fled Oakland with her daughter in October of 1977 in fear of Newton's wrath, she now remembered him as "a hero who sparked a dream of freedom in all of us runaway slaves."[23] Newton's wife Fredrika told the gathering that she planned to have her husband cremated and someday sprinkle his ashes across the city — perhaps signaling that the expensive coffin had been used for display purposes only.

Father Earl Neil lambasted the mainstream press for focusing only on Newton's misdeeds. Neil urged his listeners to see his most famous congregant as he did — a brilliant visionary and courageous prophet, "our Moses" battling modern day pharaohs. Reverend Smith ended the eulogies by asking the congregation to repeat the old familiar chant from 1968: "Free Huey, Free Huey" and then added, "Well, let me tell you, he's free!! He's free!!!"[24] One elderly woman reportedly shook her head in disbelief at all the lavish praise for a "plain old thug." "All these fools are trying to make him into a saint, but he was a real life sinner. Comparing him to Dr. King or Malcolm [X] is downright blasphemy."[25]

Yet, starting in early 1967, Huey Newton took to the streets at high risk to himself to ensure that West Oakland arrestees were afforded their new constitutional rights to *Miranda* warnings. And, as Melvin Newton pointed out, it was Huey's decision to put America on trial in 1968 with his own life on the line that launched the Panther Party as an international phenomenon. Otherwise, they would likely have disappeared within a year: "These were very young people. If you were twenty-six years old in the Panther Party, you were an elder. These were people who were in their teens and early twenties, and they went about the business of sacrificing themselves and they didn't necessarily expect to come out of it alive, and some of them didn't. I believe Huey was idealistic . . . he saw himself planting the seed. . . . [It is] the people who see things a little bit differently than everyone else that foster change and often make for a better society. . . . The people who hear another drum . . . are very, very important to all of us."

Early 1970s photo of Melvin and Huey Newton after Huey's release from prison.

20. THE ARC OF THE MORAL UNIVERSE

The only reason that they advanced is when the blacks pushed from the bottom. . ... But the black who actually was the perpetrator of the disturbance gets nothing but maybe a jail sentence.

— HUEY NEWTON

Most of us associate the familiar quote "The arc of the moral universe is long, but it bends toward justice" with a 1967 speech given by Reverend Martin Luther King. Actually, King was paraphrasing a statement first made by 19th century white abolitionist Theodore Parker, an influential Unitarian minister. Parker relished newspaper accounts of the riveting Lincoln-Douglas debates over slavery, but died in 1860. He did not live long enough to witness Lincoln's election, or the freeing of all slaves after the North and South suffered more than 650,000 casualties in a bloody civil war. And yet Reverend Parker was convinced that slavery would end someday because the preacher considered it the only just outcome of an evolving society. But that did not happen without constant agitation for change. It took an enormous number of motivated activists over the following century to pay the moral argument forward to King's day. Progress came at a very high price.

Since the 1960s, the martyrdom of Martin Luther King, Jr., undoubtedly helped galvanize major reforms. So, too, did black militants like Malcolm X and the Black Panther Party. Over the years, at key moments in the American 20th century, the catalyst that bent the arc further toward justice was activism embracing the powerful story of a life-or-death court case: Sacco and Vanzetti, the Scottsboro Boys, the Port Chicago mutiny trial, Willie McGee, and the Huey Newton trial among them.

As Melvin Newton observed, the Black Panthers would likely have disappeared within a year but for the 1968 death penalty trial that became the centerpiece of the Party to showcase its platform. The Panthers were organizers in the traditional mold defined by civil rights historian Professor Barbara Ransby of the University of Illinois: "bringing people together for sustained, coordinated, strategic action for change."[1] David Hilliard remains extraordinarily proud of what the Panthers accomplished. When interviewed in 2014, he boasted: "We were the student movement of the world. We were in 48 states in America, and eight communities broad. We were in Europe. We were in Africa."

The United States takes great pride as the world's most successful constitutional democracy. We all pledge to support "liberty and justice for all." But what do we mean? In *One Man's Freedom*, Washington super lawyer Edward Bennett Williams described how the individual civil liberties we so cherish in the United States evolved in our criminal courtrooms, where the government often prosecutes "the weak and friendless, the scorned and degraded, or the nonconformist and the unorthodox."[2] The Bill of Rights guarantees those accused of crime a trial before an "impartial jury," following the British historic practice of trial before a "jury of one's peers." Yet for most of our country's history, such juries consisted of white men only while the defendants were disproportionately minorities — at least those who escaped lynch mobs.

Over time, as activists raised arguments for equal treatment, the courts could not help but interpret the lofty, inclusive language of our Declaration of Independence and Constitution expansively. The pronouncement of the Declaration of Independence on which our nation was founded — that all men are created equal and endowed with certain inalienable rights — and the promises of the Bill of Rights embedded in our Constitution ring hollow if they exclude minorities and women. And though these rights were supposed to be "self-evident," suffragettes had to lobby for more than half a century — organizing high-profile parades and hunger strikes — to win those rights. When Martin Luther King took his sermons to the streets, hordes of followers marched with life and limb at risk and endured jail sentences for refusing to honor segregation laws. And at one memorable time in our history, defiant young Black Panthers openly picked up the gun to demand *Miranda* warnings for arrestees, and get their political platform heard, including a demand for ethnic studies programs so that minorities could learn history told from their ancestors' perspective. As feminists like Gloria Steinem readily acknowledge, those programs helped pave the way for women's studies programs and gay and lesbian studies. Free government breakfasts and free clinics are another lasting part of the Panther legacy.

David Hilliard remains particularly proud of what the Black Panthers achieved to diversify juries "of one's peers." "We were influential in making certain that if you go to trial you get — and it's in our 10-point program — a jury of your own peers." They did not get all they wanted because they defined peers "as being someone of the same historical, economic, cultural background." Even now, true equality remains elusive. Poor people still find it difficult to serve on juries because of the financial hardship it would cause. Jury expert Karen Jo Koonan observes that jurors still receive paltry compensation and the working poor, like the self-employed, rarely can afford the lost time from work on a trial of any length.

Yet Hilliard notes that, all too often in Oakland's courts, white male jurors used to come down from the hills of wealthy Piedmont to try black defendants: "We changed that dynamic." Ann Ginger's book detailing the jury selection strategy allowed the accomplishments of the Newton trial to have national impact. Today, Hilliard observes: "I think that every young guy that now has to go before a jury will make sure that there is somebody on the jury that understands him culturally, historically, economically and to make sure that that jury panel reflects who he is, the person that's being tried. . . . That's very, very clear . . . one of the most valuable . . . gains from the Black Panther Party's work . . . a major, major benefit of our work."

Melvin Newton has a similar message to convey about the Panther

Party's lasting influence: "The legacy of Huey and Bobby and the Black Panther Party lends itself to the pride that youth can take . . . looking at the examples of their leaders and their sacrifice." But youth today can also learn from the Panthers' mistakes and the price they paid. Their militarism put them in pitched battles with local police across the country and on J. Edgar Hoover's hit list. Hilliard acknowledges: "We were very young, calling for revolution in the streets and stuff like that — well, young people make mistakes, and we were not so adept and not so well-versed in the art of making revolution and change in society. But we weathered the storm, we learned, we grew, we did very well because most of our programs are now public policy." By the end of 1969 Hilliard tallied 29 Panthers who had died at the hands of law enforcement. Earl Anthony counted another 3,000 out of 5,000 Panthers nationwide who went to prison; 300 suspected informants killed by the Panthers themselves; and three Panthers who died warring over turf with US in Los Angeles. Anthony counted six more fatalities from the deadly split between Cleaver and Newton in 1971.

Hilliard says: "We all went to prison, especially if you were in leadership. You either went to prison or [were] dead. We paid a very heavy price. . . . The FBI was pretty much at its ugliest game to discredit and . . . to disqualify the Black Panther Party and its legitimate claim for freedom and justice, equality, and to . . . initiate programs around schools, educations and stuff like that for our children. . ... Most people think the Black Panther Party was limited to their own self-defense, period . . . with the guns and the patrol and the police, but it was so much more than that."

A number of Panthers remain in prison serving long sentences to this day, arguing they have been persecuted for their political agenda. The most famous former Black Panther still serving out life without the possibility of parole is author Mumia Abu-Jamal, who spent 25 years on death row — mostly in solitary confinement — before a federal court overturned his original sentence for constitutional deficiencies. Abu-Jamal was convicted in 1982 of killing a Philadelphia policeman in a case with facts eerily similar to Huey Newton's. Critics vigorously dispute Abu-Jamal's guilt and the fairness of his trial although the judgment has been repeatedly affirmed on review.

Had Huey Newton been convicted of first degree murder, he, too, would now be serving out a life sentence as one of the beneficiaries, like Charles Manson, of the 1972 California Supreme Court decision overturning the state's death penalty. Newton would undoubtedly have become an even more potent international cause célèbre than Abu-Jamal has become, as well as an even more toxic symbol to law enforcement organizations of the devil incarnate. How toxic? In 2014, President Obama nominated to head the Department of Justice's Civil Rights Division lawyer Debo Adegbile, a man with impeccable credentials, only to see the Senate reject him solely because his office played a role in the successful federal appeal asserting Abu-Jamal's constitutional rights.[3] That office — head of the country's civil rights enforcement — remains vacant to this day. What does it say about a democratic society where large numbers of politicians and law enforcement personnel still believe, essentially, in Nixon's and J. Edgar Hoover's view that U.S. citizens they consider political enemies are not entitled to any constitutional protections?

Nearly a half century ago with the whole world watching, a judge, prosecutor and unusually diverse jury led by a pioneering black foreman had a different idea in mind. They became invested in showcasing our democracy to avoid a deadly clash between black militants outraged at a racist criminal justice system and "law and order" defenders of that seriously flawed criminal justice system. They sought to achieve as fair a trial as possible for a self-proclaimed black revolutionary. To paraphrase Lowell Jensen, justice is the result of a fair process; it is not always in getting the outcome you desire. Civil rights lawyer Ann Ginger noted that the commitment of the judge, prosecutor and Newton jury to a fair trial undermined the central tenet of the Panther Party — it proved that racism was less pervasive than the Panthers argued and that trust in the system could work to produce justice. And the verdict avoided national riots just as foreman David Harper hoped to accomplish — no "sky's the limit" reprisals for a hero the Panthers would proclaim was railroaded.

David Horowitz believes there could have been a holocaust if the

Newton jury had returned a death penalty verdict and Cleaver carried out his threats to get angry young blacks to engage in guerilla warfare in city streets across America.[4] The government's response would certainly have been brutal. Suppression of major uprisings in 1968 could only have polarized society far more than it already was. If Newton remained in prison all these years condemned to die, he would undoubtedly have rallied huge numbers of supporters around the world to his cause, just as Sacco and Vanzetti did. In 1972, when the California Supreme Court outlawed the state's death penalty, Newton would have had his sentence converted to life imprisonment, just as that ruling benefited others then on death row. Then, instead of a downward tailspin leading to an ignoble end at the hands of a crack dealer, Newton could have remained a Movement star, an untarnished leftist hero for the rest of his life, as new generations of followers projected their own ideals on the revolutionary prisoner.

Yet, what did happen in 1968 — putting the United States on trial for its history of racial injustice — had a major impact to this day both on the diversity of juries of one's peers and in providing a world stage for other demands in the Panther Party platform. The results included widespread ethnic studies programs, creating a model of black activism that helped empower not only African-Americans but other minority interest groups. Kathleen Cleaver credits her generation of activists for seizing a pivotal moment when America was ripe for change: "The Black Panther Party was a phenomenon of black history that came at a time of a transition in which blacks were leaving the status of second class citizens, demanding that they be full-fledged U.S. citizens, or," she adds ominously, "maybe something else."

Hilliard takes pride in former Party members who went on to elected office. "We can claim those victories, because we were part and parcel responsible for making that stuff happen." Those who lent their voices in support of the efforts to "Free Huey" continued to leave their mark. When Panther supporter Ron Dellums left his long congressional career, he was succeeded by his protégée Barbara Lee, a self-described renegade who got her start in politics as a staffer in Shirley Chisholm's grassroots 1972 presidential campaign as the first

African-American to run for the nation's highest office. Lee was close to Newton in the early '70s and a key fund-raiser for Seale's unsuccessful 1973 Oakland mayoral campaign. Long vilified for her strong leftist views, Lee needed bodyguards in the aftermath of 9/11 for casting the lone vote against the congressional resolution to give President Bush broad power to conduct a borderless war on terror. By 2008 a growing number of Americans agreed with her, including Barack Obama, who named her a Western Regional Co-Chair of his presidential campaign.

Chicago Congressman Bobby Rush is a veteran of SNCC who grew up on Chicago's streets and helped Fred Hampton found the Illinois Black Panther Party. Thrust into a more prominent role on Hampton's death, Rush became the local chapter's Minister of Defense and named his son after Huey Newton, before Rush quit the Party and went back to school. After Rush's son Huey was killed by robbers, Rush represented the authentic voice who shared the community's pain. No white congressman would likely have had the same impact as Rush did on March 28, 2012, putting on a hoodie in Trayvon Martin's honor to address the House on racial profiling.[5]

The Panthers also played a broader role in accelerating the rising number of black mayors in cities across the country. As white flight to the suburbs accelerated, black politicians became more attractive candidates to the diverse city dwellers who remained. The greater acceptance of black candidates by white voters later enabled break-through elections of black senators and governors. President George W. Bush's appointment of retired General Colin Powell as the first black Secretary of State also paved the way for Republicans to consider Powell potential presidential timber more than a decade before Obama's successful bid for the White House in 2008.

Obama's historic victory in 2008 prompted "Wee Pals" creator Morrie Turner to circulate an exuberant cartoon with the caption, "ROSA SAT . . . SO MARTIN COULD WALK . . . SO OBAMA COULD RUN . . . SO OUR KIDS COULD FLY!" Indeed, Turner later acknowledged another milestone of achievement bridging the gap between King and Obama. Having been an observer of the 1968 Huey Newton death penalty trial, Turner reflected in 2012: "I truly believe that had

Newton received a death sentence, we would not have Obama in the White House today."

Perhaps in his decades in prison Newton would have written more books, as Black Panther Abu-Jamal has done. To his admirers, Newton might have drawn continued comparisons to South African states-man Nelson Mandela, whose political influence grew exponentially in twenty-seven years of imprisonment. Mandela was himself one of the leading international voices who came to Mumia Abu-Jamal's defense as a political prisoner.

Had Newton remained in prison as a cop-killing revolutionary, would America have elected a black community organizer President in 2008, who, as a college student identified with the goals of the Black Panther Party? Assuming Huey Newton remained an imprisoned revo-lutionary in 2008, of all the political efforts to discredit Obama as a can-didate for President, any link to Newton and the Black Panther Party would presumably have been toxic. In the 1980s and 1990s, Newton would only have been middle-aged. One can easily imagine Reverend Jeremiah Wright, Jr., circulating "Free Huey" petitions at his Trinity Church of Christ in Chicago — as was done by black churches nation-wide in the two years Newton remained behind bars for his 1968 man-slaughter conviction. It is easy to envision Barack Obama, as Wright's protégé, signing such a petition thirty years ago when his college days as a Panther fan were not that far behind him. Yet by 1995, Obama would harbor growing misgivings about the efficacy of black militants. He then dismissed "the politics of black rage . . . which exhorts but does not organize ordinary folks or create realistic agendas for change."[6]

Assume that Huey Newton, like Mumia Abu-Jamal, still remained an aging radical prisoner in 2008 when Newton would have been 66. If Obama had denounced the Black Panther founder in public, just as he distanced himself from Reverend Wright's angry rhetoric and emphati-cally rejected the militancy of Louis Farrakhan in a debate with Senator Clinton, these statements would not have satisfied his critics. Rather, Obama's political enemies would have searched the many "Free Huey" petitions over the years looking for one with the future presidential can-didate's signature. If these foes of Obama found such a signature, they would have wasted no time painting Obama as a traitor to law, order and democracy, and doing their utmost to frighten hordes of voters.

Indeed, twice during a key period of the presidential race in August and September of 2008, the Federal Bureau of Prisons publicly objected to another high-profile prisoner's request just *to read* Obama's two bestselling books, *Dreams from My Father* and *The Audacity of Hope*. At the time, Al Qaeda member Ahmed Omar Abu Ali was serving thirty years in a "super-maximum" security federal prison for attempting to assassinate President Bush. While vice-presidential candidate Sarah Palin repeatedly accused Obama of "pallin' around with terrorists," prison authorities bizarrely reported that the FBI considered some passages of Obama's widely disseminated autobiographies "potentially detrimental to national security." The Bureau of Prisons quietly withdrew this extraordinary attack on Obama's patriotism just after his election.[7]

If Newton remained in prison in 2008, it is difficult to imagine Democrats taking the risk of anointing Barack Obama as their candidate or, if he were nominated, how the Obama campaign could have persuaded swing voters to disregard qualms about electing a black community organizer as President. While civil rights advocates celebrate how far the nation has come since the 1960s, the powerful negatives associated with the Black Panthers a half century ago still reverberate — as illustrated by the vehement reaction to Beyoncé's half-time tribute at Super Bowl Fifty.

So one can add to Kathleen Cleaver's comment about the amazing trajectory from the advent of the Panthers to the election of a black President and appointment of a black Attorney General. The judge, prosecutor and pioneering jury in Alameda County, California, in 1968 who rose to the challenge to provide a black revolutionary a fair trial deserve a large share of the credit — they showcased American democracy at its finest. But if the Panthers had not been willing to risk their lives "to the horse's brow," none of their platform would have gained an international audience.

Many pillars in Oakland's black community agree with Cleaver and Hilliard that the Panthers deserve recognition for courting death to accelerate the pace of race progress. Among them is Lionel Wilson's protégé, Bill Patterson, who, since his service as the first black foreman of the Alameda County Grand Jury, has repeatedly been elected to regional office and as a trustee of local community colleges. Looking back in 2013, he observed: "I think the Black Panther Party, and what they aspired to do and their programs, if they were implemented righteously today, it'd make a great difference. And overall, I think that's why we go back and now reassess what they did. . . .[T]he negative side I think is almost drowned out by the positive side because what they advocated and what they actually did on the positive side, it's what we ought to have."

In various ways, the Panthers have gained broader recognition for their accomplishments. One dramatic example is a bronzed replica of the wicker throne that Newton sat in for the iconic photograph in the spring of 1967 that still circulates widely today. The bronzed replica sits in permanent display in the Oakland Museum of California just above the garage where police hid out the weekend after Labor Day in September of 1968, while preparing to bash heads of protesters if rioting erupted following the expected death penalty verdict.

Kathleen Cleaver sees how the Panthers' efforts back in the late 1960s started that political evolution: "Now we are two generations, if not three generations, behind that. So we can see how that all shaped out. So you have reason for more disappointment, but you also have reason for more enthusiasm. Who would have thought . . . in our life-time, I would see a black president and a black attorney general in Washington, D.C.? To me, the black attorney general is the most phenomenal change, even more so than a black president. So things are moving. They are moving to get better. They are moving to get worse."

What has clearly gotten worse over the last half century is the huge racial disparity in incarceration rates that author Michelle Alexander exposed so forcefully in her 2010 bestseller, *The New Jim Crow: Mass Incarceration in the Age of Color Blindness*. The Panthers bear some responsibility for that turn of events, too. As Jean Genet observed, the Panthers' tactic of attacking enemies "by sight" created enormous public fear which has fueled political campaigns for decades. Consider the infamous example of felon Willie Horton in the 1980s. Horton, an African-American convicted murderer, escaped while on a weekend furlough from prison and raped a woman before he was caught. George H. W. Bush featured Horton in an enormously successful (and racist) 1988 presidential campaign ad accusing his opponent Michael Dukakis of being soft on crime, even though Dukakis had not released Horton. The message was that anyone who endorsed releasing any felons on parole or furlough put the public at too much risk.

To win election for the last several decades, politicians increasingly promoted "three-strikes laws" and tough-on-crime legislation and enforcement policies. As a result of the general public's appetite to elect representatives promising to be even tougher on crime than their predecessors, the Chair of the White House Council of Economic Advisers reported that in 2015 our country's incarceration rate exceeded four times the average around the globe — even though violent crime had plummeted. The typical cost today of keeping a juvenile in prison for a year is more than $110,000 — way more than the staggering cost per year of college that is mortgaging the futures of so many of today's students. Investing in lock-ups comes at the expense of public funding for higher education. A similar dilemma faces the Department of Justice as it seeks to be more proactive in addressing systemic bias in law enforcement in cities besides Ferguson — more than a quarter of the Justice Department's current budget is consumed by the Bureau of Prisons.[8]

Congress now has before it a bipartisan bill to reform sentencing laws to reduce nonviolent prison populations. This is a shared goal of both leading Democrats and of stalwart Republicans like Newt Gingrich and former Attorney General Ed Meese. Some Congress members remain skeptical that tough sentencing for nonviolent crimes doesn't work and resist efforts to ratchet incarceration rates downward. At the same time, Black Lives Matter, Black Youth Project 100 (BYP100) and other activist groups have forced national focus on race discrimination in police practices and in government provision of essential services like clean water. As Charles Blow recognized in 2009, "Blacks are living a tale of two Americas — one of the ascension of the first black president . . .; the other of a collapsing quality of life and amplified racial tensions."[9] Indeed, the tensions Blow observed during Obama's first year in office pale in comparison to the open vitriol dividing our nation in 2016.

What does seeing how the 1968 Newton trial played out tell us today? Janice Garrett Forte has a message for younger generations: "I am very proud that I was in the Black Panther Party and I let my children know, I let my grandchild know that what we did during the '60s and the '70s was very key to . . . their freedoms that they have today. . . . The free breakfasts that they have instituted throughout the United States started with the Black Panther Party [and] free clinics that they have throughout the United States." She adds, "What we did was so key and significant for black people in the United States . . . but for all people, because the people had the power. . . . [W]e used to say, 'Power to the people' and that's exactly what happened. There was power with the people."

Jury consultant Karen Jo Koonan underscores Forte's point:

> The slogan "Power to the People" changed everything. . . . [I]t rejected the old assumptions. It set a new standard. It said that people get to make the independent decisions and not just go along with the prosecution and the system. It said that Black Panthers could follow the police around and monitor their behavior, which put a damper on their ability to abuse people in the same way that video cameras are starting to do now. . . . That "Power to the People" notion is . . . at the heart also of . . . Black Lives Matter because it says . . . you can't just function in the old way and get away with it without someone seeing it. . . . "Power to the People" is the ability to shine the light.

Comparing American society today with the 1960s, Forte notes:

> It's sad to say that the things that we fought for during the trial for Huey are still very relevant today. . . . I see it played out every day in the news. What's happening in South Carolina . . . the burning of the churches and everything that's going on. . . . Things . . . change for a period of time. But we still have an awful lot of work to do.

She urges young people as she was in the late 1960s:

> not to give up. . . .. You can get things done if you persevere and keep at it . . . The children are seeing a lot of hopelessness now . . . . I would like to let them know [to] just learn from what has happened in the past and they can go forward and create the type of society that they want.

Sixties radical Louis Armmond adds: "The one truism that we all held was that we never lost faith in the masses of the American people. And I think that our faith has been well placed and well-demonstrated. . . . We haven't won all our victories and all of our struggles, but we have never lost the faith that at some point in time, if not in our generation, future generations would carry on. And I think that's what the Newton trial demonstrated in great respect. I think the same thing in Ferguson. Out of that will grow a new movement with even broader participation than was the case in my day."

Like Kathleen Cleaver, Janice Garrett Forte and other Panther Party activists, civil rights activists today can already see some fruits of their protests — Ferguson, Missouri, now has a black chief of police. In Baltimore, a year after wide-scale protests followed Freddie Gray's death, the family reached a large settlement with the city and six city police officers soon faced criminal charges for their alleged misconduct. In the first four trials, when all the evidence was presented, no convictions resulted. All charges against the remaining officers were then dismissed. Yet Baltimore will undoubtedly continue a higher level of scrutiny of police conduct going forward than it did before Freddie Gray died. Meanwhile, the new chief of police is giving out weekly awards to officers demonstrating guardianship by finding ways to bond with community members rather than focusing on arrests. As Chief Kevin Davis acknowledges, "Would that have happened before Freddie Gray? Probably not."[10]

Now in her nineties, Ann Ginger sees an opportunity today for major progress: "This is an exciting moment for people to pick up on what Huey Newton did long ago, what Charles Garry did in defending him, and what many, many people have done from then until now."

Bryan Stevenson sums up the challenges we currently face: "We are continuing to suffer from what the Panthers could not achieve, from what the Civil Rights movement did not achieve, and from what our system of justice has yet to achieve." But Stevenson believes lack of diversity remains a daunting obstacle. "Today, in America, 90-some percent of all prosecutors are all white. . . . There is a perception that our system treats you better if you are rich and guilty than if you are poor and innocent. We've never had more people of color in jails and prisons than we have today."

Sociologist Karen Jo Koonan adds her own note of caution: "We've made some progress, but until we address that fundamental assumption that black lives are worth less than white lives — which I think is still alive and well in our society — until we address that, the progress is limited."

Indeed, with all the talk today of criminal justice reform hardly anyone in politics wants to address the scarcity of funds for public defenders. Criminal law expert Professor John Pfaff at Fordham Law School describes public defenders' offices across America today as "starved of resources while facing impossible caseloads that mock the idea of justice for the poor." With four-fifths of all state criminal defendants entitled under the Constitution to a government lawyer, Professor Pfaff suggests that the federal government should provide far more funding to state and local governments toward the cost of indigent defense.[11]

Professor Stevenson points out that the nation's judges also remain mostly white male. Women are gaining seats faster than minorities, but no state yet has as many women judges as men. A study published in 2016 called "The Gavel Gap" showed that as of 2014 in state courts — where nine out of ten cases are tried — minorities totaled two-fifths of the overall population and one-fifth of judges. This data included a handful of states where the number of minority judges matched their percentage of the population and sixteen states where not even one in ten judges was a person of color. In five states, the survey found that minority judges were "nearly absent." The researchers concluded that on the whole: "The courts are not representative of the people whom they serve."[12]

There is obviously much that is currently broken in our criminal justice system and a split among our citizenry how best to go forward. David Hilliard believes "it's a very tenuous moment that we live in now." With national attention refocused on civil rights issues, President Obama encourages activists to form coalitions to accomplish reforms. Kathleen Cleaver observes that organizations that rely primarily on social media to reach constituents "have more access, but probably less impact" than the Panthers did with education sessions, face-to-face development of infrastructure and a Party platform that members all pledged to support. That type of thinking appears to be behind BYP100's organizational efforts and recent issuance of a 50-page "Agenda to Build Black Futures." In August of 2016 over fifty civil rights groups supporting Black Lives Matter issued a detailed plan for economic justice, including reparations.[13] Opposition to these agendas is also on the rise.

Professor Stevenson remains cautiously optimistic about various reform efforts. "I am hopeful that in the last year or two, we've pushed hard enough that maybe there will be a new opportunity to talk about these issues of racial inequality in our criminal justice system. We have seen young people take to the streets in response to police violence against unarmed black men and boys . . . that has forced a conversation that was long overdue." He adds: "We now have people from both political parties, all talking about the need to end mass incarceration. So that gives me some hope that perhaps we can turn a corner. I am hopeful that social media, in the documentation of some of these acts of violence by the police towards people of color, will allow us to turn a corner. But it won't happen by itself."

Cameron Sterling, the 15-year-old son of Alton Sterling, whom Baton Rouge police shot to death on July 5, 2016, recognized the same need for thoughtful concerted action going forward. Demonstrating wisdom beyond his years a week after the July 9, 2016 sniper attack in Dallas at a protest rally honoring his father and Minnesotan Philando Castile, the grieving youth took his sudden public platform to say: "I feel that people in general no matter what their race is should come together as one united family. Yes, you can protest, but I want everyone to protest the right way. Protest in peace, not guns, not drugs, not alcohol, not violence."[14]

Shockingly, just four days later, police in Baton Rouge were attacked by a gunman, killing three officers and wounding several others. Sterling's plea could not prevent that horrendous gun violence, but it will hopefully persuade many more Americans of his underlying point. The teenager echoed the eulogies of President Obama and former President George W. Bush at the joint funeral service for the five slain policemen in Dallas that had just taken place the day before. President Bush noted: "At times, it seems like the forces pulling us apart are stronger than the forces binding us together. . . . Too often we judge other groups by their worst examples, while judging ourselves by our best intentions. And this has strained our bonds of understanding and common purpose. But Americans, I think, have a great advantage. To renew our unity, we only need to remember our values. We have never been held together by blood or background. We are bound by things of the spirit – by shared commitments to common ideals." President Obama summed up our challenge as a nation: "In the end . . . it's about forging consensus and fighting cynicism and finding the will to make change." He then asked: "Can we find the character, as Americans, to open our hearts to each other? Can we see in each other a common humanity and shared dignity?"[15] That is how we bend the arc of the moral universe toward justice.

EPILOGUE

*"If you are not at the table,
you are on the menu."*

— NANCY O'MALLEY,
ALAMEDA COUNTY'S FIRST FEMALE DISTRICT ATTORNEY

Where is Alameda County today and how much of that reflects the Panthers' influence? Today, Alameda County has a diverse population of more than 1.5 million people: 42% white, 26% Asian, 22% Latino, 12% black, 6% self-identified as multi-racial, and the rest list other races. Oakland remains its county seat and is far more diverse than any other part of the county. As its first Asian-American Mayor Jean Quan pointed out in 2014, "We're a city that speaks 130 languages." Though Oakland's population has declined somewhat from its peak, in 2015 the census showed about 390,000 residents. Slightly more than a third were white, 28 percent black, a quarter Latino, 16 percent Asian and 13 percent identified as other races. (In contrast, neighboring Berkeley — long dominated by Cal students and faculty — is almost 60% white and has nearly twice as many Asians as blacks.)

The Newton trial was a highlight of a particularly pivotal moment — the turbulent 1960s — that stood out in the history of Oakland, Alameda County and America as a whole. It had a lasting impact across the decades, reverberating on a local as well as national level. In looking back at the Panthers' imprint over the past fifty years, let's start with how City Hall and the police relate to expected protests. In anticipation of BART Officer Johannes Mehserle's possible acquittal for the January 2009 death of Oscar Grant III, long-time Panther affiliate Mayor Ron Dellums and other city officials worked with community leaders, churches and nonprofit mediators coordinated by Fania Davis

— the head of Restorative Justice for Oakland Youth — to minimize the risk and severity of violence. (Fania Davis is the younger sister of Angela Davis and helped lead fund-raising efforts for the defense of Angela's murder trial in 1972.) In 2010, for the protests following the Mehserle verdict, Oakland's black police chief enlisted diverse reinforcements from fifteen other agencies, all trained to effectuate by-the-book arrests of suspected vandals and other miscreants while giving broad scope to those exercising their First Amendment rights.[1] Volunteers kept vandalism to a minimum by providing forums for speakers to vent their frustration. Afterward, Fania Davis credited the Oakland police for their restrained behavior even when provoked by aggressive demonstrators.

Mayor Dellums presided over a diverse city council that supported these coordinated efforts to balance free speech rights against the protection of property and the public from unlawful activity. How did that happen? The Panthers played a prominent role lobbying in the 1970s and early '80s to amend Oakland's city charter to hold district elections instead of citywide elections for the school board and all but one seat on the city council. This guaranteed East and West Oakland seats at the table. Dellum's successor Jean Quan, as the city's first Asian and first female mayor, would publicly acknowledge at her inauguration in 2011 that she and other women and minorities in city office "stood on the shoulders of a lot of pioneers in Oakland, including the Black Panthers." Quan had first been elected to represent the Oakland hills district on the school board and then the same district on the city council before she was elected mayor. She realized that by pushing for district rather than citywide elections, the Panthers helped transform council control from white men "to the point when I got elected we [minorities and women] were actually the majority of the City Council for the first time in history."

The Panthers also influenced the hiring of more minority police recruits in the early '70s — the substantial increase of black officers on the beat made all officers look and act less like an army of occupation to those who lived in Oakland's flatlands. Hilliard said that was what point 7 of their platform was all about: "Who were these racist white men who lived 50, 60 miles [away] . . . who had no understanding of the average

[man] in the black community? So we were going to change that. We called for police officers that looked like us, that were from the same education, historical, cultural background. [We were] not against police officers. We want police officers that look like us, that understand our culture, including hiring more women. So we were responsible for that."

To acknowledge the Panthers' prominent role is not to diminish the collaboration of many other local activists in instigating these progressive changes. Organized efforts to improve the relationship between the black community and the police had been underway since at least the late 1940s. They gained traction in 1967 when NAACP leaders found a sympathetic ear in newly-installed Chief Charles Gain. Gain was quick to implement major policy changes such as banning the shooting of fleeing suspects who posed no threat of harm to others, stopping the use of mace against protesters, and enforcing rules forbidding racial slurs. He also sought to hire and train new officers with more diverse backgrounds, who were more likely to empathize with residents in Oakland's flatlands. His efforts matched the strong recommendation of the 1968 blue ribbon *Kerner Report* to defuse the mounting racial tension in inner cities across country.

Among other reforms, Gain instituted at the police academy a week of African-American studies and another on Latin American culture, bringing in sociology and history professors to lecture new recruits so they could be better informed about minorities and the poor. This new curriculum could also be seen as a byproduct of the Panthers' aggressive tactics in 1967–68 to get San Francisco State to offer ethnic studies — point 5 of their Party platform — that quickly revolutionized history and sociology departments nationwide.

Bobby Seale had been involved in getting black history books and literature into the library at Oakland City College back in 1965, the year before he and Huey Newton formed the Party. Huey's brother Melvin Newton soon became the college's first chair of ethnic studies: "We probably were the first ones in the country to become a department. I chaired the department and taught in the department and helped to hire, recommend the hire of faculty. . . . A lot of that started with Don Warden, Huey, Bobby Seale. . . ." Today, Oakland City College has changed its

name to Merritt College and has moved to the Oakland Hills. Yet its ties
to Panther Party history remain strong. Merritt College proudly features
a student lounge dedicated to Bobby Seale and Huey Newton.

To many others, the Panthers remain polarizing. Conservative
whites who remember the events of the late 1960s and early 1970s consider the Panthers' impact far more negative than positive. Back then,
alarmed city officials and Oakland business owners considered Chief
Gain too soft on crime and opposed his efforts to erase the image of
the OPD as an army of occupation. Yet, despite such resistance, gradual
progress in police-community relations occurred over time.

One example of the seesawing forward motion arose out of the
prickly relationship between Charles Gain and the police officers'
union that mirrored the relationship of conservatives in Sacramento to
the state's then liberal Supreme Court. By 1972, Gain replaced black-
and-white patrol cars because they filled black community members
with fear and loathing. When Gain ordered a fleet of less intimidating
light blue cars, the police union rebelled. Driving "baby blue" vehicles
when on duty was the last straw. Their progressive chief infuriated them
as much as the California Supreme Court's ruling in February of 1972
throwing out the state's death penalty. The police union issued a vote
of no confidence in their chief, and, at the urging of Attorney General
George Deukmejian, many policemen used their off hours to gather
signatures for a successful petition to reinstate the death penalty.

Gain's successor, George Hart, was also a progressive, who hired the
first woman beat cop in 1974. (For the prior two decades there had been
a small number of women in low level jobs on the police force.) Hart
was also committed to recruiting more minorities — the percentage of
black recruits under Gain had still been less than half the percentage of
blacks in the community. While still hiring graduates from police academies and military veterans, Hart also actively sought college graduates
in sociology whose community relations skills could help improve the
department's interaction with residents of minority neighborhoods.

Though Chief Hart was appointed in late 1973 during Mayor
Reading's tenure, he also established a good working relationship with
Mayor Lionel Wilson. Hart remained chief of police for nearly two

decades before he retired in 1992: "For years I gave the same speech to every recruit class, every graduating Oakland Police Academy. . . . And the paramount theme was always [that] you are in fact a public servant and you exist in your public role and your police role solely for the purpose of serving others; and you have to do that in a manner that reflects dignity and respect, consideration and, above all, fairness for everybody, without a consideration for any [other] factor. And I believe that to my soul . . . and I practiced that wholeheartedly."

As someone who ascended through the ranks of the OPD during the time the Panthers and the police were openly at war with each other, Chief Hart is remarkably restrained in evaluating the Panthers' impact. In looking back, Chief Hart believes that, on the whole, the Panthers did "more harm than good," because they were so confrontational. He disliked seeing Beyoncé's 50th Super Bowl half-time tribute and the example it sets for the broader Black Lives Matter movement. He wants black youths today "to understand that the system can work for them, does work for them, will work for them, but they cannot hope to resolve issues on the street and you don't do it by taking on the cops. . . . The street is not the place to resolve conflict. The street is not the place to decide whether or not you're going to comply with what a police officer says to do."

There is a good lesson Chief Hart thinks youth today can learn from the 1968 Huey Newton death penalty case: "One of the things we're witnessing in the Black Lives Matter . . . activity is that we're all having a tendency to rush to judgment [on police shootings caught on video] and somehow we need that under control, because it's inflammatory, to be sure. People are reacting . . . based on sound bites, and we all know how that can work out — both ways. . . . I'm making no judgment who's right, who's wrong, simply that we all need to take a deep breath and let the system work. Guess what? It worked for Newton."

Under Hart's leadership, his department won national recognition among law enforcement for innovative policing. Standards keep evolving, but, unlike many of his contemporaries, he was an early advocate of transparency:

We tried to develop the use of tape recorders . . . and we did so with
the support and understanding of the police officers who understood that they needed to have testimony to their activities that they
were not the bad guys that frequently they were accused [of having]
been . . .. [It] is very difficult to defend yourself against inappropriate allegations . . . and the easiest way to do that sometimes is some
technology — we just didn't have the technology. So, when it came
along years later, . . . that was exactly the right thing to do and I bless
them for doing that. It was a great, great thing to do.

Chief Hart adds, "In retrospect . . . it would be nice as an example
. . . if Officer Frey, if back in that era, . . . had had the technology. . . .
Body camera or even recordings of some sort, dash cams, for example,
would have been a great thing because, if nothing else, we'd certainly
know without doubt what had occurred at that scene."

* * * * *

In Oakland, far better mechanisms are now in place for addressing policing issues raised by minorities than there were back in the
1960s. The Panthers' repeated demands to hold police accountable to
the community had particular impact. Among the youths the Panthers
inspired was civil rights lawyer John Burris, co-author in 1999 of *Blue vs.
Black: Let's End the Conflict Between Cops and Minorities.* Burris switched
to law school from a planned career in accounting after absorbing the
twin impacts of King's assassination and the 1968 Huey Newton trial.
He considers his entire law practice focused on police abuse cases to
stand on the shoulders of the Panthers. His high-profile clients have
included Rodney King and the family of Oscar Grant III.

Burris launched his own practice in March of 1979 after six years
honing his skills as a deputy district attorney under Lowell Jensen.
Burris's first major police abuse case involved an investigation requested
by Mayor Lionel Wilson into the death of a 15-year-old African-
American boy named Melvin Black. Black had been shot eight times by
two Oakland policemen responding to reports of a sniper shooting at
cars from a hill abutting a dead-end street near the freeway. When the

deceased youth turned out to be unarmed — his pellet gun abandoned on a car hood — public outcry in the black community prompted Mayor Wilson to appoint Burris as an independent investigator.

Burris spent months on the assignment — even reenacting one night the police officers' account of the shooting — and ultimately sent City Hall a far more scathing report than anticipated, several hundred pages detailing a number of violations of OPD policy in connection with Black's death. That highly publicized 1979 incident prompted creation in 1980 of Oakland's Citizens Police Review Board — fourteen years after Wilson had unsuccessfully lobbied for such a board as head of the city's anti-poverty program. Burris gives a lot of the credit to ground-work laid by the Black Panthers, who pushed for community control of abusive police as a major focus of their widely disseminated newspaper and political campaigns. For more than 15 years, the Board would have an advisory role only, but that changed after "The Riders" scandal came to light in 2000. The scandal not only gave teeth to the Police Review Board, it led to a complete overhaul of the police department — another ripple effect attributable in substantial part to the Panthers.

The Riders were a group of four rogue policemen led by a veteran Latino officer known on the streets as "the choker." In the 1990s these officers won praise for their arrest rate on the dangerous late night shift in West Oakland only to be exposed in 2000 for engaging in a pattern of planting drugs on arrestees, severely beating them into false confessions and lying about what happened on their write-ups. A rookie cop who worked under one of the Riders broke the scandal after he could no longer stomach his boss's advice to forget everything he learned in the police academy and do as they did. Once exposed, the Riders' ring-leader fled to Mexico, never to return. The other three went on trial: two veteran Filipino officers and one young white follower.

The chief of police at the time was its first African-American chief, Joseph Samuels. The office would have a succession of black chiefs over the next twenty years. Former chief George Hart considers the blame for the scandal to rest not on their shoulders, but on short-sighted budget cuts. When he was chief, "we had the resources and the staffing and the physical structure as well as the professional capability to ensure that we were properly staffed at the commanding supervisory level that never would there be an opportunity for [such] systemic kind of failure." But during the prolonged drug wars of the 1980s the department became chronically understaffed to handle the burgeoning crime rate.

Judge Leo Dorado presided over the fourteen-month Rider jury trial — the longest in county history. The Oakland-raised Latino judge had his own interest in the law awakened by the surprising result in the 1968 Newton trial when Dorado was a college freshman. Dorado was in fact part of the first wave of new judicial appointees by Governor Jerry Brown in the 1980s, intended to diversify the face of California's judiciary. From a nearly all-white-male bench through the 1960s, Alameda County emerged with a higher percentage of women and minorities than any other county bench in the state.

Both sides of the Rider case considered Judge Dorado the ideal choice because of his evenhanded approach and low-key demeanor. The Rider trial ended with the exoneration of the youngest policeman; the jury deadlocked on most of the remaining charges against the two Filipino officers. (That year, Judge Dorado won the first Judicial Distinguished Service Award ever awarded by the Alameda County Bar Association.) No conviction resulted, but the scandal led to the Police Review Board gaining subpoena powers and jurisdiction to mediate complaints of excessive use of force and police bias.

The community found that the board was an improvement, but not a panacea. Even today, with its powers increased, the review board disappoints many citizens who have greater expectations than it can deliver. The city still gets criticism for the number of policemen accused of misconduct who wind up keeping their jobs. But the number of complaints against police have gone down, which sets a good example for other jurisdictions. Shortly after BART officer Mehserle killed Oscar Grant, the BART board invited the legislature to create a similar civilian police review board for BART officers. A growing number of cities across American now have their own civilian review boards, but many remain advisory only — with no enforcement mechanisms. Few have any funding to support independent investigations as Oakland now has, though it still lacks the power to oversee the police department.

The most significant impact of the Rider scandal came out of the civil rights case that John Burris then brought on behalf of many of the rogue officers' victims. By random assignment, the case landed in the courtroom of Judge Thelton Henderson, who in the 1990s became the first African-American Chief Judge in Northern California. As a tribute to his own extraordinary career, Henderson's alma mater Boalt Hall later created a center for social justice in his name; its mission is to "prepare the next generation of lawyers to challenge race, gender, and income inequality in law and society."[2] (Judge Henderson was also the subject of an acclaimed 2005 documentary, *Soul of Justice* by filmmaker Abby Ginzberg.)

In settling the Rider civil rights suit in 2003, the OPD agreed to undertake a series of reforms supervised by a court-appointed monitor under Judge Henderson's ongoing oversight. But the department was slow to comply with the settlement, with much left undone after years of prodding by the monitor. Judge Henderson observed in the fall of 2013: "There are people in Oakland who still believe that the Oakland Police Department is not friendly to the black community. That they aren't there to serve the black community's needs, but they're there rather to suppress the black community and keep them under control. I hear that. I get letters . . . to that effect all the time."

In the spring of 2014, black City Administrator Fred Blackwell and Chinese-American Mayor Jean Quan selected then Acting Chief Sean Whent as the new head of the OPD. The choice of a white veteran Oakland police officer in competition with twenty-seven candidates from across the country illustrated not only how much Oakland had changed in fifty years, but how pivotal a role the Panthers played in that transformation. Blackwell knew what qualities he was looking for: "In order to be effective in this job someone has to be committed to constitutional policing. They have to be committed to public safety. They have to be strategic. They have to put together a good team and they have to have integrity, and the chief rose to the top of a very competitive pool because he possesses all of those qualities."[3]

Just 39 when he was appointed, Whent spent nearly two decades working his way up the ladder from a cadet to head of the internal

affairs department. In 2013, as interim chief, Whent oversaw a drastic
reduction of violent crime as well as pushing the OPD to comply at long
last with Judge Henderson's 2003 order in the Rider case.[4] Whent also
reached out to community leaders, criminal defense counsel and clergy
in Oakland and won enthusiastic support. Most amazing was the history
of both officials at City Hall who collaborated on the white police chief's
appointment. Jean Quan — whose immigrant mother had never even
been taught to read — was the first Chinese-American elected mayor
of a major American city, and only got to the city's helm through district elections the Panthers helped inaugurate. City Administrator Fred
Blackwell as a youth attended the Black Panther Community School.
Mayor Quan marveled, "And so it just was in a generation he goes from
the child of protesters against police brutality to the person who is now
running the city and hires the police chief."

For more than five years, the department has required police to
wear body cams when making arrests. It has also adopted Operation
Cease Fire, a program that involves county and city officials sitting
down with gang leaders and offering help in getting them high school
diplomas, jobs and health insurance if they give up criminal activities.
Oakland's police force now includes more minorities and women in
key roles. The department has community liaisons, including one designated to reach out to the LGBT community. These efforts to increase
the OPD's diversity are ongoing.

Oakland-born Paul Figueroa, who has a Ph.D. and briefly served as
acting OPD chief in June 2016, exemplifies its evolution over the past
fifty years. Figueroa points to more inclusion of women and minorities
as a key factor: "Diversity in the police department is a good and necessary thing because you want to be able to reach all communities. And
oftentimes, there [are] the nuances of culture . . . the nuances of language. . . . You absolutely want a broad spectrum of people within your
department to reach all communities because ultimately the police are
the community and the community are the police."

Paul Figueroa grew up in the Fruitvale District of Oakland. His
older brothers were fans of the Brown Berets, a Chicano version of the
Black Panthers. In 1976 Brown Berets helped organize Latinos in the

Fruitvale District to lobby for police reform after a much-publicized shooting, much as West Oakland had organized in response to controversial police killings a decade earlier. Figueroa's African-American wife also was raised in Oakland. Her uncles admired the Black Panthers. Her mild-mannered, law-abiding father shared stories with Figueroa of his anxiety when Oakland police stopped him more than once in the 1960s because they mistook him for Huey Newton. What prompted police to pull him over? Seeing a young black man driving a VW sedan that was the same model Newton frequently drove — LaVerne Williams' used car that wound up impounded after the shootout on October 28,1967.

Fifty years ago, Oakland Police Chief Charlie Gain was a strong believer in community policing; his successors have embraced that model of policing, too, but have had too few officers over decades of under-staffing to make community policing work effectively. Figueroa acknowledges that, ideally, many more officers would walk the beat than the department has been able to afford. His biggest concern is the chronic lack of resources. "We get somewhere between 650,000 to even 800,000 911 calls a year. . . . And we just can't get to all of those. And it's very frustrating because the community is calling. . . . In Oakland, [the Police Department] always had that strain of not enough officers to meet the calls for service."

For the past several years the OPD's management has embraced as its model the view now taught in national law enforcement conferences that police are guardians of the community instead of their historic self-image as warriors primarily protecting property owners and their families. Chief Hart still believes the best view is to recognize police duties as a mix of guardian and warrior roles. Figueroa observes: "What it comes down to is that the departments have to be connected to their communities. And they've got to be connected in a way that they understand what are the root causes of what is causing crime in a community." Figueroa notes that: "We've always recruited heavily from military jobs. . . . And what's interesting is the military has even shifted to kind of the guardian mentality when they are dealing with individuals in other countries."

Civil rights and criminal defense attorneys monitoring the OPD noted substantial improvements under Whent's leadership. Veteran

Oakland trial lawyer Jim Chanin observed in June 2016: "There's been a 40 percent decline in complaints, there's been a decline in serious lawsuits, there's been a successful implementation of body cameras, there's been a decline in use of force . . . while arrests have gone up, indicating there's no de-policing."[5] Federal oversight was on a course to end within the year. But all that quickly changed in mid-June 2016 when the OPD's progress was overshadowed by a new scandal akin to the Riders' fiasco that originally resulted in that lengthy oversight.

The suicide of an OPD officer and accusations of a teenage prostitute prompted an ongoing investigation into alleged sexual misconduct with a minor by a number of men in local law enforcement agencies, including several OPD officers. Investigations have since also begun into unrelated accusations against some additional OPD officers. But external accountability is now the norm, not the exception that it was fifty years ago. Seven men now face serious charges. Although himself not the subject of any investigation, Chief Whent came under criticism for his handling of the OPD's internal investigation into the sexual misconduct charges. Whent tendered his resignation to allow Mayor Libby Schaaf to conduct a national search for a new police chief, even as she praised Whent for significant progress in achieving most of the reforms ordered by Judge Henderson. That commitment to reform is expected to continue under new leadership.

Figueroa notes that a key goal is to continue to expand the broad racial and ethnic mix of OPD recruits, but that requires perseverance: "Building diversity within the organization so that it reflects the community and the population they serve has been difficult for many law enforcement agencies around the country. We recruit in high schools. We are working as hard as we can, and one of the struggles and challenges in Oakland, in particular, has been . . . recruiting Oaklanders of color. . . . It's certainly something we're better at. There is much more diversity in the department than there was in the '70s."

Although the relationship of the OPD to its minority communities has improved over the decades in a number of respects, many in the black community remain critical of its record. Paul Figueroa acknowledges that "abuses have happened and abuses may likely occur in the future." Judge Henderson notes that the one thorny remaining issue among all the reforms he ordered is racial profiling. At his direction, experts at Stanford University conducted an independent study of the OPD; they analyzed 28,000 stops and two thousand body cam video clips of arrests during the 13-month period from April 1, 2013 to April 30, 2014.

In mid-June of 2016, after extensive review, the Stanford study produced more bad news just as the unrelated sex scandal was precipitating changes in the OPD's leadership. The study's results vindicated ongoing complaints of racial profiling. Although officers displayed little intentional discrimination, the researchers found major disparities in how the OPD treated black men even after adjusting for neighborhood crime rates — strong evidence of implicit bias. Among persons that police stopped but did not arrest, one in four black men were handcuffed compared to one in 15 white men. Black men were also four times as likely to be searched, despite no racial difference in the results of such searches. Stanford psychologist Jennifer Eberhardt led the study: "Racial disparities are real. As this research shows, differences exist in how police officers treated African Americans compared to those of other ethnic groups. . . . Transparency and data will set you free."[6]

Then newly appointed as acting Oakland Police Chief, Paul Figueroa welcomed the Stanford analysis for providing "a roadmap forward. . . . Oakland has already implemented many of the recommendations in the report and will move quickly to implement the remaining items." Psychologist Rebecca Hetey, who co-led the research, praised Figueroa's response: "We give credit to the Oakland Police Department. They have a rough path in this area but they're open to reimagining what policing is."[7]

The rough path forward is just beginning. What remains a serious problem in the OPD — one that is far from unique across the country — is a persistent macho subculture that Mayor Schaaf characterized as "toxic." Rashida Grinage, long-time leader of PUEBLO — an Oakland organization focused on police accountability — voiced similar harsh criticism. But Grinage also pointed out that the problem is not reflective of the entire department. When a reporter interviewed her in June after the sex scandal hit the headlines, Grinage empathized with other

OPD personnel who "really take their job seriously . . . [and] have to suffer this [negative] reputation through no fault of their own."[8]

As someone who came up through the ranks, Figueroa quickly decided that an outsider was far better suited to effectively oversee the department in a time of intense scrutiny and demand for major house-cleaning. Within days of his appointment, he resigned as acting chief and asked to be demoted.[9] The ramifications are still unfolding. As of this writing the OPD has no acting chief while Mayor Schaaf undertakes a several-month national search for a permanent leader. Efforts are also underway to ask the voters to amend the city charter to create a civilian police commission to oversee the OPD going forward.

Pastor Michael McBride, who has served on Department of Justice and White House task forces on racial justice, is among the OPD's critics impatient for results: "I don't care if it's implicit or explicit. I want bias gone. I want it managed, and I want people held accountable. And the people have the right to be able to live in a community where bias is not over-determining their lives."[10] Of greatest concern nationally is the statistic that black men, though only 6 percent of the population, constitute 40% of the unarmed people killed by police.[11]

There is much room for dialogue on how to best proceed. As Dallas Police Chief David Brown pointed out, we also have to realize as a society we often ask too much of our police — understaffing them and saddling them with unmet social work, parenting and drug abuse problems together with their law enforcement responsibilities. Meanwhile, the OPD's recent management should be credited for collaborating in exposing the implicit bias problems that clearly plague many other departments across the nation. Though it may take some time before Oakland's police-community relations reach the point where a monitor is no longer deemed necessary, Stanford Professor Hetey believes that the collaborative approach taken in the Stanford study can help many other police departments address their own racial profiling issues: "I think [the approach we took] will have a national impact."[12] The study includes fifty recommendations in its "Strategies for Change" that serve as a model not just for Oakland but for police departments elsewhere to review and evaluate their policies and procedures on a regular basis for disparate impact. California is at the forefront of this new approach; it now mandates collection of similar underlying data from police departments throughout the state.

The advent of body cams heralds greater transparency in how arrests take place — offering opportunities for scrutiny that have never before been available. The battle in the California legislature — as already underway in other states — is now over the timing and extent of public access to police recording data and to records of complaints about police misconduct. As the prospect looms of a new era of police-community accountability, it remains to be seen how many police departments will voluntarily collaborate on studies like that conducted by Stanford researchers in Oakland, knowing they risk faring poorly under a microscope. The approach taken under Judge Henderson's mandate is truly revolutionary. It seems likely that the U.S. Attorney General and federal courts will continue to be asked to play major roles in implementing any similar reforms in cities across the country.

* * * * *

Today, the recruitment policy of Alameda County is like that of the City of Oakland: "[to] establish a qualified and diverse candidate pool . . . which enables County departments to provide excellent public services."[13] In 1987, incoming Sheriff Charlie Plummer put in place tough new rules against "Cardinal Sins." When Plummer became Sheriff, the list of serious offenses potentially resulting in termination went well beyond employees caught taking bribes or using drugs. It included: "Making disparaging utterings or writing disparaging ethnic remarks, whether or not intended as humor; misrepresenting or lying in instances involving official County business, either orally or in writing; . . . engaging in any form of sexual harassment; this includes any unwanted comments or contact as defined in sexual harassment policy."[14]

Back on the day of Newton's release from prison in August of 1970, Sheriff Frank Madigan likened some "Free Huey" demonstrators to foxes who should be shot for raiding the chicken coop. Among the most amazing recent changes in the Sheriff's Office is the innovative

community work being done by African-American Deputy Sheriff Jinho
Ferreira. Besides his efforts to reach out to redirect juvenile offend-
ers in the county off the pipeline to prison, Ferreira is a cross-cultural
trainer for his own and other law enforcement agencies seeking to
improve their relationships with minority communities and to understand more about the Black Lives Matter movement. Ferreira's mother
is African-American and his father is from Brazil. Inspired by his father,
Ferreira learned Portugese from his Brazilian relatives and from books,
music and movies.

When he first showed up, many sheriff's departments would not
have considered Ferreira a good prospect in whom to invest their
resources. He was born in a rough section of West Oakland during
the height of the 1980s crack cocaine epidemic that devastated inner
city neighborhoods across the country. Not surprisingly, he wound up
with an arrest record. His parents divorced when he was seven and his
mother raised her three children on her own through the 1990s.

Jinho's mother taught him a passion for reading about black history.
But her full-time job made it difficult for her to keep a watchful eye on a
young teenager lured by life on the streets of West Oakland. Jinho idol-
ized infamous drug dealers and saw some of his buddies become runners.
But Ferreira also watched many friends and acquaintances die before
they reached adulthood and others wind up with long prison sentences.
Later, he became deeply affected when a childhood friend was ambushed
and killed while driving an armored car as a security guard. The friend
was Mexican-American; the suspect was black. The robbery had been set
up by his friend's work partner. Jinho and his mother came to the murder
trial to support the victim's family — never before had Ferreira's sense of
justice cried out for a black man to serve time behind bars.

With Mama Ferreira's strong encouragement, all three of her children went to college. Jinho inherited her work ethic: he became a juvenile hall counselor, wrote advertising copy and made the Dean's list at
San Francisco State University as a Black Studies major. Ferreira studied the 1968 Newton trial and read *Revolutionary Suicide* among other
influential books. He also polished his extraordinary musical talent. By
the time he graduated in 2004, Ferreira had already launched his own

political hip-hop/Latin rock band. The unique inter-racial trio Flypside defied easy categorization. It achieved its greatest success internationally — highlights included having two of their biggest hits — "Someday" and "Champion" — featured as theme songs at the 2006 and 2008 Olympics, and touring as the opening act for Snoop Dogg and the Black Eyed Peas. By 2009, the Oakland-based band had released two albums, starting with the hugely popular "We the People" and saw Flipsyde singles become commercial successes in film, video games and television.

Yet, to the surprise of friends and family, Ferreira (whose nickname is "The Piper") took a leave from the entertainment world in 2010 to enroll in the Alameda County Sheriff's Academy. Why? The Piper and his wife Dawn Williams Ferreira (an educator then studying for her Ph.D.) found themselves in a large crowd gathered outside Fruitvale Station in January of 2009 to vent their anger and frustration at the death of Oscar Grant III — yet another young black man killed by yet another white policeman. Never shy of the microphone, the renowned entertainer told a reporter that Oscar Grant symbolized too many minority kids who suffered from abusive policing. What Oakland needed were fewer police from the suburbs and more local recruits who understood and empathized with the community.[15]

When asked what Flypside planned to do to help, the Piper experienced an epiphany. The truth was that protest songs had limited reach; he realized he could have far greater impact in uniform than on stage. He decided to pay his way through the rigorous training. Skeptics expected him to fail in his efforts, but he graduated at the top of his class and, despite his background, got hired as a deputy by the Alameda County Sheriff's office. He has worked there ever since.

In 2012, Ferreira drew on his unique perspective on American justice to create his own play — *Cops and Robbers,* a fictionalized shooting incident in a warehouse involving an Oakland policeman and a crime suspect.[16] Ferreira plays 17 roles in that production, approaching the confrontation from all angles. He calls it, "a revolutionary look at the relationship between law enforcement, the media and the black community."[17] The play ends with viewers being left to determine for themselves — like the jury panel in the 1968 Newton trial — who was the aggressor, who was the victim, and to revisit their own concepts of right and wrong. Ferreira and his wife published a companion teaching guide to the phenomenally successful one-man show — *Cops and Robbers: The Past, The Present and the Future.* Their purpose is to engage kids raised in inner cities to focus on the thorny relationship their communities too often have with the police, and to encourage young people to join the effort to change that hostile pattern. As the Ferreiras say, "The time is now."[18]

* * * * *

The Alameda County District Attorney's Office has long enjoyed a reputation as one of the top district attorney's offices in the nation, dating back to when Earl Warren headed the office. Under Lowell Jensen, it was the first District Attorney's office in the country to have a victim/witness assistance program. By 2014, it would have more than 40 people who worked only with victims of crime, helping address the psycho-social impact of having been preyed upon. This staff focuses on the steps victims might take to try to heal themselves, as well as what protections the government can offer them from continued threats. The current District Attorney, Nancy O'Malley, is very proud of the department's four-decade history of offering those essential services.

It was O'Malley's mentor and predecessor, District Attorney Tom Orloff, who brought murder charges against BART policeman Johannes Mehserle in 2009. O'Malley notes:

> We have our own officer-involved shooting team that [does] separate and independent investigations any time a police officer uses a firearm and somebody dies as a result of that. And we do a thorough investigation to evaluate whether or not there is a crime that's committed. We look at what the law says and what the facts are. . . . [W]e have prosecuted other police officers for different crimes. . . . Since I have been here Officer Mehserle was the only one who got prosecuted [for murder] and I think that's relatively rare across the state, as well — still a rarity nationwide.

O'Malley, who took office in 2009 as the county's first female

District Attorney, remains among a small minority of women elected to that office across the country. Yet, by the time she graduated law school in 1983, more than half of her classmates were women. She also had female role models in the Alameda County District Attorney's office handling major felony trials. O'Malley got to know both Lowell Jensen and Ed Meese when they came back to visit the Department occasionally. Among Meese's anecdotes from the 1960s was how Huey Newton distinguished himself as a star pupil in Meese's blindly graded criminal law class. But the one and only time O'Malley saw Newton in court in the late 1980s was shortly before his death: "He was pretty strung out on drugs. . . . Crack cocaine had a very, very devastating impact on Oakland. And Huey . . . was brought in as someone who was selling drugs and looked . . . like somebody who had been abusing crack cocaine."

In March of 2009, O'Malley flew to Washington, D.C., to represent her office when President Obama honored the four officers murdered by ex-felon Lovelle Mixon. The names of the Oakland officers had just been inscribed on the wall of the national police officer memorial. Each May, Alameda County performs a similar tribute at its Memorial Wall. The City of Oakland also pays its respects; in the lobby of the Police Department, a plaque lists more than fifty officers killed in the line of duty in the city's history. Like her predecessors, every year since heading the District Attorney's office O'Malley has been invited to say a few words in praise of the work that they do: "I urge everyone to remember about officer safety, to keep the peace, and to honor those who died and gave up their lives in the line of duty. And Officer Frey's name is, of course, one of the officers whose name is inscribed on the wall." His daughter Kimberly Frey, now in her early fifties, regularly attends those ceremonies, still scarred by the loss of her father, who never lived to meet his two grandchildren who share his grin.[19]

Back in 1967, when John Frey died, O'Malley had been a young child also growing up in neighboring Contra Costa County where Frey had gone to school. O'Malley's father was a career prosecutor about to head the county office as its district attorney. She later came to know how the Oakland police and the Panthers were bitterly divided back then and how the black community mistrusted the white police. But she also realized when she joined the Alameda County District Attorney's office that residents of black communities suffer disproportionately as victims of violent crime.

Today, O'Malley sees a major focus by law enforcement in "building communities of trust. . . . The Oakland Police Department, my office, the District Attorney's office, the probation department, health care — all of the county agencies and all of the city offices — really focus on bringing equity to its citizens, to working towards reducing crime." These agencies have joined together on a pioneering program with Fania Davis's Restorative Justice for Oakland Youth and similar community organizations to reduce youth violence, suspensions and expulsions. Their aim is to break the school-to-prison pipeline in Oakland that historically led so often to a life of recidivism. O'Malley notes that the officials have also encouraged social activities to promote greater mutual trust: "We now have barbecues where the police officers go out and meet the community."

O'Malley sees many signs of success from this outreach. "We have the community who feel like they have trust and confidence in the police to come in and say, I think that you are not looking at this particular area of crime close enough." Her office also works with mothers whose sons were murdered in unsolved cases. They come to work with the police and her office in hopes of bringing the perpetrators to justice. "And that's the motivation of police officers in modern policing. The community-oriented policing that gets police out of their car and walking down the street and meeting the community is very apparent in Oakland and in all of our communities, and it's the same with my office. We're very engaged with our community to first prevent crime from happening."

O'Malley recognizes that, "Oakland still is identified as having one of the highest violent crime rates in the country. And yet at the same time we're all trying to balance providing services, providing opportunities, providing alternatives to crime and then addressing the violent crime, as well." She sees a direct correlation between the goals of local law enforcers and their hiring policies. "Look at the Oakland Police Department, it is very, very diverse. If you look at my office, it's very diverse. The police department and my office look like the communities we serve."

O'Malley is also the past President of California Women Lawyers (CWL) which Fay Stender helped found in the mid-1970s. Every year since 1982 CWL has given out a prestigious Fay Stender Award at a dinner celebrating women lawyers that quickly became a highlight of the annual meeting of the State Bar. It was representation of Huey Newton that launched Fay Stender as an internationally acclaimed criminal lawyer for social justice. The award goes to a "feminist attorney who, like Fay Stender, is committed to the representation of women, disadvantaged groups and unpopular causes, and whose courage, zest for life and demonstrated ability to effect change as a single individual make her a role model for women attorneys."[20] As much as O'Malley admires dedicated police officers who lost their lives, she greatly admires the late Fay Stender, too. "Fay Stender set that tone for advocating for an unpopular cause, standing firm, changing society, helping to change policy, and not getting a lot of recognition for it at the time that she was a strong advocate. And that's what we look for in the recipient of the award every year."

O'Malley notes that in 2009, the year she was CWL's president, the recipient of the award was someone from her own office, Sharmin Eshraghi Bock, who had become a leading advocate to increase public awareness of human trafficking. "People didn't recognize or didn't want to believe that what was happening in our society with our children was that they were being trafficked into sex slaves and sex trafficking. . . . And now my office is really seen as the leader in the country on our anti-human-trafficking efforts, both in child sex trafficking, in domestic trafficking, and in labor trafficking."

* * * * *

The Alameda County Public Defenders' office has long been recognized for the high caliber of its diverse staff. Like the District Attorney's office, its commitment to diversity has evolved enormously since Penny Cooper left it in 1969. In 2000 the County Board of

Supervisors appointed veteran Assistant Public Defender Diane Bellas the first woman Public Defender in Alameda County. Bellas appointed African-American office supervisor Brendon Woods to be the office-wide recruitment officer. In 2012, on Bellas's retirement, the Board of Supervisors appointed Woods the first African-American Public Defender in the county. Like all other Public Defenders' offices, its main challenge is a budget too small to address all the needs of its high caseload, but that is a different battle.

* * * * *

Among the causes still commanding the dedicated efforts of civil rights advocates in 2016 is guaranteeing criminal defendants a jury of one's peers. In the Supreme Court's 2015–16 term, at the request of the Southern Center for Human Rights, the high court reviewed an all-white Georgia jury who sentenced eighteen-year-old African-American Timothy Foster to death in 1987. After using challenges on all the potential black jury members, the prosecutor convinced a dozen white jurors to impose the death penalty to "deter other people out there in the projects."[21]

How did this happen a year after the landmark Supreme Court decision in *Batson* outlawed the practice of dismissing jurors based on race? The Constitution has never been interpreted to guarantee diverse juries, but only to preclude *eliminating* jurors based solely on race. So a jury of all one race — or sex for that matter — can result for a variety of reasons. But the sorry truth is that exclusion of blacks purely based on their race can still easily happen if the prosecutors do not act in good faith and the judges let them get away with racial prejudice.

When challenged, Foster's prosecutor acted as if the all-white composition of the jury was just happenstance. The challenge to this jury had legs on appeal only because the prosecutor's notes came to light years later, showing that every name of a black person on the jury panel had been circled before excusing them from the panel. A number of former prosecutors from across country were so appalled at the obvious racism documented in the *Foster* case that they wrote to the Supreme Court: "We recognize, and refuse to condone, the blatant unconstitutionality of the prosecutorial misconduct in this case."[22]

In its 7-to-1 reversal (Justice Thomas dissenting), the Supreme Court made no change in the standard that shields most peremptory challenges from review for lack of evidence of racial bias in their exercise. This issue remains of national significance today. An Equal Justice Initiative study in 2010 of eight states in the Deep South found a suspiciously high percentage of blacks kicked off juries by prosecutors as compared to prospective whites. A chapter in Michelle Alexander's *The New Jim Crow* discusses how the *Batson* decision has frequently been circumvented. When challenged, the prosecutors invariably invoke "race-neutral" reasons even when the explanations make no sense. Prosecutors share with each other "acceptable reasons for striking potential jurors, like body language, attitude and other factors," which sometimes reflect genuine concerns, but are also too often used to shield race-based decisions from judicial scrutiny.[23] While increasing numbers of prosecutors today welcome a cross-section of jurors — including Brooklyn's Ken Thompson and Alameda County's Nancy O'Malley — in many other jurisdictions racism in jury selection *still* prevails. In the wake of its decision in the *Foster* case, the Supreme Court has ordered lower courts to reexamine the record of three death penalty convictions in Alabama, Louisiana and Mississippi for evidence of intentional exclusion of black jurors.[24] If you are not at the table, you are on the menu.

* * * * *

Despite substantial progress in the last half century, Bryan Stevenson warns, "If we are not vigilant, if we are not pushing, if we don't articulate what the goal should be, we'll be having this conversation in another fifty years." As Dallas Police Chief David Brown underscored, the divide between police and minority communities must stop. Just before he left for the private sector, outgoing New York Police Commissioner William Bratton echoed Chief Brown's sentiment.

Other law enforcement leaders in major cities across country have done so as well. Shortly after news in August 2016 of the scathing federal report detailing the history of racist policing practices in Baltimore, Los Angeles Police Chief Charlie Beck wrote a joint op-ed piece in the *New York Times* with civil rights lawyer Connie Rice, a long-time police adversary. The pair described the positive results of collaboration under federal court supervision begun back in 2002 to achieve meaningful reforms of Los Angeles police practices. Those concerted efforts resulted in an experimental Community Safety Partnership unit designed to transform policing in Watts and other hotbeds of community discontent:

> Call it guardian policing, trust policing, problem-solving policing, relationship-based policing, community policing or partnership policing. We believed this approach could reduce bad policing, bolster law enforcement and increase public safety. We went out to prove it, and 15 years later, we think we have. ... We have much to do before most poor neighborhoods in Los Angeles see the Police Department through a lens of trust. But it is solid evidence that ... guardian policing is part of the solution to conflict between police and community. If it works for the housing projects of Los Angeles, it can work anywhere."[25]

The City of Oakland and the Oakland Museum of California are now partnering with former leaders of the Black Panther Party to revisit the issue of racial injustice that prompted the Party's formation — inviting the world to the Panthers' golden anniversary October 20–23, 2016, when the city will dedicate Bobby Hutton Grove at DeFremery Park. They want to both recognize the profound impact of the Panther Party over the past fifty years and also ask, "Where do we go from here for the next fifty years?"

I hope that this book and the companion documentary project, *American Justice On Trial: People v. Newton,* furthers this much-needed conversation. I invite you to follow the film project's progress on the web at www.americanjusticeontrial.com.

Certificate signed by Huey Newton and Bobby Seale given by the Panthers to lawyer Guy Saperstein in lieu of monetary payment for his legal work. The certificate is among the artifacts gathered for display in the Oakland Museum's 50th Anniversary Exhibit on the Panthers.

SOURCES

Individuals:

Many people graciously gave of their time for interviews and background information in person, by telephone and via e-mail for *The Sky's The Limit: People v. Newton, The Real Trial of the 20th Century?* [Regent Press, 2012] much of which material I have relied upon in this book as well. The sources include: Robert Blauner, Thomas Broome, Allan Brotsky, Malcolm Burnstein, Deborah Chase, Kathleen Cleaver, Kate Coleman, Penny Cooper, Fania Davis, Joan De La Sceaux, Peter Franck, Gordon Gaines, Ann Fagan Ginger, David Lance Goines, Brian Gluss, Milton Hare, Hon. Thelton Henderson, Hilde Stern Hein, Ezra Herndon, David Hilliard, Alex Hoffmann, David Horowitz, Howard Janssen, Don Jelinek, Hon. D. Lowell Jensen, Don Kerson, Ying Lee Kelley, Sandra Levinson, Michael Magbie, Marling Mast, Michael McCarthy, Jerrie Meadows, Melvin Newton, Hon. Marilyn Patel, William B. Patterson, Charles Plummer, Dru Stender Ramey, Robert Richter, Jae Scharlin, Bobby Seale, Dan Siegel, Hon. Richard Silver, Damon Silvers, Marvin Stender, Elise Stone, Peter Sussman, Hon. John Sutter (ret.), Hon. Jacqueline Taber, Michael Tigar, Morrie Turner, Karen Lee Wald, Doris Brin Walker, Doron Weinberg, David Wellman, John Wells, Jayne Williams and Philip Ziegler.

Special Collections:

Arc of Justice Productions, Inc., Oakland, California. Included in the text are quotes from new interviews of Newton trial participants and observers and of experts on criminal law, jury trials and civil rights by Director Robert Richter and myself as Co-Director for the Arc of Justice Productions, Inc. film project *American Justice on Trial: People v. Newton.* These interviews were conducted from July 2013 through February 2016, mostly in California, with two taking place in New York, one in St. Louis, Missouri, and one in Atlanta, Georgia. All direct quotations from the following individuals included in this book are from these interviews unless otherwise indicated in the notes below: Louis Armmond, Robert Blauner, James Brosnahan, John Burris, Kathleen Cleaver, Penny Cooper, Belva Davis, Leo Dorado, Emory Douglas, Paul Figueroa, Janice Garrett Forte, Mary Gallegos, Ann Fagan Ginger, Steve Hanson, David Harper, George Hart, Hon. Thelton Henderson, David Hilliard, Thomas Hofmann, David Horowitz, D. Lowell Jensen, Karen Jo Koonan, Melvin Newton, Nancy O'Malley, Bill Patterson, Seth Rosenberg, Barry Scheck, Bryan Stevenson, John Sutter, Morrie Turner and Doron Weinberg.

Black Panther Collection, archives of the African American Museum and Library, Oakland, California.

Department of Justice FBI FOIA Files: The Black Panther Party, Huey Newton, Fay Stender, Student Nonviolent Coordinating Committee.

Don Hausler, unpublished manuscript, *Blacks in Oakland 1852–1987,* Vol. 3, 113, 116. Oakland Public Library History Room.

Dr. Huey P. Newton Foundation, Inc. Collection 1968–1994, M864. California: Green Library Special Collections, Stanford University.

U.C. Berkeley Bancroft Library: Meiklejohn Civil Liberties Archives; Elsa Knight Thompson papers.

Private Collections:

Trial notes of Prof. Robert Blauner from *People v. Newton,* 1968; Peter Sussman collection of unpublished letters of Jessica Mitford; Melvin Newton scrapbook on the Newton trial.

Principal Newspaper and Periodical Sources:

American Civil Liberties Northern California News, Bay Area News Group. Berkeley Barb, Black Panther newspaper, *The Guardian, Los Angeles Times, Newsweek, New York Times, Oakland Post, Oakland Tribune, Ramparts* magazine, *San Francisco Chronicle, San Francisco Examiner, TIME, Wall Street Journal.*

Books:

Acker, James R., *Scottsboro and Its Legacy* (Westport, Connecticut: Praeger, 2008).

Alexander, M., *The New Jim Crow: Mass Incarceration in the Age of Color Blindness* (New York: New Press, 2010).

Anderson, T., *The Movement and the Sixties: Protest in America from Greensboro to Wounded Knee* (New York: Oxford Univ. Press, 1995).

Anthony, Earl, *Picking Up the Gun: A Report on the Black Panthers* (New York: The Dial Press, 1970).

_____ , *Spitting in the Wind: The True Story Behind the Violent Legacy of the Black Panther Party* (Malibu, California, Roundtable, 1990).

Aptheker, Bettina, *The Morning Breaks: The Trial of Angela Davis* (New York: International Publishers, 1975).

Armstrong, Gregory, *The Dragon Has Come* (New York: Harper & Row, 1974).

Auerbach, Jerold S., *Unequal Justice: Lawyers and Social Change in Modern America* (New York: Oxford Univ. Press, 1976).

Austin, Curtis, J., *Up Against the Wall* (Fayetteville: Univ. of Arkansas Press, 2006).

Avrich, Paul, *Sacco and Vanzetti: The Anarchist Background* (Princeton: Princeton Univ. Press, 1991).

Bingham, Clara, *Witness to the Revolution: Radicals, Resistors, Vets, Hippies and the Year America Lost Its Mind and Found Its Soul* (New York: Random House, 2016).

Bingham, Howard, *Black Panthers 1968* (Los Angeles: Ammo Books, 2009).

Bloom, Joshua, and Martin, Jr., Waldo, *Black Against Empire: The History and Politics of the Black Panther Party* (Berkeley: University of California Press, 2013).

Bradford, Amory, *Oakland's Not for Burning* (New York: David McKay, 1968).

Broussard, A. S., *Black San Francisco: The Struggle for Racial Equality in the West, 1900–1954* (Lawrence, Kansas: University of Kansas Press, 1993).

Brown, Elaine, *A Taste of Power: A Black Woman's Story* (New York: Anchor

Books, 1992).

Bugliosi, Vincent, and Gentry, Curt, *Helter Skelter: The True Story of the Manson Murders* (New York: W. W. Norton, 1974).

Burris, John, *Blue v. Black: Let's End the Conflict Between Cops and Minorities* (New York: St. Martin's Press, 1997).

Carr, James, *Bad: The Autobiography of James Carr* (Oakland, California: Nabat/AK Press, 2000).

Carroll, P. N., and Noble, D. W., *The Free and the Unfree: A Progressive History of the United States, 3d rev. ed.* (New York: Penguin Books, 2001).

Carson, C., Garrow, D. J., Gill, G., Harding, V., and Hine, D. C., *The Eyes on the Prize Civil Rights Reader* (New York: Penguin Books, 1991).

Carson, Clayborne, *In Struggle: SNCC and the Black Awakening of the 1960s* (Cambridge, Massachusetts: Harvard Univ. Press, 1981, 1995).

Churchill, W., and Vanderwall, J., *Agents of Repression: The FBI's Secret Wars Against the Black Panther Party and the American Indian Movement* (Boston: South End Press, 1988, 1990).

_____ , *The COINTELPRO Papers: Documents from the FBI's Secret War Against Dissidents* (Boston: South End Press, 1980).

Cleaver, Eldridge, *Target Zero: A Life in Writing* (New York: Palgrave Macmillan, 2006).

Clinton, Bill, *My Life* (New York: Alfred A. Knopf, 2004).

Collier, Peter, and Horowitz, David, *Destructive Generation: A Second Look at the Sixties* (New York: Summit Books, 1989).

Darrow, Clarence, *The Story of My Life* (New York: Da Capo, 1996 Davies, David R. (ed.), *The Press and Race* (Jackson, Mississippi: Univ. Press of Mississippi, 2001).

Davis, Belva, and Haddock, Vicki, *Never In My Wildest Dreams: A Black Woman's Life in Journalism* (San Francisco; Berrett-Koehler Publishers, Kindle Ed., 2010).

Dellums, R. V., and Halterman, H. L., *Lying Down with the Lions* (Boston: Beacon Press, 2000).

Dershowitz, A. M., *America on Trial: Inside The Legal Battles That Transformed Our Nation* (New York: Warner Books, 2004).

Dudziak, M. L., *Cold War Civil Rights* (Princeton, New Jersey: Princeton

Univ. Press, 2000).

Durden-Smith, Jo, *Who Killed George Jackson? Fantasies, Paranoia and the Revolution* (New York: Alfred A. Knopf, 1976).

Eberhardt, Jennifer L. (ed.), "Strategies for Change: Research Initiatives and Recommendations to Improve Police-Community Relations in Oakland, Calif." June 17, 2016, https://stanford.app.box.com/v/Strategies-for-Change.

Fanon, Frantz, *The Wretched of the Earth* (English translation: Constance Farrington, New York: Grove Press, 1963).

Foner, P. S., *The Black Panthers Speak* (Cambridge, Massachusetts: Da Capo Press, 1970).

Forbes, Flores, *Will You Die With Me? My Life in the Black Panther Party* (New York: Washington Square Press, 2006).

Foxworth, Marlin, and Gordon, Ralph, *The Black/White Divide . . . Still* (Berkeley: Regent Press, 2008).

Garry, Charles, and Goldberg, Arthur, *Streetfighter in the Courtroom: The People's Advocate* (New York: E. P. Dutton, 1977).

Geis, Gilbert, and Beinen, Leigh, *Crimes of the Century* (Boston: Northeastern Univ. Press, 1998).

Gilmore, Glenda Elizabeth, *Gender and Jim Crow: Women and the Politics of White Supremacy in North Carolina, 1896–1920* (Durham: Univ. of North Carolina Press, 1996).

Ginger, Ann Fagan, *Landmark Cases Left Out of Your Textbooks* (Berkeley: Meiklejohn Civil Liberties Institute, 2006).

——— , *Minimizing Racism in Jury Trials* (New York: National Lawyers Guild, 1969).

——— , *The Relevant Lawyers: Conversations out of court on their clients, their practice, their politics, their life style* (New York: Simon & Schuster, 1973).

Goodman, James, *Stories of Scottsboro* (New York: Pantheon Books, 1994).

Grant, Robert, and Katz, Joseph, *The Great Trials of the Twenties: The Watershed Decade in America's Courtrooms* (New York: Sarpedon, 1998).

Halperin, Mark, and Heileman, John, *Game Change: Obama and the Clintons, McCain and Palin, and the Race of a Lifetime* (HarperCollins Ebooks, 2010).

Hilliard, D., *Huey: Spirit of the Panther* (New York: Thunder's Mouth Press, 2006).

Hilliard, D., and Cole, L., *This Side of Glory* (New York: Little, Brown & Co, 1993).

Hinckle, W., *If You Have a Lemon, Make Lemonade* (New York: W. W. Norton & Co, 1973).

Horowitz, David, *Hating Whitey and Other Progressive Causes* (Dallas, Texas: Spence Publishing, 1999).

—————— , *Left Illusions: An Intellectual Odyssey* (Dallas, Texas: Spence Publishing, 2003).

—————— , *Radical Son: A Generational Odyssey* (New York: Touchstone, 1997).

Ifill, G., *The Breakthrough: Politics and Race in the Age of Obama* (New York: Anchor Books, 2009).

James, Joy, *The Angela Y. Davis Reader* (Malden, Massachusetts: Blackwell Publishers, 1998).

Jackson, George, *Blood in My Eye* (Baltimore: Black Classic Press, 1990).

—————— , *Soledad Brother: The Prison Letters of George Jackson* (Chicago: Lawrence Hill Books, 1994).

Jones, Charles E. (ed.), *The Black Panther Party [Reconsidered]* (Baltimore, Maryland: Black Classic Press, 1998).

Keating, Edward M., *Free Huey!* (Palo Alto, California: Ramparts Press, 1971).

Knappman, E. W., *Great American Trials From Salem Witchcraft to Rodney King* (Detroit, Michigan: Visible Ink Press, 1994).

Krassner, Paul, "Double Agent" http://www.emptymirrorbooks.com/thirdpage/doubleagent.html.

Lanahan, D. J., *Justice For All: Legendary Trials of the Twentieth Century* (Bloomington, Indiana: Author House, 2006).

Lee, Barbara, *Renegade for Peace and Justice: Barbara Lee Speaks for Me* (Landham, Maryland: Rowman & Littlefield, 2008).

Levine, M., McNamee, G., and Greenberg, D., *The Tales of Hoffman* (New York: Bantam Books, 1970).

Liberatore, Paul, *The Road to Hell: The True Story of George Jackson, Stephen Bingham, and the San Quentin Massacre* (New York: The Atlantic

Monthly Press, 1996).

Lukas, J. Anthony, *Big Trouble* (New York: Touchstone, 1997).

Major, Reginald, *Justice in the Round: The Trial of Angela Davis* (New York: Joseph Okpaku, 1973).

Mann, Eric, *Comrade George; an Investigation into the Life, Political Thought, and Assassination of George Jackson* (New York; Harper & Row, 1972, 1974).

Middleton, N., *The I.F. Stone's Weekly Reader* (New York: Vintage Books, 1953).

Minton, Robert, Jr. (ed.), *Inside: Prison American Style* (New York: Random House, 1971).

Mitford, Jessica, *A Fine Old Conflict* (New York: Vintage Books, 1956, 1977).

Moore, Gilbert, *Rage* (New York: Carroll & Graf, 1993).

_____ , *A Special Rage* (New York: Harper & Row, 1971).

Newton, H., and Blake, J. H., *Revolutionary Suicide* (New York: Harcourt, Brace, Jovanovich, 1973).

Newton, Huey, *To Die For the People* (New York: Random House, 1972).

Obama, Barack, *Dreams from My Father: A Story of Race and Inheritance* (New York: Three Rivers Press, 1995, 2004).

Ogletree, Charles J., Jr., and Sarat, Austin (eds.), *From Lynch Mobs to the Killing State: Race and the Death Penalty in America* (New York: New York Univ. Press, 2006).

Ogletree, Charles J., Jr. (ed.), *When Law Fails: Making Sense of Miscarriages of Justice* (New York: New York Univ. Press, 2009).

Olson, Keith W., *Watergate: The Presidential Scandal That Shook America* (Lawrence, Kansas: University of Kansas Press, 2003).

Pearson, Hugh, *The Shadow of the Panther* (New York: Perseus Books, 1995).

Pell, Eve (ed.), *Maximum Security: Letters from Prison* (New York: E. P. Dutton, 1972).

Radosh, Ronald, and Milton, Joyce, *The Rosenberg File* (New Haven: Yale Univ. Press, 2003).

Raiford, Leigh, *Imprisoned in a Luminous Glare: Photography and the African-American Freedom Struggle* (Chapel Hill: Univ. of North Carolina Press, 2011).

Remnick, David, *The Bridge: The Life and Rise of Barack Obama* (New York: Alfred Knopf, 2010).

Rhodes, Jayne, *Framing the Black Panthers: The Spectacular Rise of a Black Power Icon* (New York: The New Press, 2008).

Rhomberg, Chris, *No There There: Race, Class, and Political Community in Oakland* (Berkeley: Univ. of California Press, 2004).

Rosenfeld, Seth, *Subversives: The FBI's War on Student Radicals and Reagan's Rise to Power* (New York: Farrar, Straus & Giroux, 2012).

Russell, F., *Sacco and Vanzetti: The Case Resolved* (New York: Harper & Row, 1986).

Scheck, Barry, Neufeld, Peter Dwyer, Jim, *Actual Innocence: Five Days to Execution, and Ot, and her Dispatches from the Wrongly Convicted* (New York: Doubleday, 2000).

Seale, Bobby, *Seize the Time: The Story of the Black Panther Party and Huey P. Newton* (New York: Black Classic Press, 1970, 1991).

Stone, Irving, *Clarence Darrow for the Defense* (New York: Signet Books, 1941, 1969).

Sussman, P. Y. (ed.), *Decca: The Letters of Jessica Mitford* (New York: Alfred A. Knopf, 2006).

Tackwood, Louis., and The Citizens Research and Investigation Committee, *The Glasshouse Tapes, The Story of an Agent-Provocateur and the New Police-Intelligence Complex* (New York: Avon, 1973) 114.

Temkin, Moshik, *The Sacco-Vanzetti Affair* (New Haven, Connecticut: Yale University Press, 2009).

Timothy, Mary, *Jury Woman: The Story of the Trial of Angela Y. Davis— written by a member of the jury* (San Francisco: Glide Publications, 1974,1975).

Uelmen, Gerald., *Lessons from the Trial: The People v. O. J. Simpson* (Kansas City, Missouri: Andrews and McMeel, 1996).

Wilson, T., *Headline Justice: Inside the Courtroom—The Country's Most Controversial Trials* (New York: Thunder's Mouth Press, 1996).

Winkler, Adam, *Gunfight: The Battle Over the Right to Bear Arms in America* (New York: W. W. Norton, Kindle edition, 2013.)

The Whole World's Watching: Peace and Social Justice Movements of the 1960s & 1970s (Berkeley: Berkeley Art Center Association, 2001).

Web Sources:

(Unless otherwise noted, all web sources were accessible as of September 12, 2016.)

Alameda County Sheriff's Office, https://www.alamedacountysheriff. org. Alexander, Michelle, "Obama's America and the New Jim Crow: The Recurring Racial Nightmare, The Cyclical Rebirth of Caste," http://nathaniel turner.com/obamasamericaandnewjim crow.htm.

"Analysis of the O. J. Simpson Murder Trial: Time to Go Home " Crime Library truTV.com: Actuality.http:// www.trutv.com/li [accessed June 14, 2011].

Anderson, Gene, "Our Oakland.net.," http://blog.ouroakland.net/ Associated Press, "Supreme Court orders new look at race of jurors in three convictions," *New Orleans Times Picayune*, June 21, 2016, http://s.nola.com/02yk3te.[accessed June 22, 2016].

"Austin Criminal Defense Lawyer" www.austincriminalde fenselawyer.com.Austin Criminal Defense Lawyer; www. austincriminaldefenselawyer.com. http:// www. austincriminaldefenselawyer.com/2010/04/07/the-bernie-goetz- story -25-years- later.html. [accessed June 14-15, 2011].

Bass, Jack, "Documenting the Orangeburg Massacre," Nieman Report. nie manreports.org/articles/documenting-the- orangeburg-massacre.

Batt, Marissa N., "*Ms. Magazine* | Just Verdicts? History of Women and Jury Service." Ms. Magazine Online, http:// www.msmagazine. com/summer2004/justver-dicts.asp.

"Biography of Richard Aoki, The Asian-American Black Panther," http://racerelations.about.com/od/trailblazers/a/Biography- Of-Richard-Aoki-The-Asian-American-Black-Panther.htm.

Briker, Jason, "Rosenberg Executions." Facts On File Online Databases, http://2facts.es.vrc.scoolaid.net/icah_story. aspx?PIN=haa00001190.

Burris, John L., *Blue vs. Black*, http://www.johnburrislaw.com.

California Women Lawyers, "Fay Stender," http://www.cwl.org/about_ cwl/fay_stender.aspx.

Coleman, Kate, "Elmer 'Geronimo' Pratt: The Untold Story of the Black

Panther Leader, Dead At 63," *The New Republic*, June 27, 2011,
https://newrepublic.com/article/90735/black-panther-geron-
imo-pratt-murder-conviction-prison-huey-newton.

_____"The Party's Over, " Center for Investigative Reporting,
http://cironline.org/reports/partys-over-1276.

Crime Magazine, "The Scottsboro Boys: Jim Crow on Trial," http://
crimemagazine. com/scottsboro-boys-jim-crow-trial.

Crouch, Stanley. "The Joy of Goetz." New York http://nymag.com/
nymetro/news/anniversary/35th/n_8601/.

FBI, "COINTELPRO." What Really Happened, http://www.
whatreallyhappened.com/RANCHO/POLITICS/
COINTELPRO/COINTELRPO-FBI.docs.html.

Feinman, Mark S., "The New York City Transit Authority in the 1980s,"
http://www.nycsubway.org/wiki/The_New_York_Transit_
Authority_in_the_1980s.

Ferreira, Dawn, and Ferreira, Jinho, *Cops and Robbers: The Past,
The Present, The Future* (Amazon 2014), dedication, http://
www.amazon.com/ Cops-Robbers-Past-Present-Future/
dp/0991533402.

Ferreira, Jinho, "Cops and Robbers," http://themarsh.org/cops_and_
robbers/jinho-the-piper-ferreira Interview: https:///www.you-
tube.com/watch?v=Wu-NSij9wDk.

"Flipsyde" http://flipsyde.com/about/.

Flynn, Dan, "Panther Leader Seale Confesses, "*Front Page*, April
23, 2002, http://archive.front- pagemag.com/read Article
.aspx?ARTID=24216.

Fox News, "McVeigh Considered Assassination of Reno, Other Officials,"
http://www.foxnews.com/story/2001/04/27/mcveigh-consid-
ered-assassination-reno-other-officials.html.

Freeman, Jo, "Social Protest in the Sixties," http://www.jofreeman.
com/sixtiesprotest/ sixties.htm.

Frontline, "Two Nations of Black America," PBS, Frontline http://
www.pbs.org/PBS, "Two Nations of Black America," http://
wwww.pbs.org/wgbh/pages/frotnline/shows. Race.interviews/
ecleaver.htmlwgbh/pages/frontline/shows/race/interviews/

ecleaver.html.

Garay, Ronald, "Watergate," The Museum of Broadcast Communications, www. museum.tv/eotv/watergate.htm.

Gerstein, Josh, "Hillary Clinton's Radical Summer: A Season of Love and Leftists," *New York Sun*, Nov. 26, 2007, www.nysun.com/ national/hillary-clintons -radical-summer/66933/.

Griffey, Trevor, "When celebrated activist turns out to be informant: making sense of Richard Aoki's FBI file," May 5, 2012, http:// www.truth-out.org/news/item/12555-when-celebrated-activist-turns-out-to-be-informant-making-sense-of-richard-aokis-fbi-file.

Hanlon, Gregg, "Police Chief David Brown on Dallas Ambush of Officers: 'All I Know Is This Must Stop,'" http://www.people.com/ article/dallas-ambush-police-chief-david-brown-this-must-stop.

Hennessey, Kathleen, "Obama asks Americans not to fear a return to a dark past," Associated Press, July 10, 2016, http://www. seattlepi. com/news/texas/article/Obama-to-take-questions-on-Dallas- attack-race-8349610.php [accessed July 10, 2010].

"The History Makers," The HistoryMakers.com – African American history archive, www.thehistorymakers.com.

Hoffman, Abbie, "Conspiracy in the Streets" Haymarket Books, http://www.haymarketbooks.org/product_info. php?products_id=1187.

Hoffman, Jan, "Goetz Defense Opens, Calls Jimmy Breslin and a Psychiatrist, Then Closes," New York Times, http://www.nytimes. com/1996/04/18/nyregion/goetz-defense-opens-calls-jimmy-breslin-and-a-psychiatrist-thencloses.html.

Iaconangelo, David, "What Oakland Police's 'Implicit Bias' could mean for police reform, *Christian Science Monitor*, June 16, 2016. http:// www.csmonitor.com/.

"Impeachment: Richard Nixon." The History Place. http:// www. historyplace.com/unitedstates/impeachments/ nixon.htm.

Kahn, Jeffery, "Ronald Reagan launched political career using the Berkeley campus as a political target," University of California, Berkeley, http://www.berkeley.edu./news/media/releases/2004/06/08_reagan.shtml.

Kane, Will, "Sean Whent named Permanent Oakland Police Chief," May
     14, 2014," *SF Gate*, http://www.sfgate.com/bayarea/article/Sean-
     Whent-named-permanent-Oakland-police-chief-5477982.php.

King, Jamilah, "Why Do Progressive Activists Become FBI Informants,"
     Colorlines, Sept. 13, 2012, http://www.colorlines.com/articles/
     why-do-progressive-activists-become-fbi-informants-its-complicated.

King, Jr., Martin Luther, "Beyond Vietnam: A Time To Break
     Silence," April 4, 1967. [Full speech   www.youtube.com/
     watch?v=OC1Ru2p8OfU].

Laird, Lorelei, "Study finds a 'gavel gap' between diversity of judges
     and that of the populations they serve," *ABA Journal*, June 23,
     2016, www. abajournal.com.

Linder, Douglas O., "Famous Trials" School of Law University of Mis-
     souri–Kansas City, http://law2.umkc.edu/faculty/projects/FTri-
     als/ftrials.htm.

Linderman, Juliet, "1 year after Freddie Gray, police work to heal
     city's wounds" Live 5 News, Balitomore, Maryland, April 10,
     2016, http://www.live5news. com/story/31686177/1-year-after-
     freddie-gray-police-work-to- heal-citys-wounds.

Lyall, Sarah, "N.A.A.C.P. Leader Seeks Federal Case On Goetz-
     New York Times" New York Times. http://www.nytimes.
     com/1987/06/20/ nyregion/naacp-leader-seeks-federal-case-on-
     goetz.html.

Madison, Lucie, "Dem Rep Bobby Rush escorted from House floor
     for wearing hoodie in honor of Trayvon Martin," CBS News, March
     28, 2012, http://www.cbsnews.com/news/dem-rep-bobby-rush-
     escorted-from-house-floor-for-wearing-hoodie-in-honor-of-trayvon-
     martin/http://.

McClain, Dani, "Black Lives Matter Was Born on Twitter – Will it Die
     There?" *The Nation*, April 19, 2016, thenation.com/article/
     black-lives-matter-was-born-on-twitter-will-it-die-there.

"The Militia Movement – Extremism in America" ADL: Fighting Anti-
     Semitism, Bigotry and Extremism, http://archive.adl.org/learn/
     ext_us/militia_m.html.

Mullins, Curtis, "Ruchell Cinque Magee – Political Prisoner" It's About

Time – Black Panther Party Legacy & Alumni 45th Year Reunion http://www.itsabouttimebpp.com/Political_Prisoners/Release_Ruchell_Cinque_Magee.html.

"My Grandfather's Execution", WBUR FM. May 7, 2010, http://www.wbur.org/npr/126539134; link to Radio Diaries, "Willie McGee and the Traveling Electric Chair."

NBC News Poll: 10 years after Simpson verdict – Dateline NBC. msnbc.com. http://www.msnbc.msn. com/id/5139346/.

The Negro in Chicago: A Study of Race Relations and A Race Riot, Chicago Commission on Race Relations, Chicago, Illinois: University of Chicago Press, 1922).

"New Book on McVeigh Makes Him a Martyr, Victim's Mother Says," *LAT,* March 30, 2001, http://articles.latimes.com/2001/mar/30/ news/mn-44634.

Nittle, Nadra Karim, "Biography of Richard Aoki, The Asian-American Black Panther," January 8, 2016, http://racerelations.about.com/od/trailblazers/a/Biography-Of-Richard-Aoki-The-Asian-American-Black-Panther.htm.

Occupational Health & Safety, "Fewer Officers Killed in Line of Duty in 2008," December 31, 2008, https://ohsonline.com/Articles/2008/12/31/31-Fewer-Police-Officers-Killed-in-Line-of-Duty-in-2008.aspx.

"Oklahoma City Police Department Alfred Pi Murrah Building Bomb- ing After Action Report," Oklahoma City Police Dept., https://www.ok.gov/OEM/documents/Bombing%20After%20Action%20 Report.pdf.

Obeidallah, Dean, "Trump — 'Call Oregon Siege Terrorism,'" *CNN*, January 5, 2016, http://www.cnn.com/2016/01/05/opinion/obeidallah-oregon-trump-terrorism/index.html. App_C.pdf.

Pacifica radio, Huey P. Newton funeral transcripts, KPFA, http://www.lib.berkeley.edu/MRC/newtonfuneraltranscripts.html.

Parker, Clifton B., "Stanford big data study finds racial disparities in Oakland, California, police behavior, offers solutions," http://news.stanford.edu/2016/06/15/stanford-big-data-study-finds-racial-disparities-oakland-calif-police-behavior-offers-solutions/

Parks, Sheri, "Black women's cries that roused the world," *Washington Post,* November 21, 2010, http://www.washingtonpost.com/wp- dyn/content/article/2010/11/19/AR2010111906689.html.

Prince, Richard, "What if the 'Militants' Were Not White," Jan. 27, 2016, Maynard Institute, http://mije.org/richard- prince/what-if-militants-were-blackkcfr_App_C.pdf.

Pyle, Richard, "50 years later Rosenberg brother admits lie," *The Berkeley Daily Planet.* http://www.berkeleydaily- planet.com/issue/2001-12-06/article/8732?status=301.

Report of the Select Committee to Study Governmental Operations with Respect to Intelligence Activities, United States Senate ("The Church Committee Report"), https://archive.org/details/finalreportofsel01unit.

Rosenfeld, Seth, "Richard Aoki, Man Who Armed Black Panthers, was FBI Informant" (video) August 20, 2012, updated October 20, 2012, http://www.huffingtonpost.com/2012/08/20/richard-aoki_n_1812167.html.

Rosenmann, Alexandra, "Gun Rights, Police Brutality and the Case of the Century," AlterNet, July 7, 2016, http://withinwww.alternet.org/civil-liberties/gun-rights-police-brutality-and-case-century-video. "The San Francisco State College Strike Collection," J. Paul Leonard Library, http://library.sfsu.edu/sf-state-strike-collection.

Southern Poverty Law Center Report, "Hate groups increase ranks in 2015," SPLC Report, Spring 2016, Vol. 46, Activities, https://www.splcenter.org/news/2016/02/17/splcs-intelligence-report-amid-year-lethal-violence-extremist-groups-expanded-ranks-2015.

"Stanford Study Finds Oakland Cops Practicing Racial Profiling," June 16, 2016, http://sanfrancisco.cbslocal.com/2016/06/16/stanford-study-finds-oakland-cops-practicing-racial-profiling.

"Study slams troubled Oakland police department for racial bias," PBS, June 15, 2016, http://www.pbs.org/video/2365784451/.

Thomas, Robert McGill, Jr., "Lionel Wilson, 82, A Mayor of Oakland for Three Terms," *New York Times,* Jan. 31, 1998. http://www.nytimes.com/1998/01/31/us/ lionel-wilson-82-a-mayor-of-oakland-for-three-terms.html.

Thompson, Larry D., "How America Tolerates Racism in Jury Selection," October 30, 2015, http://digitalcommons.law.uga.edu/fac_pm/228/.

TIME, "The Nation: Odyssey of Huey Newton", Nov. 13, 1978, http://content.time.com/time/magazine/article/0,9171,946144,00.html.

"Professor on Ice," TIME, Sept. 27, 1968. http://www.time.com /time/magazine/article/0,9171,902310,00.html.

"Truman Library Desegregation of the Armed Forces Online Research File," Harry S. Truman Library and Museum, http://www.trumanlibrary.org/whistlestop /study_collections/desegregation/large/index.php?action=chronology. (Univ. of Washington Press 1982).

"Waco Siege: The Final Assault," Museum Stuff. Com, http://www.museumstuff.com/learn/topics/Waco_ Siege::sub::The_ Final_ Assault.

Weir, Stan, "Oakland: The Last General Strike," November 5, 2005, http:// libcom.org/library/oakland-general-strike-stan-weir; http:// socialistworker.org/2011/12/12/the-last-oakland-general-strike.

Weiss, Joanna, "How Obama and the radical became news – The Boston Globe." Boston.com http://www.boston.com/news/nation/arti- cles/2008/04/18/how_obama_and_the_radical_became_news/.

Wing, Nick, "Here's How The Nation Responded When A Black Militia Group Occupied A Government Building," *Huffington Post*, January 6, 2016 (updated Jan. 9, 2016), http://www.huffingtonpost.com/entry/black-panthers-california-1967_us_568accfce4b014efe0db2f40.

Zirin, Dave, "Dave Zirin: An Interview with John Carlos" Counter-Punch: http://www.counter- punch.org/2003/11/01/an-interview-with-john-carlos/.

Zuru, Deena, "Beyoncé gets political at Super Bowl, pays tribute to 'Black Lives Matter'", CNN, http://www.cnn.com/2016/02/08/politics/beyonce-super-bowl-black-lives-matter/index.htm.

Journal Articles and Pamphlets:

"America: 1968-2015; What has changed, what hasn't?" *TIME* cover
    story, May 11, 2015.

Cleaver, Eldridge," Newton On Trial" *Ramparts*, Fall 1968.

Frankfurter, Felix, "The Case of Sacco and Vanzetti," *The Atlantic
    Monthly*, March 1927.

Palmer, L. F., "Out to Get the Panthers" *The Nation*, July 28, 1969, 80.
    Pleskan, Shirl, and Marsh, Matt. "It's Not How You Draw; It's
    What You Draw: An Interview with David Lance Goines" *Pressing
    Times* 7, no. 2 (2006).

"Report from Black America." *Newsweek*, June–July 1969.

Rosebury, Celia, "Black Liberation on Trial: The Case of Huey
    Newton," *The People's World*, Summer 1968. Reprint by the
    Bay Area Committee to Defend Political Freedom, Berkeley,
    California, 1968, from articles originally appearing during the
    summer of 1968 in *The People's World*. Archives of the Oakland,
    California African-American Museum and Library, Black
    Panther Collection.

Stern, Sol, "The Call of the Black Panthers," *New York Times Magazine*,
    August 6, 1967, 11.

Wald, Karen, "Jury is selected for Newton trial," *The Guardian*, August
    3, 1968.

ENDNOTES

Unless otherwise noted all web sources were accessible as of September 12, 2016.

ABBREVIATIONS USED IN THE NOTES

BB   *The Berkeley Barb*

BP   **The Black Panther newspaper**

HPN   **Dr. Huey P. Newton Foundation, Inc. Collection, 1968–1994, M864, Green Library Special Collections, Stanford University, Series**

LAT   *The Los Angeles Times*

NY   *The New York Times*

OP   *The Oakland Post*

OT   *The Oakland Tribune*

SFC   *The San Francisco Chronicle*

SFE   *The San Francisco Examiner*

AMERICAN JUSTICE ON TRIAL, 1968--2016 [Author's Note]

1. Alexandra Rosenmann, "Gun Rights, Police Brutality and the Case of the Century," Alternet, July 7, http://www.alternet.org/civil-liberties/gun-rights-police-brutality-and-case-century-video.

2. Kathleen Hennessey, "Obama asks Americans not to fear a return to a dark past," Associated Press, July 10, 2016, http://bigstory.ap.org/article/ad7321415b1d4e6a91d2f98e2f9ba81d/obama-take-questions-dallas-attack-race-relations.

3. Greg Hanlon, "Police Chief David Brown on Dallas Ambush of Officers: 'All I Know Is This Must Stop,'" *People: True Crime,* http://www.people.com/article/dallas-ambush-police-chief-david-brown-this-must-stop, (quoting Dallas Police Chief David Brown. July 7, 2016).

 The Bill Patterson quote, like other unfootnoted quotes in this book, is from his interview for the film project "American Justice on Trial: People v. Newton." See Special Collections.

INTRODUCTION

1. Douglas Linder, "Famous Trials: The Oklahoma City Bombing & The Trial of Timothy McVeigh" (2006) http://law2.umkc.edu/faculty/projects/ftrials/mcveigh/mcveighaccount.html.

2. "New Book on McVeigh Makes Him a Martyr, Victim's Mother Says," *LAT,* March 30, 2001, http://articles.latimes.com/2001/mar/30/news/mn-

44634 ("Terrorism: 'Every person who buys this book is an accomplice to murder,' says woman whose 4-year-old died in Oklahoma City").

3.   "Hate groups increase ranks in 2015," SPLC Report, Southern Poverty Law Center, Spring 2016, Vol 46, No. 1, 1.

4.   Dean Obeidallah, "Trump — 'Call Oregon Siege Terrorism'" *CNN*, January 5, 2016,http://www.cnn.com/2016/01/05/opinions/obeidallah-oregon-trump-terrorism/index.html; Richard Prince, "What if the "Militants" Were Not White," Jan. 27, 2016 , Maynard Institute, http://mije.org/richardprince/what-if-militants-were-black.

5.   Prince, *supra, note 4,* "What if the 'Militants' Were Not White?" Jan. 27, 2016, Maynard Institute, http://mije.org/richardprince/what-if-militants-were-black.

6.   Nick Wing, "Here's How the Nation Responded When a Black Militia Group Occupied a Government Building," *The Huffington Post,* January 6, 2016 (updated Jan. 9, 2016), http://www.huffingtonpost.com/entry/black-panthers-california-1967_us_568accfce4b014efe0db2f40.

7.   Dave Zirin, "The Living Legacy of Mexico City: Interview with John Carlos," Counterpunch, October 31, 2003, http://www.counterpunch.org/2003/11/01/an-interview-with-john-carlos/. The pair of American athletes were later honored with a 22-foot statue erected in 2005 at their alma mater, San Jose State University and the 2008 ESPY Arthur Ashe Courage Award. [See https://www.flickr.com/photos/cherrilakey/54108623/ and "Salute at ESPYs: Smith and Carlos to receive Arthur Ashe Courage Award'" May 29, 2008, espn.go.com/espn/news/story?id=3417048.

8.   Deena Zuru, CNN, "Beyoncé gets political at Super Bowl, pays tribute to 'Black Lives Matter'," http://www.cnn.com/2016/02/08/politics/beyonce-super-bowl-black-lives-matter/.

9.   Occupational Health & Safety, "Fewer Officers Killed in Line of Duty in 2008," December 31, 2008, https://ohsonline.com/Articles/2008/12/31/31-Fewer-Police-Officers-Killed-in-Line-of-Duty-in-2008.aspx.

10. SFC, March 28, 2009, A11.

11. *Ibid.*

12. David Von Drehle, *TIME* magazine, May 11, 2015, cover story, "America 1968, 2015, What Has Changed, What Hasn't? The Roots of a Riot," 34.

13. Jim Salter, "Judge Approves Ferguson Deal," Associated Press, *OT* April 20, 2016, A4.

14. Amory Bradford, *Oakland's Not for Burning* (New York: David McKay Company 1968) 2.

15. *Ibid.,* 9.

16. Report Select Committee to Study Governmental Operations with respect to Intelligence Activities, United States Senate ("The Church Committee Report"), http://www.intelligence.senate.gov/resources/intelligence-related-commissions); see also Ward Churchill and Jim Vander Wall, *The*

COINTELPRO Papers: Documents from the FBI's Secret War Against Dissidents (Boston: South End Press, 1980).

17. Seth Rosenfeld, *Subversives: The FBI's War on Student Radicals, and Reagan's Rise to Power* (New York: Farrar, Straus & Giroux, 2012).

18. Leigh Raiford, *Imprisoned in a Luminous Glare: Photography and the African-American Freedom Struggle* (Chapel Hill: North Carolina Univ. Press, 2011), 119.

19. Jamil Abdullah Al-Amin (a.k.a. H. Rap Brown), "Discover the Networks. org, A Guide to the Political Left," http://www.discoverthenetworks.org/ individualProfile.asp?indid=1308.

20. Clayborne Carson, *In Struggle: SNCC and the Black Awakening of the 1960s* (Cambridge, Massachusetts: Harvard Univ. Press, 1981, 1995).256 and fn. 29.

21. Huey P. Newton, "In Defense of Self Defense," *BP,* June 20, 1967, 3-4.

22. Sol Stern, "The Call of the Black Panthers," *NYT* Magazine, August 6, 1967, 11, 63.

23. "Lasting Rift in American Society," *The Wall Street Journal,* Monday April 8, 1968, 1.

24. Ekwueme Michael Thelwell, Introduction to Moore, *Rage* (New York: Carroll & Graff , 1993) xi.

25. Huey Newton interview, *Eyes on the Prize: The American Civil Rights Movement 1954–1985,* "American Experience Blackside," http://www.pbs.org/wgbh/ amex/eyesontheprize/about/pt_203.html.

26. "Nation's Life at Stake," *BB,* July 19–25, 1968, 3.

27. Edward Jay Epstein, "The Black Panthers and the Police: A Pattern of Genocide?" *The New Yorker,* Feb. 13, 1971, http://www.edwardjayepstein. com/archived/panthers.htm.

28. Joshua Bloom and Waldo E. Martin, Jr., *Black Against Empire: The History and Politics of the Black Panther Party* (Berkeley: University of California Press, 2013) 263, quoting an editorial of the *Chicago Daily Defender.*

29. Curtis J. Austin, *Up Against the Wall* (Fayetteville, Arkansas: University of Arkansas Press, 2006), 92 and fn. 8.

30. Eugene Rostow, Dean, Yale Law School, Introduction to Edward Bennett Williams, *One Man's Freedom* (New York: Atheneum, 1962) ix.

31. Ann Fagan Ginger (ed.) *Minimizing Racism in Jury Trials: The Voir Dire Conducted by Charles R. Garry in People of California v. Huey P. Newton* (New York: National Lawyers Guild, 1969).

32. J. Anthony Lukas, *Big Trouble* (New York: Simon & Schuster Touchstone Books, 1997), 634.

33. Robert Kirsch, "Black Panther Assignment," *LAT*, May 17, 1971, E10.

34. Moore, *Rage, supra,* back-cover quote.

35. Jane Rhodes, *Framing the Black Panthers: The Spectacular Rise of a Black Power* Icon (New York: The New Press, 2007), 3.

36. "Universes: The Revolution Will Be Live!!!! Among its many posted

reviews on its web page "What They Say" is a quote from former Panther Party Chairman Bobby Seale: "This play is . . . crucial to an understanding of that turbulent time . . . This play captures us . . . trying to make change." http://www.universes.us/page11/page18/index.html.

37. Professors Alan Dershowitz and Gerald Uelmen—both members of the O. J. Simpson defense "dream team"— compiled separate, overlapping lists of 40 top trials of the 20th century. Neither listed the Newton trial. Nor did journalist Theo Wilson, *Headline Justice: Inside the Courtroom — The Country's Most Controversial Trials* (New York: Thunder's Mouth Press, 1996) or Daniel J. Lanahan, *Justice for All: Legendary Trials of the Twentieth Century* (Bloomington, Indiana: Author House, 2006). Prof. Douglas Linder of the University of Missouri launched a website "Famous Trials" that also excluded the Newton trial from his top picks, http://law2.umkc.edu/faculty/projects/ftrials/ftrials2printable.htm. A 1999 NBC poll on "the" trial of the 20th century also left the Newton trial off the list. *Great American Trials: From Salem Witchcraft to Rodney King* (Detroit: Visible Ink Press, 1994) notes that the Newton trial was one where the "potential jury's racial balance [was] central to the [Newton defense] trial strategy" and represented "one of the most politically charged trials of its era." But the editors found the 1969 Chicago Seven Trial more significant. Other authors disagreed. In *Destructive Generation: A Second Look at the Sixties* (New York: Summit Books, 1989), David Horowitz and Peter Collier noted that the 1968 Newton trial provided the model for the Chicago Seven trial. Ann Fagan Ginger cites the Newton trial in a 2006 handbook as among forty plus *Landmark Trials Left Out of Your Textbooks* (Berkeley: Meiklejohn Civil Liberties Institute, 2006). Prof. Bryan Stevenson teaches the Newton trial as one of three key 20th century cases focused on racism (along with the Scottsboro Boys and the O. J. Simpson trial).

38. *TIME* magazine cover story, May 11, 2015.

1. FREE HUEY NOW!

1. Earl Anthony, *Spitting in the Wind: The True Story Behind the Violent Legacy of the Black Panther Party* (Malibu, California Roundtable Publishing, 1990) 41, citing his 1970 book *Picking Up the Gun: A Report on the Black Panthers* (New York: The Dial Press, 1970).

2. Anthony, *Spitting in the Wind, supra*, 40.

3. See diagram in Douglas Linder, "The Trials of the Scottsboro Boys", http://law2.umkc.edu/faculty/projects/ftrials/scottsboro/SB_train.html.

4. Ruby Bates, the younger of the two prostitutes, first corroborated her companion Victoria Price's story and later recanted. "The Scottsboro Boys: Jim Crow on Trial," *Crime Magazine, An Encyclopedia of Crime,* July 13, 2009, http://www.crimemagazine.com/scottsboro-boys-jim-crow-trial.

5. James Goodman, *Stories of Scottsboro* (New York: Pantheon Books, 1994), 16.

6. James R. Acker, *Scottsboro and Its Legacy* (Westport, Ct.: Praeger Publishing, 2008), 26; see also David Aretha, *The Trial of the Scottsboro Boys*

(Greensboro, North Carolina: Morgan Reynolds Publishing, 2008).

7.   Irving Stone, *Clarence Darrow for the Defense* (New York: Doubleday & Co. Signet Books, 1941, 1969) 559.

8.   Linder, "Famous Trials: The Scottsboro Boys," "Excerpts from the summation of Wade Wright," http://law2.umkc.edu/faculty/projects/FTrials/scottsboro/wr-summations.html.

9.   F. Raymond Daniell, "Roosevelt Is Asked to Intervene to Protect Scottsboro Negroes; Warning of 'Massacre' of Seven Prisoners and Their Lawyers at Decatur (Ala.) Coart Today, Defense Counsel Wire President a Plea to Obtain State Troops, "ASK ROOSEVELT AID IN ALABAMA CASE" *NYT*, Nov. 20, 1933, 1.

10. In 1976, Alabama Governor George Wallace pardoned Clarence Norris, the last of the Scottsboro Boys. In 2013, three others received posthumous pardons from the state.

11. Sheri Parks, "Black women's cries that roused the world" *Washington Post,* November 21, 2010, http://www.washingtonpost.com/wp-dyn/content/article/2010/11/19/AR2010111906689.html. Parks' review of *At the Dark End of the Street,* by Danielle L. McGuire, recounts how the book reveals that white men raped black women and girls "with alarming regularity and stunning uniformity." Rape was used as a weapon of terror in the subjugation not only of black women, but their families and whole communities.

12. Jessica Mitford, *A Fine Old Conflict* (New York: Vintage Books 1956, 1977), 193.

13. Leslie Brody, *Irrepressible: The Life and Times of Jessica Mitford* (Berkeley, California: Counterpoint, 2010), 174.

14. In a 2010 NPR radio program, the son of McGee's prosecutor revealed that his father had shared a bottle of whiskey with McGee and asked if he had done it. McGee reportedly said, "Yes, but she wanted it just as much as I did." "My Grandfather's Execution," NPR May 7, 2010, http://www.wbur.org/npr/126539134/my-grandfathers-execution; see link to Radio Diaries "Willie McGee and the Traveling Electric Chair."

15. *Ibid.*

16. Ann Fagan Ginger, *The Relevant Lawyers: Conversations out of court on their clients, their practice, their politics, their* life style (New York: Simon & Schuster, 1973), 69.

17. David Hilliard, *Huey: Spirit of the Panther* (New York: Thunder's Mouth Press, 2006), 32–33.

18. "Oakland Policeman Slain: 2 Hurt in Panther Shootout," *SFE*, October 28, 1967, 1.

19. David Hilliard and Lewis Cole, *This Side of Glory* (Boston: Little, Brown & Co., 1993), 147–148.

20. Thelwell, Introduction to Moore, *Rage, supra,* xvi.

21. Raiford, *Imprisoned in a Luminous Glare, Introduction, note 18, supra,*

144–145, 153.

22. Austin, *Up Against the Wall*, Introduction, note 27, *supra, 35*.

2. OAKLAND – THE MAKINGS OF A RACIAL TINDERBOX

1. Amory Bradford, *Oakland's Not for Burning*, Introduction, note 14, *supra*.
2. *Ibid.*, 61.
3. Gene Anderson, Our Oakland.net, https://localwiki.org/oakland/Our_Oakland.
4. Thomas Fleming, "'Raincoat' Jones, black businessman extraordinaire," The Columbus Free Press "Reflections on Black History," March 17,1999, http://freepress.org/fleming/flemng72.html; Lloyd Boyles, 'Raincoat' Jones—A Man Who Outlived His Heyday," OT, Jan. 16, 1968, 1.
5. Harry Johanesen, "California Negro History: War Brought Negro Influx to S.F. and Changing Status," *SFE*, August 2, 1968, 52.
6. Don Hausler, unpublished manuscript, *Blacks in Oakland 1852–1987*, Vol. 3, 113, 116, Oakland Public Library History Room.
7. *Ibid.*, Vol. 3, 174.
8. A. S. Broussard, *Black San Francisco: The Struggle for Racial Equality in the West, 1900–1954* (Lawrence: University Press of Kansas, 1993) 50–51, 134.
9. Stan Weir, "Oakland: The Last General Strike," November 5, 2005, libcom.org/library/oakland-general-strike-stan-weir; http://socialistworker.org/2011/12/12/the-last-oakland-general-strike.
10. Bradford, *Oakland's Not For Burning*, *supra*, 6-7.
11. *Ibid.* 45-47.
12. *Ibid.* 36.
13. *Ibid.* 49-50.
14. *Ibid.* 18.
15. *Ibid.* 127.
16. *Ibid.* 27.
17. *Ibid.* 88.
18. *Ibid.* 122, 130.
19. *Report of the National Advisory Commission on Civil Disorders* (New York: Bantam Books, 1968) 10 [a.k.a. "the Kerner Report," after its chair, Illinois Gov. Otto Kerner].
20. *Ibid.*
21. Rev. Martin Luther King, Jr., "Beyond Vietnam: A Time To Break Silence," April 4, 1967, [full speech www.youtube.com/watch?v=OC1Ru2p8OfU].
22. Stokely Carmichael, "Let Another World Be Born," speech given on or about April 22,1967, quoted in Terry Anderson, *The Movement and the Sixties* (New York: Oxford University Press, 1995), 158–59 and fn. 22.
23. Executive Mandate No. 1, Huey Newton, *To Die For the People* (City Light

Books: San Francisco, 2009), 7.

24. Belva Davis with Vicki Haddock, *Never In My Wildest Dreams: A Black Woman's Life in Journalism* (San Francisco; Berrett-Koehler Publishers, Kindle Ed. , 2010), location 1848.

25. Bradford, *Oakland's Not for Burning, supra,* 201. 26.

26. *Ibid.,* 200-201.

3. THE PANTHERS' ROOTS

1. Mary L. Dudziak, *Cold War Civil Rights* (Princeton, New Jersey: Princeton Univ. Press, 2000) 12.

2. Pamphlet distributed at memorial service for Thelma Traylor Seale, Oakland, Feb. 1, 2008, author's collection.

3. Hugh Pearson, *The Shadow of the Panther* (New York: Perseus Books, 1995), 330.

4. Davis and Haddock, *Never In My Wildest Dreams, supra.* Belva's' uncle Ezra obtained an uncollected judgment for $2000 in damages. When Ezra's white lawyer learned of plans for Ezra to be tarred and feathered as a warning to other black men not to bring suit, all the men in the family feared reprisals and took off for California. Kindle Location 405-421. When interviewed later for the Newton trial documentary project, Belva said her father carried a gun and had a reputation as a hothead, so friends and family were glad to see him leave town safely.

5. Hilliard, *Huey: Spirit of the Panther, supra,* 9.

6. *Ibid.*

7. Bobby Seale, *Seize the Time: The Story of the Black Panther Party and Huey P. Newton,* (Baltimore, Maryland: Black Classic Press 1991) "Growing Up Before the Party: "Who I Am," *3. ,*

8. Hilliard, *Huey: Spirit of the Panther,* 21.

9. *Ibid.*

10. HPN Box 14, Folder 11, Probation Report, 9. Letter of Deputy Probation Officer Thomas Broome.

11. Huey Newton and J. Herman Blake, *Revolutionary Suicide* (New York: Harcourt, Brace, Jovanovich, 1973), chapter 14.

12. Seale, *Seize the Time, supra,* "Growing Up Before the Party: Who I Am," 3.

13. Frantz Fanon, *The Wretched of the Earth* (English translation Constance Farrington, Grove Press, 1963), chapter one, "On Violence." [Originally published in French under the title, *Les Damnés de la Terre,* 1961].

14. When Foley returned to Washington in the summer of 1966, he quickly discovered the extent of FBI overreach. Mark Comfort was obviously on their list, likely since the time he worked with Stokely Carmichael and CORE in Alabama. Just by visiting Comfort in jail, Foley became a person of interest to the FBI, which opened a file on him. The Assistant Secretary of Commerce stopped that investigation with a call to the

Attorney General. Bradford, *Oakland's Not for Burning, supra,* 155.

15.   Hilliard, Huey: *Spirit of the Panther, supra,* 46.

4. TAKIN' CARE OF BUSINESS

1.   Nittle, Kareem Nadro, Trailblazers: "Biography of Richard Aoki, The Asian-American Black Panther." About Race Relations, January 8, 2016, http://racerelations.about.com/od/trailblazers/a/Biography-Of-Richard-Aoki-The-Asian-American-Black-Panther.htm.

2.   Griffey, Trevor. "When celebrated activist turns out to be informant: making sense of Richard Aoki's FBI file," May 5, 2012, http://www.truth-out.org/news/item/12555-when-celebrated-activists-turns-out-to-be-informant-making-sense-of-richard-aoki%E2%80%99s-fbi-file?tsk=adminpreview; Seth Rosenfeld, "Richard Aoki, Man Who Armed Black Panthers, Was FBI Informant" (video), August 20, 2012, updated October 20, 2012, http://www.huffingtonpost.com/2012/08/20/richard-aoki_n_1812167.html.

3.   King, Colorlines "Why Do Progressive Activists Become FBI Informants" Sept. 13, 2012, http://www.colorlines.com/articles/why-do-progressive-activists-become-fbi-informants-its-complicated.

4.   Seth Rosenfeld, "Richard Aoki, Man Who Armed Black Panthers, Was FBI Informant," *supra.*

5.   Mitford, *A Fine Old Conflict, supra,* 108.

6.   *People v. Newson*) 37 Cal. 2d. 34, 38 (1951).

7.   Bradford, *Oakland's Not for Burning, supra,* 140.

8.   Kate Coleman, with Paul Avery, "The Party's Over: How Huey Newton created a street gang at the center of the Black Panther Party," NYT, July 10, 1978, 23, 25; John Burris, *Blue v. Black: Let's End The Conflict Between Cops and Minorities* (New York: St.Martin's Press, 1999) 210.

9.   David R. Davies, ed., *The Press and Race* (Jackson, Mississippi: Univ. Press of Mississippi, 2001), 41, quoting *The Jackson Daily News* and *The Meridian Star.*

10.   Bradford, *Oakland's Not for Burning, supra,* 192.

11.   Warren Hinckle, *If You Have A Lemon, Make Lemonade* (New York: W. W. Norton, 1973), 30.

12.   Nadra Karim Nittle, "Biography of Richard Aoki, The Asian-American Black Panther," January 8, 2016, http://racerelations.about.com/od/trailblazers/a/Biography-Of-Richard-Aoki-The-Asian-American-Black-Panther.htm.

13.   Raiford, *Imprisoned in a Luminous Glare, supra,* 149.

14.   Bobby Seale, *Seize the Time, supra,* 129.

15.   Terry Anderson, *The Movement and the Sixties: Protest in America from Greensboro to Wounded Knee* (New York: Oxford Univ. Press, 1995), 11 and fn. 35.

16.   Carson, *In Struggle, supra,* 254, fn. 23.

17.   Hilliard and Zimmerman, *Huey: Spirit of the Panther, supra,* 58.

18. Philip Foner, ed., *The Black Panthers Speak* (Cambridge, Massachusetts: Da Capo Press, 1970) 40.

19. Raiford, *Imprisoned in a Luminous Glare, supra,* 153–154.

20. David Hilliard and Lewis Cole, *This Side of Glory,* (Boston: Little, Brown & Co., 1993) 123.

21. Foner, *The Black Panthers Speak, supra,* 5–6.

22. Anthony, *Spitting in the Wind, supra, 40.*

23. Hilliard, *Huey: Spirit of the Panther, supra,* 38.

24. Howard L. Bingham, *The Black Panthers 1968 (Los Angeles, California: Ammo Books, 2009),* Gilbert Moore, "The Black Panthers," 65.

25. Declaration of Jessica Mitford, July 14, 1977, People v. Newton, Oakland Municipal Court, Alameda County No. 64624A and 65919, HPN Series 1, Box 15, Folder 5.

5. THE DEFENSE TEAM

1. Ginger, *The Relevant Lawyers, supra,* 69.

2. Jessica Mitford, foreword to Garry and Goldberg, *Streetfighter in the Courtroom: The People's Advocate* (New York: E. P. Dutton, 1977) ix.

3. *Ibid.*

4. Susan Berman, "Meet Fay: Huey Newton's Attorney," Bay Area newspaper clipping, circa Nov. 1970, 1C.

5. Ann Fagan Ginger, ed., *Minimizing Racism in Jury Trials* (New York: National Lawyers Guild, 1969), xv.

6. Jerold S. Auerbach, *Unequal Justice: Lawyers and Social Change in Modern America* (New York: Oxford University Press, 1976), 284.

7. Eldridge Cleaver, (Kathleen Cleaver, ed.), *Target Zero: A Life in Writing (New York: St. Martin's Press, 2006),* 77–78 [manuscript for "Uptight in Babylon"].

8. *The Black Panther,* Vol. I, No. 6, Nov. 25, 1967, 1.

9. "1967: Aaron Mitchell, Ronald Reagan's first and only execution" April 12, 2011, http://www.executedtoday.com/2011/04/12/1967-aaron-mitchell-ronald-reagan/.

10. Franklin H. Williams, "The Death Penalty and the Negro," *The Crisis,* Oct. 1960, 3, HPN Box 14, Folder 1.

11. Tribute by Justice Matthew Tobriner to Barney Dreyfus, June 3, 1979, testimonial dinner, Lawyers Guild program.

12. Charles Garry and Art Goldberg, *Streetfighter in the Courtroom: The People's Advocate* (New York: E. P. Dutton, 1977) , 1.

13. HPN, Box 11, Grand Jury Transcript.

14. "Incompetent, Irrelevant and Immaterial," Inter-City Express, undated news clipping, HPN Box 11, Folder 8.

15. Jahna Berry, "Legal World Says Farewell to White," The Recorder, June 29, 2001, 1, quoting then San Francisco Mayor, Willie Brown.

6. WHO DO YOU TRUST?

1. Anthony, *Spitting in the Wind, supra,* 43.
2. Cleaver, *Target Zero*, supra, 77–78, quoting from "Uptight in Babylon".
3. Hilliard and Cole, *This Side of Glory,* 148–149.
4. Cleaver, *Target Zero,* "Bunchy," 130.
5. "FBI War LA Chapter," *It's About Time,* http://www.itsabouttimebpp.com/Chapter_History/FBI_War_LA_Chapter.html .
6. Anthony, *Spitting in the Wind, supra,* 46-47.
7. Garry and Goldberg, *Streetfighter in the Courtroom, supra,* 25.
8. The diminished capacity defense was abolished in California by a 1982 ballot initiative that amended the state's penal code after former San Francisco Supervisor Dan White was convicted of only voluntary manslaughter, not murder, for the November 1978 assassination of Mayor George Moscone and the city's first gay Supervisor, Harvey Milk. See California Penal Code § 25 (a).
9. "Charles Garry Closing Argument," Ann Fagan Ginger, ed., *Minimizing Racism in Jury Trials, supra,* 203.
10. Seale, *Seize the Time, supra, 204.*

7. HONKIES FOR HUEY

1. Peniel Joseph, "Ali helped make black power into global political brand," Bay Area News Group, June 9, 2016, A8. (Prof. Joseph is the Barbara Jordan Chair in Ethics and Political Values and director of the Center for the Study of Race and Democracy in the LBJ School of Public Affairs and a history professor at the University of Texas at Austin).
2. Under current California Rules of Professional Conduct — not applicable in 1967 — a fee agreement granting the attorney a percentage of a client's literary rights would require approval of an independent lawyer for the client. See Cal. Rule 3-300.
3. Henry Louis Gates, "Interview of Eldridge Cleaver," Frontline, Spring, 1997 http://www.pbs.org/wgbh/pages/frontline/shows/race/interviews/ecleaver.html
4. "Panther Calls For Violence," *The Richmond Independent,* Dec. 23, 1967, HPN Box 19, Folder 12.
5. "Incompetent, Irrelevant and Immaterial," The Inter-City Express, HPN Box 19, *Folder 12.*
6. HPN Box 11, Folder 7, telephone message.

8. THE SMELL OF REVOLUTION

1. Newton, *To Die for the People* (New York: Random House, 1972), 10, Executive Mandate No. 2, June 29, 1967.
2. Newton and Blake, *Revolutionary Suicide, supra,* 195.
3. Seale, *Seize the Time, supra,* 222.

4. Claude McKay, *Harlem Shadows* (New York: Harcourt Brace, 1922).

5. *Seale, Seize the Time, supra,* 182.

6. Thelwell, "To Die For the People?" Introduction to Gilbert Moore, *Rage,* supra, xxvi–xxvii.

7. Earl Anthony, *Picking Up the Gun* (New York: The Dial Press, 1970) , 77.

8. Carson, *In Struggle, supra,* 282 and note 51.

9. *Ibid.*, 282 and note 52.

10. Editorial "The Other Side of the Coin" *OP,* Feb. 21, 1968.

9. CLIENT OR COMRADE?

1. California Constitution, Article 1, Section 6.

2. Newton, *To Die for the People,* supra, 11–13, Executive Mandate No. 3, March 1, 1968.

3. HPN, Box 11, File 8, Grand Jury Testimony of Dell Ross.

4. *Ibid., Newsweek* clipping.

10. POWER TO THE PEOPLE

1. Foner, ed., *The Black Panthers Speak, supra,* 62, quoting Huey Newton, "Huey Newton Talks to the Movement About the Black Panther Party, Cultural Nationalism, SNCC, Liberals and White Revolutionaries."

2   *OP,* editorial, April 17, 1968.

3. Joshua Bloom and Waldo Martin Jr., *Blacks Against Empire: The History and Politics of the Black Panther Party* (Berkeley, California: University of California Press, 2013), 134.

4   "1st Negro to Have Flag At Half Staff," *SFE,* April 8, 1968, 2.

5. "King's Dream Is Not Dead—LBJ," *SFE,* April 5, 1968, 4. At the same time, the FBI stepped up its efforts to discredit King. As noted by the Church Committee: "The depth of Director Hoover's bitterness toward Dr. King . . . was apparent from the FBI's attempts to sully Dr. King's reputation . . . . to prevent the passage of a 'Martin Luther King Day.' In 1970, Director Hoover told reporters that Dr. King was the 'last one in the world who should ever have received the Nobel Peace Prize.'" *Church Committee Final Report, Dr. Martin Luther King, Jr. Case Study,* (Washington, D.C., U.S. Printing Office, April 23, 1976), Intro., 1. The Justice Department cleared the FBI of any role in King's assassination, but failed to convince skeptics. Investigative reporter Michael Newton notes in his book, *The Encyclopedia of Unsolved Crimes* (New York: Checkmark Books, 2004) that: "There was evidence of an accomplice in King's murder from the beginning . . . . There is persuasive evidence that G-men never seriously looked for evidence of a conspiracy in King's death [and] . . . were actively discouraged from reporting conspiracy leads." *Ibid.,* 164-165. See also Ward Churchill and Jim Van der Wall, *Agents of Repression: The FBI's Secret Wars Against the Black Panther Party and the American Indian Movement*

(Boston: South End Press, 1988, 1990), 395, fn. 53 and cited sources.

6.   *See, e. g.,* "6000 at King Memorial in Civic Center Plaza; Whites Get Blame
     for Race Crisis,'" *SFE,* April 5, 1968, 1, 14; Harry Johanesen, "Grieving
     City Deplores 'Senseless' Murder," *SFE,* April 5, 1968, 14.

7.   The award bested Anne Bancroft's stellar performance as the mother in
     The Graduate, Audrey Hepburn as the blind protagonist in the thriller
     Wait Until Dark, and Faye Dunaway's unforgettable gun moll in *Bonnie and
     Clyde.*

8.   "Carmichael Reaction to King's Murder, *SFE,* April 5, 1968, 5.

9.   Cleaver, *Target Zero, supra,* 78–79, quoting from "Uptight in Babylon."

10. Anthony, *Spitting in the Wind, supra,* 59.

11. Jones, ed., *The Black Panther Party [Reconsidered],* supra, 33, fn. 35.

12. Thelwell, "Afterword," to Gilbert Moore, *Rage, supra,* 288.

13. "Eldridge Cleaver, 'Recalled to Life,' Plans Huey March," *OP,* Vol. 5 No.
     10, Wed., July 10, 1968, 1.

14. *Witherspoon v. Illinois* 391 U.S.510, 520–21 (1968).

15. United Press International, "Screams of Joy on Death Rows" *OT,* June 4,
     1968, 1.

16. The California Supreme Court was then considering an ACLU and
     NAACP Legal Defense Fund suit challenging the death penalty
     as cruel and unusual punishment. In the interim, it had stayed all
     executions. On November 18, 1968, the California high court upheld
     the constitutionality of the death penalty, but followed *Witherspoon v.
     Illinois,* 391 U.S. 510 (1968) to uphold the right to new penalty trials for
     defendants in cases where potential jurors opposed to the death penalty
     had been improperly dismissed. (In *re Anderson,* 69 Cal. 2d. 613 (1968).)
     The California Supreme Court would revisit the constitutional argument
     in 1972.

17. Hans Zeisel, "Some Insights into the Operation of Criminal Juries," 42
     (Confidential First Draft, Univ. of Chicago, Nov. 1957), cited in fn. 10,
     Witherspoon v. Illinois, 391 U.S. 510 (1968).

18. *Witherspoon v. Illinois,* 391 U.S. 510, 523, fn. 21 (1968). By week's end, the
     California Attorney General sent a letter to district attorneys throughout
     the state interpreting the new mandate's impact on capital cases as
     follows: "We conclude from the opinion that no prospective juror
     should be challenged and excused for cause on account of his views in
     opposition to the death penalty unless he answers affirmatively one or
     more of the following three questions:

     1. Are your views on the death penalty such as would prevent you
         from making an impartial decision as to the defendant's guilt?

     2. Are your views such that you could never vote to impose the
         death penalty?

     3. Are your views such that you would refuse even to consider
         imposing the death penalty in this case?" "Each Death Row

Case to Get Reviewed," *OT*, June 7, 1968, 1.

19. Moore, *Rage*, supra, 118, quoting "Defendant's Memo in support of Motion to Quash Jury Panel."

20. Blacks in Berkeley and Oakland had been divided. Senator Kennedy, in a debate the week before with Senator McCarthy, had alienated some of them with comments indicating that suburban integration should proceed slowly. John George, who was running for Congress, had endorsed Eugene McCarthy. George later attributed his failure to win the Democratic nomination, which would have ensured his election to Congress in a decidedly Democratic district, to write-in votes urged by the Peace and Freedom Party for his former client Huey Newton.

21. Quoted in *OT*, June 6, 1968, 1.

22. See, e.g., Joseph L. Myler, Washington UPI "The American Way — Is It??" *OT*, June 8, 1968, 1.

23. "Shades of Diogenes: Huey Newton Trial Delayed 'Til July 8," *OP*, June 14, 1968, 3.

24. Robert Scheer, "Eldridge Cleaver Defense," letter to the editors of *The New York Review of Books*, Vol. 11, No. 9, Nov. 21, 1968.

25. "Superior Court Orders Eldridge Cleaver Freed," *OT*, June 12, 1968, 1–2, quoting Arlo Smith, Chief Assistant Attorney General.

11. THE QUEST FOR A JURY OF HIS PEERS

1. Pearson, *The Shadow of the Panther*, supra, 166.

2. Editorial, *OP*, April 17, 1968.

3. Bradford, *Oakland's Not for Burning*, supra, 201.

4. Frank Piazzi, East Bay Bureau, "Oakland Mayor Disenchanted, May Bow Out," *SFE*, July 21, 1968, 6.

5. Justice Shenk dissenting in *Perez v. Sharp*, 32 Cal. 2d 711 (1948), 743–44, 750.

6. David Greenberg, "Civil Rights: Let 'Em Wiretap!" George Mason University History News Network, July 6, 2002, http://historynewsnetwork.org/article/366.

7. Carolyn Anspacher, "A Landmark Ruling on Juries' Racial Composition," *SFC*, July 10, 1968. The United States Supreme Court would not reach the same conclusion for almost another two decades in *Batson v. Kentucky*, 476 U.S. 79 (1986). In practice, after Batson, prosecutors retained wide latitude to excuse any and all black jurors by giving the court a race-neutral explanation. See study cited in Michelle Alexander, *The New Jim Crow: Mass Incarceration in the Age of Color Blindness* (New York: New Press, 2010), Kindle location 1620, fn. 72. See also Larry D. Thompson, "Racism in Jury Selection" *NYT* Opinion page, November 2, 2015. See http://www.nytimes.com/2015/11/02/opinion/how-america-tolerates-racism-in-jury-selection.html?_r=0)

8. Despite being labeled a "pinko," Bob Treuhaft had garnered 30% of

the votes in his race for Alameda County District Attorney, largely from
Berkeley and Oakland's flatlands. On learning the vote count, Coakley
had quipped: "I didn't realize there were that many Commies in Alameda
County." Jessica Mitford, *A Fine Old Conflict, supra,* 125.

9. Moore, *Rage, supra,* 95.

10. "As Aid to Newton — Lysistrata '68," *SFE,* July 21, 1968, A 23.

11. Thelwell, Introduction to Moore, *Rage,* supra, xxxi, citing the files of
    Prof. C. E. "Bud" Schultz, Trinity College, Hartford, Connecticut.

12. "Decks Cleared for Newton Trial: Both Sides Expect to Go to Trial," *OP,*
    July 10, 1968, 1.

13. Moore, *Rage, supra,* 118.

14. "Newton Attorneys Seek New Delays," *OT,* July 12, 1968, 14.

15. Moore, *Rage, supra,* 79.

16. *Ibid.,* 27.

17. Bingham, *Black Panthers 1968,* supra, 66, Moore, "The Black Panthers,"
    66.

18. *Ibid.*

19. Bingham, *Black Panthers 1968,* supra, Introduction, 20.

20. *Ibid.,* Gilbert Moore essay "The Black Panthers," 69.

21. *Ibid.,* 76.

22. Moore, *Rage, supra,* 97.

23. *Ibid.,* 108.

24. "Newton Attorneys Seek New Delays," *OT,* July 12, 1968, 14.

25. Moore, "The Black Panthers" in Bingham, *The Black Panthers 1968, supra,* 76.

26. *OT,* July 16, 1968, 1.

27. "Bombs and Bombast," *OP,* Vol. 5. No. 11, July 17, 1968, 1.

28. Moore, *Rage, supra,* 120, 153.

29. "Newton Trial Starts, Then Hits Delay," *OT,* July 15, 1968,1, 6.

30. Moore, *Rage, supra,* 192.

31. Almea Lomax, "Newton Trial Gets Down to Cases; Guard Tighter—
    Defense Sobered as Eyewitness Claimed," *OP,* August 7, 1968, 1.

32. "Pst-st-st . . . UC Student Sours on Panthers," *OP,* Aug. 14, 1968, 1, 6, quoting
    an Aug. 2, 1968 editorial column by Thomas Brom in t*he Daily Californian.*

33. *BB,* July 19–25, 1968, 3.

34. "U.S. Supreme Court Plea for Newton," *OT,* July 16, 1968, 1.

35. Carson, *In Struggle, supra,* 160.

36. The Panthers tracked Forman down in New York in late July 1968 when
    they were presenting their grievance petition to the United Nations.
    According to Earl Anthony, the Panthers threatened to kill Forman
    and also had their sights on Carmichael and H. Rap Brown for their
    defection, but decided against it for fear of starting an all-out war with
    SNCC and the Black Muslims. All of this was well known to the FBI which

then had all the Panther leaders and Forman bugged. Anthony, *Spitting in the Wind, supra,* 48-49.

37. "Negro Joins Newton Jury; Another Dismissed," *SFE*, July 18, 1968, 1, 16.
38. "Challenge to Newton Jury" *OT,* July 17, 1968, 6.
39. Fay Stender, letter dated July 24, 1968, to Prof. Hans Zeisel, HPN, Box 11, Folder 7.
40. *OP,* July 22, 1968, 1.
41. "Jacks Is Black," *OT,* July 18, 1968, TV page.
42. "Report from Black America," *Newsweek,* June 30, 1969, 20.
43. "Newton On Stand, Says He's Broke," *OT,* July 17, 1968, 1.
44. Moore, *Rage, supra,* 153.
45. William O'Brien, "Only Hope: Courtroom Revolution—Newton," *SFE,* July 17, 1968, 8.

12. A MINORITY OF ONE

1. Sam Blumenfeld, "1st Negro Joins Newton Jurors," *SFE*, July 18, 1968, 1, 16.
2. Pearson, *The Shadow of the Panther, supra,* 166.
3. Sam Blumenfeld, "Newton Defense Will Charge Plot," *SFE*, July 25, 1968, 1.
4. Sam Blumenfeld, "Newton's Challenge List Empty," *SFE*, July 29, 1968, 1.
5. Charles Garry, Introduction, Ginger, ed., *Minimizing Racism in Jury Trials,* supra, xxii.
6. Moore, *Rage, supra,* 138.
7. *OP,* "Newton Trial Gets Down to Cases; Guard Tighter—Defense Sobered as Eyewitness Claimed," August 7, 1968, 1,6.
8. Moore, *Rage, supra,* 140–41.
9. *Ibid.,* 145.
10. *Ibid.,* 142.
11. Robert Blauner, "Sociology in the Courtroom: The Search for White Racism," Ginger, ed., *Minimizing Racism in Jury Trials, supra,* 59.
12. *Ibid.*
13. Excerpt from transcript, Huey P. Newton testimony, HPN, Box 11, Folder 3.
14. *OP,* July 24, 1968, 1.
15. Moore, *Rage, supra,* 134.
16. "Newton Jury Selection Goes On," *OT,* July 19, 1968, 6.
17. Ginger, *Minimizing Racism in Jury Trials, supra,* 93–94.
18. Karen Wald, "Jury is selected for Newton trial," *The Guardian,* August 3, 1968, 3.
19. Moore, *Rage, supra,* 139.
20. Wald, "Jury is selected for Newton trial," *supra.*
21. Garry and Goldberg, *Streetfighter in the Courtroom, supra,* 109.

22. Ginger, *Minimizing Racism in Jury Trials, supra,* xxi.
23. Laughlin McDonald, ACLU March 18, 2011, *"A Jury of One's Peers," https://www.aclu.org/blog/speakeasy/jury-ones-peers*
24. *Hoyt v. Florida,* 368 U.S. 57, 67 (1961).
25. See Marissa N. Batt, "Just Verdicts? A Prosecutor Extols Jury Service for Women," *Ms. Magazine,* Summer 2004, http://www.msmagazine.com/summer2004/justverdicts.asp.
26. In *Taylor v. Louisiana,* 419 U.S. 522, 537, the still all-male high court concluded: "If there was ever the case that women were unqualified to sit on juries or were so situated that none of them should be required to perform jury service, that time has long since passed."
27. Sam Blumenfeld, "Opening Newton Trial Arguments Today," *SFE,* July 31, 1968, 3.
28. Ginger, *Minimizing Racism in Jury Trials, supra, 195.*
29. Blumenfeld, "New Panel Called in Newton Trial," *SFE,* July 23, 1968, 1, 1 4.

13. ON TRIAL — NEWTON OR AMERICAN SOCIETY?

1. "Cleaver Warns on Huey Trial," *OT,* July 24, 1968, 8.
2. Rush Greenlee, "Newton's Dad: Guilty? 'That's a Fool Question,'" *SFE* Aug. 6, 1968, 6.
3. Moore, *Rage, supra,* 154.
4. Greenlee, "Newton's Dad: Guilty? That's a Fool Question," *op. cit.,* 6.
5. HPN Box 11, "Oakland Police Department Radio-Transcript of Tape October 28, 1967.
6. "Newton Trial Defense: 'Police Radio Tapes Prove Bias,'" *SFE,* Aug. 6, 1968, 1, 6.
7. Jeff Morgan, "Re-Enactment of Officer's Murder," *OT,* Aug. 7, 1968, 7.
8. *Ibid.*
9. Morgan, "'Gun Under Pillow,' Newton Jury Told," *OT,* Aug. 7, 1968, 3.
10. Morgan, "Re-Enactment of Officer's Murder, *OT,* Aug. 7, 1968, 7.
11. "Witness Saw Frey Killed," *OT,* Aug. 8, 1968, 2.
12. Morgan, "Defense in Newton Trial Fires Back," *OT,* Aug. 8, 1968, 1.
13. Garry and Goldberg, *Streetfighter in the Courtroom, supra,* 121.
14. Ross Defies the Court — Won't Talk," *OT,* Aug. 13, 1968, 1, 6.
15. "Threatened Deadlock in Newton Trial Broken: See No Evil, Tell None 'Try' Fails," *OP,* August 14, 1968, 4.
16. *Ibid.*
17. *Ibid.*
18. "Ross Defies The Court—Won't Talk," *OT,* Aug. 13, 1968, 1, 6.
19. *Ibid.*
20. "Newton Jury Hears Ballistics Expert," *OT,* Aug. 14, 1968, 1, 6.

21. *Ibid.*

22. *Ibid.*

23. Blumenfeld and Greenlee, "Newton May Go on Stand Last—in Next Week?" *SFE*, Aug.16, 1968, 8.

24. Unpublished manuscript and notes of Prof. Robert Blauner.

25. *Ibid.*

14. THE BURDEN SHIFTS

1. The "Dear Nigger Lover" letter commenced: "I guess you will get that murdering coon off because the judge, jury and witnesses have all been intimidated to the extent that nobody would dare convict him. I hope he will be gunned down in the street by some friends of the poor policeman he killed . . . It's too bad we ever stopped lynching. At least the damn niggers knew their place in those days and didn't cause any trouble. I remember reading about how one time they strung up coons and pulled out pieces of their flesh with corkscrews. That must have been a lot of fun. I wish I'd been there to take part in the good work." (HPN, Box 11, File 10).

2. "Witnesses Recall a Happy Newton," *OT*, Aug. 21, 1968, 7.

3. Keating, *Free Huey!, supra,* 129–30.

4. Garry and Goldberg, *Streetfighter in the Courtroom, supra,* ix.

5. The Secretary of State refused to accept Cleaver's name on the ballot because Cleaver was only 33, two years below the minimum age to serve as President. The Peace and Freedom Party sued for a court order to require Cleaver's name to be listed on the ballot even if he could not serve as President. No one expected him to win, after all. The suit was rejected.

6. Hilliard, *Huey: Spirit of the Panther, supra,* 156.

7. Moore, *Rage, supra,* 191.

8. Newton and Blake, *Revolutionary Suicide, supra,* 292.

9. Hilliard and Cole, *This Side of Glory, supra,* 130.

10. Almena Lomar, "Newton Talks Peace as Panthers Shout Defiance," *OP,* Aug. 28, 1968, 3.

11. "40 Whites Parade at Newton Trial," *SFE,* Aug. 22, 1968, 8.

12. "Stokely at Newton Trial—'Political,'" *SFE,* Aug. 22, 1968, 8.

13. Sam Blumenfeld and Rush Greenlee, "D.A. Ends Newton Grilling," *SFE,* Aug. 26, 1968, 1.

14. "Huey Relates His Story of Shooting," *OT,* Aug. 23, 1968, 1, 9.

15. Foner, *The Black Panthers Speak, supra,* 41–42.

16. Garry and Goldberg, *Streetfighter in the Courtroom, supra,* 141.

17. Bingham, *The Black Panthers* 1968, *supra,* Moore, "The Black Panthers" 61.

18. Anthony, *Spitting in the Wind, supra,* 23.

19. *OT,* Aug. 27, 1968, 3.

20. Eldridge Cleaver, "Newton On Trial," *Ramparts,* Fall 1968, 23.

21. Rush Greenlee, "Newton Casts a Long Shadow," *SFE,* Aug. 27, 1968, 16.

22. HPN, Series 1, Box 11, File 9 [letter, dated Aug. 28, 1968, from J. Herman Blake to Huey Newton].

23. Moore, *Rage, supra,* 204.

24. Greenlee, "Newton Casts a Long Shadow," *SFE,* Aug. 27, 1968, 16.

15. THE DAY OF RECKONING ARRIVES

1. HPN, Box 11, File 10.

2. HPN Box 19, Folder 1, transcript direct examination of Dr. Diamond, 3397 at 3405–3407.

3. "Defense Winds Up Case in Newton Murder Trial," *OT,* Aug. 27, 1968, 3.

4. Anthony, *Spitting in the Wind, supra, 57.*

5. "Huey Newton Trial Enters Final Phase," *OT,* Sept. 3, 1968, 1.

6. *Ibid.*

7. "Newton Case to Jury," *OT,* Sept. 3, 1968.

8. "Huey Newton Trial Enters Final Phase," *OT,* Sept. 3, 1968, 5.

9. Jeff Morgan, "Jury Given Newton Murder Case: Jurors Select Negro Foreman," *OT,* Sept. 5, 1968, 1.

10. Moore, *Rage, supra,* 211.

11. Ginger, ed., *Minimizing Racism in Jury Trials, supra,* 216 (excerpt from defense closing argument, *People v. Newton*).

12. *Ibid.,* 199-200.

13. *Ibid.,* 201.

14. *Ibid.,* 204.

15. Blumenfield, "Newton Attorney: Witness a Liar — Or Psychopath," *SFE,* Sept. 3, 1968, 1.

16. Blumenfeld and Greenlee, "Newton Jury Hears Closing Arguments," *SFE,* Sept. 4, 1968, 1.

17. Blumenfeld and Greenlee, "Newton Fate Up To Jury," *SFE,* Sept. 5, 1968, 1, 4. At the Barristers Club, Cleaver had told the audience of white liberals that he loved the handful who supported him. But as for the rest, he said, "Fuck you, all of you. I hope a nigger gets you on a dark street and kills you, takes your fat wallets and your credit cards and cuts your throats." Quoted in Bingham, *The Black Panthers 1968, supra,* Moore, "The Black Panthers," 73.

18. Greenlee, "Row on Newton Evidence: Judge Refuses Defense Plea," *SFE,* Sept. 6, 1968, 1, 4.

19. *Ibid.*

20. Anderson, *The Movement and the Sixties, supra,* 225 and n. 32, quoting one gleeful Yippie calling the Chicago debacle "a revolutionary wet dream

come true."

21. Blauner, unpublished manuscript, Chapter Two, 10.

22. Greenlee, "How the Jury Decided; Puzzling Newton Verdict," *SFE*, Sept. 9, 1968.

23. Moore, *Rage, supra*, 229.

24. Montgomery, "Newton Is Guilty Of Manslaughter," *OT*, Sept. 9, 1968, 1.

25. "Huey Says He Ordered 'Keep Cool'," *OT*, Sept. 12, 1968, 7.

26. Austin, *Up Against the Wall*, 115 and fn. , citing Cox's unpublished manuscript.

27. Moore, *Rage, supra*, 231.

28. Montgomery, "Newton Is Guilty of Manslaughter," *supra*, 1.

16. AFTERMATH

1. Gaile Russ, "Juror in Newton Trial Talks," *OT*, Sept. 10, 1968, 1, 5.

2. Sam Blumenfeld and Rush Lee, "Oakland Reaction Parallels Race," *SFE*, Sept. 10, 1968, 6.

3. Editorial, "The 'Free Huey' Demonstrations, *SFE*, Sept. 10, 1968, 32.

4. The Jury and Democracy Project citing Mapping Police Violence, https://jurydemocracy.wordpress.com/2016/01/23/only-one-black-juror-chosen-in-akai-gurley-shooting-case/.

5. Thomas Tracy, Christina Carrega-Woody, John Marzulli, Denis Slattery, Stephen Rex Brown, "NYPD Officer Peter Liang found guilty of manslaughter in fatal shooting of Akai Gurley in Brooklyn housing development," *New York Daily News*, Feb. 12, 2016, 10:40 A.M. http://www.nydailynews.com/new-york/nyc-crime/nypd-peter-liang-guilty-fatal-shooting-akai-gurley-article-1.2528827. See also http://www.newsday.com/news/new-york/peter-liang-trial-jury-deliberations-begin-1.11454031.

6. Alan Feuer, "Shrewd Victor in Police Case" *NYT* March 25, 2016, 1, A21, http://www.nytimes.com/2016/03/25/nyregion/brooklyn-prosecutor-emerges-as-shrewd-victor-in-akai-gurley-case.html?_r=0. Vinegard helped convict NYPD officers for their infamous misconduct against Haitian security guard Abner Louima in 1997, sodmizing Louima with a broom. Louima later obtained the largest damage award for police brutality in New York's history.

7. Alan Feuer, "Former Officer Avoids Jail for Brooklyn Killing." *NYT*, April 20, 2016, 1, A21.

8. *Ibid.*, 1.

9. Alan Feuer, "Liberal District Attorney is Facing Unlikely Critics: Activists on the Left." *NYT*, May 17,2016, A18, A19.

10. Bingham, *The Black Panthers 1968, supra*, 20.

11. *Ibid.*, 79.

12. Moore, *Rage, supra*, 268.

13. Bingham, *Black Panthers 1968, supra*, 79.

14 Brief of Appellant Huey Newton to the Court of Appeal, 1969, Appendix C.

15 Moore, *Rage, supra, 246.*

16 Lorenzo Ferrigno, "Ex-NYPD Office Peter Liang's Manslaughter
    Conviction Sticks" CNN April 14, 2016, http://www.cnn.com/2016/04/14/us/
    officer-peter-liang-shooting-conviction/index.html.

17 Juror Questionnaire for Criminal Cases," Form MC-002 (Optional Form
    Code of Civil Procedure section 205(c)-(d) (California 2006), http://
    www.courts.ca.gov/documents/mc002.pdf., Question 1.33.

18 Otto Friedrich, Roger Kaplan and Raji Samgaba, "Not Guilty,"
    TIME, June 29, 1987, http://content.time.com/time/magazine/
    article/0,9171,964773,00.html.

19 Jan Hoffman, "Goetz Defense Opens, Calls Jimmy Breslin and a
    Psychiatrist, Then Closes," *NYT,* April 18, 1996, http://www.nytimes.
    com/1996/04/18/nyregion/goetz-defense-opens-calls-jimmy-breslin-and-a-
    psychiatrist-thencloses.html.

20 Stanley Crouch, "The Joy of Goetz: There Was A Moment In Bullied-By-
    Thugs, Pre-Rudy New York When Even This Creep Was A Hero," http://
    nymag.com/nymetro/news/anniversary/35th/n_8601/.

21 *The People of the State of New York v. Bernhard Goetz,* 68 N.Y. 2d 96, 101 (July
    8, 1986).

22 Associated Press, "Bail Slashed for Man Who Shot Four on Subway" *LAT,*
    Feb. 7, 1985, http://articles.latimes.com/1985-02-07/news/mn-5137_1_
    bernhard-Goetz.

23 Robert McFadden, "Poll Indicates half of New Yorkers See Crime as City's
    Chief Problem," *NYT,* January 14, 1985, 1.

24 Otto Friedrich, Roger Franklin, Raji Samghabad "Not Guilty: a jury
    acquits the subway gunman, but the argument goes on," *TIME,* June
    29, 1987, http://content.time.com/time/magazine/article/0,9171,964773-1,00.
    html. "Goetz Verdict Will Endanger Young Black Males, Leaders Say," *Jet
    Magazine,* Vol. 72, No. 15, July 6,1987, 18; see also David Pitt, "Blacks See
    Goetz Verdict as Blow to Race Relations," *NYT,* June 18, 1987, A1, 33.

25 Pitt, *"Blacks See Goetz Verdict as Blow To Race Relations,"* supra.

26 Friedrich et al., "Not Guilty," *supra.*

27 Sarah Lyall, "N.A.A.C.P. Leader Seeks Federal Case on Goetz," *NYT,* June
    20, 1987, http://www.nytimes.com/1987/06/20/nyregion/naacp-leader-seeks-
    federal-case-on-goetz.html.

28 Nancy Grace, Larry King Live, "Interview with 'Subway Vigilante'
    Bernard Goetz" aired Dec. 17, 2004, http://transcripts.cnn.com/
    TRANSCRIPTS/0412/17/lkl.01.html.

29 Janet Gilmore, "New research reveals historic 1990s US crime decline,"
    Feb. 16, 2007, citing Frank Zimring, *The Great American Crime Decline,*
    http://www.eurekalert.org/pub_releases/2007-02/uoc–nrr021207.php.
    See also "What Reduced Crime in New York City," http://www.nber.org/
    digest/jan03/w9061.html.

30. Mark Lesly with Charles Shuttleworth, *Subway Gunman: A Juror's Account of the Bernhard Goetz Trial* (New York: Farrar, Straus & Giroux, 1988).

31. *The Austin Criminal Defense Lawyer*, "The Bernie Goetz Story: 25 Years Later," April 7, 2010, http://www.austincriminaldefenselawyer. com/2010/04/07/ the-bernie-goetz-story-25-years-later.html accessed June 14, 2011.

32. "NBC Today Show," transcript of broadcast of debate on "THE" Trial of the Century, National Broadcast Co., Inc., Feb. 2, 1999, 29. Prof. Charles Ogletree argued that the O. J. Simpson trial was "the" trial of the 20th century; San Francisco attorney James Brosnahan argued that it was the then pending Senate trial following the impeachment of President Bill Clinton.

33. Gerald Uelmen, *Lessons from the Trial: The People v. O. J. Simpson* (Kansas City, Missouri: Andrews and McMeel, 1996), 55. Prof. Uelmen was the proud author of "if it doesn't fit, you must acquit." Uelmen, *Lessons From the Trial, supra,* 2.

34. After the California Supreme Court overturned the state's death penalty in 1972, it was reinstated by a 1976 initiative led by the state's Attorney General. The death penalty remains in effect to this day, although renewed efforts are being made to get it repealed.

35. Linder, *Famous Trials:* "The O. J. Simpson Jury," http://law2.umkc.edu/ faculty/projects/ftrials/Simpson/Jurypage.html. Armanda Cooley, the forewoman, and two other jurors, Carrie Bess and Marsha Rubin-Jackson, wrote a book about their experience: *Madam Foreman* (New York: Dove, 1996.)

36. Vincent Bugliosi, *OUTRAGE: The Five Reasons Why O.J. Simpson Got Away with Murder* (New York: W.W. Norton & Co, 1996) 170.

37. Linder, *Famous Trials: "The O. J. Simpson Trial," http://* law2.umkc.edu/ faculty/projects/ftrials/Simpson/poll.html.

38. "NBC News Poll 10 years after Simpson verdict: issue of race still figures prominently in public opinion," http://www.nbcnews.com/id/5139346/#. V9dU7igrLIU.

39. "Most Black People Now Think O. J. Simpson was Guilty," FiveThirtyEight. com, http://fivethirtyeight.com/features/most-black-people-now-think-oj-simpson-was-guilty/.

40. Bingham, *Black Panthers 1968, supra,* 79.

41. Frank Newport, "Gallup Review: Black and White Attitudes Toward Police," Gallup, August 20, 2014 http://www.gallup.com/poll/175088/ gallup-review-black-white-attitudes-toward-police.aspx.

42. Emily Swanson, "George Zimmerman Poll Finds Divide Over Not Guilty Verdict," The Huffington Post, July 13, 2013, http://www.huffingtonpost. com/2013/07/17/george-zimmerman-poll_n_3612308.html.

43. "In U.S., 24% of Young Black Men Say Police Dealings Unfair," July 16, 2013 http://www.gallup.com/poll/163523/one-four-young-black-men-say-police-dealings-unfair.aspx.

44. Daryl E. Lembke, "Newton Case Strains Nerves of Police," *the Vallejo Times Herald,* Sept. 25, 1968, HPN, Series 1, Box 23 [publicity clipping].

45. Terry A. Reim, "Cops' Panther Shoot Blows 1000-year Cover," *BB,* Sept. 19, 1968, 1.

46. "Panther HQ Shot Up: 2 Police Fired," *SFE,* Sept. 10, 1968.

17. WINNING NEWTON'S FREEDOM

1. HPN Collection, Box 11, Folder 5, Probation Report, 4, M864.

2. "Huey Says He Ordered 'Keep Cool'" *Oakland Tribune,* Sept 12, 1968, 7.

3. *Ibid.*7.

4. HPN, Series 1, Box 11, Folder 5, Probation Report, 4, M864.

5. Ronald Stevenson, "Black Community Reacts to Verdict, HPN Box 23, Folder 1 [undated clipping].

6. "Tensions, Martyrdom and Where Causes Lie," *San Raphael Independent Journal* editorial, HPN, Series 1, Box 23, Folder 1 [clipping of editorial].

7. Terry Ryan, "Mrs. Cleaver criticizes white men," *The Redwood City Gazette,* Oct. 2, 1968; HPN Box 23, Folder 1 [clipping].

8. "Hoffer Rows with Negro at Hearing," Washington, D.C., Oct. 26, 1968; Allen News Service, HPN, Box 23, Folder 1 [clipping].

9. "Newton Predicts Bloodshed," *The Redwood City Tribune,* Oct. 25, 1968, HPN Box 23, Folder 1 [clipping].

10. Lawrence J. Kirshbaum, "Militant Head of New Left Moves HQ Here," *The San Francisco Sunday Examiner and Chronicle,* Sept. 29, 1968, Section A, 10 [*Newsweek* Service].

11. "The San Francisco State College Strike Collection," http://jpllweb.sfsu. edu/about/collections/strike/periodical-article.html.

12. "Races: Professor on Ice," *TIME,* Sept. 27, 1968, http://content.time.com/ time/magazine/article/0,9171,902310,00.html.

13. "At State: That Ole Cleaver Rhythm," *BB,* Oct. 17, 1968, HPN, Box 23, Folder 1.

14. Cleaver, *Target Zero,* supra, 146, 148–49.

15. *U.S. Senate Select Committee to Study Governmental Operations with respect to Intelligence Activities* (The Church Committee), "The FBI's Covert Action Program to Destroy the Black Panther Party," April 23, 1976.

16. Anthony, *Spitting in the Wind, supra,* 60.

17. Kurt Gentry, *J. Edgar Hoover: The Man and the Secrets (New York:* W. W. Norton, 1991), 442.

18. Frontline: "Interview Eldridge Cleaver," Spring 1997, http://www.pbs.org/ wgbh/pages/frontline/shows/race/interviews/ecleaver.html.

19. Anthony, *Spitting in the Wind, supra,* 62-63.

20. "Bloodbath 'Figure of Speech,'" *OT,* April 8, 1970, 1. Although Governor Reagan publicly retracted his statement about a blood bath, within a month he launched a violent confrontation with Berkeley activists just as

he originally threatened to do.

21. Hilliard, *Huey: Spirit of the Panther, supra,* 126.

22. Ward Churchill and Jim Vander Wall, *Agents of Repression: The FBI's Secret Wars Against the Black Panther Party and the American Indian Movement* (Boston: South End Press, 1988, 1990) 63, quoting Noam Chomsky and a June 1970 special report to President Nixon.

23. *Ibid.,* 175.

24. L. F. Palmer, "Out to Get the Panthers," *The Nation,* July 28, 1969, 80.

25. J. Edgar Hoover, letter to the head of the San Francisco FBI office, June 9,1969. Counterintelligence and Special Operations (1970), https://groups.google.com/forum/#!topic/misc.activism.progressive/1DeDX9JMKKw.

26. "Supplementary Detailed Staff Reports on Intelligence Activities and the Rights of Americans, Book II, Final Report, April 23, 1976," The Committee staff noted "little or no apparent evidence of violations [by the targets] of state or Federal Law." http://aarclibrary.org/publib/contents/church/contents_church_reports.htm , Book II, p. 220, fn. 156, p. 128.

27. Mark Levine, George McNamee, Daniel Greenberg, *The Tales of Hoffman* (New York: Bantam Books, 1970), quote from the cover.

28. *Ibid.,* xix. Jessica Mitford covered the trial and then wrote the book, *The Trial of Dr. Spock* (New York: Alfred A. Knopf, 1969).

29. Garry and Goldberg, *Streetfighter in the Courtroom, supra,* 178.

30. *Ibid.,* 176.

31. I. L. F. Palmer, "Out to Get the Panthers," *The Nation,* July 28, 1969, 78.

32. Levine et al., *The Tales of Hoffman, supra,* 55-57, 62, 68-69.

33. Associated Press, "Chief 'Was Astonished' By Indictment of Seale," April 4, 1972, *SFC,* 1.

34. Hilliard and Cole, *This Side of Glory, supra,* 264-265.

35. Fred Hampton 1948–1969, http://www.hartford-hwp.com/archives/45a/715.html; see also "Today in Counterculture History, The Murder of Fred Hampton," https://www.shroomery.org/forums/showflat.php/Number/13580978.

36. Cecil Levinson, "Huey is My BROTHER TOO!," *BP,* Jan. 25, 1969, 7.

37. Roland Young, "Huey's Appeal," *BP,* Feb. 28, 1970, 2.

38. Clara Bingham, *Witness to the Revolution: Radicals, Resisters, Vets, Hippies and the Year America Lost Its Mind and Found its Soul* (New York: Random House, 2016) 242.

39. "Yale U. and the Panthers," *Chicago Daily Defender,* May 7, 1970, 19, quoted in Bloom and Martin, *Black Against Empire, supra,* 263, n.69.

40. Stender's private notes on her copy of the proposed jury instructions indicated "agree one or the other" next to the unconsciousness instruction and marked that instruction "out.")30.

41. *People v. Newton* (1970) 8 Cal. App. 3d. 359, 375.

42. "Huey: 'BPP Will Go to UN'," *BB*, June 5-11, 1970, 4.

43. Mark Lane, "Exclusive: Mark Lane interviews Huey Newton in jail," *Los Angeles Free Press*, July 24, 1970, 4, 18.

44. *OT*, Aug. 5, 1970, 1; *SFC*, Aug. 4, 1970, 1; *SFC*, Aug. 5, 1970, 1.

45. Branning, "Newton Warns Establishment: Free 'Political Captives,'" *SFE*, Aug. 6, 1970, 1.

46. "Alameda Sheriff on Panthers and OEO," *SFC*, Oct. 16, 1970, 3.

18. TO WHAT END?

1. Richard Branning, "Newton Warns Establishment: Free 'Political Captives," *SFE* August 6, 1970, 1.

2. Earl Anthony, *Picking Up the Gun,* supra, 90-91.

3. J. Durden-Smith, *Who Killed George Jackson? Fantasies, Paranoia and the Revolution* (New York: Alfred A. Knopf, 1976) 142–44; Paul Liberatore, *The Road to Hell: The True Story of George Jackson, Stephen Bingham, and the San Quentin Massacre* (New York: The Atlantic Monthly Press, 1996) 93–94. Newton's older brother Sonny Boy was one of his sources. Newton was so skeptical of Pratt that Hilliard had Pratt submit to an injection of truth serum to prove he was not an undercover agent. Newton remained unsatisfied, assuming that Pratt had been trained by the Army to pass that type of test. Hilliard and Cole, *This Side of Glory,* supra, 310–312.

4. Citizens Research and Investigation Committee and Louis Tackwood, *The Glasshouse Tapes, The Story of an Agent-Provocateur and the New Police-Intelligence Complex* (New York: Avon, 1973) 114.

5. Angela Davis put together a dream team of mostly black lawyers headed by "the black Perry Mason," Leo Brant, Jr., and former SNCC General Counsel Howard Moore. The team obtained a change of venue from Marin County where the deadly kidnapping took place, only to wind up in Santa Clara County, which also had a tiny black population. A month before her death penalty trial began in the spring of 1972, the California Supreme Court issued its ground-breaking ruling in *People v. Anderson,* 6 Cal. 3d 628 (1972), declaring the state's death penalty unconstitutional. The ruling permitted Davis to be released from prison on bond during the headline trial. In picking the jury, the Davis defense team was among the first to invest in professional jury consultants, like the volunteer sociology professors Fay Stender worked with for the Newton jury selection. Surprisingly, the polls conducted by the Davis team showed that the Communist scholar was viewed more favorably by educated, upper class whites in Santa Clara County than by the working class and the poor. The lawyers seated a mostly female jury, all of whom had some college classes. Eleven were white, one man was Latino. The jury chose Mary Timothy, a 51-year-old lawyer's wife, as the foreperson. She called herself "Fore-Ms." in honor of the new women's magazine. After Timothy led the sequestered panel to a surprising acquittal, she wrote a book describing the deliberations in detail: *Jury Woman: The Story of the Trial of Angela Davis*

– written by a member of the jury (San Francisco: Glide, 1974, 1975).

6.   "The FBI vs. Jean Seberg," *TIME*, Sept. 24, 1979.

7.   Garry and Goldberg, *Streetfighter in the Courtroom*, supra, 216. Donald Freed published his book the following year, *Agony at New Haven: The Trial of Bobby Seale and Ericka Huggins* (New York: Simon & Schuster, 1973).

8.   J. Durden-Smith, *Who Killed George Jackson? supra,* 155. The journalist presumed this happened in August, but according to Hilliard, Newton reluctantly okayed Pratt's move underground to Alabama and did not banish his group from the Party until several months later, at the same time as the Panther 21. Hilliard and Cole, *This Side of Glory, supra,* 320.

9.   "Supplementary Detailed Staff Reports on Intelligence Activities and the Rights of Americans Book II Final Report April 23, 1976," www.icdc.com/~paulwolf/churchfinalreportIIIb.htm. The Committee staff noted "little or no apparent evidence of violations [by the targets] of state or Federal Law." *Id.*, Book II, p. 220 fn.156, p. 128.

10. "Jury Hopelessly Deadlocked in Newton's Trial," *SFC*, August 9, 1971, 1.

11. Durden-Smith, *Who Killed George Jackson, supra,* 142-144. Liberatore, *The Road to Hell, supra,* 93-94.

12. Durden-Smith, *supra,* 243, fn.5.

13. "House Probers Split on Panther Study," *OT*, Aug. 24, 1971, 36 E.

14. Drew McKillips, "Huey Newton Free—Case Dismissed," *SFC*, December 16, 1971, 1.

15. Lloyd Boles and Gaile Russ, "Huey Free As Charge Dismissed," *OT*, December 15, 1971, 1.

16. Boles and Russ, "Huey Free As Charge Dismissed," *OT*, December 15, 1971, 24.

17. Larry D. Thompson, "How America Tolerates Racism in Jury Selection" *NYT*, October 30, 2015, http://www.nytimes.com/2015/11/02/opinion/how-america-tolerates-racism-in-jury-selection.html?_r=1NYT.

19. REVOLUTIONARY SUICIDE

1.   David Hilliard, *Huey: Spirit of the Panther, supra,* 292.

2.   Durden-Smith, *Who Killed George Jackson?, supra,* 216-217 and fn. 21.

3.   Tim Findley, "A Grim Finale for Prison Inmates," *SFC,* May 25, 1973, 6.

4.   *Ibid.*

5.   John Kifner, "Cinque: A Dropout Who Has Been in Constant Trouble; School Dropout On Welfare Wanted to Sell Bombs Recommendation Ignored Cooperation Indicated Charges Dropped," *NYT, May 17, 1974;* Paul Krassner, "Double Agent" http://www.emptymirrorbooks.com/thirdpage/doubleagent.html.

6.   These homegrown white terrorists headed by a black ex-felon later kidnapped newspaper family heiress Patti Hearst, who grew to identify with their cause. She then became the defendant in a sensational

criminal trial in 1976 for her participation in an armed robbery for which she later won a presidential pardon.

7. "Newton: 'Panthers Have Put Down Their Guns,'" *Berkeley Daily Gazette*, Jan. 13, 1972, 1.

8. Kate Coleman with Paul Avery, "The Party's Over: How Huey Newton created a street gang at the center of the Black Panther Party," *New Times*, July 10, 1978, 29–30. See also Flores Forbes, *Will You Die with Me? My Life in the Black Panther Party* (New York: Washington Square Press, 2006).

9. See e.g., Coleman and Avery, "The Party's Over," *supra*, n. 8, and Peter Collier and David Horowitz, *Destructive Generation: Second Thoughts About the Sixties* (New York: Encounter Books 1989, 2006), Chap. 5, "Baddest: The Life and Times of Huey P. Newton."

10. Robert McGill Thomas, Jr., "Lionel Wilson, 82, A Mayor of Oakland for Three Terms," *NYT,* Jan. 31, 1998, http://www.nytimes.com/1998/01/31/us/lionel-wilson-82-a-mayor-of-oakland-for-three-terms.html.

11. See Pearson, *The Shadow of the Panther*, supra, 292, quoting Newton's Ph.D. advisor Bob Trivors interviewed after Newton's death.

12. Garry died in 1991. In 2007 Armenian filmmaker Hrag Yedalian completed the biopic *The People's Advocate: The Life & Times of Charles R. Garry*.

13. Don Martinez, "Stender: She was shot for the wrong reason," *SFE,* January 19, 1980, 3.

14. In 1987, PBS aired the first part of its award-winning miniseries *Eyes on the Prize*, reviewing the history of the Civil Rights Movement. It was instantly acclaimed by civil rights educators as "the principal film account of the most important American social justice movement of the 20th century." Three years later, in 1990, PBS aired *Eyes on the Prize II: America at the Racial Crossroads 1965–1985*. Episode 12, "A Nation of Law? (1968–1971)," focused in large part on COINTELPRO's efforts to destroy the Black Panther Party in Chicago and murder Fred Hampton.

15. Pearson, *The Shadow of the Panther, supra*, 286, 288. The thesis was republished with a foreword by his widow several years after his death: Huey Newton, *War Against the Panthers: A Study of Repression in America* (New York & London: Harlem River Press, 1996).

16. Hilliard, *This Side of Glory, supra*, 1.

17. William Brand and Larry Spears, "Friends and foes remember Newton 'visionary,' 'thug,'" *OT,* Aug. 23, 1989, 2.

18. Brenda Payton "Black Panthers failed to learn lessons of history," *OT,* Aug. 23, 1989, 1, 2.

19. Hilliard, *Huey: Spirit of the Panther, supra*, 157.

20. Anthony, *Spitting in the Wind, supra*, 178, 180.

21. Dan Flynn, "Panther Leader Seale Confesses," FrontPageMagazine.com, April 23, 2002, http://archive.frontpagemag.com/readArticle.aspx?ARTID=24216.

22. Pearson, *The Shadow of the Panther, supra*, 322–324.

23. Bill Snyder and Michael Collier, "Newton laid to rest: Many former Black Panthers attend rites," *OT,* Aug. 29, 1989, 1.

24. KPFA, Huey P. Newton funeral transcripts, http://www.lib.berkeley.edu/MRC/newtonfuneraltranscripts.html.

25. Pearson, *The Shadow of the Panther, supra,* 322–324.

20. THE ARC OF THE MORAL UNIVERSE

1. Professor Ramsby is quoted in Dani McClain, "Black Lives Matter Was Born on Twitter – Will it Die There?" *The Nation,* April 19, 2016, https://www.thenation.com/article/black-lives-matter-was-born-on-twitter-will-it-die-there/.

2. Williams, *One Man's Freedom, supra,* 6-7.

3. Susan Davis, "Senate blocks Obama nominee over cop-killer case," *USA Today,* March 5, 2014.

4. David Horowitz, *Hating Whitey and other Progressive Causes* (Dallas: Spence Publishing, 1999), 213.

5. Lucie Madison, "Dem Rep Bobby Rush Escorted from house floor for wearing hoodie in honor of Trayvon Martin," March 28, 2012, http://www.cbsnews.com/news/dem-rep-bobby-rush-escorted-from-house-floor-for-wearing-hoodie-in-honor-of-trayvon-martin/.

6. Hank deSutter, "What Makes Obama Run? *Chicago Reader,* Dec. 8, 1995, http://www.chicagoreader.com/chicago/what-makes-obama-run/Content?oid=889221.

7. Matthew Barakat, "Al-Qaeda inmate gets access to Obama's books," Associated Press, July 20, 2009, www.denverpost.com/.../09/al-qaida-inmate-gets-access-to-obamas-books; "Obama's books Ok'd for inmates," *Los Angeles Times,* July 11, 1990, A14.

8. Jason Furman and Douglas Holtz-Eakin, "Why Mass Incarceration Doesn't Pay," NYT, April 21, 2016, Op Ed A27.

9. Charles M. Blow, "Black in the Age of Obama," *NYT,* Dec. 5, 2009, A 19.

10. Juliet Linderman, "1 year after Freddie Gray, police work to heal city's wounds," Live 5 News, Baltimore, Maryland, April 10, 2016, http://bigstory.ap.org/article/743e92689ffa4d59b1bb6328b9d8cdea/1-year-after-freddie-gray-police-work-heal-citys-wounds.

11. John Pfaff, "A Mockery of Justice for the Poor," *NYT* Op Ed page, April 29, 2016, http://www.nytimes.com/2016/04/30/opinion/a-mockery-of-justice-for-the-poor.html.

12. "The Gavel Gap," http://gavelgap.org/.

13. Tanzira, Vega, "The next battle for Black Lives Matter: Economic Justice," August 2, 2016, http://money.cnn.com/2016/08/02/news/economy/black-lives-matter-the-economy/index.html.

14. Charles Pulliam Moore, *FUSION,* July 13, 2016, "Alton Sterling's 15 year old son just gave a powerful speech about violence, protests, and unity," http://fusion.net/story/324621/alton-sterling-son-cameron-sterling-

speech/.

15. Full transcript of former president Bush's speech at memorial service, WFAA News, http://www.wfaa.com/news/local/dallas-ambush/read-full-transcript-of-former-president-bushs-speech-at-memorial-service/270770750; "Read President Obama's Speech From the Dallas Memorial Service" *TIME* July 12, 2016, https://www.yahoo.com/news/read-president-obama-speech-dallas-203011684.html.

EPILOGUE

1. Paul T. Rosynsky, "Mehserle now a free man," *OT*, June 14, 2011, 1, 7.

2. Thelton Henderson Center for Social Justice, https://www.law.berkeley.edu/research/thelton-e-henderson-center-for-social-justice/.

3. Will Kane, "Sean Whent named Permanent Oakland Police Chief, May 14, 2014, *SF Gate*, http://www.sfgate.com/bayarea/article/Sean-Whent-named-permanent-Oakland-police-chief-5477982.php.

4. *Ibid.*, quoting an East Oakland church leader with a congregation of 6,000: "We just didn't expect him to be as good a leader as he turned out to be. He blossomed into it, he really did. We were all skeptical of him coming from (internal affairs). But he was ready to turn the corner and gain the respect of the men, and the morale has picked up. He seems to really be doing a great job." Yet two years later he surprised the community with his resignation amid speculation that he was pressured to step aside. David DeBolt, "Was chief pushed out?" *East Bay Times,* June 11, 2016, 1; Gary Peterson, "Police chief's exit raises questions," *East Bay Times,* Local News, Section B1,2. Mayor Schaaf assured the press that the ongoing investigation into a sex scandal in the OPD did not include allegations against Chief Whent. Commenting on his resignation, Schaaf praised Whent for having taken "incredible strides to build community trust in the department."

5. David DeBolt, "Trust eroded in new scandal: Former chief calls it 'Riders 2.0 on steroids'; progress of reforms shatters," *East Bay Times,* Local News B1, B7.

6. "Stanford Study Finds Oakland Cops Practicing Racial Profiling," June 16, 2016. http://sanfrancisco.cbslocal.com/2016/06/16/stanford-study-finds-oakland-cops-practicing-racial-profiling/.

7. Clifton B. Parker, "Stanford big data study finds racial disparities in Oakland, Calif., police behavior, offers solutions." June 15, 2016. For the complete report. See https://sparq.stanford.edu/opd-reports.

8. DeBolt, "Trust eroded in new scandal," *supra.*

9. David DeBolt and Matthew Artz, "Latest OPD Chief Quits," *East Bay Times,* June 18, 2016, 1.

10. "Study slams troubled Oakland police department for racial bias," PBS, June 15, 2016, http://www.pbs.org/video/2365784451/.

11. Sandhya Somashekhar, Wesley Lowery, Keith L. Alexander, Kimberly

Kindy, Julie Tate, "Black and Unarmed," The *Washington Post,* August 8, 2015, http://www.washingtonpost.com/sf/national/2015/08/08/black-and-unarmed/.

12. David Iaconangelo, "What Oakland Police's 'Implicit Bias' could mean for police reform, *Christian Science Monitor,* June 16, 2016, http://www. csmonitor. com/.

13. Alameda County Sheriff's Office, https://www.alamedacountysheriff.org.

14. Alameda Court's Sheriff's Office, https://www.alamedacountysheriff.org/history.php.

15. The Piper's interview at the January 2009 protest can be viewed on You-Tube, https:///www.youtube.com/watch?v=Wu-NSij9wDk.

16. Jinho Ferreira, "Cops and Robbers" http://themarsh.org/cops_and_robbers/jinho-the-piper-ferreira.

17. "Flipsyde," http://flipsyde.com/about/.

18. Dawn Ferreira and Jinho Ferreira, *Cops and Robbers: The Past, The Present, The Future* (Amazon 2014) dedication, http://www.amazon.com/Cops-Robbers-Past-Present-Future/dp/0991533402.

19. Kimberly Frey is among more than a score of those wishing to honor her father who have posted notes at the website, Officer Down Memorial Page http://www.odmp.org/officer/reflections/5125-police-officer-john-f-frey,

20. California Women Lawyers, "Fay Stender," http://www.cwl.org/about_cwl/fay_stender.aspx.

21. Larry D. Thompson, "Racism in Jury Selection," *NYT,* Opinion page, November 2, 2015. See http://digitalcommons.law.uga.edu/fac_pm/228/.

22. *Ibid.*

23. *Ibid.*

24. Associated Press, "Supreme Court orders new look at race of jurors in three convictions," *New Orleans Times Picayune,* June 21, 2016.

25. Charlie Beck and Connie Rice, Op. Ed., "How Community Policing Can Work," *NYT,* August 12, 2016, A21.

INDEX

ACKNOWLEDGEMENTS

First of all, I want to offer my profuse thanks to my good friend and long-time neighbor David Alexander, who first suggested that I would reach a wider audience if I wrote a second, shorter book on the Newton trial and then took time from his tireless efforts to free his death-penalty client Kevin Cooper (www.savekevincooper.org) to provide me with a steady stream of ideas to bring my new book to market and to offer his help in reaching that goal. My deep appreciation also to everyone who gave of their time and materials as sources for this book. I would like to specially thank photographer Ilka Hartmann (www.ilkahartmann.com), three of whose many extraordinary Panther photos appear in this volume. Ilka generously opened doors to important contacts when I was writing my first book and has since become a good friend. Thanks also to my extraordinary editor Dan White (The Cactus Eaters *and* Under the Stars)*, to Mark Weiman of Regent Press and Suzanne Waligore for all their hard work and for believing so wholeheartedly in this project, and to Christopher Bernard for his proofreading talents. Special thanks as well to the Board of Arc of Justice Productions, Inc. for allowing me to use excerpts from transcripts of its filmed interviews for the documentary project* American Justice on Trial: People v. Newton *[www.americanjusticeontrial.com] to help me retell the story of the Newton trial more vividly from different perspectives. Thanks again — always — to my wonderful family: my daughters Anna Benvenutti Hoffmann, Jamie Benvenutti and Mali Benvenutti for their invaluable assistance and feedback, my sister Leslie Pearlman for her proofreading skills and editing suggestions and my husband Peter Benvenutti — for being a sounding board, astute and meticulous editor and constant source of support in launching this project.*

CPSIA information can be obtained
at www.ICGtesting.com
Printed in the USA
FSOW02n0447270517
34494FS